BORA LASKIN

Bringing Law to Life

BORA LASKIN

Bringing Law to Life

PHILIP GIRARD

Published for The Osgoode Society for Canadian Legal History by
University of Toronto Press
Toronto Buffalo London

Printed in Canada

ISBN-13 978-0-8020-9044-7
ISBN-10 0-8020-9044-3

Printed on acid-free paper

Library and Archives Canada Cataloguing in Publication

Girard, Philip
Bora Laskin : bringing law to life / Philip Girard.

Includes bibliographical references and index.
ISBN 0-8020-9044-3

1. Laskin, Bora.   2. Canada. Supreme Court – Biography.   3. Judges –
Canada – Biography.   I. Osgoode Society for Canadian Legal History
II. Title

KE8248.L38G57 2005   347.71'03534   C2005-903122-0
KF345.Z9L38 G57 2005

University of Toronto Press acknowledges the financial assistance to its publishing program of the Canada Council for the Arts and the Ontario Arts Council.

University of Toronto Press acknowledges the financial support for its publishing activities of the Government of Canada through the Book Publishing Industry Development Program (BPIDP).

For my parents
and for Sheila, Daniel, and Gabriel

You are not required to complete the work,
but neither are you free to desist from it. (Avot 2:15)
Rabbi Tarfon, 2nd century CE

Contents

Foreword

THE OSGOODE SOCIETY
FOR CANADIAN LEGAL HISTORY

In the history of Canadian law in the twentieth century, Bora Laskin is a major figure and a biography of him is definitely overdue. In his account of Laskin's long and distinguished career, Professor Philip Girard of Dalhousie University explores in vivid detail what he describes as the life and times of 'a restless man on a mission.' In assessing many of Laskin's significant contributions, Professor Girard delves into his 'first career,' which included his work as a human rights activist, university professor, and labour arbitrator. In a compelling analysis Girard demonstrates how Laskin used the law to make Canada a better place for workers, racial and ethnic minorities, and the disadvantaged. These efforts are fully chronicled, revealing the contribution of a dedicated academic and legal scholar in a Canada which was changing for the better. Then, in what Laskin himself called his 'accidental career' as a judge on the Ontario Court of Appeal, a member of the Supreme Court of Canada, and Chief Justice of Canada, Laskin continued these efforts. In his quest to make the judiciary more responsive to changing expectations related to justice and fundamental rights, Laskin demonstrated how a great judge could contribute to the development of a modern Canada. Professor Girard's biography of Chief Justice Laskin adds significantly to our understanding of Canada's evolution in an age of social change and increasing liberalization.

The purpose of The Osgoode Society for Canadian Legal History is to encourage research and writing in the history of Canadian law. The

Society, which was incorporated in 1979 and is registered as a charity, was founded at the initiative of the Honourable R. Roy McMurtry, a former attorney general for Ontario, now chief justice of Ontario, and officials of the Law Society of Upper Canada. Its efforts to stimulate the study of legal history in Canada include a research-support program, a graduate student research-assistance program, and work in the fields of oral history and legal archives. The Society publishes volumes of interest to the Society's members that contribute to legal-historical scholarship in Canada, including studies of the courts, the judiciary, and the legal profession, biographies, collections of documents, studies in criminology and penology, accounts of significant trials, and work in the social and economic history of the law.

Current directors of The Osgoode Society for Canadian Legal History are Robert Armstrong, Kenneth Binks, Patrick Brode, Michael Bryant, Brian Bucknall, Archie Campbell, David Chernos, Kirby Chown, J. Douglas Ewart, Martin Friedland, Elizabeth Goldberg, John Honsberger, Horace Krever, Virginia MacLean, Frank Marrocco, Roy McMurtry, Brendan O'Brien, Peter Oliver, Paul Reinhardt, Joel Richler, William Ross, James Spence, and Richard Tinsley.

The annual report and information about membership may be obtained by writing: The Osgoode Society for Canadian Legal History, Osgoode Hall, 130 Queen Street West, Toronto, Ontario, M5H 2N6. Telephone: 416-947-3321. E-mail: mmacfarl@lsuc.on.ca. Website: Osgoodesociety.ca

R. Roy McMurtry
President

Peter N. Oliver
Editor-in-Chief

Acknowledgments

I would like to thank the following people who read and commented on draft versions of various chapters: Eric Adams, Constance Backhouse, Michiel Horn, Jean Milner, Bruce Muirhead, Dianne Pothier, Audrey Samson, Shirley Tillotson, David Warrington, and Sheila Zurbrigg. I owe particular thanks to Harry Arthurs, Blake Brown, Joyce Miller, Jim Phillips, and Dick Risk for reading large chunks of the manuscript, and to Peter Oliver and two anonymous reviewers for commenting on the entire work. A number of research assistants have worked on this project over the years, and I am most grateful to Eric Adams, Nicolas Barr, Luke Cragg, Kerri-Ann Gillis, and Adam Newman for their excellent work. All errors remain my own. I acknowledge research funding from the Dalhousie Research Development Fund (Humanities and Social Sciences), the Osgoode Society, and Dalhousie Law School, and I wish to thank Dalhousie University for two six-month sabbaticals, in 2001–2 and 2004–5, without which I could not have completed the writing of the manuscript.

This is an unauthorized biography. After some initial discussion the Laskin family declined to be involved with my proposed work. They have not seen this manuscript and cannot be held responsible for any views expressed herein. Bora Laskin's children, the Hon. John I. Laskin and Barbara Laskin Plumptre, have considered writing about their father, and I hope that one day they will publish a memoir of him. He looms large in Canadian life and this biography should not be the last word on the subject.

I initially planned to write this book with my colleague Wayne MacKay, who clerked for Bora Laskin in 1978–9. Other responsibilities intervened to prevent Wayne from collaborating on this volume, but he generously shared with me extensive research materials he had collected over the years. The research for this book involved much more travel than I had at first anticipated, and many friends welcomed me while I ransacked archives in one city after another. For their hospitality I thank Patti Allen and Peter Swan in Ottawa; Rosemary Gartner, Jim Phillips, and Grant Wedge in Toronto; Ruth Thompson in Saskatoon; Jacqui Shumiatcher in Regina; and Sandi Witherspoon and Pete Chamberlain in Vancouver. Librarians and archivists in many places were of great assistance, beginning with the Sir James Dunn Law Library at Dalhousie University. I wish also to thank those at the following institutions: Dalhousie University Archives, the Canadian Jewish Congress Archives, the National Archives of Canada, the University of Toronto Archives, York University Archives, the Ontario Jewish Archives, the Holy Blossom Temple Archives, the Archives of Ontario, the Thunder Bay Historical Museum, Thunder Bay Public Library (Fort William branch), Thunder Bay City Archives, Lakehead University Archives, the University of Manitoba Archives, the Jewish Heritage Centre of Western Canada, the University of Saskatchewan Archives, the Saskatchewan Archives Board, the University of British Columbia Archives, the Institute for Advanced Legal Studies (London), the University of Edinburgh Archives, Harvard University Archives, New York University Archives, and Yeshiva University Archives. The Osgoode Society provided access to many transcripts of interviews with legal figures whose careers intersected with Laskin's. I also thank the registrar of the Supreme Court of Canada, Anne Roland, for allowing me access to some materials held by her office. For service above and beyond the call of duty I would like to thank Susan Lewthwaite of the Law Society of Upper Canada Archives, who responded to innumerable requests for information about Laskin's contemporaries; David Warrington at Special Collections, Harvard University Library, who went out of his way to assist me during my visit there; and Yael Wyant of the Faculty of Law, Hebrew University of Jerusalem, who provided information regarding Laskin's visits to Israel. Special thanks to Esther Leven of Winnipeg for translating from the Yiddish the account of Bora Laskin's bar mitzvah found in the *Israelite Press*.

I was very fortunate to establish contact with Jacqui Shumiatcher, the spouse of one of Laskin's oldest friends, Morris Shumiatcher. Morris was Bora's first graduate student in law, and the Shumiatchers and the Laskins remained close friends for many years. Jacqui allowed me access to relevant portions of the Shumiatcher Papers held by the Saskatchewan Archives Board, and to further correspondence between the two men (and occasionally their spouses) still in her possession. She generously hosted me in her Regina home for several days to allow me to consult the correspondence. I thank her for granting permission to quote from the letters of her late husband, who died on 23 September 2004. Jean Milner, the widow of Laskin's former colleague and friend James B. Milner, generously provided extracts from her diary from the 1950s through the 1970s. Both Jacqui and Jean helped to give me some insight into Bora and Peggy's relationship. The Milners and the Laskins were good friends from 1950, when James joined the Faculty of Law, until his sudden death in 1969, and often met while holidaying in Britain in the 1960s. I thank Jean for allowing me to quote from her diary and also from the letters of her late husband. Laskin's correspondence with F.R. Scott is found in the latter's papers at the National Archives, and I thank William Toye, Scott's literary executor, for permission to quote from Scott's letters.

Earlier versions of some chapters were presented in various venues, and I thank those who provided comments at the Canadian Law and Society Association annual conference (Lake Louise, June 2000), a Dalhousie Law School faculty seminar and History Department seminar, the Brock University conference on Canadian Biography (November 2002), the Toronto Legal History Group seminar (March 2003), the McCord Museum conference entitled 'The Sixties – Style and Substance' (November 2003), and the Canadian Association of Law Teachers annual conference (Winnipeg, June 2004). I also thank John McLaren and Ian Holloway for inviting me to address the Australia–New Zealand Legal History Society meeting in Canberra in July 2000 on the topic of judicial biography.

It was a pleasure to work with Marilyn Macfarlane at the Osgoode Society, and Len Husband and Allyson May at the University of Toronto Press. Roberta Osborne provided invaluable help with the photos. Geordie Lounsbury, Molly Ross, and Sheila Wile at Dalhousie Law School provided technical assistance of various kinds, for which I am most grateful.

When I told my parents that I was undertaking a biography of Bora Laskin, my mother's comment was 'he was such a fair man.' She then went and found a copy of an article from *Chatelaine* she had saved for twenty-five years. It was a story about Irene Murdoch, of the famous case *Murdoch v. Murdoch,* in which Laskin had dissented in 1973. Like Irene Murdoch, my mother was and is married to a farmer, but unlike her she did not endure a divorce that left her bereft of any significant share of the property acquired by her and my father during their marriage. My mother's instant sense of connection with Laskin was one I encountered again and again when I told people of my research. I have not found a single layperson who has been able to identify any of Laskin's successors as chief justice of Canada, but many people over the age of forty know of him. Such anecdotal evidence tends to confirm my view, developed at greater length herein, that Laskin was a pivotal figure in the transition to a more rights-oriented Canada. Whether one looks with approval or regret on the emergence of the judiciary as a major actor in Canadian social and political life in the wake of the Charter, Bora Laskin's role in that historic transformation cannot be denied.

BORA LASKIN

Bringing Law to Life

Introduction

When I entered law school in 1975 Bora Laskin was at the height of his powers and his fame. Chief justice of Canada for less than two years, he was the first Jew and the first academic named to the Supreme Court of Canada. Belonging to neither of Canada's European founding nations, and known for his rigorous commitment to the highest ethical and intellectual standards on the part of the judiciary, he symbolized a new spirit of openness and transformation in Canadian society and law. In spite of his position at the summit of the Canadian judiciary he remained a passionate and well-known dissenter, especially in cases involving federalism, civil liberties, and claims to equality under the Canadian Bill of Rights. Sometimes he actually talked about what interests the law protected and why, whereas most other judges of the time recited long strings of precedents in a fashion intelligible only to the initiated. For the younger generation of legal academics, including my professor of constitutional law at McGill, Irwin Cotler, Bora Laskin was a hero, a role model, an inspiration. The only figure who had provided similar intellectual leadership on the Supreme Court was Ivan Rand, who had long since departed. We read lots of Rand judgments as well as many of Laskin's, but mostly we read impenetrable decisions by a strange group of long-dead British men called the Judicial Committee of the Privy Council. They were strange to me, at any rate, as I had studied little Canadian history at the time, but I learned that they formed the final court of appeal for Canada as late as 1949.

I graduated from law school in 1979, having taken a year out to travel, and clerked for Justice Willard Estey at the Supreme Court in 1979–80. In that short time, the Laskin legend had undergone a marked shift. Laskin missed the entire fall term of 1979, having come close to death as a result of multiple health problems. When he returned to the Court in early 1980 he arranged to meet with the clerks as a group, and apologized for not having been able to welcome us in September (Justice Martland had done so in his stead). I was shocked. In the mid-1970s Bora Laskin cut a dashing image in the media, even in the red Santa Claus suit (as Estey called it) worn by the judges on ceremonial occasions. Those piercing eyes, the mane of silver hair swept back from the high forehead, the slightly ironic smile – he appeared intelligent, handsome, physically fit, *bien dans sa peau*. The man before us now appeared at least a dozen years older than the images of a few years earlier. He seemed physically smaller, he was cautious in his movements, gaunt, his eyes now shielded behind large unattractive glasses. So he appeared on national television during that disastrous attempt to broadcast the release of the decision in the *Patriation Reference* on 28 September 1981 (all video, no audio). We had set up a large television in a classroom at the faculty of law at the University of Western Ontario, where I was then teaching, and a throng of students and professors witnessed the debacle. Not only was Laskin's health in decline at this time, but his heroic reputation seemed somewhat tarnished by a perceived conservative turn in his judicial decisions, symbolized by his very public battle with Justice Thomas Berger in 1982 over the limits of judicial free speech.

The Canadian Charter of Rights and Freedoms arrived in the spring of 1982. Laskin had never embraced an entrenched bill of rights while an academic, but his increasingly aggressive approach to the Canadian Bill of Rights on the bench suggested he was ready for the more expansive role expected of the courts after the advent of the Charter. It took a while for cases involving Charter issues to percolate up from the lower courts. The first was *Hunter v. Southam*, a case involving the guarantee against unreasonable search and seizure contained in section 7 of the Charter.[1] It was heard on 22 November 1983 by the full court, but Laskin was unable to take part in the subsequent decision-making process. He did not return to the court in the new year, and died on 26 March 1984. It seemed a cruel twist of fate that prevented Laskin from expressing his views on the Charter in a single decision.

Bora Laskin died at the very dawn of the Age of the Charter, and the very end of the Trudeau era. (The public careers of the two men in the judiciary and politics coincided to an uncanny degree, beginning in the same month in 1965 and ending within months of one another in 1984.) Within a very short time Canadian law and politics seemed launched on a totally new course. A more conciliatory prime minister sought harmony in federal-provincial affairs, and the frequent constitutional references to the courts diminished. As the courts' federalism docket dried up, the Charter side of the ledger took on added significance. Within legal education, the profession, and even within ministries of justice, federalism quickly became yesterday's news as Charter-mania swept the land. The current state of play is succinctly summed up in a recent article by Wayne MacKay: 'The Supreme Court of Canada and Federalism: Does/Should Anyone Care Anymore?'[2] Laskin's decisions on federalism now seem almost as obscure as the Privy Council's. His decisions on the Canadian Bill of Rights, which might have served as a repository of ideas about how to interpret constitutionally guaranteed rights under the Charter, have been referred to by his successors in a perfunctory manner, if at all. Even in the field of civil liberties, Robert Sharpe predicted in 1985 that one would be 'hard pressed to think of any judgment which will stand as a landmark.'[3] This was confirmed for me indirectly during an interview I conducted with a distinguished Canadian jurist. When asked to identify a particularly memorable Laskin decision, the jurist replied, 'Oh, that would have to be *Drybones*.' *Drybones*, in which the Supreme Court held inoperative a law making it an offence for an Indian to be found inebriated off a reserve, was decided before Laskin joined the Supreme Court; the majority decision was in fact written by Justice Roland Ritchie.

The current preoccupation with the Charter makes a biography of Bora Laskin all the more necessary. The recent spate of judicial biography in Canada has been inspired primarily by those judges who are associated with the early years of the Charter: Chief Justice Brian Dickson, and Justices Bertha Wilson and William McIntyre.[4] This biography of Bora Laskin functions as a prequel to those of his Charter-era colleagues already published, and in some sense a sequel to the recently published biography of his friend and colleague Emmett Hall.[5] It will argue that Bora Laskin made a signal contribution to Canadian society and law in two ways. He articulated, popularized, and symbolized a new rights-oriented discourse in post-war Canada, and he helped to prepare the Canadian judiciary for the challenge of a fundamental constitutional reform. It is ironic that his enduring contribution to Canadian law has not been in the field of the division of powers, to which he devoted so much of his intellectual energy and his passion. Rather, it has been to the development of the constitution in the eighteenth-century sense: to the whole complex of institutions, customs, conventions, and attitudes, both lay and professional, that enable a society to elaborate and enforce norms and cohere over time. Expressed in another way, the Laskin stamp is impressed on Canadian legal culture.

This was a contribution that began long before Laskin became a judge, indeed even before he became a professor. In the 1930s Laskin developed a set of ideas about law and its role in society which I call 'legal modernism.' This is a neologism, one I have coined consciously so as to avoid using American or British labels for similar trends in contemporary legal thought. Laskin did not invent legal modernism nor was he alone in espousing it, but he was unusual in the persistence and force with which he continued to advocate his views, and the chance he got to translate them into Canadian law both as a labour arbitrator and a judge. At the core of these ideas was the notion of responsive law, law as an instrument through which society seeks to achieve its goals. Both of Laskin's mentors, W.P.M. Kennedy at the University of Toronto and Cecil A. Wright at Osgoode Hall Law School, spoke of 'bringing law to life' rather than 'life to law.' By this they meant ensuring that human needs and aspirations shaped the domain of law, instead of requiring human experience to squeeze into the pigeonholes of legal doctrine.

In insisting that precedent and past practice constituted the beginning, not the end, of legal inquiry, legal modernism tried to orient jurists towards the future rather than the past, the 'ought' rather than the 'is' of law. It advocated a more active role for legislation in responding to social ills, and dismissed the traditional bias against interfering with the common law, itself seen as unduly biased towards the powerful. Only legislation could provide for a proper 'adjustment' of the respective rights of disputing parties who started from highly unequal positions. Legal modernism also re-examined the role of judges both in interpreting legislation and in applying the common law. Laskin accepted that judges exercised a quasi-legislative function, because the ambiguous language of legislation and previous decisions always left some room for judicial choice and creativity. The study of jurisprudence thus needed to go beyond the analytical positivism of English legal thought and the legal formalist, 'law as science' tradition of the late-nineteenth-century United States. But rather than adopt some of the more radical critical stances of the day, such as legal realism, Laskin steered a middle course. He did not accept that the indeterminacy of legal language necessarily led to arbitrariness; instead, he agreed with the position of Benjamin Cardozo that the judge was constrained by a web of customary practices, expectations, and mental habits (including respect for precedent), which limited the range of possible outcomes.[6] There was a role for judicial boldness and innovation in Laskin's worldview, but it was carefully circumscribed by respect for the legislature, by the weight of judicial tradition, and by the calculus of judicial legitimacy.

When appeals to the Judicial Committee of the Privy Council were abolished in 1949, Laskin was quick off the mark in urging the Supreme Court of Canada to embrace his version of legal modernism. In a 1951 article he urged the Court not 'to walk in the shadow of the Privy Council' but to strike out on its own by engaging in 'the same free range of inquiry which animated the Court in the early days of its existence, especially in constitutional cases when it took its inspiration from Canadian sources.'[7] His writing took on a more nationalistic hue as he encouraged the Canadian judiciary to develop law in a manner responsive to Canadian needs and conditions. In the post-war period the claims of nation largely replaced the claims of class which had animated Laskin's pre-war writings, but he remained rather vague about what 'Canadian needs and conditions' actually were.

Always a devoted supporter of British-style political institutions, Laskin was initially more ambivalent about the content of the English legal heritage. Before 1960, he sought to introduce into Canada's highly Anglophilic legal culture a recognition of its North American situation, and frequently advocated the adoption of particular U.S. laws or judicial decisions as more suitable than domestic or English precedents. After direct exposure to the British legal scene during a sabbatical in London in 1961–2, Laskin became more positive about English law, though he insisted that 'English decisions will have to compete on merit for consideration with decisions in Canada as well as decisions elsewhere.'[8] Persuasiveness, not deference to tradition, was the key.

The varied nature of Laskin's achievements has dictated the shape of this book. He was known across Canada for his contributions to university affairs, legal education, labour arbitration, constitutional law, and the advancement of civil liberties before he ever went to the bench. His role in the development of anti-discrimination law in the post-war period was not as well known outside the Jewish community, but is no less important for that. All these activities were significant in their own right, both in Laskin's life and in a larger historical sense. I have accordingly treated them at some length, not as a simple 'prelude' to his judicial career. When discussing Laskin's judicial role, I have not sought to provide a comprehensive account of his contributions to all areas of law. I have chosen to focus principally on the public law decisions – in criminal law, administrative law, and constitutional law – as these were the areas he cared most about, and where his legal modernism was most influential. I have been much more selective about his private law decisions, treating only those which possessed special biographical significance.

Tracking Laskin's public career was not difficult, given its relative recency. Laskin the private man was much more elusive. As the narrator of Alistair MacLeod's *No Great Mischief* says, 'It is hard when looking at the pasts of other people to understand the fine points of their lives. It is difficult to know the exact shading of dates which were never written down and to know the intricacies of events which we have not lived through ourselves but only viewed from the distances of time and space.'[9] Biographers have traditionally relied on private letters to bridge this gap. I have had no access to any familial correspondence, but in letters to friends Laskin often seemed to have taken to heart Joseph Kennedy's famous dictum that you should never put on paper anything you would not be content to see on the front page of the *New York Times*. Even with close friends such as Morris Shumiatcher, Laskin did not unburden himself on paper. He did not gossip, rarely passed judgment on the actions of others, and even more rarely wrote about his own feelings. His letters are brisk and businesslike, squeezed in, one feels, amidst many other pressing obligations. His mind is already on the next task before he closes the letter. In person, Laskin could be much more forthcoming. His closest friends found him warm and generous in personal encounters, but outside of his family and a small circle of intimates he could appear cold, hyper-rational, unyielding, and intimidating. I have tried to keep both facets of Laskin in view but the focus on his public career inevitably gives precedence to his formal and assertive side.

This division between a tough, businesslike public demeanour and a more sensitive private side revealed only to family and close friends was a common feature of twentieth-century masculinity. Laskin's lack of self-revelation was rooted both in his status as a Jewish outsider for much of his life, and in his very masculine persona.[10] From the moment when he first emerges in the public record as a high school sports hero and public speaker in Fort William, his masculine qualities are in the forefront. He is tough, confident, competitive, a rugged individualist. As a scholar he early on developed an aggressive analytical style, to which he would later add strong flourishes of irony and sarcasm. His combative nature was forever burned into his public image when he, Cecil Wright, and John Willis resigned in protest from Osgoode Hall Law School as a result of their conflict with the benchers of the Law Society of Upper Canada. From this point on, Laskin was able to add personal courage to his list of masculine attributes, and to overcome a certain stigma he encountered as a result of his decision not to volunteer for the war effort. His reputation as an alpha male was entrenched even further after his sensational report for the Canadian Association of University Teachers on the firing of Professor Harry Crowe from Winnipeg's United College in 1958, which the press covered as if it were a gladiatorial contest between university governors and the professoriate.

Laskin's masculine identity was also framed by his Judaism. In Toronto, he had to confront a number of often contradictory stereotypes of Jewish males: they could be pushy and loud, but also too passive, too sensitive, too effete and bookish. Laskin had ambitions beyond the established network of Jewish fraternities, law firms, and social clubs, but gaining acceptance in the Gentile world was not an easy task in the 1930s and '40s. By adopting a confident demeanour of North American Anglo masculinity, oriented around sports, emotional reserve, and hard work, Laskin was able to negotiate the obstacles to successful integration. His outsider status as a Jew reinforced his tendency to separate his public persona and his private life. There was nothing to be gained by speaking to Gentiles about your background or family life; such talk would only tend to reinforce an impression of difference and possibly reveal something that could be used against you later on. This habit became deeply ingrained. Even after Laskin became chief justice, when there was considerable public curiosity about him, and Laskin himself was encouraging the media to take an interest in both himself and the Court, he would not speak directly about his own past. A long feature article in *Maclean's* in July 1974 gained all its information about Laskin's youth from his brother Saul. Through a kind of fraternal ventriloquism, Laskin could communicate to the public without putting himself on the record. He would speak a little more openly with Jewish publications, such as the *Canadian Jewish News*, which avidly claimed him as a Jewish hero towards the end of his life. But even there one has the sense he is telling the interviewer what he thinks the audience wants to hear.[11]

It was not just the Gentile world in general that Laskin had to negotiate, however, but the world of the legal profession, which presented conflicting codes of masculine behaviour. Although often highly competitive in their one-on-one interactions, lawyers' collective self-identity in the first half of the twentieth century still focused on the ideal of the lawyer-gentleman. (Female lawyers were still such a rarity that their lack of fit with this ideal could be safely ignored, and it is worth recalling that Laskin experienced the legal worlds of student, professor, arbitrator, and judge as almost entirely male preserves.) Christopher Moore characterizes the governors of the Law Society of Upper Canada in this era as 'the last patricians,' and notes the continuing influence of prominent Anglophiles in setting the tone for lawyers in the province.[12] The essential attribute of the gentleman was, to put it baldly, that he did not sweat too much. He should not be seen to strive, nor to compete too obviously, nor should he be overly concerned with money. John Cartwright, known as 'gentle John,' epitomized this code of behaviour, both as a lawyer and as a judge. Laskin worked closely with him on various human rights cases in the 1940s, before Cartwright's appointment to the Supreme Court of Canada in 1949, and succeeded to the vacancy created when Cartwright retired as chief justice in 1970. Gérald Fauteux, Laskin's immediate predecessor as chief justice of Canada, represented the francophone manifestation of this ideal: *le gentilhomme parfait*. Such an ethos tended to assist those who were already well established through family connections or seniority, and to work against those, such as Laskin, who lacked such advantages.

Although somewhat insulated from these expectations as an academic, Laskin nonetheless seemed able to straddle their inconsistent demands. He was a hard-working, competitive North American male but at the same time displayed a certain sense of decorum and demanded civility from those with whom he interacted. Laskin's reputation for honesty and integrity perhaps helped him to transcend this dialectic, along with his transparent concern for the disadvantaged. When he was appointed to the bench, he tended to emphasize the gentlemanly side of his persona, and to reinterpret his past as a rather bland story of merit duly recognized from which all trace of personal ambition and striving was effaced. There was some truth in this account with regard to his initial appointment to the Ontario Court of Appeal, which neither he nor his friends had sought out. The government of the day had come to him, for reasons of its own. But Laskin's career as a whole was characterized by an intense drive for recognition as part of his quest to reshape Canadian law and through it, Canadian society. There is nothing objectively wrong with this, but as he ascended through the ranks of the judiciary, Laskin felt it would reflect badly on him to admit it. And he was probably right. Canadians have traditionally not responded well to stories of personal ambition rewarded. We seem to prefer tragic failures or quirky, unexpected successes.[13]

In spite of his attempt to project a gentlemanly aura while on the bench, at times Laskin's competitive side reasserted itself. The common denominator in his public confrontations with Chief Justice Wilbur Jackett of the Federal Court, with Justice Thomas Berger of British Columbia, and with his old academic rival William Lederman seems to be a sense of threat on Laskin's part. When faced with men whose positions were at odds with his own but apparently attracting some public or professional support, Laskin seemed to lose the sense of decorum he normally prized, and to lash out in a manner quite inappropriate for someone in his position. Some have attributed Laskin's clash with Berger to his illness, but I do not believe illness to have played a major role, even though his health had begun to decline by then. Rather, the Berger affair can be explained as part of the larger pattern I have just described.

It was commonly said after Laskin's death that he would be better remembered if he had retired several years before he did. In not doing so, he exhibited a very human flaw, that of believing one is indispensable. But it would be wrong to dwell on those final years to the exclusion of all that went before. Few people have contributed to the public weal for so long and in so many different capacities as Bora Laskin. If I have succeeded in capturing even a small part of that contribution, I will be content.

PART I

Starting Out

1

The Lakehead

Thwack! The baseball soared into the summer sky. Spectators craned their necks and shaded their eyes against the sun, trying to follow the arc of the vanishing sphere. Bora 'Home-Run' Laskin paused, tried to locate the ball in the vast expanse of blue, slowly released his bat, and began to lope around the dusty diamond. He had just hit the longest home run in the history of Fort William.

Many years later law professor Harry Arthurs visited the Lakehead. He asked his taxi driver to pass by the Laskin furniture store, now run by Saul Laskin, who was soon to be the first mayor of the new city of Thunder Bay. Did the cabbie remember Saul's brother Bora Laskin? He paused, then replied: 'Oh yeah, I knew Bora. He was a helluva baseball player. I wonder whatever happened to him?'[1]

In 1906 twenty-five-year-old Mendel Laskin stepped off the train in Winnipeg after a long and arduous journey halfway around the world from his home in Russia. He spoke little English and had never been outside Russia. Fortunately, the strangeness of the New World was tempered by the burgeoning Jewish community then establishing itself in Winnipeg's North End. Only a few hundred individuals in 1901, the community now numbered some six thousand. It would swell to ten thousand by 1910, a tenth of the Canadian Jewish population. Mendel soon found employment in a scrap metal yard, where he worked for fifty cents a day. It was not much, but enough to sustain himself and to put some money aside to bring his intended bride to join him. After long tiring days at work Mendel could at least relax briefly with his own people, who spoke his language, practised his religion, and ate his kind of food. And he could dream of his future under these endless new skies, where the burden of anti-Jewish laws and prejudice lay less heavily than in his homeland.

Mendel Laskin's life history was similar to that of hundreds of thousands of his fellow Jews who fled to the New World to escape persecution in the Old. The origins of this epic migration lay in imperial Russia's efforts to deal with its 'Jewish Question.' No sooner had it expelled its tiny native Jewish population in 1742 than it acquired some 400,000 Jews as a result of the partitions of Poland in 1772, 1793, and 1795. In order to prevent this 'foreign' group from spreading throughout the empire, successive tsars established a zone called the Pale of Settlement to which Jewish settlement would be restricted. This vast rectangle, bounded by the Baltic provinces, the Black Sea, the European border, and the Urals, was home to 95 per cent of Russia's Jews and perhaps half of all Jews in the world by the end of the nineteenth century. Outside it, Jewish activities were highly regulated, but even inside it restrictions could be onerous. By the mid-nineteenth century, a spate of liberal reforms began to ease the plight of the Jews and other oppressed groups. On his accession to the imperial throne in 1856 Tsar Alexander II exempted Jews from military service, ending his predecessor's practice of conscripting Jewish boys at age twelve in a clumsy attempt at forced assimilation. Within a few years he emancipated the peasantry, introduced wide-ranging reforms in the courts and the professions, and removed some of the major restrictions on Jewish social and geographic mobility. Jews could now qualify for the legal profession and some Jewish mechanics and craftsmen could circulate freely beyond the Pale. At last this vast empire seemed to be moving slowly in a more enlightened direction.[2]

The assassination of Alexander II by a group of revolutionaries in 1881 abruptly halted this flirtation with liberalism, and unleashed a major reaction. Alexander III began to dismantle his father's reforms, and the Jews were scapegoated in a wave of pogroms that swept across Russia that year. After several decades of relatively harmonious relations with their neighbours, this violent persecution came as a shock. In its wake, many Jews began to emigrate; the few who found their way to the small settlement of Winnipeg in 1882 were part of this first group of refugees. Into this tense and dangerous atmosphere Mendel Laskin was born in the Pale province of Mogilev (now Belarus) in 1881. Mendel and his siblings would emigrate in their turn when they reached adulthood, but in the meantime life went on. Mendel received a traditional Jewish education, becoming literate in Yiddish and Hebrew. In 1894, the same year as his bar mitzvah, a new tsar came to the throne of all the Russias, Nicholas II. Many Jews were expecting a relaxation of restrictions after the iron reign of Alexander III, but they were to be gravely disappointed in this last scion of the house of Romanov.

As Mendel reached young manhood, networks of kin and acquaintance were mobilized in the usual way to find him a bride. The Zingel family belonged to the Jewish community in nearby Latvia, then the Russian province of Livonia. Although outside the Pale of Settlement, the Jews of Riga and its environs were exempt from most of the restrictions of tsarist rule.[3] They could own land, for example, and according to the family story the Zingels were farmers near Riga.[4] It was decided – what role the young couple had in this process is unclear – that Bluma Zingel and Mendel Laskin would suit one another. Bluma, born in 1886, was somewhat younger than the groom-elect, and marriage was out of the question in any case until Mendel had completed his stint in the army. Universal military conscription had been imposed in 1874, but length of service varied according to one's education and literacy in Russian. Those educated in Russian-language secondary schools were obliged to serve only two or three years, while those with no schooling in Russian had to serve as long as six or seven years. In 1886 the proportion of Jewish students attending Russian secondary schools in the Pale of Settlement was limited to 10 per cent while outside it they were limited to 3 to 5 per cent. If Mendel received none of his education in Russian, as seems likely, he faced a lengthy period of military service when he entered the tsar's army at age twenty-one in 1902. Evading enlistment was not a realistic option, as heavy fines were imposed on the families of those who did not report for service. Mendel later told his children that he played the cornet in the army band, but spared them the grim details of his military career.[5]

The year 1905 was a portentous one in Russian history for anyone with a taste for prophecy. In the war between Japan and Russia over their respective influence in Manchuria, the emergent island empire dealt the continental one a stunning defeat, capturing Port Arthur (then leased by the Russians from China) and destroying Russia's Baltic Fleet. Meanwhile, a near-revolution bubbled on the domestic front. A young

Vladimir Lenin accurately linked the two events, predicting that 'the capitulation of Port Arthur is the prologue to the capitulation of tsarism.'[6] In one of those ironies that seemed to be lost on Russia's autocrats, the Russian state expelled the indigenous Jews of Port Arthur in 1903, then sent 30,000 conscript Jews from European Russia to defend a city in which they would not have been allowed to settle.[7] The usual accompaniment to political turbulence in Russia resumed its course: pogroms spread across the empire again, stimulating another mass exodus of Jews. While 37,000 (mostly Russian) Jews had emigrated to the United States in 1900, more than 125,000 did so in 1906, and over 6,000 Russian Jews entered Canada that year.[8] This time Mendel decided to join the growing tide. According to the family story he deserted from the tsarist army and set out eastward on the long sea and rail route to the heart of another continent.

Once in Winnipeg, Mendel's hard work paid off: within a year or two he had saved enough for Bluma's passage. They married upon her arrival in Winnipeg, and about 1908 set off for the Lakehead.[9] Winnipeg had a large Jewish population, but it was inundated with refugees for whom there was little work. Mendel and Bluma must have felt that the rapidly growing community at the head of Lake Superior, then near the height of its pre-war boom, offered better opportunities for economic advancement. The family story is to the effect that they were attracted to the Lakehead by the possibility of grants of Crown land, but if so, they were to be disappointed. The land around the twin cities of Port Arthur and Fort William had been granted away decades before. When Mendel acquired land in due course, he purchased it in the usual way, from other individuals or from the Hudson's Bay Company.

Human settlement at the Lakehead was very old and very new. The spot where the Kaministiquia River emptied into Lake Superior had long been known to the aboriginal peoples of the region. It was the hub of a network of transcontinental trade routes that pre-dated European arrival by several millennia. Tools and weapons fashioned from Lakehead copper six thousand years ago have shown up in archaeological sites in a vast arc from the St Lawrence River to the Saskatchewan River. These commercial relations are also attested to in the oral traditions and ancient birchbark scrolls maintained by the descendants of the original inhabitants, the Anishinabeg or Ojibwa people (known as Chippewa in the United States). When the French and English began to penetrate the area in the second half of the seventeenth century in search of furs, they followed the same trade routes traditionally used by the native peoples. As the English established a presence in the Hudson Bay area, assisted by the royal charter granted by Charles II in 1670 to the Hudson's Bay Company, the French carried on the fur trade in the upper Great Lakes. Daniel Greysolon Dulhut established a trading post in 1679 near the mouth of the Kaministiquia, on the site of the later town of Fort William, and used it as a site for further westward expansion. After the defeat of the French in 1760, British traders took over this network of outposts (though Fort Kaministiquia itself had been abandoned by that point), often operating in partnership with the French who were familiar with the trade.

One of the first fur traders to operate under British auspices in the region was Ezekiel Solomon, a Jewish trader who had supplied British troops in New York. Established at Michilimackinac by 1761, by 1780 he controlled the trade in a large area around Lake Nipigon. A small-pox epidemic in 1782–3 devastated the aboriginal population, destroying Solomon's business and changing forever the balance of power in the region.[10] Earlier political and economic relations between native and newcomer had been on a basis of relative equality. A weakened Ojibwa people henceforth had to be content with a subordinate role. They opposed the plan of the Northwest Company to relocate its main entrepot to the site of the old French trading post at Kaministiquia, but were unable to prevent the move. In a placatory gesture, the company agreed to purchase an area of ten by twelve miles at the mouth of the river from the Ojibwa for three hundred pounds. It constructed a new trading post there in 1803, naming it Fort William after William McGillivray, the company's chief director.

Until 1821, when the Northwest Company merged with the Hudson's Bay Company, Fort William was the crux of the Canadian fur trade. Every spring trade goods arrived from Montreal via canoe, while company factors brought in the tons of pelts purchased over the course of the previous winter at outposts in the northwestern hinterland. The factors then returned to their lonely stations with renewed supplies, leaving the furs to be transported on to Montreal over the inland route. After the merger, this route was mostly abandoned for the James Bay route through York Factory favoured by the Hudson's Bay Company. In the wake of Fort William's decline the trading post was closed in 1883, the last remaining store demolished in 1902 to make way for a Canadian Pacific Railway terminal. Meanwhile, the Ojibwa had lost much of their influence after they adhered to the Robinson-Superior Treaty of 1850, by which 19,000,000 acres of land were surrendered.[11]

The railway that brought Mendel and Bluma Laskin to Fort William opened a new chapter in the history of the region. The area's mineral and forest resources could now be transported to southern and western markets, while prairie wheat could be shipped by rail to the Lakehead and loaded on ships for transportation around the world. By 1909, three major railways – the Canadian Pacific, Canadian Northern, and Grand Trunk Pacific – connected the Lakehead to the Atlantic and Pacific coasts. Fort William and Port Arthur had been incorporated as towns in 1892, shortly after completion of the CPR. Both were recreated as cities in 1906 and 1907 respectively, as Laurier-era optimism about the future growth of the 'Chicago of the North' reached its apogee. Mendel and Bluma must have absorbed some of the spirit of boosterism evident in *Henderson's Fort William City Directory for 1907*: 'It is one of the most interesting sights in the country to travel up the river past the giant cranes taking the coal from the large lake freighters, along the line of mammoth grain elevators, by the long docks piled high with steel rails for railway expansion, past the line upon line of cars awaiting their turns to hurry west to supply a waiting country or to speed eastward with the wealth of the Great West.' Not to be outdone, Port Arthur's publicists boldly predicted 'the development of the city to be one of the largest centres of Canada.' They lauded the municipally owned water-works, electrical supply, telephone and street railway systems, which were indeed pioneering achievements in Canada, before alluding to the city's egalitarian ethos: 'This prosperous city is democratic in all things – there is no aristocracy, and no hoarding of wealth – her people have faith in the future of the place, and have worked in unison to make it what it is, the "Queen City of Ontario."'[12] In spite of this supposedly democratic outlook, the city went wild when Queen Victoria's youngest son Arthur, the Duke of Connaught, visited the city named after him on his first rail tour as governor-general of Canada in August 1912.[13] The duchess noted in her diary: 'Very much impressed by marvellous growth and development of this place – beautifully laid out – golf course in construction and Country Club and showing signs everywhere of rapid development and prosperity.'[14] The duchess's sunny vision was not so much wrong as blinkered: she was shielded from the ethnically tinged class conflict and substantial pockets of poverty that plagued an industrializing Lakehead.

The railway not only brought resources in and out of the Lakehead, it also funnelled in an entirely new population. The population mix of the fur trade era – Anglo-Celtic, French-Canadian, and Ojibwa, with much intermarriage between white men and native women – was soon over-laid with a crazy quilt of European ethnicities. Mendel and Bluma joined an influx of Finns, Norwegians, Czechs, Slovaks, Germans, Ukrainians, Poles, Rumanians, Greeks, and Italians. Their muscle and sinew laid the rails, felled the trees, built the roads, shovelled the grain and coal, mined the iron, and erected the factories upon which the economy of the new cities was founded. The population of Fort William was 2,000 when the town was incorporated in 1892. By the time of the Laskins' arrival it was 12,500, and it would nearly double again by 1914. With Port Arthur home to about 15,000 in 1914, the Lakehead could boast a population larger than many cities in southern Ontario.[15]

This surge in population created an instant demand for food. Max Laskin – once in Fort William, Mendel would adopt the anglicized version of his first name – was involved mostly in the provisioning trade during his first dozen years at the Lakehead. He and Bluma rented a house in semi-rural Westfort at the southern edge of the city, near the CPR rail line which followed the north bank of the Kaministiquia River.[16] The south bank of the river rose almost vertically to form Mount McKay, which dominated the city like a Norman fortress. At Westfort Max and Bluma kept some cows and chickens, but Max operated principally as an itinerant middleman, a New World version of Tevye in *Fiddler on the Roof*. He collected milk, eggs, butter, and cheese from local farmers and resold them both retail and wholesale. Initially described in local records as a 'dairyman,' by 1913/14 he is a 'cattle dealer' and 'meatcutter.' By 1910/11 Max had saved enough to make his first forays into the real estate market, purchasing a small rural property, also in Westfort, for $1,500. Although Max was making some progress, life at Westfort was arduous and isolated, especially for Bluma. Her husband's peregrinations with horse and cart meant long lonely days for her, and neighbours were few. There were as yet no sewage or water facilities or garbage collection services in this part of the city. More Jewish families were moving into the Lakehead by 1910, but they did not live in this raw transitional zone between city and country. Two little girls born to Max and Bluma during this time did not survive, and these tragic losses only added to Bluma's sense of isolation.[17]

The neighbourhood, criss-crossed by two major railways, was industrializing rapidly. In 1912 the Canadian Car and Foundry Company bought up all the vacant lots in the vicinity, as well as the few lots occupied by tenants. The Laskins were uprooted, but Bluma at least, now pregnant again, undoubtedly welcomed the move. They rented a house in the city proper, at 325 Brodie Street South. Now they were at the heart of bustling Fort William at the zenith of its pre-war prosperity. Just two blocks north, $50,000 of Carnegie money had endowed the proudly classical edifice housing the new city library. The new Orpheum Theatre provided an opulent venue for vaudeville acts, soon to be superseded by silent films. A new city courthouse boasted an imposing pillared façade, while the massive red-brick YMCA and several large new commercial buildings gave Fort William a skyline to supplement its serried ranks of grain silos.

More important for Max and Bluma than any of these structures was the erection of the city's first synagogue, just a fifteen-minute walk away from their Brodie Street residence. Services began in 1908 in a small building in the east end of Fort William, and in Port Arthur in a private home, but these had been too far for the Laskins to reach on foot as required by Orthodox tradition.[18] They had been among the earliest Jewish settlers in the city when they arrived in 1908; the 1901 census recorded only thirteen Jews at the Lakehead. In 1909 a group of families coalesced into the Shaarey Shomayim congregation, purchased land for a small cemetery, and began planning to build a place of worship in the east end of Fort William. It was a synagogue on the Orthodox plan, with the women seated separately in a screened-in balcony, so as not to disturb the prayer of the men seated below. The congregation was fortunate in being able to attract a rabbi, Abraham Katz, who could also serve as *shochet*, a butcher versed in the ritual slaughter of animals required by Orthodox tradition. By the fall of 1912, when the Laskins attended Rosh Hashannah services at the new synagogue, the *Daily Times-Journal* reported that there were about one hundred Jewish families in Fort William, and some one hundred visitors were also expected for the two-day celebration.[19] For Max and Bluma, joy at finally being able to worship in a proper synagogue was mingled with apprehension about the child to come, now close to term. Having buried two children already in their new country, they yearned for a healthy baby.

Max and Bluma's eldest son was born on 5 October 1912, a Saturday, the Jewish Sabbath. The weather was fair and warm, another propitious sign. Presumably the child was born in the house at 325 Brodie, since only dire emergency caused a woman to deliver her baby in a hospital at this time. The baby boy would have been named at the *bris* ceremony on the eighth day after his birth, when he was circumcised. Naming is important in all cultures, but in Jewish tradition it is enmeshed in a particularly dense thicket of cultural prescriptions. Every child must have a Hebrew name, on the theory that heavenly administration is monolingual: at the time of the resurrection, the dead will be called only by their Hebrew names. In the diaspora, however, children are also given a name in the local language for official purposes, which may or may not be a simulacrum of their Hebrew name. The Midrash teaches that 'one should examine names carefully in order to give his son [sic] a name that is worthy, so that the son may become a righteous person, for sometimes the name is a contributing factor for good as for evil.' Among the Ashkenazim, the Hebrew name is often that of a deceased relative, but it need not be. In the Middle Ages the Jews adopted the Christian practice of naming children after angels. Raphael, Michael, and Gabriel were those most commonly invoked, and among these Raphael ('God shall heal') was a particular favourite. The name was engraved in amulets worn by pregnant women in the hope of producing a healthy child. A child of hope after searing loss, the little boy would be named Raphael.[20]

The Hebrew name Raphael is often rendered as Ralph in English, but the new Laskin child would come to be known by the name Bora. There are differing family stories about who decided upon this name, but agreement that it derived from Senator William E. Borah of Idaho. A senator since 1907, Borah was a pillar of the Progressive movement in the pre-war years and perceived as a defender of the Jewish people in the United States in the early twentieth century.[21] One story is that in elementary school some childhood friends found the young Laskin a little self-important and said, 'Look, there goes Senator Borah' as he strutted by. Such precocity strains credulity, and the second story is more plausible. It attributes the name to Bluma, who admired the senator so much that she began calling her son by the same name. This accords with what we know of Bluma's empathy for the poor and oppressed and her lively interest in the world around her. In most respects Borah lived up to Bluma's heroic image of him. He fought against large corporate monopolies, and opposed the confirmation of Louis Brandeis on the Supreme Court because he judged him insufficiently concerned about corporate power in America. He later regretted his decision, and in 1932 he was a strong supporter of Benjamin Cardozo's elevation to the Supreme Court to replace Oliver Wendell Holmes. It is said that President Hoover handed Borah a list of possible candidates for the vacancy in descending order of preference with Cardozo's name at the bottom. Borah replied that 'your list is all right but you handed it to me upside down.'[22] Later, however, Borah opposed changes to the immigration laws that would have made it easier for Jewish refugees from Nazi oppression to enter the United States.

One thing is certain: Bora Laskin himself did not use Raphael, his 'official' name, and always referred himself as Bora. He attracted a variety of nicknames in high school and university, but none of them stuck into adulthood. When a professor asked him for his full name for some official purpose in 1937, Laskin replied that he had 'only one Christian [sic] name' – Bora.[23]

Children with unusual names are said to 'grow into them,' and something like that happened to Bora Laskin. His unique name seemed to mark him out for some special destiny. Rather than sheltering behind a more familiar name, as he might have insisted upon, from an early age the Laskins' eldest son embraced this distinctive identity with its whiff of mystery. It was a mixed blessing, short and euphonious, to be sure, but also liable to be taken for a woman's name. In later years Professor Laskin would get occasional letters addressed to Miss Cora Laskin, and in 1973 an Israeli news correspondent unfamiliar with the name reported the appointment of Canada's first Jewish and female chief justice: 'Dora' Laskin.[24]

Even as Max and Bluma were founding their own family, they were helping Max's siblings to come to Canada. Brother William came out around 1909 and settled in the town of Goodeve in southeastern Saskatchewan. The youngest brother of the family, Bures, was twenty years younger than Max, born in 1901. Sent out alone by boat in 1911 to join his brothers, he was prevented by the authorities at Glasgow from proceeding until an adult could be found to accompany him – a process which took fourteen months. When he finally arrived, he went on to stay with brother William in Saskatchewan. Bures settled in Humboldt, where he ran a general store and served as mayor of the town for ten years.[25] Max's sisters Rose and Sonia would also leave Russia, settling with their husbands in Vancouver and Chicago respectively, while Bluma would assist her own sister and several cousins to come to Canada.

Just over a year after Bora's birth, Max bought the home in which he and Bluma would raise their family. It was a large two-storey frame home at 138 Heron Street, at the corner of McKenzie and Heron in the east end of Fort William.[26] The area was initially developed to house CPR workers after the railway moved its operations from Westfort to this area. In fact, the Laskins bought the house from two brothers who were brakemen for the CPR. It was not inexpensive at $3,100, but a major attraction of the site was its location next door to the synagogue and its proximity to Ogden Street School. The new Laskin home was just a block from the shops of Simpson Street, a major artery paralleling the lake but cut off from it by rail lines. A little to the north were the coal docks and finally, row upon row of the port's iconic grain elevators. While there were some Jewish families in the vicinity, it was not a Jewish neighbourhood, but rather a polyglot community of people of French-Canadian, Swedish, Polish, Finnish, Ukrainian, Slovak, and Hungarian origins, as well as considerable numbers of Anglo-Celtic households. Other parts of Fort William were more ethnically homogeneous – there were whole neighbourhoods of Italians, Slovaks, Finns, and Ukrainians, for example – but this part of the east end was 'a little United Nations,' as Bora's younger brother Saul later remembered it. Over time it would become more solidly 'ethnic' as the Anglo-Celtic families slowly moved out and were replaced by others of various European origins. By the time Bora left to attend university, there would be virtually no English names left in the neighbourhood.

The respectable Anglo-Celtic population were ambivalent about the strong alien presence in their city. A 1913 social survey of Fort William by representatives of the Methodist and Presbyterian churches defined the 'immigrant problem' as insufficient Canadianization of adult immigrants at one point, only to laud the public library at another for providing lists of foreign-language books to a variety of ethnic groups. Discussion of the squalid living conditions of the Finnish colony settled near the coal docks was aimed partly at obtaining better sanitation and housing, but implicitly placed the blame for the Finns' substandard housing on their way of life.[27] The local English-language newspapers played an important educative function, describing the customs and traditions of various ethnic groups on the occasion of their festivals or religious holidays. After the infamous *Komagata Maru* incident, when a boatload of Sikhs was turned away from Vancouver in 1912, the *Daily Times-Journal* lamented that 'not a little prejudice [towards] Great Britain's eastern subjects' had been shown, and urged Canadians to give 'the most kindly and attentive hearing' to those presenting the Indians' point of view.[28]

Faraway Indians were one thing, local Indians another. If the Lakehead could claim with some justice to represent an ongoing transition from cultural hierarchy to cultural mosaic, that mosaic was definitely made in Europe. The local native population existed on the furthest fringes of

Lakehead society. Mythical Indians dominated the landscape, while real ones were conveniently ignored. When Port Arthurians looked out at Lake Superior they saw a large peninsula known as the Sleeping Giant, resembling the profile of an Indian brave serenely floating on the water. For Fort William residents, Indian legends rather than political controversy swirled round Mount McKay, home to the remaining rump of the Fort William Indian reservation. Its heart, 1,600 acres on the north side of the river, had been expropriated by the Grand Trunk Pacific in 1905–6, forcing the relocation of some three hundred Ojibwa across the river.[29] They tried to mix casual labour at the docks and grain elevators with traditional hunting in the winter, but the combination proved unsustainable. Constant encroachment on the reservation and outlying areas made hunting increasingly difficult, while after the First World War a formalization of labour relations worked against casual labourers.[30]

In the purely cultural sphere, the leaders of Fort William society could be reasonably tolerant if not particularly inclusive. In matters of politics and labour, the immigrant population was perceived as more threatening.[31] A significant property qualification for voters and candidates helped to diminish the influence of the labouring and immigrant population in municipal politics, although Ward One, in which the Laskins lived, regularly voted Labourites on to city council. The interweaving of class and ethnicity gave a particular 'ethnic edge' to labour relations at the Lakehead. A bitter freight handlers' strike at Fort William in 1909 pitted Greek and Italian workers against CPR management. During the week of Bora Laskin's birth, Dominic and Niccolo Durenzo were on trial for a 'murderous assault' against Port Arthur police chief Joseph McLellan arising out of the CNR coal handlers' strike. The next year witnessed brutal confrontations between police and Canadian Car and Foundry workers in Fort William and street railway workers in Port Arthur.[32]

As the Laskins moved into their new home in the fall of 1913, the region was hit with the abrupt nationwide recession that ended the Laurier boom years. Large numbers of unskilled workers who had helped to build the factories were discharged upon their completion. When they left to seek work elsewhere they took their purchasing power with them. The new industries struggled to find markets, and many failed. The economy shuddered and chunked, like the trains passing along the waterfront when the brakeman tried to stop too quickly. When the war came a year later, it created many jobs elsewhere in the country but few in northwestern Ontario. The population of Fort William declined by a third between 1914 and 1917 and although the city recovered slowly in the 1920s, it would never again experience the heady days of the pre-war boom.[33]

This was not the most auspicious time to invest in real estate, but in 1914 Max bought a bare lot on a street a few blocks away and built a house on it with the aid of a three-thousand-dollar mortgage from the Canada Permanent Mortgage Corporation. Presumably the idea was that the rental income would help pay off the mortgage, but it never quite worked out that way and Canada Permanent would dispose of the property under its power of sale in 1930.[34] The property at Westfort also had to be given up in 1916 when Max could not meet the mortgage payments. Chastened by these early experiences, Max never again speculated in real estate.

Meanwhile, the Laskin family was growing. Charles was born in 1915, and a third son, Saul, in 1918. During the lean war years, the provisioning trade was not bringing in enough money to support the household adequately. According to Saul's account, it was Bluma who urged Max to enter a more remunerative line of business. In 1919 Max opened a furniture and dry goods store at 89 Cumberland Street in Port Arthur, a business he would run for the rest of his life. It is not clear why he chose Fort William's twin city, rather than a location closer to his own home. The commute was reasonably easy on the electric street railway – except that you had to change trains at the city limits, there being no through line connecting the two rival cities.

Port Arthur had emerged as a settlement in the 1860s with the discovery of silver nearby. It was perceived to be the less advantaged of the two cities in the early twentieth century: smaller, more working class in outlook, and less prosperous. Port Arthur and Fort William engaged in a no-holds-barred sibling rivalry for much of the twentieth century. The cities, only three kilometres apart, competed fiercely to attract industry, railways, and investment, and each developed totally separate municipal services and facilities. It was a point of pride for residents of one city to claim they had never set foot in the other. In 1926, when there was talk of establishing a local university affiliated with the University of Toronto or McMaster, professors were brought in to give a few classes on an experimental basis. When municipal elders could not agree where the infant institution should be located, the visitors were obliged to give each lecture twice, once in each city. They did not return. Max Laskin was unusual, living in one city and working in the other, but he and his family could never see what all the fuss was about. It was Saul Laskin who tirelessly advocated municipal union and ultimately became the first mayor of the united city of Thunder Bay in 1970.

A family photo taken about 1920 portrays the Laskins at this time of transition. It is suffused with anxiety – about looking right for the camera, certainly, but also about their position in the world. In their fine studio attire they appear prosperous, but nothing is guaranteed. Max works very hard to earn the modest income that supports them, and there is no safety net if he should become ill, if the economy should falter again, if the store should not succeed. Bluma and Max look wary, skittish. An attractive couple they are, he with his high forehead, finely arched eyebrows, and bushy moustache, she with her short dark curly hair and fair complexion. The parents and the two younger boys look obediently in the direction indicated by the photographer. Eight-year-old Bora looks intently in the opposite direction, his eye fixed on something unseen by the viewer. His stance is emblematic of his position in the family: while a dutiful and loving son, he will go his own way, his questing eye always on the far horizon.

The Ogden Street Public School attended by Bora, Charles, and Saul was meant to be the crucible in which the children of the immigrant masses would be acculturated in Canadian traditions and values. In 1917, according to the Board of Trade, '27 distinct dialects are spoken in [Fort William's] foreign quarters but, thanks to an efficient system and teachers, all these races are being rapidly Canadianized.'[35] This was a heavy responsibility to place on the shoulders of the dozen unmarried Anglo-Celtic women (supervised, of course, by a male principal and vice-principal) who taught at Ogden Street. In spite of an average class size of forty-three at city schools, they seem to have acquitted themselves well, in no small measure because parents of all backgrounds supported the school's efforts. The 1913 Social Survey noted with approval a truancy rate at Ogden of only 2 per cent, and this in spite of the fact that a majority of its students came from the very poor Finnish colony.

Bora received a good education at Ogden if his later success at high school is any indication, but like other Jewish children he also attended a second shift at Hebrew school, the Talmud Torah. While in public school they would study the Hebrew language and Jewish scripture from 4:30 until dinner time; in high school, they switched to a night shift, from 9:00 until 10:30 p.m., or even later. Bora thus became trilingual in Yiddish (his first language), English, and Hebrew. To say that education was highly valued in the Laskin household would be an understatement. Not only were Bora and his brothers encouraged in their academic pursuits, but Sundays in their house were given over to discussion as well as entertainment. Their father did not believe in corporal punishment: reason was the best way to deal with mistakes and transgressions once children were past infancy. Max subscribed to Yiddish newspapers from Winnipeg, Chicago, and New York and discussed the editorials with family and friends who might be visiting. A connoisseur of cantorial singing, he also ensured a musical education for the Laskin boys. Bora played the violin, Charles the piano, and Saul the clarinet, and all three might be prevailed upon to perform for visitors on a Sunday afternoon in the Laskin parlour, while Bluma passed around the coffee cake and glasses of tea.

Sunday was the only day of rest for Max, and the only day the children saw much of him. He was able to attend Friday evening services at the synagogue, but seldom went to Saturday morning Sabbath services with his family because of the demands of the store. In later years Bora Laskin sometimes spoke of the influence of his mother, but very seldom of his father. Laskin's emotional bond was clearly with Bluma, who was constantly present, while Max was a more distant, albeit respected, figure for his eldest son.[36]

Max rented the store premises for nearly twenty years from an expatriate English landlord who did not believe in maintenance. The building was not insulated, and the old box stove kept the place barely habitable during the fierce Lakehead winters. Max stumped about in boots and a camel-hair coat all day long. He sold new and second-hand furniture, and tools and work clothes for the hundreds of miners and lumbermen who streamed into the city on their riotous days off. They passed by Max's store on the way to the Hoito, the Finnish cooperative where all-you-can-eat meals were served bush-camp style at trestle tables for twenty-five cents.[37] Max worked long hours, often not returning until midnight. Nonetheless, he somehow found time to participate in communal affairs and in the broader community. An ardent Zionist, he was active in local societies that sought to assist the creation of a Jewish homeland in Palestine, and organized fund-raising events to relieve the suffering of Jews elsewhere.[38] With his knowledge of Russian and smattering of Ukrainian, he sometimes provided informal interpretation in court when charges against immigrant Slavs were heard.

The Jewish religion and way of life were of consuming importance for Max and Bluma, but their devotion was to the ideals and values of Judaism rather than dogma. Bluma constantly reached out to those in need in the community, and taught her children to do likewise. The needs of others sometimes took precedence over one's own, as Bora discovered when his bedroom was given over for two years to a Hebrew scholar in need of accommodation. Max and Bluma were not narrowly focused on the affairs of the Jewish community, but took an active interest in all that went on at the Lakehead. Bluma felt it was important for her children to understand the faith of the majority, and took them to the church services of various Christian denominations.[39] The Judaism of Bora Laskin's youth was a living faith, not a mere set of textual prescriptions.

Bora Laskin observed two rites of passage in 1925: his bar mitzvah, and graduation from Ogden Street School. The account of Laskin's bar mitzvah in Winnipeg's Yiddish newspaper, the *Israelite Press*, provides an indication of early professorial tendencies. 'The Bar Mitzvah recited the *maftir* very well. Then he delivered a forty-five minute sermon in Hebrew which greatly impressed the congregation.' Max and Bluma's prominence ensured a large attendance at the ensuing festivities held next door at their home. The Lakehead Jewish community functioned as a kind of extended family, and bar mitzvah ceremonies provided a means of communal self-affirmation as well as an opportunity to recognize and embrace members of the rising generation. At thirteen, young Bora's leadership skills were already in evidence, and he was an accomplished showman to boot. 'The Bar Mitzvah played "Hatikvah" on the violin accompanied by his younger brother and also delivered a fine speech. His father followed with a speech in Yiddish and the two younger brothers also spoke. Then the Bar Mitzvah spoke again (in Yiddish) thanking his mother and the guests, especially the ladies, were touched by this tribute.' Before the evening was over, the guests were reminded of their obligation to the Jewish homeland. Mr Kessler, president of the congregation, 'appealed to the guests to contribute thirteen trees in the Herzl Forest in [Laskin's] name and also to subscribe his name in the Golden Book. Money for these contributions was immediately raised. The party lasted till two in the morning.'[40] Bora's place in the local Jewish community was secure. As he entered high school, it remained to be seen how he would function in a rather more exclusive and demanding environment, far removed from the 'little United Nations' of Ogden Street School.

Most of Laskin's classmates ended their formal education when they graduated from Ogden, or at best after a year or two of high school. Figures for the 1920s do not seem to be available, but as late as 1948 over half of Ontario school entrants had dropped out by age sixteen, only 20 per cent completed grade twelve, and only 4 per cent went on to university.[41] There was no question about the Laskin boys, though: all three would complete high school and the two elder boys would go on to university.[42] The closest high school, a good twenty-minute walk away, was Fort William Collegiate and Technical Institute (FWCI). When the twin cities were in their expansive phase in the early twentieth century, each had invested in a stunningly impressive temple of higher education. Port Arthur housed its Collegiate Institute in an enormous Gothic stone pile perched atop the old Lake Superior shoreline. Fort William Collegiate possessed a monumental main entrance, with a neo-Gothic style stone arch surmounted by enormous fluted columns and pilasters topped by elaborate Corinthian capitals.[43] The High School Inspector for Ontario was pleased to note in 1925 that '[t]he building, as now completed, presents an attractive appearance, provides much needed accommodation, and is an eloquent testimony to the high regard in which secondary education is held in the community.'[44]

Concern about secondary education was not limited to the school's physical quarters. Virtually all the teachers had BA degrees and a number of them had MAs. Visiting university professors gave occasional lectures, and the school's aspirations were summed up in its motto *Agimus meliora* (let us do better). It was home to three different streams, the matriculant (aimed at university entrance), the commercial, and the technical, accommodating some 1,200 students in all.[45] The school may have been walking distance from Laskin's home, but in social and cultural terms it was a planet away from the densely populated ethnic quarter where he had been raised. The area was graced with large homes, ample lots, and wide, shaded streets. The students were almost exclusively of Anglo-Celtic background, with only three or four Jews and a smattering of 'ethnic' students in the matriculant stream in any given year. For the first time, Bora Laskin would be thoroughly exposed to the manners and mores of the Anglo-Celtic middle and upper classes. He not only adapted socially, but excelled academically and athletically in this new environment. Already, for reasons he himself could not explain fully, he had decided to become a lawyer. Later in life he would say only that he decided on his future profession around the age of twelve, 'perhaps influenced by the lawyers who acted for my father in legal matters.'[46]

In most things, students were expected to submit to the benign super-intendence of their peers in the two senior years. Those in the fourth and fifth forms (later known as grades twelve and thirteen) dominated the sports teams, the yearbook (known as the *Oracle*), the students' administrative council, and more generally, the social life of the school. For a fifth-form Bora Laskin, this was only as it should be. He observed in Burkean fashion that 'First Formers, Seconds and even Thirds know too little about affairs to be allowed active participation in matters of paramount interest to the whole Collegiate.'[47] The school yearbook gave short shrift to students in their first three years; only in his last two years of high school does Bora Laskin emerge with any clarity from the general student body. In his fourth year (1928–9) the *Oracle* described him as 'a rugby star [who] also plays basketball, in addition to his brilliant class reports. Sports Editor of the *Oracle*; he takes a consider-able interest in school affairs. Since he has fallen in love no more great achievements are expected of him.' The young lady in question re-mains, alas, unidentified. The fourth form was divided into two classes of thirty each, but they socialized together. Skiing and snow-shoeing parties to Shuniah and Point de Meuron were popular activities, as was dancing to the new jazz music deplored by Principal E.E. Wood as noisy and superficial.

Rugby was the most popular sport at the school, and Laskin was a half-back on the senior team when it won the city championship in 1929 and 1930. He and Sam Katz, the rabbi's son, also made a formidable defensive pair. The team celebrated the end of the 1930 season with a grand banquet at the Avenue Hotel, where Laskin made a presentation to coach H.F. Moran of 'a fine pen and pencil set, as a token of the high esteem with which he is regarded.'[48] In addition, he played basketball and in his final year joined the track team, where he competed in javelin, shot put and discus. Of average height at about five feet eight inches, Laskin had matured into a powerfully built natural athlete. 'He is keen on sports and has the physique that means prowess,' enthused the *Times-Journal*.[49] Two photos in the *Oracle* disclose different sides of a many-faceted young man. One, Laskin's official photo as *Oracle* editor, reveals a strikingly handsome adolescent, with his mother's full fea-tures and deeply set, sensitive eyes, wavy hair carefully brushed back from an intellectual brow. In a photo of the rugby team, by contrast, Laskin stares steely-eyed at the camera, hands on hips, aggressive, truculent. The competitive rugby player would always remain coiled beneath the façade of Laskin the legal intellectual, ready to spring when provoked.

Although well known locally for his triumphs on the track and the rugby field, it was on the baseball diamond that Bora Laskin made the greatest impression. The sport was enormously popular at the Lakehead. The week after Laskin was born, the headline in the *Times-Journal* was 'Montenegro declares war on Turkey' but above that was a banner with the real news: 'RED SOX WIN, 4 TO 3' in the first game of the World Series. The next year, a group of Fort William businessmen bought the St Cloud, Minnesota, professional baseball club franchise and entered Fort William in the Northern League, competing against teams from Winnipeg to Duluth. The First World War unfortunately brought an end to professional baseball at the Lakehead.[50] Laskin played softball for the Belmonts in the senior league for two seasons and baseball for the CNR team in his final year at FWCI. His presence was unusual: the sport was dominated by Anglo-Canadians, and Laskin had no Jewish or ethnic team-mates. The games at McKellar Park were well attended all during the hot Fort William summers and breathlessly written up in the local press. The exploits of 'Home-Run Laskin' at the bat, in left field, and on third base gave rise to an enduring Laskin legend at the Lakehead. Winter sports were never Laskin's favourites, however, and the Great White North held little appeal for him.

Bora Laskin exulted in competition, whether intellectual or athletic, and constantly pushed himself to the limit of his abilities. During his senior two years at high school he exerted himself as never before, juggling many commitments and excelling in all of them – setting the pattern for the rest of his life. Principal Wood encouraged the academic side of this talented young man, who graduated as class valedictorian. On top of his academic and sporting triumphs, Laskin edited the *Oracle* in his final year, participated in regional debating competitions, and took over the teaching at the Fort William Talmud Torah for two years after the sudden departure of its teacher. He was also president of the Young Judaea club, a Zionist youth organization, following in his father's footsteps in this regard. Max and Bluma fully supported their golden boy in all his endeavours, though Bluma sometimes thought he overdid it on sports.

For his brothers, Bora was definitely a hard act to follow. The nearly six years separating Saul from Bora allowed him to hero-worship his older brother without jeopardizing his own sense of identity. At first, according to his own account, Bluma treated Saul as a replacement for the little girls she had lost. When he started school he had a Buster Brown haircut and luxuriant curls. Brother Charles felt this was highly inappropriate and lopped off the offending hair, to his mother's chagrin. Although perhaps subject to less lofty expectations as the youngest child, Saul quickly became a mainstay for his parents as his older brothers went to university and established careers in Toronto and Winnipeg. He remained rooted in Thunder Bay and flourished. As the middle brother, a little more than two years younger than Bora, Charles did not have such an easy time of it. He seems to have taken refuge in denigrating his own abilities and playing the class clown. In fourth form at FWCI, 'Goggy' was known as 'IV-A's curly-haired fat man. He provides the amusement for the class. A bad man with the females. Distinguished by a high, shrill, feminine giggle. Sometimes answers to the name "unconscious."' In his final year he played rugby and basketball but did not achieve the heroic status of his brother. His classmates noted that he was 'extremely lazy, but can be quite clever when he wants to.' Charles overcame his high school image, graduated in commerce from the University of Toronto, and emerged as a handsome, stylish man. He would eventually settle into the clothing business in Winnipeg and later Toronto, but never sought the public career achieved by both his brothers. Three brothers, three very different personalities: earnest, over-achieving Bora; coolly urbane Charles; folksy and flamboyant Saul.

Bora Laskin's oratorical triumphs in his final year at Fort William Collegiate pointed clearly to a career in advocacy or politics. First he captured the gold medal in the intramural competition in public speaking. The finals were held in the evening and attracted a large crowd, as such events often did in the days before television. A ten-year-old boy in attendance that evening reminisced forty years later that the two most exceptional speakers he heard in his youth were Bora Laskin and J.S. Woodsworth, founder of the CCF. The lad was Douglas Fisher, later to become the CCF MP for the constituency and a columnist for the *Toronto Sun*.[51] Laskin's initial success made him eligible to enter the northern Ontario competition for the *Toronto Star* cup, which he won with a speech on 'Canada and Empire Free Trade.' On returning with the cup from the final round in Fort Frances, he 'was met at the CN station ... by members of the UPA fraternity of the collegiate institution who gave him a rousing reception.'[52]

Non-Christians and non-Anglos were in a definite minority at Fort

William Collegiate, but they seem to have been well accepted and integrated into the student body. Anti-Semitism appears not to have been a major problem for the young Laskins, who mixed easily and left no account of negative experiences in later interviews. One litmus test of this integration is that dating sometimes occurred between Jewish and Christian students, a practice highly discouraged in Canadian metropolitan centres. Peer respect came from a variety of sources, and Bora Laskin scored high in virtually all of them. He was widely admired by his classmates for his combination of academic excellence, sportsmanship, leadership ability, and outgoing personality, but he was not alone among those from outside the mainstream. Bernard Shaffer, a fellow Jew and future lawyer a year behind Laskin, was on the Students' Administrative Council, and student activities do not seem to have been the preserve of an Anglo-Celtic élite. FWCI students may have created 'fraternities' to mimic those they knew existed at university, but these were not chapters of existing fraternities and did not observe their racial and religious exclusivity. The emergent youth culture of the 1920s was more democratic, less inclined to judge people solely on the basis of ascribed characteristics, than earlier generations had been. Jazz (Laskin would be a lifelong Duke Ellington fan), dancing, mass sporting events, and films created new forms of sociability where young people could meet across class and religious lines in ways not previously possible.[53]

The year 1929–30 was one of unalloyed success for Bora Laskin. His academic, athletic, and oratorical successes had given him a public presence in Fort William unusual for someone of his age and background. He was one of the earliest of the first generation of 'New Canadians' to assume such a prominent leadership role in his community. Many others would follow, at the Lakehead and elsewhere in Canada, but in each local environment someone had to show that it could be done. At the Lakehead, Bora Laskin was that one. He was now ready to test himself in a larger pond, and relished the challenge. According to his own testimony later in life, he 'was attracted by the programme of the newly established department of law under W.P.M. Kennedy, [partly] because with my ... fairly respectable Grade XIII standing I was admissible to the second year of the honours programme instead of beginning in the first year.'[54] This decision caused him to set his sights on the University of Toronto rather than the University of Manitoba, which attracted many Lakehead students.

Bora's aspirations posed serious problems for the Laskin household.

By the summer of 1930 it was clear that the stock market crash of 1929 was not simply a passing cloud: the Depression was beginning in earnest. Already Max had lost his 'income' property to the finance company. How would his retail business endure when consumer spending power was starting to plummet? Charles had one more year at FWCI before he too would be ready for university. Saul was entering his last year at Ogden Street School. In a few years he would also want to attend university. Max and Bluma could not imagine how all this higher education was going to be paid for when the family resources seemed to be shrinking daily.

On the broader political scene, there were troubling signs on the horizon. That last summer in Fort William, a federal election was underway. On 28 July the Bennett Conservatives received a majority, and the Conservative incumbent at the Lakehead, Dr Robert Manion, was returned with an enhanced majority. A backlash against 'radical' immigrants and the unemployed was not far behind. While Bora Laskin was earning his oratorical spurs in April, the bodies of two Finnish union organizers were discovered in a shallow creek outside Port Arthur. John Voutilainen and Viljo Rosvall of the Lumber Workers Industrial Union had disappeared the previous November during a strike against the Pigeon River Timber Company. The condition of their remains suggested the possibility of foul play, but the coroner's jury ruled the deaths accidental. The lawyer for the union at the inquest was a man who would cross Laskin's path years later in Toronto: radical labour advocate J.L. Cohen.[55]

Another omen: the day after 'Home-Run Laskin slammed out a circuit cloud' in one of his last ball games of the season, the Fort William police commission decided that in future permits would be required for all parades, and required the Union Jack to be flown at them.[56] Parades of communists the previous year had alarmed some city residents, who raised questions about the legality of such demonstrations. As economic distress grew and protest movements emerged in response, police forces across the province began to crack down on dissent of all kinds, but particularly that with a communist flavour.

At the end of August Bora Laskin and a few classmates travelled to Hamilton to participate in the all-Ontario amateur track and field championship. The young athlete 'had tough luck in the intermediate discus, fouling what would have been the winning throw' and finishing third.[57] His team-mates did better, capturing a first and two seconds, but this minor setback was not enough to dampen Laskin's spirits. The British Empire games were being held at Hamilton during the same week, providing a source of excitement second only to the Olympics. And already the young collegian was enjoying the fruits of his new-found independence. Classes did not begin until the end of September, but Bora Laskin stayed in Toronto after the track meet rather than return home to the Lakehead. He would use those precious weeks to get the lay of the land in this exciting but somewhat intimidating metropolis.

Bora Laskin left Fort William with the confidence to aspire, the ambition to succeed, the discipline to achieve, and the independence of mind to pursue his own way. He was now ready to move on to greater challenges. His family and his community had provided him with the best start in life anyone could have. From his parents he received love, encouragement, and a strong awareness of his Jewish heritage. By their example in both business relations and daily life, Max and Bluma instilled in their sons a sense of ethics and altruism, and a hatred of injustice. Money was never the main thing for Max and Bluma; doing the right thing was, and people at the Lakehead revered them for it. Fortunately, at the Lakehead one could be a Jew and still participate fully in the larger community. No one stopped Laskin from exercising leadership in high school activities or on the local sports scene. His teachers urged him to go to university. His efforts were welcomed, his successes applauded in the local newspapers. The 'Chicago of the North,' Laskin would soon find, was more accepting of cultural diversity than the provincial capital. In Toronto, he would encounter a much more rigid social code than he was used to at home. Where he should live, which fraternity he should join, whom he should date, how he should behave in 'mixed' settings, all were subject to a very definite set of prescriptions. Perhaps the greatest lesson Fort William taught Laskin was that *it did not have to be that way*. Where the operative presumption in Fort William was one of cooperation between Jew and Gentile, in Toronto it was one of mutual avoidance and isolation. In spite of this tension, Bora Laskin took quickly to the city that would be his home for the next four decades and, in an emotional sense, for the rest of his life. Fort William always retained a certain place in his heart, but that place was filled with nostalgia rather than longing.

2

Law School

On Tuesday 23 September 1930 Bora Laskin made his way to the gloomy brick house at 43 St George Street, where he entered the second year of the honour course in law at the University of Toronto. The course had been created in 1924 by a professor in the department of political economy, W.P.M. Kennedy, and was somewhat unusual in the Canadian context. In all other provinces except Prince Edward Island and British Columbia, one or more universities had a distinct law faculty granting an LLB degree recognized by the local bar. The LLB degree was not yet required in those provinces in order to article and be called to the bar, but it was in fact held by a large majority of candidates seeking admission to the bar by the 1930s. The governing body of the Ontario bar, the Law Society of Upper Canada, did not recognize any law program except that run by its own proprietary law school, the Osgoode Hall Law School, attendance at which was compulsory. Thus the University of Toronto had created its law program in the faculty of arts, and in 1930 law had just been constituted as a separate unit within the department of political economy, with Kennedy as its chairman. The program was conceived as a joint arts and law course leading to an honours BA in law, with classes in philosophy, economics, history, and political science required alongside those in legal subjects.

All law classes were held in the old house at 43, then 45 St George Street, while students would attend other buildings on campus for their arts subjects. The facilities were primitive by later standards. Laskin remembered sitting on hard wooden kitchen chairs and writing on his knees because there were no desks.[1] Law classes were taught exclusively in the morning, and in the afternoon there might be lectures in other subjects. If not, students either studied at home or in the university library, as there was no library in the law building itself.

In spite of the small, virtually all-male classes, relations between students were cordial but not necessarily warm. Social life revolved more around college or fraternity than a student's classes or degree program, and religion was thus a predominant factor in delimiting social circles. Laskin had enrolled at University College, home to many Jewish students and some tepid Protestants. Jewish students had to be very careful about trying to strike up friendships with Gentiles, for fear of appearing pushy or forward. David Vanek, two years behind Laskin in the honour law course, described his Gentile classmates as 'good companions during incidental contacts at school, but [they] otherwise extended no association on a social basis.'[2] Laskin himself glossed over this aspect of student life in later interviews, referring to his classmates as 'good friends' and relationships in the department as 'very cordial,' but providing no details.[3] There was one other Jewish student in Laskin's year, Abe Acker from Guelph. Both were academically inclined and became good friends during these university years and later at Osgoode. Abe had been born at the Lakehead, where his parents knew the Laskins, but the family had moved to Guelph when Abe was a baby.[4] Among his Gentile classmates Laskin had most in common with a tall, lanky, cerebral student named Moffatt Hancock, who would also become a career law professor.

While intergroup relations in the law program may have been marginally better than those elsewhere on campus, relations between Jew and Gentile were chilly at best when Laskin arrived. Non-Jewish sororities banned Jewish men from attending their dances, reminiscent of the anti-miscegenation practices of the old South. 'It is notorious on the Campus,' observed the *Varsity*'s editors, 'that the Jewish students and the Gentile mix to an almost negligible extent. They belong to and meet in the same groups, and clubs, and societies; but cases of friendship are so rare as to excite comment.' The *Varsity*'s response to this state of affairs was to propose a separate Jewish college, hoping that 'recognition might in the end become acceptance.'[5] The proposal was made in good faith, but illustrates how integration of the two groups was felt to be totally unfeasible. Some writers even feared violence might erupt between the largely Jewish University College sports teams and those of other colleges.[6] Their fears were not far-fetched: sports rivalry would trigger the anti-Semitic riot at Christie Pits in 1933.

There were virtually no Jewish faculty, and Jewish students were beginning to ask why not.[7] Jewish women could not be hired by public school boards because they were thought to be undesirable role models, and similar objections were raised in the case of university lecturers. As a matter of law and social expectation the university acted *in loco parentis* to its students, giving the objectors considerable leverage. Jews were slightly under-represented in the university's general student population, but over-represented in some professional faculties, this being partly a function of their de facto exclusion from many careers in finance and banking. In spite of this, no formal quotas were placed on Jewish applicants, although informal exclusionary practices were attempted, particularly in medicine and dentistry.[8] Laskin would be fortunate to be taught by Jacob Finkelman, the university's first Jewish lecturer, hired just months before Laskin's arrival on campus. Their relationship began as one of mentor-apprentice and would end as a lifelong friendship.

Jewish students joined a variety of 'mixed' university clubs and societies, but the most important social institutions of the day, the fraternities and sororities, remained strictly segregated by religion. One of the first things Bora Laskin did in Toronto was to join one of the two, soon to be three, Jewish fraternities on campus, Sigma Alpha Mu.[9] In 1920 it had established a branch at the University of Toronto and by 1927 it had enough money to purchase a house at 8 Willcocks St.[10] Prior to the construction of university residences on a large scale, fraternities provided an indispensable source of affordable housing for students in North American cities.[11] They also provided an excellent means for out-of-town students to develop a circle of friends who could assist with their integration into university and city life, and ultimately, through the involvement of fraternity alumni,[12] into the employment market. Fortunately for aspirant lawyers, Osgoode Hall Law School was also considered a university for purposes of fraternity membership. Through their *fratres in aule Osgoode* Jewish law students at the University of Toronto could develop contacts to help them find articles and develop a clientele. Fraternity acquaintances would provide critical support to Bora Laskin during the early stages of his legal career, as well as some 'home-grown' entertainment. Fraternity brother Maurice Solway achieved fame as a violinist, and would later compose a 'Judicial Polka' for his friend. Laskin did not care for the silliness of fraternity etiquette, however, and resisted attempts to involve him in his fraternity in later life.[13]

Like Gentile fraternities, Jewish ones were also delimited by social class. The Pi Lambda Phi fraternity stood at the tip of the social pyramid. Sigma Alpha Mu came next. Founded at City College of New York in 1909, it was made up largely of Russian Jewish immigrants or their children and grew to become the largest Jewish fraternity in North America over the next twenty years. Those who were not accepted as 'Sammies,' as they were known, formed a branch of the Beta Sigma Rho fraternity on campus in 1932. Laskin also joined the Avukah Society, the only officially recognized Jewish organization on campus aside from the fraternities.[14] From the outset, Bora Laskin quickly became aware that life on campus, as elsewhere in the big city, was circumscribed by lines of ethnicity and class in spite of the uneasy surface egalitarianism of student life. Gender lines were important, too, but less obvious because of their seeming 'naturalness.' One would like to know what early impressions Laskin conveyed in the letters he apparently wrote in Yiddish to his father, but then again children tend to tell their parents what they want to hear in such missives.[15]

Laskin probably spent his first year in Toronto living at the fraternity house on 8 Willcocks Street. As the year 1931 wore on and the Depression began to bite deeper, his parents faced a difficult decision as they contemplated Charles attending university as well. The creative solution to their problem illustrated the extraordinary commitment to higher education among early-twentieth-century immigrant Jewry. The family home in Fort William would be leased out and Max would move into a rented room. Bluma and the three boys would move to Toronto where Bora would continue his studies, Charles would begin university, and Saul would attend high school at Harbord Collegiate.[16] Bora may have chafed at this sudden loss of independence, but he had little choice in the matter.

The family rented a flat at 378 Markham Street, near College Street, in the heart of the downtown Jewish enclave known as the Ward. In an area of large and solid single family homes, the Mulgrave Apartments still stand out as one of the few buildings in the area initially constructed as an apartment building. A long, rambling four-storey building, it held ten apartments in the 1930s. From here it was a pleasant walk to the law school, and later to Osgoode Hall. It would be home to the fatherless Laskin family until 1936, when Bora went to Harvard, Charles graduated from the University of Toronto, and Bluma and Saul returned home to Fort William. The move to Toronto allowed Bluma to become reacquainted with the Ackers. She would sometimes take the train to Guelph to visit Mrs Acker, where they no doubt shared their dreams about their brilliant boys. While at university Laskin returned with his family to the Lakehead to work during the long summer break. To cover his train fare he entered into an agreement with CN for a free berth in return for serving as an 'escort' to the cattle car, making sure the cattle were fed and watered.[17]

The Ward was an island of Yiddish culture in a very British city. Defined by Spadina on the east, Bloor on the north, Ossington on the west, and Dundas on the south, it sheltered most of the city's Jews, who were largely recent immigrants from eastern Europe and Russia. A trickle of Jewish immigration in the nineteenth century had left small clusters of English and German Jews more dispersed through the city. The first generation of East European Jews, used to an intense communal life in the Old World, found comfort in recreating it in the New. In the Ward you could read the daily *Yiddisher Zhurnal*, take in the smells wafting from the Jewish bakeries, and hear the bittersweet music of the *shtetl* on a summer night. Here was Jewish life on a scale such as Laskin had never experienced it in Fort William. It was exciting, but almost overwhelming to a young man used to a community where Jew and Gentile lived side by side. The Jews were by far Toronto's largest ethnic group in the 1930s, comprising 7.2 per cent of the city's population. A smattering of other ethnic groups such as Italians, Poles, and Ukrainians also inhabited this zone of the city, but in numbers none compared to the Jews.

There was safety in numbers, but geographic concentration had its drawbacks too. To the Anglo-Celtic majority the Ward symbolized a growing invasion by large groups of seemingly unassimilable aliens, who could be avoided physically but not imaginatively. Unlike the southern Europeans who seemed content with their assigned place in the class structure, second-generation Jews actively sought advancement on terrain the majority regarded as their own: the universities, professional associations, even the legislature. The immigrant generation of Jews was inured to a certain amount of anti-Semitism, having experienced much worse in the old country. Their children were less patient, determinedly seeking respect and equal treatment with Gentiles. Their quest, carried on with dignity but meagre success before the war, would drive Canada's rights revolution in the post-war era.

With the continuing dramatic decline in the birth rate of Anglo-

Canadians, the presence of a large Jewish community constantly nourished by immigration seemed all the more threatening. In the fall of 1930
R.B. Bennett's Minister of Immigration, W.A. Gordon, told the Toronto
Canadian Club that 'the past has revealed in a large measure an undisci-
plined encouragement of the entry into Canada of people, many of
whom I am afraid are incapable of being assimilated into and of understanding the social, the religious and political structure that has been
built up in our country.'[18] At the national level, the doors would be closed
to further immigration. At the civic level, Anglo-Celtic Toronto wanted
to shut its doors too, trying with varying degrees of success to maintain
exclusive spheres of social, professional, and cultural activity.

The Depression greatly exacerbated the tensions latent in the encounter of the Jewish minority with the Anglo-Celtic majority in the Queen
City. The Toronto in which Bora Laskin arrived at the end of the first
year of the Depression was an economic Goliath staggered by an unknown assailant's missile. Contemporaries struggled to understand
how boom had turned to gloom so quickly. The boosterism of the
Lakehead in the 1910s paled beside the civic bravado of 1920s Toronto.
In that decade the population increased from 600,000 to 825,000, and
the value of new construction doubled, from $25 million annually to
$50 million in 1928. The first generation of skyscrapers began to rede-
fine the city skyline. The completion of the thirty-four-storey Canadian
Bank of Commerce building in 1930 made it the tallest building in the
British Empire, but the value of new construction had plummeted to
less than $7 million by 1932. The loss of employment and spin-off
effects from reduced consumption were devastating. The panhandlers
who would become a fixture of urban life for the next decade were
already working the streets of Toronto as Laskin arrived.

Physically and economically the city was an integrated unit. A network of newly paved streets served growing numbers of automobiles,
and the merger of a tangle of private street railways produced a city-
owned one-fare system in 1923. Socially and ethnically, however, Toronto
was anything but a seamless whole. With 80 per cent of its people of
British origin, Toronto was known as the Belfast of Canada for its mix of
aggressive Orangeism, dour Presbyterianism, and fervent imperialism.
The motion 'Toronto is deserving of her reputation for intolerance' was
duly sustained by a vote of 211 to 56 at a Hart House debate in November 1929. Swings in public parks were padlocked on Sundays, and
Prohibition had only recently been tempered through the sale of spirits
in government-owned stores in 1927.

The Belfast label was appropriate in another way too. Toronto's Protestant majority was determined to dominate the city as their counterparts in northern Ireland lorded it over the Catholics. Toronto dowager Auntie Muriel in Margaret Atwood's novel *Life Before Man* is the perfect archetype of the Protestant elite. Auntie Muriel's personal Great Chain of Being puts God at the top, followed by Auntie Muriel herself and the Queen. 'Then come about five members of the Timothy Eaton Memorial Church, which Auntie Muriel attends. After this there is a large gap. Then white, non-Jewish Canadians, Englishmen, and white non-Jewish Americans, in that order. Then there's another large gap, followed by all other human beings on a descending scale, graded according to skin colour and religion. Then cockroaches, clothes moths, silverfish and germs.'[19] Auntie Muriel and those of her ilk were at the height of their powers in the 1930s, but ultimately they would prove more flexible and less unified than their Belfast counterparts in the face of continuing resistance to their project of rule.

The University of Toronto taught law courses in a desultory way in the nineteenth century, and established a faculty of law on paper in 1887, but as we have seen, until the 1920s there was no organized program. Authorities at the University of Toronto were not insensible to this gap in their curriculum. In a 1913 address to the Ontario Bar Association President Robert Falconer lamented that '[w]e have lost a very great deal by the fact that we have had no faculty of law. Many of our ablest men in arts are drifted off into another environment entirely; we lose a great deal of the contributory influence that comes from the strength and precision of men who have been highly trained, and whose very study stimulates intellect and power of thinking – and all the maturity of intellectual thought that gathers around the faculty of law has been lost to the University of Toronto.'[20] Falconer could not have known that the man who would begin to remedy this state of affairs at Toronto had arrived in Canada that very year from Britain. William Paul McClure Kennedy was, at first blush, a most unlikely candidate for the task. Born in Northern Ireland in 1879, he held three degrees from Trinity College, Dublin, where he studied English and history. For a quarter-century Kennedy pursued his interest in Tudor ecclesiastical history, culminating in his largest work, *Elizabethan Episcopal Administration*. Along the way, this son of an Ulster Presbyterian minister converted to Roman Catholicism; perhaps the fallout from that radical act propelled him to the new world. (He later shifted again, to the Anglican communion in

1922.) In 1913 Kennedy took up a position at St Francis Xavier College in Antigonish, Nova Scotia, then moved to St Michael's College at the University of Toronto in 1914. In 1924 he was charged with developing a curriculum in law in the faculty of arts. With the aid of a young professor named James Forrester Davison, replaced in 1927 by Norman A.M. MacKenzie, Kennedy put together an honours BA in law and an LLB program.[21]

Kennedy possessed undoubted intellectual gifts, but his success, and that of his law course, were also a function of his shrewdness and talent for promoting himself and his program. If Bora Laskin in far-off Fort William had heard about the honour course in law, Kennedy must have targeted his publicity extremely well; he was remarkably successful in attracting high-quality students and faculty to his program in the 1920s and '30s. Kennedy was also able to create a sense of excitement about the program by attracting a parade of high-profile visitors to the school, by his own active scholarship and that of his colleagues, and by the creation of the *University of Toronto Law Journal* in 1935. His support would be critical in launching Laskin's academic career.

Now about fifty years of age, Kennedy was a man of medium height, bald, ascetic, wiry. Champion billiards player, ecclesiastical historian, legal scholar, and constitutional adviser to the mighty, he topped off all these roles with a charisma that attracted many but left others sceptical. Like many people of a theatrical disposition, Kennedy was a hypochondriac who lived to an advanced age. As chair of the department, he was the sun around whom revolved three lesser planets. Two of these were Maritimers almost a generation younger than himself, both veterans of the Great War. Frederick Clyde Auld, from Canoe Cove, Prince Edward Island, possessed the dry wit one might associate with the Oxford-trained classical scholar that he was; he had joined the department the year before Laskin arrived and taught Roman law, jurisprudence, and various private law subjects. Norman ('Larry') A.M. MacKenzie, a child of the manse from Pugwash, Nova Scotia, had obtained degrees in arts and law from Dalhousie. As hearty and physically imposing as Auld was spare and austere, he had followed his passion for international law to the new International Labour Organization at Geneva for two years before joining Kennedy.[22]

Finally there was Jacob Finkelman, who had just joined the department that summer. Here was a man only five years Laskin's senior, with a very similar background. Born in Russia, Finkelman had come to Canada as an infant with his parents, who settled in Hamilton. One of the earliest graduates of Kennedy's program, he had gone on to Osgoode and was about to pursue graduate work at Harvard when Kennedy persuaded him to stay and teach. In recommending Finkelman to the president, Kennedy observed bluntly that '[h]e is not much to look at; but he is humble, gentlemanly, scholarly and has a facility of putting clearly his ideas, and of grasping the limitation of a subject.' Finkelman had a withered arm as result of childhood polio but neither his appearance nor his religion concerned Kennedy; the candidate was 'a Hebrew, [but] as far as I am concerned this is no objection.'[23] He was the first Jewish lecturer hired at Toronto and probably the first at any Canadian university. His initial, non-tenured lectureship did not create waves. By contrast, Kennedy's recommendation in 1934 that Finkelman be promoted to associate professor with tenure aroused opposition in some quarters of the board of governors on the ground of the candidate's religion. Kennedy dug in his heels, as did President H.J. Cody, and Finkelman got his professorship.[24] He would remain fiercely loyal to Kennedy until the latter's death.

An interesting, disparate, almost quirky group of men. None was a Torontonian. All were outsiders to the mainstream of Ontario society. And all were engaged in the common enterprise of trying to build up a department of law with a vision different from that of any existing Canadian law faculty, and from the Law Society of Upper Canada's professional school at Osgoode Hall. The Canadian law faculties outside Ontario modelled on Dalhousie (created in 1883) had been inspired by the American style of university legal education offered at Harvard, Columbia, and Michigan, where the acquisition of substantive legal knowledge and skills useful to the practising lawyer was accompanied by critical academic reflection on the law. The course at Osgoode Hall Law School concentrated on the former to the virtual exclusion of the latter.

Kennedy's vision was on the surface closer to the Oxbridge and Dublin tradition of legal studies as an aspect of a liberal education. In his department, he said, 'the emphasis on [legal subjects] is on educational and legal analyses as a function of *Society*: in the professional school [i.e., Osgoode Hall] the emphasis must necessarily be on the function of *practice*.'[25] But Kennedy's goal was more cutting-edge than the ambitions of either Oxbridge or Osgoode. He wanted to introduce students not just to large theories about law, which could be done adequately in a philosophy and political science program; nor just to law as a technical system for the resolution of private disputes, which was the prerogative of Osgoode Hall Law School. Rather, he wished to unite and transcend both these approaches in order to study law as a living entity, intimately connected to the resolution of modern social problems, whether familial, municipal, national, or international. 'We are concerned,' he declared, 'to create a body of citizens endowed with an insight into law as the basic social science, and capable of making ... it the finest of all instruments in the service of mankind.'[26] This noble ideal was reflected in the department's pedagogy, its undergraduate curriculum, and its emphasis on research and graduate study.

Kennedy and his colleagues did not restrict their teaching to the transmission of general principles and ideas about law. They were also concerned to teach students how to deal with traditional sources of law, especially cases and statutes, in the detailed analytical way that legal professionals do. To do so, they focused on the dissection of case law in particular. Replying to a student inquiry, Kennedy stated, 'I do not in the least work along lecture lines. The entire subject is worked by cases.'[27] Kennedy was in fact noted for his magisterial lectures, but the lectures themselves were based on extensive analysis of judicial decisions. In this Kennedy and his colleagues followed North American traditions much more than the British, where lectures on large legal themes and principles were the norm. And whatever the pedagogical style, students were encouraged to reflect critically on the 'why' of the law, not just the 'what' and the 'how.' Kennedy's curriculum also departed from British models with its novel emphasis on public law, especially in the new courses in administrative law and industrial law created by Jacob Finkelman. Larry MacKenzie's approach to international law was also non-traditional: in his class you were as apt to discuss the rise of Hitler or the implications of Britain going off the gold standard as the law of treaties or consular privilege. The ultimate goal was to create a cadre of legal scholars capable of doing graduate work in law, preferably at the University of Toronto. Graduate work 'at home' was necessary, according to Kennedy, to stem the 'deplorable' brain drain to the United States, 'at a time when the complexities of modern life and the growing vastness of legal problems demand more than ever before legal research in Canada.'[28]

When Laskin entered the University of Toronto, the BA degree in law was the principal degree, with the LLB functioning as a graduate degree. An MA and a PhD in law were also on offer, but the latter was soon superseded by the D.Jur. degree. Laskin was part of the last class to be granted an exemption from the first year. After 1930 students with

Ontario grade thirteen were no longer allowed to begin in the second year, as the university tried to raise admission standards. The Kennedy curriculum, as we have seen, involved some legal subjects and some liberal arts subjects in each year. Laskin recalled taking lectures in history from G. deT. Glazebrook and Frank Underhill, and a special course in legal philosophy prepared by departmental chair G.S. Brett. There were also courses in economics, one in psychology, and a program in political theory given by Alex Brady, whom Laskin remembered 'with great affection.'[29] On the legal side there were courses in the history of English law, 'legal science' (an introduction to the basic elements of the common law and to legal reasoning), contracts, torts, criminal law, real property, commercial law, public and private international law, Roman Law, Canadian constitutional law and history, comparative federalism, administrative law, municipal law, and jurisprudence. In Laskin's third year, Finkelman's new course in 'industrial law' was added, which was described as 'a sociological study of legal relationships in industry.'

This was a demanding curriculum for students straight out of high school, too demanding for some if the attrition rate is any indication. Laskin's class began with some thirty students but finished with only eighteen graduates. And the class of '33 was relatively large: only a dozen graduated in 1932, and only eight in 1934. No women graduated in Laskin's class, and only one, Clara Halperin, graduated in 1932. For those who remained and rose to the challenge, it was an exhilarating, if at times frustrating, intellectual experience. Kennedy spoke often of the necessity of teaching law 'amid the intellectual clash of university activities as well as in relation to the other social sciences.'[30] The martial metaphor was all very well for mature university professors, but the adolescents participating in this experiment must have felt at times like child warriors conscripted into an obscure cause. Kennedy assumed that students had read and understood the materials on their own and went on with his own advanced analysis. Laskin and a number of his classmates enjoyed the challenge of keeping up with him, but others were not equal to the task.

As R.C.B. Risk has pointed out, Kennedy's reach exceeded his grasp.[31] The legal and the social science streams within the honour law course followed separate paths and were not pedagogically integrated. Nor did the extant intellectual resources of the University of Toronto permit the exposure to sociology, anthropology, and psychology necessary to ground the complete 'law in social context' program that Kennedy wanted. Still, realizing Kennedy's ideals was going to be a long-term project. Given severe resource restraints, it is surprising how much he and his colleagues accomplished. And even if the program's goals were not always achieved, individual talented students might seize the initiative on their own. On his elevation to the Supreme Court of Canada in 1970 Laskin replied to a letter of congratulations from Larry MacKenzie; even more important than the law he had learned at MacKenzie's feet, he said, was what he learned 'about things that affected the law.'[32] He later reminisced that all of his Toronto professors 'gave you a feeling that law was something more than a narrow discipline. I knew something about Holmes and Brandeis and Cardozo long ahead of [the] people who didn't take the law programme [or] people at Osgoode Hall ... [T]he interest in law as a social science, and indeed as a humanity, was aroused in me by the teachers at the University of Toronto.'[33]

In spite of his airy denials that the faculty of arts was providing 'vocational education,' Kennedy went to some lengths to maintain good relations with Osgoode Hall and with leading members of the bench and bar in Ontario and elsewhere in the Empire. In 1930 he helped to create the Law Club as a forum where distinguished legal speakers might address the student body. The initiative seems to have come from the students, who saw it as a vehicle for 'bridg[ing] the gap between the members of the Law course and the older members of the profession,' and the association rapidly became 'one of the most active ... at the University.'[34] For Kennedy this was a way of publicizing his program nationally and internationally; his correspondence is full of invitations to prominent legal and political figures in Canada and abroad to speak at the Law Club. Kennedy's choice of a young and iconoclastic Osgoode professor as the inaugural speaker for the Law Club was a fateful one. On the evening of 21 January 1931, in the University College common room, eighteen-year-old Bora Laskin fell under the spell of one Cecil Augustus Wright.

It is symbolic of Wright's particular vision of the law that he baulked when Kennedy suggested he call his talk 'Tendencies in Jurisprudence' and insisted on calling it simply 'The Modern Approach to Law, or Recent Tendencies in the Law.'[35] In spite of his noted advocacy in the cause of university legal education, he had recently 'killed' the Jurisprudence course at Osgoode Hall. A London boy, gold medallist at both the University of Western Ontario and at Osgoode in 1926, Wright was the first Ontarian to receive a doctoral degree in law from Harvard.

There he had absorbed the gospel of Roscoe Pound, regarded as the father of an intellectual movement known as sociological jurisprudence. This doctrine represented the legal version of the flight from nineteenth-century formalism common to many disciplines at the time; it advocated the resolution of legal disputes through a balancing of interests rather than an abstract dissection of competing rights. Law was not an end in itself but rather a means of ordering society, and it was incumbent on lawyers to bring law to life, rather than the other way round. 'The end of law must always be found outside the law itself, and as our opinions of that end change, so must change the content of the law,' Wright told his young audience.[36]

For much of the history of the common law this was merely stating the obvious. In the late nineteenth century, however, a rigorous legal formalism constructed by judges and intellectuals fearful of the impact of universal male suffrage had obscured this basic point. It was this relatively recent ossification of legal thought that Pound, Wright, and others attacked. Wright's biographers call this talk his 'challenge to the legal profession,' and so it was. Wright's radical (in the eyes of the benchers of the Law Society) views on legal education and law reform, overlaid with a feisty and combative personality, guaranteed his notoriety in a highly conservative legal community.

Wright's views were shared in large measure by all Laskin's professors at the law school, where the intellectual atmosphere was changing rapidly. Previously, the role of the legal scholars was to synthesize doctrine in a respectful way that discouraged criticism and limited it to inconsistencies in discrete corners of the doctrine.[37] Now, Canadian legal academics were beginning to challenge received ideas, to question the goals of law rather than simply study its techniques, to try to work out Canadian solutions to Canadian problems. The Depression had a stimulant effect on this new critical spirit but the latter had already been provoked by a growing Canadian nationalism evident since the Great War. With the passage of the Statute of Westminster in 1931 Canada was released from virtually all vestiges of colonial status. This seems to have shocked legal scholars into the realization that the British model need no longer be treated as sacred: Canadian conditions might call for legal reforms unsuitable or even unthinkable in Britain. Kennedy delivered his own challenge to the status quo in a series of lectures at Lafayette College in 1931, wherein he clearly rejected nineteenth-century positivists such as Austin and Holland, and called for a major effort of state, society, and the legal profession to make law 'serve social ends.'[38] Like Wright, he agreed that the ends of law had to be found outside law, and like Pound, he called for legislation to be preceded by 'comprehensive survey[s] of social values' and a 'carefully sifted examination of social facts.' He pleaded with younger lawyers to become a 'vast social advance-guard of legal reform.' An idealistic, earnest, restless Bora Laskin was only too happy to pick up the gauntlet.

These new approaches to law also entailed reforms to legal education. Lawyers had to learn new skills, said Kennedy, 'to save us from the black-letter lawyer ... at a time when ... we are still so ill-fitted to mold law to social ends.'[39] One might have thought that Wright, who would fight a decades-long battle to force the benchers to release their stranglehold on legal education in Ontario, would find a natural ally in W.P.M. Kennedy. Nothing of the sort. Their differences were one part ideological to three parts temperamental. Wright and Kennedy were in accord on many fundamentals, and at one level the disagreement between the two men related to means rather than ends. For 'Caesar' Wright, the Harvard Law School model, with its pre-requisite university degree, was sacrosanct, and he reproached Kennedy for his seeming Anglophile tendencies. In 1933 he wrote to his friend and former professor at Osgoode Hall, Sidney Smith, then dean at Dalhousie Law School, expressing deep scepticism about Kennedy's intentions. 'K. has for some time past, been blowing off steam about his working arrangements with Oxford and Cambridge. As a matter of fact, he is, and has been, shooting all his best men to England for their law ... [His] scheme is to establish this English connection, and then, as I see it, use the Ontario ultra-enthusiasm for all things English for the acceptance of his own school.' Wright was also dead set against Kennedy's joint program in arts and law, on the ground that students needed a few years of university before any exposure to law. He also professed to be less than impressed with the students Kennedy was attracting:

The man who is to spend the rest of his life at law, needs some stimulus to his interests other than more law. To take a High School student and begin to teach him substantive law seems to me to be absolutely contrary to everything that has been gained in the last few years. You ask me for my opinion of the Toronto law student. It is exactly what you might expect from such a catapulting of immature minds into law. They come down here [i.e., to Osgoode] with a few half-baked principles which, for example, in Contracts, they have memorized from Anson. That to them is the law. They want no more, nor are they interested in anything like a through-going analysis until perhaps after Christmas, when they find to their amazement, that they did not do very well in the examinations. With one or two exceptions, who of course do well, and to my way of thinking, would have done well anyway ... I have found that the graduates of K's course are entitled to no consideration whatsoever. On the contrary, due to their attitude of self-satisfaction, they are not able to appreciate that what they have taken, for example in Contracts, in about 20 lectures, I should worry them with for 90. It is of course the old story. If you tell a youngster something emphatically enough just after he graduates from High School, it's the devil's own job to try and get him to qualify his idea.[40]

Wright believed that Kennedy was 'out to get his own law school,' but did not blame him for that, because he agreed that 'the only solution of legal education in Ontario is to establish University schools.' His fear was that Kennedy would exploit the benchers' evident Anglophilia to ensure the adoption of his 'bastard' model of concurrent arts and law in preference to Wright's Harvard-based model where law would be taken as a second degree.

In retrospect the differences between the two men seem slight enough that one is compelled to ask why they could not have compromised on a scheme to present to the benchers. A five-year university degree with a predominance of arts courses in the early years and law courses in the later years would seem to have been an obvious solution, and is the principal mode of legal education in Australia today. Such a scheme might have overcome the drawbacks of both Kennedy's honour law course, which was probably overly ambitious for many entrants coming directly from high school, and Wright's desired university LLB, which isolated law from the intellectual 'clash' with other disciplines. Other people might have been able to resolve these differences, but both men clung tenaciously to the one point of principle that separated them: Kennedy to his vision of law as integrated with other university disciplines, and Wright to his goal of a hard-edged professional law faculty. In personality Wright and Kennedy were too similar to cooperate. Both had elevated notions of their own importance, demanded absolute loyalty from their own acolytes, and liked to run their own show. Kennedy could no more have worked in the same department as Wright than Wright could have worked with him. Ultimately, Bora Laskin would be forced to choose between the two men, and he chose Wright.

Just days before Wright's lecture to the Law Club foreshadowed the development of Laskin's legal philosophy, another university event centred on an issue that would be one of Laskin's central preoccupations later in life: academic freedom. On 15 and 16 January 1931 four Toronto newspapers carried a letter signed by sixty-eight professors at the University of Toronto, complaining that the attitude of the Toronto Police Commission towards public discussion of political and social problems made it clear that 'the right of free speech and free assembly is in danger of suppression in this city.' It was the 'plain duty of the citizen to protest publicly against such curtailment of his [sic] rights,' and free expression of opinions, 'however unpopular or erroneous' had to be safeguarded. Professors Auld and MacKenzie were among the signatories, Kennedy and Finkelman were not.[41] In a related development, when the *Varsity* carried a story in February claiming that a good number of faculty and students were atheists and agnostics, the editor was forced to resign.

The police campaign that goaded the professors into action began with a January 1929 edict of the Toronto Police Commission prohibiting all political meetings held in languages other than English, Yiddish being the principal target. This and other police actions, such as the fingerprinting of taxi-drivers, led to the scheduling of a debate at the Empire Theatre for 11 January on the resolution 'that the Toronto Police Commission is justified in its attitude in regard to free speech.' Two members of the commission, Police Chief Denis Draper and Police Magistrate Emerson Coatsworth, were invited to argue the affirmative and the Rev. Salem Bland, a United Churchman and prominent Social Gospel adherent, was to argue the negative along with a lecturer from Trinity College. The debate was never held because police agents urged the theatre owner to cancel the booking, while Coatsworth and Draper charged that the occasion was to be 'a communistic meeting under a thin disguise.' Some professors perceived this as a public insult and solicited support among their colleagues for the letter sent to the newspapers a few days later.

The largely negative public reaction to the professors' letter illustrated the narrow confines within which academic freedom was expected to be exercised. Expressing views on subjects of contemporary controversy even within the classroom was thought to be inappropriate, but for professors to take a public stand on political issues was viewed by most as illegitimate. Professors were analogized to judges and senior civil servants, who were understood to have accepted certain restrictions on their freedom of speech along with their positions. In the end, the action of the gang of sixty-eight helped to expand the notion of academic freedom. The board of governors considered whether to censure the professors, but in the end decided not to do so. Sir William Mulock, chancellor of the university and chief justice of Ontario, was felt to have publicly rebuked the signatories at a public meeting in February, and with that public opinion appeared to be assuaged. Bora Laskin could hardly have failed to become aware of this controversy involving two of his professors, as it raged across the pages of the *Varsity* and the city newspapers. That he joined the staff of the *Varsity* for the next two years suggests an early commitment to the cause of free speech and a spirited resistance to intimidation.

Extra-curricular activities such as service on the *Varsity* also provided one means of interacting with Gentile students, an important goal for Laskin from the outset of his university career. He was a member of the University College Track Team in his second year and joined the rowing team in his third year. There were three teams, the 'heavy eights,' the middle-weight (150-lb.) team, and the 'tack-weight' (140-lb.) team. Laskin was on the middle-weight team, and was apparently the only Jewish student involved in rowing in those years. The heavy eights competed in the famous McGill Varsity race on the Lachine Canal, while the other teams aimed for the Toronto Dominion Day regattas or the Henley Regatta in St Catharines. During seasonable weather the men were out on the water for practice sessions daily at 6:30 a.m. and 6:30 p.m., using sculls they stored in a boathouse rented from the Toronto Harbour Police. As the ice crept in, they retreated indoors for long toughening-up sessions at the rowing machines in Hart House over the winter. The coxswain of the heavy eights was history student Samuel Hughes, later Laskin's student at Osgoode Hall and a High Court of Ontario judge, who remembered Laskin as a powerful oarsman.[42]

In his third year Laskin also served on the executive of the UC Literary and Athletic Society.[43] Thanks to its interdenominational character, the University College 'Lit' was one of the few social clubs on campus where religious integration was close to being a reality. In his year on the executive Laskin was joined by fellow law students Sydney Hermant and Nathan Pivnick. As 'literary director' Laskin was responsible for planning a series of speakers, which attracted 'a larger attendance than has been noted for many years.' The most popular speaker was Agnes Macphail, the sole woman MP in the House of Commons. In her address to the students in November 1932 she 'flayed pet Canadian institutions,' arguing for increased state control over finance, trade, and industry in order to remedy the horrors of the Depression. The occasion was historic: the all-male Lit had never invited a 'lady' speaker before, but her presence 'met with the approbation of all.'[44] In December, 'a further surrender to the female of the species took place when the Women's Undergraduate Assocation were for the second time in history the guests of the Society.'[45]

One of Laskin's main accomplishments was to help the Lit to revive the University College Parliamentary Club (essentially a debating society), moribund since 1928. In October 1932 he was elected speaker, though the *Varsity* reported that a 'Miss Laskin' had topped the polls.[46] Where most young men yearned for the combative political posts, already Laskin displayed a preference for the role of neutral arbiter. Assisted by deputy speaker Richard Bell, he presided over a session of the UC Parliament in which Prime Minister Marvin Gelber and Opposition Leader Richard Reville debated the motion 'that this house will have confidence in the idea of a League of Nations.' The club upheld the Lit's reputation as a nursery of leaders. Reville was Laskin's classmate and would become a prominent lawyer and county court judge. Bell, who was a year behind, would become a member of Diefenbaker's cabinet, while Gelber became a Liberal MP and Canadian delegate to the UN.

The rage for debating continued when UC issued a challenge to the Osgoode Hall team. Laskin and fellow UC student N.H. Shaw took the negative position on the resolution 'that this House approves of the Japanese occupation of Manchuria.' Political economy lecturer A.F.W. Plumptre chaired the debate, while Larry MacKenzie was expected to 'clarify the Canadian position with respect to the Eastern imbroglio.'[47] The Parliamentary Club concluded its program with yet another debate on foreign policy, this time on the resolution 'that Ottawa is nearer Washington than London.'[48]

Laskin and his debating colleagues conceived an elaborate (and sexist) joke involving a mock lawsuit against the *Varsity* for having attributed to Sydney Hermant the following opinion on the establishment of co-educational residences: 'What the hell and why not? It would save time, money, and effort.' Hermant denied making the statement, and a 'writ' for libel was served on three *Varsity* staff members by Hermant's 'counsel,' the firm of Bell, Laskin, and Singer. The 'trial' was put on as a moot court exercise before a packed house. The seven-hour-long proceeding provided a good test of forensic skill for the participants, but 'dragged out until it became wearisome and tedious' for the audience.[49]

Laskin described the moot as originating in 'a spontaneous feeling among the staff and students that a grounding in the actual practice of judicial proceedings is of parallel importance to the student in law with a knowledge of the substantive branch of that study.' He noted that the court was in its third year of existence, which points to his class as the prime mover behind this addition to the law course. Far from rejecting it as foreign to their high-concept curriculum, the moot court was embraced by the faculty, 'who have succeeded in instilling in their students that seriousness towards judicial practice which is so essential in the training of law students.'[50]

Laskin returned to the Lakehead after completing his exams at the end of third year, and did not attend his graduation ceremony on 9 June.[51] He did well, if not as spectacularly as he might have hoped. Moffatt Hancock and Richard Reville were the only two students who graduated with first class honours. Laskin and Abe Acker came at or near the top of the sixteen remaining graduates, who all had second class honours – the exact order is not known. Judging from their subsequent encouragement of Laskin's academic interests, the faculty had already identified him as someone to watch. The next hurdle he had to overcome on his own: finding a lawyer to serve as principal for his articling period. The Law Society of Upper Canada's training program involved concurrent service in a law office while following lectures at Osgoode Hall Law School. Those without an articling position could not enrol. Abe Acker's political activity had provided useful contacts, including a Gentile lawyer who served as his principal. Having chosen to avoid partisan political activity, Laskin had to rely on other networks in this regard.

The lad from Fort William had not carried off the highest honours, but perhaps more importantly he had earned the respect of the small faculty and of his classmates. While learning legal skills and concepts, he had also been afforded a solid grounding in British and Canadian constitutional history, in Roman law, international law, and in legal theory; nor was he a stranger to American law or legal thought. Laskin had taken the only courses in administrative law and labour relations law existing anywhere in Canada. He was familiar with the flight from laissez-faire, positivism, and formalism and the emergence of new functionalist theories emphasizing the incorporation of social facts into legal decision making. In short, he was well-prepared for the graduate work he would undertake at the University of Toronto and later at Harvard.

Just as important as his academic success was Laskin's ability to hone his social skills, in particular to negotiate the twin perils, faced by all Jews, of being too insular or too extroverted. In spite of the ambient anti-Semitism on campus, Laskin had found a way to play a leadership role in mixed activities without alienating non-Jewish students or denying his own Jewish identity. His election as speaker of the Parliamentary Club was an eloquent testimonial to the respect he inspired in Jewish and non-Jewish students alike. He could be firm without appearing strident, forceful without seeming pushy. Laskin conducted himself according to a code of civility containing enough Anglo-Saxon content to assure his non-Jewish associates he would do nothing unpredictable, but in turn subtly enjoined them to accord him the same respect. Whether Laskin 'naturally' behaved this way as a result of growing up in Fort William, or whether he consciously adapted his behaviour in Toronto, it is impossible to say. Either way, his combination of assertiveness and civility was key to his future successes.

During his first three years at the University of Toronto, Bora Laskin tested his body against the waters of Lake Ontario, his mind against the expectations of his professors, and his leadership abilities through his academic and extra-curricular contributions. These activities brought him as close to the mainstream of university life as Jews were permitted to get, and gave him a perspective on the institution as an organic whole. With the occasional hiatus, it would remain his citadel for the next thirty-two years.

3

Articling

On 16 August 1933, the largest riot in twentieth-century Toronto broke out at the park known as Christie Pits, a short walk from the Laskin residence. Provoked by the overt display of the swastika symbol at a local baseball game, the clash between nativist and Jewish youth gangs spiralled out of control until some eight thousand people were embroiled in the melée. Scores were injured but miraculously, no one was killed.[1] The riot at Christie Pits challenged the complacent self-image of 'Toronto the Good' as no event in recent memory had done.

The tension had been building for months. After Adolf Hitler came to power in January 1933, the ensuing crescendo of anti-Semitic invective and violence in Germany received detailed coverage in Toronto newspapers. The German spark ignited the social anti-Semitism that smouldered like a subterranean bog fire in Canada. In Quebec, Adrien Arcand's deliriously anti-Semitic Fascist movement was invigorated by the events in Germany, while brown-shirted militants organized the Canadian Nationalist Party in Winnipeg and German propaganda fell on fertile soil across the prairies. In Toronto, swastika clubs sprang up among disaffected and largely unemployed Anglo-Canadian youth. Their use of Hitler's symbol did not imply adoption of his political program, but was a convenient means of intimidating Jews and other ethnic groups. Clashes occurred in the summer of 1933 in the Beaches area of eastern Toronto, where a newly constructed boardwalk had attracted many Jewish and immigrant families for lakeside outings. The conflict between the cultural norms of the local Anglo-Canadians and the new-comers might have been comic but for the extreme nativist reaction it inspired, as swastika club members harassed Jewish bathers and sought to 'clean up' the area.

These tensions found a perfect breeding ground in the local sports scene, which pitted a few largely Jewish teams against mainly non-Jewish teams. On the night of 14 August, a crowd of youths had un-veiled a huge swastika emblem at the end of a game at Willowvale Park (now better known as Christie Pits) between the Jewish-identified Harbord Playground team and the St Peter's Church team. Tensions ran high but no fighting ensued. Later that night a large swastika and the words 'Hail [sic] Hitler' were painted on the Willowvale Park club-house. Two nights later, when the teams met again, the game was punc-tuated with shouts of 'Heil Hitler' and loud anti-Semitic remarks. When several youths unveiled a large white blanket emblazoned with a black swastika at the end of the game, all hell broke loose. Jewish youths attacked the blanket bearers and soon bats, lead pipes, and rocks were being brandished on both sides. In a display of inter-ethnic solidarity, some Italians and Ukrainians assisted the Jews in the fray. Mayor Stewart immediately issued an order that anyone displaying the swastika em-blem would be liable to prosecution. Removing the cause of provocation worked: Toronto was spared further disturbances of this nature.

When the riot occurred Bora Laskin was in Fort William, but he did not have to be present to see in Christie Pits a symbol of the overt hostility encountered by Jews in virtually all walks of life. Laskin had experienced this subtly at the University of Toronto, and now had to face it in not-so-subtle form as he prepared to attend Osgoode Hall Law School and qualify as a lawyer. To be sure, Osgoode Hall Law School itself imposed no quotas and did not discriminate overtly against Jews in its admission process, but the concurrent system of articling and lectures obliged all students to find a principal in Toronto willing to supervise them for three years. Aspirant lawyers from outside Toronto without contacts in the capital had always found this a problem, but for those whose gender or race put them outside the mainstream the bar-rier was well-nigh insuperable. When one of the first black lawyers, Delos Rogest Davis, found it impossible to obtain an articling position in the 1880s, a special act had to be passed enabling him to be called to the bar. Ontario's first woman lawyer, Clara Brett Martin, also de-spaired of finding a principal until the chivalrous barrister William Mulock cast his cloak over that particular puddle in 1893.

Laskin's Jewish background and Fort William origins defined him as an outsider in an employment market where ties of family, faith, class, and community were crucial to getting established. A few Canadian-born Jews from the old English and German communities, comparatively assimilated and well-off, had made it into the legal profession in the early twentieth century with relative ease, but the post-war influx of Polish and Russian Jews had a totally different experience.[2] Even as prejudice against women, blacks, and Catholics ebbed somewhat within the profession, that against Jews intensified. The response by Jewish law students was naturally to seek out Jewish principals, but Laskin was an outsider even to the Toronto Jewish community, and had no obvious mentor or patron. In an interview forty years later, Laskin made no reference to these difficulties, stating simply that he had articled with W.C. Davidson, an alderman in the City of Toronto.[3] This reticence is in itself not surprising. As Christopher Moore has noted, many Jewish lawyers who began their careers before the war prefer to stress their good fortune rather than dwell on the obstacles they faced.[4] Laskin's route to the bar was not as straightforward as he made it out to be. The real story of his articling experience reveals just how vulnerable he was as he tried to enter the legal profession in the depths of the Depression.

Bora Laskin managed to put his first step on the professional ladder by relying on one of the few social networks open to him: the fraternity. His fraternity brother Samuel Gotfrid of Sigma Alpha Mu had been called to the bar only the year before and had virtually no practice, but agreed to sign Laskin's papers in order to assist his confrere.[5] Articles-on-paper were perhaps more the rule than the exception in the 1930s, when the Law Society's educational system plunged into a crisis which it barely weathered.[6] The actual articles of indenture show Max Laskin as a party of the first part, since his son was just under the age of twenty-one on 18 September 1933 when the contract was concluded. The requisite certificates of respectability were signed by Bathurst Street dentist Bernard Schaffer and Jay Kasler, president of Mercantile Finance Corp. Ltd.[7] Samuel Gotfrid, himself the son of an immigrant Polish tailor, began his legal career in the same way as Laskin. A fraternity brother served as his principal of record but Gotfrid worked mainly for other lawyers, including a small non-Jewish firm. When he asked if he could stay on after his call to the bar, one of the partners replied, 'I don't know how my clients would like the idea of having a Jewish boy in the firm.' Gotfrid then returned to his Sigma Alpha Mu contacts, and found a small office in a building owned by the family of a fraternity brother, J.M. Bennett.[8] Echoing Robert Frost's words about the family, Gotfrid explained that he 'was there because I had nowhere else to go.'[9] The fraternity functioned as a kind of extended family, an invaluable support network for those on the fringes of mainstream society.

During the ten months that Gotfrid served as Laskin's principal of record, his practice consisted of a couple of clients in the dress business, a little estate work, and some criminal work. Gotfrid's work came not via the Jewish community as such, but once again through fraternity connections. His practice exposed Laskin to some of the more unsavoury aspects of legal work during the dying days of Ontario's restrictive liquor laws. The Conservative government of G. Howard Ferguson had allowed the sale of spirits, but not beer, in government stores in 1927. Just before their electoral defeat in June 1934, the Conservatives had passed a law providing for the sale of beer and wine (Ontario wine only!) by the glass in hotels and restaurants, but it was the victorious Liberals under Mitch Hepburn who proclaimed it into force. Until that time there was a brisk illicit trade in the distribution of beer. Gotfrid frequently defended bootleggers in court on a retainer from the brewery supplying them, which was content to treat the minimal fines as a kind of licence fee.

Gotfrid's act of generosity to a fellow Jew would be repeated with another minority lawyer some years later. When a student telephoned seeking an articling position, the caller warned Gotfrid that he was a 'Negro.' Gotfrid reacted strongly: 'it bothered me that a fellow had to demean himself in that way to apply for a job.' He interviewed the caller and hired him: the man was Lincoln Alexander, a future federal cabinet minister and lieutenant-governor of Ontario.[10] Through such acts of private resistance, as well as their well-known public advocacy of stronger human rights codes, Jewish lawyers played a key role in fighting discrimination in the inter-war and post-war years.

After a year of doing nothing, Laskin was impatient to get some real experience. His articles were formally transferred to a new principal on 26 July 1934. Exactly how Laskin made contact with W.C. Davidson is not known, but his firm's location a few floors above Gotfrid's office provides an obvious connection. In 1934 W.C. Davidson was forty-six years old, a King's Counsel (K.C.) with an established practice in commercial and real estate law. Raised in Simcoe County, Davidson had lost his left arm in a farm accident at the age of fifteen.[11] This misfortune was commemorated in a poignant and darkly comic ritual. Through a strange coincidence, another Toronto lawyer named W.W. Davidson (no relation to Laskin's principal) had lost his right arm in the First World War. Every Christmas each Davidson would purchase a pair of gloves and send to the other's office a parcel containing only the glove fitting the recipient's hand. And each year the juniors and staff would scan the mail as Christmas approached, anxious to see if the mysterious and faintly titillating package had arrived.[12] Perhaps this experience of personal difference explains Davidson's unusual willingness to take on a woman, Beatrice Van Wart, as an associate and the Jewish Bora Laskin as an articling student.[13] Whatever his motivation, it reveals an important element in Laskin's success: his determination to break into the WASP legal establishment instead of confining himself to the Jewish legal community.

Davidson's wide real estate practice occasioned Laskin's initiation into the mysteries of title searching at the registry office. Some articling students in the 1930s complained of being confined to the registry office during their entire apprenticeship. In later years firms would hire paralegal title searchers, but even into the 1960s articling students almost invariably did it. Most title searching was utterly routine, but it always carried a certain potential for drama because of the possible discovery of some previously unnoticed blot on the title. Laskin always retained a certain fondness for the mathematical and puzzlelike nature of real property law; he would teach it for over two decades, eventually publishing the first Canadian casebook on the subject. The political aspect of property law was no doubt also revealed to Laskin during this time. Articling students usually served the writs of possession on behalf of foreclosing mortgagees, notifying homeowners that the lender was about to repossess the premises.[14]

The professional community Laskin sought to join was uniquely Canadian in some respects, but still very Anglophile in others. Ontario lawyers, like their counterparts in the other common law provinces, were all admitted as both barristers and solicitors, unlike England where the two groups retained separate professional identities. A specialized litigation bar existed in Canada, but on a de facto rather than de jure basis. Promotion to the bench in England occurred almost exclusively from the ranks of senior barristers who had been awarded a K.C. as a result of recognized professional merit. In Canada both the K.C. designation and promotion to the provincial benches were heavily influenced by religious and political affiliation, with professional merit a sometimes overlooked factor. Ontario lawyers conveyed their own idea of who were appropriate leaders of the profession when they founded the Lawyers' Club in 1922: its constitution excluded from membership women, non-whites, and non-Christians. *En revanche,* Jewish lawyers founded the Reading Club, named after the first Jewish lord chief justice of England.[15]

Near the end of his articles Laskin had occasion to observe the Anglophilic elements of the Ontario bar on full display. On 20 January 1936 George V died at Sandringham. As soon as the news was received by telegraph the great bell in City Hall began to toll, continuing its melancholy music for an hour until the sound filled the entire city. Lawyers in the British tradition are considered officers of the monarch's courts; hence Ontario lawyers and judges donned official mourning costume for some months. This consisted of large white cuffs over their jackets, and 'weepers' – pleated tabs hanging down over the chest, instead of the usual unpleated ones.[16] Loyalty to all things British seemed solidly entrenched, but some Anglo-Canadian legal ties were already beginning to fray. The legislation abolishing appeals to the Privy Council was passed in 1939, though it did not become effective for another decade, and when George VI died in 1952 it is not clear whether the bar observed mourning at all. The attenuation of these formal ties did not immediately affect the dominant influence of the British legal tradition, which abated only slowly over subsequent decades.[17]

Forty years later Chief Justice Bora Laskin could afford to be critical of his articling experience with Davidson:

to say that I read law with him [Davidson] was really a euphemism of the worst kind ...

I was paid $2 a week and I was mostly in debt to the petty cash throughout the whole three years of my service under articles. We were still under, to a degree, ... the English tradition ... where you paid your principal for the privilege of – what – of being educated by him in the intricacies of the law. Well, I think that I was worth a hell of a lot more than $2 a week, but perhaps I was lucky. A good many of my friends got nothing, but then of course, they were articled in other law offices maybe some more prestigious, some larger.[18]

Seen from the perspective of the young Bora Laskin in the mid-1930s these critiques are quite inapposite. Given the Depression and his own lack of connections in Toronto, Laskin was fortunate to obtain 'real' articles. In stating that he was 'worth a hell of a lot more than $2 a week,' he implies that he actually did some work, and thus gained some experience, while under articles to Davidson. This was more than many of his contemporaries could say. Samuel Gotfrid had been paid five to seven dollars weekly during the late 1920s, but lawyers' incomes had fallen sharply after 1930. In 1936 partners at the respectable firm of Raymond and Honsberger took home two hundred dollars each, or four dollars per week, only twice Laskin's wage.[19]

Laskin's comments should be read as an indictment of the entire articling system rather than a personal criticism of Davidson. During his apprenticeship Laskin became a vociferous critic of the Osgoode concurrent program. By its end he was advocating a full-time university course of three years' duration followed by a period of practical training as the only proper preparation for the legal profession. This prescription was based on his diagnosis that the articling system was terminally ill. A few lucky students did a variety of work and received excellent preparation in many aspects of legal practice, doctrine, and ethics; some even read law in the literal sense with their principals. Most received no instruction at all, and did little office work that a well-trained adolescent could not have done equally well. The benchers constantly preached the benefits of exposure to law office work while refusing to put in place any mechanism to monitor its quality.

In this account of his articling experience Laskin presents a highly edited version of his past, one he saw as appropriate for public consumption in light of the position he held at the time. He portrays himself as a chief-justice-in-embryo whose abilities were unrecognized by those about him, rather than a vulnerable articling student struggling to survive in a harsh social and economic environment. Laskin's masculine self-image always made him reluctant to admit to experiences of vulnerability. His unwillingness to dwell on this point may explain his failure to mention his first year of articles with Gotfrid, either in the 1976 interview or in any other given during his lifetime. The way he chose to tell his story differs markedly from the reminiscences of U.S. Supreme Court judges who faced similar obstacles, such as Felix Frankfurter and Thurgood Marshall. Both were quite open about their experiences with discrimination and their determination to penetrate a hitherto unresponsive legal establishment.[20] Laskin's future Supreme Court colleague Bertha Wilson also spoke of her difficulties as a woman in the legal profession and on the bench.[21] Tales of personal success in the face of grave obstacles are highly prized in American culture. Canadians have traditionally preferred their life stories to be told in a different key, one which downplays personal ambition. People should be rewarded not because they strove for advancement but because some beneficent higher authority recognized their merit. Laskin's omission of his association with Gotfrid suggests a need to reshape his past to fit comfortably within a familiar Anglo-Canadian narrative of success. He could have told a story of triumph over adversity or ambition achieved, but chose not to. Rather, he tells it as a bland tale of merit recognized and rewarded (or, in the case of his articling experience, under-rewarded), in which everything 'just happened' to him.[22] While there is some truth to this in the context of his judicial appointments, it is difficult to believe that Laskin was hired by Davidson by mere chance. He was a man of great personal ambition but emphasizing it would have conflicted with the gentlemanly image he wanted to convey as chief justice. Cultural norms around privacy in Canada may also help to explain Laskin's reticence, and he probably did not wish to appear ungrateful to the country that had ultimately showered him with recognition. Frankfurter, Marshall, and Wilson, by contrast, must have hoped that open discussion of their experiences would serve a cathartic and educative function.

During the first two years of his articles Laskin attended lectures in the morning at Osgoode Hall and spent the afternoon in his principal's office if there was any work for him to do. Office work was supplemented by lectures on fields of substantive law and procedure. These were meant to be essentially positivist in nature, covering the major legal rules currently applied in Ontario. Jurisprudence, comparative law, and international law were seen as academic luxuries with no place in the Osgoode Hall curriculum.[23]

There were still only three full-time professors at the school, even though the student body was much larger than that at the University of Toronto. The dean, John Delatre Falconbridge, was a gentleman of the old school, befitting both his age (he was called to the bar in 1899) and his position as the son of Sir Glenholme Falconbridge, a former chief justice of the Court of King's Bench of Ontario. Dean since 1924, Falconbridge was arguably the most productive Canadian legal scholar of his generation. While his scholarship was always aimed at practising professionals, it often displayed impressive historical research and a search for principle that permitted him a certain amount of critical analysis. His large volumes on the law of banking and bills of exchange,

mortgages, and the conflict of laws, all notoriously intricate and difficult topics, were among the most-thumbed texts on any lawyer's shelf.
Falconbridge on Mortgages is still current in its fifth edition (2003).[24]

Falconbridge cautiously tried to nudge Osgoode Hall Law School in a
more academic direction. Before 1924 the law school had no official
name, nor any graduation ceremony: Falconbridge secured both. He
asked for and was granted the title of 'dean,' as opposed to 'principal,'
the title of his predecessors. After increasing the number of teaching
hours, he improved the teaching staff by hiring serious scholars committed to academic legal education. Dean Falconbridge and the two
men whom he brought on in the 1920s, Donald A. MacRae and Cecil A.
Wright, constituted the entire full-time complement during the 1930s,
along with a number of part-timers. A native of Prince Edward Island,
MacRae had taken degrees in classics at Dalhousie and Cornell, then
taught Greek at Princeton. After a brief stint as a lawyer in Toronto he
returned to the Maritimes to take up the deanship at Dalhousie. Laskin
respected MacRae as a teacher and advocate of the cause of university
legal education, but felt his major scholarly contribution lay behind him
by the time he came to Osgoode.[25]

In 1925 Falconbridge hired Sidney E. Smith, a Cape Bretoner who
had studied law at Dalhousie and Harvard and taught at Dalhousie
before following his mentor MacRae to Osgoode. He would return to
Dalhousie as dean in 1929, and thus did not teach Bora Laskin, but he
did teach the next addition to Osgoode's complement, Cecil Augustus
Wright. Their long-standing friendship would play a crucial role in the
unfolding drama of legal education in Ontario two decades later. In
1927 Falconbridge made the most fateful personnel decision of his
deanship by hiring Wright. 'Caesar' would come into repeated conflict
with the Law Society over his feisty advocacy of the cause of university
legal education in Ontario. At Osgoode Wright was the *enfant terrible*:
he was energetic, he was fiery, he was iconoclastic, and he made an
indelible impression on Bora Laskin. Laskin had heard him lecture once
or twice at the University of Toronto, but he now thrived on a steady
diet of Wright. Wright in turn grew to admire this highly intelligent and
rather combative student from Fort William. While all Laskin's professors at the University of Toronto guided him in some way, Caesar
Wright became Laskin's chief mentor. Both were impatient with the
entire Upper Canadian legal and judicial superstructure, from the complacent antediluvianism of the benchers to the smug Anglophilia of the
judiciary. Both shared a commitment to modernity, and saw Ontario as

mired in a faded Victorian liberalism no longer appropriate in an economy increasingly dominated by big government and big corporations. Laskin was perhaps more concerned than Wright to contribute to what we would now call public policy. To that end he began to work under Jacob Finkelman's guidance with the Workers' Educational Association, an organization aimed at providing continuing education for working people and securing better legislative protection for workers.

Perhaps the greatest gift that Wright gave to Bora Laskin was the permission to be himself. In Wright's classroom, only ideas mattered, though you had to have enough *chutzpah* – and Laskin did – to challenge the master if you wanted to be noticed. Wright and Laskin were similar enough to become lifelong friends, but different enough to be able to challenge each other intellectually. They were also quite different in personality. Wright 'was a big man with a powerful booming voice and a personality that hit you in the face like a fist.'[26] Along with this combative exterior there went a certain jovial camaraderie, at least with other males. He could come up behind a student at a party, slap him on the back, and have a drink with him, having terrorized him in class the day before. Laskin, though warm and personable with people he knew well, was rather guarded in gatherings of non-intimates, ill at ease making small talk and (unlike Caesar) not fond of the alcohol that fuelled many a Gentile social gathering.

Laskin studied contracts with Wright in first year, agency and partnership in second year, and wills and trusts in third year.[27] In later years Laskin remembered Wright as 'a man of unusual quality, [with] a capacity ... for stimulation ... unexcelled in any teacher I have had.'[28] In spite of Wright's championing of the 'case method' of legal instruction, Laskin found him to be 'more of a lecturer than a Socratic interrogator[:] usually [he] became so wound up in his exposition, [and] threw out so many ideas, that hardly any time was left to question students unless they were brave enough – and some of us were – to interrupt his flow.'[29] Wright taught to the top 10 per cent of the class, leaving the rest scrambling to fit together the shards from his kaleidoscopic imagination.

Laskin's other courses at Osgoode were pretty dreary, with the possible exception of real property in second year and mortgages in third year. These were taught by J.J. Robinette, the gold medallist at the University of Toronto and Osgoode who was immediately asked back to teach in 1929. He went part-time in 1932, teaching the two courses in question until his resignation in 1937. There is no record of what Laskin thought of him but he is universally remembered as a brilliant teacher by those who were his students.[30] Laskin's future Supreme Court of Canada colleague Wishart F. Spence taught him bankruptcy in third year, and in each year the students were treated to a stultifying course on procedure taught by the ineffectual but endearing Col. Harold Foster.

Aside from a first-year course on the history of English law, the courses at Osgoode were uniformly *in* law rather than *about* law. No course was offered on comparative law, or sociology of law, or jurisprudence. There is a curious twist to the story of jurisprudence at Osgoode, however. Samuel Bradford had taught such a course for many years, and it was assigned to Caesar Wright in his very first year of teaching. He chose not to use the classic texts, Holland and Salmond, but created his own materials based on Roscoe Pound's *Outlines of Lectures on Jurisprudence*. The course was a fiasco, probably because Wright's heart was not in it. The next year he wrote to Francis Bohlen at Pennsylvania, 'This year, Jurisprudence – Thank God – is gone – in fact, I like to think that perhaps I killed it.'[31] The course was promptly replaced by Crimes in the first year. Bora Laskin was told a totally inverted version of this story, as he recounted years later: '[T]here was no jurisprudence at Osgoode Hall. I learned later that Caesar Wright had tried to introduce jurisprudence at Osgoode in 1928, and after a year the programme was dropped – he simply gave up the programme – so that the very narrow professionalism of Osgoode Hall Law School left a very, very large gap which the department of law [at the University of Toronto] tried to fill.'[32] Paradoxically, the legal education Wright so desperately sought to locate in a university was not much broader than the 'narrow professionalism' of Osgoode he so stridently decried. Even Laskin had to admit this. 'I think in looking back at it now that he was essentially ... of a fairly conservative nature in terms of his approach to legal education. He saw legal education geared to the production not of philosophers, but of good professional practitioners.'[33] Wright differed with the benchers mostly in his insistence on a full-time legal education. The concurrent system always left academic study in second place as students tried to satisfy their office demands while squeezing in class preparation around the edges. Wright's model was definitely more ambitious than the benchers' even if the content was not dramatically different.

Laskin's academic record at Osgoode Hall was impressive, but as at the University of Toronto he never stood at the top of the class. Given his competitive nature, this must have been rather a disappointment. In first year he stood fifth, netting him a scholarship of forty dollars, in second year his second place earned him sixty dollars, and in third year he was eighth out of a class of one hundred.[34] Moffatt Hancock usually stood ahead of him, as did Abe Acker, who graduated at the head of the class and carried off most of the prizes. In second and third year Laskin received the first prize of $100 in the Wallace Nesbitt essay competition, and together with his scholarships was able to cover his $150 annual tuition in two of his three years at Osgoode – a considerable relief to his cash-strapped family. In second year Laskin wrote on a labour law topic, 'The Law Relating to Collective Bargaining Agreements in Canada,' and in third year on statutory interpretation, 'The Protection of Interests by Statute and the Problem of Contracting Out.' The latter was published at Caesar Wright's urging in the *Canadian Bar Review* in 1938. There was no course in labour law at Osgoode Hall, but Laskin was concurrently pursuing graduate degrees at the University of Toronto with Osgoode's permission. The first essay was probably written for the MA degree in law, completed in 1935 under the supervision of Clyde Auld.

Laskin also enrolled in the LLB program at Toronto. Both degrees involved directed study courses and a major paper, along with a few seminars.[35] Before 1941 all candidates for the LLB in a given year wrote a major paper on a set topic. The choice for 1935–6 was highly pertinent in the turbulent inter-war years: 'the jurisdiction of the Permanent Court of International Justice and the source and development of the principles of law which it applies.' Laskin was never very interested in international law, but the exercise served him in good stead a few years later when he was obliged to teach public international law on short notice after Larry MacKenzie's departure from Toronto. Kennedy was keen to advance graduate study at Toronto and by encouraging Laskin to pursue higher degrees was clearly grooming him as possible faculty material.

The late 1920s saw an attempt to revive a certain esprit de corps at Osgoode many felt had disappeared after the First World War. As in many law schools throughout the twentieth century, one element in this campaign was the mounting of a student newspaper. *Obiter Dicta* came out monthly during the academic year and served as a kind of *omnium gatherum* of law school news, gossip, humour, serious discussion of law, politics, and legal education, and even legal scholarship. It reflected the trials and triumphs of student life in the 1930s and '40s, was suspended during the war, then re-emerged as a much less ambitious publication. In 'Presenting First Year Personalities' editor Ralph Standish singled out thirty incoming students, including three women, for notice. Bora Laskin was noted for neither academic nor sporting prowess, but for his roles as literary director and speaker of the Parliamentary Club at University College, and as *Varsity* staff. Abe Acker, meanwhile, 'led first year law at Varsity, wrestled, was a finalist in the Robinette Trophy debates and took an active part in moot courts.'[36]

Both Laskin's prize-winning essays, plus a piece by him entitled 'The Dominion-Provincial Conflict In Relation to Judicial Competence,' were published in *Obiter Dicta* as part of its mission to transform itself into an intellectually respectable review. As of 1934 the *Canadian Bar Review* was the principal outlet for academic writing about law outside Quebec, where the civilian university tradition had fostered the growth of a handful of law reviews. The editors of *Obiter Dicta* mused hopefully that 'under the right direction and with the necessary stimulus there could be developed a law journal that would be of great value to the School, and the profession.'[37] Articles on topical subjects such as divorce law reform, unemployment insurance, and the need for legal aid in civil cases appeared regularly in the early 1930s, alongside more esoteric contributions on 'The Theory of Law and its Development in the 13th Century.'[38]

Unfortunately for the ambitious students at Osgoode Hall, their efforts were sidelined by the appearance of the new *University of Toronto Law Journal* in 1935. W.P.M. Kennedy had had lined up well-known legal figures from around Canada and the Empire as contributors, and his journal created a buzz almost instantly. Honour Law graduate and Rhodes Scholar Kenneth Macalister reported in 1939 that 'the Law Journal continues to keep its high reputation at Oxford,'[39] while Laskin later called the *Journal* a 'monumental achievement' for Kennedy.[40] Even the *Canadian Bar Review*, much to Caesar Wright's chagrin (he had become editor in 1936), was unable to attract articles equal to Kennedy's. The competition between these two journals was another manifestation of the Wright-Kennedy rivalry, which continued to reverberate like a strong bass line under the surface dissonance between Wright and the benchers.

As at the University of Toronto, Laskin took advantage of whatever extra-curricular activities were offered. In February 1934 he and Abe Acker spoke against the motion 'that the organization and maintenance of trade unions should be discouraged' in a competition against a team from McMaster University. Sadly, his campaign to become secretary treasurer of the Osgoode Legal and Literary Society failed in March 1935. A number of politically oriented clubs were established at Osgoode during these years, such as the Gladstone Club (Liberal) and the Mansfield Club, which aimed 'to provide a socialistic approach to law and politics otherwise lacking at Osgoode Hall.' Laskin avoided overt political affiliation and did not join them. Nor did he join a club affiliated with the newly formed League for Social Reconstruction, an academic group aimed at educating the public about socialism and modelled on the British Fabian Society.

The atmosphere at Osgoode was heavily inflected with an air of male camaraderie. There were a few women students in each of the three years – two in Laskin's class of one hundred – but their presence had not made much of an impact. In the late 1920s the position of first vice-president of the Osgoode Hall Legal & Literary Society was reserved for a woman, but the (male) commentary on elections for this post usually framed it as a beauty contest. Any change was perhaps more evident in the enhanced consciousness of the women students than in male attitudes. In 1935 when an instructor declared that he could not tell a certain joke because of the presence of women, the seven women in the class walked out in protest. As Cecilia Morgan has observed of this period, women (like native people at the Lakehead) were simultaneously highly visible and yet constantly overlooked and ignored.[41] They were obliged to sit together in the front two rows of the lecture theatre, for example, but could not be seen by the instructor because of the height of his dais and the angle of the seating. Nearly forty years after Clara Brett Martin's call to the bar, and five years after the Privy Council's decision in the famous 'Persons' case, women still had no robing room at Osgoode Hall. Even as they left Osgoode, their second-class status was confirmed: the graduation dinner in the 1930s was an all-male affair.

During his time as a student-at-law, Laskin was less concerned with the women inside Osgoode Hall than a certain woman outside of it. Her name was Gertrude Tenenbaum but she was always known as Peggy. Her background was similar to that of many Jewish families who migrated from smaller centres to provincial capitals across Canada for a combination of cultural, educational, and economic reasons. The Tenenbaums moved from Campbellford, a small town in eastern Ontario, to Toronto about 1930 when the time came for the children to attend university. Peggy's father had died at an early age but his widow

Rebecca sent two of their children to the University of Toronto even during the depths of the Depression. Peggy graduated with her Bachelor of Household Science degree in 1933 and her brother Sam two years later with a Bachelor of Science.[42] The family lived at 59 Clinton Street, not far from the Laskins, in an extended family household that included Peggy's uncle and aunt.

The young men of Sigma Alpha Mu cultivated a particular reputation as ladies' men, and dating a 'Sammy' was considered quite an accomplishment for young Jewish women of the day. Peggy must have been the envy of her peers as one of the three official organizers of the annual Sigma Alpha Mu dance in February 1936, held at the Crystal Ballroom of the King Edward Hotel.[43] This was no mere social gathering but a community event patronized by local rabbis and Jewish business and professional leaders, with the proceeds going to assist the work of the Jewish Big Brothers and Sisters. The evening was particularly poignant as Bora and Peggy contemplated the coming year of separation when Bora would pursue graduate work at Harvard.

Bora Laskin's years at Osgoode Hall Law School coincided with the high-water mark of the inter-war campaign to reform legal education in Ontario. The benchers' decision to create a part-time law school as a supplement to the apprenticeship experience had been a progressive move when taken in 1889, but even at that time bolder initiatives were being taken elsewhere. A reform movement favouring full-time university legal education had taken shape in the United States after the Civil War, as part of a general gravitation of professional education towards the increasingly prestigious halls of higher learning. Reforms at Harvard Law School undertaken by Dean Christopher Columbus Langdell provided a beacon for legal educators across North America. Appointed in 1870, Langdell had raised admission standards, introduced the 'case method' of instruction, and emphasized the importance of legal scholarship by his faculty members. The cause of full-time university legal education was taken up in Canada at Dalhousie (1883), and in New Brunswick (1892), Alberta (1912), Saskatchewan (1913), and Manitoba (1914), while it had been available in Quebec since 1848. Receiving one's call to the bar after articling only, without a university degree in law, was increasingly perceived as a 'second-best' alternative. By the 1930s well over 80 per cent of those called to the bar in Nova Scotia each year held an LLB from Dalhousie, for example, and in some years this rose to 100 per cent.[44] The Law Society of Upper Canada remained isolated in its determination to require attendance at its own law school as the sole recognized method of joining the legal profession.

A variety of constituencies expressed concern about the Law Society's methods with increasing vehemence after the First World War. The Canadian Bar Association (CBA), founded in 1914, was active in pressing for full-time university legal education, and in this it was joined by the handful of full-time legal academics teaching outside Ontario, men such as Dalhousians John Read, Horace Read, Donald MacRae, and Sidney Smith, and F.C. Cronkite and Malcolm McIntyre in the west. In 1923 MacRae, then dean at Dalhousie and chair of the CBA's Legal Education Committee, presented a report to the CBA highly critical of the situation at Osgoode Hall. In 1928 a Carnegie-funded study of legal education in Canada could barely conceal its disdain for the 'antiquated' concurrent system of lawyer training and the low standard of admission to legal education in Ontario.[45] All these critiques took for granted two major premises: that university education, both pre-legal and legal, would produce 'better' lawyers, and that one could define with some precision what 'good' lawyers should be.

The Law Society was not entirely deaf to these criticisms. Dean Falconbridge was able to persuade the benchers to raise the standard of admission in 1927 to two years of university, and to increase the hours of instruction. With the advent of the Depression, however, the benchers backtracked: in 1932 the standard for admission was returned to senior matriculation (Ontario grade thirteen or first-year university). Any suggestion that the benchers were concerned about impecunious law entrants was countered by their 1933 decision to double the admission fee to $100 and raise tuition from $100 to $150. As a piece of student doggerel put it,

> They raised the fees and lowered the standards
> To get the poor boy within the portal
> And then when exam time came around
> They slaughtered them with many a chortle.[46]

The Depression posed a grave threat to the Law Society's continuing reliance on articling as the cornerstone of its legal education strategy. Established lawyers were reluctant to take on students even on a voluntary basis because of the lack of legal work, resulting in many instances of 'articling on paper.' Such problems had always existed but their scale was seen to be greatly magnified during the Depression.

Critics of the Law Society's monopoly over legal education saw these developments as proof that the articling system was broken, could not be fixed, and should be supplanted by university legal education. In June 1933 the benchers responded by creating a special committee to study legal education in Ontario. Students at Osgoode Hall were asked to provide their views, and did so in a separate report published in the *Canadian Bar Review*.[47] The students agreed with the points made by the most passionate of the reformers: a university education should be the minimum entrance standard, and a full-time law school was needed. Yet, the benchers' committee 1935 report strongly defended the status quo, lamenting 'the tendency ... to emphasize unduly the academic training at the expense of efficient office training.'[48] This was consistent with the reaction of the benchers to nearly every issue brought before them during the 1930s: 'significant change would be both impractical and wrong in principle.'[49] The benchers did propose an alteration to the existing regime, but it only added insult to injury; lectures should be squeezed in first thing in the morning and last thing in the afternoon, so that the bulk of the day could be spent in a law office, and the overall number of hours of instruction was to be reduced while the topics covered would remain the same.

The new regime began in Laskin's last year of articling, 1935–6. After a one-hour lecture at 9:00 a.m., students went to the office until a final lecture from 4:40 to 5:30 p.m. rounded out the day. A year into the new dispensation the students once again protested. A committee chaired by Bora Laskin, now possessed of a certain leadership profile at Osgoode, lectured the benchers one last time on the unsuitability of their approach to legal education. One could not call their report an attempt to persuade. It shows little appreciation of some of the problems with which the benchers were, at least partly in good faith, attempting to grapple at a time of unprecedented economic turmoil. Rather, it is a last attempt to state for the record the unshakeable conviction of its authors that the benchers were wrong. Officially the product of a six-man committee including G. Arthur Martin and Moffatt Hancock, the report is written in a style clearly identifiable as Bora Laskin's. This was the first occasion on which he practised publicly the kind of unflinching critique he would later direct at courts, university administrations, and governments.

The report opened with the authors' view of the role of the legal profession and the goals of legal education: '[M]embers of the Bar in Ontario belong to a learned profession (rather than a trade craft), which is most intimately conceived [sic] with the regulation of the social relations among all members of the community. Such being the case, methods of legal education should be directed towards the enhancement of the prestige of the profession. The object of legal education must be to [produce] a cultured class of well-trained men and women, having a deep insight into the history and spirit of the law, and a knowledge of the trend of the social conditions to which it must be made applicable.'[50] To replace the concurrent system, the committee promoted a full-time law school run by academics at arms' length from the benchers, followed by practical training of some kind. Thinking of law as a social science was key: 'the almost abysmal ignorance of the social sciences that exists among lawyers ... has reduced the profession, in the mind of the ordinary layman, to the status of a trade.' The necessity of a rapprochement with the social sciences was founded on the notion, articulated in Caesar Wright's 1932 article 'An Extra-Legal Approach to Law,' that 'the impetus to all important law reforms has come from outside rather than inside the legal profession.'[51] This need was particularly obvious in Ontario, 'which has been content to travel in the ruts of traditional technique, oblivious of changes in the social scene.'[52]

Earlier student reports had advocated a university education for its ability to 'overcome the bad habits of intellectual passivity contracted under the spoon feeding methods of our primary and secondary educational system.'[53] Laskin's report, by contrast, stated quite baldly that 'entrance to the law school course ... should be [restricted to] those men and women ... who seem most likely, in the long run, to make better lawyers and citizens.' Graduation from university was in itself a badge of the 'better citizen.' By allowing matriculants to enter, the benchers were only encouraging 'heedless persons who, with no special taste or aptitude for law, are anxious to enter that profession which will honour them with its credentials at the lowest price.' It is not clear why university graduates are automatically assumed to have a 'special taste or aptitude for law,' while non-graduates are not. Nor is it clear why university graduates should make better citizens. Attempts were made by others to show that matriculants were disbarred in greater proportions than lawyers who had attended university, but some leaders of the profession had admittedly entered as matriculants.

This concern about the type of lawyer being created was inextricably bound up with the issue of how many of them were being produced. The Laskin report was in no doubt on this point: 'the legal profession is admittedly and indubitably overcrowded ... [S]ome sort of limitations on the annual output of lawyers has become a drastic necessity.'[54] It has been argued in the U.S. context that admissions standards were raised in the 1920s in order to keep members of newly landed ethnic groups away from the bar,[55] an argument cautiously refuted for Ontario.[56] Of the two steps taken by the Law Society that might be seen as exclusive – the new requirement of certificates of respectability of articling students in 1929, and the raising of the admission standard to two years of university in 1927 – the first rapidly became meaningless and the second was revoked in 1932. The Laskin report shows that any concerns about limiting entry came from students-at-law as well as the bar. It is a predictable response by insecure young proto-lawyers at a time of economic crisis. The concern about the format of legal education is not so easily analysed. In hindsight, the insistence on pre-law university education and university-based legal education looks like a blatant attempt to limit the bar to middle-class entrants; in turn, this would likely render legal education disproportionately inaccessible to women and members of some minority groups. At first glance the benchers seem more democratic than the student critics in their insistence in admitting all who applied; the poor but talented matriculant who survived the dreaded first-year cull stood a good chance of entering the profession.

Yet it is likely that Laskin had in mind exactly the opposite outcome. His own entry into the profession had almost been short-circuited by his difficulty in finding a principal. His goal in transferring legal education to the university was in part to create a more meritocratic entry process for the profession, removing the bar's collective power to refuse entry to members of disadvantaged groups by refusing them articles. For Laskin, the point about matriculants was that only those with sufficient connection to find a principal got in the door, while university graduates such as himself without those connections might well not. He did not say this openly in the report; one did not openly accuse the bar of discrimination in 1936. Laskin's preference for university legal education was motivated not only by intellectual and public relations concerns but also by a sense that the university was a less arbitrary gatekeeper to the bar than the legal profession itself. As Caesar Wright noted a few years later, while he believed in some form of practical training, 'it should be a uniform training open to all students regardless of race, creed or colour and that is a practical impossibility under the existing system. We have found this out this year with the difficulty attendant on admitting a negro lawyer to a respectable office.'[57] The invocation of the culture and image of the profession in Laskin's report appear to be calculated to appeal to the bar on the basis of self-interest. Some of his gravest concerns he chose not to voice in the report.

The benchers weathered the storm of criticism of the early 1930s seemingly unscathed. The public were concerned with far graver issues and, unlike the situation a dozen years later, there was little media interest in this tempest in the juridical teapot. The benchers' uncompromising stance in the 1935 report ushered in a 'decade of frustration' for those committed to reform: the Laskin report would be the last gasp in the reform campaign until after the war. In the short term, it was a parting shot by some disgruntled students. Over the long haul, it would be the opening volley in what Laskin himself called 'the fiercest debate' in the history of the Ontario legal profession.

In the spring of 1936 Laskin's anger at the intransigence of the benchers mingled with excitement at the prospect of graduation and moving on to Harvard. Male members of the class were exhorted to attend the graduation dinner at the Piccadilly Hotel on 19 March. 'It represents the last function at which all [sic] the members of the year will foregather before spreading out all over the Province ... Publicity is scorned and events are treated with the utmost secrecy and confidence ... It is not a party nor a mere dinner: it is a ritual.'[58]

As Laskin's class prepared to graduate in the spring of 1936, the editors of *Obiter Dicta* ran sketches of sixteen of those felt to be class leaders (all male, needless to say). These portraits leaned towards the light-hearted, replete with references to wine, women, and eccentric behaviour, leavened with occasional predictions of future greatness. Bora Laskin's began with a couplet from Wordsworth's *The Oak and the Broom*: 'And he is oft the wisest man, Who is not wise at all.' Laskin's memorialist chose to focus on his keen mind and his politics:

We do not remember associating with anyone who is more truly wise, or one who flees more vigorously from the appellation 'wise' than Bora, or 'Butch,' as he is familiarly called. For 'Butch' is no mere 'gatherer and disposer of other men's stuff,' no mere human dictaphone, as are so many so-called students at Osgoode. 'Butch' has a keen mind, an originality and literary flair that mark him out from the common run of fact-grinders. He is widely read, has a vigorous vocabulary, and speaks in the Burkian tradition. Politically, 'Butch' is mildly socialistic. We have often heard him expatiate, calmly and dispassionately, on the absurd paradox of people starving in the midst of plenty, and the inhuman gulf that exists in society between extreme penury and extreme opulence. We have approved his sane views on the need for reform and the means by which reform can be sanely introduced. 'Butch' is not a bombastic Bolshevik with a bomb, but rather a sane sage with a sedative. We predict that he will be Canada's belated but much needed 'first' statesman.[59]

In equating Laskin's expression of political views with a desire for political office (he seems to be predicting that Laskin will become the first Jewish prime minister of Canada), the author misunderstood Laskin's ambitions. He was passionate about politics in the broadest sense but shrank from partisan political activity. A number of young Jewish lawyers were beginning to find that joining a political party was one way to do an end run around the prejudice they faced in the private sector. Liberal Premier Mitch Hepburn rewarded Jewish lawyers active in the party with patronage appointments and, notably, invited David Croll into his cabinet as minister of public welfare in 1934, making him the first Jewish cabinet minister in Canada. Such rewards held little temptation for Laskin.

This description of Laskin's public persona shows why the aura of leadership clung to him. He could speak effectively about injustice but was not a strident exponent of the causes he espoused. Rather he speaks 'calmly and dispassionately' and – three times! – 'sanely.' He was not arrogant, fleeing from the appellation 'wise.' Laskin had found the right mix of conviction, humility, and assertiveness to move people without alienating them. On paper, as in the student report, he could sound harsh and unyielding, but this was balanced by a less threatening and more moderated personal presence.

The summer of 1936 witnessed a realignment of the Laskin household. Charles graduated with his Bachelor of Commerce degree and went off to seek employment in Winnipeg. Bluma and Saul returned to Fort William while Bora relished the thought of completing his legal education at Harvard. Probably he relished as well the prospect of some personal independence, long delayed by his lack of income. For years he had been dependent even for spending money on brother Chuck, whose winnings at pool brought in more than Bora's articling wages. That summer he earned a little money teaching at the Workers' Educational Association summer school at Pickering College, Newmarket, where he and Finkelman and Auld lectured on the new *Industrial*

Standards Act passed by Mitch Hepburn's government the previous year.[60] The Act allowed the minister of labour to enforce standard hours and wages in particular industries after a conference of interested parties, and was seen by some as a stepping stone to some kind of collective bargaining legislation.

In his first six years in Toronto Bora Laskin had achieved everything he had aspired to upon leaving Fort William as an eager seventeen-year-old – and more. He had departed planning to become a lawyer, but somehow had shifted on to a career path as a legal academic along the way. Undoubtedly his own success and the encouragement of his professors had something to do with this switch. What cannot be known – what Laskin himself could probably not have known – is whether, had there been fewer barriers to entering mainstream law firms, he might have embarked on a more traditional legal career. Given his preoccupation with legal scholarship from the outset of his engagement with the law, it would seem not. Laskin had set his course as an 'ideas man' from a very early date, but the type of scholar he became owed much to the support and influence of Caesar Wright and the faculty members at the University of Toronto. All of them provided excellent role models for Laskin, combining a passion for ideas with real-world engagement across a spectrum of broadly progressive causes. Laskin would never pursue theory for the sake of theory. Like his mentors, he was always happiest when bringing legal theory to bear on some knotty problem in real life, whether it was the regulation of collective bargaining, the division of property on marriage breakdown, or constitutional reform.

4

Harvard

Bora Laskin's education at Toronto and Osgoode had provided a solid, perhaps even a superior, intellectual preparation for the work he would undertake at Harvard Law School. Where Toronto paled in comparison with Harvard was in the sheer scale and scope of the legal education enterprise. After three years in the decrepit old house on St George Street, Laskin was in awe of the templelike edifice inhabited by the Harvard Law School.[1] Langdell Hall's severe classical façade of fifteen enormous Ionic columns rivalled the U.S. Supreme Court itself for sheer majesty. The interior was no less daunting. In the lofty-ceilinged library, students scuttled among book stacks under the baleful gaze of dead Supreme Court judges and Harvard professors whose portraits ringed the room. In Langdell and nearby Austin Hall some fourteen hundred students were taught by a full-time faculty of thirty-five supplemented by casual lecturers – a professorial complement larger than the total number of law professors in Canada at the time.

The large student body was diverse geographically, but in few other respects. Women were not admitted. There were exactly two blacks, no Asians and few from ethnic minorities except for a small Jewish contingent. Roughly 80 per cent of the LLB students came from Harvard itself, Yale, and Princeton, the rest from a select group of colleges whose standards Harvard trusted. Even so, Laskin was exposed to a certain cross-section of the American population: 'brilliant Jewish graduates of City College of New York, ramrod-straight products of West Point,

earnest day-trippers from Dorchester and Arlington, ... sons of the farm
from Kansas, graduates of Ole Miss with broad Southern accents, tweed-
jacketed fashion plates from Williams, wearing button-downs and fou-
lards ... and snap brim, felt hats[,] ... direct descendants of the Pilgrim
settlers and second-generation citizens whose parents had arrived from
Russia only decades before.'[2] Graduate students in law mingled with
the LLB population because they usually took only two purely graduate courses, with the other three chosen from the LLB curriculum. The
LLB degree was the main attraction, the graduate program very much a
sideshow. There were only about forty graduate students, including a
number doing independent research as well as the LLM and SJD
students, with few from outside the United States. Only seventeen
students graduated in Laskin's LLM class in 1937, of whom three were
German, one was English, and the rest were American.

Securing admission to Harvard was not too difficult with Caesar
Wright's letter of recommendation.[3] Finances were the possible stum-
bling block. Laskin had virtually no savings, and probably deferred his
call to the bar to 1937 because it cost $161. Tuition fees alone would be
$400, but fortunately Harvard was able to offer Laskin a scholarship in
that amount.[4] Basic living expenses in Cambridge amounted to at least
$15 per week over some nine or ten months, and there would be
occasional trips to Toronto – a year without seeing each other was more
than Bora and Peggy could tolerate.[5] A family caucus was called, and it
was decided to give Bora the nest egg set aside for Saul's university
education.[6] This decision clearly illustrated Bora's dominance within
the family, but if Saul resented it he never let it interfere with their close
fraternal relationship. Now eighteen, Saul would return to the Lakehead,
look for work, and help his father around the store. In due course Bora,
Max, and Bluma planned to assist Saul with his university education,
but with the war's intervention his turn never came.

Laskin found a room at 65 Hammond Street, in a large frame house
just five minutes from the law school. Classes began on 28 September,
when Laskin enrolled in five courses: Administrative Law with Felix
Frankfurter, Jurisprudence with Roscoe Pound and Sidney Post Simpson,
both graduate courses, Labor Law with Livingston Hall, Equity III with
Zechariah Chafee, and Government Control of Business with James
Angell McLaughlin. Three of these courses were tested by examination,
one by a major research paper, and one by a master's thesis, which
Laskin chose to do in Frankfurter's course. Caesar Wright's ongoing ties
with some of the faculty undoubtedly eased his entry into this intimi-

dating world. Warren Seavey graciously afforded Laskin a personal interview early on and reminisced that Wright's thesis defence was the first he had attended.[7]

In spite of its magnificent facilities, most students found Harvard Law offered a truly 'Spartan education.'[8] This was especially true at the LLB level, where the rigorous pruning of the class from around six hundred entrants to four hundred graduates left few feeling they could afford any leisure time. Laskin's straitened finances and his desire to excel ensured that a brisk walk along the Charles River was his main distraction. He recalled living on two meals a day and spending 'most of my time in the library because that was the most secure place I could be away from whatever temptations Cambridge or Boston offered.'[9] Like any good Canadian, Laskin was surprised to find the library open on Sunday. He soon met fellow Canadian Fred Fraser, who had earned his master's degree the year before and was staying on with the aid of a research fellowship.[10] Fraser came from an elite Halifax family – his father Sir Frederick Fraser was well known for his work with the blind – and the two men did not move beyond a superficial acquaintance. It is not known whether Laskin ran across a young Nova Scotian named Robert Stanfield, then in the first year of his LLB course at Harvard, or the only other Canadian, a second-year student from Vancouver named Herbert Barclay. Stanfield achieved notoriety at the end of his first year for being the only student in living memory to decline a place on the prestigious *Harvard Law Review* when it was offered to him.[11]

Laskin's one lasting friendship from his Harvard days was with an American, Albert Salisbury Abel, with whom he took Felix Frankfurter's course. Abel was raised in Iowa, graduated with his first law degree from Harvard in 1930, and returned to do his LLM in the same year as Laskin. He completed a doctorate in law at Harvard in 1943 and later taught at the West Virginia College of Law. So close was their bond that Laskin took the unusual step of persuading Caesar Wright to offer Abel a position at Toronto in 1955, and Abel took the even more unusual step (for an American scholar of constitutional law) of accepting. The single most significant legacy from Laskin's Harvard days was a personal as well as intellectual one: his encounter with Al Abel.

Given the dominance of the Harvard model in the thinking of both Caesar Wright and Bora Laskin and in Canadian legal education gener-ally, it is worth examining exactly what Harvard Law School stood for in the mid-1930s.[12] Harvard's pre-eminence had long rested on the efforts of Dean Christopher Langdell (1870–95) to transform legal education and scholarship in North America by using the more interactive case method of teaching instead of the grand lecture, and drawing explicitly on models from the natural sciences. By the 1930s, however, the law school had lost its previously undisputed place as 'the' national law school, and tensions bubbled among the faculty. Laskin's first day of classes in 1936 was the last day of Roscoe Pound's twenty-year deanship, and many laid the blame for Harvard's perceived decline at his feet. All Pound's successes in fund-raising and library expansion could not allay the sense of malaise plaguing the faculty in the 1930s.

Even as some other Ivy League schools experimented with the curriculum and with new teaching methodologies, Dean Pound kept Harvard's educational methods true to Langdell's vision: the case method, the dominance of private law, large classes rather than clinics or small seminars, and the sink-or-swim approach to legal education. The famous aphorism of nineteenth-century English legal historian F.W. Maitland became Pound's mantra: 'taught law is tough law.' And tough law was for men only: women were determinedly kept out. The first two years of the curriculum were devoted entirely to private law. Only in third year did students take Constitutional Law, and Administrative Law was a third-year option. Until 1927 the 'mission statement' of the faculty was contained in one sentence: 'the design of this School is to afford such a training in the fundamental principles of English and American Law as will constitute the best preparation for the practice of the profession in any place where that system of law prevails.' Only in that year was the training of law teachers (a function of the tiny graduate program) added to the mission, and an oblique reference made to legal scholarship.[13]

A few professors of public law, such as Felix Frankfurter, James Landis, and Edmund Morgan, innovated to a modest extent by creating courses such as Public Utilities and Government Control of Business, but for the most part legal education remained ossified at Harvard. Meanwhile, the realists at Chicago and Yale were experimenting with curricular change based on the idea that factual patterns rather than legal concepts should determine legal categorization. Chicago created a four-year optional curriculum in 1937 aimed at evaluating 'the social workings of the law,' and including courses in psychology, economic and political theory, and accounting.[14] Yale incorporated agency, partnership, and corporation law into courses on business organizations, and offered a sequence of three courses on business losses, management, and finance. Even if Yale realists did not always incorporate their theory into their pedagogy, there was a liveliness, a willingness to question received ideas about legal education at Yale.[15] As Abe Fortas, later a Supreme Court justice but then teaching at Yale, recalled, 'Harvard people tended to look at us as unsound maniacs, and we in turn looked upon them as antiques who time had passed by.'[16]

As for legal scholarship, Harvard had many men who authored major texts in their fields, but only two who were asking the big questions about the role of law in society. Roscoe Pound and Felix Frankfurter were the brightest stars on faculty, and both had already influenced Bora Laskin through their writings as he developed his own legal philosophy. Pound, however, seemed to be retreating further every day from the implications of 'sociological jurisprudence,' the school of thought he had founded early in the century. He remains nonetheless a major figure in legal theory. Trained as a botanist before studying law, Pound was able to translate the relativistic and evolutionary features of post-Darwinian science into a modern theory of law. Legal sceptics such as Oliver Wendell Holmes had helped to undermine legal conceptualism (or formalism) and the 'discovery' theory of law in the late nineteenth century, but Pound went beyond criticism to reconstruction. A key element in his theory was the embrace of pragmatism as an antidote to formalism. 'The sociological movement in jurisprudence,' he declared, 'is a movement for pragmatism as a philosophy of law; for the adjustment of principles and doctrines to the human conditions they are to govern rather than to assumed first principles; for putting the human factor in the central place and relegating logic to its true position as an instrument.'[17] Like logic, legal ideas too were merely instruments and should be judged by the adequacy of the results they produced. Sociological jurisprudents were willing to accept a more creative and somewhat experimental role for the judiciary, to encourage a functionalist approach to statutory interpretation and to law in general, and to look to other disciplines to enrich and inform the law and legal education.

Avant-garde in some of his ideas, Pound was no revolutionary. He remained a devotee of the common law and revered its organicism with an almost mystical zeal. Indeed, Pound's spidery runic script made one imagine a gaunt Druidic figure holding the pen, but in fact he looked more like a Midwestern version of Santa Claus. Pound's retreat from the implications of his theory, his nostalgic Anglophilia, and his fortress mentality were all on full display in a conference he organized at Harvard the month before Bora Laskin arrived. As part of the 1936

celebrations of Harvard's tercentenary, the law school held a 'Conference on the Future of the Common Law,' where jurists from Britain,
Canada, and the Irish Free State joined their American colleagues for
three days of discussion in August.[18] The pace was leisurely: two papers given in the morning, lunch al fresco on the lawn in front of
Langdell Hall, and discussion in the afternoon. The speakers (all judges,
with Supreme Court judge Henry Davis representing Canada) all addressed the history of the common law in their own jurisdictions, and
none addressed the role of law in the current crisis. Like W.P.M. Kennedy
in Toronto, Pound was keen to stress the common law heritage linking
the United States to Britain and the Dominions, a connection increasingly imperilled by divergences in public law among the common law
countries. Ironically, Pound's conference may be regarded as the last
major expression of this kind of thought, as the Anglo-American legal
community that had flourished since the end of the Civil War fragmented and largely disappeared after 1939.[19]

The emergence of a rival school of thought, legal realism, threatened
much of what Pound held dear. He and his acolytes typically spoke of
the 'adjustment' of legal rules and competing interests, a purposefully
vague word that provided little assistance in determining how judges
did or should go about their work. Into this gap rushed the legal
realists, first at Columbia, then at Yale. They agreed with Pound that
abstract formal analysis did not explain the results of judicial decisions,
but pushed the agenda further. The role of Pound in legal thought can
be analogized to that of Henry James in the history of the novel; both
broke with the prevailing canons of formal representation and authorial omniscience, but still adhered to a recognizable 'story line.' The
realists play the role of James Joyce or Virginia Woolf, whose full-blown
subjectivism undermined the formal narrative structure employed by
their predecessors.[20] Realists such as Karl Llewellyn, Jerome Frank, and
Thurman Arnold denied that the formal reasons articulated by judges
explained anything useful about their actual decisions. A judge's discretion in finding 'facts,' and the inherent indeterminacy of language
and thus of legal rules, meant that judicial decisions were simply manifestations of personal preferences, not objective applications of clear
legal principles. Broad legal rules that ignored factual context, they
said, led to confusion. Thus Leon Green, in applying the realist approach to torts, 'said the question should be whether a railroad engi-
neer or restaurant owner committed a negligent act instead of the legal
ingredients of negligence.'[21]

Pound had kept the realists out of Harvard, but still felt on the defensive. '[M]y chief reason for giving up the Deanship,' he wrote to a friend, 'is that I do not care to be responsible for teaching that law is simply a pious fraud to cover up decisions of cases according to personal inclinations or that there is nothing in the way of reason back of the legal order but it is simply a pulling and hauling of interests with a camouflage of authoritative precepts.'[22] The more radical version of legal realism would quickly run out of steam, but it was at the peak of its strength in the mid-1930s. A less threatening variety, more similar to Pound's functionalism, would prove more enduring.

After two decades of Pound's deanship the law school was also in need of an administrative makeover. In 1933 Harvard appointed a new president, James Bryant Conant, who complained of Pound's 'almost pathological ... inability ... to carry on any sort of decent administration.'[23] The university's most recent historians argue that Conant used the professional schools as the cutting edge of his mission to transform Harvard from a Brahmin to a meritocratic institution of learning. This was in sharp contrast to Conant's predecessor A. Lawrence Lowell, who had tried to impose Jewish quotas in the 1920s and to keep blacks out of Harvard dormitories. Professor Edmund Morgan served as acting dean for the year until Pound's replacement was confirmed. Laskin reported to Caesar Wright early in the new year that the appointment of James Landis, while popular, had caused some surprise because he was seen as a protégé of Felix Frankfurter.[24] Landis had not in fact been Frankfurter's first choice, but the two men were usually paired because of their closeness to the Roosevelt administration and their role in the New Deal. Indeed, Landis had been on leave as chair of the Securities Exchange Commission when named dean. He was a much abler administrator than Pound and hired men such as Paul Freund, Milton Katz, and Lon Fuller, who would become the law school's best- known scholars of the next generation.

Felix Frankfurter's Jewish immigrant background was similar to Laskin's, though Frankfurter was himself an immigrant, arriving in the United States from Austria at the age of twelve. Quick, mercurial, ambitious, Frankfurter spoke non-stop but revealed very little about himself; a law clerk called him 'a very private public person.'[25] Alluding to his course in Public Utilities, students declared

> You learn no law in Public U.
> That is its fascination,
> But Felix gives a point of view
> And pleasant conversation.[26]

Frankfurter's 'insider-outsider' status has continued to fascinate biographers, who have puzzled over the contradictions between his public radicalism as a professor and his seemingly over-eager embrace of traditional American values when on the Supreme Court.[27] There is more than a faint echo of Frankfurter's struggles to be accepted by the Boston Brahmins in Bora Laskin's experiences in Toronto. Frankfurter had pursued a varied career in government service and academe, and attracted public attention for his bold and unpopular defence of the anarchists and convicted murderers Sacco and Vanzetti in the late 1920s. He became an intimate of Franklin D. Roosevelt, who offered him the solicitor-generalship shortly after his inauguration as president in 1932, but Frankfurter preferred to remain at Harvard as an 'unofficial adviser, without being bound to the inexorable demands of an exacting office.'[28] Like Laskin, Frankfurter valued his independence as a public intellectual, but he was much more publicly aligned with a particular administration than Laskin would ever be. In January 1939 Roosevelt would appoint Frankfurter to the Supreme Court to replace Benjamin Cardozo. For a young Canadian Jewish lawyer with academic aspirations, Frankfurter was an awe-inspiring role model, and the chance to study with him a magnificent boon. Laskin's career as academic, government adviser, activist, public intellectual, and finally judge, paralleled Frankfurter's in striking fashion. In some ways Laskin went Frankfurter one better, achieving the public respect and sense of fulfilment at the Supreme Court of Canada that eluded Frankfurter during his own judicial career.

Unlike Pound, Frankfurter did not create an entire new school of legal thought, but his public law scholarship and government service carried the concerns of what might be called a critical functionalism directly into the legal lifeblood of America. Nowhere was this more evident than in his book *The Labor Injunction*, co-authored with Nathan Greene in 1930.[29] Harry Arthurs has acknowledged this 'early realist/ empiricist muckracking classic' as profoundly formative for him in the 1950s, when he was introduced to it in Bora Laskin's Labour Law class. It clearly made an impact on Laskin, who cited it in some of his earliest publications.[30] In the decades before labour unions were certified and collective bargaining protected by legislation, U.S. employers often sought to enjoin the activities of striking employees as an illegal interference with the employer's business or trade. Such injunctions were regularly granted on an ex parte basis, and breach was punished by contempt proceedings before a single judge rather than a jury. Frankfurter and Greene documented beyond any reasonable doubt that the labour injunction was deployed abusively by an anti-union judiciary to shore up the prerogatives of capital. Their solution, adopted in federal legislation two years later, was much tighter regulation of the process by which such injunctions could be granted.

Once very close, Frankfurter and Pound initially became estranged over Pound's seeming appeasement of Lawrence Lowell's anti-Semitic tendencies. Pound himself travelled to Germany in June 1934, came to regard Hitler as a leader who could create order out of agitated central Europe, and accepted an honorary degree from the University of Berlin that fall. The awarding of the degree at Harvard itself by the German ambassador caused considerable consternation. James Bryant Conant refused to be photographed with the party and Frankfurter lamented that Langdell Hall was being 'turned into a Nazi holiday.'[31] The rift widened further as Pound sought to curtail Felix Frankfurter's activities in Washington even though he himself had been very active in advising the Hoover administration a dozen years earlier. He grew distrustful of the broad discretion granted to administrative agencies, sceptical of their claims of expertise and ever more reverential towards the common law, even as Frankfurter was helping to build the new administrative state and directing dozens of Harvard's best students to positions in the New Deal agencies.

The debate over anti-Semitic practices at Harvard resumed during Laskin's year there, precipitated by President Conant's determination to move the university in a more meritocratic direction. Admissions practices at the law school until the end of Pound's deanship seem to have incorporated informal quotas for some ethno-religious groups. In December 1936 the faculty assembly decided that in future, academic standing would be the only relevant criterion for admission. The motion passed with little debate but in January some faculty moved to reopen the question. The new rules, observed J.A. McLaughlin, 'would have the effect of excluding many men from Catholic schools and from Southern Colleges and would exclude very few Jews.' Frankfurter's own notes of the debate record McLaughlin as attributing a good deal of anti-Semitism in the student body 'to jealousy of the Jewish students; many of the men from Princeton, Harvard and Yale, whose way had been greased by prep schools and who had gotten through college with a "gentleman's C" found, upon coming to the Law School, that there was stiff competition for the first time, and that with Jewish students.'[32] Felix Frankfurter reminded his colleagues that in 1923 'the Governing Boards of the University by solemn vote had declared against any such discrimination' and the meeting concluded by maintaining the standards set in December. The impact was sudden: the failure rate of the class entering in 1937 was only 20 per cent, 10 per cent less than the rate of the previous class. The higher standards also aroused controversy: when interviewed by the *Harvard Crimson* Acting Dean Morgan 'regretted that many Harvard seniors were protesting against the stiffer entrance requirements to be introduced next fall.'[33]

Pound's departure also allowed more sustained attention to curriculum matters. The issue of adding a fourth year to the LLB had been discussed in a desultory way in previous years. There was a vague sense that students needed exposure to broader comparative and historical perspectives on law, but no consensus on whether a fourth year of such material should be compulsory or optional, or whether it should be recognized as an 'enriched' LLB or as an LLM in its own right. Frankfurter was adamant that 'it was impossible to mix fourth-year work, which included large numbers of students, with graduate work as conceived now by the Graduate Committee.' For him, graduate work was about contributing to legal scholarship, not taking more courses, and it involved an 'intimate companionship' between the faculty member and the student. Those who shared his romantic vision had proposed getting rid of graduate degrees altogether when the faculty reviewed its graduate program a few years earlier, in order to avoid the tendency to 'stifling standardization' in modern universities. In Frankfurter's view, the social sciences proceeded on the basis that men were capable of giving direction to social organization, and the furtherance of these efforts 'in those aspects of social control which we call law is ... the aim and the justification of our graduate work.'[34]

W.P.M. Kennedy's aims for graduate work in law at the University of Toronto in the 1930s and '40s were expressed in virtually identical terms, and in the 'fourth-year debate' of the late 1930s Harvard unwittingly contemplated moving its LLB curriculum closer to his model. Although exposure to other disciplines and broader juridical vistas would not be incorporated throughout the law program, as at Toronto, the faculty voted to study an enriched optional fourth-year program that would include compulsory courses in jurisprudence and comparative law, choices from a suite of courses in public law, international law, and legal history, plus joint seminars with students in other disciplines.[35] The course was to be introduced in 1941–2, but never materialized in view of the more utilitarian demands of the war years and the post-war period.

In comparison to other programs at Yale, Columbia, and Pennsylvania, the Harvard that Caesar Wright and Bora Laskin chose as their model of legal education was in many ways a bastion of traditionalism and certainly an island of male privilege.[36] This did not stop them from representing it to Canadians as the cutting edge of legal education. In their defence, it may be observed that foreign graduate students under Felix Frankfurter's tutelage (as most Canadians were in the 1920s and '30s) probably had a better experience of Harvard than most LLB students.[37] Wright and Laskin would continue to recommend graduate work at Harvard to their most talented students throughout their careers, and Harvard regained some of its lost prestige in the post-war years. They were not alone in their embrace of Harvard. Dozens of Maritimers had attended Harvard Law School in the nineteenth century for their first law degree, and it was Dalhousie LLB holders who began doing graduate work in law at Harvard in the early 1920s when the LLM degree began to be offered.[38] Wright was himself encouraged to attend Harvard by Dalhousian Sidney Smith, who had studied there (though only as a special non-degree student), and by Donald MacRae. MacRae had transformed Dalhousie's curriculum along Harvard lines after succeeding Richard Chapman Weldon, a Yale-trained political scientist, in 1914, and persuaded Harvard to recognize the Dalhousie degree for purposes of graduate work. The 'MacRae curriculum' in turn was adopted by the Canadian Bar Association in 1920 as a standard suggested for adoption in all the common law provinces.[39]

The appeal of the Harvard model in early twentieth-century Canada is easily explained. As a small coterie of legal academics and some members of the bar aimed at selling the university model to provincial bar societies (and especially to the Law Society of Upper Canada), Harvard's large competitive classes, private law-oriented curriculum, exclusively masculine atmosphere, and professionally successful alumni could be portrayed as largely in tune with the values and needs of the legal profession. The fact that Harvard was doing some serious soul-searching about its own approach to legal education in the 1930s went unreported and unremarked in Canada. Wright would have found it simply unbelievable that Harvard was seriously contemplating moving in a direction similar to Kennedy's law school, which he despised so heartily.

Wright and Laskin enjoyed Harvard for its stimulating intellectual atmosphere, but were especially impressed with the kind of cross-fertilization among the practising bar, emerging administrative agencies, the judiciary, and legal academe found there. In the United States, the professoriate at the Ivy League law schools formed a respected and independent 'third branch' of the legal profession alongside the judiciary and the practising profession, feeding ideas to the policy establishments in Washington and the state capitals. Law professors did not just teach and produce scholarship, they were *important*. In Canada, legal academics were still a tiny and beleaguered band of idealists, bit players in the great theatre of the law. At Harvard Laskin had a vision of how a law professor might stride to the centre-stage of national life. Later, he went on to live it.

For someone with Laskin's interests and political views, it was a turbulent and exciting time to be doing graduate work in the United States. As Eric Hobsbawm has said, the America of the 1920s and early 1930s 'was a watch-word for the hard-faced pursuit of profit, for injustice, for ruthless, unscrupulous and brutal repression. But F.D.R.'s U.S.A. not only disclaimed this reputation: it turned it sharply to the left. It visibly became a government for the poor and the unions.'[40] The *National Labor Relations Act* had been passed in 1935, mandating collective bargaining between employers and unions for the first time and providing machinery for the supervision of a union certification process, but it and other pieces of Roosevelt's New Deal legislation were under attack in the courts. A conservative bloc on the Supreme Court had already struck down a number of key statutes, including the *National Industrial Recovery Act*. The low point was reached in June 1936 with the invalidation of a New York minimum wage law. As Bora Laskin arrived at Harvard, the fate of Roosevelt's 'sharp left turn' was by no means certain.

The Court's continuing hostility to the New Deal led to Roosevelt's ill-fated court-packing plan, unveiled on 5 February 1937. The bill presented to Congress proposed that when a federal judge failed to retire within six months of reaching the age of seventy, the president would be able to appoint an additional judge to that court, to a maximum of fifteen. In March 1937 the Supreme Court upheld a Washington state law substantially similar to the one it had invalidated the previous year, when Justice Owen Roberts changed his vote. This new five-four majority went on to uphold other key pieces of New Deal legislation, in what Abe Fortas called the 'switch in time that served nine.'[41] Roosevelt's controversial plan suddenly seemed less necessary, and his bill failed in the Senate.

At almost exactly the same time, the Supreme Court of Canada and the Privy Council were invalidating Canada's equivalent to the New Deal, a move that provoked the final campaign to abolish transatlantic appeals. Soon after his defeat of R.B. Bennett in 1935, Mackenzie King had referred Bennett's whole package of social legislation to the Supreme Court of Canada. Acts creating a Dominion Marketing Board to see to the orderly marketing and grading of all manner of farm products, an unemployment insurance scheme with levies on employer, employee, and government contributions, and a rudimentary health insurance scheme were all found invalid by the Supreme Court, and these decisions were affirmed by the Privy Council. In *Re Weekly Rest in Industrial Undertakings Act, Minimum Wages Act and Limitation of Hours of Work Act*, the Supreme Court held the legislation valid as entered into pursuant to a British Empire treaty under section 132 of the *British North America Act*, but the Privy Council reversed their decision. Only the *Farmers' Creditors' Arrangements Act*, aimed at dealing with the prairie farm crisis, was upheld both in Ottawa and London as within the federal power relating to bankruptcy. Years later, Laskin spoke of the effect of reading Frank Scott's 1937 article castigating the Privy Council for these decisions: 'I had just graduated in law at the time and still recall the impact that this piece of writing made upon me.'[42]

Back at Langdell Hall, the court-packing plan aroused considerable interest, and exposed important divisions. Four hundred law students signed a petition opposing the plan, while a bare majority of the faculty signed a public letter decrying the plan's impact on judicial independence. The non-signatories registered their discontent with their colleagues' action behind the closed doors of a faculty meeting. Dean-designate James Landis came out strongly in favour of the plan on the basis that the Court's actions imperilled democracy, while President Conant came out equally strongly against it. A public debate between two teams of law faculty members held at Langdell Hall further explored the issue on 26 March.

Amidst all this agitation, Felix Frankfurter found himself unusually quiet. He had a long history of speaking out publicly on all manner of legal and political issues, and he opposed the plan, but Roosevelt had given his confidant advance warning and exacted a pledge of silence from him. Al Abel recalled Frankfurter's statement to the class on 8 February, the Monday after the court-packing plan was introduced. After announcing 'that there was no occasion to take notes on what he was about to say, ... he proceeded to elaborate on the importance of hallowed institutions and the risks involved in tampering with them. After a prose elegy of some twenty minutes, we took up the assigned cases ... Neither the class nor the President ever got an unequivocal statement of his reaction; but the depth of Frankfurter's feeling when he made the remarks and the depth of his silence thereafter are memorable facts.' When Frankfurter gamely tried to justify his silence to his colleagues on the ground that signing the letter might actually have an effect opposite to that intended, few were convinced. His colleague Ed Warren wrote starkly, 'I think the less of you for this, that is all I care to say.'[43]

A poignant footnote to this debate over the public role of the law professor and the law school occurred the year after Laskin left. In the fall of 1938 the faculty of law of the University of Amsterdam sent an urgent appeal to all faculties of law in the British Empire, the United States, France, and northern Europe, asking them to protest the 'inhuman treatment' and 'violation of the basic principles of justice' occurring in Nazi Germany. The Dutch professors asked the faculties to publish the resolution and to communicate their protest to their respective governments. At a meeting on 6 December 1938 the faculty decided not to support the resolution. Frankfurter sent out a memo of regret to all his colleagues the next day, saying 'I shall sign the proposed protest as an individual member of this faculty, but I shall sign it deeply regretful that the Law School as such is committed to a policy of silence. Of course I agree that this school should not form a habit of protesting against every sort of injustice, [but] the present occasion is unique in the history of the last 1000 years ... Germany is avowedly repudiating by word and deed that conception of the unity of civilization as a whole and of Occidental civilization in particular which is the peculiar function of universities to preserve and cherish.'[44]

The headline events of 1936–7 did not figure in the correspondence Laskin carried on with Caesar Wright and Jacob Finkelman during his year at Harvard; unsurprisingly, it was more concerned with Laskin's prospects for the coming year, laced with a bit of Harvard gossip. With Finkelman, Laskin discussed his writing projects, while Finkelman reported on his – ultimately unsuccessful – efforts to secure Laskin a postgraduate fellowship from the Royal Society of Canada. There was nonetheless some good news: the Burroughs Company would need someone full-time for its *Canadian Abridgment* project in the next year, and Clyde Auld was going to recommend Laskin. 'You will be taken care of for the next year,' wrote Finkelman, to which Laskin replied that he would be delighted to take the job.[45]

The correspondence with Wright was more wide-ranging. At one point Wright thought he might be asked for an opinion on the controversial Millar will case, rumoured to be going on appeal to the Privy Council. The professor was not above asking his protégé to do a little research for him and even requested that when Laskin got an opportunity he 'might quietly attempt to draw Roscoe on the question.'[46] Millar was a wealthy and eccentric barrister who died without issue in 1926, leaving the bulk of his estate to the Toronto woman who, in the ten years after his death, should have the largest number of children. Some of Millar's relatives sought to have the will declared invalid as contrary to public policy in order to inherit on an intestacy. This doctrine declares invalid certain stipulations in wills and contracts if they contravene core values or interests ordinarily protected by law. The courts had reluctantly admitted that determinations of public policy had to move with the times, suggesting that a balancing of interests was permitted – in *Millar*, for example, freedom of testation versus the possible risks to health posed to poor women who sought the prize.[47] While he was not able to provide much assistance to Wright on this occasion, Laskin would return to the issue eight years later in the famous case of *Drummond Wren*, where he successfully urged the doctrine on the Ontario High Court in order to invalidate a discriminatory restrictive covenant.[48]

During second term the Administrative Law thesis loomed, but Laskin did not get much individual guidance. 'Frankfurter, of course, at that time, was terribly busy running back and forth to Washington, but I must say for him that he always met his classes in the graduate programme. He was a hard man ... for me to see personally and indeed for anyone, so one had to correspond with him ... I wrote a note to Frankfurter suggesting that I would like to do my thesis on the Ontario Municipal Board [and asking] "What would you think of my doing my thesis on this subject?" And I can still recall his answer ... "Dear Laskin: you yourself should know whether this is worth doing. F.F."'[49] So much for the romantic ideal of the graduate student-mentor relationship earlier advocated by Frankfurter. Perhaps his familiarity with Kennedy's program in Toronto inspired his confidence in Laskin: Frankfurter had co-authored one of the first casebooks on U.S. administrative law in 1932 with one of Kennedy's former colleagues. James Forrester Davison was one of the first two Canadians to undertake a master's degree in law at Harvard (1924) after his Dalhousie LLB. He taught with Kennedy until 1927 before returning to Harvard for his doctorate, then was hired by George Washington University where he spent the rest of his career. Kennedy and Frankfurter had carried on a correspondence until the latter, according to Davison, 'found himself unable to cope with such a frequent and voluminous correspondent.'[50]

Although a substantial study of 250 pages, and somewhat novel in dealing with the actual work of the tribunal as well as the interpretation of its constituent legislation by the courts, Laskin's study of the Ontario Municipal Board rarely rises above the descriptive. He acknowledged as much in a letter to Finkelman, admitting that its main attraction was its size.[51] Adopting a historical approach, Laskin traced the rather haphazard growth of the board's jurisdiction from its creation in 1906 down to a major revision of its organic act in 1932; provided tables showing the number of cases dealt with over time by the board in its various areas of responsibility; and followed the judicial interpretation of the relevant legislation. In a brief introduction Laskin set his topic within the new literature on the rise of the administrative state and distanced himself from Diceyan 'rule of law' thought. Tribunals were here to stay, and the main question now was 'reconciling the maximum of administrative regulation required by the necessities of government with the minimum of arbitrary interference in the life of the ordinary citizen.'[52] In the body of his thesis, however, Laskin did not provide any criteria by which one could assess whether the proper balance between these two goals had been achieved. Nor did he provide more than a tentative conclusion: invoking Frankfurter's theme of avoiding 'premature synthesis,' Laskin declared that it was too early to come to any conclusions about administrative law.

That Laskin himself was not entirely satisfied with the product of his work may be deduced from his failure to publish any portion of it. The decision shows Laskin's maturity of judgment: he did not make the mistake of the immature scholar by racing heedlessly into print with an unworthy product. His thesis was part of an important shift by legal academics towards the empirical study of the work of administrative agencies, but this brave new world of scholarship ran out of steam by the later 1940s.[53] Once they had completed their descriptive work, these scholars, Laskin included, lacked the ability to interrogate their material in a critical and probing way. They simply did not know what to do next, with the result that such work was effectively absent from legal scholarship for decades thereafter.

After a brief visit to Toronto during the Harvard break in late April, Laskin returned to Cambridge for the final push. He must have been pleased with his results: 86 in Equity III and Government Control of Business, 78 in Jurisprudence, and 75 on his thesis in Administrative Law. The mark in Labor Law on his transcript is illegible, but his average of 77 was good enough to allow him to graduate *cum laude*. He and Al Abel were the only two to do so among the seventeen LLM graduands. *Magna cum laude* honours were given only to LLB students, and one of the few awarded that year went to a tall courtly Yankee named Archibald Cox. In future years Laskin would send his best students to study labour law with Cox at Harvard. Cox served as solicitor-general under John F. Kennedy but is remembered most as the special Watergate prosecutor fired by Richard Nixon in 1973, the man who got the U.S. Supreme Court to force the troubled president to surrender the incriminating Watergate tapes.

If Laskin was less than happy with his performance for Frankfurter, it appears the converse was not true. There is a family story to the effect that Laskin was offered a chance to work with one of the New Deal agencies in Washington, an opportunity which could only have come courtesy of Felix Frankfurter. Why he should have refused such an apparently attractive offer has been a matter of some speculation, when all he could look forward to in the short term back in Toronto was writing headnotes for the Burroughs Company.[54] Peggy's presence was undoubtedly part of what drew Laskin back. Yet aside from the boost to his self-confidence and the challenge of the position itself, how attractive was it for a young Canadian Jew without connections to work in the U.S. capital? Interesting and exciting in the short term, over the long term such a move was risky. At home nothing was assured, and the Toronto legal community was rife with anti-Semitism; but at least Laskin was known there and highly thought of in the circles he cared about. Besides, he was looking for much more than employment. Bora Laskin wanted to make his mark, to contribute to public discourse, and he only stood a chance of doing so in the country he knew best: Canada.

Laskin's earliest published articles illustrate how he absorbed the dominant legal philosophies of the day, re-articulated them, and then applied them to current Canadian problems. Although published in the later 1930s, some were written in the two years before Laskin went to Harvard and merely polished there, though two seem to have been written while he was at Harvard. They reveal the influence of Pound and Frankfurter as refracted through his teachers at Toronto and Osgoode, with a dash of Cardozo thrown in. These writings situate

Laskin squarely within the first group of Canadian legal academics to challenge the dominant conceptualism and formalism of Canadian law, who included Herbert Smith at McGill, Alex Corry at Queen's, E.R. Hopkins at Saskatchewan, and John Willis at Dalhousie, in addition to Laskin's teachers Jacob Finkelman, W.P.M. Kennedy, and Caesar Wright.[55] Laskin was the youngest of the crew by a significant margin and the only one not to hold a university faculty position at the time of writing. Aside from Smith's precocious effort in 1926, the writings of Corry, Laskin, Hopkins, and Willis on new approaches to statutory interpretation were virtually contemporaneous, all appearing between 1936 and 1938.

Laskin did not add anything distinctive to the reservoir of ideas drawn on by these Canadian scholars, but he articulated them so clearly and insistently that R.C.B. Risk has used him to illustrate 'the state of the art of legal thinking at the end of the 1930s.'[56] As one of a group whom we may label 'Canadian legal modernists,' Laskin drew on various schools of American legal thought but added other elements to the mix. Before describing his thought, it will be useful to outline what he was reacting against. Like his professors in Toronto, Laskin found the late-nineteenth-century approach to law unsatisfactory. That tradition, whether in England, the United States, or Canada, took the common law (i.e., the judge-made law) as the 'essence and foundation' of all law, 'pervading the day-to-day work of lawyers, their courts, their constitution, their ceremonial speeches, and their ways of understanding their work and their world.'[57] The common law itself was composed of principles that evolved slowly over time under the watchful eye of the judges. Statute law was exceptional and to be interpreted narrowly lest it interfere with these principles. The job of lawyers and judges was to find the appropriate principle and apply it to the facts of a given dispute, using the tools of logic and 'ordinary' grammatical interpretation, but never considering context or social desirability. Law was said to exist in a completely autonomous and apolitical realm of artificial reason, but in fact expressed clear political values: those of Victorian liberalism. As R.C.B. Risk has said, 'these ways of thinking ... continued to be virtually the only way of thinking from the late nineteenth century to the late 1920s.'[58]

Laskin and his contemporaries turned this approach to law on its head. In its Canadian version, the central tenet of legal modernism was simple: law must be responsive to the society it serves. Law was not primarily a historical artifact, a set of fixed principles, or a professional monopoly; it was a dynamic tool of social organization and social engineering, promulgated by the legislature and fine-tuned by the courts. The legislature was the primary body through which social consensus was achieved and implemented, and the role of the courts was to assist in the process of implementation through a careful study of a statute's policy goals and attention to the ambient social conditions.

Where the common law was concerned, the court was to ensure that it conformed to current societal needs, rather than to logical or historical consistency. Laskin was fond of quoting Oliver Wendell Holmes's statement that '[t]he very considerations which judges most rarely mention, and always with an apology, are the secret root from which the law draws all the juices of life. I mean, of course, considerations of what is expedient for the community concerned.'[59] Courts could and should thus play a modest quasi-legislative role, wherein the adjustment or balancing of interests was more important than the declaration of rights. The modernists rejected the dominant tradition of Canadian academic writing, that of English analytical positivism. They repeatedly invoked American approaches to law, but did not replicate the jurisprudential struggles apparent in the United States. In typically eclectic fashion, the Canadian modernists took what they needed from American theory and ignored the rest. Finally, the modernists were distinctive in their bracing criticism of some judicial decisions, breaking with a Canadian academic tradition based on synthesis rather than critical analysis of the law.

Two articles written at Harvard, 'Picketing: A Comparison of Certain Canadian and American Doctrines.'[60] and 'The Labour Injunction in Canada: A Caveat,'[61] along with 'The Protection of Interests by Statute and the Problem of "Contracting Out,"'[62] published in 1938 but written in 1935, illustrate the main tenets of Laskin's legal modernism. In 'Picketing,' Laskin took issue with the judicial use of the historical method of legal analysis as 'the one unchallengeable approach to the solution of legal problems.' He was particularly irked by the tendency of Canadian courts to apply English common law precedents even where they had been overruled by statute in England. In such cases, he asserted, courts would be well advised 'to mark the legislative departures ... as giving a new direction to judicial reasoning on the problems with which they deal.' The evolution of the common law was slow, Laskin observed impatiently, and 'the demand of social interests for recognition often cannot await the judicial march of history.'[63]

The substance of 'Picketing' was a comment on two Manitoba decisions granting employers injunctions to prevent peaceful union picketing. In the first case, *Allied Amusements*, the injunction was granted even though no members of the union were employees of the employer.[64] Unless the union had some 'immediate interest' in the business affected, Justice Donovan concluded, picketing was per se unlawful. Why, Laskin asked, was the union's general interest in improving the conditions of work not sufficient to justify its activity? While admitting that many U.S. courts had come to the same conclusion as Donovan, he was able to cite a 1927 decision of the Supreme Court of New York agreeing with his own position. In *Exchange Bakery v. Rifkin*, the New York court pointed out that wages and conditions of work in a particular trade were inseparable from general wage rates and working conditions, and thus took an expansive view of the legitimate province of union activity.[65] England was the preferred metropole for the Ontario legal profession, but Laskin always urged lawyers to look to the quality of the reasoning rather than its source. He also found fault with a second decision by Justice Donovan, *Kershaw Theatres v. Reaney*, where the carrying of signs containing statements of opinion was held to be a common nuisance.[66] Laskin found the failure of the judge to take freedom of expression into account inexcusable.

Laskin returned to the issue in 'The Labour Injunction in Canada: A Caveat.' While noting that its use 'as a coercive weapon in labour disputes has been relatively infrequent,' he was concerned that a recent decision of the Ontario Court of Appeal granting such an injunction might represent a change of heart, one he was keen to preempt. The 'caveat' of the title was essentially a warning to Canadian lawyers and judges to look at the grim American experience as set out in Frankfurter and Greene's book, which had resulted in legislation restraining curial powers to grant preliminary injunctions and to dispose of contempt charges. 'There can be little doubt,' Laskin warned, 'that Canadian courts will find themselves similarly circumscribed by legislative enactments if they fail to infuse their equitable jurisdiction in labour injunction decrees and contempts, with a spirit of social understanding.'[67] Legislative enactments were not contemplated until three decades later when employer recourse to injunctions precipitated a labour relations crisis in Ontario in the mid-1960s. Retired justice Ivan Rand was appointed to a royal commission to investigate the problem, and both the Ontario Federation of Labour and the Textile Workers of America cited Laskin's article and reproduced its arguments *in extenso* in their briefs.[68]

In 'Contracting Out,' Laskin examined the general problem of when benefits or immunities conferred by a statute could be validly released by private contract. In response to socially oriented legislation of the early twentieth century, economically powerful interests had sometimes required vulnerable parties to surrender benefits conferred by statute as a condition of employment, or of entering a contract. For example, a lender might require that a potential borrower contract out of exemptions provided by statute, so that the lender could foreclose against property of the debtor declared by statute to be exempt from seizure. The general rule was that anyone could waive benefits provided by statute, unless such waiver was found, on interpreting the statute, to be contrary to public policy. There were masses of inconsistent decisions on when a statute did or did not show a sufficient intent to disallow waiver of its benefits, and Laskin sought to put the whole question on a new footing.

He began his exploration of this question with an assertion of the primacy of the legislative role in adapting law to the needs of a changing society, while admitting that the judiciary played such a role 'within narrower limits.' In particular, 'the experience of recent years has proved the absolute necessity of the law reorientating itself to meet the demand ... for more positive protection of the status and capacity of its constituent members than the haphazard and meagre shelter afforded by reliance on the individual will.' Laskin did not end his analysis with a general exhortation to curial deference, however. Rather, he launched on a more far-reaching critique of existing techniques of interpretation. 'The policy of a statute depends ... on more than a literal interpretation of the words used in it ... Some consideration must hence be given to the question of how the sense of a statute is arrived at.' Laskin cited Cardozo, Alex Corry, and U.S. legal philosopher Morris Cohen to the effect that 'the intention of the legislature is a fiction, [but] the purpose or object of the legislation is very real.' That object was in turn 'the result of social pressure on the government of the day.' A judge should 'take cognizance of the trend of social forces and treat the statute as a means to the realization of a social end.' Thus courts should look not only at parliamentary debates but at the history of legislative measures in the broadest possible context. If such a process were followed, 'there would be less danger of the judge substituting his own views of policy than under an adherence to the literal doctrine of interpretation.'

In accepting some of the realists' observations about the indeterminacy of language, Laskin was not prepared to follow them into the minefield of judicial subjectivism. One work conspicuous by its absence from Laskin's references was Jerome Frank's *Law and the Modern Mind* (1930). Frank took the same point of departure as Laskin, but concluded that the discretion afforded a judge both by the vagueness of language and by the finding of 'facts' would be exercised primarily in accordance with the judge's own psychological make-up. Such a position was totally unacceptable to Laskin, but he did not need to refute Frank's view because no one in Canada espoused it anyway.[69] Only much later did he elaborate on his theory that judges could be made to 'behave,' even contrary to their personal inclinations, by a web of institutional conventions, public expectations, self-discipline, and the need for reasoned elaboration of their decisions.[70] Laskin invoked in support of this position Benjamin Cardozo's *The Nature of the Judicial Process*, a work he cited many times in the 1930s. For him this was a key text from an admired judge who accepted much of the critique of nineteenth-century formalism but still insisted that the existence of principled judicial reasoning was both desirable and possible.[71]

It was no coincidence that Canadian advocates of new strategies of statutory interpretation all emerged in the depths of the Depression. All were concerned about the consequences of a possible judicial emasculation of new social legislation, and were for the most part the same scholars incensed by the Privy Council decisions of 1937 holding much of Bennett's New Deal legislation unconstitutional. When Laskin invoked in passing 'the experience of recent years' in 'Contracting Out,' it was one of the few overt references to the Depression in his published work, but his experience of the misery of the 1930s was the 'secret root' of much of his writing in the 1930s and '40s and beyond. His extensive involvement with the Workers' Educational Association in the 1930s (considered in the next chapter) reveals more obviously than his scholarship his concern to respond to the assault on the dignity of labour. None of the Canadian legal modernists was concerned with theory for its own sake, but rather as a tool, a lever for moving society forward during a time of economic crisis and social conflict. American legal realism did not appeal largely because it provided no political purchase for these action-oriented scholars. For these reasons, Laskin resists easy labelling as belonging to one 'school' of legal thought or another.[72]

Out of Pound's conception of responsive law, Frankfurter's analysis of competing interests in labour law and public law generally, Cardozo's conception of the judicial function, and the realists' insights on law and language, Laskin fashioned his legal modernism. He also added some distinct Canadian elements. As Denise Réaume has pointed out, Laskin's advocacy of close cooperation between the judiciary and the legislature was not one found in American scholarship of the period.[73] Perhaps because the separation of powers doctrine is woven so tightly into its constitutional life, courts and legislatures are seen as inherently antagonistic bodies in the United States, Laskin saw courts and legislatures as partners in the task of governance, with different roles to be sure, but partners nonetheless. While influenced by American ideas, Laskin did not lose sight of the distinctiveness of his own society, nor was he an uncritical admirer of the United States. In 'Contracting Out' he deprecated attempts made in the States 'to canonize liberties by writing them into constitutions' (referring here to economic liberties). Such practices paid 'homage to rigidity and [made] change difficult in a society in which conditions [were] constantly changing.' If it was hard to impose reasonable limitations on freedom of contract in Canada and England, '[a]n infinitely harder battle [was] being fought in the United States.'[74]

Among the Canadian legal modernists Laskin was not radical, but when set against the mainstream of professional and judicial opinion he was definitely a dissenter. The perception of him as an iconoclast was always somewhat misguided, however, a function of the reaction of the bar and the judiciary to Laskin's somewhat acerbic style, and perhaps his outsider status as a Jew. For all his espousal of legal modernism in the 1930s, Laskin remained anchored to the fundamental values and institutions associated with the common law.[75] He was preoccupied with the question of how to maximize liberty without unduly jeopardizing social order or moral values. In this context, the organicism of the common law increasingly appealed to him as a kind of societal ballast. The reason he sought so forcefully to reform judicial attitudes was precisely because the judiciary mattered so much to him as an institution. If the judiciary remained out of touch with the needs of a changing society, it risked losing its legitimacy and its key role 'in the polity of a self-governing people,' as Pound would have said. These characteristics were more latent than patent in Laskin's scholarship of the 1930s, but they would assert themselves more strongly in the coming decades as the sharper edges of his legal modernism were rounded off.

5

Waiting

In June of 1937 Bora Laskin returned to Toronto. The Depression had relaxed its grip slightly, but by year's end the economy worsened again. Fortunately Laskin had a paying position to which he could return while searching for something better. He was about to begin work for the *Canadian Abridgment* project as arranged by Clyde Auld, but postponed that when an opportunity arose to work with the provincial legislative counsel on the Revised Statutes of Ontario 1937. This task had always been contracted out to a single judge or a small committee of judges working under commission from the provincial government. The Revised Statutes of Ontario 1927 were the child of Mr Justice Middleton, but they would be the last supervised by a judge.[1] With the appointment of Eric Silk as the first legislative counsel in 1936, the provincial government was at last prepared to take direct responsibility for producing authoritative versions of its own legislation.

At the same time, the attorney-general's office was preparing to compile in one volume all provincial government regulations, that is, the detailed rules prepared by cabinet or by government departments under the authority of particular statutes. Or rather, W.P.M. Kennedy had volunteered the services of the law department to do so. Attorney-General A.W. Roebuck informed his fellow ministers in May 1935 that 'Prof. Kennedy and his associates are giving their services without charge, other than clerical out of pocket expenses.'[2] Kennedy promptly threw the project into the lap of Jacob Finkelman, who had begun to conduct empirical studies of the work of particular administrative decision makers. These connections put Finkelman into regular contact with Eric Silk, and Bora Laskin's contract undoubtedly arose from his teacher's recommendation. The work was rather tedious, involving careful tracing of the legislative history of particular statutes, but at $131 per month it paid decently and gave Laskin a glimpse of the legal bureaucracy ensconced at Queen's Park.[3]

When the contract ended early in 1938 Laskin shifted over to the position at the Burroughs Company. The *Canadian Abridgment* was a vast publishing project that aimed to create the first topically organized digest of all Canadian case law. In the early twentieth century, Canadian lawyers were obliged to turn to two non-native publications for encyclopaedic views of the common law. They might consult the *England and Empire Digest* – a compilation of English judicial decisions with footnote references to authorities from the colonies and dominions – or the American *Corpus Juris Secundum*, named after the original *Corpus Juris*, a digest of Roman law compiled under the direction of the sixth-century emperor Justinian. Sixty years after Confederation, Burroughs gambled on there being sufficient Canadian law and an adequate market for an indigenous publication along these lines, and they succeeded. The *Canadian Abridgment*, with its annual supplements, became an indispensable resource for anyone working with Canadian law.

Such a work required the production of case summaries on a heroic scale. Several lawyers toiled away in the Burroughs Company offices at 204 Richmond Street, digesting cases on everything from Absent Debtors to Zoning. These 'rookies' would pass on their summaries for review by more senior staff, who in turn transmitted them to Auld for approval.[4] At the very summit of this editorial pyramid stood the formidable Mr Justice William Renwick Riddell, a prolific writer on the history of Canadian law, but his association with the project was essentially for public relations purposes. The front-line digesters worked at a piecework basis of fifty cents per headnote. Laskin would produce up to two hundred per week, giving him an effective salary of up to four hundred dollars per month, or close to five thousand dollars per annum if he kept up that pace. Given his other activities, three to four thousand dollars is probably a more reliable estimate. Burroughs wanted the work done quickly, so 'it didn't matter to them how hard I worked or the hours that I put in.'[5] Laskin would start teaching at about half his Burroughs wage and would not earn more than four thousand dollars from his academic salary until after the war.

Later observers have portrayed these years as a low point in Laskin's life, assuming that he 'deserved better' than the job at Burroughs in view of his later success. He was of course upset about the anti-Semitism he faced in the legal profession at large. Yet that made him even more grateful to get this position, and he always spoke with pride in later life about his ability to work hard and quickly, and to earn a substantial wage at it. To earn a good living, even at work that involved a less than ideal intellectual challenge, at a time when many of his peers were unemployed or underemployed, was a triumph of sorts. It affirmed Laskin's masculine role as breadwinner and enabled him to contemplate marriage, something many of his contemporaries were forced to postpone indefinitely. For intellectual stimulus he turned to his teaching and writing for the Workers' Educational Association, to which he devoted a good deal of time and energy during these years.

If Bora had found a niche for himself, so had Peggy, who was employed with the cosmetics department at Eaton's. As the first Jewish woman to be hired by Eaton's, she had the right combination of good looks, engaging personality, and modern outlook. Peggy embraced modernity in life as Bora embraced it in law. Not for her the sad tales and historical baggage of Old World Judaism. She managed to escape from the toils of a traditionalist mother and define a different life for herself in modern North American terms, shedding her birth name Gertrude and reinventing herself as Peggy – not Gert or Trudi, but something entirely different. Like her future husband, she asserted control over her name as a fundamental aspect of her identity. Peggy observed some of the cultural traditions of Judaism but in adult life, unlike her husband, did not attend synagogue. In Bora she found someone who shared her desire to enter the mainstream of North American society, with its excitement, its secularism, its encouragement of individual aspiration and promise of upward mobility. She did not reject her heritage entirely, but found it easy to leave behind those parts of it that posed barriers to integration in the majority culture. She chose, in short, the life most North American Jews of her generation chose.

Luckily, the Burroughs Company office was not far from Eaton's. Sending Bora five dollars for a contribution to the *Canadian Bar Review* in January 1938, Caesar Wright added in a jocular vein, 'I authorize you to spend [it] on the charming young lady with whom you were lunching in Eaton's.'[6] When Max Cohen, a friend from Winnipeg who was also aiming to be a legal academic, was passing through Toronto, Bora couldn't wait to bring him by Eaton's to show off his beautiful girlfriend.[7] In June 1938, a year after his return from Harvard, Bora and Peggy were married. After a brief honeymoon at Niagara Falls they moved to a flat in the west end of the city at 191 Howard Park Avenue. Their choice of location proclaimed their independence not only from Peggy's family but also from the whole Ward-based Jewish community. The opening a year earlier of the magnificent new Holy Blossom Temple at the northern edge of the city confirmed the status of nearby Forest Hill as a beacon for Jewish families seeking a more suburban life, but the Laskins would not move there until 1951. For the moment, Howard Park was the next best thing. Only two blocks west of High Park, it offered fresh air, open spaces, and ample greenery to offset the sweltering heat of Toronto's summers; two blocks east was Roncesvalles, a busy street full of small shops containing everything a carless young couple might need. Downtown was easily accessible via the nearby Dundas streetcar.

However attractive the financial rewards in the short term, Laskin did not intend to stay in legal publishing for very long. In Caesar Wright's words, he was 'anxious for an opportunity to really work.'[8] From the safety of his citadel on Richmond Street, he began a determined assault on the private, public, and academic job markets soon after returning from Harvard. Both Wright and W.P.M. Kennedy provided superb references for their former student, but to little effect. Wright recommended Laskin as 'extremely sound [and] industrious' to his old friend Sidney Smith, who had left the deanship at Dalhousie Law School to become president of the University of Manitoba in 1934. 'Unfortunately,' he continued, 'he is a Jew. This may be fatal regarding his chances with you. I do not know. His race is, of course, proving a difficulty facing him in Toronto so far as obtaining a good office is concerned ... Laskin is not one of those flashy Jews, and the highest recommendation which I could give him is to say that, in the absence of any overwhelming prejudice and if I had control of a decent faculty, I would have no hesitation in placing Laskin.'[9]

Presumably Sidney Smith did not feel able to foist a Jew on his law school, which did not hire one on the full-time faculty until 1965 in spite of the presence of a large local Jewish community. Jewish members of the local bar were hired as part-time lecturers only, beginning in 1941 with Samuel Freedman – who became Manitoba's first Jewish judge when he was appointed to the Court of Queen's Bench in 1952. The public service proved no more receptive. When Laskin applied for a job as junior advisory counsel in the federal Department of Justice, Kennedy wrote him a glowing letter of recommendation: 'During the several years of his legal studies in this University he disclosed that he was a man of most exceptional ability. He possesses a keen analytical mind, a careful and balanced judgment and a fine sense of practical legal scholarship. From his earliest years as a student he has given himself unreservedly to legal studies fortified by training in Political Science and Economics, Canadian Constitutional History, and Philosophy in which he obtained honours. I have no hesitation in saying that he is a man of outstanding qualifications.' More diplomatic than Caesar Wright in alluding to Laskin's Judaism and yet trying to allay anticipated concerns about it, Kennedy continued: 'These university qualifications speak for themselves. I would not, however, leave them without pointing out that Mr. Laskin combines them with a fine personality and a character of the highest integrity ... [S]eldom have I recommended a man more confidently. He is a scholar, a practical lawyer and a gentleman, the possessor in an eminent degree of adaptability and the quality of getting on with people.'[10] With over one hundred applicants for this position, it is difficult to attribute categorically Laskin's lack of success to anti-Semitism. The code words in Kennedy's letter suggest he at least saw it as a potential problem and tried to deflect it by emphasizing Laskin's ability to fit in. At a time when Mackenzie King's government adamantly refused to accept Jewish refugees from Hitler's Europe, it is hard to believe such attitudes did not colour departmental decision making. Attitudes were just beginning to change, however. Max Cohen was hired by the Department of Labour in 1938 as the first full-time lawyer employed by the Combines Investigation Commission – probably the first Jewish lawyer in the federal civil service.

Laskin lost out in this competition to Wilbur Jackett, a Saskatchewan native who rose to deputy minister of justice and ultimately to be chief justice of the Federal Court of Canada, where he and Laskin would cross swords many years later. Jackett had stood first in his graduating class at the University of Saskatchewan in 1933 and was the province's Rhodes Scholar for 1934. He returned from Oxford with disappointing seconds at his BA and BCL, then worked for a well-known Saskatoon lawyer before taking up the post in Ottawa.[11] Laskin had not stood first either at the University of Toronto or Osgoode, though he was near the top of the class at both institutions. His graduate work was more rigorous than Jackett's, but in the nostalgic Canada of the inter-war years it was hard to beat the cachet of an Oxford BCL and a Rhodes Scholarship.

Even in the midst of the Depression, Wilbur Jackett was able to find a position with a respected lawyer in Sasktoon. Laskin sought out positions with Toronto firms but to no avail. Like Max Cohen and many other Jewish lawyers of the day, he encountered a wall of prejudice. Laskin never spoke about it publicly, stating many years later that he preferred the *Canadian Abridgment* work to that in a law firm because it paid better. 'In any event,' he remarked in passing, 'I had no particular contacts in Toronto that would bring me into any prestigious law firm.'[12] Within the family circle he would sometimes unburden himself. His brother Saul 'recalls the bitterness of the first rejections, the shattering disillusionment with the profession he loved and in which he hoped to make his career. In later years, Laskin would occasionally remind his family how "waspy" a city Toronto once was and how he was shunned by the large law firms.'[13] He could probably have found a niche in one of the smaller Jewish law firms, but his goal was to work in a more integrated environment and he was prepared to wait until something came along.

Whether that 'something' would be a post at the University of Toronto remained to be seen. In January 1938 Kennedy begged President Cody for an additional lecturer and mentioned Laskin in the warmest terms, but Cody refused.[14] As an 'extra' hire Kennedy would have snapped up Laskin, but on several occasions when a vacancy in an existing spot arose, he did not offer Laskin the post. Kennedy had his own vision for the law department, and made a careful assessment of its needs when an existing position was vacated. In July 1936 lecturer E.R. Hopkins resigned to take up a much better paying position at the Saskatchewan law faculty after only a year at Toronto. When Dean Cronkite wrote to apologize for poaching Hopkins, Kennedy replied with a hint of sour grapes. Hopkins was good, allowed Kennedy, but 'you must keep him tuned up to scholarship and productive work. He ought to finish his Oxford doctorate and see that he writes that article for me on Quasi Contract.'[15] To replace Hopkins, Auld advised hiring Laskin: 'all things considered, [he] is familiar more than any other candidate whose name presents itself, with our work and our ideals; and his enthusiasm and loyalty, with his capacity for hard work, make his claims as a candidate exceedingly weighty.'[16] Kennedy had other ideas. 'I am in hopes of getting one of our own distinguished graduates who has had a fine career at Osgoode and done well at the bar for a few years. Then, if this fails or falls through, I intend to approach Laskin; but not before I am certain of the other's decision ... [B]roken-down lawyers are beginning to worry me,' he lamented, 'and I have to steer a careful course.'[17] A relatively secure job at the law department looked extremely attractive to lawyers in private practice battered by the Depression.

Kennedy had his eye on J.M. Gage, who had graduated in the political science and law course with first class honours, gone on to win numerous scholarships and a gold medal at Osgoode, and then established a flourishing practice in Hamilton. His concern with hiring someone known at the bar reflected his desire to position his department for closer relations with Osgoode Hall and possible recognition by the benchers, but not at the expense of scholarship. He made his ordering of priorities absolutely clear to Gage: 'The teaching is important indeed and the general advancement of our purposes; but most important are scholarship and productive work. The life is a happy and creative one and has compensations which are inestimable.'[18]

Gage spent the year 1936–7 at the department but decided early on that either academe or Kennedy or both were not for him. This time Moffatt Hancock edged out Laskin to replace Gage. Hancock had entered the doctoral program in law at the University of Michigan the same year Laskin went to Harvard, with the aid of a princely thousand-dollar scholarship. Initially he had planned, like Laskin, to study Canadian administrative law but when this proved impractical he shifted to the field of private international law. This is the body of law invoked when disputes arise with connections to more than one jurisdiction: for example, when a resident of Nova Scotia injures a national of France in a car accident in Vermont. Hancock developed a lifelong passion for the subject and became an international authority on it after leaving for California in 1949. Hancock and Laskin would be colleagues under Kennedy from 1940 to 1945, when both departed (Hancock to Dalhousie, Laskin to Osgoode), but for the moment they were competitors and Laskin had lost out yet again.

Kennedy's 1938 initiative with President Cody having failed, Laskin would have to wait for another vacancy. Already another competitor was looming on the horizon, with academic achievements and personal qualifications so brilliant as to cast even Laskin's impressive record into the shadows. John Kenneth Macalister achieved the highest honours of any graduate in Kennedy's program during its entire existence: first class honours in *every* subject in *every* year, along with a cascade of prizes, scholarships, and medals. He entered the law program in the fall of 1933, just after Laskin's graduation, and was named one of Ontario's two Rhodes Scholars for 1937. At Oxford Macalister proved he was not just a big fish from a tiny colonial pond. Graduating with one of only six firsts among two hundred degree candidates in 1939, he topped even this the next year by standing first at the bar exams in London. Kennedy began a campaign to lure him back to teach at Toronto. Laskin must have been aware that Macalister represented a dire threat to his job prospects at the University of Toronto. When another opening presented itself in the summer of 1940, the two men made up Kennedy's short list of candidates.

In the meantime, Laskin pursued a variety of opportunities during his off hours. He began to help Caesar Wright as de facto associate editor of the *Canadian Bar Review*, and also privately tutored a half-dozen Osgoode students Wright sent his way. One of these became a friend for life. David Spencer's family owned the Woodward chain of department stores which were to the west coast what Eaton's was to central Canada. Spencer had no real interest in or aptitude for law but had been sentenced to it by parental decree. His real passions were opera, antiques, and men, not necessarily in that order. After enrolling as a student-at-law in Vancouver, he received permission from the benchers to transfer his articles to Ontario and enrol at Osgoode Hall, a highly unusual step at the time. Whether the move represented a flight from familial oversight, a banishment by parents disconcerted by their son's proclivities, or both is not known. Spencer returned to Vancouver and was called to the bar in 1943 but forsook the law for a career as a patron of the arts. He provided for the Laskins an exposure to Canada's haute WASP elite they would have been hard pressed to find through any other channel. Later in life Spencer would initiate Peggy into the mysteries of antique collecting, and the trio would meet from time to time in Vancouver, Toronto, or London.

During these years Laskin strengthened his connections to the labour movement. His timing could not have been better. The Depression had spawned a more militant and aggressive industrial trade union movement, which the state – once it gave up on total suppression – wished to channel into some framework of legal regulation. In the United States the Committee for Industrial Organization (CIO) was founded by John L. Lewis in late 1935 as an umbrella for unions frustrated with the craft bias of the American Federation of Labor (a bias mirrored in Canada by the Trades and Labour Congress). Auto workers defected from the AFL to form a new union, the United Auto Workers, under the wing of the CIO. The spring 1937 strike by four thousand workers at General Motors' Oshawa plant, carried on under the aegis of the CIO though without any financial support from it, was the acid test for industrial unionism in Canada. It succeeded in spite of extraordinary concerted efforts by Premier Mitch Hepburn, the company, and the press to stop it. Hepburn's anti-CIO stand won him the 1937 election, but his anti-labour stance soon contributed to 'the strange death of Liberal Ontario' by creating a political vacuum for more moderate leaders.[19]

Many in the union movement welcomed the respectability legal recognition would provide and sought to participate in the public debate about the form and limits of that recognition. An important vehicle for raising the consciousness of working people in the 1930s was the Workers' Educational Association (WEA), with the charismatic Scot Drummond Wren at its helm as secretary-general. Based on a similar British organization, the WEA collaborated with the University of Toronto to offer non-credit, inexpensive evening classes to workers. Courses were offered by university faculty (called 'tutors') at a university standard, and attracted professors sympathetic to the labour movement. By the late 1930s the WEA was a force to be reckoned with. It had expanded from 230 members in two district associations in 1929–30 to 2,200 members in twenty-nine associations across Canada by 1937–8, but its publications, radio programs, film strips, and course offerings reached many thousands more. Wren had also created an entity called the Labour Research Institute supported by unions through a check-off of four cents per member in return for receiving copies of all WEA publications. Under Wren the somewhat paternalistic set-up of the WEA was harnessed to a more analytical and critical agenda aimed at helping workers and the unemployed understand and respond to the crisis of the Depression.[20]

Laskin came to know Wren through their association with the Industrial Law Research Council (ILRC). This body was a joint creation of the WEA, the law department, and the Toronto District Trades and Labor Council, 'formed for the scientific and objective study of legal problems affecting organized industry.'[21] Kennedy was the official chair, but it was Finkelman, Auld, and increasingly Laskin who provided the contacts and the brainpower. Finkelman and Laskin wrote a number of reports on new labour legislation in various parts of Canada, beginning with one on Quebec's new *Collective Labour Agreements Extension Act* Laskin wrote while still at Osgoode Hall. Through this writing and his first foray into teaching at the WEA summer school in August 1936, Laskin began to develop a profile within the labour movement. Wren and Laskin became close friends and Wren would later be a key figure in Laskin's entry into the practice of labour arbitration. The two men shared very similar views both on the direction labour legislation should take and on the nature of the role to be played by the WEA. Wren always insisted that the WEA was non-partisan, non-denominational, and not the creature of any particular union or group. A large grant from the Carnegie Foundation paid Wren's salary during the 1930s and allowed him to preserve the WEA's much-prized independence.[22] With his traditional distrust of partisan affiliation of any kind, Laskin found Wren's views echoed his own.

Upon his return from Harvard Laskin's involvement with the WEA shifted into a major key, and included research, teaching, and broadcasting. He addressed the Labour Research Institute on the subject of the *Wagner Act* in June 1937, just days after returning from Harvard, and wrote a short pamphlet entitled 'The Wagner Act and Collective Bargaining' published by the ILRC in December. Laskin strongly urged the U.S. model on Canada. It represented 'an advanced step in defining more rationally, in the light of experience, the relations of capital and labour.' The very survival of democracy required both sides to accept 'in good faith canons of conduct under which they may act on equal terms in the promotion of industry.' Acceptance of the Act would, in the words of Harvard law professor Calvin Magruder, mean a final farewell to 'yellow dogs, company unions, blacklists, deputy sheriffs in the pay of employers, barricades, tear gas, machine guns, vigilante outrages, espionage and all that miserable brood of union-smashing detective agencies.' It was, agreed Laskin, 'time for an act of faith.'

No sooner had Laskin finished this pamphlet than he agreed to rewrite a short book on trade unionism for the WEA. The original manuscript by Leo Warshaw was considered too strident in tone and insufficiently objective, and the WEA asked Laskin to rewrite it.[23] He had volunteered in mid-December to finish the work by 1 January 1938 and on 8 January the committee voted him payment of fifty dollars. This work was published as *The Trade Unionist's Handbook*, a succinct but holistic account of trade unions in their historical, political, social, economic, and legal dimensions. Here was W.P.M. Kennedy's vision of law as a social science put into practice – significantly, though, where the intended audience did not include lawyers. Laskin insisted that trade unions represented 'not so much a class interest as a vocational or functional interest.'[24] They had become 'so vital ... in the daily activities of workers, that they may be truly designated as a school of life, teaching in action the principles and spirit of co-operation for the social welfare within the necessary framework of democracy.'[25] If respect for democracy enjoined unions to accept occasional subordination of their interests to those more urgently in need of protection, in return 'the rights of labour may not be tampered with by the government until trade unionism has been consulted.'[26] Castigating both business unionism and revolutionary unionism, Laskin believed 'a more comprehensive unionism than either [was] necessary to withstand the business cycle unimpaired. It must be sought in a combined policy of dealing with daily problems with business efficiency and of pressing forward with a broad social program, integrally related to the welfare of the general labour movement.'[27] Service to the twin goals of business efficacy and social responsibility would characterize Laskin's later career as a labour arbitrator and informed his approach to law in general.

Laskin gave the first classes on trade unionism ever offered by the WEA in Ontario, and probably in Canada, beginning in October 1937.[28] From this he progressed to giving short WEA courses in Oshawa and Hamilton as well as Toronto, where his students included rising labour leaders such as Charlie Millard, leader of the Oshawa strikers, George Burt, later head of the United Auto Workers in Canada, and Russell Harvey of the American Federation of Labour. In later life Laskin reflected in a jocular and self-deprecating way on this experience: 'I look back in some amazement and maybe some amusement to think that here was I at about 23 years of age, you know, pretending that I could give lectures to these people on problems that were beginning to affect them in their union-management activities. At any rate, I had a lot of fun doing that in addition to which, of course, I got paid, I think it was $200 a course.'[29]

By portraying his teaching as a fun activity that brought in a little cash on the side, Laskin underplayed the nature and significance of his WEA connections in this period. Some contemporaries saw him as crossing the line from education into activism. This was particularly the case with his participation in a series of lectures on trade unions and the law broadcast on CBC radio as part of a WEA-sponsored series called the Workers' Educational Series. There were twelve half-hour broadcasts in the series. The first four, on the history of the labour movement, were given by Professor Lorne Morgan, a political economist at the University of Toronto and WEA tutor. Laskin gave the next four in December 1937, entitled 'what is a trade union?', 'the functions of a trade union,' 'trade union principles and the state,' and 'some aspects of trade unionism.' These broadcasts were intended as an adjunct to the WEA's study circles, which functioned with the aid of written materials prepared by the WEA and discussed under the guidance of group leaders.[30]

Laskin was auditioned in October by Charles Jennings. His voice was found to be suitable for radio but CBC staff were less than impressed with his radio debut. 'After listening to several of Mr. Lasker's [sic] broadcasts,' observed D.W. Buchanan of the program department, 'I feel that he could make these much more interesting if he brought in more specific illustrations. His broadcasts deal so much with law and principles of labour organization that the theories he expounds are very difficult to follow, especially when he allows his talk to proceed for ten or fifteen minutes without any description of an actual labour dispute or court proceeding to which the question at issue relates. Otherwise the broadcasts continue to be excellent.'[31] Later broadcasts incorporated a question-and-answer format to break the tedium of the straight lecture.

In the broadcasts Laskin undertook a spirited advocacy of the legitimacy of the trade union movement. Unions did not exist just to lobby for improvement in the standards of employment. They safeguarded their members' vocational interest, defined as 'an economic relation [which] leaves very little of [one's] life untouched.' Trade unions developed 'self-respect and independence ... in their members' and ultimately should be involved in the management of industry. To the charge that trade unionism involved undue interference with liberty of contract, Laskin responded with his favourite quotation from Oliver Wendell Holmes: unionism merely established 'that equality between the parties in which liberty of contract begins.' The state should encourage and respect trade union activity as long as it did not threaten the state itself, and the state should function as an impartial umpire when disputes between labour and capital threatened to disrupt social order. 'The democratic principle is preserved only in so far as both the state and the groups within it are willing to compose their demands so as to give as much recognition as is possible to all with the least sacrifice of any of them.' When pressed about the legitimacy of a general strike, Laskin was much more willing to talk about the English general strike of 1926, which had no overt political aims, than the Winnipeg General Strike of 1919, which did. Laskin contented himself with reporting that the Manitoba courts found participation in a general strike could amount to seditious conspiracy, and was not pressed any further by his interlocutors.

Laskin's advocacy of the union cause was generally moderate; he was not a defender of the closed shop, for example, which he saw as threatening the individual's right to earn a living. He did stray into controversy when he discussed the relationship of the courts and trade unions, particularly with respect to the labour injunction. In such cases, he asserted, 'unconscious partiality' existed on the part of the judges. The theory of an injunction was to protect the status quo, 'but when an order is given by a law court to prevent labour activity, that is not a case of preserving the status quo, but an invitation to nullify trade union activity.' These comments in his last lecture on 29 December 1937 provoked an angry response from J.B. Macpherson, K.C., of Montreal, who fired off a letter to the CBC the next day protesting 'the attack on the fairness and impartiality of the Canadian courts made by one Boris [sic] Laskin ... last night ... Mr Laskin is preaching class warfare of the worst type, ... and [encourages] labour to seize every opportunity to fight and embarrass the employer. [These broadcasts] are pure propaganda and should be labelled as such and not classed as "educational."' Mr Macpherson concluded his tirade with the observation that '[t]his week's and last week's speaker on this hour was Mr. Boris Laskin, next week we are to be treated to Mr. Moses Finkelstein.' (He confused Finkelstein, a Winnipeg alderman, with Professor Jacob Finkelman.) The implication was clear: only Jews would stir up trouble in this way, and the CBC should not be providing a platform for such undesirables. Such casual anti-Semitism by a leading member of the legal profession speaks volumes about the atmosphere in which Laskin was trying to get ahead. D.W. Buchanan responded calmly that 'there was no intention to introduce any propaganda in those broadcasts and the careful selection of the principal authorities, to be found in the University of Toronto, on the subject of labour history and law, should be a sufficient indication of the extent to which we have tried to ensure accuracy.'[32]

Closer to home, others were upset with the broadcasts as well. The WEA carried on its activities under the aegis of the Extension Department of the University of Toronto, from which it received a substantial grant. The WEA's political activities were thus carefully monitored by university authorities, and the RCMP also kept an eye on the group.[33] In 1939 the university cut the WEA grant from eight to two thousand dollars, and attempted to impose conditions on WEA activities, including the cessation of its radio programs. Laskin was upset but assured Drummond Wren he would continue his involvement.[34] Agitation from various sources eventually led to Mitch Hepburn's government restoring the grant in 1942 outside the university context.

Laskin's knowledge of labour law and his association with Finkelman secured him an invitation to speak at the prestigious Couchiching Conference, held annually by the Canadian Institute on Economics and Politics at a lakeside resort near Orillia, Ontario. In August 1938 the theme was 'Problems in Canadian Unity,' but 'Labour and Unionization' joined the more familiar fare of federal-provincial tensions. Laskin spoke on the legal status of trade unions in Canada, drawing on his recently published WEA study. He noted that neither decriminalization of trade union activity nor mere legislative declarations of the right to organize was sufficient to ensure industrial peace. Where an employer refused to treat with his employees, 'only the wasteful industrial sanctions of strikes and picketing' remained available to unions; the law on these topics was so uncertain as to invite litigation in each and every case.[35] He concluded with a nod towards the reign of industrial experts that would inform his thinking ever after. 'Social legislation today depends for its efficacy not so much on its terms as on its administration. The whole emphasis in law is shifting to administration, and in this connection personnel is of vital moment.'[36] Another conference speaker was Laskin's former professor Frank Underhill who, even as he lamented the dominance of regional thinking in Canada, accurately predicted that Canada was on the eve of a new wave of nationalism.

Bora Laskin's fundamental ideas about labour relations and labour law were formed in the double helix of activism and academe at a particularly momentous historical conjuncture in the 1930s. His academic work at the University of Toronto and Harvard had exposed him to the ferment of new ideas in the labour field, while his work with the WEA allowed him to hear directly the concerns of workers and prominent labour leaders. Laskin was no armchair theorist, nor just a detached professional observer, as he tended to portray himself later in life. His engagement with labour was very much within a liberal rather than socialistic framework, but engagement it was, and it was unusual enough at a time when the vast majority of lawyers had little use for unions. It was unusual too among legal academics, who might be broadly sympathetic to the rights of labour but who, aside from Jacob Finkelman, seldom wrote on the topic. In his radio broadcasts and his educational work for the WEA, Laskin attempted to popularize the idea that the imposition of compulsory collective bargaining on the employer, while leaving employees the right to strike, aimed only to redress a prior situation of inequality between capital and labour, and portrayed it as a necessary step in the progress of humanity. Such legislation was another way in which 'the government equalizes the conditions under which liberty becomes more than an empty symbol,' thus implementing its 'primary duty of enlarging individual liberty.'[37]

Laskin's commitment to labour did not arise out of any familial tradition of union activity or leftist politics, as was the case with his contemporary David Lewis, for example. The Laskin family were comfortably petit bourgeois, usually the most politically conservative element in any community. Laskin shared this conservatism in his lifelong search for order and discipline, at both the personal and political level, but it was tempered by his passionate concern for civil liberties, for enlarging the sphere of individual aspiration, action, and fulfilment. This was ultimately the product of his ethical position, grounded both in his Judaism and in his reaction to the Great Depression. He retained a lifelong commitment to fostering the dignity of labour and the intrinsic worth of the individual, while advocating the need for state intervention to enable individuals to make a contribution to society.[38]

If the 'rights of labour' were very much on the public agenda in the 1930s, the discourse of 'human rights' was virtually unknown. A 1939 Supreme Court of Canada decision, commented on briefly by Laskin, illustrated the lack of interest in racial discrimination in the dying days of the pre-war world.[39] On 11 July 1936 Fred Christie was refused a drink in the York Tavern in Montreal because the operator had a policy of not serving blacks. With some assistance from the local black community Christie challenged in the courts what he saw as a discriminatory act.[40] He succeeded at trial but lost both on appeal to the Court of King's Bench and at the Supreme Court of Canada, though there was a dissenting judge on each appellate court. For the judiciary the matter was a simple issue of freedom of contract. Aside from a few exceptional cases such as that of the innkeeper, anyone offering services to the public could decline to treat with any member of the public for any reason or no reason. Laskin seems to have accepted that as an accurate statement of the common law but argued for the adoption of the reasoning advanced by Supreme Court Justice Henry Davis in his dissent. Davis's reasoning echoed Laskin's own legal modernism: 'In the changed and changing social and economic conditions, different principles must necessarily be applied to the new conditions ... The doctrine that any merchant is free to deal with the public as he chooses had a very definite place in the older economy and still applies to the case of an ordinary merchant, but when the state enters the field and takes exclusive control of the sale to the public of such a commodity as liquor, the old doctrine ... has in my view no application to a person to whom the state has given a special privilege to sell to the public.'[41] Where the statute already specified the classes of people to whom licensees could not sell, it should be interpreted to preclude further discrimination unless specifically authorized. Laskin's suggested solution of '[a]dministrative oversight by a licensing authority of discriminatory practices by imposing conditions upon the grant of a licence or by exercising a right to refuse renewal' was taken up by a number of Ontario municipalities during and immediately after the war, before provincial legislation made such by-laws unnecessary. The comment was brief, only two pages long, but it was the only one to appear on this decision in any legal forum; only a laconic factual account would appear in the newspapers.[42] The only other faint protest was a two-sentence editorial note to the case when reported in the *Dominion Law Reports*, probably penned by Caesar Wright.[43] The decision contributed to Laskin's increasingly jaundiced view of the quality of Supreme Court jurisprudence.

As matters went from bad to worse on the international front in the summer of 1940, a sudden movement on the domestic scene promised to break the logjam Laskin had faced at the University of Toronto for three years. In the spring of 1940 the University of New Brunswick was looking for a president and settled on Larry MacKenzie, but the final step in the appointment could not be arranged until 30 July. This late exit caused some anxiety to W.P.M. Kennedy, who would have only two months to arrange a replacement before the beginning of classes. From his Muskoka redoubt he swung into epistolary action. In a worst-case scenario, assuming no replacement could be found on such short notice, MacKenzie's subjects would be parcelled out to existing staff: Hancock would take conflicts of laws, Kennedy constitutional law, and Auld public international law, which he admitted 'rather dismayed' him.[44] Kennedy's alternative strategy involved going after Kenneth Macalister and persuading him to return to Canada before he succeeded in enlisting in the British army; if that didn't work, he would go to Bora Laskin. He seemed to assume Laskin would not volunteer, and in fact Laskin stayed in Toronto throughout the war.

  Macalister was not only a man of rare intelligence, but of high ideals and admirable character.[45] He had become acutely aware of Hitler's persecution of Jews and dissenting Christians while on a trip to Europe in 1934. Just before the outbreak of war he married a Frenchwoman, and through Jeannine and her family he was bound to the fate of Europe. In fact he volunteered for the French army while visiting her in France before the Occupation, but the authorities rejected the offer of the *étranger* in disbelief. Rejected by the Canadian army as well on account of myopia, he turned to the British army as the Nazi juggernaut rolled over Western Europe. On 22 June 1940 Macalister wrote to Kennedy. 'For a week or so now, ... the complacency has gone. Oxford has not yet been bombed but that is bound to come one of these nights. We are all hoping that the colleges will be spared. I have been trying for two months to get into the British army ... I have an interview in London on July 1 as the final hope. If I am not accepted then I suppose the only thing to do then will be to go home ... I'd like to teach for a while or get some government work.'[46]

Kennedy was definitely interested but seems to have waffled between Macalister and Laskin as late as mid-August. On the eleventh he wrote to Cody that he had Laskin in mind as MacKenzie's replacement, but would discuss the matter with Cody on his return to Toronto in early September. He did not mention Macalister's name at all, possibly because he felt his acceptance was a long shot, possibly because he briefly contemplated offering the position to Laskin first before changing his mind.[47] In early September the army finally gave Macalister a definite offer. He was to show up at the Winchester training depot, but no sooner had he left Oxford than his landlady received word that W.P.M. Kennedy was trying to contact him to offer him a lectureship. She telephoned the War Office in London and the Winchester depot to try and get his enlistment rescinded – in vain. Macalister received his commission on 16 September and the next day cabled Kennedy 'IN ARMY SINCE YESTERDAY SORRY MANY THANKS.'[48] With the beginning of term only days away, Kennedy contacted Laskin immediately, offered him the position, and wrote to President Cody on the twentieth urgently recommending his appointment.[49] From Winchester Macalister wrote Kennedy a brief note thanking him for the offer of a lectureship, to which Kennedy replied 'I do not see any opening here in the near future, as of course I had to fill the appointment when you could not take it.'[50]

Macalister's subsequent fate is now the stuff of myth, the subject of a poignant memoir-poem by Douglas LePan.[51] In the winter of 1941 his unit was assigned to protect the training schools of the Special Operations Executive (SOE), a new and highly secret intelligence unit created after the fall of France to promote sabotage and subversion behind enemy lines. Macalister and his friend Frank Pickersgill volunteered for

SOE duty and were parachuted into France on 15 June 1943.[52] Within days they were betrayed by a French double agent, imprisoned in Paris and tortured. In the final months of the Third Reich they were transferred to Buchenwald, where they were executed on Hitler's direct orders in September 1944.

It is not clear whether Bora Laskin ever knew of the intense behind-the-scenes activity preceding his own appointment at the University of Toronto. Certainly he knew of MacKenzie's appointment as he wrote the new president a letter of congratulations on 27 August.[53] As the weeks of August and September ticked by with no definite offer from Kennedy he would have experienced a crescendo of anxiety. Did Kennedy alert him to the possibility of an appointment? In 1976 Laskin recalled having 'about two to three weeks notice of the opening of term following my appointment. All I ... can remember ... is that I was working at the department seven days a week, all day Sunday, in order to get ready for my lectures which were three weeks off.'[54] Term started on the fourth Tuesday in September, which in 1940 was the twenty-fourth. If Kennedy had contacted Laskin directly after receiving Macalister's telegram on the seventeenth, Laskin would have had one week's notice before the beginning of term. If Laskin's recollection is literally correct, he must have had some intimation of a possible offer before the seventeenth, but this seems unlikely in light of other evidence. Kennedy went out of his way to try and keep the Macalister offer under wraps, writing afterwards to Larry MacKenzie: 'For some years I have been looking forward to the appointment of Mr. Bora Laskin and I had no one else in mind at all when you retired, as I had set my heart on him. All sorts of rumours flew about that various people were being appointed. Naturally I could afford to laugh at them as the appointment lay in my hands.'[55] If Kennedy was trying to keep the information from MacKenzie, he was even less likely to have told Laskin. Whether Laskin guessed what was going on is something we shall never know.

In any case, secrecy within such a small circle of intimates was virtually impossible. Finkelman revealed all in a letter to MacKenzie on 15 October: 'You may have heard that Macalister received a commission and has, therefore, been unable to accept the appointment. Bora Laskin has joined us and is lecturing in your subjects with the exception of private international law.'[56] MacKenzie's reply throws another sidelight on the Laskin appointment. He feared that a second Jewish appointment in a unit of only five faculty members would undermine the department and Finkelman's position by making it appear as if Jews were taking over: 'You and I both know that even in Canada anti-Semiticism [sic] is a threat that has to be kept in mind and in check. One of the most effective ways of doing this is by never allowing oneself to get in a weak position or one that is difficult to defend. You will realize from the inaccuracies that have been published about the percentages of Jews in University College and the consequent statement that it was therefore undesirable to send one's sons and daughters there what I have in mind. It may be that I am over cautious and unduly fearful on this point and I certainly hope so for both your sakes and for the sake of the course in Law ...'[57] This position had obviously caused Finkelman some anxiety: he replied that MacKenzie's letter had set his mind at ease on a number of matters.[58] Exactly the same concerns had been raised in 1932 in the United States, when it was assumed that a second Jew would not be appointed to the Supreme Court with Louis Brandeis still there. Herbert Hoover nonetheless appointed Benjamin Cardozo, and on his death in 1938 Roosevelt ignored similar sentiment to replace him with Felix Frankfurter. W.P.M. Kennedy too ignored the cautious counsels of those such as Larry MacKenzie, thereby striking an important blow against anti-Semitism. He had had his fight with the board of governors over Finkelman's appointment as a professor in 1934 and was prepared to go to bat again if necessary. After Laskin left Toronto for Osgoode in 1945, Kennedy would appoint another Jew, David Vanek, to the staff.

In light of these actions, it is worth taking a close look at Kennedy's letter recommending Laskin's appointment to President Cody, a letter that has gained a certain notoriety. In it he nervously told Cody that he had 'made all the private enquiries possible ... about [Laskin's] political opinions and publications and I had to ask him to declare unequivo-cally that he has no connections public or private, expressly or implic-itly, with organized or unorganized communism, fascism or any subversive movements; and he has *categorically made* such declaration and repeated it in the presence of a witness ... I have told him ... that his duties are to teach Law and not to make any public statements – oral or written – on political or public questions' (emphasis in original).

Many have been quick to see evidence of anti-Semitism in this letter, and certainly the prejudice associating Jews with political subversion was a long-standing one. The ex-president of Harvard University, Charles William Eliot, had casually observed to Laskin's mentor Felix Frankfurter in 1924: 'Many Harvard men are worried because they think you are a Socialist. I observe that educated Jews easily entertain

Socialistic views. In what sense are you a Socialist? Marxian, pink, parlor, or red?'[59] An alternative reading might see Kennedy as trying to anticipate and deflect anti-Semitic responses in the recipient, but President Cody seems to have been on good terms with the Jewish community. He defended a Jewish lecturer attacked by a Toronto lawyer for offering a course on Marx as a 'wise and competent teacher,' welcomed a number of Jewish refugee professors to the university, and received high praise from Rabbi Maurice Eisendrath in 1938 for his support of the Jewish community.[60]

Only recently has this letter been analysed in its proper historical context.[61] The reference to 'public statements ... on political or public questions' is clearly to the Frank Underhill crisis that was convulsing the university at this very moment. Professor Underhill had courted dismissal the previous year when an earlier article of his advocating Canadian isolationism in the case of a European war had come to light.[62] Then on 23 August 1940, at the annual Couchiching Conference where he and Laskin had both spoken two years earlier, Underhill made a speech interpreted by some as advocating that Canada stand aloof from Britain during her hour of need. As Cody's biographer has noted, the atmosphere in the late summer of 1940 was 'infinitely more tense' after the German advance and the fall of France, than that of 1939. After Underhill's remarks were reported in the Toronto *Telegram*, Cody's telephone never stopped ringing. He was under immense pressure from the board of governors and the public to fire the outspoken professor, but recommended no action against him when the board met on 16 September.[63] It was at the very peak of this controversy that Kennedy found himself writing to Cody recommending Laskin's appointment. Kennedy undoubtedly thought Laskin's very public association with labour leaders and the WEA, in this wartime atmosphere when anxieties about loyalty ran high, might trouble Cody. The university did not need another faculty member making controversial statements to the media at this particular moment. In January 1938 Kennedy had recommended Laskin to President Cody in the warmest terms, with none of the caveats present in his 1940 letter.[64] Kennedy's concern about Laskin's loyalty may seem over the top today, but he was acting at a time of immense concern about the war effort, reflected in the enormous outcry around the Underhill affair. The loyalty oaths required of Laskin had little to do with his Judaism and everything to do with his very public association with the cause of labour and the left, now seen in a more suspicious light as a result of the war.

In 1976 interviewer Robin Harris asked Chief Justice Laskin about the 'loyalty oath' referred to in Kennedy's letter, expressing doubt whether Kennedy had ever made such inquiries. Laskin replied 'I know. [Chuckle] Well, I have no recollection at all of these enquiries having been made ... If these questions had been put to me at the time I suppose I would have resented any implication, any pejorative implication, but I ... just have no recollection of it ever having been said.'[65] Yet a decade before the interview Laskin spoke to a friend of the embarrassment of having these questions put to him in 1940.[66] It is unlikely that he should have forgotten, in the interim, such an extraordinary incident connected with his long-sought first academic post. Rather, he preferred not to appear ungrateful to his alma mater by confirming the incident, and possibly wished to avoid any imputation of unworthiness by having complied. Taking the oath rankled, but there was no choice. With that, Laskin barely skimmed over the last remaining hurdle to an academic post days before the beginning of term. The waiting was over.

PART II

The Academy

6

Professor

There was no time to lose. With only days before the beginning of term on 24 September, Laskin plunged into preparing classes. He would teach MacKenzie's courses in public international law and Canadian constitutional law, as well as two introductory courses to non-law students in the faculty of arts. MacKenzie passed on an odd legacy to Laskin: one subject in which he had no interest whatsoever, and one that became the abiding passion of his life. He had told Larry MacKenzie in 1938 that international law was a 'pipe dream,' with no impact on the current problems between nations.[1] In this Laskin shared the prejudices of the traditional common law lawyer who saw international law as hardly law at all, just a vague set of pious ideals with no clear enforcement mechanism. Common law was hard law, analytical, instrumental, masculine. International law was soft law, holistic, idealistic, feminine: definitely not Laskin's cup of tea. As he said in a 1943 book review, '[a] great deal of the disdain of the present system of international law stems from its duality in the sense that it looks with equal dispassion on action and inaction in relation to international delinquencies. The man in the street is justly sceptical when told of what action international law permits, when he remembers that inaction preceding the present war was likewise said to be consistent with international law.'[2] Fortunately for Laskin, W.P.M. Kennedy was himself wary of international lawyers. He 'proposed to appoint a thoroughly trained common lawyer,' he wrote to Dean Vincent MacDonald at Dalhousie, 'who can take one course in International Law as part of his general teaching load. ... I do not believe that the policy of having a specialist in any subject, apart from a thorough capacity to handle the Common Law, is a sound policy.'[3]

Laskin's law classes were sizeable but not huge – about fifty in constitutional law and thirty in public international law – but the courses for non-law students were rather larger. The figure of fifty is somewhat misleading as there was considerable attrition from the law program. Only twenty-four students graduated with the BA in Law in 1941, for example, and even fewer thereafter: ten in 1942, eighteen in 1943, thirteen in 1944, and ten in 1945. Unlike the First World War experience, when women entered Osgoode Hall in unusual numbers, their numbers did not increase this time. Three women graduated in 1941, none in 1942 or 1944, and one in each of 1943 and 1945. Probably better employment opportunities for women during the Second World War dampened their enthusiasm for legal studies.

Laskin's teaching experience with the Workers' Educational Association came in handy. Appearing before senior trade union officials was more intimidating than facing a group of young and deferential law students. The WEA experience had spared him the usual anxiety of the novice teacher, Laskin wrote to Drummond Wren.[4] Clyde Auld reported to Larry MacKenzie that 'Laskin is doing a thoroughly good job [and] making ... an excellent impression on the students.'[5] Auld might have discerned a less euphoric student reaction after the examination marks appeared. Laskin quickly developed a reputation as a demanding professor and a ferociously hard marker. Of fifty students in constitutional law in 1942 only one obtained a mark over 80 per cent, and nearly half the class had marks in the fifties. In the international law class a third of the class found themselves barely passing.[6]

Some young academics cultivate a reputation for tough grading out of insecurity, as a way of marking their turf and discouraging challenges to their authority. This seems unlikely in Laskin's case. He always set the highest standards for himself, and genuinely expected no less of others. In intellectual life as in sports Laskin thrived on competition, even though his in-class competition with students was necessarily one-sided. He engaged in some verbal sparring with his students when dissecting individual cases, but relied fairly heavily on lecturing and was not a devotee of the 'Socratic method.' Laskin's lectures always had a critical edge, however, probing the logical foundations and social suitability of the judicial decisions that formed a large part of the curriculum. Predictably, many of the brightest students found his approach challenging and exhilarating, while those of average ability sometimes found it alienating or discouraging.

Laskin's relations with the student body were a little more distant than those of some of his contemporaries. Moffatt Hancock could often be found enjoying himself at student parties, unlike Laskin. Then again, Hancock was single and Laskin was married and became a father during his second year on faculty, when Peggy gave birth to their first child, John. 'Moff' cut an unforgettable figure, tall, lanky, striking rather than handsome of face, with his shock of straw-blonde hair and Coke-bottle glasses. He was a brilliant teacher whose classroom performances dazzled students. Laskin was not especially gregarious, but befriended a few selected students. Charles Dubin, for example, eight years younger than Laskin and in his final year of the honour law course in 1940–1, became one of his closest friends. Laskin took a paternal interest in all his students, however, and was famous for being able to recall their names and significant personal facts when meeting them years later during chance encounters on the streets of Toronto.

Relations between students and faculty were expected to be cordial but somewhat distant. The main quasi-social events at which students and faculty mingled were meetings of the Law Club, where the speakers could sometimes supply unexpected entertainment. In December 1940 Sergeant McKinney of the Morality Department of the Toronto Police 'explained the operations of the red light district, gaming-houses, flop-houses, dope-joints, and, generally, the high spots of criminal life in this pious city.' Clyde Auld reported that '[i]t was one of the most successful and undoubtedly the spiciest lecture we have heard in a very long time, and completely eclipsed a recent and much more pedestrian effort of the Chief Justice of Ontario.'[7] Kennedy managed to attract high-profile speakers for the annual Law Club banquet in spite of wartime constraints, including Professor Samuel Williston of Harvard and Sir Owen Dixon, on leave from the High Court of Australia for a wartime diplomatic mission to Washington.

Laskin's starting salary at the University of Toronto was $1,800, or $150 per month, rising to $2,000 in 1942 and $2,500 in 1943. This was adequate to support a family of three but did not provide the degree of security and comfort Laskin desired. Kennedy had agreed that he could continue doing headnotes for the *Canadian Abridgment* on a piece-work basis, and he picked up some extra money doing evening and summer courses for the WEA. In late 1942, as the *Canadian Abridgment* work was ending, Laskin, Moffatt Hancock, and Laskin's Osgoode classmate G. Arthur Martin were appointed associate editors of the *Dominion Law Reports,* then under the general editorship of Caesar Wright.[8] Laskin would retain this position until he went on the bench in 1965, and would also serve as editor of other case reports. The work paid more than a nominal stipend but consumed a lot of time: the headnotes were a nightly part-time job added on to his full-time job.

In a sense Laskin owed his position at the University of Toronto to the war, and its impact was omnipresent during his first five-year stint there. In contrast to the year of the 'phony war,' by the fall of 1940 the University of Toronto was transforming itself to assist the war effort. By 1941 all male students over eighteen – some 3,500 – were receiving military training either in the Officers' Training Corps or in the Training Centre Battalion, and many students attended class in uniform. A new drill hall just down from the law building at 119 St George Street served as the headquarters for on-campus military training, with the adjacent grounds in continuous use for parades and exercises. A whole variety of special courses for armed forces personnel were on offer, including one in military law given by Clyde Auld. A dozen departments were engaged in war-related research, including highly secret work on chemical and biological warfare. By the spring of 1941 lectures outlining air raid precautions had commenced.[9]

The academic atmosphere continued to be dominated by the Underhill affair. Cody initially resisted pressures to fire Underhill. By December he had changed his mind and recommended his dismissal to the board, but the motion was deferred to June 1941. In private the board gave him the alternative of resigning quietly but he refused.[10] Most of the professoriate supported Underhill, but W.P.M. Kennedy did not. Arguing that 'common sense is the basis of freedom,' Kennedy found Underhill singularly deficient in that commodity. Harold Innis prophesied that the firing of Underhill would imperil the university's reputation as a defender of academic freedom, and perhaps this influenced the president. By the time a majority of the board voted for Underhill's dismissal on 26 June Cody had had a change of heart and refused to assent as required by the university's Act. Underhill went off to New York on a Guggenheim Fellowship while the university heaved a collective sigh of relief. The battle for academic freedom ended with a whimper rather than a bang.[11]

With his own loyalty tested at the time of his appointment, it is hard to believe that Laskin did not empathize with Underhill. But as a mere neophyte lecturer without any form of job security, Laskin did not sound off about the affair. In other contexts where freedom of expression was imperilled, he did speak out. At the very outset of the war Mackenzie King's government proclaimed the Defence of Canada Regulations (DOCR) under the *War Measures Act*, seen by some as 'the most serious restrictions upon the civil liberties of Canadians since Confederation.'[12] They gave the government extensive powers of press censorship and preventive detention, and later added a list of proscribed organizations which included the Communist Party. The regulations did not explicitly refer to trade union activities, but the police were often quick to equate these with subversion.

An early example was the December 1939 arrest of Bora Laskin's old WEA student Charles Millard, now leader of the Steel Workers Organizing Committee in Ontario. His crime? He had made a speech in Timmins condemning investors for resisting the government's tax on wartime profits. The charges were dropped after a public outcry, but in November 1940 another of Laskin's former students ran afoul of the DOCR. George Burt, now leader of the UAW in Canada, was convicted by a magistrate of having violated a prohibition on 'loitering' merely by peacefully picketing the Chrysler plant in Windsor. When the High Court affirmed the decision,[13] Laskin vented his outrage in a highly critical case comment.[14] The ban on loitering, he noted, was contained in a section of the regulations headed 'Espionage and Acts likely to Assist the Enemy.' Justice F.D. Hogg found the prohibition was, indeed, 'for the purpose of preventing spying upon and obtaining information of activities carried out in premises' such as the Chrysler plant, which were deemed 'essential services' by regulation, but found Burt guilty nonetheless. Laskin observed with some asperity that '[o]rganized labour is not likely to react favourably to even an implication that legitimate trade union activities are being [equated with] "spying."' In February 1941 the government amended the regulation so as to exclude strike-related activities more clearly.

With the door closed on the Underhill affair, the academic year 1940–1 stumbled to a close. When Laskin had finished his grading he and Peggy could look forward to a respite from Toronto's heat at Kennedy's cottage.[15] In 1940 Kennedy purchased 'Narrow Waters' at Kearney, on a lake near Algonquin Park. The heavily wooded property possessed a substantial waterfront, two houses, a huge barn and icehouse, but lacked electricity.[16] Whether visitors such as Bora and Peggy found their stay as idyllic as the setting warranted may be doubted. Laskin's successor at the law school, David Vanek, recalled the spartan regime that prevailed in the Kennedy household. Jacob Finkelman had cautioned Vanek that 'the Dean directed his family like a commander of a military establishment. An atmosphere of strict discipline prevailed. Activities were regulated for each segment of the day. Meals were frugal. "You will be hungry," he warned, "so take along some chocolate bars. There will be no snacks between meals and no food after dinner, which will be held early. After dinner, the Dean will turn on the radio for the news. When the news is over, he will examine his pocket watch and announce it is time for bed."'[17] Vanek found Finkelman's predictions entirely accurate, and was glad of his smuggled snacks.

Kennedy relied heavily on Laskin, writing to President Cody, 'I could not possibly work without Mr. Laskin's assistance.'[18] The number of students continued to diminish, but the war also brought to Toronto students from an unexpected source: the West Indies. The route to the bar in the English Caribbean lay, as it had for centuries, through the Inns of Court. With transatlantic travel rendered dangerous by the war, the English Council of Legal Education conceded that Toronto could substitute for an Inn for West Indian students. Dispensation from Part I of the English bar exams was granted to those students obtaining a degree from the school of law at Toronto. Laskin handled these arrangements as secretary to the faculty, a post to which Kennedy had appointed him at the end of his first year on staff; he welcomed the first two students, Charles Bourne from Barbados and Gloria Carpenter from Jamaica, in the fall of 1941.[19]

The West Indian students were well received in Toronto. Bourne became president of the Law Club, and Telford Georges of Dominica was voted the recipient of the Maurice Cody Award in 1947 for his contributions to college activities.[20] Laskin thought the West Indian students gave the law school good publicity and enjoyed their time in Toronto.[21] With Moffatt Hancock as their guardian angel, one can understand why. Gloria Carpenter provided Clyde Auld with the opportunity to display his dry wit. One Monday afternoon she was lamenting to Auld about what a dreadful day she had had, rushing around and not accomplishing anything. To which Auld retorted: 'Sic transit Gloria Monday.'[22] A few of the students, such as Charles Bourne, later a professor of law at the University of British Columbia, stayed in Canada, but most returned to the Caribbean. Many rose to prominence in their home countries: Eugenia Charles became prime minister of Dominica, Noor Hassanali president of Trinidad and Tobago, and Louis Fox served on the Jamaica Court of Appeal. Telford Georges, gold medallist in 1947, had the unique distinction of serving as chief justice of Tanzania, Zimbabwe, and the Bahamas.

These mostly black students (Bourne was white) were probably the first of their race to study at the University of Toronto law school. A number of black lawyers had been called to the bar in Ontario by this point, but none had done the law course at the University of Toronto. The small indigenous black population was still too poor, generally speaking, to be able to send their children to university in addition to the long years at Osgoode Hall. Two exceptions were Lincoln Alexander from Hamilton and Leonard Braithwaite from Toronto, but they received BA and B.Com. degrees from McMaster (1949) and Toronto (1950) respectively before attending Osgoode Hall, and hence did not attend Kennedy's school. In the decades after the war the number of black students at the University of Toronto law school declined again, to one every few years.

For Canadians, the shock of Japan's attack on Pearl Harbor in December 1941 was followed closely by the crushing defeat a few weeks later of the Canadian Expeditionary Force sent to assist British Forces in Hong Kong, and Japan's lightning strike through southeast Asia. In a spring plebiscite a majority of Canadians (though a minority of Québécois) voted to release the King government from its no-conscription pledge, and in July the drafting of young Canadian men for home defence began. Fortunately the Toronto Laskins were able to spend a few weeks in Port Arthur early in the summer before Bora's two younger brothers were called up.[23] Saul, aged twenty-four, had been working with his father in the family business after finishing high school, while Charles, aged twenty-seven, had been working in the clothing business in Winnipeg. During the war years the Toronto Laskins spent three to four weeks of the summer visiting Max and Bluma, who had left Fort William in 1938 to move into accommodation above the store in Port Arthur. They were not old in years, but Bluma's weak heart required the installation of an elevator chair to carry her to their second-floor living quarters. Her homeland was blighted by the Holocaust: in 1942 virtually the entire Latvian Jewish population was exterminated by the Nazi occupiers in concert with Latvian Fascists.

Laskin's age and marital status exempted him from call-up throughout the war (only married men born in 1916 or after were later called up). Still, one might ask why he did not volunteer for the armed forces.

All of his colleagues at the law school were unfit for war service. Auld was in his fifties, Kennedy older. Finkelman had a withered arm, Hancock a severe visual disability, and Gilbert Kennedy, hired in 1943, was epileptic. Possibly Laskin had some occult medical condition rendering him unsuitable for service, but this seems unlikely. In the early days of the war there was no great rush to enlist, and it was only the fall of France in the spring of 1940 that triggered a large influx into the armed forces. Did Laskin, like Frank Scott, initially oppose the war as an imperialist venture? It seems improbable. By the autumn, Laskin had a position at the faculty of law, and contrary to the First World War experience, the authorities were not encouraging academics to enlist. Certainly Kennedy would have been desperate to have him stay on staff and not go running off to the front. Perhaps Laskin saw his labour work as providing more 'value added' to Canadian society than anything he might have done in uniform. He was in the vanguard of those fighting the war for better living and working conditions on the home front, but his contribution in this regard pales beside that of people such as Kenneth Macalister, who made the ultimate sacrifice. Once Laskin's brothers were called up, his decision not to enlist might be justified, but nearly three years of the war had gone by at that point. The fact is, there is no evidence of Laskin's motivation. Even if his decision can be justified as an ethical one, his ability to advance his career during the war gave him an enormous advantage in the post-war years. Some in the legal profession held it against him for a very long time.

The war provoked enormous changes in the field of labour relations. Laskin had a ringside seat from which to observe the demise of industrial voluntarism and the emergence of a new mode of regulating industrial relations: industrial legality. Under the old order, the state acted in theory as an impartial umpire laying down the basic rules of engagement for capital and labour, but not imposing any substantive results. In reality, the coercive power of the criminal law, the civil courts (through the labour injunction and a variety of anti-labour doctrines with deep roots in the common law), the police, and the military were always waiting in the wings to discipline labour when industrial conflict passed a certain threshold of tolerance. Under the new model the state would supervise more directly labour-capital relations, in effect reducing the scope for independent action by both.

It took the enhanced bargaining power of labour during the war years to bring forth a new paradigm of industrial relations in Canada.

This new system centred on certified trade unions, compulsory recognition by employers, and mandatory collective bargaining. It also included penalties for unfair labour practices and a process for the final and binding settlement of disputes arising out of collective agreements. Bora Laskin had advocated such a transformation ever since his student days. During the early war years he continued his role as critic of the old order, while after 1943 he became a publicist for the new system and a participant in its institutional mechanisms. Before 1940 Laskin was an outsider, trying to interpret the demands of labour to civil society, the state, the courts, and the legal profession; afterwards, his position at the University of Toronto gave his pleas an aura of legitimacy they had previously lacked.

The federal government's labour policies seemed to go from bad to worse during the early years of the war.[24] December 1941 saw the promulgation of wage and price controls, effectively removing wages as a subject of bargaining and making it more difficult for unions to demonstrate their utility to their members. In the long and bitter Kirkland Lake gold mine strike, the government refused to compel the mine owners to bargain with the union, resulting in the failure of the strike in February 1942. Labour was also incensed by federal advocacy of plant-level 'employee committees,' which were perceived as company unions.[25] By 1943 'one out of three workers across the country engaged in some form of collective action to protest both the government's wage and labour policies and their treatment by their employers.'[26] The translation of this resentment into political action finally caused Canadian governments to abandon the voluntarist mantra, as CCF electoral support rose dramatically both provincially and federally in 1942–3.

At Queen's Park, Minister of Labour Peter Heenan promised a collective bargaining bill shortly after the end of the Kirkland Lake strike, and secretly hired radical labour lawyer Jacob L. Cohen to draft one. Cohen's book *Collective Bargaining in Canada*, favouring a compulsory collective bargaining process supervised by an administrative tribunal, had appeared in 1941. None of his draft bills went this far, but the government rejected them all and decided to appoint a select committee of the legislature to hold hearings and draft a law. Jacob Finkelman was appointed counsel to the committee, while Laskin appeared on behalf of the Amalgamated Clothing Workers of America and the International Ladies Garment Workers' Union. He also appeared as counsel for the upstart Canadian Congress of Labour (CCL). The CCL had recently absorbed the CIO in Canada and now, with its

265,000 members, rivalled the traditionally craft-oriented Trades and Labour Congress.[27]

Laskin summarized the provisions of the new law in an article published in the fall of 1943, 'Collective Bargaining in Ontario: A New Legislative Approach,' and gave a brief account of some of the jurisprudence of the Labour Court handed down in the first few months of its operation.[28] The *Collective Bargaining Act, 1943* obliged employers to bargain collectively with unions certified by the Labour Court to have the support of a majority of workers in the particular bargaining unit.[29] In return, strikes were prohibited during the currency of a collective agreement; all disputes were to be referred compulsorily to arbitration. At last the need for costly and wasteful recognition strikes was avoided, though the new system did nothing to guarantee a fair first contract once a union was certified. Curiously, Laskin had no comment on the decision to confide the administration of this ground-breaking law to a division of the Supreme Court of Ontario rather than a government department or an administrative tribunal, beyond noting that the Select Committee of the Legislature had recommended the latter. He warned that it would be 'unfortunate if the strictly legalistic approach stultifies the aim of the Act to establish peaceful collective bargaining relations,' but saw in the court's power to 'make such orders as appear to it just and agreeable to equity' a signal opportunity 'to develop a flexible technique in terms of sound labour relations policy.'[30] Labour leaders, including Aaron Mosher of the CCL, were much more sceptical, complaining that the Labour Court was 'nothing more than a picnic for the lawyers.'[31]

Decisions of the Labour Court came in for criticism only on one major point. In spite of strong language in the Act aimed at preventing employer interference with unions, the Labour Court had certified a number of company unions; in fact, by the end of 1943 about half of all certifications went to independent company unions.[32] Laskin castigated the Court's formal procedures as 'hardly adequate instruments for discovering whether, in the words of s. 1(b) of the Act, [the union was] "dominated, coerced or improperly influenced by the employer in any manner whether by way of financial aid or otherwise."'[33] He also queried the Court's high threshold for a finding of domination, as it was not replicated in the rulings of the U.S. National Labor Relations Board (NLRB). On this and other points of interpretation, Laskin found the NLRB's decisions were 'the only precedents of value.' A year later, he delivered a benign judgment of the Labour Court's work: its decisions 'comprised a body of labour law which was, on the whole, acclaimed both by employers and employees alike as a significant contribution to industrial peace.'[34] This second article was based on a talk Laskin gave to a coal and steel industry conference at Sydney, Cape Breton, in September 1944; his views were clearly beginning to attract national attention.

A year after the Ontario government acted (British Columbia and Alberta also amended their legislation to similar effect in 1943), the federal government finally brought in a comprehensive labour relations law in the form of the War-time Labour Relations Regulations (usually known collectively as PC 1003), which became effective on 20 March 1944. PC 1003 followed the main lines of the Ontario Act, obliging employers to bargain collectively with certified bargaining representatives, and providing for a no-strike clause during the currency of collective agreements. Unlike the Ontario Act, it provided that if the parties were unable to agree on the terms of a collective agreement they could refer the matter to a conciliation board, which had the power to recommend but not enforce a settlement. (Laskin served on many of these, as we shall see.) PC 1003 also differed from the Ontario Act in confiding its administration not to a court but to a War-time Labour Relations Board, representative of employers and employees and headed by two non-partisans who happened to be judges. The board's non-expert, part-time character and its unwieldy size offended Laskin's legal modernism. 'These factors, along with the bipartisan character of the boards, tend to produce loose administration, militate against the building up of a body of labour jurisprudence since written decisions are rare, and result in interpretations which proceed not so much on principle as on compromise.'[35]

Why was the reasoned elaboration of precedent so important? Laskin constantly sought to bring labour relations into the mainstream of the law, to create a true 'labour law' where neither union violence nor blatant economic coercion by the employer could force the other side to submit. For him, this was the dividing line between civilization and barbarity. This went totally against the traditions of labour relations, where 'getting to yes' was the dominant consideration and expediency the only yardstick. Laskin saw clearly that the state's involvement in collective bargaining would be a hollow victory for labour – and probably resisted by management – unless the rules of engagement were clearly articulated through a transparent process. It was crucial that the exact nature of the parties' rights and obligations be fine-tuned through reasoned discussion and debate before appropriately qualified decision makers.

Lawyers would play a key role in framing and contributing to that debate. Laskin was perfectly placed to play a direct role, but in the early 1940s he was overshadowed by Jacob L. Cohen. Cohen was a generation older, a gritty, brilliant advocate in the cause of labour, the politically radical and the disadvantaged. His intellect and his popularity with labour were such that the King and Hepburn governments were forced to seek his services in spite of his close association with Communist groups. In February 1943 Mackenzie King appointed Cohen to a reconstituted National War Labour Board, but fired him in September when his outspoken reports on the need for far-reaching labour reforms were perceived as too partisan. Along with Cohen, Andrew Brewin, Ted Jolliffe, Jacob Finkelman (who was named registrar of the new Labour Court), and a few others, Laskin was one of a small circle of legal advisers whom labour leaders trusted. When George Burt became Canadian regional director of the United Auto Workers in 1943, he promptly hired his former WEA tutor as general counsel for the UAW. Soon Laskin found himself before the Labour Court on a dozen applications for certification, and was obliged to hire a stenographer who worked in an attic office in the law building.[36]

In one of these, Massey-Harris resisted attempts by the UAW to unionize its Toronto branch, arguing that its plant industrial council represented a majority of the 2,700 plant workers and no vote need be taken. Laskin was up against the cream of the Toronto bar on this one: J.S.D. Tory represented the company, while J.J. Robinette appeared for the intervenor plant council. He sought a ruling from Justice Barlow that if a vote were ordered, the votes of older employees should count more than those of newer ones. Older employees were likely to remain at the plant after the war, asserted Robinette, while younger ones would probably leave. He also sought to have the Labour Court provide the five hundred or so employees in the armed services with a chance to vote. Barlow agreed with Laskin that distinguishing between employees on length of service was both dangerous and impractical, while polling the servicemen was out of the question. He also agreed with Laskin that the existing contract with the plant council was no bar to the holding of a vote, and ordered one to be taken.[37]

When Laskin's courtroom appearances on this file were reported in the newspapers, they elicited a strong response from W.P.M. Kennedy, who advised President Cody that 'there has arisen a very awkward and indeed amazing situation in the school of law.' Kennedy accused Laskin of not asking his permission and saying he would have refused it in any case, as 'the School is built on *full-time* men [who] understand, as well as Laskin, that while they may do private work, they must not appear before the courts. This is our condition of appointment of permanent members of the school and ... Laskin is the first person who has (wilfully) broken it.' Kennedy was concerned about the appearance of salaried faculty members competing with the school's own struggling graduates, and about fairness to other faculty members both inside and outside the law school.[38]

Unbeknownst to Kennedy, Laskin had already sought the consent of President Cody and the Law Society of Upper Canada before appearing in court. The fact that Laskin had gone over Kennedy's head suggests that he anticipated some resistance on that front. Cody had simply told Laskin to use his own judgment and the Law Society had said it had no objection.[39] In his 1976 interview, Laskin said he had told Kennedy when he joined the faculty that he would like to continue doing some labour work and secured his consent to do so, and expressed surprise at Kennedy's letter to Cody. It is possible that Kennedy had given consent in a general way years before but became alarmed when he saw accounts of Laskin working for the CIO, letters which at that time, as Laskin put it, 'would perhaps raise the hackles of sections of the community' – including, no doubt, members of the board of governors.[40] Laskin's desire to forestall any adverse reaction by board members may explain his concern to clear his actions with Cody and not just Kennedy alone. In any case, he agreed to stop appearing in court and turned over all his Labour Court work to Jacob Cohen.

Laskin's and Finkelman's increasingly high-profile engagement with the labour cause gave rise to adverse comment by some high-powered lawyers and business people whose opinion counted at the University of Toronto. Harold Fox, the Canadian copyright expert who taught part-time at the law school, complained to Kennedy about this in 1944. 'To take any action,' he replied, 'would mean that every solitary avenue of public work would have to be closed to the staff of the entire University ... in order to avoid invidious distinction.' Kennedy assured Fox 'most emphatically that there is nothing tendentious or of the nature of advocacy in' Laskin's or Finkelman's lectures. Anyone familiar with legal academe in the 1980s and '90s will recognize a familiar cycle: professor speaks publicly on controversial issue; professor labelled as advocate rather than objective academic; concern expressed by professional and business leaders about quality of education being provided; university administration receptive to concerns; attempts made to quiet controversy. The only difference is that the causes of the 1980s and '90s were feminism, racial discrimination, and native rights, while in the 1940s, the rights of labour were at issue. To his credit, Kennedy did not try to muzzle his staff, and concluded his letter to Fox by saying he could not carry on, 'nor could anyone, if we were at the mercy of every complaint.'[41]

The endeavours of the WEA reached their peak during the war years, and Laskin's talents were much in demand as workers and unions struggled to keep abreast of the sudden burst of reforms in labour law. He gave evening courses, taught in the WEA summer school at Port Hope, and spent numerous weekends in southern Ontario's industrial centres on WEA 'institutes' devoted to the new labour laws, wage and price controls, the handling of grievances, and the like. The WEA contracted with the unions for some of its services, the UAW and the communist-led unions being its biggest clients.[42]

In 1942 the WEA purchased the former home of the Ontario College of Art, an old millhouse at Port Hope. There it created 'Canada's First Labour College, where working men and women can enjoy a holiday "with a purpose".' Two-week-long WEA courses were offered to eighty or ninety participants at a time, and some unions held their own summer programs there. Women formed a quarter to a third of the enrolment, and three female tutors, M. Winspear, Idele Wilson, and Cynthia Barrett, were on staff along with Laskin and Professor Lorne Morgan. Mildly erotic photos of young participants enjoying the bathing facilities were prominent in the school's publicity, as were outdoor lectures in sylvan surroundings. The humanistic roots of the WEA were evident in courses in 'recent literature' and 'modern dance' alongside offerings on Fascism, collective bargaining, and union-management cooperation; surviving film footage shows a class on racial discrimination. The school embodied a vision of working-class culture that perceived the worker as a complex human being with a variety of material, emotional, and spiritual needs, and a participant in a broader social project aimed at eliminating injustice.[43]

The WEA model of eclectic, critical, and transformative labour education would barely outlast the war. The large unions began to develop their own in-house educational capacity, focused more on nuts-and-bolts training for shop stewards and grievance officers, and the Canadian Congress of Labour also developed its own programs. The WEA's non-partisan stance became difficult to sustain with the rise of the CCF and the advent of the Cold War. Laskin's good friend Drummond Wren was persuaded to become the head of the UAW's educational department in 1943, but stayed on as voluntary executive secretary of the WEA. In 1947 he was fired by the UAW's anti-communist president Walter Reuther, foreshadowing further difficulties for Wren on the home front. The WEA's greatest challenge was the enormous transformation in Canadian society between 1930 and 1950: the demand by workers and the unemployed for critical analysis of their place in society, so urgent during the Depression, waned considerably in the triumphantly prosperous post-war years.

The fast-moving changes in the field of labour law soon affected Laskin's academic career. Jacob Finkelman took a leave of absence to become registrar of the Labour Court in July 1943, leaving Kennedy with some courses to cover on short notice. In his peremptory way Kennedy informed Laskin that he would take over his friend's courses in labour law and administrative law. This was in addition to his teaching constitutional law, international law, real property, and two law courses for arts students. Laskin recalled summoning up the courage to ask 'if I am going to take on Finkelman's courses, shouldn't I have an increase in salary?' When Kennedy said there was no money, Laskin replied, with some *chutzpah*, that he had 'got a pretty full load and perhaps we had better just leave it at that.' A few days later Kennedy returned with an offer of a $500 increase.[44] Laskin does not say so in his 1976 interview, but it may be that another part of the *quid pro quo* was Kennedy's recommendation for a promotion from lecturer to the rank of assistant professor, which at the time included a grant of tenure. In any case, Laskin was promoted as of 1 July 1943. Finkelman's other courses were taken by Gilbert Kennedy, W.P.M.'s son, who was hired to teach torts and criminal law on a half-time basis. Gilbert's qualifications were excellent and there were few competitors given wartime labour shortages.

The Labour Court experiment was short-lived, and it was replaced in 1944 by an administrative tribunal, the Ontario Labour Relations Board. Appointed chair of the board on a part-time basis in 1944, Finkelman continued to shuttle between it and the law school until 1947, when he returned to the law school full-time. Kennedy needed another lieutenant in Finkelman's absence and immediately chose Laskin. Why not Hancock, Laskin's senior on staff? Perhaps Kennedy agreed with Cae-

sar Wright: Hancock was more brilliant but he 'lacked ballast,' which
Laskin possessed.[45] Laskin had a keen sense of practicalities and the
energy to get things done, but serving a commanding officer as domi-
neering as Kennedy was no picnic. It meant receiving letters such as
this one in August 1943: 'It will be necessary for someone to be in the
School of Law every day from Sept 9 or so as I or Finkelman was, since
you will have to see inquirers and guide them into law. In fact our first
year *depends on this*. Put up a notice *at once* headed *Interviews with
students* and give date and times and room, and state that all students
considering the study of law may have an interview.'[46] Kennedy's
acolytes, such as Jacob Finkelman, and later Eugene La Brie, were
prepared to shrug off his imperious ways as simple personality quirks.
Bora Laskin had already shown that he was prepared to stand up to
Kennedy to defend his own interests, and it may be doubted whether
he was fully comfortable in this new role.

The war years saw important structural and curricular changes within
the law program. As a result of Kennedy's determined advocacy
and his very good relationship with President Cody, three important
steps were taken in quick succession. The first was the emergence of
the department of law as a separate school of law, independent of the
department of political economy, under Kennedy as chairman. In the
following year the Senate authorized the offering of a doctoral program
leading to the degree of Doctor Juris (D.Jur.), and in 1944 Kennedy was
appointed dean of the School of Law. With these institutional changes
the structure of 'Kennedy's School' came to resemble more and more
that of other North American law schools.[47]

Curricular reforms followed the same pattern. The labyrinthine requirements of the LLB degree were simplified so that as of 1943 students with the Honours BA in Law could achieve the LLB with only one
more year of study, for a total of five years. In effect, the school now
offered a joint BA-LLB degree. And the balance within the Honours BA
itself shifted away from the arts courses and towards law. By the mid-
1940s students took only two arts courses in each of the four years;
when Laskin began in 1930, the first year (which he had been able to
skip because of his senior matriculation) had been almost entirely arts,
with two to four arts courses in upper years. A new direct-entry three-
year LLB program was also created in 1943, containing only law courses
and no arts courses, for those possessing BA degrees or equivalent
qualifications. In the first year there were six compulsory courses: Contracts, Torts, Criminal Law, Property Law I, Commercial Law I, and

Judicial Remedies. In the second year students took seven out of a possible eleven course offerings, three in private law, six in public law, and two in comparative law and jurisprudence. The third year was devoted to intensive work in small seminars rather than lectures in five courses out of a possible nine. Except for the format of the third year, the new program fell into line with LLB programs at other North American universities.[48] The LLB accordingly became a much more popular course in the 1940s than it had been in the 1930s, when it was still an academic curiosity.

In one significant respect Kennedy's law school still diverged from the North American mainstream, and that was in its nurturing of graduate study in law. Aside from programs at a handful of Ivy League schools, graduate work in law was unavailable in North America outside Quebec. Manitoba had wanted to offer a graduate degree in law in 1939 but then-president Sidney Smith found the proposed program insufficiently rigorous, and one was not established until 1949.[49] In Kennedy's vision the University of Toronto would supply the postgraduate experience that aspirant Canadian legal academics could then seek only outside Canada. Laskin gave him 'full credit for foresight and perhaps for pushing things ahead of their time' in fostering graduate legal study.[50] Kennedy was convinced 'that the most important legal fields for many years will be in Canadian social legislation and Canadian administrative law, [but it was] utterly impossible for graduate students in law to get ... these Canadian law subjects in the graduate law schools in the U.S.'[51] Such sentiments highlight Kennedy's nationalism and his attempts to create a niche for his graduate law program. He also secured funds for student support in the form of the Newton Wesley Rowell Fellowship of five hundred dollars for graduate study in law, offered for the first time in 1943.

A surprising number of students came to Toronto for graduate work in law in the 1940s, and Laskin supervised many of them. Two were from China, W.H. Chin and Han du Pei. Han du Pei returned to Wuhan University in time to see China's law faculties decimated by the revolution's reaction against the bourgeois concept of law. Having survived the long twilight of legal studies in China, he re-emerged as head of the department of international law at Wuhan in the early 1980s. When representatives of the Canadian Institute for the Administration of Justice visited Wuhan in 1982, they were met by a wizened little man who greeted them with the query, 'And how is my old friend Bora Laskin?' When informed of Professor Han's greetings, Chief Justice Laskin immediately arranged for a shipment of supernumerary books from the Supreme Court library to be sent to Wuhan's law library to assist in its reconstitution.[52]

A Canadian LLM student had a more tortuous route into the program. George Tamaki was a Japanese-Canadian from British Columbia who had graduated from Dalhousie near the top of his class in the spring of 1941. Upon completion of his articles in Halifax he joined his family, recently interned in the interior of British Columbia. While teaching in the camp schools, he applied to do graduate work at Toronto. The board's policy in 1942 was to not accept any Japanese-Canadian applicants, but in June 1943 it reversed itself to the great relief of the faculty at the law school, who were keen to accept Tamaki. A list of Japanese-Canadian applicants for 1943–4 was approved for admission provided they were British subjects and not under RCMP suspicion. Tamaki completed a thesis under Laskin on the law relating to nationality in Canada and went on to become one of Canada's premier tax lawyers, first in Montreal and later in Toronto.[53]

Once the doctoral program in law was approved in 1942, three candidates for the degree were accepted almost immediately, and Laskin supervised all of them. James Northey of New Zealand did a dissertation on the office of governor-general in New Zealand; later, as dean, he took the University of Auckland law school from a part-time night-school to a full-time professional school.[54] The two other doctoral candidates were from Alberta, Morris Shumiatcher and Eugene La Brie. 'Shumy' was a slightly younger variant of Laskin himself, and the two became lifelong friends. The son of a Jewish lawyer in Calgary, Shumiatcher's own legal career was very much his second choice: he had wanted to become an English professor but was told he would have no chance as a Jew. A man of enormous energy and zest for life, he became a highly successful lawyer and author of the province's 1947 Bill of Rights, the first such Act in Canada. Shumiatcher spent the year 1940–1 on a Rotary scholarship to Japan before coming east to do an LLM at the University of Toronto. As the first candidate accepted into the D.Jur. program in 1942, he was the inaugural recipient of the Rowell Fellowship. The title of his dissertation shows a close fit with the vision of the Kennedy school and with Laskin's own graduate work at Harvard: *A Study in Canadian Administrative Law: The Farmers' Creditors Arrangement Acts.*

Like Tamaki, La Brie was interested in the new field of taxation and would teach it after joining the faculty in 1945.[55] Laskin described their relationship in disarming fashion many years later: 'Now I didn't know anything about taxation. La Brie didn't know anything about taxation. La Brie later ... established a reputation in the tax field. But here we were, teacher and student, really two graduate students, if you like, trying to work up some interest in a ... field which of course today is so extremely important.'[56] Laskin's frank admission of his lack of expertise in his student's area of interest, coupled with Kennedy's vehement opposition to hiring 'specialists,' may lead one to ask whether the Kennedy School was a credible place to do graduate work in the 1940s. Graduate study in law usually involved primary research in judicial decisions and legislation on the topic of choice, followed by exposition and critical analysis of the results. Under this model, the specialist credentials of the supervisor were not crucial; the professor's role related to more general matters of legal method and argumentation, and to helping the student situate the chosen topic in related fields of law and legal theory. A 'bootstrap' operation it may have been, but the graduate program at Kennedy's law school was none the worse for that.

By the middle of the war Laskin was feeling restive under Kennedy, increasingly of the view that the law school needed reshaping. It was, he said in 1976, 'very difficult to straddle two fences ... on the one hand to try to teach students in a broad liberal way and on the other hand to give them some insight ... into a professional discipline. Maybe Oxford and Cambridge have succeeded in marrying those two things. But it was difficult in Canada because there were professional schools ... [F]rom 1930, you felt almost an irresistible pressure to professionalize the department of law in the faculty of arts.'[57] It was this philosophical difference, Laskin states, that precipitated his move to Osgoode Hall Law School in 1945. Accepting these as Laskin's genuine recollections as of 1976, they are difficult to square with what was actually happening in Kennedy's school. By 1943 the arts content of the Honours BA in law had been dramatically reduced, and a new direct-entry three-year LLB had been created for those already possessing BA degrees. Its curriculum was scarcely distinguishable from the one Laskin would help Wright establish when he returned to the University of Toronto in 1949. Why was that not sufficient for Laskin? Why could the school not have focused on the new LLB program and let the Honours BA in law wither away? Laskin's move in 1945 may have been motivated in part by certain perceived philosophical differences between the Kennedy school and Osgoode, but strategic considerations on his part and the interplay of personalities were also important.

Obtaining the ear of the legal profession was very important for Bora Laskin. It is striking that virtually everything he published in the first decade of his scholarly life (1937–47) appeared in the *Canadian Bar Review*. He did not publish in the *University of Toronto Law Journal* (UTLJ), which was the better regarded academic journal, until 1947, and even then contributed only annual reviews of legislation. Not until 1955 did he publish a 'real' article in the UTLJ.[58] In fact, Laskin almost became editor of the *Canadian Bar Review* in the fall of 1945, after Wright gave it up, but in the end begged off because of the demands of more students and new courses at Osgoode.[59] For Bora Laskin, the *Canadian Bar Review* 'counted' in a way that the UTLJ did not. Ideas appearing there had a good chance of circulating within the bar and the judiciary, whereas the UTLJ had a more diffuse readership. Even Laskin's curriculum vitae reflects this concern: it includes articles in the *Canadian Bar Review*, the UTLJ, and a few other Canadian law journals, but virtually none of his publications in non-law journals or chapters in edited collections.[60]

Through the *Canadian Bar Review* Bora Laskin could lecture the members of his profession who would not admit him as a full member because of his Jewish heritage. It was the bar, the judiciary, and to some extent government policy makers, not the tiny legal academic community or the broader university community, whom Laskin wished to reach at this point in his career. In that sense, teaching at Kennedy's school had always been a detour for Laskin, but it was the only place where he stood a chance of being hired when he returned from Harvard. Even with Caesar Wright's support, which he clearly would have had, Laskin knew his chances of being hired at Osgoode Hall Law School in 1938–40 were nil because of his faith, should a position fall vacant. What a sea change the war brought! Knowledge of the Holocaust undermined the fortress of Canadian anti-Semitism, seemingly so impregnable in the 1930s. In his 1976 interview Laskin and his interviewer generally steered clear of issues related to Judaism, but Laskin volunteered that 'there were a couple of interesting features' about his being hired at Osgoode. 'First, they had never had a person of the Jewish faith on the faculty of Osgoode Hall. And that in itself was probably a revolution.'[61]

Throughout his time at Kennedy's school, Laskin remained in constant contact with Caesar Wright, with whom he became linked ever more closely. First and foremost, he was Wright's (formally unrecognized) assistant editor at the *Canadian Bar Review*. In 1942 Wright arranged for Laskin's appointment as associate editor of the *Dominion Law Reports*, a very prestigious position at the time. After the passage in March 1944 of PC 1003, Laskin sat as labour nominee on many conciliation boards chaired by Wright. And, he later recalled, while at Kennedy's school 'I would be over there [at Osgoode] having lunch with [Wright and Dean Falconbridge] ... and we used to have long talks, especially Wright and myself, about the future of legal education in this country.'[62]

In any migration there are always 'push' and 'pull' factors. The 'pull' factors to Osgoode were very strong: the ability to work with the iconic Caesar Wright, the automatic legitimacy and influence with the provincial bar that teaching at its own school would convey, the possibility of reshaping professional legal education, and, not insignificantly, quite a lot more money. Laskin would start at Osgoode at four thousand dollars per year, 60 per cent more than at Toronto. There were 'push' factors besides the supposed philosophical difference between Osgoode and Toronto: Kennedy was not an easy man to work under, and while he might retire soon, he might stay on forever. He had tried to overload Laskin with courses once and might try to do it again. Laskin and Finkelman were good friends but Finkelman was more at home than Laskin in the school Kennedy had created. With Hancock looking elsewhere and Auld distracted by a tragic family life, there was rather little to excite Laskin about staying on at the University of Toronto.

Laskin's scholarship during his five years at Kennedy's school was not especially impressive in either quality or quantity compared to his publications in the late 1930s or those from 1947 onwards. Clearly the extra-curricular activities were taking their toll. Aside from the articles on the new developments in labour law discussed earlier, he wrote a number of very brief case comments and book reviews in the *Canadian Bar Review*, and an article on the determination of the situs of corporate shares for taxation purposes.[63] The latter added little to the existing literature on the subject and has the air of a legal opinion turned into an article. More curious is Laskin's absence from the scholarship in administrative law appearing during the war years.[64] One of the most important books on Canadian law to that date, *Canadian Boards at Work*, was published in 1941.[65] Edited by Laskin's future colleague John Willis, then of Dalhousie, it was a collection of empirical case studies of individual agencies. One might have expected to see a condensed version of Laskin's Harvard LLM thesis in this volume, but it was not there. It appears that Laskin and Jacob Finkelman were working on a book-length version of the thesis to be published by the University of Toronto

Press but abandoned the project after the Ontario government announced a major restructuring of the Ontario Municipal Board in 1942.[66] The decision reflects the priority they gave to legal scholarship as a vehicle for urgent law reform rather than cool reflection on past experience.

While Laskin did not ignore his scholarship during these early years, it was not uppermost in his mind. His main priorities were teaching and labour activism. Laskin's connections in the labour field meant he was well placed to get in on the ground floor in the brave new world of industrial pluralism. Any number of career paths would have been open to him, either alone or in combination with academics, had he chosen to pursue them. Most obviously, he could easily have set up a lucrative labour law practice. Jacob Cohen's personal demons were about to destroy him; he would be disbarred in 1946, leaving a large gap Laskin could have filled. The path to a political career was also clearly visible, as CCF support grew in the later years of the war. Labour advocates Andrew Brewin, Ted Jolliffe and, a little later, David Lewis, all went this route. Or Laskin could have followed Jacob Finkelman's lead, providing advice on labour relations policy and legislation, and perhaps becoming a high-level civil servant in a nascent labour bureaucracy.

None of these options appealed to him. Laskin would never practise law again (aside from some opinion work) after his brief stint in the early 1940s. Nor did a political career interest him; although always perceived as being on the centre-left of the political spectrum, Laskin remained publicly non-partisan all his life. He was not part of the group of self-identified socialist academics in the League for Social Reconstruction such as Frank Scott, Eugene Forsey, and Frank Underhill, nor did he contribute to the de facto League journal, the *Canadian Forum*. And while Laskin provided occasional advice to governments on labour, and later constitutional matters, he did not want to become a civil servant. He did not wish to be beholden to anyone: clients, the labour movement, a political party, organized religion, or the government. Aside from his post-war involvement with the Canadian Jewish Congress and later Holy Blossom Temple, what Kennedy reported to President Cody in 1940 remained substantially true: 'Laskin informs me that he has not been connected, and is not connected, with any type of organization, even of a social nature.'[67]

The university was the only environment in which Laskin's primordial desire for independence, influence, and security could be satisfied.

Even there, given the jarring ritual on his appointment, his independence was clearly subject to some constraints. At least there were fewer in the university than elsewhere. Motivated by a strong sense of injustice, Laskin wanted to see major changes in his society. He felt he could do this best by developing a reputation for exercising independent judgment, free of the claims of class, religion, and partisanship. His post-war popularity as a labour arbitrator suggests a high degree of success in this respect. Engaged in the world, but aloof from traditional group claims – that is how Bora Laskin wished to represent himself. Wrapping his message in the mantle of scholarship, Laskin gambled that it would have to be taken seriously. From the university base, shielded by a concept of academic freedom he himself would later help to define, Bora Laskin began to carve out an identity as a public intellectual, one who could speak authoritatively on some of the major issues of post-war society. It was a difficult niche in which to position himself, and an unusual choice for a young Jewish man of his era, but he would make it his own. The waiting had been worth it.

7

Osgoode

The last years of the war saw a revival of interest in the question of legal education at Osgoode Hall. Even the benchers of the Law Society could not ignore the enormous legal and administrative changes the war had wrought in Canadian life. All of a sudden powerful boards and tribunals were everywhere, allocating housing, setting prices, reshaping labour relations, commandeering resources of every description. In January 1943 the Law Society offered a special course of lectures for lawyers on 'Wartime Emergency Orders and Administrative Tribunals'[1] and struck a committee to recommend changes to the Osgoode curriculum. In January 1944 the committee accepted several recommendations by Dean Falconbridge: income tax, administrative law, and labour law would be added to the curriculum; a new full-time faculty member would be hired, and the hours of instruction would increase from 900 to 1,050 over the three years of the law course. The new man turned out to be John Willis of Dalhousie, who inaugurated the courses in income tax and administrative law upon his arrival that fall; labour law was deferred for a year. In the spring of 1945 'Daddy' MacRae announced his retirement, and on 6 July 1945 Bora Laskin was appointed to teach labour law, constitutional law, real property, and the history of English law at Osgoode Hall Law School.

This bare recitation of facts glosses over an enormous amount of backstage manoeuvring, occasionally flaring into public drama, over the future of legal education in Ontario in the closing years of the war.

At Osgoode, Wright, and less dramatically Falconbridge, were committed to a full-time three-year law course taught to students already
possessing a university degree. Kennedy and his colleagues at the
University of Toronto had in practice already achieved this, although
they did not make a prior university degree an absolute prerequisite,
and of course their BA degree in law was not recognized by the Law
Society. Sidney Smith, president of the University of Toronto as of
1 July 1945, also supported the full-time university model. The benchers,
while accepting some modernization of the curriculum and hiring two
men, Willis and Laskin, known for their passionate commitment to the
full-time university model of legal education, remained wedded to the
concurrent system of articling and lectures. After nearly a decade of
frustration following the benchers' 1935 decision to forestall any sys-
temic reform, Caesar Wright and his allies were getting restive indeed.[2]

The first public skirmish in the renewed war over legal education
occurred at a meeting of the Ontario section of the Canadian Bar Association held in Toronto in February 1944. The treasurer of the Law
Society, D'Alton Lally McCarthy, chose this occasion to make a public
attack on university legal education in general and the University of
Toronto in particular. Wright rose to the provocation and 'speaking as
he said as a member of the profession and not as a member of the Law
School staff, made a virulent attack upon the [Osgoode Hall] Law
School as at present constituted. The gist of his remarks was that it was
no damned good.'[3] Unprotected by tenure or any concept of academic
freedom at the Law Society's proprietary law school, Wright displayed
considerable courage, if also a good deal of imprudence, in crossing
swords with his employer in public. He might well have been disciplined or even fired except that he agreed to an apology which allowed
both men to save face.[4] The incident was only a harbinger of things to
come.

Beating the well-worn drum of the 'lad o' parts,' McCarthy had said
that matriculants performed just as well in law school as university
graduates, and that 'the head man in the last three years at Osgoode
Hall was a matriculant.' He was wildly wrong on both counts. Only one
of seven medallists had been a matriculant over the previous three
years. As for the general performance of the two groups, W.P.M.
Kennedy compared them over the years 1930–43 in a report prepared
for his faculty council. He calculated that University of Toronto students constituted 11.5 per cent of all Osgoode students over that period,
but comprised only 2 per cent of all failures and 6 per cent of all

supplementals, while gaining one-third of the honours.[5] The myth of the heroic matriculant died hard: the benchers were not about to change their views because of a few inconvenient facts.

Behind the scenes, Sidney Smith, Caesar Wright, and Bora Laskin were pondering how they might advance the cause of university legal education. Was it best to try and reshape the University of Toronto on the mainstream North American model, or should Osgoode itself be reformed? Now one, now the other of these possibilities came to the fore. In the wake of the Wright-McCarthy imbroglio it looked as if the University of Toronto were going to try and force the benchers' hand. President Cody created Kennedy dean of the law school, suggesting an enhancement of its status, but Kennedy immediately offered to retire if Wright were to be brought in as his successor. Cody offered Wright a position at the University of Toronto in 1944, but he did not accept it. Wright's friend Sidney Smith, as president in waiting, was not keen on confronting the benchers at this early point in his tenure, and Wright may have felt he needed his friend's unqualified support before making a move.

As the University of Toronto backed off, Wright became more aggressive about transforming Osgoode into the type of law school he wanted to see. An important component in his plan was filling up the Osgoode faculty with men who thought like himself. John Willis was the perfect choice for Wright in ideological terms. An English immigrant and Oxford graduate, Willis had spent a year as a non-degree student at Harvard and written a highly regarded book, *The Parliamentary Powers of English Government Departments*, published by Harvard University Press in 1933. Willis had been a professor since 1933 at Dalhousie, perceived as the sheet anchor of university legal education in Canada. Willis and Wright were not personally close, and in fact kept each other at arm's length, but they were prepared to work together to advance the ideas they shared.

There remained only to lure Bora Laskin to Osgoode. When D.A. MacRae announced his retirement in the spring of 1945, the way was open. The prospect of Laskin's shift to Osgoode set off a tug of war between Wright and Falconbridge on the one hand, and Kennedy and Sidney Smith on the other, which mirrored a certain conflict of loyalties in Laskin's own mind. Laskin was grateful to Kennedy and Auld for their mentorship, and enjoyed the friendship of Finkelman and Hancock at Toronto. Yet he had come increasingly within Wright's orbit and was bound to him through a dense network of professional and academic ties. Most importantly, he and Wright were in total agreement about what was wrong with legal education in Ontario and what was required to fix it. If Wright's presence made a shift to Osgoode attractive, the addition of Willis to the staff in 1944 made it almost irresistible. Laskin respected Willis enormously, observing later that his time at Osgoode had provided him with 'a kind of postgraduate education [as] the junior member of [a] faculty consisting of Falconbridge, Wright and Willis ... [t]he three most eminent legal scholars that we had in Canada.'[6]

When Kennedy heard of the overture to Laskin in early July he was already upset by the news that Moffatt Hancock had just accepted a position at Dalhousie. Kennedy quickly conferred with incoming President Smith, who immediately understood what the loss of these two talented and energetic young scholars would mean for the law program. Smith tried to persuade Wright that Laskin should stay at Toronto and made him a counter-offer: Wright should himself come to Toronto and replace Kennedy in 1946. Then Smith would go to the benchers with a plan to cooperate in the provision of legal education. Laskin, for his part, discussed his options first with Jacob Finkelman, on Friday and Saturday, 6 and 7 July; but he also wanted to consult both Wright and Kennedy before making a final decision. On Monday the ninth he visited Wright at his cottage on Lake Ahmic near Magnetawan and discussed the matter with him. They continued their discussions on Tuesday, when Wright agreed to accompany Laskin to visit Kennedy the next day at Beaver Lake, some thirty miles away.[7]

While walking along a path through the woods near Beaver Lake, Wright and Laskin tried to persuade Kennedy that Laskin's departure was for the best. At first Kennedy 'raved about.' The two men emphasized that with the addition of Laskin and Willis all the staff at Osgoode would now be university oriented. Not only that, Laskin would be the first University of Toronto professor hired at Osgoode, itself a big shift for the benchers. Laskin could act as a bridge between Osgoode and Toronto, between the benchers and the university authorities, with a view to establishing a professional university-based law school. Kennedy began to thaw a little, and made Laskin promise to stop in and see Sidney Smith at his cottage on his way back to Toronto. He gave Laskin a note for Smith which showed he had not given up hope yet; in it Kennedy asked Smith to make Laskin 'the very highest offer possible ... to retain him.' He went on to say, 'my chief aim has been and will always be to improve and benefit legal education and scholarship and I feel that if Laskin's going would help that purpose, I shall be satisfied indeed.' As it turned out, Smith was not at his cottage when Laskin called, and he left the note with Mrs Smith. When the two men met on Friday the thirteenth at Smith's Simcoe Hall office at the university, Smith was without the benefit of Kennedy's note. He offered Laskin more money anyway, only to be told that money was not the only issue: Laskin wanted 'to cut his teeth on a new job.' Reluctantly Smith accepted Laskin's resignation and wished him well, expressing the hope that he would 'play a part in a finer and better and bigger scheme for legal education in Ontario.' Laskin cabled Kennedy later that day to report his decision. The die was cast.

Wright and Smith saw the shift in personnel at Osgoode and Toronto from different perspectives. For his part, Wright thought it was ideal that he, Laskin, and Willis were all in a position where they might leave en masse for the university. To Smith he wrote: 'with Laskin at Osgoode ready to move with Willis and myself we strengthen rather than weaken the bargaining position.'[8] Wright was predicting the scenario that would play itself out four years later, although under more explosive circumstances than he might have foreseen. Smith saw only a decimated law school, bereft of Laskin and Hancock, and possibly of Finkelman too in the near future. In the short term it would be impossible to find replacements of the same experience and calibre. How was he to extol the benefits of a university law school to the benchers or anyone else when he had so few cards in his hand? In any event, Smith, Wright, and Laskin agreed to begin talking to key people in the university, the Law Society, and the judiciary with a view to amalgamating the two law schools. Kennedy gave Smith a free hand: 'I trust that Cecil and [Laskin] are right and the *consolidated* and *firm* action by the three may do much ... I want you at once to know that, if it is wise, if changes *come*, I am willing indeed to do only my teaching and writing and serve under anyone else as Dean. I am alone interested in the School of Law and the administration is freely and gladly in your hands. I am not worrying.'[9] This magnanimous stance was not replicated by Caesar Wright when he ultimately succeeded Kennedy. Once in power, Wright would do all he could to exclude Kennedy from the life of the law school and to erase and obscure his place in the collective memory of the institution.

As the war had shaped Bora Laskin's career while at the University of Toronto, so the societal adjustments of the post-war period would affect his stint at Osgoode. The most obvious of these was the dramatic increase in students numbers: it put enormous strains on Osgoode Hall Law School while hardly affecting Kennedy's school at all. The returning veterans were men and women in a hurry, anxious to establish themselves in civilian careers as quickly as possible. Few were willing, or financially able, to amble through a university degree in law as a prelude to their three years at Osgoode, though many had had some university education before the war. They beat a broad path to Queen Street West: from a total enrolment in all three years of about 100 during the last two years of the war, the numbers soared to 445 in 1945–6 and 703 in 1947–8. The first year classes of 1945–6 (300) and 1946–7 (352) were ten times the size of the 1943 first-year class – a mere thirty-three students. The teaching loads were brutal. Then as now, law teachers did not use teaching assistants and marked all assignments and exam papers personally. Laskin would correct some six hundred exams in *each* of two terms during his years at Osgoode. No wonder he wrote in 1947 to his Harvard friend Albert Abel, now teaching law at the University of West Virginia, that he had been unable to do much writing in the past two years.[10]

The post-war classes were different not just in quantity but also qualitatively. The veterans were older, feistier, less deferential than the classes of the pre-war years. They also had a greater sense of entitlement. Having sacrificed much for their country, they were less disposed to accept failure: the loss of some fifty classmates, about one-sixth of the 1945 entering class, was a great shock. To some it was especially galling to be failed or marked down by someone like Bora Laskin, who had chosen not serve in the war. 'Here were the returning soldiers being slashed and routed by what looked to us to be a mean little bunch who had not seen any of the hardships we had seen during the war,' recalled one veteran years later.[11] In one class Laskin was criticizing a number of judicial decisions as being out of touch with modern conditions when he asked rhetorically, 'where have these judges been for the last ten years?' A student called out from the back of the class: 'and where have you been for the last ten years?'[12] Few students would have dared to draw attention to Laskin's lack of war service so pointedly, but others held it against him silently.

Some students also complained about what they saw as Laskin's left-of-centre views, especially as he articulated them in labour law. A disgruntled judge with a son at Osgoode wrote to the benchers in 1949 that 'Laskin had a very stormy time with the Third Year class last winter, when he expressed some of his "Social" views. In B.C. a Communist is not knowingly admitted to the Law Society, let alone to act as Lecturer.'[13] Laskin's students a decade later recalled him as very balanced as between labour and management perspectives in his labour law classes. It is difficult to know whether the more critical responses of the 1940s reflect a bolder, more partisan style by Laskin which mellowed over time, or simply a more impatient and conservative student body in the later 1940s who wanted to be taught 'the law' without any digressions into policy. Probably some mellowing did occur, but Laskin always remained identified with a left-of-centre political stance.

Many students met with Laskin over a failed exam or a low mark, but he was unlikely to budge. Samuel Hughes, Laskin's former rowing companion from the early 1930s and later a judge of the High Court of Ontario, recalled one such incident. Hughes had spent two years at Osgoode from 1939 to 1941, then four and a half years overseas in England and Italy. In 1946–7, his final year at Osgoode, he took constitutional law from Bora Laskin. In his final examination Hughes had, somewhat blithely given Laskin's well-known federalist leanings, 'followed the leads of Lords Watson and Haldane in their [provincialist] interpretation of the British North America Act.' Upset at receiving a mark of fifty-one, he remonstrated with Professor Laskin. Caesar Wright happened to enter Laskin's office at that point, and 'reproached Bora [in a jocular manner] for trying to be a crusader rather than an impartial examiner,' but Hughes's mark was not changed.[14] While it is not clear whether Hughes was marked down for explaining the Watson-Haldane interpretation poorly, or for espousing it at all, the incident suggests a perception of Laskin as a less than impartial marker in his early years. Students who tried to do an end run around their professors by appealing to the benchers' legal education committee were likely to receive a sympathetic ear, much to the consternation of the faculty. In the fall of 1946 they complained at length to the benchers about 'the reduction of examination standards to the vanishing point' if they continued to allow such appeals.[15]

In quantity Laskin's published scholarship tapered off during his Osgoode years, but in quality it improved considerably. Laskin withdrew entirely from the field of case comments,[16] and in 1947 made his first major contribution to Canadian legal scholarship since the late 1930s. In '"Peace, Order and Good Government" Re-examined' Laskin erupted on to the field of constitutional law with both fists flying.[17] The reputation of an academic is often launched with a 'break-through' article that catches the attention of a generation largely because of good timing. '"Peace, Order and Good Government" Re-examined' was such a piece; it probably remains Laskin's best-known article.[18] The article is set in the context of Laskin's thinking on federalism in chapter nine. Here it is sufficient to note that it contained a stinging critique of the Privy Council's role in interpreting the division of powers under the Canadian constitution – not just of the political results of their decisions, as the 1930s scholars had done, but of the actual interpretive process employed by the law lords. Instead of merely lamenting the Privy Council's decisions Laskin sought actively to undermine them by exposing their technical inadequacy.

'"Peace, Order and Good Government" Re-examined' marked a highly significant shift for Bora Laskin. The field of labour law, in which he had been so intimately involved almost since his arrival in Toronto, had been transformed largely along the lines he had so long advocated. The new system was up and running; it now needed fine-tuning rather than fundamental reform. From now on constitutional law would be his main scholarly preoccupation, and it would increasingly project him from the provincial stage onto the national one. Constitutional law's gain was definitely labour law's loss. Laskin's scholarship on labour law was shaped by advocacy and the desire to resolve immediate problems; once those problems were resolved, his scholarship became of largely historical value, with little to contribute to future developments. He never produced the major article or 'big book' on labour law that might have anchored future scholarship. Yet his contribution to the domain of labour law, as opposed to labour law scholarship, was profound. It consisted principally of legitimating the entire field, helping to articulate it as an object of state policy, professional interest, and public concern. In teaching labour law Laskin taught generations of students, future lawyers, and policy makers to think critically about the balancing of interests involved The *ends* of labour law – not just 'industrial peace' but the securing of a fair share of the social product to workers – were of fundamental concern to him. Laskin's arbitral jurisprudence too played a critical intellectual role at a foundational moment in the emergence of modern labour arbitration.[19]

One wonders if Laskin sometimes regretted his shift from the University of Toronto, where the law program did not experience anything like the same upward trend in numbers as did Osgoode Hall after the war. After the loss of Hancock and Laskin, Kennedy tried to rebuild his faculty, but was initially so discouraged at the lack of suitable recruits that he and Finkelman briefly contemplated closing the law school. If they did close, Finkelman wrote in July 1945, they had to hire a full-time lecturer for the next few years: 'even at the very worst, we would be committed to carry on the course for at least 4–5 more years to discharge our obligations to those who would be entering this year. It would be impossible to continue with part-time people over that period of time ...'[20] Prospects for the school did not look very bright, but with Finkelman's help the show went on. Doctoral candidate Eugene La Brie was hired as a full-time lecturer in 1945 to teach taxation and take over Laskin's course in constitutional law, and Laskin's former student Charles Dubin taught property and conflicts of laws on a part-time basis. Gilbert Kennedy, probably wisely, decided to escape the academic environment so heavily dominated by his father's presence. When he decamped to the new law school at the University of British Columbia in 1946, his father hired an alumnus recently returned from the war, David Vanek. These three young men had excellent records as students but were totally untested as teachers. For the moment Osgoode had cornered the Toronto market on mid-career legal academics.

Kennedy gradually got over his post-war depression and decided to hold a great fête to give his struggling faculty some profile. He seized on the 1947 annual banquet of the Law Club to celebrate the sixtieth 'diamond' anniversary of the faculty of law, counting from the establishment of the faculty on paper in 1887. The Crystal Ball Room of the King Edward was filled with graduates and representatives of the bench and bar, including the chief justice of Ontario, for the event. After receiving many flattering tributes, Kennedy replied and 'laid the success of the Faculty to the fact of its modern approach to legal education as a scheme of human engineering and to the atmosphere of broad humane learning.'[21] Ever the publicist, Kennedy arranged for a cross-country CBC broadcast of the proceedings, and a similar one to the British West Indies.

If Laskin missed the smaller class sizes at Toronto, he presumably did not miss his $2,500 salary there. He started at Osgoode at $4,000 and soon discovered that Dean Falconbridge had been authorized to go as high as $5,000. Laskin recalled that he was 'damn well annoyed at this and so I had enough crust and I was angry enough ... to go to the head of the legal education committee of the Law Society [Hamilton ('Laddy') Cassels] ... When Laddy learned of this, of course he immediately raised my salary a thousand dollars and at the same time raised the salaries of the other members of the staff.'[22] (Relations between

Laskin and Cassels, who supported the status quo in legal education, would not always be so amicable.) In fact the $1,000 increment was paid in two instalments, a $500 increase as of 1 June 1946 and a second one as of 1 January 1947. In July 1948 Laskin's salary was raised to $6,500. With the additional revenue earned from his editorial positions, his growing labour arbitration practice, and some opinion work for law firms, Laskin's total annual income must have been in the $9,000 to $10,000 range by the late 1940s. At a time when the working poor subsisted on $1,100 per annum and a High Court judge's salary was $12,000, this was a very respectable income.

Laskin's summers while at Osgoode were divided between longish sojourns at Port Arthur with his family, sitting on conciliation boards and labour arbitration panels, and trying to get some writing done once his enormous mounds of marking were completed. In 1948 he managed largely to escape an erupting marks controversy by spending five weeks away from Osgoode, mostly in Port Arthur with a side trip to Winnipeg to visit Charles. Life was returning to normal after the convulsions of the war years. Saul and Charles were demobilized, married, and began their families. Saul transformed the family furniture business into a much larger operation, filling the needs of an increasingly affluent generation intent on acquiring the consumer durables their parents were unable to afford. The one source of worry was Bluma, whose health declined steadily in the post-war years.

By 1947–8 Osgoode was a pressure cooker. Too many students, too few staff, too many conflicting ideas about legal education, and excessive expectations by all parties made for an extremely tense atmosphere. Wright, Laskin, and Willis raised the stakes considerably when they failed an unprecedented one-third of the class at the spring 1948 examinations, and required another third to write supplementals. The students were outraged. They took their case to the media, the Ontario government, and the Department of Veterans Affairs, and contemplated taking it to the courts, but no change resulted. Some of the benchers saw this as an attempt by the academics to bully the Law Society into accepting their views, and did not hesitate to say so to the newspapers. As it turned out, this media skirmish was only the prelude to a larger battle soon to erupt.[23]

The veterans felt caught between the rising expectations of their professors and those of their principals. As a student editorial in *Obiter Dicta* put it in the fall of 1948:

The new Osgoode Hall, with its 'Harvard Law School complex,' is regarded almost with scorn by many practising lawyers. In turn the burden of work prescribed by an increasingly heavy syllabus certainly disregards the time which must be devoted to 'practical training.' ... We have talented instructors lecturing on an inadequate time schedule to overly large groups of students who in most cases have not prepared their work. We have hard-working principals demanding an equal standard of industry in their offices, and howls of protest go up when time off is asked to study for examinations ... We admire the enlightened efforts to improve the standards of teaching. We admit the incontrovertible necessity of practical training in a law office; we heartily condemn the increasingly unworkable system of inflicting both on a student simultaneously.[24]

There is respect for the vision and the teaching skills of Wright, Laskin, and Willis, but also frustration with their failure to moderate their academic demands to accommodate the framework within which they had to operate. The editorial pleas fell on deaf ears. This ambitious trio had no intention of trying to accommodate themselves to what they saw as a wrong-headed and antiquarian model of legal education. Rather, they wished to 'heighten the contradictions' in order to help hasten its demise, and to 'prove' to the benchers that their low admission standards allowed in weak students who could not succeed as lawyers. They had no qualms about the slashing that had to be done to make their point.

The sheer volume of numbers was also undermining the existing model in another way. When class size outstripped the capacity of Convocation Hall, the benchers simply rented space in the Metropolitan United Church down the street – but providing a seat in a lecture hall was easier than finding one in a law office. There were simply not enough articling positions in Toronto for all aspirant lawyers in postwar Ontario. The benchers, ever ready with band-aids while always avoiding the scalpel, responded to the problem by setting up 'practice groups' for first-year students who had not found articling positions. These were small-group tutorials conducted by practising lawyers, usually recently called to the bar, that attempted to familiarize students with office routines, title searches, and the like. They were so successful that they were made compulsory for all first-year students in 1947 and replaced office training during the school year.

Among the dozen tutorial leaders was the first (and only) woman ever hired as an instructor at the old Osgoode Hall Law School, Eileen

Mitchell (later Thomas). Mitchell's appointment was probably inspired by the larger numbers of women in post-war classes. She was assigned all fourteen women who entered Osgoode in 1947, including a young veteran named Judy La Marsh. (As a member of Pearson's cabinet, La Marsh would later play a role in Laskin's appointment to the Ontario Court of Appeal.) At first, Mitchell recalled, 'we were kind of mad, that they had ... put all the women in one bag ... And we had a discussion about it, and we all decided that it was not very smart of them.' Mitchell tried to get the women distributed to other groups, but after a few sessions 'we had such fun in the thing, that we all decided ... perhaps it would be a better idea if we did stay together.'[25] Mitchell left after only one term, and Osgoode remained an all-male enclave thereafter as long as the benchers controlled it.

Almost without realizing it, the benchers had instituted a full-time 'academic' first year at Osgoode Hall Law School. This may have appeared to be a major step on the road to a full-time university legal education, but the benchers did not see it that way. They went through the motions of discussing some sort of cooperative scheme with the University of Toronto, but persisted in seeing the legal education problem as one which would go away when the bulge of veterans had passed through Osgoode. In 1946 Sidney Smith managed to get the chair of his board of governors, W. Eric Phillips, to approach his close friend, Premier George Drew, with a view to getting Drew to nudge the benchers into cooperation with the university. Out of this initiative came a joint committee with five representatives from the benchers and five from the university's board of governors. Chief Justice of Ontario Robert S. Robertson, a former treasurer of the Law Society known to be open-minded about university legal education, agreed to chair the committee as of March 1947. The Law Society, meanwhile, had appointed its own special committee to look into ways of improving the law school. Its members, who also served as the Law Society representatives on the joint committee, were 'heavy hitters' by any standard: treasurer Shirley Denison, treasurer-elect Gershom Mason, Percy Wilson, the Official Guardian of Ontario, and two very prominent litigators, Cyril Carson and John Cartwright.[26]

Initially matters seemed to go smoothly. Robertson appointed a member from each constituency to try and agree on a plan for a cooperative model of legal education, and Sidney Smith and Percy Wilson came up with one by late summer. Wilson, a New Brunswicker by origin and McGill graduate, represented a soft spot in the Law Society's armour.

At first the benchers stalled when the Smith-Wilson proposal came forward, but in January 1948 it was repudiated by convocation. The joint committee quietly disbanded and an impasse loomed yet again. But this was not be a simple replay of 1935. At this key moment Dean Falconbridge announced his 'urgent' desire to resign. Some have speculated that this was a final, characteristically quiet, protest by Falconbridge, who had spent his entire academic life at odds with his employers over the nature of legal education. Falconbridge recommended Caesar Wright as his successor, and the benchers appointed him dean on 1 March.

With Wright at the helm at last, Laskin felt that matters would now evolve in a more satisfactory fashion. There was, he said 'a sense of elation on the part of all of us that progressively we were going to establish Osgoode Hall Law School on a very firm academically oriented foundation.'[27] When the special committee met with Wright shortly after his appointment they declared a full-time law school to be neither practicable nor desirable 'at this time,' but agreed to maintain the substitution of practice groups for articles in first year and authorized Wright to hire two more full-time faculty. He promptly got civil procedure expert Walter Williston on a one-year contract, but failed in his attempt to hire Horace Read, who was comfortably ensconced at Minnesota.[28] Wright re-hired John Willis, who had gone off to the International Monetary Fund in New York for 1947–8. The faculty had now expanded to six: Falconbridge stayed on for some years and a young lecturer in tax, Stan Edwards, hired initially to replace Willis, was kept on. In spite of these moves, Wright still fumed in private that the 'signs of development all seem to be in reverse [and in] another two months I shall probably be sweeping the floors of the classrooms.'[29]

Typically, Wright could not refrain from speaking publicly about the ills of legal education as he saw them. On 14 January 1949 he attacked 'a narrow professionalism that only wants to teach existing techniques' at a meeting of the York County Law Association, and was hauled on the carpet by his employers. The benchers were tired of these guerilla tactics and were moving towards a more global resolution (as they thought) of the legal education wars, one that would silence (they hoped) Wright and his followers for good. After the disbanding of the joint University-Law Society committee in January 1948, the Law Society's own special committee had continued to meet, and by early 1949 its work was done. The fractured committee in fact produced three reports: a 'majority' report prepared by the traditionalists, Hamilton

Cassels, Gershom Mason, Cyril Carson, and H.J. McLaughlin; a minority report sympathetic to Wright, prepared by Percy Wilson and concurred in by John Cartwright; and a third report somewhere in between prepared by Park Jamieson and Reid Bowlby. The Cassels group made up only half the committee members but their report came to be termed the majority report. On 20 January convocation considered the three reports.

Cassels's report unapologetically defended the status quo: there was, he said, 'no fundamental difference in the situation since the report of a Special committee was adopted by Convocation on February 21st, 1935.' The dearth of articling positions was a temporary problem created by the war, and it would soon pass. The increase in hours of instruction that had crept in during the war should be rolled back, and students should return to the old routine of one class at 9:00 a.m. and one at 4:10 p.m., with the bulk of the day spent in their principal's office. Any conflict was 'largely due to the attitude of the full-time staff in regard to the present system of concurrent Law School and practical training'; this would have to stop as the Legal Education Committee 'must be able to count on the loyal co-operation of the staff appointed by Convocation.' Cassels's admonishment of the staff did not stop there. In remarks some have seen as aimed at Bora Laskin, Cassels lamented that '[w]e think it doubtful whether under present conditions students are being taught to have a proper respect for the Bench. We have always been able to take a real pride in our Bench and probably the standing of the Bench has never been higher than at the present time. If the complaints in this regard from both students and members of the profession which have been brought to our attention are warranted we feel that steps should be taken to remedy the situation.' The disagreement between a significant portion of the benchers and their staff could not have been revealed more starkly. Not only did they differ over the structure of legal education, but also over the role of critical analysis within the academic component of that education. For Bora Laskin, a lifelong champion of the academic's right and duty to pursue intellectual inquiry unfettered by institutional restraints, this was really the last straw.

The Wilson-Cartwright minority report was much more sympathetic to the goals of Wright and Laskin. Wilson wanted Osgoode Hall Law School to transform itself into a full-time institution modelled on a university, with a similar degree of autonomy accorded to the staff. Given the deep convictions of those supporting Cassels, Laskin later lauded Wilson's 'tremendous courage in dissenting.'[30] Jamieson's minority report recommended a full-time program interspersed with periods of full-time articling but rejected the university analogy, seeing Osgoode as 'a vocational or trade school.' If the staff could not accept this basic fact, he implied, they should resign. Within twenty-four hours, they would take the hint.

After discussion, Convocation accepted the Cassels report with some minor amendments. Meanwhile, Wright, Laskin, and the other staff were going about their usual business in the educational wing of Osgoode Hall. They had not been told that the special committee had completed its reports, or that they would be discussed at Convocation that day. No one afforded the staff the elementary courtesy of informing them personally of the final decision. The first they heard of it was by reading the newspapers the next morning. Even then, the full Cassels report was never released to the public, nor did the benchers acknowledge publicly the existence of the minority reports, in an effort to present a bland façade of unanimity. Only the summary recommendations accepted by Convocation appeared in the newspapers, and it was over twenty-five years later before Laskin saw a copy of the complete report.[31]

After reading the *Globe and Mail* on the morning of 21 January, Laskin recalled, all the full-time teachers rushed into work that morning as if shot out of a cannon.[32] It 'didn't take us very long ... simply to ... all toss in our resignations, that is, Wright, Willis and myself, Falconbridge [being] well on in years and there was no reason why he should ... do that, and so we resigned effective at the end of the year, although some of us were angry enough to have made our resignations effective immediately.'[33] Concern for the students kept the three on site for the remainder of the academic year, though it also provided them with a brief respite when they could pursue other alternatives. Williston had decided to return to practice in any case, and Edwards decided that he would do so too. Osgoode was now virtually bereft of full-time staff.

Past treasurer Shirley Denison was apoplectic. In Victoria on business, he followed the debacle at a day or two's delay through the *Globe and Mail*. From the Empress Hotel he wrote to his successor Gershom Mason on 24 January, enclosing a copy of the *Globe*'s 22 January coverage 'with pictures of the 4 glamorous beauties who somehow found their photos on the front page of this paper.' Airing their dirty linen in public was bad enough, but Denison also bitterly reproached Wright for, as he saw it, going back on his word. 'As I understand it,' wrote

Denison, 'he [Wright] solemnly promised you and Mr. Cassels to abide by the decision of the Benchers and now we find what looks very like a plot to bring the wreck of the Law School to Toronto University with Wright and the other 3 beauties as professors.'[34] Denison voiced what many others thought – that the mass resignation had the air of a strategy cunningly planned for some time. Wright and Sidney Smith were known to be close friends of very long standing who shared identical views on legal education. If Smith had not wished to antagonize the benchers in his very first year as president of the University of Toronto, when a similar move was suggested by Wright, he had been able to solidify his position in the interim and was now prepared to take the risk.

If the Denison interpretation was current in the aftermath of the resignations, in interviews many years later Willis (implicitly) and Laskin (explicitly) denied that any such 'plot' had existed. For several weeks the status of the resignations remained in limbo. As John Willis recalled in 1979, the three men did not expect their resignations to be accepted; the three academics felt the benchers would have to take them back because they would not be able to find alternates.[35] This is not inconsistent with a 'plan B' scenario where the men might have arranged to go to Toronto only if the benchers did not take them back, but it is not affirmative evidence of such a plan either. Laskin said nothing on this point in his 1977 interview, stating merely '[a]s far as I was concerned, I didn't have a job. I didn't know where I was going to go. I suppose I could have gone into practice ... [b]ut it wasn't until all efforts ... were made at composing the differences had failed that we then started to look around and then Sidney Smith came to us, I think it was somewhere around the end of March ...'[36] Earlier in the interview, Robin Harris had said 'I get the impression that the University of Toronto acted properly, in institutional terms. Until your resignations, there, I gather, was no contact,' to which Laskin replied, 'No, not at all.'[37]

Was there a plot? Was Laskin involved in it? If so, what does it tell us about him? The evidence in favour of a plot is mainly circumstantial, based on the close relationship between Wright and Smith, except for one solid and highly significant piece of evidence. As we saw earlier, in July 1945 Wright had written to Smith that 'with Laskin at Osgoode *ready to move* with Willis and myself we strengthen rather than weaken the bargaining position' (emphasis added). He added, '[w]hen I talked to Cody a year ago I would have had to go alone – and would have. Are we not better with three?' Earlier in the letter he said, 'WPM [Kennedy] ... will go if I indicate that I will come up [to the University] ... I *will go* –

provided there is hope – and enough money to live on – and I am sure I can take Laskin and Willis – both of whom should be there. On this basis, my suggestion would be to attempt to obtain a temporary senior man for this year at Toronto ...' Wright was in effect proposing that Smith keep Kennedy's school in a holding pattern pending the arrival of himself, Willis, and Laskin, and confirming that he *'will go'* to the university. Wright's reference to 'the bargaining position' clearly refers to his position vis-à-vis the benchers. If one needs a smoking gun to substantiate the plot theory, this is clearly it.[38]

Did Laskin know of it? There is no positive evidence that he did, and he denied it many years later. It is possible that Wright kept this all to himself, but even if Laskin and Willis were fully aware of Wright's discussions with Smith, and agreed to resign as part of an overall plan to force change in legal education, does it reflect badly on them? Some contemporaries clearly thought so, and recent scholarship curiously avoids the topic. For the benchers there were two issues, a general one concerning the 'loyalty' of the three men to the Law Society as employer, and a more precise concern about whether Wright had broken his word in resigning. The latter is easily dealt with. Treasurer Gershom Mason's view was that when Wright was appointed dean he had agreed to cooperate with the benchers in spite of his disagreement with some of their policies. In his letter of resignation Wright stated, 'I indicated that it was unsatisfactory to appoint a Dean unless policies had been clearly settled, but I did say that I would co-operate with the Benchers until such time as their actions became completely incompatible and inconsistent with my views, at which time I would resign.'[39] Letters of resignation are notoriously self-serving, but in this case there is good reason to believe that Wright had put some kind of caveat on the limits of his cooperation with the benchers when appointed dean of Osgoode Hall Law School in March 1948. It strains credulity that after all the years of adversarial relations, Wright would suddenly agree to cease and desist without reservation. In the over-heated world of Law Society gossip in early 1949, the caveat was conveniently forgotten or ignored, the better to paint Wright as a faithless traitor.

The 'loyalty' issue was based in the Law Society's view of the law school as a proprietary enterprise, and its teachers as 'staff' rather than 'faculty.' They were not thought to have the same freedom of inquiry as university faculty, and as employees, were thought to have a duty of loyalty that precluded public criticism of their employer. Wright clearly breached this duty several times, but each time the Law Society chose to waive its right to discipline or even dismiss him. It is less clear whether Laskin ever breached his duty of loyalty while a member of the staff at Osgoode. The benchers clearly thought that if the three men had resigned as part of a plot to force their employer to change its collective ways, or had previous discussions with another employer as part of this strategy, they were behaving in an illicit fashion. This belief reflected an almost medieval conception of the employment relationship. Accepting that law school staff owed a duty of loyalty during their contracts, they were clearly not forbidden from seeking employment elsewhere. And even if they were seeking to exert pressure on their employer through a mass resignation, there was nothing illegal or unethical about such an act. Through their actions Wright, Willis, and Laskin declared they could no longer remain at Osgoode because they were so opposed to its educational policies. Their resignations were motivated by principle, and whether or not they had worked out alternate employment beforehand was simply irrelevant in legal and ethical terms.

The existence of a pre-arranged exit to the University of Toronto becomes relevant in a larger assessment of Laskin's resignation. If he resigned on principle without having previously arranged alternate employment, his action appears truly courageous. If Laskin resigned knowing that he could expect a soft landing at the university, his action looks more calculating, but it was still not without courage given his family responsibilities. As it turned out, Laskin's starting salary at Toronto, $6,650, was in step with what he was earning at Osgoode ($6,500 in 1948–9). Nonetheless, doing public battle with the Law Society, with all its resources and prestige, was not an easy thing to do even with a job offer from the U of T in one's back pocket. His action entailed a real risk of alienating those with power and influence in the legal profession, of being labelled a troublemaker. Being the first Jew and the first University of Toronto academic hired at Osgoode Hall Law School had been an enormous coup for Bora Laskin four years earlier – he himself called it 'a revolution.' Whether Sidney Smith was on side or not, Laskin's action imperilled the professional capital he had laboriously accumulated.

Fortunately for Laskin, time, public opinion, and a significant portion of the legal profession were with him and his colleagues. The contrast with the lack of public interest in the Law Society's resistance to reform in 1935 could not have been greater. The benchers' refusal to release the committee's report did not sit well in post-war Ontario, a society less attuned than previously to *raisons d'état* and *ex cathedra* pronouncements. As the perception and role of universities changed substantially, from bastions of class privilege to gateways to middle-class prosperity, the benchers appeared out of step in their resistance to post-secondary legal education. The *Globe and Mail* reminded the benchers that the public was interested in legal education because the Law Society's powers 'spring from an Ontario statute, not from divine right'; furthermore, the editorial writer hinted heavily, 'this statute is amendable.'[40]

This sudden stirring of the public against the Law Society was unprecedented. Christopher Moore has called it 'the first substantial, and greatest single, blow to the hegemony of the benchers over governance of the legal profession in Ontario,' the first effective challenge to the 'almost sacrosanct authority of Osgoode Hall' in a century and a half. The Law Society found its legitimacy forever tainted by its inability to accept reform of one of its key functions.[41] If the story had a villain, it also had its trio of heroes. Willis soon returned to Halifax and faded from public view. Wright's public profile remained high but he was already fairly well known. It was Laskin who gained the most from the emergent heroic myth of '49. He was becoming well known within the legal community both for educating hundreds of its newest entrants and for his arbitration work, but the resignations propelled him to wider public notice in dramatic fashion.

The well-known *Globe and Mail* photo of March 1949 centres on Laskin reading his letter of resignation. He looks serious, youthful but not young like Stan Edwards on the left, perfectly groomed and entirely credible. John Willis looks like a prematurely aged English schoolboy who has forgotten to comb his hair, while Wright appears vaguely paternal and almost uninvolved, standing a little removed from the others with his nonchalant cigarette dangling. Laskin looks the part of the hero more than any of the others, and as his dark hair gradually turned silver, he seemed even more suited to the role. For the next generation of students, cocooned in the complacent consensus of the 1950s, the actions of Wright and Laskin seemed larger than life. The slight tarnish Laskin's reputation had suffered through his lack of war service disappeared and he was recreated almost as some righteous Jewish prophet of old, fearlessly affirming the true belief against the dogma of the worldly and corrupt Pharisees.

In hindsight, the 1950s deluge of students made the benchers' delegation of legal education to the universities inevitable. The blow-up was probably unnecessary, but the participants could not have foreseen that. The trio would never admit that without their decision to confront the benchers, events would soon have unfolded in a broadly similar way. If Laskin and Wright's actions were invested with mythical status by later generations of students, so were they too in Laskin's own mind. He, Wright, and Willis had dared to take on the seemingly all-powerful benchers and won. Laskin had missed the real war but the events of 1949 became his own personal war story, one that became even more dramatic in his recollection in the ensuing decades. In his last years it became the privileged subject of passionate reminiscence with his law clerks who, thirty years on, were unfamiliar with the tale and somewhat nonplussed by the chief justice's intensity on the topic. In one of his last writings, his memoir of Caesar Wright published in 1983, Laskin writes of the events of 1949 as if they had occurred the week before, his interpretation of them altered not one iota over the years.

The battle over legal education in Ontario has been wrongly considered as a unique situation simply because it came to public attention in a highly dramatic way. Elsewhere in post-war Canada, even in those provinces with university law schools, the struggle between a local professional elite focused on training for the corporate bar and a professoriate with more critical academic aspirations or leftist tendencies played out more quietly (as it does today). The descent of the Cold War gave this tension a sharp political edge that was not overtly on display in the Osgoode imbroglio, though it may well have been present below the surface. Certainly it existed elsewhere. At McGill, where the warring factions were represented by two brothers, the conflict possessed a Shakespearean intensity. William B. Scott, dean of the St James Street bar, member of McGill's governing board, and future chief justice of Quebec, represented everything that his younger brother Frank, socialist, poet, and academic, detested. Due to the machinations of the elder Scott and his fellow board member J.W. McConnell, owner and publisher of the *Montreal Star*, university benefactor and Duplessis supporter, the McGill law faculty went through no fewer than five deans between 1946 and 1950 as the board sought to prevent socialists and free thinkers such as Frank Scott and John Humphrey from assuming the position. Given McConnell's control of the English press in Montreal, it was left to the *Winnipeg Free Press* and *Saturday Night* to inform the public of McGill's vendetta against Frank Scott. Laskin heard of it through the legal academic grapevine in January 1948 and wrote Scott to say that he hoped the proposed association of Canadian law teachers, once it was up and running, might be able to come to his aid. It does not, however, appear to have done so.[42]

The political tensions running through legal education in these post-war years can also be seen in the careers of E.K. Williams and Gérald Fauteux. Both were counsel to the Royal Commission on Espionage appointed to investigate the existence of the Soviet spy ring revealed by the defection of Soviet embassy cipher clerk Igor Gouzenko in Ottawa in September 1945. Supreme Court of Canada judges Roy Kellock and Robert Taschereau presided as co-chairs of the inquiry with the assistance of Williams and Fauteux, but its hearings were held in camera and witnesses were denied many of their rights, including being forced to testify without benefit of counsel and without notification that their testimony could be used against them in subsequent prosecutions. Outrage at these practices launched the post-war civil liberties movement, and a motion to condemn them was hotly debated at the Canadian Bar Association (CBA) annual meeting in 1946. Williams, a Winnipeg lawyer, happened to be president of the CBA, and a majority of the Association rejected any criticism of the conduct of the Royal Commission. Williams was shortly thereafter named chief justice of the Manitoba Court of King's Bench, and soon after that, was elected chair of the board of trustees of the Manitoba Law School, an Osgoode-type school run by the profession.[43] Fauteux, for his part, was soon to become one of the brief-tenured McGill law deans, appointed in June 1949 but elevated to the Supreme Court of Canada in December of that year. (Laskin would succeed him as chief justice of Canada.) Such anti-communist credentials were considered appropriate for those providing leadership in Canadian legal education in the early years of the Cold War.

The media battle of 1949 was easily won, but the dispute with the benchers turned into a long war of attrition that preoccupied Wright and Laskin for the next eight years. For the moment, however, anything seemed possible as Wright was installed as dean, in succession to Kennedy, at the University of Toronto school of law, and Willis and Laskin joined him as full professors on 1 July 1949.

8

Revolution

When the members of the law school at the University of Toronto heard they were to be joined by John Willis, Bora Laskin, and Caesar Wright, they were ecstatic. Kennedy was glad of the chance to retire, and gracefully handed over the reins to Wright. In May he wrote to welcome Wright 'to a faculty which has been my life's work,' adding 'I can think of no one whom I could desire more to be my successor and play out my hand.' Finkelman, La Brie, and Vanek looked forward to a reinvigorated faculty with the addition of this talented triumvirate. They soon realized Wright had no intention of playing out Kennedy's hand at all. What had happened was not so much a merger of Osgoode and Toronto as a hostile takeover of the latter.[1] Wright had long wanted to create 'an honest to God law school,' and he set about the task with all the zeal of the true revolutionary. Willis and Laskin agreed with Wright's vision even if they may not always have agreed with his methods. Gone was the idea of Laskin acting as a 'bridge' between Osgoode and Toronto. He was now universally seen as first lieutenant in Caesar Wright's campaign to reconstruct the University of Toronto School of Law as a professional law faculty on the Harvard model.

The campaign took place on all levels: physical, intellectual, and ideological. Wright immediately transformed Kennedy's ascetic book-lined study into a more businesslike office. Away went the blinds, bookshelves, and army folding chairs, in came thick drapes, a large intimidating desk, and a separate new reception area. Kennedy's secre-

tary had been on the third floor, and there had been only one telephone
line for the whole law school. Wright installed Joyce McClellan, who
had migrated from Osgoode with him, in a newly renovated space
outside his office, and had a second phone line installed for his exclusive use.[2] A new geography of administrative power supplanted the
casual eclecticism of the Kennedy era.

With physical reconstruction underway, Wright moved on to the
second task of any revolution: the rewriting of history. The Toronto
calendar for 1949–50 had been prepared by Kennedy early in 1949
before the migration of Wright, Willis, and Laskin was confirmed.
Wright immediately set about creating a new calendar to trumpet to the
world the arrival of a new regime at the University of Toronto law
school. The new calendar announced that the existing three-year LLB
and the five-year BA-LLB were 'discontinued' and 'a new Bachelor of
Laws course is established in the School of Law.' A new mission statement – lifted almost verbatim from the pre-1927 Harvard Law School
calendar – declared that the program was 'designed to furnish an
adequate liberal and professional education for persons contemplating
the practice of law or dealing in public and private affairs where a
sound knowledge of law and legal method is indispensable.'[3] Eugene
La Brie was so upset with Wright's revisionism that he managed to
contact the dean by telephone at his cottage (not an easy thing in those
days) to remonstrate with him. Kennedy had already created a new
three-year LLB in 1943, La Brie reminded Wright, 'and you haven't
done anything but change the men who are teaching.'[4] La Brie at first
refused to publish the calendar, but acquiesced after Finkelman advised he had no choice. In spite of Wright's elaboration of a creation
myth, his LLB curriculum scarcely deviated from Kennedy's, which
had gravitated towards the North American norm in the 1940s. Wright's
biographers concede that 'his attitudes still reflected the thinking of the
Harvard professors of the late 1920s.'[5]

Wright did not preserve everything though: he got rid of Kennedy's
five-year BA/LLB, which might in time have developed into a more
scholarly and interdisciplinary type of legal education. Under Kennedy's
model, law and the other university disciplines occupied distinct rooms
separated by lattice-work screens. Each had its own space but could see
and hear, albeit not perfectly, what was going on in the other rooms. All
could participate in a conversation, or even a heated debate, without
leaving their home base. Under Wright's model, law occupied a closed
room with only one door. Law professors might go out and mingle with

scholars in other disciplines, but those scholars in turn would have to be invited in to the law room if they wished to join the conversation. They could not enter and exit freely, and might not feel very comfortable debating their hosts in the law room.[6]

Where Wright did introduce something new, some thought he was trying to 'out-Osgoode' Osgoode itself. In his first year the new dean hired six (the number later doubled) 'demonstrators in trial practice' (young practising lawyers) who conducted tours of the courts and various legal offices for three weeks in January. These looked very like the practice groups initiated at Osgoode in the later 1940s to substitute for the shortage of articling positions, but at Toronto there was no such imperative for adopting them. The terminology was deliberate: analogizing these instructors to lab demonstrators and the law library to a laboratory was a constant theme in Wright's correspondence with the university administration. Wright regularly invoked the 'law as science' metaphor, where for Kennedy the humanities and social sciences had been the model.

Another task of revolutions is to remove members of the old regime, lest they become a focus for insurrection. Wright put Kennedy under a kind of reverse house arrest, where his contact with his erstwhile domain was strictly controlled. The former dean was not to have an office at the law school, and in the early 1950s he was put on a ration of two lectures per year on constitutional law, when he had offered to give substantially more. Wright fobbed him off with a graduate student in 1953–4, and thereafter his involvement ceased. The Kennedy-Wright correspondence of these years reflects well on neither man, though worse on Wright because he was the more powerful of the two. Kennedy's letters have a wheedling quality: 'My troubles last winter arose mostly from having nothing to do. Syd [Smith] was in and he promised to talk to you when he could ... It's up to you! No legal obligation, but *moral* – far more demanding. I trust you will take this up with Bora and see if something can be done.' Wright replied with brusque formality.[7] He appeared to pay tribute to Kennedy by naming the new moot court room after him when the law faculty moved to Flavelle House in 1962, but failed to install any sign or portrait of Kennedy in the room; the name did not stick.[8]

The old regime's festivals also had to go. Kennedy's choice of 1887 as the foundational moment of the law school was over-ruled, and 1 July 1949 became the equivalent of the first of *vendémiaire* under the new revolutionary calendar. When the faculty observed the 'fiftieth' anniversary of 'modern legal education' in 1999, no one noted that it had already celebrated its 'diamond' anniversary in 1947.[9] The one shrine to Kennedy's memory was the *University of Toronto Law Journal*, whose editors remained Kennedy loyalists: Jacob Finkelman until 1956, then Eugene La Brie until 1961, when new appointee Ronald St John Macdonald took over. La Brie paid warm tribute to Kennedy in the pages of the journal on the occasion of the latter's eightieth birthday in 1959. The journal of the 1950s had a rather tired and cloistered air, though, publishing almost exclusively the work of Toronto professors. It demonstrated little of the sparkle or dynamism of the Kennedy years, but in this it reflected a larger shift in North American legal scholarship from the politicized ferment of the 1930s to a more technocratic genre.

Kennedy's pleading with Wright to 'take this up with Bora' suggests he saw his former student as a possible ally. Yet Laskin acquiesced in the new myth-making and participated in the erasure of Kennedy's efforts in an article he contributed to a British legal academic journal. It aimed to introduce its audience to the recently established Canadian Association of Law Teachers, of which Laskin was then president, but provided a brief sketch of the history of university legal education in Canada by way of background. Laskin paid tribute to many leading figures from coast to coast who had furthered the cause, but W.P.M. Kennedy's name was conspicuously absent from this list, and the pre-1949 program at the University of Toronto was barely mentioned.[10] Gilbert Kennedy saw this 'conspiracy of silence' as a cruel betrayal of his father, fired off an acerbic letter to the editor, and sent a copy to Laskin. The covering letter was curt: 'Bora, I am shocked and more than disappointed in you.'[11] It is hard to believe Laskin did not feel some pangs of guilt in glossing over the contributions of his one-time mentor. For all that Laskin insisted on acting according to his own conscience, he felt obliged to 'toe the line' drawn by Wright in certain matters.[12] The fact Laskin did so says much about both the force of Wright's personality and the strongly ingrained sense of hierarchy permeating academic life in the 1950s. If Laskin bowed to Wright's interpretation of Kennedy in the public sphere, he remained loyal in the private sphere: Bora and Peggy continued to visit W.P.M. and Pauline Kennedy on a social basis until the former's death in 1963.

While the rivalry between Kennedy and Wright was a fact of life for Bora Laskin, in retrospect it is time to acknowledge that both played a significant role in legal education at the University of Toronto and elsewhere in Canada. If in the 1950s it seemed as if the two men offered competing visions of legal education, in later years these would slowly blend into a model which sought to draw on the best of both worlds. The professional element so important to Wright still dominates Canadian legal education more than Kennedy would have preferred, but he would have enjoyed the flourishing of Canadian socio-legal scholarship of the last thirty years, and the diverse perspectives available to students of Canadian law. Wright built on Kennedy's foundations even if he refused to acknowledge doing so, and one of the best products of that joint endeavour was Bora Laskin himself.

Having neutralized Kennedy, Wright also felt obliged to draw sharp distinctions with Osgoode. The benchers had managed to find a successor to Wright in an expatriate New Brunswicker who had been dean of law at the University of Birmingham for over twenty years. C.E. Smalley-Baker was not a star appointment but he provided the benchers with some academic respectability when it was sorely needed. His request to his old friend Clyde Auld to assist him in co-marking his first set of Osgoode exam papers gave Wright the perfect excuse to administer a royal dressing-down to the rival dean. When he learned of the request, Wright ordered Auld to return the papers immediately. He would not, he lectured Smalley-Baker, allow such cooperation to 'give countenance in some quarters to an impression ... that we at the University had any part in the administration of your School or your exam standards.' The Osgoode dean meekly replied that such co-marking was customary 'in the great professional law schools in England' and it did not occur to him to ask permission.[13] Secure in their superiority, the faculty at Toronto mostly ignored Osgoode for the next decade, except when it became necessary to defend their turf. Ian Scott, a future attorney-general of Ontario and Osgoode student in the 1950s, recalled being persuaded by friends to attend some first-year lectures by Dean Wright in torts and Jim Milner in contracts. His presence was soon detected, upon which the dean summoned the trespasser to his office 'and with little formal ceremony, threw me out. He made plain that the intellectual deficiencies I had elected to bear by enrolling at Osgoode were not to be offset by surreptitious attendance at his university.'[14]

At the very moment of his apparent victory over the benchers, Bora Laskin had to face the most difficult loss of his life. Throughout the fall of 1949 he was increasingly preoccupied with the state of his mother's health. Bluma's heart condition grew steadily worse, and she died in Port Arthur on 23 January 1950 at the age of sixty-three, a year almost to the day after her son's dramatic resignation from Osgoode Hall Law

School. Fortunately Bora had arrived in the city prior to her death, as that evening the season's worst blizzard swept into the Lakehead, disrupting air and train travel.[15] The funeral service was held in the old Finlayson Street synagogue, the centre of Bluma's spiritual life and the Laskin boys' second home. The decrepitude of the old wooden building symbolized the decline of the Lakehead Jewish community: it would soon be succeeded by a new suburban synagogue built for a much smaller congregation. Revered by community and family, Bluma had passed on to her sons, especially Bora and Saul, a strong sense of public duty and of commitment to her adopted land. Unfortunately she did not live to see most of her grandchildren, including Bora and Peggy's second child Barbara, born later that year.

With Bluma's passing, Max lost interest in life and died on 5 July 1955. His will reveals a man of modest means: he left two-hundred-dollar legacies to a few Jewish institutions and a life insurance policy of a thousand dollars to be divided among his grandchildren. The furniture business went to Saul, the land to the three sons but to be rented back to Saul at a fixed rent of not more than seventy-five dollars per month.[16] If the newspapers lauded Max Laskin as a 'prominent businessman,' it was likely because the worth of a businessman in that time and place was measured as much by his contribution to the betterment of the community as by his accumulation of material assets.[17] While Bora lost his father, he in a sense regained his brother Charles, who moved with his family from Winnipeg to Toronto the year before Max died. With the loss of the senior Laskins, Bora and Peggy began to orient their family vacations away from the Lakehead. In the later 1950s and early 1960s they favoured Cape Cod for summer holidays. They would sometimes visit Caesar Wright at his cottage at Magnetawan, but did not rent or acquire their own summer place, concerned perhaps about lingering anti-Semitic prejudice at Muskoka resorts. When inquiring about a summer cottage she had seen advertised, Rabbi Feinberg's wife Ruth was told '[w]e just don't rent to Jews ... It isn't that *I* have feeling against *you* [but] the *neighbours* in our little colony would be upset!'[18]

On the law school front, the euphoria of 1949–50 soon ebbed away. The situation might be summed up in the old 1960s expression: what if they held a revolution and no one came? For some years after Laskin's return the very survival of the law school was a matter of doubt as the numbers of incoming students slowed to a trickle. The benchers had played the one trump card left in their hand. In the wake of the resignations, Park Jamieson's intermediate solution found favour with a chastened Convocation. Osgoode would extend its three-year program to four, with the first two years full-time, the third spent in full-time articles, and the fourth in concurrent office work and lectures. In May the university's board of governors asked the Law Society to recognize the Toronto LLB as 'at least equivalent to the first two years' of the new Osgoode program. This may have appealed to the university as an apparent compromise, but it gave away their bottom line too early in the game. The Law Society promptly accepted the university's minimum position, leaving Toronto LLB candidates in the position of having to complete one year more than Osgoode students before being called to the bar.

The results of this policy were predictable. In 1951 the number of entering students actually fell below twenty, with the entire enrolment in the faculty dipping below 60 students in subsequent years before rebounding to 116 (87 of those being in first year) in 1957, when the settlement with the Law Society was finally reached. It was well known that a desperate 'Caesar would take anything that could walk through the door' during these years.[19] Laskin was not one to suffer in silence. '[N]othing favourable can be said,' he observed, 'about [the Law Society's] policy of discriminating in favour of its own school in Osgoode Hall against all university law schools whose graduates are given but partial recognition for their university LL.B. degree.'[20] Laskin and his colleagues questioned why they had been good enough to teach at Osgoode, but 'somehow coming to the University of Toronto, our qualifications for teaching seemed ... to have dropped.'[21] If Laskin expected that the Law Society was going to make life easier for the three professors who had publicly humiliated the benchers, he was sorely mistaken.

In the fall of 1951 John Willis dropped a bombshell: he was returning at the end of the academic year to Halifax to practise law with the firm of Burchell Jost. His letter of resignation paints a bleak picture of conditions at the school. 'Just two years after it started up as a professional school,' Willis observed bitterly, 'the School of Law is to all intents and purposes dead.' The 'pitiful handful' of students in attendance had nothing to do with 'the potential excellence of the School,' he thought, but resulted from the impasse on the recognition issue. In a chilling aside, he conceded that the university's governors might have 'tried mild persuasion, but power does not yield to persuasion – it only yields only to force.'[22] Wright himself had been tempted to leave in 1950 when

offered a position at the University of California at Los Angeles. He
went so far as to write his friend and counterpart Erwin Griswold at
Harvard to ask for advice, but in the end decided he could not leave
with matters still unsettled with the Law Society.[23]

The nadir of the school's fortunes was probably reached in 1953,
when Laskin stood in for an absent Caesar and presented LLB degrees
to a mere thirteen men. Even then Caesar managed to put a brave face
on things. He and Marie decided to attend the coronation in June, but
left in April to permit Caesar to embark on a lecture tour of English
universities. The *Globe and Mail* noted their plans under the headline
'Toronto's Caesar Sails for Conquest of Britain,' and reported the dean
to be 'confident that the University of Toronto, the University of British
Columbia and Dalhousie University law schools can now be compared
on reasonably favourable terms with the schools at Harvard, Yale and
the University of Chicago.'[24]

Laskin and Willis seemed to think that when they swept back into the
University of Toronto, the administration was duty-bound to provide
the best possible facilities regardless of the number of students enrolled
and in spite of the uncertainty hovering over the whole enterprise
of university legal education in Ontario. Wright had more of an
administrator's mind and while not always happy with the pace of
change at the U of T, understood the big picture rather better than his
more impatient colleagues. In his 1977 interview Laskin was highly
critical of what he saw as the inadequate efforts made by the university
to accommodate the 'new' faculty in its midst. One can agree with him
that the university's board of governors pursued the recognition issue
too mildly, owing to the divided loyalties of some prominent lawyers
on the board who shared the benchers' point of view. On other issues
Willis and Laskin were unfair to the university, which continued to
provide a budget and status to the law school far beyond that which its
tiny enrolment warranted.

In 1952 the law school moved to larger quarters in Baldwin House on
the southwest edge of the campus, replacing the history department.
Built in 1861 and showing its age ninety years later, the house was still
an improvement over the cramped quarters at 45 St George St.[25] For the
first time the law school was able to house a law library, with space for
forty students.[26] With enrolment increasing modestly (forty-three entered in 1953, fifty in 1954), the law school was promoted to the status of
a full faculty in 1955. The university allowed Wright to hire new professors until the complement of full-time faculty in 1950–1 was no fewer

than eight: Wright, Laskin, Willis, Auld, Finkelman, La Brie, and new-comers Jim Milner and Wolfgang Friedmann. (Wright had dismissed the untenured David Vanek in 1950 as an unwelcome relic of the Kennedy era.) After Willis resigned, two more younger men, David Kilgour and Robert MacKay, were taken on in 1952. This was an extraordinary vote of confidence in the law school at a time when it was not at all clear how, or even whether, the recognition issue would ever be settled.

Milner was a Nova Scotian, the gold medallist at Dalhousie when he graduated in 1939. He joined Moffatt Hancock on the teaching staff at Dalhousie in 1945 but they both left in 1949, along with roughly a quarter of the university's entire faculty, over President Kerr's refusal to increase salaries adequately in these inflationary post-war years. When Jim's wife Jean, an assistant in the faculty of medicine, was grudgingly granted a five-hundred-dollar raise, Kerr promptly reduced her husband's salary by a like amount. That was the last straw. Jim went off to Harvard for his LLM and was snapped up by the University of Toronto. Bora and Peggy would become quite close to the Milners, and Peggy and Jean organized a faculty wives' group along with Marie Wright, though Marie did not approve of Jean's continuing employ-ment with the Ontario Research Foundation.[27] Jim Milner became an expert in the law of land use planning, a much-needed specialty in the heyday of 1950s urban growth and one very much in tune with Laskin's own interest in the development of the administrative state.

Friedmann was a jurist in the continental tradition, with broad inter-ests in legal theory, international law, and comparative law – an exotic indeed among the hard-nosed common lawyers in Caesar Wright's faculty. A Berlin-born Jew, he had the great good fortune to escape the Third Reich through his appointment to a lecturership at the University of London in 1938. After the war he emigrated to Australia, whence he was lured to Toronto. Friedmann owed his appointment to a Carnegie Corporation grant of $50,000 secured by Wright, an unheard-of amount for research in Canadian law faculties at the time. Oriented around the theme of comparative law, the grant paid much of Friedmann's salary; subsidized the publication of a University of Toronto Comparative Law series; provided an annual scholarship for a Quebec graduate student to study at Toronto; and funded occasional exchanges of law professors between Toronto and Quebec. It was an ambitious and far-sighted enterprise for a faculty still preoccupied with its own struggles. While their interests diverged significantly, Laskin admired his new colleague's intellect and verve. Before long Friedmann became a kind of media star through his appearances on a law-and-public affairs program on CBC television. After five years at Toronto he left for Columbia, where he remained until his premature death in 1972. Dramatic in death as he was in life, Friedmann was murdered by a mugger while taking one of his customary walks near the campus.

Laskin never took any particular interest in Quebec and remained on the fringes of the Carnegie project, except for arranging an exchange between himself and Frank Scott at McGill. Laskin went first, lecturing to Scott's class at McGill in the winter months of 1952 while Scott was providing technical assistance to the UN in Burma, and Scott returned the favour in 1953–4. One legacy of Laskin's visit to McGill was his friendship with student Fred Kaufman, later of the Quebec Court of Appeal. Scott was thirteen years older than Laskin, but the strength of their shared convictions nourished a lifelong friendship. Strong civil libertarians and federalists, both men found much to criticize in Canadian society in the complacent 1950s.

After the enormous classes at Osgoode, Laskin now taught classes of twenty and thirty students at the University of Toronto. Initially his teaching load comprised real property in first year, and real estate transactions and constitutional law in second year. In 1953 Laskin reclaimed labour law when Jacob Finkelman took a one-year leave to act as full-time chair of the Ontario Labour Relations Board. When Finkelman resigned from the university the following year, Laskin continued with labour law and dropped real estate transactions. In two of these fields Laskin would publish student casebooks: constitutional law in 1951, and land law in 1958. He would never publish the labour law casebook he had first compiled at Osgoode in 1947, probably because the Canadian market was too small. While these texts consisted primarily of extracts from leading cases connected by notes and questions written by Laskin, they were frequently used by lawyers and judges, given the small numbers of Canadian works on these subjects. Laskin's casebook on constitutional law in particular was adopted widely at law schools outside Ontario, enhancing his reputation and eliciting requests for opinions from parties across the country. His renown as a scholar of constitutional law probably played a role in his appointment as Queen's Counsel in 1956.

These small classes of the 1950s enjoyed a particular esprit de corps for a variety of reasons. Students who chose to take the University of Toronto LLB before 1957 and brave the extra year of legal education were likely to incline already to the academic side of law. (A number of them would go on to become well-known pillars of Canadian legal education.) They also felt rather daring in following the heroic trio who had stood up to the benchers. 'Wright and Laskin were really Olympic heroes to us, they were mythical,' recalled former student Stanley Schiff.[28] For those with left-of-centre policial views, Laskin's identification with progressive causes was attractive. In short, the University of Toronto was now the 'alternative' law school, whose students fancied themselves a cut above the pettifogging Osgoode crowd. With his rugged good looks, stylish suits (unlike the perpetually rumpled Caesar Wright), and rather confrontational stance, Laskin's physical presence affirmed the aura of myth surrounding him. Occasionally students could persuade him to retell the 1949 tale over lunch while they listened in rapt attention. While momentarily satisfying, recounting the story only reminded Laskin of his own frustration with the ongoing absence of a settlement with the Law Society.

It would be more apt to call Laskin a role model than a mentor to his students, for the simple reason that he was always ferociously busy. He had dramatically fewer students and far less marking than at Osgoode, but Laskin simply filled the vacated hours with other work, both paid and *pro bono*. In addition to his scholarly writing, which resumed its momentum after he left Osgoode, Laskin was conducting frequent labour arbitrations, writing headnotes for law reports, and doing some opinion work for law firms. He also devoted a good deal of time to the Canadian Jewish Congress campaign for better human rights legislation, and to the affairs of Holy Blossom Temple. If you went to visit him in his office, his head would be bent over at his desk and he would be writing madly. As former student Martin Friedland recalled, 'he would tell you exactly what you needed to know, and you were out of there in three minutes, because he had this immense workload.'[29] If this sounds rather chilly on Laskin's part, such an impression is belied by other evidence of continuing amicable relationships with students. Friedland invited the Laskins to his wedding, as did Jerry Grafstein and Harry Arthurs, who recalled that his graduation present from Laskin was being addressed by his first name. If he did not spare time for fireside chats, Laskin nonetheless assisted many of his students at crucial moments as they launched their careers. Years later he recalled the 'extraordinary personal relationship with our students'[30] during this period.

This sense of commonality was enhanced by the nature of the student body. They were almost all young white males from southern Ontario, many of whom had known each other as undergraduates. Athletics played a significant role in this male bonding; in fact, athletics would never again dominate the student identity at the University of Toronto as it did in the 1950s. In both 1954 and 1955 law won the Reed Trophy for Division B athletics, with the same group of men doing triple service as the soccer team, the hockey team, and the basketball team.[31] The only substantial minority were the Jewish students; there were no aboriginal students, and visible minority students and women were barely present. In sixteen years Laskin would teach four black men, two Asian students, and fifteen women. On average, one lonely woman per year graduated, and several classes had no women at all.

A second shift in location reinforced the law school's sense of its identity. With enrolment on the rise again by the mid-1950s, the faculty quickly outgrew Baldwin House. Administrators turned their eyes north, to the large estate bequeathed to the university by philanthropist Euphemia Woods in 1949. Ensconced in eighty-odd acres of woods, Glendon Hall was a Canadian version of an English country house with a magnificent view over the Don Valley. Rather austere on the outside, with its grey stucco walls and black shutters, its interior decor featured elaborately carved cornices, imposing marble fireplaces, and a huge oval skylight above the main staircase. The portico was wreathed in mauve when flowering almond blossomed in the spring, and to the south spread roseries, parterres, ponds, and privet hedges.

The physical separation from the main campus meant that the faculty could no longer make do with the bare-bones collection of law books available at Baldwin House. Wright demanded a 'wholesale transfer from the central stacks of everything classed as law' – an assault stoutly resisted by the historians and political scientists. An attempted solution saw the university librarian, Robert Blackburn, Bora Laskin, and political economist James Eayrs reduced to 'inspect[ing] the shelves within the contested area, book by book.' Unfortunately, 'Bora's [assumption] was that anything that smelt of law should be transferred to Glendon Hall, Jim's that anything of possible interest to non-lawyers should stay where it was.' After three rancorous days, 'the subcommittee ended in a minor explosion.' A lively memo war ensued, with historian Donald Creighton accusing Wright of 'impertinence,' while Wright's reply reached 'new heights of intemperance and invective.' Blackburn finally invoked closure and declared the status quo would prevail – though by this point Wright had obtained most of what he wanted.[32]

The new building would also house new colleagues. In 1955 Friedmann was replaced by Ted McWhinney, a young Australian scholar fresh from a doctorate in international law and an assistant professorship at Yale. A second Australian, the flamboyant A.B. Weston, was hired to teach jurisprudence but proved to be rather too unconventional for his colleagues and stayed only six years. Laskin also persuaded his old friend Albert Abel to join the faculty. Other faculties at Canadian universities have at times been staffed by a majority of Americans, but they are rarely encountered in Canadian law faculties. Then again Albert Abel was an unusual American: his brother was heard to remark with some bemusement that 'Al' had 'never owned a car and never owned a gun.'[33] Rather shy and a lifelong bachelor, Abel gradually took on an avuncular role in the Laskin family. His birthday and those of Bora and Barbara Laskin all coincided in early October, and they usually had a joint celebration at the Laskins' house. Abel would pay his friend the ultimate tribute of editing the fourth edition of *Laskin's Canadian Constitutional Law* after its author went to the bench.

With its highly qualified faculty and small classes the Wright law school might have expanded the graduate program, but it was preoccupied almost exclusively with the LLB. Few students were admitted to the LLM program and no doctorates were awarded until the 1960s. Those enrolled were mostly Quebec students doing comparative law work, who tended to use the LLM degree as an introduction to the common law rather than for advanced study. One of these, Louis Lebel, took labour law with Laskin during his graduate work in 1962–3 before returning to Quebec. In 2000 he became the first labour lawyer since Laskin to be named to the Supreme Court of Canada.

Laskin emphasized his singular commitment to LLB students in a heated exchange of views with Professor Alan Mewett. Responding to the 1956 report of the CBA's Committee on Legal Research, Mewett advocated an Institute for Advanced Legal Studies on the British model for Canada. A recent English import, he acknowledged 'the most urgent need for research in Canada on Canadian law,' but lamented the lack of 'facilities of the most elementary kind' to support it. For those aspiring to do graduate work in law, 'the last place they should consider is Canada.'[34] Laskin was 'horrified to think that the finest facilities and the highest calibre faculty should be wasted upon an unaffiliated institute when they would better serve the cause of research ... by being placed at the service of the undergraduate law student.' It was at the undergraduate (i.e., the LLB) level that 'the disciplined work habits and mental stirrings that underlie useful inquiry into ... the legal solutions to the problems of our social order [had to] be inculcated.' Thus, '[r]esearch at the graduate level should be merely a specialized projection of the undergraduate school.'[35] Laskin's opposition to the institute model was arguably appropriate for the environment of scarcity in law schools in the Canada of the 1950s. Law libraries were expensive investments and should be pressed to serve as wide a clientele as possible, among whom LLB students were a key group. Alongside this economic rationale lay a political one: the idea of a rarefied research library restricted to specialists offended Laskin's democratic instincts.

While Laskin denied that English graduate programs in law surpassed those found in Canada, he admitted that some U.S. schools offered superb facilities for graduate study. Canada could not at present match the best the United States could offer, but this time would only come when 'we have poured as much energy and money into the improvement of undergraduate training as the United States has done and are able to show similar results (on a comparative basis) in the existence of a large number of excellent first-law-degree schools.'[36] Laskin's statements on graduate studies in law contained mixed messages. Given his emphasis on improving existing LLB programs, did he think Canadian law schools should not offer graduate programs? Well, no. Four Canadian law schools offered adequate (in his view), if not yet 'first-class' graduate programs in law. In spite of this tepid defence of Canadian graduate programs in law, Laskin and his colleagues put little energy into their own graduate program, and encouraged talented students to continue their studies at Harvard. This decision had important consequences in the 1960s and '70s, when law schools in Canada were constantly seeking new personnel. A large majority of these newly minted law professors received their graduate degrees in the United States rather than Canada, where they studied Canadian problems principally through the lens of U.S. models, assumptions, and theories. This exposure was undoubtedly beneficial in many ways, but in other respects it hindered advanced study in Canadian law.

If Laskin and his colleagues were preoccupied in the years before 1957 by their own struggle for recognition by the bar, they also took heart in the expansion of university legal education everywhere in Canada. By 1950 Canadian university law schools, like Canadian universities in general, were embarked on an expansionist phase that would not halt until the early 1970s. They were growing into a more confident, more securely funded, and larger set of institutions whose personnel were anxious to discuss the challenges of the post-war world. When Laskin began teaching in 1940 there were only thirty or so full-time law professors in Canada. By 1952 there were fifty-six, teaching some 2,400 students. In 1947 Frank Scott and George Curtis, dean of the new law school at the University of British Columbia, arranged for an informal meeting of some Canadian law teachers to be held in conjunction with the CBA annual meeting in Ottawa. A 1948 meeting at McGill was attended by sixteen law professors from eight law schools, including Laskin from Osgoode and Jacob Finkelman from the University of Toronto.[37] It would turn out to be the effective founding meeting of the Association of Law Teachers (later changed to the Canadian Association of Law Teachers, or CALT), even though a constitution was not adopted until 1951.

The CALT provided the first venue where academics from the civil law and common law traditions could meet regularly, and a forum for the exchange of ideas about teaching, library resources, and research. The members of the early CALT were highly self-conscious, keen to promote the idea of the law schools as a 'third branch' of the legal profession along with the bench and bar, and to seek a status commensurate with that role. While believing the organization to be a good idea in and of itself, Laskin thought it could only help in the struggle with the Law Society, and he invested considerable energy in the CALT in its early years.

The small group of law professors who met at Banff in 1949 was the last to meet with the CBA's annual convention. In 1950 the CALT joined the annual gathering of Canadian learned societies, held that year at the Royal Military College, Kingston. The symbolism of the new arrangements was important: the law teachers wanted to emphasize that they were not just an appendage of the bar. Laskin, Wright, and Willis all attended the 1950 meeting, forming nearly a third of the meagre attendance of ten, but the 1951 meeting at McGill was the biggest yet: twenty-five law professors attended, nearly half the full-time law teachers in Canada. For the first time research and graduate studies were a major focus, a sign of the growing maturation of legal studies within the academy. Frank Scott and George Curtis recruited Laskin as vice-president in 1952, during the presidential tenure of Albert Mayrand of the Université de Montréal. Erwin Griswold, the dean of Harvard Law School, bestowed his blessing on the infant organization at the conference on 4 June. Griswold's long tenure as dean (1946–67) overlapped almost exactly with Caesar Wright's, with whom he remained in regular contact. He visited Canada frequently both for business and pleasure, was on close terms with Ivan Rand, and knew many of the Canadian law deans personally. The smaller, more personal world of the 1940s and '50s allowed him to acquaint himself thoroughly with the world of Canadian legal education, but this intimate relationship between Harvard and the Canadian legal academy was not replicated after Griswold's departure to become solicitor-general under Lyndon Johnson.

The 1952 CALT meeting at Université Laval was probably Bora Laskin's first direct exposure to the traditional ideas and culture of French Canada, hitherto mediated for him through Frank Scott and McGill. Monseigneur Vandry, the rector, startled his guests with an impassioned plea for the unity of Canada and the building of a Christian democracy, noting that Laval's mission was to make use of the French culture for the grandeur and enrichment of Canadian civilization. After a further discourse by part-time lecturer Louis-Philippe Pigeon about the problem of *stare decisis* in Quebec, the rapporteur of the meeting recorded that 'Mr. Laskin tried to bring the discussion back to a practical level.' Laskin saw the two main challenges as being the preparation of teaching materials, which posed problems of both resources and coordination, and the production of scholarship, without which 'the University Law Schools in Canada have no business functioning in the long run.' Here again he pointed to lack of funds as a major difficulty. In a session devoted to library issues, Laskin proposed that 'the organization should fix a minimum budget for library needs ... which the organization would endorse.' CALT should then use 'what weight it had to back schools having difficulties in securing minimum requirements' – a kind of equalization formula for law libraries.[38]

Social activities at Laval included a tour of Quebec city and a visit to a lecturer's 'peasant cottage' on Ile d'Orléans. This French-Canadian focus on the glories of the past contrasted strangely with the after-dinner speech given that evening by Professor Mathews, a representative of the Association of American Law Schools (AALS). Mathews spoke of the threats to civil liberties posed by the McCarthyite hysteria then gripping the United States, and to the problem of racially segregated legal education. The U.S. situation in these years just before the groundbreaking decisions in *Brown v. Board of Education* (decided in May 1954) astonished the Canadian audience. When individual blacks had dared to apply to southern law schools in the late 1940s, the universities had responded by establishing segregated programs. The University of Oklahoma, for example, assigned three instructors to Ada Sipuel, who taught her in a roped-off section of the state capitol building. The NAACP attacked these practices and their counsel Thurgood Marshall argued the cases before the U.S. Supreme Court. The Court found the facilities provided to the individual blacks were not equal and ordered them admitted to the law schools in question, but failed to overturn *Plessy v. Ferguson*, the key precedent legitimating the provision of 'separate but equal' facilities.[39]

Laskin had further opportunities to broaden his exposure to Quebec and the civil law over the next year, when he worked with Albert Mayrand on the 1953 meeting in Montreal.[40] One of the topics discussed there was of special interest to Laskin. Should the Supreme Court of Canada adopt a one-judgment rule such as that observed by the Judicial Committee of the Privy Council? No dissents were allowed because in strict theory the 'judgment' was actually advice to the monarch tendered by the judges: a constitutional wrinkle with no parallel in Canada. When Chief Justice Thibaudeau Rinfret pronounced himself nonetheless attracted by the idea, which mirrored the practice of the French Cour de cassation, the Canadian Bar Association decided to investigate the question. Neither the CBA nor the Supreme Court had solicited the opinion of the CALT, but it decided to issue a statement anyway, in spite of the chief justice's less than gracious observation that 'he could not see what concern Canadian law teachers had with the practice of the Supreme Court.'[41] Clearly Canadian law professors had a long way to go in persuading the legal establishment of the validity of their claim to be a 'third branch' of the legal profession.

Foreshadowing his role as a judge known, and in some cases celebrated for, his dissents, Bora Laskin took a prominent role in marshalling the arguments against the one-judgment rule. Forbidding dissents and adopting a corporate judgment in which each judge was effectively anonymous struck at Laskin's most basic concerns: freedom of expression, individual responsibility, and the constant need for growth and adaptation of the judge-made law. He described the anonymity implicit in a compulsory one-judgment rule as an invitation to individual irresponsibility of judges as well as a denial of their individuality. Laskin pointed out that such a rule assumed either that there was only one solution to any problem or, that only one should be revealed. It denied the litigants, lawyers, and the public the opportunity to know what alternative arguments recommended themselves to the court. The recording of reasoned dissents gave precision to a majority judgment and stimulated growth in the law by the reception of conflicting ideas. 'The history of law shows that no one generation can permanently bottle up the social pressures that determine our legal rules.'[42] Laskin cited the careers of Oliver Wendell Holmes and Lord Atkin as evidence of the vital role played by dissents in the growth of the common law.

The law teachers found Laskin's arguments persuasive, and resolved unanimously that the existing right of each justice to issue his own opinion should be maintained, but that wherever possible a 'judgment of the court' should be issued defining the extent of majority agreement among the justices upon the reason for disposition of the points at issue. The CBA eventually recommended the maintenance of the status quo, which was more or less the CALT position. Contrary to the opinion of the chief justice of Canada, perhaps Canadian law teachers did have something to contribute to the discussion of judging in the country's highest court.

The meeting at Montreal was a great success, as much for its social side as for its academic content. The university hosted a magnificent dinner on 4 June, featuring a tongue-in-cheek menu with dishes named after well-known jurists:

> Hors d'oeuvre à la Laurent
> Filet de Sole Troplong
> Consommé Dicey
> Filet Mignault[43]
> Pommes Justiniennes
> Pointes d'asperges Savigny

The quality of the cuisine and the company ensured that the Montreal dinner became something of a benchmark for future gatherings of the association, and it augured well for the upcoming year of Bora Laskin's presidency. His colleague J.B. Milner saw the 1953 meeting as evidence that 'the hope for a renaissance in legal education is not a wholly idle one.'[44] Laskin would be assisted by Bill Lederman of Dalhousie as vice-president, Wilbur Bowker of Alberta as secretary-treasurer, and an executive comprising Albert Mayrand, Frank Scott, Louis-Philippe Pigeon, and Allan Leal of Osgoode Hall Law School. Aside from Scott, they were younger men on the way up, all of whom would make their mark on Canadian law as scholars, educators, or judges.

The 1954 Winnipeg meeting had to be handled with some delicacy because Manitoba was the only province outside Ontario still adhering to the concurrent model of legal education. As Laskin observed, 'the "practical" point of view dominates in the administration of the law school,'[45] and it was actually housed in the law courts, not at the university. Wilbur Bowker wanted the association to meet at the university, but Laskin preferred a diplomatic solution. The first session should be in the law school because the leaders of the bar and Chief Justice Williams would join the law teachers on that day; as a courtesy to them the opening venue should be on their turf. Afterwards the meetings would be held at the university. On the final Saturday the Hudson's Bay Company threw a party at the Fort Garry Hotel, where Laskin stayed throughout the meetings. Four years later he would return to that hotel to conduct an inquiry for the fledgling Canadian Association of University Teachers into a controversy involving a professor at Winnipeg's United College; it would turn into the most important cause célèbre on academic freedom in twentieth-century Canada.

For the first time academic papers on subjects other than legal education were given before the thirty-five registrants. Mayrand spoke on 'the Work of the Supreme Court in Civil Law,' while Laskin spoke on the Court's recent constitutional jurisprudence, focusing on both federalism and civil liberties cases. In what was probably his first public pronouncement on the topic, he wondered aloud 'whether the Supreme Court would ultimately find an implied bill of rights that barred the provinces from passing laws abridging freedom of speech and religion.'[46] His friend Frank Scott would attempt, with some success, to flesh out this theory when arguing before the Supreme Court in several civil liberties cases of the 1950s, especially *Switzman v. Elbling*[47] and *Roncarelli v. Duplessis*.[48] At this meeting he took up Laskin's theme by referring to the experience under Quebec's notorious *Padlock Act*, and raised the more general issue of the need for a Canadian Bill of Rights. Some participants agreed with Scott but Laskin's old professor Larry MacKenzie dissented; such issues were better solved in the long run 'by a process of give and take and by education,' rather than a bill of rights.

Even as Bora Laskin became a nationally recognized figure in constitutional law and legal education in the 1950s, adding to his renown in the field of labour law, he began to play a more prominent leadership role in his own community. In the fall of 1951 the Laskins moved from the west end of the city to 301 Warren Avenue in the northern suburb of Forest Hill. The former village had become a magnet for affluent professionals and businessmen seeking relief from the crowded and noisy downtown districts, and they built very substantial homes indeed. The Laskin residence was almost uniquely modest in the neighbourhood. Nestled snugly into a small hill on the corner of Chaplin Crescent, it looked more like an English cottage with its white brick, black accents and small gables.

The proximity to Canadian Reform Judaism's nerve centre, Holy Blossom Temple, was also a likely draw for Bora, if not for Peggy. Seen from a distance, the Temple looks like nothing so much as an Italian Romanesque church. The cathedral-like architecture and occupational provenance of many of its congregants led to its irreverent nickname, 'Our Lady of the Schmattas.' Laskin served on the board of trustees from 1953 to 1960, and as vice-chair and later chair of the religious education committee during these years.[49] Neither post was a sinecure: the rapid growth of the congregation called for major building campaigns, and Laskin's dispute resolution skills were required to resolve a variety of conflicts that arose within the Holy Blossom membership. In return, he was able to participate in one of the most dynamic and socially progressive faith communities Canada has ever seen.

The decision of the congregation to move their place of worship from downtown Bond Street north to Ava Road in 1938 was prescient. The trek north, already begun in the 1930s, accelerated in the affluent postwar years. Temple membership grew from about 1,000 in the early 1940s to over 1,700 in 1955, putting such a strain on existing facilities that a moratorium on new members was seriously contemplated, and a new Reform congregation, Temple Sinai, had to be established.[50] The baby boom in turn overwhelmed the capacity of the religious school, as the number of students enrolled more than doubled from 475 in 1947 to 1,100 in 1957.[51] A Board of Education was created and the integration of the religious school with the Hebrew education program commenced. Laskin's philosophy of religious education sounded remarkably like his approach to legal education: 'the school should be able to present customs and ceremonies not merely historically,' he urged, 'but as having a place and meaning in the Jewish life of today.'[52] With Laskin as its chair the board oversaw the erection of a new school building at the same time as a new eight-hundred-seat auditorium was added to the temple facilities. The service of dedication on 5 June 1960 was presided over by lieutenant-governor Keiller Mackay, long considered the Gentile patron saint of the Jewish community, and the gala occasion was a fitting conclusion to Laskin's decade of service to Holy Blossom.[53]

Laskin's role at the temple put him in regular contact with two individuals at the very heart of the Reform Jewish community in Toronto: Heinz Warschauer, executive director of Jewish education at Holy Blossom, and Rabbi Abraham Feinberg. Warschauer was a German refugee who had escaped to England during the war, then suffered internment in a camp in Quebec. One delicate matter Laskin and Warschauer faced was the appropriate stance to adopt towards the new state of Israel. Attitudes varied within the congregation but Laskin seconded the view of Warschauer, who believed the school should give students information about Israel and try to implant emotional ties in them, but should not 'emphasize that Israel is *our* homeland. On the contrary, we emphasize that Canada is our homeland. We are proud that Israel exists ... , but we are not responsible for the autonomous state of Israel.'[54] The board eventually issued a report describing its educational program as 'historical and interpretive, not Zionistic and propagandistic.' Laskin's interest in Israel remained rather detached and intellectual. He later lent his name to various fund-raising efforts in aid of Israel while chief justice, but he and Peggy visited the country only twice, both times as a result of official invitations. Laskin and Warschauer also made uniform the ages for the bar and bat mitzvah (the age for girls was formerly twelve rather than thirteen), and encouraged parents to prepare their daughters for the bat mitzvah at a time when few did. They also tried to interest more girls in studying Hebrew, at a time when 90 per cent of the congregation's boys but only 10 per cent of its girls did so.

Feinberg was surely the most colourful figure ever to be associated with Holy Blossom Temple – and that is saying a lot. A New Yorker by birth, he had joined the rabbinate but quit in disillusionment in 1930. Feinberg reinvented himself as a radio star – 'Anthony Frome, Poet-Prince of the Air Waves' – and made a small fortune, but rejoined the rabbinate in 1935 to take part in the struggle against Fascism. Holy Blossom found him in Denver when they were seeking a successor to the redoubtable Maurice Eisendrath in 1943, and he would spend the next twenty-eight years in Toronto. From the abolition of capital punishment to the adoption of anti-discrimination laws to the advocacy of more liberal attitudes on abortion and sexuality, Feinberg was on the front lines of social radicalism.[55] It speaks volumes about Holy Blossom that its members were prepared to allow their rabbi free rein even though many might not have agreed with his stance on particular issues.

Finally, like a reef-stranded ship gradually freed by the tides, the dispute between the Law Society and the universities began to move towards a resolution. The process that brought closure to the 'fiercest debate' has been extensively chronicled elsewhere, and is not retraced here in any detail.[56] Over time the minority of benchers, who had always favoured wider university involvement in legal education, were strengthened by the replacement of old blood with newer men such as J.J. Robinette and John Arnup, who were much more receptive to change. In the end, however, the pressure of money and numbers overwhelmed the benchers. Even the most diehard opponents of the universities had to admit that the surge in student population would require extraordinary expenditure on new facilities. By 1955 a building designed to hold three hundred students was crammed with some seven hundred. Worse, the numbers were expected to double again by the mid-1960s. As it contemplated an addition to Osgoode Hall, the Law Society was faced with the prospect of borrowing money for the first time in over a century. The unthinkable was whispered in the corridors – it might be necessary to mortgage the venerable edifice itself.[57]

In January 1955 convocation created a Special Committee on Law Society Accommodation, chaired by treasurer Cyril Carson, to make recommendations about additions to Osgoode Hall. Its members soon realized that a deal would have to be struck with the universities. On 30 April Carson invited the heads of all Ontario universities to a dinner at Osgoode Hall to discuss the future of legal education, thereby initiating the process that would lead to the creation of four new faculties of law in the years ahead. Bora Laskin and Caesar Wright were elated at this turn of events but played no role in the discussions. Wright had too many enemies in the Law Society to be an acceptable negotiator, and Laskin was so identified with Wright as to disqualify him as well. Even Sidney Smith wisely took a back seat, while Queen's University produced the lead negotiators for the universities, in the person of principal W.A. Mackintosh and professor of political science J. Alexander Corry.

Though prepared to delegate a role in legal education to the universities, the Law Society was not yet ready to surrender its own law school. The Special Committee continued to meet and produced plans in the fall of 1955 for a law school addition to Osgoode Hall costing some $1.3 million, exclusive of furniture. For some, this was simply preposterous. Richard A. ('Dick') Bell, an influential Ottawa lawyer, classmate of Laskin at Kennedy's school and future minister of immigration under Diefenbaker, was elected a bencher in the spring of 1955. Upon hearing of the proposed expenditure, he wrote Cyril Carson a stinging letter exposing the folly of the benchers' plans:

> Within your lifetime & mine, this province may well have a population of 10–12 millions. The potential law school population may well be between 2000 and 3000, perhaps even more. Are we to continue to erect ever 'larger classrooms'? The medical schools at Toronto, Queen's and Western rank with the very best on the continent. Where does Osgoode Hall Law School rank with law schools on this continent? Where does it rank with Canadian law schools? Is there any reason to believe that the U of T would fail to do for legal education what it has done for medical education, for other professional courses? ... Conversely, is there any doubt that the Benchers of the Law Society of Upper Canada have failed to provide for Ontario a law school even remotely approaching the standards of our medical schools?[58]

For the old guard, questions of comparative standards were totally irrelevant – the function of a legal education was not to theorize about the law but to train practising professionals. For the post-war generation, more oriented to the North American context, the benchers' obsessive insularity on legal education was, in addition to being unaffordable, becoming an embarrassment and a distraction from other pressing concerns. A decade later, the benchers decided to turn the Osgoode Hall Law School over to a newly created York University and abandon the field of legal education altogether except for a restructured bar admission course.

The eight years after Laskin left Osgoode and returned to the University of Toronto were in some respects the most difficult of his life. Although his career took off as he gained national recognition as a labour arbitrator, a scholar of constitutional law, and a legal educator, the long war of attrition with the Law Society was debilitating. The dramatic departure from Osgoode, at first a seemingly brilliant strategic move, led only to inertia and a school so small as to be barely viable. Willis's early exit was a severe blow, though he would return in 1959.

The situation was all the more frustrating because Laskin, like a star hockey player relegated to the benches in the last period, could play no active role in the final resolution. The conflict created a cloud over the future, and Bora Laskin was a man who hated uncertainty. The same uncertainty permeated the law faculty's relationship with the university, on both the physical and the academic planes. The constant shifts in location, the petty squabbles over the library, and the seeming inability of the university to force the issue of recognition all combined in Laskin's mind to produce a strong sense of grievance and betrayal. In an unguarded moment in his 1977 interview he said, 'I don't know really how we survived those years.'[59]

9

Federalism

Every Canadian has heard the following joke. People from different countries were asked to write an essay on the elephant. The French representative wrote an elegant essay on the love life of the elephant. The German wrote an encyclopaedic treatise considering the elephant from every conceivable point of view. The American wrote an essay on the profit-making potential of the elephant. The Canadian's essay was entitled 'The Elephant: A Federal or Provincial Responsibility?' One can almost imagine Bora Laskin writing such an essay. With few exceptions, his constitutional law scholarship was narrowly focused on this central dynamic of Canadian federalism: the division of powers outlined in sections 91 and 92 of the *British North America Act, 1867*. When Laskin wrote about the Supreme Court of Canada, it was usually to examine its federalism jurisprudence or to discuss how its institutional role as the final arbiter (after 1949) of Canadian federalism could be enhanced. When he wrote about civil liberties, it was usually to discuss which level of government was constitutionally enabled to protect various kinds of fundamental freedoms. Topics such as the independence of the judiciary, the power of the executive, the position of native peoples, or minority language rights, all of which are of constitutional significance, are scarcely addressed in his scholarship. Again and again he returned to the question of the division of powers, and for the most part he aimed to shore up the federal power after a long period during which he and many others felt the Privy Council had interpreted Canada's constitution in a dangerously decentralist way.[1]

Laskin's first major foray into constitutional law was triggered by the imminent abolition of appeals to the Privy Council, an event that both exemplified and helped to launch a new wave of Canadian legal nationalism. His 1947 article '"Peace, Order and Good Government" Re-examined' was, as we have seen, his first major contribution to constitutional law.[2] The catalyst for it was provided by three recent decisions of the Privy Council: the *Reference re Privy Council Appeals*, recognizing the Canadian Parliament's authority to vest final appellate jurisdiction in all matters in the Supreme Court of Canada;[3] the *Co-operative Committee on Japanese Canadians* case, legitimating the post-war deportations of Japanese Canadian citizens;[4] and the *Canada Temperance Federation* case, upholding the validity of federal temperance legislation on the basis that its subject matter went 'beyond local or provincial concerns' and 'from its inherent nature [must] be the concern of the Dominion as a whole.'[5] These decisions, Laskin wrote, 'on one view, neutralize much of what had been said by the Judicial Committee [of the Privy Council] on the matter [i.e., the interpretation of the 'peace, order and good government' clause in s. 91 of the *British North America Act*] in the past twenty-five years, and on another view, merely add to the confusing course of judicial pronouncements on the subject.'[6] At last the Privy Council seemed to be altering its views on the Canadian constitution, moving away from the markedly provincialist stance so deplored by the scholars of the 1930s, such as Frank Scott, Vincent MacDonald, and W.P.M. Kennedy, and inviting a more active role by the federal government.

Not only that: with the Privy Council now providing itself with a dignified exit from the Canadian constitutional stage, the scene would soon shift to Ottawa, where the Supreme Court of Canada would assume final responsibility for interpreting the constitution. In 1943 the Court had marked the retirement of Chief Justice Duff, identified by Laskin as a willing collaborator in the Privy Council's provincialist subversion of the constitution. New recruits to the court during the war years included Ivan Cleveland Rand from New Brunswick and James Wilfred Estey from Saskatchewan, men of high intellectual calibre and liberal views whom Laskin would come to admire. It was almost too good to be true: Duff gone, the Privy Council on the way out, and a reinvigorated Supreme Court willing to take up the task of Canadian constitutional adjudication. Canadians suddenly had a chance for a new beginning, and in '"Peace, Order and Good Government" Re-examined' Laskin set out to educate the legal community about how to achieve it.

The first step was a blistering attack on the Privy Council's progressive diminution of federal powers from the *Local Prohibition* case in 1896 down to the decisions invalidating most of the federal government's New Deal legislation in the 1930s. This was not new in substance – the scholars of the thirties had made similar complaints. What was new in Laskin's approach was his method. He privileged detailed doctrinal analysis over the more broadly political approach taken by the previous generation of scholars to questions of constitutional interpretation. The impact of major decisions on political actors and on the country at large were their main preoccupations, rather than the interpretive maze through which the courts travelled.[7] Laskin's starting point was the obverse. He took it for granted that the results of the Watson-Haldane view of the Canadian constitution were unacceptable in a socio-political sense; that is, that most Canadians wanted to see the federal government play a larger role in economic policy and in building the welfare state. Rather, Laskin was concerned to expose what he saw as the inadequacy of the legal reasoning underlying the Watson-Haldane view, so as to liberate future courts, if possible, from the necessity of following it. His audience was much more precisely targeted than that of the 1930s scholars, who tended to publish in broad-circulation journals such as the *Queen's Quarterly* as well as in the *Canadian Bar Review*. Judges, lawyers, and law students, in that order: these were Laskin's intended audience.

For the 1930s scholars, the ability to legislate for the 'peace, order and good government of Canada' mentioned in the opening words of section 91 was meant, both as a matter of original intent and of ordinary grammatical construction, to be a plenary grant of power to the Dominion, with the enumerated heads of that section (criminal law, divorce, copyright and patents, and so on) merely illustrations. The Privy Council, to the contrary, had regarded the opening words as a mere preamble, and given the federal government little room to manoeuvre beyond the specific heads of power mentioned later in the section. Only in emergency situations or those clearly extending beyond the borders of a single province, such as aeronautics or radio broadcasting, could the opening clause justify an exercise of federal power. Laskin agreed with the critique of the 1930s scholars but argued it had been over-stressed to the detriment of another doctrine that might have been used to validate federal legislation. Here and throughout his career, Laskin was a champion of the 'aspect' doctrine, which states that a given matter of legislative concern may have both federal and provincial facets validating measures by both levels of government. For example, provincial highway traffic legislation may impose penalties for careless driving while federal law criminalizes the negligent operation of a motor vehicle. Only in the case of a direct conflict would federal legislation prevail; otherwise each could remain valid on its own terms. Although later identified as a centralist, Laskin was here advocating a form of cooperative federalism, in which the provinces would have an important role to play along with the federal government in resolving socio-economic problems that spilled over jurisdictional boundaries.

Although the aspect doctrine had its origins as early as *Hodge v. The Queen* in 1883, it was rather at odds with the late-nineteenth-century approach to adjudication, built on a legal theory defining rights as absolute within their boundaries but meaningless outside them. It was much more in harmony with modernist theories stressing pragmatism, subjectivity, and the fragmented and multifarious nature of reality. The beauty of the aspect doctrine was that it allowed Canadian courts to do an end run around the Privy Council jurisprudence, without openly disagreeing with their decisions. In fact it would be resorted to with increasing frequency by the Supreme Court of Canada in the 1950s and '60s, as the rapid expansion of both provincial and federal government activities rendered the Privy Council's 'watertight compartments' approach to federalism unworkable.

For those Privy Council decisions that would be more difficult to avoid using the aspect doctrine, Laskin advocated taking a more flexible approach to binding precedent. Here he could point to the Privy Council's own decision in the *Canada Temperance Federation* case, which he saw as a 'fresh beginning,' likening it to 'the removal of shutters from a house which has been kept dark for many years.'[8] The shutters were of course the restrictions placed by the Privy Council on the Dominion's power to legislate for the 'peace, order and good government of Canada.' In *Canada Temperance Federation* the Privy Council had accepted the validity of federal legislation under this clause pursuant to an 'inherently national' test that was difficult to square with its earlier jurisprudence.

Laskin's substantive points were easily stated. It was the harsh and sarcastic language he directed at the Privy Council, particularly at the late Lord Haldane's decisions of the 1920s and '30s, that made readers sit up and take notice. This was not traditional in Canadian legal academic writing of the day. Even Frank Scott, the *enfant terrible* of the generation ahead of Laskin, did not personalize his criticism in this way. W.P.M. Kennedy might send off an acidic rhetorical volley, but it was usually very general and not directed at individuals. Laskin, by contrast, hammered relentlessly at the judges. Viscount Haldane's reasoning in the *Board of Commerce* case had a 'sham quality.'[9] In *Snider* it was replete with 'barren comment,' and made for 'despair.'[10] Lord Watson was 'a constitutional "Houdini"' who reduced the opening clause of section 91 merely to a supplementary position; 'Viscount Haldane's magic is strong enough to make it disappear altogether.' In the *Employment and Social Insurance Act* reference, the Judicial Committee gave a 'short opinion, almost shocking in its casualness,' with '[n]ot even a pretence at analysis.'[11] The emphasis on abstract logical formulae and the ignoring of social facts in the 1937 decisions were especially distressing. The Judicial Committee failed to give 'explicit consideration to the effects of years of national unemployment in the 1930's, [or] to the need for legislating preventively as well as curatively.' Overall, its jurisprudence was a 'monument to judicial rigidity and to a complacence which admits of no respectable explanation.' Laskin virtually accused the law lords of bad faith; his analysis revealed a 'conscious and deliberate choice of a policy which required, for its advancement, manipulations which can only with difficulty be represented as ordinary judicial techniques.'

For Laskin the federal nature of Canada's constitution was the core feature distinguishing Canadian law from that of the English parent state. His frustration with the Judicial Committee arose from his conviction that the law lords, all trained in a unitary state, simply did not understand federalism. He would have heartily agreed with the critiques voiced by Australian Chief Justice Owen Dixon in a 1956 judgment:

[F]ederalism is a form of government the nature of which is seldom adequately understood in all its bearings by those whose fortune it is to live under a unitary system. The problems of federalism and the considerations governing their solution assume a different aspect to those whose lives are spent under the operation of a federal Constitution, particularly if by education, practice and study they have been brought to think about the constitutional conceptions and modes of reasoning which belong to federalism as commonplace and familiar ideas. A unitary system presents no analogies and indeed, on the contrary, it forms a background against which many of the conceptions and distinctions inherent in federalism must strike the mind as strange and exotic.[12]

Dixon agreed with prominent Australian barrister Douglas Menzies, who reproached the law lords for doing 'no work behind the scenes.' Worse, said Menzies, they treated it 'as bad form to do so,' relying on 'facility of expression & finality of a decision.'[13] Even a highly conservative jurist like Dixon could agree with the substance of Laskin's strictures on the insufficiency of the Judicial Committee's understandings of federalism.

Although the Privy Council was the main focus of Laskin's critiques in his 1947 article, he did not think Canadian judges were doing a very good job of constitutional interpretation either. Osgoode student Harriet Clark noted that 'Laskin doesn't think our judges have any conception of their role under the BNA Act. The consequences of invalidating Bennett's social reforms in 1935 [were] well-nigh disastrous.' And even though the Persons case of 1929 'gave promise of a new principle of flexible interpretation, [it had] little kick, [as] the case had no bearing on the legislative authority of the provinces. Subsequent interpretation showed [one must] still interpret the BNA Act narrowly – with provinces autonomous within their sphere.' Contrary to British traditions of total parliamentary supremacy, Clark recorded, there was 'necessarily more legalism' in Canadian constitutional law as a result of its federalist foundation.[14]

More strident in his criticisms of the Privy Council than other commentators, Laskin was actually less radical in his proposed solutions. In a sense he could afford to be: the despair of the 1930s commentators had given way to the buoyant optimism of the post-war years. Laskin agreed with Kennedy, MacDonald, Scott, and many others that abolition of Privy Council appeals was one step in solving Canada's constitutional problem. He was not as sanguine as they about the political prospects of amending the Canadian constitution in the near future (amendment was, in the closing words of the 1947 article, a 'final refuge'), nor did he consider it desirable as an end in itself. 'It is clearly preferable that the constitution be kept fluid through judicial interpretation than through repeated amendment, and the 'aspect' doctrine is a ready tool for the purpose.' He foresaw the crucial role to be played by the Supreme Court of Canada in constitutional adjudication, and sought to provide a how-to (and how-not-to) manual for interested players. The real job was to educate legal actors, especially judges, about their true roles and responsibilities: judicial review was inevitable in a federal system and '[w]e ought not to forego the opportunity of trying to place it on the higher level of constitutional interpretation as opposed to keeping it on the lower level of statutory interpretation.' Here he challenged decades of Privy Council decisions stating that the *British North America Act* was to be interpreted just like any other statute. The exercise was at any rate 'worth a fair trial with a Canadian court operating in a Canadian climate of opinion.' The civil liberties cases of the 1950s would show that Laskin's exhortations were not entirely in vain.

'"Peace, Order and Good Government" Re-examined' marked a turning point for Bora Laskin. Labour law, the focus of his energies for a decade and more, had been transformed largely along the modernist lines he had so long advocated. Laskin's main contribution to labour law henceforth would be his arbitral jurisprudence, not his scholarship. From now on constitutional law would be his main scholarly preoccupation, and it would increasingly project him from the provincial stage onto the national one.

For the short term, Laskin was preoccupied with other matters. The very large classes at Osgoode, the battle with the benchers and the return to the University of Toronto consumed much of his time and energy until 1951, when he published both his constitutional law casebook and an article entitled 'The Supreme Court of Canada: A Final Court of and for Canadians.'[15] Both of them expressed the confidence, optimism, and nationalism of post-war Canada. At last Canadian problems could be addressed by Canadians with Canadian goals and values in mind. The *Statute of Westminster* of 1931 had ended Canadian legislative subordination to Britain (except for amendment of the constitution itself), and now the abolition of Privy Council appeals had finally done away with Canadian judicial subordination. The 'captive court,' as Laskin called the Supreme Court of Canada, would at last be set free.

In the 1951 article he sketched a history of the Court, described and analysed its internal organization for the despatch of business, and provided an overview of its constitutional jurisprudence. At the outset, Laskin lamented the absence of virtually any scholarship on the Court as an institution, on its doctrine or its judges. His article marks the beginning of serious scholarship on the history, jurisprudence, and contemporary organization of the Court, and treats all three topics in a holistic and interconnected fashion. Laskin's analysis of the Court's inner workings is of interest in view of his later opportunity to shape its modus operandi as chief justice. His main concerns related to the need for greater efficiency in the use of judicial time, and the adoption of practices that would enhance the clarity and quality of the decisions rendered. Thus the Court should reconsider allowing unlimited time for oral argument, and allowing oral argument at all for motions for leave to appeal (in contrast to the U.S. practice of written submissions).

It should also consider the American practice of hiring law clerks to provide '[p]rofessional assistance in devilling, and in research generally, [which] would certainly give the judges more time for reflection.' These administrative changes were phrased as respectful suggestions rather than urgently needed reforms. Laskin adopted a firmer tone on the need for the Court, and counsel pleading before it, to refer both to periodical literature and to judicial decisions from other countries in both the common law and civil law traditions. The flourishing of Canadian law had been hampered by 'the conservative tradition of the Canadian legal profession reinforced by the awe and timidity of a colonial outlook, and in the late development of university law schools where free inquiry grounded in Canadian experience' could be undertaken. By considering comparative jurisprudence in light of Canadian needs and conditions, a 'distinctively Canadian contribution to the common law system [sic]' might be achieved – a development 'long overdue when one considers that in art, in literature, in drama and in science Canadians have already shown that they can do better than merely copy: they can be original.' Here Laskin clearly distinguished the respective positions of the American and Canadian Supreme Courts. Whereas the former, constitutional cases aside, accepted state law as defined by the state courts, Canada's highest court was 'in a stronger position to develop a unified common law' across the country – a task to which it has gradually warmed over the years.

Laskin contrasted unfavourably the Supreme Court's irregular use of judicial conferences with the U.S. Supreme Court practice of regular 'weekly conferences at which cases are discussed, a justice is given the assignment of writing the opinion of the Court, and a draft is then circulated among the justices for approval and comment.' The result in Canada was 'a conspicuous waste of time and an unnecessary cluttering of the reports with separate reasons by individual judges amounting to mere repetition.' It is not clear whether Laskin knew that for many years judicial conferences were inhibited by Mr Justice Locke's practice of leaving immediately after hearings to attend his invalid wife.[16] In this as with many of Laskin's other suggestions, change would have to await his own arrival at the court.

Turning to the Court's constitutional law decisions, Laskin found that in its early years the Court had been much more open about interpreting the *British North America Act* in light of what it perceived to be Canadian needs and values, and much more likely to uphold federal power, until the late-nineteenth-century shift in direction engineered in

London. In his closing paragraph he urged the Court both to strike out on its own, free of an excessive reliance on *stare decisis*, and to return to its roots. 'What is required is the same free range of inquiry which animated the Court in the early days of its existence, especially in constitutional cases where it took its inspiration from Canadian sources.' Then, in a much-quoted phrase, he urged the Court to develop Canadian law in accordance with Canadian aspirations. 'Empiricism not dogmatism, imagination rather than literalness, are the qualities through which the judges can give the Court the stamp of personality.'

Laskin's Anglo-Canadian legal nationalism was not without its dangers. Francophone jurists in Quebec had generally supported the direction of the Privy Council decisions favouring provincial autonomy, and were much less enthusiastic than Laskin about what a Canadian law developed in accordance with Canadian aspirations would look like. Laskin's plea for a more flexible judicial technique and a more vigorous Supreme Court looked like a thinly veiled attempt to promote a more centralized vision of the Canadian constitution, one that would not necessarily accord with Quebec's interests. Louis-Philippe Pigeon, Laskin's future Supreme Court colleague, said as much in a 1951 article. He agreed that 'tests of constitutional validity cannot be rigidly devised' and should rest not on technical constructions but on 'broad principles and on a general conception of what the B.N.A. Act intended to secure to the provinces and to the federal authority.'[17] But he parted company with Laskin in his characterization of the Privy Council and Supreme Court decisions hostile to federal power. For Pigeon, the law lords 'recognize[d] the implicit fluidity of any constitution by allowing for emergencies and by resting distinctions on questions of degree. At the same time they firmly uphold the fundamental principle of provincial autonomy.'[18] Pigeon was vague about the tests the courts should use to resolve these 'questions of degree' but seemed to be groping towards the approach that William Lederman would eventually call 'balanced federalism.' Scholar Paul Gérin-Lajoie also took issue with Laskin's approach to the constitution, in particular with his approach to the need (or lack of need) for provincial approval of constitutional amendments.[19]

To some extent the Supreme Court fulfilled Laskin's aspirations in the 1950s under the intellectual leadership of Ivan Rand, but Laskin himself did little to assist the Court in fleshing out how Canadian conditions might be invoked to develop Canadian law. The whole thrust of his 1947 article had been, in a sense, to arm Canadian judges with technical legal tools rather than, say, a more overtly policy-oriented approach to constitutional adjudication. Laskin never ceased to urge the relevance of Canadian conditions upon the judiciary, but never showed them how to incorporate such considerations in their judgments. The more he urged Canadian courts to take *stare decisis* less seriously, the more diligently he parsed cases he disagreed with in order to undermine them in terms of inconsistency with previous precedents, logical flaws, or doctrinal error – not in terms of their inadequacy on policy grounds. The one place where Laskin demonstrated clearly, sometimes brilliantly, how an understanding of 'local context' and an overt and sensitive balancing of interests could advance the law was in his labour arbitration decisions, but these always existed in a separate compartment from his legal scholarship. As a judge Laskin could also be creative in this way, but seldom in the field he cared most about, constitutional law. His division of powers decisions are the most opaque, doctrinal, and unsatisfying of his entire judicial repertoire. It is almost as if he felt unable to justify openly in policy terms his preference for federal jurisdiction, and was thereby reduced to the kind of judicial formalism he decried in others.

Laskin's judicial approach was foreshadowed in his constitutional law casebook, first published in 1951. The book was a significant achievement in its day, and solidified its author's reputation as an expert in the field. It gathered extracts of all the leading cases on the interpretation of the *British North America Act*, organized them by subject along with extracts from relevant academic articles, and tied the whole package together with connecting bits of text and occasional questions and observations. But these authorial interventions did not provide any extended justification for Laskin's clear preference for federal jurisdiction. There was little discussion of what factors should be taken into account in assigning a particular matter to federal or provincial authority. In its intellectual orientation, the book was based principally on Laskin's 1947 article, which was liberally excerpted throughout.

The subtitle of the text, 'Cases and Notes on Distribution of Legislative Power,' revealed its rather constricted approach to constitutional law. Virtually the whole volume was taken up with the interpretation of sections 91 and 92. There was little on constitutional history, and nothing on the meaning of responsible government, the separation of powers doctrine, language rights, or numerous other topics of constitutional law. There was however a concluding section entitled 'Constitutional Guarantees,' in which Laskin included some reference to the privileges for denominational schools found in section 93 of the Act, and a brief discussion of civil liberties, the first to be found in any Canadian constitutional text.[20] In the second (1960) edition of his text, this section was expanded to nearly one hundred pages and retitled 'Civil Liberties and Constitutional Guarantees.' The book was widely consulted at the time, but some contemporaries lamented its format. While useful as a teaching tool, a reviewer observed, '[a]s a textbook for lawyers, it sacrifices much to its first purpose ... [T]his book does not give what is badly needed, a textbook of Canadian constitutional law defining and discussing in the author's words what the law is and what its implications are [for] constitutional development today. That is the crying need in Canadian legal literature.'[21] While the reviewer suggested that this effort 'show[ed] clearly that [Laskin] could write such a book,' he would never do so. Laskin was too practically oriented, too busy with extra-curricular commitments, and too restless to commit to such a sustained work of scholarship. His articles were widely read at the time, but if assembled they would not add up to a major oeuvre, such as William Lederman's *Continuing Canadian Constitutional Dilemmas: Essays on the Constitutional History, Public Law and Federal System of Canada.*[22]

Laskin's other writings in constitutional law usually but not invariably supported broad national powers rather than provincial autonomy. When he wrote about the treaty-making power he lamented the orthodox theory as laid down by the Privy Council in the *Labour Conventions* case: the government of Canada had plenary authority to make treaties but their implementation had to follow the allocation of legislative authority in sections 91 and 92.[23] It was 'risking stultification in international intercourse to have the limitations of law added to those of politics and economics operating on the central government in Canada.'[24] Laskin was predictably categorical on the inability of provinces to enter treaties with foreign nations, and even took part in a radio debate on the topic with Professor Jacques-Yvan Morin of the Université de Montréal.[25] A book review of Alexander Smith's *The Commerce Power in Canada and the United States* provides a pithy summary of his thinking on the interpretation of the trade and commerce clause.[26] On the issue of paramountcy, which arises when two independently valid provincial and federal enactments touching on the same activity come into conflict, Laskin advocated a fairly narrow definition of conflict. This approach allowed considerable scope for the co-existence of federal and provincial legislation on the same subject, and was in tune with the emergent cooperative federalism of post-war Canada.[27] In a paper he was invited to write on jurisdiction over water resources in Canada, he concluded that the constitution gave both the provinces and the federal government significant powers, and advocated cooperation between the two levels of government.[28]

In matters outside the heart of the division of powers in sections 91 and 92, Laskin could sometimes be more benign towards provincial authority. The case law on section 96 of the *British North America Act* was one such example. On its face the section states simply that the federal government shall appoint the judges of the provincial superior courts and those of the county and district courts. Over the years, however, the section had been interpreted so as to prevent provinces from depriving the superior courts of jurisdiction to the benefit of provincially appointed boards or tribunals such as the Workers' Compensation Board or the Ontario Municipal Board (OMB).[29] Laskin's colleague John Willis had written a brilliant article in the *Harvard Law Review* years before pointing out how the courts had transformed section 96 into a kind of common law bill of rights favouring property-owners and capital.[30] There were some risks in according too much latitude to the provinces, but also risks to the integrity of provincial administrative processes in adopting too rigid an interpretation of section 96. As with so many legal matters, the exercise involved some rather unscientific line-drawing. When Laskin was on the Supreme Court he and his colleagues would bring some clarity to the law, but in the 1950s and '60s it was in a rather sorry state.

Laskin was very critical of the Supreme Court's decision in *Toronto v. Olympia Edward Recreation Club*, in which it had struck down Ontario's scheme of property assessment for municipal taxation purposes on the basis of a section 96 argument.[31] The scheme provided numerous opportunities to challenge the initial assessment: the taxpayer could appeal first to a court of revision (provincially appointed); then to a county court judge; then to the Ontario Municipal Board; and finally to the Ontario Court of Appeal. A majority of the Supreme Court of Canada held that section 96 prevented the province from vesting final authority to determine assessability in a provincially appointed tribunal (here, the OMB), and that the provision of an appeal to the federally appointed Court of Appeal could not cure this defect. The Court based its decision on the 'frozen jurisdiction' theory that had come to be associated with section 96. If the province tried to vest in a tribunal an adjudicative function broadly similar to one exercised by superior courts at Confederation, the attempt would be struck down. Laskin the legal modernist was predictably opposed to any doctrine that acted as 'a straitjacket on adaptability and innovation in governmental administration,'[32] and wanted the provinces to be masters of their own house with regard to administrative organization on equal terms with the Dominion. He was probably also wary of the possibility of section 96 being used to challenge the constitutionality of labour boards, an issue he would explore further as a judge.[33]

All judicial interpretation of sections 91 and 92 of the *British North America Act* hinged on how the legislation in question was characterized, what its 'matter' was in legal terms. But how exactly was one to decide what the 'matter' of a particular statute was? Laskin and Toronto lawyer D.W. Mundell disagreed violently with each other over this issue in a series of articles. Mundell, who would later work for the Ontario attorney-general's office and argue a number of cases before Laskin at the Supreme Court, was almost an ideal representative of the formalist approach to law so decried by the legal modernists of the 1930s. In his legal world-view there was a clear and unbridgeable division between law and politics. The courts had always acted in an objective and apolitical way, using only the tools of logic and grammar to interpret the law, and this was as it should be. 'Matters' were simply 'objective descriptions of fields of practical human relations that may be regulated or controlled by law ... [and in another sense, the] motives for legislative action.' Deciding the 'matter' of legislation was thus a two-pronged exercise in fact-finding. It was easy enough for Laskin to critique Mundell's view by showing the extent to which judicial choice rather than a mechanical application of formulae governed the results in various cases. Laskin's own positive account of how to characterize the matter of legislation, however, was less clear. At times he seemed to take refuge in a kind of legal realism he had spent much of his career avoiding; there were, he averred, cases where there were 'few if any familiar landmarks, and the course must be set by the light of the particular judge's mind.' This begged the question of what the judge might legitimately take into account in reaching a decision in such a case.[34] In spite of these problems, Frank Scott was jubilant about the article: 'Bravo! Bravo! Your article in the UTLJ is one of the best you have ever done. You have marshalled the essential material in relentless fashion. I only wish you had been printed in the [Canadian] Bar Review so that more members of the profession might read it.'[35]

Mundell represented a segment of the Ontario bar who found Laskin's approach to law not only heretical but dangerous (Mundell found William Lederman equally heretical in his rejection of logic as the ultimate tool of classification in constitutional law). This attitude extended even to Laskin's students, as Harry Arthurs found out some years later. Arthurs was hired to teach labour at Osgoode Hall Law School but was also given to understand that he would teach constitutional law in due course. For some reason this never happened, and Arthurs discovered that Mundell had persuaded Dean Leal that he (Arthurs) was unsound because he was too 'Laskinite': too social policy-oriented and not doctrinal enough. One evening at a party, when Mundell was rather in his cups, he revealed that he had other problems with Arthurs: he was a 'sensitive Jew' (too quick to take offence) and this had held him back.[36]

The Mundell-Laskin exchange did point to a larger problem in Laskin's federalism scholarship: the absence of any clearly articulated foundation for his assumption that the Canadian constitution meant to confer broad powers on the federal government to deal with all important issues, and of any discussion of what role the provinces were meant to play, other than perhaps as large municipalities. Laskin did invoke history in support of his argument once, in his 1951 article on the Supreme Court, and he occasionally referred to the grammatical construction of sections 91 and 92, but by and large he treated it as axiomatic that the constitution leaned towards the Dominion. After Laskin had gone to the bench, Al Abel published a brilliant article entitled 'The Neglected Logic of 91 and 92,' in which he used both historical and linguistic analysis to support the general thrust of constitutional interpretation favoured by his friend. Examining the powers granted in section 91 as a whole rather than as 'a congeries of specifics,' Abel argued they constituted a 'a roll call of what the then current vulgar economic doctrine recognised as standard pressure points for effectuating financial market regulation ... The central complex of federal concerns was essentially a nineteenth-century equivalent, for the British North American community, of what the Treaty of Rome gave the European Economic Community.' By contrast, 'the life of the neighbourhood, its lawsuits and weddings, its local communications facilities, and its local forms of business organization were for the provinces to deal with.' 'Broadly,' said Abel, 'the federal "classes of subjects" had regard to Canada as an economy, the provincial to Canadians as members of societies.'[37] Unfortunately the courts were unlikely to adopt an entirely new pattern of interpretation so late in the day, and Abel's insights exerted little influence. At the time, however, Frank Scott wrote to Abel to pronounce his article 'excellent. Not even Bora at his best has come in my opinion, [close] to giving us anything so penetrating.'[38]

R.C.B. Risk has referred to Laskin's scholarship as embodying a 'model of the nation,' as opposed to a new model, 'the model of balance,' being articulated by other scholars such as William R. Lederman.[39] Lederman put forward these views in a fully developed fashion in a 1965 article but his scholarship had been heading in this direction for some time.[40] A son of the prairies, the Saskatoon-born Lederman was more receptive to provincial autonomy than Laskin, and more inclined to find merit in some of the Privy Council jurisprudence on the division of powers. Lederman's idea was simple enough: a balanced constitution was one 'that maintains and develops reasonable equilibrium between centralization and provincial autonomy in subject after subject of public concern.' He agreed with Laskin that constitutional interpretation was far from pure logic and involved a considerable amount of judicial discretion, and he agreed too that judges should consult a wider range of extrinsic evidence than they were habitually used to examining. Where logic ended, the judges would have to ask: 'Is it better for the people that this thing be done on a national level, or on a provincial level? ... Such considerations as the relative value of uniformity and regional diversity, the relative merit of local versus central administration, and the justice of minority claims, would have to be weighed.'[41]

Laskin would not have disagreed with this method of proceeding; where he differed from Lederman was in his assumption that national uniformity would normally trump claims to regional diversity. In this Laskin probably reflected the views of a majority of English-Canadians in the fifteen years after the war. But as new constitutional battles erupted in the early 1960s, and assertions of provincial autonomy once more claimed centre-stage, Lederman's theory of balance would send Laskin's model of the nation into eclipse. Laskin was keenly aware of the rising of Lederman's star, and treated him as an intrusive competitor on a terrain that was rightly his. Lederman treated Laskin with respect, including his work in an edited anthology of writings on constitutional law, but this did little to assuage Laskin's ego.[42] Their academic rivalry intensified after Laskin's appointment to the bench. He seemed to relish using his judicial position to pronounce some of Lederman's theories wrong, and engaged in very spirited arguments with him when he appeared before the court.[43] As the final blow, Lederman's casebook on constitutional law, first published in 1975, would largely supersede Laskin's.[44]

Laskin was well known to the cognoscenti of constitutional law by the mid-1950s, but it was his high-profile role in the debate over the adoption of a Bill of Rights in 1958–60 that propelled him to broader public notice. For Laskin, this debate raised fundamental issues of federalism. In a 1955 article, Laskin had argued that civil liberties were a 'matter' of legislative competence under the Canadian constitution, whereby the most fundamental civil liberties (freedom of association, speech, and religion) were exclusively assigned to federal authority. Other civil liberties, such as those associated with the legal process (freedom from arbitrary arrest and search, the right to a fair trial and to access to counsel, the procedural safeguards incorporated in criminal trials), with economic entitlements (the right to be free from arbitrary expropriation or interference with the enjoyment of property), and with equality (anti-discrimination measures and benefits derived from the welfare state) might be either a federal or provincial matter depending on the precise right involved. Laskin accepted that pursuant to the British tradition of parliamentary supremacy there were no rights beyond modification by the legislature, with the Canadian caveat that rights could only be modified by the *competent* legislature, whether federal or provincial. His attempted assignment of the political civil liberties to the federal power achieved, as Robert Sharpe has noted, their 'partial entrenchment' insofar as they lay beyond provincial competence.[45]

Laskin drew his inspiration for this view from a number of Supreme Court decisions, but especially from Justice Rand's decision in *Winner v. S.M.T. (Eastern) Ltd.*[46] Indeed, Rand's remarks in *Winner* may have been the trigger for Laskin's 1955 article. In this case Rand elaborated what W.R. Lederman later called 'the most comprehensive and definitive statement concerning the significance of Canadian citizenship that we have in the Law Reports.'[47] The context was perhaps not auspicious for this kind of declaration. In *Winner* a U.S. bus company contested the refusal of the province of New Brunswick to issue it a permit to carry on its international and interprovincial bus service. The province claimed it could do so as part of its jurisdiction to regulate provincial highways. No province, Rand replied, could prevent a Canadian citizen resident in another province from entering or leaving (except for temporary reasons such as health), or deprive a citizen from the means of working so as to force his or her exit, or deny a citizen the use of provincial highways, which would 'destroy the fundamental liberty of action of the individual.' For Rand, Canadian citizenship embodied 'certain inherent or constitutive characteristics of members of the Canadian public, and it can be modified, defeated or destroyed, as for instance by outlawry, only by Parliament.'[48] From here it was only a short step for Laskin to declare that the political liberties permitting full participation in national political life were themselves attributes of Canadian citizenship which could not be abridged by provincial action. Later, he suggested that this same conception might operate to prevent provinces from incorporating racially discriminatory categories in their legislation, or from passing change of name legislation; one's name, he argued, was a fundamental aspect of citizenship.[49] This universalist conception of citizenship went hand in hand with the expanding welfare state of the post-war years, and continued to anchor Laskin's legal and political thought.

This complex and layered approach to civil liberties, with political liberties elevated to a higher plane and other rights subjected to a more fragmented regime, put Laskin somewhat at odds with friends and colleagues who preferred to see the constitutional entrenchment of all important rights, in order to place them beyond the reach of both federal and provincial legislatures. Frank Scott advocated such an approach in his 1959 Plaunt Lectures, but in reviewing them Laskin declared that he took 'a different view of the values involved in the civil liberty categories set up by Professor Scott, and would not agree that they are all equally deserving of constitutional enshrinement. Those that are, for example, the political freedoms, fall in any event within federal competence.'[50] For Laskin the 'political freedoms' were part of the federal constitution alone; their entrenchment could be achieved simply by Ottawa asking London to amend the *British North America Act* accordingly, without provincial consent.

A conference held in Ottawa to celebrate the tenth anniversary of the Universal Declaration of Human Rights in December 1958 provided Laskin with a platform to attack the first draft of the Bill of Rights presented that fall to Parliament. A variety of topics were discussed at the conference by a sparkling list of delegates who included Gérard Pelletier, Pierre Elliot Trudeau, Claude Jodoin, John Humphrey, and Frank Scott. This may well have been the first meeting between Laskin and Trudeau, who would soon find they shared a common constitutional vision. The Bill of Rights was not meant to be the principal focus of the conference, but it generated the most controversy and media interest. Much of the criticism centred on the exclusion of social and economic rights from the Bill, and on its form as a mere statute rather than a constitutional amendment. Laskin was not among those issuing a clarion call for a constitutional amendment, but he seized the occasion to 'cut the bill into bits, [calling it] a timid and tepid affirmation of a political and social tradition which for all practical purposes carries us no further than the prevailing tradition in unitary Great Britain.'[51] He concluded that '[i]t would be better that no Bill be proposed so that the common-law tradition be maintained through the unifying force of the Supreme Court of Canada.'[52] Laskin provided an advance copy of his talk to the Department of Justice, where it generated some concern. MP David Walker, parliamentary secretary to the minister of justice, had been deputed to enter the lions' den at the conference and defend Diefenbaker's bill. He asked the department for some material with which to reply to Laskin's critiques but deputy minister W.R. Jackett was not very helpful. 'I do not know Professor Laskin so there is nothing personal intended when I say that I find [his] views ... as difficult to get hold of as those put forward by other academic lawyers.'[53] Walker's lacklustre defence of the bill did not satisfy many at the conference.

When Laskin revised his talk for publication in the *Canadian Bar Review*, he remained highly critical but moderated his conclusion noticeably. Although beginning the article with the 'no bill rather than this bill' position he had taken at the conference, he concluded with a much blander statement: the proposed Bill of Rights might operate as no more than a 'political charter,' but this was 'certainly not without value, and there is always the comfort of the continuing vigilance of the courts as evidenced by the course of recent decisions.'[54] For someone who had traditionally been so critical of the courts Laskin's confidence may seem inconsistent, but his faith had been somewhat restored by the Supreme Court's civil liberties decisions of the 1950s. It was no coincidence that the decisions he most respected, *Boucher v. the King*,[55] *Saumur v. City of Quebec*,[56] *Switzman v. Elbling and Attorney-General of Quebec*,[57] and *Roncarelli v. Duplessis*,[58] all featured important contributions by Ivan Rand.[59] In *Boucher* the Court had decided that the law of sedition could only be used against someone who incited violent revolution against the state, as opposed to hurling abuse at the Catholic Church, as the defendant had done. In *Saumur* a Quebec city by-law requiring police permission for the distribution of any pamphlet was held not to apply to Jehovah's Witnesses distributing religious literature, while in *Roncarelli* the spiteful revocation by the premier of Quebec of a liquor licence held by a Jehovah's Witness restauranteur was held to be unauthorized by the licensing legislation. In *Switzman* the Supreme Court held the Quebec 'Padlock Act,' aimed at suppressing communist literature, *ultra vires* as a matter properly within the federal power over criminal law. In all of these decisions the Court had used common law techniques of interpretation to protect free speech and freedom of religion, in the absence of a bill of rights. Laskin's unbounded respect for Ivan Rand was revealed in the uncharacteristic accolade he accorded a judge 'shortly to retire from membership of a court which he has graced with dignity, humanity and a profundity in scholarship which mark him as the greatest expositor of a democratic public law which Canada has known.'[60] Unfortunately, Diefenbaker's appointments to the Supreme Court would give Laskin cause to regret the confidence he had placed in that body, as the trend of the 1950s decisions petered out with Rand's departure.

In spite of his initial scepticism Laskin appears to have gradually warmed to the Bill of Rights. In *Robertson and Rosetanni v. The Queen*, a challenge to federal Sunday observance legislation on the ground of freedom of religion as guaranteed by the Bill of Rights, the Supreme Court interpreted freedom of religion narrowly and denied the challenge, but made some observations Laskin found of interest nonetheless.[61] In a case comment, Laskin noted that the decision 'suggests that so far at least as concerns federal legislation in force at the date of its enactment, the Bill of Rights is more than an interpretation statute which must yield to a contrary expression.'[62] This left open the possibility that in future a statutory provision irreconcilable with the Bill of Rights could be declared inoperative to the extent of the inconsistency, as indeed happened some years later in *Drybones*.[63]

By the later 1950s Laskin's position as the dean of Canadian constitutional law was unassailable. Frank Scott's activities had shifted towards advocacy and away from scholarship in the 1950s, while William Lederman was still relatively new in the field and would do his best work in the 1960s and '70s. Laskin's 1955 article on the protection of civil liberties was read by Prime Minister Diefenbaker, who solicited a memorandum from him on the relevant Supreme Court decisions when he was planning to introduce the Bill of Rights. Eddie Goodman was the intermediary for this communication, and he also urged Diefenbaker to meet with Laskin before appearing in the House of Commons to present the first draft of the Bill of Rights in 1958. There is some evidence that Diefenbaker even considered Laskin for a judicial position in 1958, but was put off by his criticism of the Bill of Rights.[64] Later, Laskin's views on the proposed constitutional amending formula would be solicited by those close to Prime Minister Lester Pearson for his consideration.[65]

Just as Laskin deplored the anaemic Bill of Rights proposed by Diefenbaker, so he disapproved of the amending formula for the Canadian constitution put forward by Diefenbaker's minister of justice, Davie Fulton, on 1 December 1961. He had first of all attacked the private nature of the constitutional consultations between Fulton and the provincial attorneys-general. At the Canadian Association of Law Teachers conference in June 1961, Laskin, Albert Mayrand, and George Curtis drafted a resolution requesting both public hearings and the public release of the proposals under consideration by the politicians. Fulton replied that the provincial ministers had only agreed to *in camera* meetings. While admitting that the 'uniqueness of Canada's position as a federal state with a written constitution which contains no provision for its amendment [had] worn thin within Canada,' Laskin thought it would be 'most regrettable' to adopt an amending procedure that was 'legally as well as politically rigid.' Fulton's proposal required unanimity for all matters touching provincial powers or the use of the English or French language. For Laskin, such inflexibility was 'too high a price to pay for what would be a rather empty trapping of independence.'[66] His law teaching colleagues across Canada agreed, and unanimously supported a resolution disapproving of Fulton's draft bill at the annual CALT conference in June 1962. Laskin was no more positive about the very similar Fulton-Favreau formula that emerged in 1964.[67] For someone who had championed the cause of responsive law all his adult life, the freezing of the constitution by means of a unanimity requirement was totally wrong-headed.

Laskin's pre-eminence in constitutional law caused him to be sought out by groups, governments, and lawyers in private practice. When amending the constitution appeared on the agenda in the early 1960s, the Liberal caucus committee on the constitution invited him to address them. Rookie MP Eugene Whelan from Windsor asked him, semiseriously, how southwestern Ontario could go about seceding from Canada. According to Whelan's recollection Laskin replied in a similar vein: 'there is only one way you can do it – and don't forget I'm from northern Ontario and I don't like Toronto any better than you do – and that's by bloody revolution. But you look like the type that could lead a bloody revolution and if you're successful, I'll draw up the constitution for your new province.'[68]

Possible secession, though not from Canada, was also the root of one of Laskin's most satisfying international contacts. Caribbean lawyer Fred Phillips was cabinet secretary to the Federation of the West Indies, established in 1958 to bring together Jamaica, Trinidad and Tobago, Barbados, Grenada, and six smaller islands in a confederal union prior to independence. In 1959 he was sent to Toronto for some months to study Canada's federal constitution with Bora Laskin, paying particular attention to the position of Quebec because of Jamaica's open threats of secession. Fortunately their personal connection proved to be more durable than the Federation, which dissolved in 1962 when Jamaica withdrew after a referendum. Phillips faced yet another secession crisis in 1967 as governor of St Kitts-Nevis-Anguilla, when the minuscule island of Anguilla rebelled against the union and ultimately achieved independence. The two men carried on a regular correspondence until Laskin's death, and Sir Fred (as he became), a frequent visitor to Canada, often dropped in on Bora after his appointment to the Supreme Court.[69]

This review of Laskin's two decades of federalism scholarship raises a number of questions and problems. Why did Laskin so consistently prefer national authority over provincial autonomy in federalism disputes? In spite of his constant references to evolving social conditions, why did his repertoire of scholarly ideas on this subject remain so static? What influence did Laskin's views have on the course of Canadian constitutional scholarship and on federalism jurisprudence? On the first question especially, Laskin himself left little to assist in understanding his position.

Laskin was very much a man of his generation in his preference for federal over provincial authority in most fields of state action, and it is necessary to return to the 1930s for a moment to understand the roots of his strong commitment to federal power. Even before the notorious Privy Council decisions of 1937, intellectuals in English Canada had come to regard the federal system as a 'major impediment to the adoption of progressive policies.'[70] It seemed to them that 'rather than one government losing powers that the other gained, the courts in this period deprived both orders of government of powers that simply disappeared into a constitutional "black hole."'[71] Laskin was fond of quoting a saying of Frank Scott: 'provincial autonomy means national inactivity, and the more we have of one, the more we have of the other.'[72] And so, while hope rose in America with the adoption of the New Deal, as Laskin witnessed at Harvard, in Canada things went from bad to worse. In 1939 it was still the case that one-third of Canadians lacked sufficient income to purchase adequate food.[73] And the character of provincial governments in the 1930s – especially Mitch Hepburn's Ontario, Maurice Duplessis's Quebec, and William Aberhart's Alberta – was hardly such as to inspire confidence in a somewhat left-of-centre young intellectual. Among the group of English-Canadian intellectuals active in the 1930s and 1940s whom Douglas Owram has called 'the government generation,' it was an article of faith that only the federal government could carry out the large-scale economic planning (for the socialists) or coordination (for the liberals) required to modernize Canada.[74] This group of intellectuals saw their agenda confirmed in the Rowell-Sirois Report of 1940, with its centralizing thrust and preoccupation with national management of the economy.[75] It is no coincidence that extracts from the Report on the nature of Confederation provided the introductory pages of Laskin's text on constitutional law in all three editions edited by him.

These intellectuals welcomed the assumption by the federal government of virtually complete authority during the war years, and feared the return of provincial control after the war. Writing in 1943, the historian A.R.M. Lower worried that the 'most serious threat to any orderly kind of future for Canada lies in the nature of our Constitution.' Provincial power over property and civil rights 'will make short work of our war-time measures and will very quickly reduce us to the bedlam of provincialism again. Can any sane person believe that the competing authorities, mostly parochial, will give us anything but anarchy leading perhaps to revolution?'[76] As Louis-Philippe Pigeon observed drily, 'autonomy is deprecated here as a mark of insanity, but no other argument is advanced.'[77] It was an article of faith on the part of Anglo-Canadian modernists that the larger unit of government was to be preferred to the smaller, just as large units of industrial production had vastly increased the productive potential of humanity as compared to household and craft-based modes of production.

Seen in the light of his experience of the 1930s and early 1940s, Laskin's tirade in '"Peace, Order and Good Government" Re-examined' in 1947 becomes more understandable. The gap between 'legal justice' and 'social justice' had never been greater than in the 1930s, and

Laskin sought to realign the two as part of his legal modernist project. The inability of Depression-era provincial governments to undertake the programs required to regulate big business, ameliorate the condition of labour, and build the modern welfare state was so obvious to Laskin as to require no extended demonstration. As well, the *Trade Unionists' Handbook* Laskin had prepared for the WEA in 1939 contained the germ of the idea that classical federalism was a recipe for the continuance of laissez-faire. He would have seen that large business interests consistently opposed federal jurisdiction in economic affairs so as to be able to deal with more tractable provincial governments.[78] It is possible too that his later work was influenced by the modernization theorists of the 1950s and early 1960s, who argued that regional and linguistic conflicts could be expected to wither away under the impact of increasing prosperity and convergence of lifestyles in industrial society. J.A. Corry had argued in 1958 that traditional federalism might be dead as citizens developed new loyalties beyond those to their provinces.[79] The need for federal intervention seemed correspondingly obvious, and thus the main question for Laskin was how to reorient constitutional interpretation to achieve that goal. We may think of Laskin as an 'instrumental federalist' rather than an 'ideological federalist.' Just as law was an instrument rather than an end in itself, so was federalism. If the ultimate goal of all human organization, as Laskin saw it, was the enlargement of liberty – understood as positive support for the human capacity of self-expression – then an expansive federal government, he reasoned, was most likely to conduce to that end.

Laskin's modernism was also of a piece with his preference for city life. Bora Laskin was a very urban person, who never displayed any particular interest in or understanding of Canada beyond its cities. Even his birthplace, Fort William, was self-consciously a city, albeit a small one. When he became active in the labour movement, it was the new urban industrial unions that interested him. In music his tastes ran to jazz, in religion he was on the most liberal wing of Reform Judaism. Modernism was a product of industrial society and urban life and for Laskin, cities were the crucibles of Canadian values for the future. The city represented freedom, individuality, privacy, prosperity, and progress, while rural and small-town Canada stood for a benighted localism better relegated to the past. Under the Canadian constitution, the provinces represented these local interests and their legislatures were dominated by rural constituencies. For Laskin, only the federal government had the resources, the vision, and the power to implement a modernist agenda for Canada, to get beyond local prejudices and local magnates. Ironically, Laskin worked quite productively with the Ontario government on legislation with regard to two of his principal interests, labour relations and human rights, but this experience seems not to have affected his views on the proper nature of Canadian federalism. In his defence, it may be observed that it was only in the 1960s, well into Laskin's middle age, that the two Quiet Revolutions in Quebec and New Brunswick showed how thoroughly and quickly provincial administrations could modernize their societies once the political will to do so existed.

Laskin's nationally oriented federalism was of a piece with the tremendous surge of post-war nationalism in Canada, which in the legal sphere saw a rapid shift away from British traditions and influences and towards an emphasis on Canadian conditions and American models. Unlike W.P.M. Kennedy, who had always stressed Canada's position within the Empire and the emerging Commonwealth, Laskin was concerned almost exclusively with Canada's internal development. Post-war English-Canadian nationalism posed grave problems for the future of relations with French Canada, however. The mantra 'Canadian law for Canadians' meant defining what a Canadian was, and while it was one thing to do so in the context of the new *Citizenship Act* of 1947, it was another to do so for more ordinary domestic purposes. Paradoxically, incorporating Quebec under the rubric of 'British justice' had proved to be less problematic than subjecting it to 'Canadian justice.' 'British justice' was a set of ideals and conventions sufficiently vague that it could be rendered part of Quebec's legal order without appearing threatening. 'Canadian justice' promised to be more centralizing, more officious, and more alien. It seemed to be premised on an abstract Canadian who in fact was a thinly disguised white Anglo-Saxon non-Catholic. The English-Canadian nationalism of the post-war years often appeared to be based on the European model, with all its baggage of unity, intolerance, and assimilation of 'others.'

There was little in Laskin's published work to dissociate him from this position. Admitting that 'some flexibility is desirable in the exercise of national authority,' he accepted that Quebec might need some particular guarantees regarding language and culture. Nonetheless, he admonished that 'federal-provincial contention about the reach of law-making power should not be embarrassed by interposing ethnic-linguistic-cultural qualifications which would make the central government less one for the people of a particular Province than it is for the people of other Provinces.'[80] When the Quiet Revolution put Quebec's demands back on the table, Laskin's constitutional vision had little to offer. At the 1964 meeting of the Learned Societies in Charlottetown, Paul-André Crépeau and C.B. Macpherson, presidents of the CALT and the Canadian Political Science Association respectively, solicited papers for a day-long joint discussion of the future of Canadian federalism. The papers, subsequently published as *The Future of Canadian Federalism/L'Avenir du fédéralisme canadien,* included an outstanding essay by Pierre Elliot Trudeau on 'Federalism, Nationalism, and Reason,' as well as significant legal contributions by W.R. Lederman, Jean Beetz, Jacques-Yvan Morin, and Edward McWhinney. Laskin did not contribute, nor, more importantly, were his ideas given more than glancing reference by the essayists.

Laskin reviewed this volume as 'a recent defector from the academic world,' calling it a 'long overdue association of economists, political scientists, and lawyers in bringing their particular skills to bear on a common theme so relevant to all of them. Federalism is economics and politics and law and much more [including sociology and philosophy].' He singled out Trudeau's paper as 'a fundamental one, in my view, the most searching of all in its attempt to examine, in a federal frame of reference, the meaning of state and of nation, the role of emotion and of reason applied to those conceptions, and their political and economic consequences in Canada.'[81] There is no little irony in both these comments. If the cooperation of the various disciplinary specialists was 'long overdue' it would seem that Laskin himself should bear some of the blame. Given his stature in the field of constitutional law, he could surely have organized such a gathering if he had wished to do so. And while Laskin may have thought that Trudeau's vision mirrored his own – it did, in many respects – his essay contained both a critique of the kind of English-Canadian nationalism of which Bora Laskin was an exemplar, and a far more aggressive statement of the need for Canadian federalism to respond to the French fact than Laskin could have approved.

Laskin's attitudes on interdisciplinary scholarship were somewhat conflicted. He always encouraged scholars from other disciplines who wanted to do work on the law, but regarded the boundaries between disciplines as virtually inviolate and seldom incorporated insights from other disciplines into his own work. His relationship with a young professor in the department of political economy at the University of Toronto revealed his views. Peter Russell was interested in doing some work on the Canadian judiciary – a very unfashionable subject among political scientists in the late 1950s. He went with some trepidation to speak to Bora Laskin, who welcomed him unreservedly; intrigued, he sat in on Laskin's classes in 1960–1 and attended John Willis's the next year. By this point Russell had decided he wanted to do a law degree and went to discuss it with Laskin. At the interview, the senior professor suddenly became very stern and discouraged Russell from enrolling. When the puzzled young academic asked why, Laskin replied, 'if you do that you will lose your own particular perspective,' as if acquiring a law degree would somehow emasculate a political scientist. (Perhaps he was thinking of the old saw that political science is constitutional law with the difficult bits left out.) Russell took his advice and continued to work on Canadian courts for the next forty years, to the great benefit of the scholarly community.[82] He and Laskin remained friends even as Russell's own views on federalism shifted markedly away from Laskin's 'model of the nation' and much more towards Lederman's 'model of balance.'

It may seem curious, for someone who constantly urged courts to be responsive to changing social conditions, that Laskin's constitutional ideas remained so static over many decades. But he was not alone. Most of the 'government generation,' including Frank Scott, Brooke Claxton, and Eugene Forsey, retained the same basic constitutional commitments, Forsey famously remarking that he became a Pierre Trudeau Liberal because he was a John A. Macdonald Conservative.[83] Laskin's ideas about the necessity of a vigorous federal power seem to have been imprinted in his legal DNA by his personal experience of the 1930s and the critiques of the scholars active in that decade. In 1969, while paying tribute to Frank Scott at an event honouring his seventieth birthday, Laskin admitted that he 'owe[d] him much for the sense of direction that he has given to my own work in Canadian constitutional law.' After quoting a passage from Scott's 1937 critique of the Privy Council's New Deal decisions, one condemning the law lords as 'too remote, too little trained in our law, too casually selected, and [with] too short a tenure' to serve as a fit court of final appeal for Canadian matters, Laskin observed: 'I had just graduated in law at the time and still recall the impact that this piece of writing made upon me.'[84] He continued to press for an expanded conception of federal power and was heartened by some Supreme Court of Canada decisions in that direction in the later 1950s, even though for some observers the main problem in Canada at the time was over-centralization, not excessive provincial autonomy.

Laskin must have been aware that the federal government was hardly the hamstrung, impotent giant depicted in his scholarship. As Lester Pearson's close adviser Tom Kent observed, 'federal-provincial relations were no longer a matter, even primarily, of ensuring that each layer of government was free and able to be effective in its jurisdiction. Respect for jurisdictions remained essential, but as a base for making possible the consultation and cooperation necessary in order to ensure that what federal and provincial governments did in their respective spheres would meld in a mutually supportive way.' In fiscal and administrative terms the country had remained comparatively centralized after the end of the war. Before 1939, the federal government levied 46 per cent of Canadian taxation, the provinces 54 per cent. This balance shifted dramatically in favour of the centre during the war years, and Ottawa did not quickly give up its fiscal dominance; in 1962 the federal share still remained at 63 per cent versus 37 per cent for the provinces and municipalities. Flush with the tribute derived from postwar prosperity, Ottawa modernized quickly while provincial governments 'remained by comparison old-fashioned [in the 1950s], their public services ... poor in professional qualifications, their politics largely parochial.'[85]

This contrast may go some way to explaining Laskin's seeming distrust of the provinces and his continued favouring of federal authority, especially in economic matters. The federal government represented modernity in a way the provinces never could. It had the money, the capacity, and the vision to drag Canada into the modern era, where prosperity and security would be assured for all under the rule of law. Laskin would work with the Ontario government where necessary, as on labour law and human rights issues, but he seems to have regarded provincial politics as essentially narrow and unenlightened. Where others looked at Canadian regionalism and saw a fruitful and admirable diversity of human experience, Laskin saw petty fiefdoms, parish pump politics, and constricted horizons. Whether he could hold in check these strongly held views when appointed to the court acting as the final arbiter of federalism disputes in Canada, remained to be seen.

PART III

Extra-curricular

10

Arbitrator

In 1944 Bora Laskin observed that 'we entered this war with a system of labour relations that showed little, if any, advance over that in vogue in 1914.'[1] The provinces had not exactly raced to copy the 1935 *Wagner Act*; some had experimented with laws providing more protection for collective bargaining, but none had gone so far as to force employers to bargain with unions enjoying majority support among their workers, or to create state machinery for certifying unions or enforcing collective agreements. Laskin commented at a later date, '[a]s a matter of history, collective agreements in Canada had no legal force in their own right until the advent of compulsory collective bargaining legislation. Our Courts refused to assume original jurisdiction for their enforcement and placed them outside of the legal framework within which contractual obligations of individuals were administered.'[2] Meanwhile, the federal government invoked jurisdictional reasons to justify its inaction. The wartime demand for continuous production finally shifted the balance of power in favour of labour, as a wave of strikes in 1941–2 demonstrated. Dissatisfaction with existing labour policies, especially Mackenzie King's wage controls, provided the CCF with such electoral heft that the traditional parties had to take notice. In 1943 Ontario enacted a *Collective Bargaining Act* similar to the *Wagner Act*, except that its administration was confided to a division of the High Court rather than an administrative tribunal. Finally, the King government passed the order-in-council known as PC 1003, the War-time Labour Relations Regulations, in February 1944.

While directly applicable only to federally regulated industries, PC 1003 allowed the provinces to opt into its provisions, which most of them did. After the war they passed legislation copying its provisions, which continue to anchor Canadian labour law. PC 1003 was 'a unique amalgamation of three distinctive elements: compelling employers to bargain with unions, compelling conciliation, and compelling grievance arbitration.'³ Arbitration, the resolution of disputes by a neutral third party chosen by them, is one of the oldest forms of dispute resolution known to humankind, much older than the common law itself. It had a respectable history in North American labour relations, at a time when collective agreements were not considered enforceable in the courts. In the United States, the coal, printing, and clothing industries all adopted arbitration protocols in the decade before the First World War. In Canada, the building and needle trades were early devotees. In 1919 the newly created employers' association in the Toronto men's clothing industry negotiated its first agreement with the trade unions, outlawing all strikes and work stoppages during its currency. Instead, all disputes were to be settled by arbitration panels comprising employer and labour representatives, presided over by an impartial chair. Laskin's mentor Jacob Finkelman often served in this latter capacity in the 1930s and '40s, and the industry was distinguished by an absence of major strikes even during the Depression.

Arbitration is a dispute resolution process perched on the cusp of formal and informal law, of state and civil society. Once the process was legislatively mandated in labour matters, and arbitral decisions made enforceable in the same manner as judgments of the superior courts, arbitration might appear to be wholly state law. Yet arbitrators are not bound by precedent, at least not officially, nor by the same rules of procedure as courts. They are free to recognize local custom and to invoke considerations of equity and policy to an extent unusual among superior court judges. In short, arbitrators are local law-makers in a particular trade or industry. Labour arbitration gave Bora Laskin ample scope to implement his vision of legal modernism, to carry out the kind of sensitive balancing of interests advocated by the scholars of the 1930s. While publicly identified with the cause of labour, Laskin did not discount the interests of the employer in making a legitimate profit and in organizing production. He would quickly achieve an enviable reputation for impartiality in a highly adversarial domain.

PC 1003 harnessed the ancient process of arbitration to the modern goal of achieving industrial peace. It distinguished between two types of disputes and provided that arbitration would be mandatory for one but not the other. With regard to grievances involving the rights guaranteed to both parties under an existing collective agreement, PC 1003 required every collective agreement to include 'a procedure for final settlement, without stoppage of work, ... of differences concerning its interpretation or violation' – a clause which has become a permanent feature of post-war provincial and federal legislation. Grievance arbitration for such 'rights' disputes was thus mandatory, but 'interest' disputes involving issues such as wage scales or seniority rights, which are on the table during the bargaining leading up to a collective agreement, did not have to be submitted to arbitration. For interest disputes, PC 1003 set up a two-stage resolution process. First, conciliation would be attempted with the assistance of a representative of the minister of labour. If this proved unsuccessful, the parties moved to the second stage: the appointment of a tripartite conciliation board, with one labour nominee, one employer nominee, and an impartial chair, which would report to the minister of labour on how it thought the dispute should be resolved. The minister would have the report published, making the public aware of the merits of the parties' positions, but neither the minister nor the board could impose a settlement. Fourteen days after receipt of the report, the union would be able to strike, or the employer to lock out, if agreement had not been reached in the interim. The philosophy underlying this process was that after the issues had been publicly aired, the parties would be encouraged to conclude an agreement along the lines recommended by the conciliation board.

It was in this conciliation process under PC 1003 that Bora Laskin gained his first exposure to the resolution of labour disputes. He sat as a union nominee on some thirty-two conciliation boards between August 1944 and the end of 1946, twenty-two of them in 1945. Although the issues were different from those he later faced as an arbitrator, the conciliation process itself was very similar to labour arbitration. Labour and management representatives, sometimes lawyers and sometimes not, would present the facts and make their arguments before a tripartite panel, and the chair would write up a report (in the case of conciliation) or decision (in the case of arbitration). The majority ruled in both places, and dissents by one of the nominees were common.[4]

There was no shortage of lawyers willing to serve as employer nominees on conciliation boards, and Laskin would serve on panels with prominent counsel such as J.S.D. Tory, George Gale, and J.J. Robinette. The pool of suitable union nominees was tiny in comparison, comprising a few lawyers sympathetic to labour, such as F.A. Brewin, and the occasional progressive clergyman. Someone like Bora Laskin was a godsend to labour in its hour of need. His friend Drummond Wren was heavily involved with the United Auto Workers (UAW) and often presented the union's case before the boards. Wren recommended Laskin's appointment as labour nominee on various conciliation boards before which the UAW appeared, and no doubt supplied his name to other union officials looking for nominees. Laskin in turn recommended Caesar Wright as chair of the conciliation board whenever he could. Usually the nominees could not agree and the minister was obliged to appoint the chair, almost invariably a county court or supreme court judge. For Bora Laskin, the non-practising lawyer, this work provided a bridge to the Ontario bar and judiciary he would not otherwise have had. It also contributed powerfully to his reputation as an academic who understood intimately the power relations the law sought to regulate, and who could be trusted by the corporate elite in spite of his identification with labour.

The impression Laskin made on the corporate bar was already in evidence during the bitter Ford strike at Windsor in the fall of 1945. Laskin was the union nominee on a conciliation panel appointed to try and avert a strike, but its chances of success were nearly nil. Ford was determined to break the union, while the UAW was equally set on achieving a closed shop and compulsory dues check-off. A majority of Laskin and the chair, Justice G.B. O'Connor of Alberta, recommended a voluntary check-off and did not recommend a closed shop. The president of the UAW union local tore up the report on 12 September and announced the strike. Ninety-nine days would pass before the parties agreed to arbitration on 20 December. Supreme Court judge Ivan Rand was appointed sole arbitrator and the results of his inquiry did much to shape labour relations in the post-war world. Rand did not recommend a closed shop but he did require a compulsory dues check-off from all plant workers, whether union members or not, thus providing a clear incentive for workers to join the union if they wished to have some say over how their dues were spent. The 'Rand formula' spread rapidly throughout Canada and made the judge a heroic figure in the eyes of legal academics such as Laskin and Frank Scott.[5]

In the course of the inquiry, when the parties were discussing the identity of arbitrators to be appointed under collective agreements, George Burt complained about the practice of appointing county court judges who were perceived by labour to be unduly pro-employer.

According to Burt it was not fair to put the judge in that position: 'if he takes the side of the union he probably has to play golf all by himself because those interested in the company's side will not play with him any more.' Rand asked whether it would be preferable for the minister to appoint 'jurists of repute,' to which Ford's counsel J.B. Aylesworth readily agreed. Rand proffered the name of Caesar Wright as an example, to which Aylesworth added that of 'Morris [Bora] Laskin' as 'another jurist of repute.' Aylesworth admitted that Laskin's ideas were 'markedly different' from his own, but admitted he had 'never left a board of conciliation in which Mr. Laskin was the union nominee without feeling that I had a fair hearing by him ... [W]hen it came to dealing with a set of known facts I felt particularly confident that no matter how sympathetic he might be toward labour, he would approach the facts absolutely impartially.'[6] For Laskin to have convinced Aylesworth, the dean of corporate labour lawyers in Ontario (and a future colleague on the Ontario Court of Appeal), of his impartiality was no mean feat; it ensured that Laskin would play a major role in shaping the labour law of the post-war period.

About half of Laskin's conciliations involved the United Auto Workers, but he was nominated by many other unions, from large international unions such as the United Steelworkers of America, the United Electrical, Radio and Machine Workers of America, and the United Gas, Coke and Chemical Workers, to smaller local unions such as the Textile Workers Committee of Dunnville and the Paper Box and Specialty Workers' Union of Leaside. The hearings were usually held on site in cities and towns across southern and eastern Ontario. The automotive industry brought Laskin to Windsor, Chatham, and Oshawa a number of times (Ford and Chrysler), the farm implement industry to Brantford (Cockshutt and Canadian Car and Foundry), the home appliance industry to Hamilton (Westinghouse), and the shipbuilding industry to Midland (Midland Shipyards). Disputes at smaller companies brought him to Kitchener, Sarnia, Dunnville, Wallaceburg, and Belleville.

The most contentious cases were those in which the employer refused to grant the union's demand for a 'union shop,' that is, where union membership would be required of all employees in that particular plant. Wright and Laskin sat together on a number of such cases and Wright's decisions may be regarded as expressing a jointly held philosophy on such matters. The two academics believed that the demand for a union shop should not be granted automatically, but rather that it should be 'earned' by the union demonstrating its stability and respon-

sibility over a relatively lengthy period. Thus in one of the first conciliations in which he and Laskin sat, Wright urged the union to drop its
claim for a union shop in view of the fact that it had been the employees' representative for less than a year.[7] In a unanimous October 1945
conciliation, chair Justice W.D. Roach of the Ontario High Court put
the doctrine in theological terms: 'Management should not be asked
nor expected to rely upon "faith alone" but should have before it
something in the nature of "good works" on the part of the Union'
before being asked to accept a union shop clause.[8] In two other conciliations dealing with Oshawa companies, Wright and Laskin recommended
that the company accept a union shop clause where the union represented 82 and 100 per cent of the company's employees respectively,
and had done so for a period of seven or eight years. The approach to
union security developed in these conciliations depended on highly
context-specific assessments, but the bottom line was clear: unions that
behaved themselves would be rewarded with greater security than
those which acted unpredictably and uncooperatively.[9]

As the war approached its end, industrial plants sought a return to
'normalcy' by replacing the women they had employed during the war
years with male veterans. The Corbin Lock Co. of Belleville, for example, had employed 18 women out of a staff of some 200 at the
outbreak of the war, but counted 117 women in a similarly sized
workforce in 1945. The union and the company agreed to a clause that
would allow the company to lay off up to 30 per cent of the women
employed in 1945 in jobs formerly done by men, but disagreed over the
exact nature of the seniority rights to be enjoyed by those women who
were kept on. The conciliation board, comprising Caesar Wright, Bora
Laskin, and George Gale (a future chief justice of Ontario), agreed
unanimously on a clause that preserved some plantwide seniority rights
for remaining female employees, but without commenting on the larger
issue of the significant displacement of women by men at the plant.
What stands out in several conciliations on this issue is the assumption
that the women would be replaced, and the absence of any evidence of
the views of the women themselves. In Corbin Lock, the company was
represented by three men, the union by two men, including Drummond
Wren, but there was no evidence as to whether the female employees
acquiesced or not in their proposed replacement.[10]

Virtually all the conciliations on which Laskin sat favoured the union's
position on all issues except that of the union shop, making it unnecessary for him to dissent – in fact many of the conciliations on which he

sat featured dissents by the employer nominee. However, on occasion he was outvoted on an issue and recorded a dissent. The first of these arose in the conciliation between the UAW and the Dominion Glass Company of Wallaceburg. The majority recommended that the union accept the company's position prohibiting union activities on company premises or during working hours. Laskin agreed that the union activities could be banned during working hours, but felt that the company could 'hardly expect its employees to maintain a frigid silence during lunch hour or other periods when they are not on tours of duty, even though they may be on the company's premises.' He would also have recommended a clause allowing preferential seniority for union committee-men in connection with lay-offs, so as 'to dissipate any fears which the committee-men might have relative to their complete independence in discharging their duties on behalf of their fellow employees.'[11]

Laskin reserved his strongest language for his dissent in a 1946 conciliation involving wages at Toronto's Wellesley Hospital. Laundry workers were asking for an increase from $80 per month for a 48-hour week ($960 per annum) to $90, or $1,080 per annum. By way of comparison, the Welfare Council of Toronto had determined that a minimum of $154.17 per month at 1944 prices would be required to support a family of five including three pre-teenaged children.[12] The hospital had experienced a loss in 1945 and argued that it could not afford the increase after already increasing wages by $10 per month in August of that year. With only one exception, all other Toronto hospitals paid the same rates for such work. Laskin asserted that he could not concur 'in a conclusion that denies to underpaid workers some encouragement towards an approach to a living and respectable wage.' If the hospital were a business, he continued, 'it would deserve little sympathy in pleading inability to pay as a reason for asking its employees to subsidize its operations through the acceptance of substandard wages.' Nor should the hospital's charitable status insulate it from paying reasonable wages. 'Charity may well begin at home in this instance,' Laskin observed tartly. He urged the hospital to review its general wage structure 'in order to ascertain whether some sacrifice to charity ought not to be made by classifications of employees whose present wages are well above subsistence level.' Bluma Laskin's son was not afraid to speak out on behalf of underpaid service workers at the bottom of the employment hierarchy. The reaction was vintage Laskin: where the result was so offensive to social justice and human dignity, it was necessary to work backwards and change the institutions involved, not just accept the status quo.[13]

Occasionally the conciliation process involved more than a hearing about defined areas of disagreement. In a case involving an Oshawa auto parts company, both parties accused each other of failing to bargain in good faith and had not agreed on anything. In effect, the board was asked to negotiate a renewal agreement. The company then invited Laskin to sit in on the negotiations. Once the company's proposals were properly explained, the union was agreeable. In the end the only issues left for conciliation were union shop and voluntary dues check-off clauses, both of which the majority of the board (Wright and Laskin, as it turned out) recommended that the company accept. Such 'inside' experience of the negotiating process proved highly valuable when Laskin began presiding over labour arbitrations after the war.[14]

Laskin's service on wartime conciliation boards provided him with the experience and contacts necessary to kick-start his grievance arbitration practice after the war. It was not easy to find parties acceptable to the captains of both labour and industry, and the demand for arbitration rose quickly during the post-war boom in Canada's industrial heartland. *Faute de mieux*, county court judges tended to serve frequently as chairs of arbitration boards but were not popular with labour. University professors with an interest in labour relations were an obvious choice, but as of the late 1940s there was only a handful of candidates in the entire province of Ontario: Wright, Laskin, and Jacob Finkelman. The three of them dominated the field, accounting for 40 per cent of all arbitrations reported in volume one of *Labour Arbitration Cases* (1947–9), for example. Laskin led the trio with sixteen reported arbitrations, Wright following with eleven and Finkelman with ten. Virtually all the rest were written by county court judges and two High Court judges, J.A. Hope and W.D. Roach. Laskin's performance on conciliation boards had reassured the representatives of capital with a sense of his commitment to responsible unionism within a framework of legality. He also appeared to be an acolyte of Caesar Wright, who had already established his acceptability to labour and capital alike. When Wright engineered Laskin's appointment at the Osgoode Hall Law School, his ideological suitability was established beyond question.

Between 1947 and 1965 Laskin wrote 137 reported arbitration decisions. Undoubtedly he acted in other arbitrations where his decision was not reported, but the reported decisions constitute the core of his arbitral jurisprudence since they became easily available to other arbi-

trators and judges. He started off modestly, undertaking two arbitrations in 1947 and six in 1948. These were the years of the very large
classes of veterans at Osgoode Hall Law School, when his spare time
was at a premium. Over the next five years he did on average ten per
year, or about one a month. This dropped to five per year between 1955
and 1962, then bounced back to twelve and thirteen in 1963 and 1964,
the two years before he went on the bench. Laskin heard grievances on
every conceivable issue, but the most common were unjust dismissal
(twenty-one), job classification (seventeen), and seniority rights on lay-
off (thirteen). Others involved a miscellany of issues from holiday and
overtime pay to transfer rights to complaints by employers about unlawful strikes. Although identified as sympathetic with the labour cause,
over his whole career Laskin decided 37 per cent of the arbitrations in
favour of the union and 55 per cent in favour of the employer; 8 per cent
resulted in a split decision. Over time he decided in favour of unions
more frequently, but this trend probably reflects a more acute sense by
union advisers of which cases should be settled, rather than any shift in
Laskin's own views or sympathies.[15]

In one-quarter of his cases Laskin sat as sole arbitrator, but he usually
sat as chair of a three-person panel. Over his nearly twenty years as an
arbitrator he sat with some eighty different panelists, but most he sat
with only once or twice. There was only a handful of men (one out of
the eighty was a woman) who sat with him frequently, including Charles
Dubin. The name that stands out is Drummond Wren's. Laskin's old
friend sat with him thirty-seven times, or on every third panel. A number
of people appeared before him representing one side or the other on a
grievance, and then sat with him as a panelist on other occasions.

As in so many other areas, Laskin's timing was perfect.[16] In the late
1940s he was uniquely placed to contribute to an emergent arbitral
jurisprudence, to develop a 'common law of the shop.' In part this was
because of the effective absence of any competitors, and in part because
Laskin's earlier combination of scholarship and experience in labour
relations prepared him perfectly for the task at hand. He had developed
his own vision of how the law ought to function in the field of labour
relations, and he now had the chance to put it into action. The field was
new, and Laskin had the advantage of being able to insert his vision
and values into the very structure of labour arbitration. The techniques
for implementing this vision mirrored those found in his legal modernist scholarship of the 1930s: the break with the past; a fluid, socially
aware interpretive practice; and the balancing of interests.

Key for Laskin was the idea that the legislative entrenchment of collective bargaining represented a fundamental break with the common law:

> The change from individual to Collective Bargaining is a change in kind and not merely a difference in degree. The introduction of a Collective Bargaining regime involves the acceptance by the parties of assumptions which are entirely alien to an era of individual bargaining. Hence, any attempt to measure rights and duties in employer-employee relations by reference to pre-collective bargaining standards is an attempt to re-enter a world which has ceased to exist. Just as the period of individual bargaining had its own 'common law' worked out empirically over many years, so does a Collective Bargaining regime have a common law to be invoked to give consistency and meaning to the Collective Agreement on which it is based.[17]

Laskin himself would be the principal architect of this new common law, which he erected on the foundation of a new theory of interpretation. For him the traditional approach to statutory interpretation gave rise to two insuperable objections. First, judges treated words as vessels containing precise and discrete units of meaning, when in fact they were at best leaky and unsatisfactory containers for communicating ideas. The imprecision of language thus gave judges much more discretion than they admitted to having. Second, the common law was treated as the norm and statute as exceptional, with the result that the intended benefits of ameliorative legislation were often cut back under the guise of interpretation. In the field of collective bargaining, so dependent on its statutory foundation, the limits of the traditional approach would be nothing short of disastrous. Thus Laskin felt compelled to entrench the radical separation between the old world of individual contracts of employment and the new world of collective bargaining.[18]

In his 1930s scholarship Laskin had urged judges to approach legislation by 'tak[ing] cognizance of the trend in social forces and treat[ing] the statute as a means to the realization of a social end.'[19] This meant that decision makers should analyse, compare, and weigh the interests involved, rather than simply taking refuge in formal legal categories and abstractions, a process as applicable to collective agreements as to the legislation authorizing them. In a grievance against Canadian General Electric, for example, a conflict arose between the right to facilitate unionization through the distribution of brochures, and the property rights of the company. An employee was found to have distributed blue cards to employees on company property during the dinner hour. Employees were allowed to stay on the premises during their evening meal and were paid for this time. As they were remunerated partly by piece-work rates, they could keep on working through the meal break if they wished. Laskin dismissed the grievance because the employee in question was found to have disturbed employees who chose to continue work while she was distributing her brochures. In an elaborate *obiter*, however, Laskin stated that if the grievor had distributed the brochures on her supper hour without disturbing working employees, the employer should not be able to object.[20] In a related case he noted that 'statutory provisions for collective bargaining in force in Ontario require property owners who are employers to accommodate their rights of property to the statutory policy ... this means only that abstract property rights ought not to be put forward as barriers to communication between the Union and its members, especially when there is explicit recognition of the Union under a collective agreement.'[21] Thus union members permitted to be on company property outside working hours should be able to solicit others about union activity without the permission of the company. The possible undermining of property rights in this way was more than a little controversial in 1951, and presaged one of Laskin's more famous dissents a quarter century later, in *Harrison v. Carswell*.[22]

Another grievance against Canadian General Electric illustrated the care Laskin took in balancing the interests of the parties. Two employees were discharged for fighting at work, though one was reinstated by the company. The aggressor, who was not rehired, grieved his discharge. Laskin observed that '[o]ne might characterize discharge as capital industrial punishment ... the most extreme discipline open to the employer,' and concluded that it was too harsh under the circumstances.[23] The fight was an isolated incident, inspired no fear in other employees, caused no damage to company property, and involved no flouting of company authority (the other party was a fellow employee, not a foreman). Further, the employee had apologized to his victim and there was no ongoing hostility between the two men. Balancing the interests of both parties, the need for the company to set an example and the risk of future harm were small compared to the enormous loss suffered by the fired employee. Laskin did not explicitly invoke the criminal law maxim that the punishment should fit the crime, but it clearly underlay his decision. The company's disciplinary authority was premised on the protection of its legitimate interests, and should not be exercised arbitrarily. The employee was found to have been disciplined sufficiently by his loss of seniority during the period between his discharge and his reinstatement.

Laskin took an expansive view of the employee's interests in his or her job. As he had said in his CBC lectures years before, an employee possessed a 'vocational interest – an economic relation [that] leaves very little of one's life untouched.' Buried in some disputes others might have viewed as trivial, he saw an employee's dignity and self-esteem at stake. In a grievance against Canada Packers, the union complained about the abusive language and belligerent conduct of a foreman. The foreman's conduct had not resulted in any adverse employment consequences for the employees as employees, and Laskin found that the collective agreement did not provide any recourse for such behaviour. He nonetheless expounded at some length on the duty of supervisors and employees to behave 'decently.' 'While a meat packing plant is not a formal drawing room, and while neither employees nor supervisors must be qualified psychologists or experts in human relations, both company and union surely understand that there must be mutual respect for dignity even in a meat packing plant, albeit with recognition of the fact that this can be compatible with some elasticity and tolerance of exuberant language.' Had the preamble to the collective agreement spelled out more clearly 'a reciprocal obligation of union and company to co-operate in maintenance of proper working conditions,' he wrote, 'this board would have had no hesitation in holding that decent behaviour by a supervisor is as much a matter of proper (or safe) working conditions as is decent behaviour by employees within a bargaining unit.'[24]

In other cases dealing with absences from work, Laskin forced companies to treat workers as human beings rather than units of production. In one case Molson's had discharged the grievor for missing one day's work and failing to provide the company with proof that he was ill. The grievor had telephoned in at the appropriate time to say that he had bumped into a door on waking up, and had a serious nosebleed. When he reported for work the next day, the supervisor noted that his nose was swelled and prevented him from coming to work but did not carry out any further inquiry. The company did not dispute that the employee had been disabled from working, but said it was entitled to demand proof beyond the employee's own word. Laskin stated that it was unreasonable for the company to demand that an employee see a doctor at his or her own expense in every case of absence due to illness.

There had been some unsatisfactory absences by the employee in the past, but Laskin held that this absence was not deserving of any discipline, and could not be added to previous incidents to establish 'just cause' for dismissal.[25] Decency, civility, and mutual respect were qualities Laskin demanded of employers and supervisors no less than of employees.

In spite of Laskin's general solicitude for employees, it is striking how women employees tended not to fare so well at his hands. The 1944 conciliation at Corbin Lock Co. has already been mentioned. In 1950 Laskin was faced with a dispute over job classification at a Canadian General Electric plant. There were two types of jobs in producing radio consoles: male 'production helpers' received ninety-nine cents per hour, female 'assemblers' received eighty-four cents per hour. The union alleged that the women were doing production helper work and should get the higher pay, though curiously it did not rely on an 'equal pay' clause in the collective agreement. Laskin found that the two job categories were not watertight, and that since the 'girls' had been doing some production helper work earlier at the lower rate, the status quo should remain. While noting that the union could have raised the 'equal pay' clause, he himself did not do so. Drummond Wren dissented on this point, saying the board did not need to wait for the union to raise the equal pay clause, and that applying it would raise the women's pay as requested. Laskin himself agreed in a later article that an arbitrator could rely on arguments not raised by the parties: an arbitrator's decision 'ought not to be given to one party merely because its advocate *makes* a better case than his opponent but rather because he *has* a better case under the collective agreement.'[26] This time, at least, unlike the Corbin Lock proceeding, a woman had represented the union before the board.

Laskin's decision looks even more anomalous when contrasted with one he rendered only eight months later. A similar dispute over job classification arose at Canadian General Electric's Davenport Works in Toronto, only this time the quarrel was over 'men's' work versus 'boys.' Boys under eighteen received a lower hourly rate than men over that age for doing allegedly different work. The union denied that there was much difference in the actual work performed by the boys, and argued that they should get the higher wage. The company cited Laskin's own earlier decision to him, but he cursorily distinguished it and agreed with the union![27] This seeming tolerance of unequal treatment for women in someone highly sensitive to assaults on human dignity demonstrates how deeply gender stereotypes had become entrenched. In the post-war world racial discrimination was high on the agenda of the labour movement, which devoted not insignificant resources to educating its members about the nature of the problem and trying to remedy it. Sex discrimination, by contrast, was barely on the radar screen of either labour or the human rights movement in a society which was trying hard to re-establish the pre-war status quo in gender relations.[28] Labour arbitration during Laskin's heyday was simply not a site for female agency. Only a small percentage of unionized employees were women, so disputes involving them rarely came to arbitration. The whole process of labour arbitration itself was overwhelmingly male: the arbitrators, union and company nominees, and counsel for both parties were almost invariably men. One lone woman, Idele Wilson, whom Laskin knew from the WEA summer schools, sat a few times on panels he chaired.

One of the most important issues facing arbitrators in the 1950s was defining the nature of the interaction between the collective agreement and management rights. Was it correct to say that management reserved plenary rights to organize production saving only what it had expressly granted away in the collective agreement – the so-called reserved rights theory? Or did the statutory scheme of collective bargaining impose upon both management and labour a reciprocal duty to act in accordance with the purposes of collective bargaining? Management lawyers fought tenaciously for the 'reserved rights' theory but Laskin resisted it, calling it 'a very superficial generalization.' In the *Peterboro Lock* arbitration, he had emphasized the break with the past represented by the statutory introduction of collective bargaining precisely in order to counter the reserved rights theory. For him, collective bargaining meant revolution, not evolution – a difficult doctrine to preach to lawyers schooled in the studied incrementality of the common law. The whole rationale of collective bargaining was to redress the imbalance of economic power between employees and employers, in order to breathe some semblance of genuine equality into the formal equality recognized by the common law. The reserved rights theory threatened the very basis of collective bargaining by returning virtually all the bargaining chips to the hands of the employer. It was wrong because it 'ignore[d] completely the climate of employer-employee relations under a collective agreement.' Part of this climate was a kind of mutuality between employer and union that was meant to replace the subservience of the old master-servant relationship. Accordingly, employees should have a say when important changes to their wages or work routines were contemplated. Thus in *Peterboro Lock* Laskin forbade a company from changing a wage rate for a particular job from an incentive rate to an hourly rate in the absence of specific authorization in the collective agreement.[29]

Management nominee E. Macaulay Dillon issued a forceful dissent. With some asperity, he observed that 'if the law of the collective agreement is to be determined by the "climate of collective bargaining," rather than by the canons of construction applicable to written words, then, of course, there is ample room for wide differences of opinion.'[30] Dillon charged Laskin with going outside the parameters of the law to reach a result he favoured, but in doing so he begged the real question: what *were* the appropriate canons of construction applicable to the words of collective agreements? There was room for legitimate argument on this point, but both sides tended to assume the correctness of their views without fully articulating their reasoning. Ironically, Laskin's views were used against him by his former student Harry Arthurs in a 1966 arbitration that is generally considered to have entrenched the 'reserved rights' theory. The dispute was over whether the employer could contract out work if there was no specific clause in the collective agreement prohibiting it. If the 'climate of collective bargaining' had to be considered, Arthurs reasoned, then it was relevant to note the widespread assumption, strengthened by a steady stream of arbitration decisions (other than Laskin's), that the employer could do so in the absence of a prohibitory clause.[31]

Another issue on which Laskin was compelled to develop new law related to the remedial authority of the arbitrator. He consistently held that arbitrators had the power to fashion appropriate remedies for breach even if these were not spelled out in the collective agreement. On this issue representatives of both labour and capital tended to argue opportunistically, advocating broad remedial authority when the other side was in breach but insisting on specific authorization when their own side had contravened the collective agreement. The issue first arose in a 1948 award, where Laskin rejected an argument that he was empowered merely to issue a declaration that the collective agreement had been violated.[32] He then amplified his views in a 1950 award against the Amalgamated Electrical Company. Helen Driscoll was laid off work as an assembler and according to the collective agreement should have received a three-day trial as a factory clerk in the shipping room. The collective agreement provided for plantwide seniority, enabling senior laid-off employees to take 'jobs they are capable of doing ... provided that at the time of transfer the senior employee to be transferred can satisfactorily perform in all respects, within three working days, the job of the employee who is to be replaced.' After a cursory interview the company decided Driscoll was not capable of doing the work, did not grant her the trial, and maintained her lay-off for some six weeks. Laskin decided that provided Driscoll had an honest belief that she could do the work (which she did), and that such belief was not patently unreasonable, the company could not deny her the three-day trial. Otherwise, he reasoned, the plantwide seniority rights granted by the collective agreement could be ignored in practice. Laskin did not speculate whether Helen Driscoll's sex played a role in the company's denial of the trial period in the new job, but his decision effectively made it much more difficult for the company to discriminate on the basis of sex or race in the job allocation process.

The more difficult issue was the remedy. There was nothing specific in the collective agreement, in existing arbitral decisions, or elsewhere in Canadian law. Counsel for the company argued forcefully that an arbitrator could only provide an interpretation of the collective agreement, and not award compensation or other remedies. In the result, Laskin required the company to pay Driscoll retroactively at the shipping clerk rate for the six weeks of the lay-off. This assumed she would have passed the three days of probation, which was not a certainty, but Laskin said the employee should not have to bear the loss for the company's default – an approach consistent with the ordinary assessment of damages in civil cases. To justify his award Laskin invoked the collective agreement itself and U.S. law. The agreement provided for the 'prompt and equitable disposition of grievances' by arbitration, which was to be the 'final and binding' method of settling disputes. Leaving remedial issues to be decided in other fora would render arbitration neither prompt nor final, said Laskin. He also cited several decisions by courts and arbitrators in New York allowing compensation awards against both companies and unions.[33]

Laskin's best-known decision on the power of arbitrators to award compensation involved an award against a union for its role in an illegal walkout during the currency of a collective agreement. The walkout at the Polymer Corporation's Sarnia plant arose out of widespread dissatisfaction with the company's discharge of one Mason, a laboratory employee. On the morning of 7 February 1958 some one thousand employees did not go on shift, but picketed the company's

The Laskin family, Fort William, Ontario, ca. 1919. Back row: Max and Charles; front row: left to right, Bora, Saul, and Bluma.

Bora Laskin as the editor of the Fort William Collegiate Institute yearbook, the *Oracle*, 1929–30. In his afterword to the yearbook, Laskin extolled the noble efforts of the school's teachers in 'saving us from drowning in the Sea of Ignorance, and instead leading us step by step up the ladder of success.'

Fort William Collegiate Institute senior rugby team, 1928–9. Laskin is first on the left in the back row. The competitive rugby player always remained an important facet of Laskin's persona, giving an edge to his intellectual engagements.

University of Toronto middle-weight rowing team, 1932–3. Laskin is fifth from left.

Laskin's professors at the honour law program at the University of Toronto.
Clockwise from upper left: W.P.M. Kennedy, F.C. Auld, N.A.M. ('Larry')
MacKenzie, Jacob Finkelman. All assisted Laskin in numerous ways and
encouraged him to pursue an academic career. MacKenzie's departure in the
summer of 1940 allowed Kennedy to hire Laskin.

Moot club, in front of Burwash Hall, 1934. Back row, left to right: George Keith Drynan, Bora Laskin, John Donald Burwell. In the front row: Peter Stuart MacKenzie, Moffatt Hancock, John Kenneth Blair. Hancock would be Laskin's colleague at the University of Toronto from 1940 to 1945, before leaving for Dalhousie and eventually Stanford.

45 St George Street, home of the honour law program at the University of Toronto from the 1920s to 1952.

Baldwin House housed the law school from 1952 to 1956.

Graduating from Osgoode Hall Law School, 1936. Laskin deferred his call to
the bar until 1937 because he could not afford the fee.

Peggy Tenenbaum graduated with a Bachelor of Household Science degree
from the University of Toronto in 1933. She and Bora married in June 1938.

Harvard Law School, 1930s. Harvard had more full-time law professors in the 1930s than all Canadian law schools combined.

Felix Frankfurter, 1935. Laskin's LLM thesis on the Ontario Municipal Board was 'supervised' by Frankfurter, whose role as confidant to President Roosevelt and promoter of the New Deal left him little time for contact with students. Laskin's career path was similar to Frankfurter's in many respects.

A conciliation board on which Laskin sat as the union representative was unable to avert the bitter Ford strike that paralysed Windsor in the fall of 1945. Left to right: Laskin, Justice G.B. O'Connor (chair) of Edmonton, Stanley Springsteen, KC (employer representative).

Ford Motor Company of Canada representatives. Left to right: Wallace H. Clark, personnel manager; D.B. Greig, treasurer; John Aylesworth, company solicitor. Aylesworth was appointed to the Ontario Court of Appeal in 1946 and would be the dominant figure there when Laskin joined the court in 1965.

Constant tension with the benchers of the Law Society of Upper Canada over
the direction of legal education resulted in a mass resignation of Osgoode
Hall Law School professors in January 1949. Left to right: Stanley Edwards,
John Willis, Bora Laskin, Cecil A. Wright.

This ca. 1960 photo captures Laskin as the 'elder statesman' of Canadian law and legal education, a reputation he gained as a result of his public pronouncements on constitutional law and his ability to combine scholarship, labour arbitration, and involvement in national university affairs.

Holy Blossom Temple was the nerve centre of Reform Judaism in Toronto. Laskin played an important role in its governance, particularly in the expansion of its religious education programs during the baby boom years of the 1950s.

One of Laskin's two most memorable dissents while on the Ontario Court of Appeal involved the conviction of gallery owner Dorothy Cameron for exposing obscene material to public view. This painting by Robert Markle, 'Paramour,' now in the collection of the Art Gallery of Ontario, was one of the offending items. Laskin's colleagues thought a depiction of a 'woman in an attitude of sexual invitation' must necessarily be obscene, but he declared that 'the human figure, expressing love in any of its known forms, is a permissible theme for a novel and for a picture.'

A rare moment of relaxation at Lake O'Hara, Alberta, with friends Morris
and Jacqui Shumiatcher (early 1970s).

The 1958 report by Vernon Fowke and Bora Laskin on the Harry Crowe case became a milestone in the definition of academic freedom in Canada. Laskin's colleague J.B. Milner carried on his work, and when CAUT created the Milner Award for Academic Freedom after his death, Laskin was the first recipient in 1971. Left to right: Laskin, Jean Milner, J. Percy Smith, executive director of CAUT.

Bora and Peggy in their Ottawa apartment, shortly after the announcement of his appointment as chief justice of Canada on 27 December 1973.

Laskin agreed to be the first chair of the board of governors of the Ontario Institute for Studies in Education (OISE) when it was created in 1965. OISE thanked him by awarding him an honorary degree through the University of Toronto in 1975.

Laskin receiving an honorary doctorate from Harvard University, 1979. Others honoured at the same convocation were Desmond Tutu, Helmut Schmidt, Isaiah Berlin, and Jacques Cousteau.

Judges of the Supreme Court of Canada and their spouses, along with
Governor-General Jules Léger and Mme Léger, on the steps of the Supreme
Court building, summer 1978. Back row, left to right: Willard Estey, Paule
Pratte, Jean Beetz, Ruth Estey, Yves Pratte; middle row, Madeleine Pigeon,
Louis-Philippe Pigeon, Brian Dickson, Barbara Dickson, Wishart Spence,
Elizabeth Spence; front row, Iris Martland, Bora Laskin, Jules Léger, Gabrielle
Léger, Ronald Martland, Peggy Laskin, Roland Ritchie.

The day after Laskin received this humanitarian award from the Beth Sholom Brotherhood in Toronto, he was admitted to hospital with a heart disturbance – the prelude to a cascade of health problems over the next six years. Accompanying Laskin is Ontario Attorney-General R. Roy McMurtry, who had argued the *Anti-inflation Reference* personally before the Supreme Court; he would return to present the province's position in the *Patriation Reference* in 1981.

As the provincial premiers prepare to lobby British MPs to oppose Trudeau's patriation package in 1981, he appears to be the only politician speaking for Canada. Laskin as referee seems uncertain as to whether Canadian or British rules apply.

Prime Minister Pierre Trudeau consoling Peggy Laskin and Barbara Laskin Plumptre at Bora Laskin's funeral, 28 March 1984.

administration building to protest Mason's discharge. Two unions were involved, local 16-14 of the Oil, Chemical & Atomic Workers International Union, and the international union itself, neither of which had declared an official strike or encouraged the workers to wildcat. The matter was largely resolved by the end of the day shift, the total stoppage lasting about eight hours. The company's grievance was that union officials did not do enough to bring the workers back on the job once the walkout started. A majority of the panel ruled that the international union had used its best efforts to bring the workers back, but the local had not. In particular Laskin rebuked the local for allowing the stewards and committeemen to remain on the picket line rather than obliging them to dissociate themselves from the strike.[34]

Once the liability of the union was established, a further hearing was held on the question of an arbitrator's power to award damages. Laskin deprecated in the strongest possible terms several awards by county court judges which had denied an arbitrator's power to award damages for breach of a collective agreement obligation in the absence of explicit language to that effect. All of these arose out of union-launched grievances, where damages were being sought against the company. These decisions, said Laskin, were 'based on a fundamental misconception of jurisdiction.' If a board's remedial powers were to be treated as a question of initial jurisdiction, 'any board of arbitration must find itself stultified at the very inception of a case when the collective agreement fails to specify any course of procedure.' Taking the argument further, Laskin asked rhetorically how arbitrators could even apply rules of interpretation or law to the rules presented, when they were not expressly told to do so in the collective agreement. Finally, he could not resist an *ad hominem* attack. 'One fairly ancient legal rule is that breach of contract is compensable by damages if loss results therefrom. This is a proposition which a County or District Judge does not doubt when sitting on the bench; and he requires no legislative direction to persuade him to apply it. Why then is it doubted in arbitral jurisdiction of labour disputes?'[35]

At one level, there was an important difference between county courts and boards of arbitration: the county court was a superior court with a certain inherent jurisdiction while a board of arbitration had only the powers given to it by the parties or by statute. Laskin's question still raised a valid point: if arbitrators were not vested with a certain penumbra of inherent authority, the whole process would grind to a halt. Another distinction between courts and arbitration boards lurked in the shadows of the Polymer decision: unions could not be sued for damages in the ordinary courts because of their legal status as unincorporated associations, not corporations. This common law disability had been further entrenched in Ontario's *Rights of Labour Act* in order to prevent companies from harassing unions with tort suits. It was thus somewhat anomalous that arbitration boards should be able to award compensation against a union when the ordinary courts could not. However, Laskin believed that the status of arbitration as the lynchpin of industrial peace would be imperilled if arbitrators were denied the power to award compensation to either party where the collective agreement was breached. As was often the case in Laskin's arbitral reasoning, functional arguments prevailed over logical and conceptual ones.

There are many ironies in the *Polymer* case. Not the least of them is that it was not a case of first impression at all. Back in 1952 a board of arbitration chaired by Laskin had already found a union liable to compensate the employer where it had breached the collective agreement. When Canadian General Electric grieved an illegal work stoppage by the union, Laskin found, as in *Polymer*, that the union, although not initiating the strike, had not taken adequate steps to stop it once begun. A majority of the board assessed the company's lost profits at $9,200 and ordered the union to pay this amount.[36] For some reason this early decision did not arouse the feeling within the union movement that *Polymer* did, perhaps because two subsequent arbitrations chaired by county court judges refused to follow it. A student happened to be present at the law school when Laskin read one of these. He recalled Laskin storming out of his office shouting, 'That dirty son-of-a-bitch! He knows what happened in our case and he had the gall to do this!'[37] Laskin would have his revenge in *Polymer* as the case was appealed through the court hierarchy.

The union decided to challenge Laskin's award in *Polymer* in court, and argued it all the way to the Supreme Court of Canada, purely on the point that an arbitrator had no power to award compensation for breaches of collective agreements, absent specific authorization. The union's tenacity is curious: if it won, the result would surely have been that the union could not demand compensation from employers in breach of the collective agreement, a much more common scenario than the converse. Laskin's friend David Lewis, by now an active labour lawyer in Toronto, argued the case for the union in the Ontario High

Court before Chief Justice McRuer, where he lost; before the Court of Appeal, where Justice Aylesworth wrote the decision dismissing the appeal; and before the Supreme Court of Canada, where Justice Cartwright, writing for the Court, also dismissed the appeal. J.J. Robinette appeared for the company in all three courts, arguing in support of Laskin's award – a novel position for him.[38]

The upholding of Laskin's award in all three courts was not so surprising, given that its result was to punish a union for a wildcat strike. Had the shoe been on the other foot, one may wonder whether the courts would have been so quick to embrace an autonomous remedial power for arbitrators. While on the surface it may have appeared as a setback for trade unions, in many ways *Imbleau v. Laskin*, as it was known in the Supreme Court, represented the fulfilment of Bora Laskin's vision for labour law in general and arbitration in particular. The case affirmed the role of arbitrators as the front-line peacekeepers in the zone of industrial conflict. It also affirmed the supremacy of law rather than violence or intimidation as the ultimate authority in the unionized workplace. And it provided high legitimacy for Laskin's vision of the inherent remedial power of the arbitrator. Laskin knew that unions had given up their most powerful weapon by agreeing to forego work stoppages during the course of a collective agreement, and that capital had gained a key point by being able to insist on continued production. Unions had to remain convinced that arbitration was a prompt and fair way of resolving ongoing workplace problems, or they would repent of the bargain. Arbitration could only be effective, in Laskin's view, if knowledgeable arbitrators were given a reasonably free hand in interpreting and enforcing the collective agreement. Sensitivity to the real interests of both parties, rather than parsing the common law, should be the touchstone of the arbitrator's practice. But hanging over the whole process was the question of enforcement and remedy. If arbitrators were to be limited to issuing declarations of right, it would not be long before the parties resorted to their own extra-legal modes of enforcement. Only an independent power to grant appropriate remedies could properly anchor arbitration in the turbulent waters of labour relations.

On the merits of the case, Laskin's former student Harry Arthurs thought his professor had not only got it right but had shown how the labour arbitrator was uniquely positioned to assist in the resolution of labour disputes. After an LLM at Harvard Arthurs would take up a position teaching labour law at Osgoode in 1961, and he was quickly becoming Laskin's successor in that field. 'Professor Laskin's language is neither a literal adherence to the broad statutory ban on all strikes, nor the conceptualistic judicial imposition of liability for all interference with or breach of contract ... [H]is decisions do not merely indicate a more sophisticated handling of the facts in labour litigation. They may represent pioneering navigation through troubled waters between the courts (which can give relief but often do not understand the problems) and the Labour Board (which understands the problems but cannot make the struck employer whole).'[39]

Aside from remedial anaemia, the other threat to the effectiveness of labour arbitration was an overly aggressive practice of judicial review by the superior courts. It was no good for arbitrators or labour boards to fashion an enlightened jurisprudence if they were going to be overturned at the drop of a hat by courts invoking a literalist interpretation of collective agreements and collective bargaining legislation, and deploying expansive conceptions of management rights. Legislatures had tried to prevent this result by enacting clauses in labour legislation purporting to insulate labour relations boards and labour arbitrators from judicial review (known as 'privative clauses' and 'finality clauses' respectively), but some courts had predictably found ways of avoiding these constraints. Laskin railed against these practices early on, and consistently advocated a 'hands-off' policy by the courts towards labour boards and labour arbitrators in all but the most exceptional circumstances.[40] Deference to expert tribunals was one of the foundational tenets of legal modernism. If the legislature had recognized another set of decision makers as primary in the field of labour – or anywhere else for that matter – it was the duty of the courts to respect that allocation of responsibilities. Vincent MacDonald, who had been named to the Nova Scotia Supreme Court by the time Laskin wrote this article, disagreed with his conclusions in a letter to Caesar Wright; he doubted whether the courts were 'embarked on a deliberate attempt to expand their reviewing function or to flout the legislative will' and noted that legislators seemed to have acquiesced in the results in any case. He did agree that a system of administrative appeals would render the issue less acute. Wright confessed that he disagreed with many of Laskin's conclusions and was not too worried about 'judicial arrogance.'[41] As a judge Laskin tried to persuade his colleagues of the validity of his reasoning. He eventually succeeded in the Ontario Court of Appeal, only to find his decisions overturned by the Supreme Court of Canada.[42]

When he reached that court he began the process all over again, and once more achieved success.[43]

By the late 1950s the need for arbitrators was expanding rapidly along with the steady growth of the economy and the spread of collective agreements over large sectors of the labour market. Reliance on the judiciary was seen as increasingly problematic but it was not until 1962 that the attorney-general of Ontario struck a committee to examine the problem – chaired by Bora Laskin's old boss, Eric Silk, now deputy attorney-general. Silk's committee revealed that 84 per cent of all labour arbitrations were heard by county and district court judges in 1960–1.[44] It recommended legislation, passed in 1963, preventing judges from acting as arbitrators, but where was the new class of arbitrators to come from? In the United States the busiest arbitrators had begun to take on apprentices, although official training programs by the National Academy of Arbitrators remained controversial through the 1960s.[45] Bora Laskin in effect took responsibility for training a new generation of arbitrators. In the late 1950s and early 1960s he encouraged students who had an interest in labour law to come and sit in on several of his arbitrations. He mentored Earl Palmer and Harry Arthurs, who became active arbitrators and in turn mentored others such as Paul Weiler.[46] Law professors rapidly filled the arbitral space vacated by judges.

Laskin's arbitral experience not only gave him a certain legitimacy within the legal profession, but also served as a kind of judicial apprenticeship. He acquired extensive experience in fact-finding and assessing credibility, in running hearings, and in dealing with a whole range of counsel from the best to the least experienced. Without this crucial exposure, it is unlikely that Laskin's judicial career would have materialized. The Ontario bar had never had much time for academics, and would not have taken kindly to a 'pure' academic on the bench. Laskin's high visibility in the world of arbitration helped to make him an acceptable candidate for judicial appointment. It was fitting that the judge he replaced on the Ontario Court of Appeal, W.D. Roach, had himself been one of the few superior court judges to acquire a positive reputation as an arbitrator.

In intellectual terms, Laskin's creation of a Canadian arbitral jurisprudence was a significant achievement, while in personal terms it provided valuable training for his future judicial role in terms of fact-finding, opinion-writing, and observing procedural fairness. Using his legal modernist techniques he demonstrated how the law could be interpreted purposively and responsively, rather than as a simple cutting and pasting of dry precedents. Just as Caesar Wright had prescribed an 'extra-legal approach to law,' and W.P.M. Kennedy had insisted on the necessity of 'putting law at the service of life,' so Laskin insisted that 'the law is to be found outside the collective agreement, in principles and doctrines which must take their inspiration from the aims and purposes of collective bargaining.'[47] In his new role Laskin was free to fashion the ground rules himself, unlike his experience on the bench where he found himself caught in a web of centuries-old traditions. Laskin's arbitral decisions were, moreover, educative in the broadest sense of the word. He saw himself as not just deciding the dispute in question, but actively teaching the parties how they should behave in future, and educating a broader public about their industrial relations system. In the early years this self-appointed task appeared to be a 'solitary crusade,' as David Beatty and Brian Langille have noted. Gradually Laskin won some converts to his cause, especially when the next generation of labour arbitrators found themselves heavily dependent on the mode of analysis he had articulated in his decisions. But it was not just Laskin's legal techniques that appealed: the underlying values promoted by his decisions were perfectly in tune with those of the post-war welfare state, with its commitment to the dignity of labour and its more generous and inclusive sense of citizenship. In essence, Laskin's arbitral jurisprudence was a civics primer for life in the industrial age.[48]

11

Human Rights

As the war drew to a close, Jews outside Europe reacted with a combination of relief and horror. Even as they welcomed the end of the war they recoiled at the revelations from the newly liberated death camps of eastern Europe. Bora Laskin shared in these mixed emotions. The optimism was palpable in Canada, visible in the faces of the large class of eager veterans Laskin faced at Osgoode in the fall of 1945. Yet his connections to the Holocaust cast a dark shadow on his experience of the post-war years. The Jewish population of Bluma's Latvian homeland had been virtually eliminated, while Saul had been present at the Belsen concentration camp shortly after its liberation. Addressing the B'nai Brith lodge in Fort William on his return, he reported how he and his fellow soldiers wept upon seeing the mass graves and the thousands of orphans who had known no other life.[1] Although not a direct participant in the war, Bora experienced its horrors vicariously through his brother; this exposure in turn stimulated Laskin's involvement with the emergent human rights movement. After a decade of activism and scholarship in the field of labour relations, Laskin focused his energies on a new cause: the elimination of anti-Semitism and all forms of racial and religious discrimination.

Laskin's sole scholarly pronouncement on this issue to date was provoked by *Christie v. York Corporation*, where the Supreme Court of Canada had upheld the right of a tavern owner to refuse service to a black patron on the basis of freedom of contact.[2] His brief and prescient case comment called for the state to show leadership by forbidding discrimination on the part of those holding public licences or franchises – a direction in which several Ontario municipalities would move in the later 1940s.[3] Such a direct discussion of egalitarian human rights would remain rare in Laskin's scholarship, in contrast to his frequent treatment of traditional civil liberties such as freedom of expression and association. His anti-discrimination work involved activism and advice rather than scholarship, and took place as part of the Canadian Jewish Congress (CJC) fight against anti-Semitism. Although a key player in this campaign, Laskin chose to stay out of the limelight and his contribution has remained largely unknown.

The Joint Public Relations Committee (JPRC) was established in 1938 by the Canadian Jewish Congress and the B'nai Brith to fight anti-Semitism in all its forms. Its members, like the Congress leadership, were mainly second-generation middle-class entrepreneurs and professionals. Rabbi Abraham Feinberg, who took charge of Holy Blossom Temple in 1943, chaired the committee until 1950, when lawyer Fred Catzman succeeded him. Socially respectable – insofar as Jews could be – and middle of the road politically, these men (and a few women) were concerned to remove the remaining barriers to full participation by Jews and other minorities in Canadian social and economic life. Although the JPRC worked with other equality-seeking groups such as blacks and Japanese Canadians, trade unions, and the Canadian Association for Adult Education, it remained the nerve centre of the campaign for the elimination of discrimination in Ontario, generating the ideas, the strategies, and much of the funding. It then exported its techniques to Jewish groups from Vancouver to Halifax, and the legislation the committee successfully promoted in Ontario was copied at the federal level and by all other provinces.[4]

The trajectory of Laskin's human rights activism both reflected and reinforced his legal modernism. After a brief and unsatisfactory experience with a test-case strategy in the late 1940s, he and the JPRC pursued the legislative route in the 1950s. His goal was to supersede the courts and the common law entirely by creating statutory prohibitions on discrimination and confiding the tasks of public education and enforcement to an expert tribunal based on the labour relations model. Laskin and his colleagues pursued an incrementalist strategy reflecting both their own training as lawyers and their sense of what was politically possible at a given moment. Canada would have a rights evolution rather than a rights revolution. With the creation of the Ontario Human

Rights Commission in 1961 and the passage of the Ontario Human Rights Code in the next year Laskin saw his vision largely implemented after nearly two decades of effort.

By 1944 Laskin was deeply involved in a JRPC-sponsored legal challenge to the validity of racially and religiously exclusive restrictive covenants. By allowing the creation of white Anglo-Saxon residential enclaves these covenants symbolized the exclusion experienced by Jews in many areas of life. Thus when the Workers' Educational Association purchased a piece of land subject to a covenant prohibiting it from being 'sold to Jews or persons of objectionable nationality,' the stage was set for a head-on challenge to this much-resented legal device. In form the case was an application by Drummond Wren under the *Conveyancing and Law of Property Act* asking for a declaration that the covenant was void.[5] In fact the case was wholly conducted by the JPRC, who retained John Cartwright and Irving Himel to represent Wren and the WEA. The CJC was given intervenor status and was represented by Laskin's old fraternity friend J.M. Bennett. Laskin, Jacob Finkelman, and Charles Dubin developed and drafted the arguments but it was Laskin who largely wrote the brief Cartwright presented to the court. It advanced four grounds of invalidity: uncertainty, restraint on alienation, public policy, and a contravention of Ontario's new *Racial Discrimination Act*. The latter statute forbade the posting of discriminatory signs and notices in public places ('No Blacks or Jews allowed') but did not go so far as to prevent refusal of service on the basis of race once a person entered a public establishment. On 1 May 1945, just a week before VE Day, Justice Keiller Mackay heard argument on the application in chambers, and on Hallowe'en he released his reasons for striking down the covenant.[6]

Finding it void on the first two grounds, and declining to pronounce on the fourth argument, Justice Mackay reserved his most expansive comments for the argument on public policy. This doctrine sets some outer limits on the basic liberal principle informing the law of private agreements and property dispositions. For example, freedom of alienation does not allow property to be conveyed on condition that an unmarried grantee never marry on pain of losing her interest: the right to marry is considered more important than freedom of disposition.[7] The courts admitted public policy to be a fluid doctrine subject to historical evolution, but feared its very subjectivity and uncertain scope. Invoking precedents from the heyday of Victorian liberalism, Lord

Lindley had declared in 1902 that 'public policy was a very unstable and dangerous foundation upon which to build until made safe by decision,' and English and Canadian courts had invoked it sparingly ever since.[8] The latest word was the Millar will case, where the Supreme Court of Canada refused to strike down a clause leaving a large sum of money to the Toronto woman who should have the most children in a ten-year period.[9]

Justice Mackay not only omitted to mention *Millar* but began his reasons by invoking Justices Benjamin Cardozo and Oliver Wendell Holmes in order to lay the basis for a more expansive view of public policy. The quotation from Holmes was one Laskin had cited in a 1938 article, asserting that community needs were 'the secret root from which the law draws all the juices of life.'[10] Mackay took this as his cue to look to Canada's international commitments in the 1941 Atlantic Charter and the brand new UN Charter, and even to statements by wartime leaders Churchill, de Gaulle, and Roosevelt on the necessity of ending anti-Semitism, before turning to recent Ontario legislation such as the *Insurance Act* and the *Racial Discrimination Act* as evidence of changing attitudes to discrimination. In these diverse elements he found an emerging public policy against racial and religious discrimination sufficient to void the covenant. This rather daring argument was based on the legal modernist understanding of the judicial role found in Laskin's 1930s scholarship, and expounded in his brief to the court.[11] Mackay feared that legal endorsement of residential or commercial segregation would 'create or deepen divisions between existing religious and ethnic groups in the Province,' a result he thought was to be avoided at all costs.

Keiller Mackay was something of an outsider to the Ontario establishment, an expatriate Nova Scotian Presbyterian who had attended the Catholic St Francis Xavier University in Antigonish. An active Conservative, Mackay was appointed to the High Court by R.B. Bennett in 1935. With his tall spare frame, aquiline nose, and elegant attire, he combined an almost regal bearing with the common touch. Unmarried until the age of fifty-five, Mackay resided in the Park Plaza Hotel, and 'it was no uncommon thing to see him riding bare-headed in street cars and chatting informally with people he knew.'[12] In his eighties, Mackay would author a report, much appreciated by the Jewish community, recommending the replacement of religious teaching in public schools with moral education.

Drummond Wren was hailed as an enormous victory not only by the

Jewish community, but by many outside it. The JPRC printed a pamphlet depicting Mackay in heroic terms; the publicity likely helped secure Mackay's appointment as lieutenant-governor of Ontario eight years later.[13] In it Rabbi Feinberg put his finger on the source of the decision's widespread appeal: 'It clothes in concrete reality, for specific cases, the universally-acclaimed principles for which World War Two was pursued to a victorious end.' On 12 November *Drummond Wren* was noted in *Time*, and soon it would be cited in U.S. courts.[14] Arriving in the euphoria of the immediate post-war period, before the downward spiral into the Cold War, Keiller Mackay's innovative and inspirational decision seemed to herald a new era of social inclusiveness free of legally sanctioned prejudice.

Given the significance of *Drummond Wren* in Canadian law and in Laskin's life, it is worth looking more closely at its origins. The official story was that the WEA had purchased the lot in order to build a home on it and raffle it off as a fund-raising project. Then, when it 'discovered' the restrictive covenant, the WEA realized that this would complicate the scheme and sought to have it discharged. There is an air of unreality about this account. The 'discovery' of the restrictive covenant should have taken place during the title search when the WEA purchased the land in 1944. Wren's vendor, William Vanderbent, had taken title only in 1942, and the covenant was contained in his deed so it was not difficult to find.[15] In the normal course of events, the WEA's solicitor should have informed Wren about the covenant as a possible complicating factor in the raffle plans. The WEA did not have to accept the land with the covenant. If they were truly concerned about it, they could have withdrawn from the transaction and sought an unburdened lot elsewhere. In fact, Mr Vanderbent sold part of the same lot to a Jewish purchaser in 1944 and simply left out the obnoxious covenant in his deed.[16] As it was, the WEA likely purchased the land with full knowledge of the covenant and then sought a declaration of its invalidity. The sequence of events suggests that the WEA and the CJC were scouting out a possible test case in which the WEA could appear as the ostensible plaintiff. Neighbouring landowners were notified but none chose to participate in the hearing. In the short term this was expeditious because it put the CJC in control of the litigation: there was no adverse party, no real *lis inter partes* (legal issue between the parties). In the long term, however, this was a weakness. When the hearing came on before a sympathetic judge, it turned out to be a love-in rather than an adversarial proceeding. The public policy argument, however meritorious it might have been, was not exposed to the full blast of strong counter-arguments existing in Ontario law. A few years later those arguments would be made in earnest in a much different political climate, and they would bring *Drummond Wren* crashing to earth.

Drummond Wren was to be only the first blow in a much larger campaign, one aimed to 'ensure that the integration of Canadian Jewry into Canadian life is so complete that anti-semitism will be discredited as ... impossible nonsense.'[17] However useful common law victories might be, the JPRC had its sights set on legislative reform in two priority areas: restrictive covenants and employment discrimination. Eventually they wished to tackle discrimination in the provision of services and facilities ordinarily available to the public. Finally, Bora Laskin and Jacob Finkelman, among others, wished the Canadian Jewish Congress to pursue the ultimate prize: a national bill of rights.[18] The strategy was deliberately incrementalist, to enable the building of alliances and avoid alienating the unconverted through broad and threatening rights-based claims.

After their apparent success in *Drummond Wren*, the activists turned their attention to employment discrimination. In 1946 two sub-committees of the JPRC were formed, one on community relations chaired by Dr Reva Gerstein, and the other on law and legal research chaired alternately by Bora Laskin and Syd Harris. Both 'launched important activities in their respective fields and were preparing material which could be put to valuable use in connection with an approach to the Government for a Fair Employment Practices Bill.'[19] The concept of state intervention to redress employment discrimination had been pioneered in the United States during the war years. Under the threat of a massive black march on Washington to protest their exclusion from defence industry work, Roosevelt created a fair employment practices board by executive order. It successfully settled thousands of cases before its power expired with the end of the war. New York and New Jersey set up their own fair employment practices commissions in the closing months of the war, but further federal action was stymied by the southern Democrat lobby in Congress.[20]

With his background in labour law and extensive contacts in the union movement, Bora Laskin was a natural leader for the fair employment practices campaign. When their initial brief to the government was rebuffed in 1947, Laskin and his colleagues realized that the CJC had to develop alliances, universalize the struggle for the elimination of prejudice, and embrace issues beyond employment. His committee would work with those trying to end discrimination at the Icelandia skating rink in Toronto, which had refused entry to both blacks and Jews.[21] Similarly, the refusal of some restaurants and barber shops in Dresden, Ontario, to serve blacks would be relentlessly pursued by the JPRC along with a group of local blacks called the National Unity Association. With the hiring in April 1947 of a full-time executive director, the extraordinarily capable Ben Kayfetz, the JPRC was well-equipped to move into the vanguard of the human rights policy community in Canada.

The most fruitful strategic alliance formed by the JPRC was its November 1947 agreement with the Jewish Labour Committee (JLC). Formed in 1936 by workers in the garment industries, the JLC was resolutely social democratic and carried on a heated rivalry with communists in the labour movement. In spite of some ideological differences, the two organizations were able to cooperate under the leadership of Kalmen Kaplansky, a Polish-born Montrealer appointed national director of the JLC in April 1946. The JLC set up a national network of Joint Labour Committees to Combat Racial Intolerance, all run by volunteers except the Toronto office. In 1947 the JLC hired a full-time executive secretary in Toronto to work with the Toronto Joint Labour Committee, paid for largely out of CJC funds. She or he reported directly to Kaplansky but also worked extensively with the Toronto JPRC.[22] The secretary's weekly letters to Kaplansky chronicle in intimate detail the activities of the evolving human rights policy community through the 1940s and '50s.[23] As Patrias and Frager have noted, the JLC and the JPRC wanted to avoid 'creat[ing] the impression that the anti-discrimination campaigns were particularistically self-interested.'[24] They preferred to work with other groups such as the Joint Labour Committees, and the Canadian Association for Adult Education, with which the JPRC formed an alliance in 1949. The JPRC agreed to pay 70 per cent of the salary of a CAAE employee who would undertake educational work in human rights, and would also make common cause with a number of black groups seeking recognition of their rights.

Ironically, these earnest bourgeois Jewish activists were being monitored by the RCMP. In the post-war years the RCMP remained suspicious of Jews for their perceived allegiance to communism and of rights-seeking organizations for their susceptibility to infiltration by communists. 'It may well be said,' reported an intelligence officer in 1945, 'that Jews are the dynamic nucleus of the Communist Party in

Canada.'[25] When Rabbi Feinberg joined the advisory board of the Toronto Labour Progressive Party (the nom-de-plume of the Communist Party) in 1944, 'O' Division of the RCMP in Toronto opened a file on him; it was probably because of his presence that it maintained surveillance of the Canadian Jewish Congress and related groups. Feinberg's RCMP file contains reports on his meetings at the time of the Icelandia skating rink incidents, on Congress meetings, and on the creation of Irving Himel's Association for Civil Liberties in 1949. Just as his work with the WEA had not escaped the scrutiny of the RCMP, Bora Laskin's JPRC involvement continued to be monitored, as would his later activities with the Canadian Association of University Teachers.

The Canadian Jewish Congress campaign was given an enormous moral boost with the adoption of the Universal Declaration of Human Rights in December 1948. Though usually sceptical of the efficacy of international law, let alone a mere resolution like the Declaration, Laskin tried to harness it to his own domestic agenda. In a CJC publication, he and Finkelman put forth a proposal for implementing the Universal Declaration through an independent representative commission responsible directly to Parliament. It would examine all new and existing legislation, as well as judicial decisions, to check for compliance with the Declaration, and would also receive and investigate complaints by individuals or organizations. Canadian federalism demanded that different articles might have to be dealt with by different levels of government, and the merit of the Laskin-Finkelman scheme was to '"spotlight" the terms of the Declaration throughout Canada while leaving it open for particular legislation to be enacted as occasion arises.' The commission would have no power to take direct action but would report periodically to Parliament; it would then lie with the appropriate government to act. 'Of course, the sanction of public opinion would begin to operate immediately and would not have to await any governmental action.'[26] The proposal respected parliamentary sovereignty, and closely resembles the method recently chosen by the United Kingdom to implement the provisions of the European Convention on Human Rights. Judges may issue a 'declaration of invalidity' where a Convention right is found to be breached, but have no power strike down a law.

This proposal went nowhere, but it reveals much about Laskin's legal modernism, his faith in expertise, and his distrust of judges at this point in his life. Not only were independent experts rather than judges supposed to bring violations of the Universal Declaration to light, but judicial decisions themselves might be spotlighted as contravening human rights norms. For Laskin, the common law as declared by the judges – *Christie v. York*, for example – was often the problem, not the solution. The Universal Declaration at last provided in a highly public and solemn fashion the fundamental human rights norms towards which all states should aspire, and the commission mechanism was a way of pointing out where Canadian law fell short. If, as Mary Ann Glendon has suggested, 'one of the most common and unfortunate misunderstandings today involves the notion that the Declaration was meant to impose a single model of right conduct rather than to provide a common standard that can be brought to life in different cultures in a legitimate variety of ways,' Laskin and Finkelman did not share in this confusion.[27] They recognized the aspirational value of the Universal Declaration, and left the final translation of its broad norms into precise rights effective in domestic law to be worked out in a dialogue among Parliament, public opinion, and expert advice.

If 1948 brought welcome news on the international front, at home the news was more mixed. The provincial Conservative government was returned to power in a June election, but Premier George Drew lost his seat and resigned. His successor, chosen in April 1949, was Leslie Frost, a small-town lawyer from Lindsay. Frost's iron will was clothed in the velvet glove of down-home folksiness and avuncularity, and his leadership would be crucial in the adoption of the legislation sought by the JPRC.[28] Just days after the election, another restrictive covenant decision came down, and it threw cold water all over *Drummond Wren*. On 11 June 1948 Justice Schroeder of the High Court released his decision in *Noble v. Wolf and Alley*.[29]

Mr Noble was one of the original purchasers of a lot in a cottage subdivision on the shore of Lake Huron called Beach O'Pines, initially laid out in 1933. Each purchaser was required to sign a covenant stating that the land in question should never be transferred to, or occupied or used by, 'any person of the Jewish, Hebrew, Semitic, Negro or coloured race or blood.' Another clause required purchasers to exact the same covenants from their purchasers, and the restrictions were to last until 1962. Mr Noble's widow, Annie Maude Noble, wished to sell her cottage in 1948, and Bernard Wolf, a wealthy Jewish businessman from London, Ontario, wished to buy it for $6,800. When Wolf's solicitor Ted Richmond discovered the clause during his title search and asked Noble's solicitor to apply for an order under the *Vendor and Purchasers Act* declaring the covenant void, both lawyers fully expected the court to follow *Drummond Wren*. Mrs Noble's neighbours had other ideas, however. They hired prominent Toronto K.C. Kenneth Morden to argue for the covenant's validity, so Wolf secured the services of John Cartwright to face off against him. The legal issues would now be debated fully in a way they had not in *Drummond Wren*, before a judge who had not embraced the *zeitgeist* to the same extent as Keiller Mackay.

Schroeder differed with Mackay on both the restraint on alienation point and the certainty point, but it was over the interpretation of public policy that the battle lines between the two men were most clearly drawn. Flatly stating his disagreement with Mackay's treatment of public policy, Schroeder declared the 'paramount' principle in this case to be freedom of contract. For him, only clear evidence of legislative intent to override it would suffice to ground the Laskin/Mackay argument. The real debate between Mackay and Schroeder was about the nature of law itself. For Schroeder a bright line separated the legal from the non-legal. Only judicial decisions and legislation were 'law,' and the sources relied on by Mackay to pour content into public policy were so much fluff. Treaties were not effective in domestic law until 'incorporated' in it by the appropriate federal or provincial legislation, and no such laws had yet been passed. The statements of Allied leaders had no legal status whatsoever. For Mackay, more influenced by natural law theories which had a renewed appeal after the legalistic excesses of the Third Reich, the line was not so bright. The entire world had recoiled at Hitler's attempts to define, segregate, degrade, and ultimately exterminate the Jews and other 'lesser races.' When the nations of the world had pledged to ensure that such acts could never be repeated, Mackay asked implicitly why such solemn commitments, undertaken by the government of Canada along with others, could not be considered 'law?' Were they not at least sufficiently 'law-like' that they might be used to inform the doctrine of public policy? More generally, why could the law not nourish itself from sources 'outside' formally binding enactments? Here, Mackay echoed the writings of Wright and Laskin from the 1930s, especially Wright's 'An Extra-Legal Approach to Law' and Laskin's article on 'The Problem of "Contracting Out."'

When the JPRC learned that Wolf planned to appeal, they set up a committee, chaired by Laskin, to assist Cartwright. The Congress retained J. Shirley Denison for his expertise on real estate law, with Norman Borins assisting, to represent Mr Wolf. Laskin's committee met repeatedly in the summer and fall of 1948 to prepare their arguments. When the Court of Appeal heard the case on 10 January 1949, the five judges gave counsel for Noble and Wolf a rough ride.[30] Justice Henderson could not hide his distaste for Jews, even when one was a party to the case and another (Borins) was pleading before him.[31] Cartwright was thus 'distressed but not surprised' when the court unanimously upheld Schroeder's decision five months later. All five judges agreed that public policy was about voluntary association, freedom of contract, and healthy uncoerced plurality, not about forcing people to accept neighbours they did not want. With the Cold War now descending, the judges managed to suggest that the contrary view was totalitarian. Justice Hope was of the view that 'freedom of the individual in and under a democracy has implicit in it, as an absolute, the freedom of association[:] the activities of the people of a free nation' demanded it. The *Globe and Mail* approved, observing that 'to give any one a legal right to force himself uninvited into an association of people would be the most certain way to add to social tensions.'[32] The editorial writer, like the judges themselves, invoked the spectre of the pushy Jew, constantly poking his nose in where he was not wanted.

The *Globe*'s reaction stood out. Most newspapers were violently critical of the decision, and it gave Rabbi Feinberg the opportunity to exercise his talent for colourful prose. 'Canadian democracy,' he opined in the *Toronto Daily Star*, 'may never grow beyond a collection of isolated racial units, roped off from one another by a legalized iron curtain of snobbery and barred from the mutual acquaintance and understanding which alone can develop internal unity.'[33] The adverse decision meant Bora Laskin would spend another summer and fall meeting with his team and strategizing about an appeal to the Supreme Court of Canada.

Opinions were sharply divided on how to proceed. Saul Hayes of the CJC in Montreal had written to say that lawyers there saw no chance of winning on public policy. Cartwright the tactical litigator thought there was 'an even chance on the public policy angle and a good chance on uncertainty,' and wished to make the latter argument more prominent in the pleadings.[34] For Laskin the academic and activist, 'the most important line to be followed was that the public policy issue be given as much attention as possible in the pleadings.'[35] Eventually they agreed to stay with the same four points made in the Court of Appeal. On 22 December the team suffered a major blow: John Cartwright was appointed to the Supreme Court of Canada, along with Gérald Fauteux, as the Court expanded to nine members in view of the imminent abolition of Privy Council appeals. Congress retained J.J. Robinette to replace Cartwright as counsel for Annie Noble, with Walter Williston as his junior.

It was thus before a newly 'supreme' Supreme Court of Canada that the appeal was heard in June of 1950. Cartwright of course could not sit, and Chief Justice Rinfret sat out as well to provide an odd number of judges. Counsel for Noble and Wolf had a much more relaxed time than in Toronto. With recent changes in personnel, the Court was now stronger intellectually than it had ever been, and more liberally inclined. A few days before the argument in *Noble* it had just reheard the appeal of Aimé Boucher, a Quebec farmer convicted of seditious libel for distributing a Jehovah's Witness pamphlet entitled 'Quebec's Burning Hate for God and Christ and Freedom.' Its decision, handed down in December, would redefine the law of seditious libel and overturn his conviction in a decision containing 'the most overt statement of judicial creativity yet found in the [Court's] decisions.'[36] With men like Ivan Rand, James Estey, and Patrick Kerwin on the bench, the team was not terribly surprised when the Court of Appeal decision in *Noble* was overturned. Even so, and much to Bora Laskin's disappointment, the Court did not touch the public policy issue.[37] Rather, they seized the technical argument advanced by Laskin's old nemesis Shirley Denison – that such a covenant did not touch and concern the land because the attributes of the owners had nothing to do with land use.

From a strictly legal point of view, basing the decision on the failure of racist covenants to touch and concern the land rather than on public policy was actually a stronger result. It meant that such covenants were not true restrictive covenants at all and could never bind subsequent purchasers. Race- and religion-based zoning was over, not just in Ontario but across Canada, and with retrospective effect since such covenants had never been legally effective to begin with. While the public was ready for *Drummond Wren* – a 1949 opinion poll showed 68 per cent of Canadians would definitely not sign a covenant prohibiting sale of their property to people of colour – the legal community as a whole was arguably not ready for Mackay's creative approach to public policy.[38]

The activists had already begun to explore legislative avenues for human rights protection before *Noble v. Wolf and Alley*, but their strategic loss in the Court of Appeal effectively closed the door to further test cases. The spring of 1949 saw a third organization added to the struggle for human rights in Ontario: Irving Himel's Association for Civil Liberties (ACL). The ACL was formed in the spring of 1949 to provide a home for the non-Communist members of the Civil Liberties Association of Toronto (CLAT). As the Cold War developed, trade unions and many voluntary associations began to purge their Communist members. Bora Laskin had not belonged to CLAT but he did appear on the board of the ACL, along with other prominent progressives, both Gentile and Jewish. The ACL became 'simply a letterhead organization,' run by Himel out of his law office, with no funds or staff.[39] Himel was something of a maverick, but the JPRC and the JLC worked with him on a number of issues.

All three groups decided to coordinate their efforts to lobby the new premier for legislation on employment discrimination and restrictive covenants. When they met with Premier Frost on 24 January 1950 they had three hundred delegates on side representing some seventy church, labour, professional, fraternal, and social welfare groups. The continuing denial of service to blacks in Dresden, publicized in an article entitled 'Jim Crow Lives in Dresden' in the 1 November 1949 issue of *Maclean's*, was a 'heaven-sent opportunity' for the fledgling human rights movement in Ontario.[40] Interestingly, a *Maclean's* article by Pierre Berton entitled 'No Jews Need Apply,' published a year earlier, had not generated nearly the same political momentum.[41]

Frost appeared somewhat cool to the delegation, but a wave of editorial support for legislative action may have helped him convince those in his own caucus who were reluctant to tamper with existing property and contract relations. Some opponents also lobbied him privately. Frost's fishing companion, County Court Judge H.A. McGibbon of Lindsay, wrote to him on 17 February when the legislation was introduced. 'Surely we have not arrived at this stage of life,' he fumed, 'where the Government is going to take it upon itself to dictate to whom I must sell my property, and whom I must have as my next door neighbour. I do not want a coon or any Jew squatting beside me, and I know way down in your heart you do not.' Surely someone setting up a new subdivision should be free 'to debar all but Anglo-Saxons. Nobody would be interested in any property if they felt that a Jew or a coon could come in and buy a lot in a strictly residential area.' Frost's reply was 'even-tempered but firm': the new law would not compel anyone to do anything, it simply prohibited certain actions.[42] This was somewhat disingenuous as McGibbon could indeed be compelled to accept a Jewish neighbour in future as a result of Frost's proposed legislation.

Once the legislation was announced in the Speech from the Throne, Laskin's committee scrutinized it and recommended strengthening the language to prohibit covenants based on 'nationality, birth-place, and national origin' in addition to the grounds of race and religion found in the bill. The attorney-general accepted these suggestions and they appeared in the bill as passed.[43] Two brief but important statutes were passed by the Ontario legislature in March 1950: an Act prospectively rendering void any restrictive covenant based on race, religion, or nationality, and another forbidding discrimination on such grounds in collective agreements. In order to build on the momentum, Laskin called a meeting for 1 March to discuss drafting laws on fair employment and fair accommodation practices. The former would be based on the New York model, and for the latter Laskin drafted amendments to the *Racial Discrimination Act*, broadening its scope to deal with acts of discrimination in public accommodation. In fact, all three opposition parties (Liberals, CCF, Labour Progressive Party) introduced fair employment practices bills that spring, though none passed. None used the *Saskatchewan Bill of Rights* as a model. It had been drafted by Laskin's friend Morris Shumiatcher and passed in 1947, but the only remedy provided for breaching the rights guaranteed therein was a quasi-criminal prosecution. Laskin knew this would mean the Act remained a dead letter; he wanted a civil enforcement apparatus that would have some impact beyond the educational.

The JPRC kept up its lobbying for a fair employment practices act through the rest of 1950. There was little strong opposition; even the Canadian Manufacturers' Association accepted the principle of the bill, though the *Globe and Mail* did not. The *Fair Employment Practices Act, 1951* passed in March, as did a companion piece of legislation not sought by the JPRC, the *Female Employees Fair Remuneration Act, 1951*.[44] The lack of interest by the JPRC in gender discrimination illustrates their acceptance of prevailing ideas about the necessity of differential treatment for women and men in many areas of life. The administration of the two Acts was confided to the Department of Labour, suggesting that labour supply issues were prominent in Frost's mind. The premier was quite aware that British immigration was dropping rapidly, while that from other countries was increasing. 'Ontario was going to be host to a lot of immigrants,' he told Ben Kayfetz, and he 'didn't want them to feel like second class citizens.'[45]

For the next few years, it was not clear whether Frost would make good on his vow. When the attorney-general finally admitted in late 1953 that nothing could be done about the situation in Dresden under existing law, the JLC, the ACL, and the JPRC swung into action. Donna

Hill of the JLC coordinated a major public relations campaign, calling upon Bora Laskin, David Lewis, and others to provide the legal advice underlying the substantial brief presented to Frost in March 1954 advocating a fair accommodation practices law. In spite of efforts made by agents provocateurs to tarnish black activism as communist-inspired, Frost was receptive and the law passed in April.

Such was the close relationship between the Frost government and the Jewish activist groups that their draft bills were accepted with little amendment in 1951 and 1954. Some of the initial drafts prepared by Laskin or Syd Harris were much broader than those eventually settled on by the committee. One, for example, declared the right to freedom from discrimination in employment on the basis of race, religion and similar grounds to be a civil right.[46] The final draft adopted by the legislature was more modest, containing no rights language at all, and no direct action to sue for discriminatory acts. It began with a preamble declaring it to be 'contrary to public policy in Ontario to discriminate against men and women in respect of their employment because of race, creed' and the like, and noting such action to be 'in accord with the Universal Declaration of Human Rights as proclaimed by the United Nations.' Laskin was clearly trying to enshrine legislatively what the Court of Appeal had refused to do judicially. The 1951 Act's operative provisions were contained in three short prohibitions. No employer could discriminate in employment; no trade union could discriminate in membership; and no application or oral interview for employment could refer to any preference for candidates of a particular race or religion. On receipt of a complaint, the director of the Fair Employment Practices Branch of the Ministry of Labour could appoint a conciliation officer who would try to effect a settlement. If this failed, a commission could be appointed with all the powers of a conciliation board under the *Labour Relations Act*. After a hearing the commission could recommend reinstatement with or without compensation to the director, who in turn could recommend to the minister, whose order would be final. The *Fair Accommodation Practices Act, 1954*, which prohibited discrimination on the specified grounds in respect of 'accommodation, services or facilities available in any place to which the public is customarily admitted,' followed exactly the same pattern. So did the *Canada Fair Employment Practices Act, 1953*, shorn of the preambular statement about public policy, and subsequent legislation in other provinces.

Aside from the preamble to the Ontario statutes, the language of the new laws was reassuringly familiar. So were its procedures, based explicitly on the existing labour relations model. The titles contained motherhood sentiments. Who could be against 'fairness' in employment or accommodation? The activists were keen to portray the provincial state as a kindly parent encouraging its child-citizens to get along, not a highly coercive disciplinary apparatus. Such incrementalism and attractive packaging was important in overcoming resistance to the legislation, especially within the Conservative caucus. Frost often said that 'his job was like feeding a young child–he could no more obtain immediate acceptance of minority rights than a parent could cajole a child into eating a large meal.'[47] The fact that the Jewish organizations and their allies could present the legislation they desired as 'respectable, responsible, democratic and Canadian,' in James Walker's words, helped Frost enormously.[48]

The JPRC did not make the mistake of demanding more from Frost than he could give, and relations were smoothed by their allies in the Conservative Party. Laskin's friend Eddie Goodman tried to persuade Frost that passing a fair employment practices law was not only the right thing to do morally, but was also politically wise.[49] Would-be Conservative politician Allan Grossman needed some action by government on discrimination issues if he was going to succeed in his campaign to wrest an inner city riding with a large Jewish/ethnic population from the communist Joe Salsberg. He succeeded in 1955, the year after the *Fair Accommodations Practices Act* was passed.[50]

The activists also tried to make anti-discrimination legislation more palatable by adopting the least controversial approach available. In the field of employment discrimination, they advocated a colour-blind disparate-treatment vision of discrimination favouring individual rights, merit-based personnel decisions, and equality of opportunity. A competing philosophy, known as disparate-impact, is group-based; it assumes that 'institutional racism is so pervasive as to render individual merit meaningless, and regards group representation [i.e., quotas] as the safest guarantee of individual rights.'[51] In the United States, the latter model had some brief success before the war, but the state fair employment commissions adopted the individualized model of discriminatory behaviour in the 1940s and '50s. It was written into the U.S. *Civil Rights Act* of 1964 but by the later 1950s was being condemned as ineffective by American civil rights groups. The colour-blind model assumed that both the hypothetical white and black candidates for a particular job were equally competent, and that only the arbitrary factor of race separated them. It ignored the history of generations of unequal treatment of blacks, native peoples, and others, especially in the field of education. As Canadian journalist David McReynolds put it, 'the Civil Rights Act of 1964 is dramatic on paper but ... only guarantees that black millionaires, as well as white millionaires, may book rooms at the best American hotels. The mass of Negroes ... are more concerned with getting a job at a wage that will enable them to eat at all.'[52]

The same could have been said about the Canadian anti-discrimination laws of the 1950s. As James Walker has noted, they were based on an 'understanding of prejudice as an individual pathology within a democratic society that was fundamentally fair.'[53] The new laws eliminated some of the more public indignities suffered by members of minorities, such as refusal of service in restaurants, but had little to say about the limited educational and employment opportunities available to most blacks and native Canadians. It is not clear that an aggressive pursuit of a disparate-impact strategy was feasible in Canada, however, even if it could have been sold politically. Racial proportionalism would have been difficult when native Canadians formed only 2 per cent of the national population, and the black population only 1 per cent. In any case, alternate visions of discrimination never seem to have come up at the JPRC. Their individualistic approach to discrimination was in tune with the ethos of the post-war years, with its backdrop of anti-communism and hostility to class-based initiatives outside the carefully circumscribed domain of collective bargaining.[54] Another generation would pass before a new constellation of actors challenged the strategies of the post-war Jewish activists.

If Laskin's 'fair practices' approach to discrimination might be found insufficient with the benefit of hindsight, it should also be emphasized that his conception of human rights was in some ways more powerful than those current by the end of the century. Laskin's work in labour law cannot be dissociated from his human rights work. Both shared a common concern with the enhancement of human dignity. Being arbitrarily dismissed by an employer was just as offensive to human dignity as not being given an apartment because of one's race. All human beings were entitled to respectful treatment in their dealing with others, and it was the job of law to codify minimum standards for such treatment in numerous areas of human interaction. Laskin would have been surprised to find indignities based on race, gender, and sexual orientation as the principal focus of Canadian human rights law in the twenty-first century, while those resulting from social class or income level were virtually ignored.

The activists' efforts did not slacken after the passage of the legislation they had sought. Especially in the early years, the JPRC was concerned that the Fair Employment Practices Branch of the Ministry of Labour was too hesitant in its approach, too reliant on the voluntary cooperation of employers. The JPRC and the branch functioned as a kind of uneasy private-public partnership with respect to enforcement, with the JPRC bringing violations and administrative anomalies to light and following up on their correction.[55] After a long struggle, the recalcitrant barbers and restauranteurs of Dresden finally complied with the Act.[56] A subsequent case taken up by the JPRC presented the possibility of considerable embarrassment. A complaint by a black man that a Jewish landlord had refused to rent a vacant flat to him was found to be legitimate after investigation by the JLC. The matter was 'pursued with full rigour' by the JPRC and County Court Judge Thomas of Bracebridge eventually held a hearing. He duly found an act of discrimination had been proved, but denied the applicant relief after interpreting the Act not to apply to multiple-unit apartment buildings. These did not, in his view, provide 'accommodation ... in [a] place to which the public is customarily admitted.'[57] Thomas's exercise in statutory interpretation was a perfect example of the narrow, literalist approach Laskin had railed at in his earlier scholarship, but he had become inured to it by the 1950s.

The JPRC felt itself bound to pursue a legislative amendment in view of its prior involvement in the field. Laskin pursued his own private testing of the efficacy of the *Fair Accommodation Practices Act* with some of his law students. Julius Isaac was a black Grenadian student who entered the law school in 1955. Laskin asked Isaac to pose as a potential tenant and respond to advertisements for rental accommodation in particular buildings. When, as often happened, Isaac was told all the units had been rented, Laskin would have a white law student go and make the same inquiries, only to be shown one or more available flats.[58] In this case, however, amendment of the Act was not a foregone conclusion. It was not until 1961 that the desired change took place, and a discriminatory denial 'of any dwelling unit in any building that contains more than six self-contained dwelling units' was prohibited under the Act.[59] Presumably the Conservative government found it more difficult to resist the protests of the vocal Toronto landlord lobby than the less well-organized opponents of previous anti-discrimination laws.

Laskin also had occasion to observe discriminatory practices among law firms hiring articling students. He functioned as a placement office for law students, and he and Caesar Wright were particularly concerned to place minority students in the better-known firms. Laskin's first big success was with Stan Schiff, for whom he arranged an interview at Borden and Elliott in 1956. Schiff was delighted with his articling experience and was asked back as an associate but by that point had accepted an offer from Wright to teach.[60] His good fortune was not immediately replicated. Laskin had a harder time placing Julius Isaac, whom the larger firms did not want in spite of his excellent marks and recommendations. In the end Laskin's friend David Lewis hired Isaac as an articling student.

Anti-semitism, though generally on the wane in the 1950s, remained a strong force in some quarters of the legal profession. At the firm McCarthy and McCarthy, Laskin's book on constitutional law was not permitted in the firm library as a result of the prejudice of a senior lawyer. The firm had no Jewish lawyers even though some of its partners had a large Jewish clientele.[61] Within the Lawyers' Club, a motion to remove the requirement for members to be Christian and white was the subject of such controversy in 1945 that no one dared bring up the issue again for some years, and it was not until 1952 that the offending clauses were removed. (Not until 1966 would anyone question the gender bar.) The vote of 115 to 39 suggested a less than enthusiastic welcome for non-WASP members, and no Jews seem to have applied for membership until the mid-1960s.[62] On the positive side of the ledger, Isadore Levinter was elected the first Jewish bencher in 1956, and Dean Smalley-Baker at Osgoode agreed to move exams out of the Friday afternoon slot to accommodate observant Jews.

Even before the Thomas decision, Laskin had become disillusioned with the cumbersome enforcement procedures of the fair practices Acts. Having considered New York and New Jersey precedents, Laskin wanted a board combining conciliation powers with the authority to issue cease and desist orders.[63] For Laskin the legal modernist, the specialized expert administrative body was the proper solution. These efforts met with partial success with the creation of an Anti-Discrimination Commission in 1958, but Laskin was especially pleased when the Ontario Human Rights Commission was created in 1961 as an independent body with sole jurisdiction to enforce the rights guaranteed in the new Ontario Human Rights Code of 1962.[64] The Code replaced the separate pieces of fair practices legislation and transformed their prohibitory clauses into broad declarations of rights in the manner of a constitutional charter.

Returning to the distinction between equality rights and civil liberties introduced earlier, a striking pattern in Bora Laskin's life emerges. With regard to equality rights he functioned almost exclusively as an activist, albeit mostly behind the scenes, and almost never as a scholar or public intellectual. With regard to civil liberties he functioned almost exclusively as a scholar and public intellectual and almost never as an activist. The pattern only began to shift in the very late 1950s when, with the emergence of the Bill of Rights, these two roles began to merge. It is not surprising that Laskin would carry on his advocacy of equality rights through the JPRC. What is curious is the apparent firewall between Laskin's anti-discrimination activism and his scholarship. After the brief case comment on *Christie v. York* in 1940, the topic disappears from Laskin's published scholarship until 1959, when he discussed equality rights as a category of civil liberties in an article on the Diefenbaker Bill of Rights. When his constitutional law casebook appeared in 1951, only two paragraphs on the subject appeared on the very last page. He wrote nothing on the restrictive covenant cases, for example, nothing on the spread of the fair employment and fair accommodations practices statutes across Canada in the 1950s.

Even Laskin's activism was of a very particular kind. He was never the JPRC spokesperson to the media, nor to government during the numerous delegations to the premier's office in the 1940s and '50s. Among his fellow activists he was respected, even held in awe. A former student recalled being invited to attend a JPRC meeting in the later 1950s, and found the degree of deference afforded Laskin quite unsettling.[65] His authority was such that when a Congress delegation asked Laskin to review a brief they planned to present to the parliamentary committee on the bill of rights in 1960, they semi-jokingly but tellingly referred to his approval as a *hechscher* (rabbinical blessing).[66] Within the Congress, Laskin was highly visible, but his role was not well known outside it.

Laskin chose not to be visible as an activist or scholar in this cause about which he cared so deeply for two reasons. He was wary of being too visible as an activist because of the need to maintain the reputation for impartiality he had achieved as an arbitrator. Just as Laskin avoided all public identification with any political party, he did not wish to appear *parti pris* with regard to any particular cause. He also did not wish to appear as an advocate in his own cause. The notion that 'voice' scholarship could be a legitimate form of scholarly expression lay far in the future. Laskin wanted his ideas to be taken seriously because of their content and the quality of his reasoning, not simply on the basis of his own personal characteristics. It is revealing that he made his proposal about an independent commission to monitor the implementation of the Universal Declaration of Human Rights not in the *Canadian Bar Review* or other scholarly journal but in a Canadian Jewish Congress publication. When Laskin wanted to reach the legal profession, he knew how to do so. That he chose not to do so with this proposal illustrates his hesitancy about discussing human rights issues outside the Jewish community.

The obverse side of Laskin's equality rights activism was his lack of overt engagement in the cause of civil liberties. Laskin's friend Frank Scott was active in this field, as was Rabbi Feinberg. As the Cold War deepened there was no shortage of infringements of civil liberties at home or in the United States to be concerned about, from the treatment of the suspects during the inquiry into the Gouzenko affair in 1946 to the spread of loyalty tests in the United States.[67] In 1952 several Canadian law professors wrote an open letter to the *Canadian Bar Review* to protest the U.S. government's demand that United Nations employees convicted of a loyalty offence in their own country, or invoking the privilege against self-incrimination in the course of such an investigation, should be barred absolutely from UN employment. The signatories were Laskin's colleagues Wolfgang Friedmann, J.B. Milner, and Eugene La Brie, and his friend Frank Scott, but Laskin himself did not sign.[68] Nor did he belong to any of the major civil liberties organizations of the period. He appeared on the letterhead of Irving Himel's Association for Civil Liberties, but in spite of its name the ACL was principally about fighting anti-Semitism.[69]

What to make of these associational choices? It is true that Jews did not commonly join Gentile associations at this time, but signing the 1952 letter would not have entailed joining a group. Did Laskin fear that speaking out on civil liberties abuses would later be used against him? Was he concerned about the possibility that seemingly innocent organizations might be Communist fronts? While fear is not a word one associates with Laskin's lexicon, he may have felt somewhat vulnerable during the intense Cold War atmosphere of the post-Gouzenko decade.[70] One casualty of the anti-Communist purge was Laskin's good friend Drummond Wren, sacked as educational director of the UAW in December 1947. Wren was not identified as a Communist but was thought to be 'travelling around in that company.' The perception not only cost him his job but also gave the WEA (of which Wren was still secretary) 'a black eye from which it ... never recovered.'[71] By the early 1950s the atmosphere was uncomfortably similar to that of 1940, when amidst wartime concerns about security Laskin had been singled out to swear a 'loyalty oath' to W.P.M. Kennedy. Jews felt under the spotlight once again as a result of the participation of some of their number in the Gouzenko affair and the execution of Julius and Ethel Rosenberg in 1953 for providing atomic secrets to the Russians. As we have seen, the Jewish activists were in fact being monitored by the RCMP, and they may have suspected such surveillance. Then there was the spectacular fall of Jacob Cohen. In 1945 he was the best-known union-side lawyer in Canada, defender of Communists though not a Party member himself, and a prominent champion of many progressive causes. In 1946 he was sentenced to six months in prison for assaulting his secretary, the next year he was disbarred, and in 1950 he died mysteriously, possibly a suicide. Cohen's biographer has found that the assault did occur and that Cohen's trial was fair but there was a widespread perception in the Jewish community at the time that the decision to prosecute had been orchestrated by a vengeful legal establishment.[72]

It is useful to compare the activities of Laskin and Frank Scott in this regard. Scott could speak out on any number of issues from his unassailable position in the Canadian elite, even to the point of suing a thuggish premier who had intimidated an entire province. This is not to deny Scott's extraordinary personal courage, but his confidence was based in part on the impeccable Anglo-Quebec lineage standing behind him. There was no one but Laskin standing behind Laskin. At the end of the war he was only thirty-three, a junior professor at an institution (Osgoode) where academic tenure was not yet recognized. He had made his own way, and had to choose his battles very carefully. He also could not afford to squander the respectability he had built up so carefully. Frank Scott could commit any number of *faux pas* without losing his social capital; for a Jew, however, one false step could prove fatal.

Indirect proof of a certain self-censorship can be found in remarks Laskin made at a later date, when the worst of the McCarthy era had passed and his own position was more secure. At the second Commonwealth and Empire Law Conference held at Ottawa in September 1960, Laskin observed that '[t]here is little point in talking about legal liberty unless we associate with it a right to be adequately represented by counsel.' He reminded his audience how some of the accused were denied counsel during the investigations of the Royal Commission on Espionage in 1946. Without benefit of legal advice, they 'had not objected to answering criminating questions and hence lost the protection of the Canada Evidence Act' when their answers were admitted against them in their subsequent trials.[73] Laskin also referred to this example in his 1959 article on the Diefenbaker Bill of Rights, and in a 1962 article on the use of the Bill of Rights by the courts,[74] but he had not spoken out against it publicly at the time as far as can be determined.

Another critique by Laskin at the conference was more contemporary. 'There are, it is regrettable to say, verified cases of discrimination on the ground of religion and colour in the refusal of some firms to accept students for service under articles.' The extenuating arguments usually advanced – 'a highly personal relationship is involved,' or 'clients would object' – Laskin dismissed as 'shabby.' Such actions should be treated both 'as conduct unbecoming a barrister and solicitor and deserving of discipline by the controlling organisation,' and 'the equivalent of contempt of court.'[75] These were strong words, but Laskin chose to deliver them at an obscure conference rather than in a newspaper interview or an article in the *Canadian Bar Review*, where they would have been much more widely noticed.

Finally, when he was at the height of his fame in the mid-1960s, Laskin felt confident enough to lend his name to the reborn Canadian Civil Liberties Association. It had coalesced to oppose an Ontario government bill proposing a dramatic extension of police powers. Irving Himel's Association for Civil Liberties had won most of its battles, but Himel did not seem alert to emerging issues. Laskin, Harry Arthurs, and Julian Porter, all formally on the board of the ACL, decided Himel should resign so that the organization could be revived with a more contemporary and dynamic agenda. The men asked journalist and activist June Callwood to join them in their mission. To her astonishment, once inside Himel's door the men seemed reluctant to come to the point. After they praised Himel's accomplishments at great length, Callwood felt obliged to say 'Irving, you are wonderful but we have come here to ask for your resignation.' Later, as they left the building, Laskin expressed a surprised admiration at Callwood's *chutzpah*.[76] In its mix of Jewish and Gentile members the CCLA represented one of the first genuinely integrated activist groups; that in itself was a testament to the success of the post-war human rights movement.

Toronto became the centre of the movement for human rights protection in large part because discrimination against Jews, although already on the decline after 1945, was still widespread enough to be a constant irritant in the first ten years after the war. The existence of discrimination against other groups such as African and Japanese Canadians, and a growing awareness of human rights within the labour movement, provided allies with whom the Jewish activists could work, but without their catalytic role it is doubtful whether these small and marginalized groups would have made much headway. The post-war decade saw the adoption in Ontario of the half-dozen key pieces of legislation that would form the backbone of human rights protection across Canada for the remainder of the century. In most cases it was local JPRCs working with other local groups who galvanized the lobbying campaigns for legislative reform in other provinces, and who then kept a watching brief on enforcement of the new laws. That legislation, with its reliance on administrative rather than judicial enforcement, was heavily inflected with Bora Laskin's legal modernism. It marked a decisive shift, evident in many areas of Canadian law in the post-war world, away from the British example and towards U.S. legal models, but always adapted to a Canadian context. Even where the legislation was imperfectly enforced, its mere existence contributed powerfully to an emergent sense of Canadian identity, an inclusive identity transcending the old English-French divide and suitable for the tidal wave of non-British immigration about to sweep over the country.

Dedication, zeal, and intelligence are not enough to guarantee success in the legislative arena, however. The Toronto Jewish activists were definitely swimming with the tide. They lived in the fastest-growing city in North America, in the midst of a long period of steady economic growth. Unemployment and interest rates were low, and the standard of living for most Canadians was visibly increasing year by year. Post-war comfort and confidence generated its own tolerance. Toronto's Anglo-Celtic majority felt less threatened by the Jewish minority, who were no longer seen as a throng of unassimilable socialistic aliens but as respectable members of the white middle class keen to participate fully in Canadian society. Ontario had its pockets of non-white citizens, but the numbers of blacks, Chinese, and Japanese were small enough not to occasion alarm. The largely rural and northern native population was simply not on the radar screen for the urban Jewish activists. If Ontario, like Canada, was slowly becoming more tolerant of racial and ethnic diversity, it was also more accepting of state intervention in areas of life previously roped off as private. Leslie Frost was in the midst of recreating the provincial government as a modern administrative state, actively shaping economic development and promoting human betterment. The big breakthrough had been the remoulding of labour relations during the war, and the JPRC closely modelled their human rights legislation on that widely accepted precedent. They also espoused a mostly unthreatening 'colour-blind' philosophy of equal treatment rather than proposing more radical measures such as quotas for particular minority groups.

Laskin and his colleagues are a textbook example of what Robert Putnam has called 'the civic-minded World War II generation.'[77] Laskin may have sat out the war but he made up for it during the peace. The Toronto Jewish activists recognized Laskin's leadership by persuading him to chair numerous committees, to draft and lobby for anti-discrimination legislation, and to settle their own internal differences. In spite of many other professional commitments he went to countless meetings at the JPRC office at 150 Beverley Street. Laskin was not a Frank Scott, battling on behalf of civil liberties in high-profile courtroom dramas. While Laskin admired – perhaps was even a little envious of – Scott's courtroom successes, his own talents lay in another direction; he lent them unstintingly where they were most effective.

12

Academic Freedom

It was a mysterious beginning to an extraordinary controversy at Winnipeg's United College. On 10 April 1958 a private letter from one faculty member to another showed up in a blue envelope on the desk of principal William Cornett Lockhart. Its original envelope was missing and attached to it was an anonymous typed note: 'Found in College Hall. We think you should read it. Some staff loyalty???' The author of the misdirected missive, history professor Harry Crowe, was on leave at Queen's University. He had written to Professor William Packer of the German department inquiring about the fledgling United College Association (UCA). Packer, Crowe, and other colleagues had formed the association a few years earlier to press the college administration for better wages and faculty representation on the board of regents. In the letter Crowe criticized the board, the principal, other faculty members, and religion in general. He thought it galling that the board had tried to pressure faculty into canvassing for money for the college when they had said administration was none of the faculty's business. Principal Lockhart, a minister of the United Church, was bound to resent Crowe's statements that he 'distrust[ed] all preachers' and found religion to be 'a corrosive force.' Finally, for good measure, Crowe expressed his displeasure with the 'freeloaders' – those faculty members who had not joined the UCA.[1] When dismissed by the board of regents on the basis of the sentiments expressed in the letter, Crowe resolved to fight. The contest would test the mettle of the nascent Canadian Association of University Teachers, entrench Bora Laskin's reputation as a fearless champion of academic values, and highlight the growing conflict between boards and faculty over understandings of the university constitution.

United College was the long-delayed posthumous child of the 1925 union of the Methodist, Presbyterian, and Congregational churches that created the United Church of Canada: Winnipeg's Methodist Wesleyan College and Presbyterian Manitoba College merged in 1938 to form the new institution. Two decades later it was still a small church-affiliated college with some fifty faculty and an atmosphere of complacent 'no-frills rectitude.' The *United College Act* required that students be educated 'according to the principles of the Christian religion,' and stated that professors held their positions at the pleasure of the board.[2] Even aside from the Act, university professors were expected to share the basic ethos of their employers. For a professor at a religiously affiliated college to declare religion 'a corrosive force' – even in private – was considered a radically disloyal act.

Crowe himself accepted this at first and conveyed unofficially to the board his plan to resign after a final year at United, but warned that he would fight a dismissal.[3] At its meeting on 2 July the board decided nonetheless to dismiss the offending professor. It believed it had grounds to do so without notice but allowed Crowe to remain at the college for another year provided he reported for duty by 1 September. The board's reasons for this provocative, unnecessary, and 'astonishingly inept' action are hard to discover.[4] For his part, Crowe was far away in Kingston and received the news by letter. Whatever the motive, the dismissal appeared shockingly high-handed to faculty. Even Queen's Principal W.A. Mackintosh found it 'completely outrageous.'[5]

This emergent drama featured a cast of ill-assorted characters. The two dominant personalities were Allan Watson, the chairman of the board, and Crowe himself. Watson was a retired banker 'of conservative views and decisive habits.'[6] Crowe, a recipient of the Military Cross, was a tough man with an air of disreputability and rebelliousness; even friends thought him 'a very smearable person.'[7] He was not about to conform to the Sunday school picnic vision of life that supposedly animated the denizens of United College. Principal Lockhart was something of a cypher caught between these two forceful men, though his wife Eileen 'showed some personality resemblance to Marie-Antoinette' in Kenneth McNaught's estimation.[8] Well-meaning and liberal-minded, Lockhart had arrived at United four years earlier after a successful pastoral career in Toronto, but remained rather in the shadow of the local notables represented in the board of regents. The Crowe case would be his baptism of fire.

When Crowe informed the Queen's faculty association (to which he still belonged) of the situation, it immediately requested the Canadian Association of University Teachers (CAUT) to set up an inquiry. A few days later three professors were given a mandate 'to investigate carefully all relevant circumstances surrounding Professor Crowe's dismissal and attempt to determine to what extent issues of academic freedom and tenure are involved,' to make such recommendations as they saw fit, and to report to the CAUT council in November. This was a bold move for the CAUT, established only seven years earlier as a result of the same kind of discontent with salaries and benefits that had provoked the creation of the UCA. The CAUT had never conducted such an inquiry, and did not even have a central office. President Clarence Barber, an economist at the University of Manitoba, asked two other economists to conduct the inquiry: Vernon Fowke of the University of Saskatchewan, and David Slater of Queen's. Rounding out the trio was Martin Johns, a physicist at McMaster. Fowke was a Fellow of the Royal Society of Canada, and past president of the CAUT.

United College challenged the choice of Slater on the ground of apprehended bias, and Bora Laskin's name was suggested to Barber as a substitute by H.D. 'Buzz' Woods, director of the Industrial Relations Centre at McGill.[9] Woods had initially encouraged Barber to settle the case if at all possible 'because the conflict will encourage a lot of muckraking against [Harry].' Laskin had learned of the case at the June Learned Societies meeting in Edmonton, which had been 'awash in discussions of United College,'[10] and eagerly accepted Barber's offer. On 17 September he advised Woods that he had already met with Fowke and Johns in Toronto to consider the procedure to be followed.[11] The inquiry was given an added fillip on 15 September when the board dismissed Crowe a second time, with a year's salary in lieu of notice.

Martin Johns nearly threw the whole inquiry off the rails when he attended the meetings of the General Council of the United Church in Ottawa in late September. The United College situation was discussed at some length (although only Lockhart supporters were heard from) and the council voted almost unanimously to approve of the actions of the administration.[12] Barber persuaded a compromised Johns to withdraw from the inquiry. Frank Scott in turn was appalled at what he called the 'whitewash' of the college administration by the United

Church, writing to Laskin that this 'complete acquittal of the college authorities seems to suggest that all questions of justice are set aside and power interests have taken over. I think your committee has a chance of doing something of lasting value for the teaching profession, and it is strange that the opportunity should have arisen in the same year in which we have our first draft of a Bill of Rights.'[13]

The CAUT executive decided there was no time to replace Johns and went ahead with a two-person panel. This led to the criticism that the inquiry was not properly constituted, but Fowke and Laskin faced down the objection and proceeded. The board of United College pressed strongly upon the CAUT its desire to be represented on the panel, suggesting a tripartite body on the labour arbitration model: two CAUT representatives and two board representatives, with the chair chosen by agreement. The CAUT refused, rightly: the arbitration analogy was flawed. The CAUT had no legal power to affect the rights of Crowe or of the College, and had created the panel primarily to investigate the actions of the board of regents. Why should the board have a role in investigating itself? The process was purely voluntary, and the panel had no power to subpoena witnesses or enforce attendance. From the CAUT's point of view, the decision to maintain exclusive control of the inquiry process was crucial to its success, even though it soon led to the board's withdrawal. Meanwhile, back at United College, Stewart Reid of the history department and UCA president Kenneth McNaught led the pro-Crowe movement, but the campus was badly divided.

The inquiry began on 6 October in the Fort Garry Hotel. Principal Lockhart, board of regents chair Allan Watson, the board's lawyer D.C. McGavin, Crowe, Barber, and Kenneth McNaught all attended, primarily to discuss procedural questions. Laskin had earlier suggested to Fowke that they confer with each of the witnesses separately, letting each of them know at the conclusion of their interview what had been noted from their testimony.[14] Neither direct questioning nor cross-examination as such would be allowed, but adverse parties could propose questions to be put to the witnesses through the panel. Proceeding in this way would obviate the need for shorthand reporters and expedite production of the report. The prohibition on cross-examination was unacceptable to the board and surprised some observers, but it was the method followed by the American Association of University Professors in similar inquiries. It flowed from the premise that the panel was investigatory only, and was not about 'to umpire or referee a contest in forensic skill,' as Laskin put it in the report.[15] The board was also not happy with the panel's decision to allow Crowe and McNaught to attend the entire in camera hearing, even though the president and the board of regents were afforded the same privilege. For their part, Fowke and Laskin were insulted by McGavin's request that they sign affidavits of impartiality (they reluctantly complied). The tension in the room rose steadily over the course of the day, and was not relieved by news of the death of O.T. Anderson, United's dean of arts and science, in a car accident that morning.

At the opening of Tuesday's proceedings D.C. McGavin delivered an ultimatum: either accept the proposed five-person panel, or the board would boycott the hearing. Fowke firmly rejected this attack, and informed Watson that the inquiry would proceed whether the board participated or not. Fowke's stance that morning, said Laskin later, 'was to me one of the things which dignified the whole affair.'[16] Of Laskin's role, Kenneth McNaught recalled that '[f]rom beneath heavy brows, his extraordinarily sharp glance missed no nuance in the attempts to obstruct and invalidate the committee' made by McGavin.[17] The board's absence admittedly left the inquiry listing to port. The eleven men and women who testified were all on Crowe's side, but the panel's hearings were in fact 'the least important part of its work' since the lengthy paper trail was the main source of evidence. Still, Fowke and Laskin heard some disturbing testimony. Peggy Morrison, recently appointed registrar by Lockhart, had written a strong letter of protest as a graduate of the College to Watson with a copy to the principal. Lockhart censured her, she stated, accused her of writing the letter at McNaught's behest (which she denied), and implied that her job was at risk. Fowke and Laskin found such behaviour especially unacceptable where a woman was concerned.[18]

Once home, the two men parcelled out the sections and exchanged them by mail, but each made only minor corrections to the other's work. Fowke sketched in the factual background and wrote the section on tenure, while Laskin wrote the rest.[19] How he must have savoured this opportunity to air his views on the moral economy of the university – not just in an abstract essay, but in the more compelling context of a real dispute. The Crowe case was such a perfect vehicle for Bora Laskin, it was almost as if the hand of Yahweh had intervened to redirect the notorious letter to Principal Lockhart's in-box. Finally he had the seniority and the moral authority to articulate a ringing defence of the value of free inquiry and speech in the university context, and the ideal platform from which to proclaim his message.

Laskin was merciless in his castigation of the actions of the board of regents and of Principal Lockhart. The board's lawyer 'was determined to treat the investigation as if it arose out of a labour relations dispute between an employer and a trade union. The concept of a University as a community of scholars, as an integrated body of civilized men and women (composed of administrative heads, teaching faculty and students) dedicated to the pursuit of knowledge and development of wisdom, was completely absent from his presentation.' The president and the board were respectively 'tactless and arbitrary in their handling of a situation which they themselves had created.' Lockhart 'did not make even the minimum efforts which might reasonably have been regarded as his responsibility,' and he had been forced or permitted 'to occupy a position of docile subservience to the governing board.' Unlike the principal, Crowe had behaved in appropriately manly fashion (Laskin implied) in protesting the invasion of his private correspondence and the violation of his perceived rights.

The panel saw itself as 'assessing the conduct and treatment of Professor Crowe against a postulate of academic freedom and tenure and against a conception of procedural fairness.' Laskin immediately denied that the common law and statute law could be 'the sole measure of academic freedom and tenure or of procedural fairness in discipline of faculty members.' A board might be within its legal rights in dismissing a professor, but commit a moral wrong by breaching the conventions and expectations of the Canadian university community regarding academic freedom and tenure. The panel's very lack of legal foundation was actually liberating: since it was not a court of law it was not restricted to interpreting the positive law contained in university statutes and court decisions. It was free to examine the moral economy of labour relations in the university context.

Laskin and Fowke agreed on the existence of a set of fundamental unwritten principles governing academic freedom and tenure, a customary law of the university constitution. Thus the *United College Act*, stipulating that tenure, 'unless otherwise provided, shall be at the pleasure of the Board' was not determinative, especially in view of Crowe's original contract with the college. It stated that after a year's probation, his position would become 'permanent.' '[E]ven the most elementary understanding of security of academic tenure excludes arbitrary dismissal without just cause' and a prior opportunity to meet the charges being tendered, Laskin noted. The link to academic freedom was, in his view, straightforward: 'cause of dismissal which is a denial of academic freedom cannot be just cause.'

Was there a denial of academic freedom here? According to Laskin, a professor's privilege 'to utter and publish opinions in the course of teaching and research and to exchange opinions with faculty colleagues without liability to official censure or discipline is the commonly understood substance of academic freedom.' While conceding that 'particular institutions may require some kind of conformity [amounting] to acceptance of a limitation on academic freedom as otherwise generally understood,' the validity of such restrictions depended on their being clearly specified in advance and accepted by the faculty member. Crowe had not accepted any such limitation, and even if he had, Laskin continued, it could not be relied on to justify Crowe's dismissal. The principal should have first afforded him an opportunity to explain what he meant before taking any action. Here Laskin quoted his younger self on the indeterminacy of language: 'Persons in academic life are well aware that words do not always illuminate thoughts; that the reader may easily miss the point made by the writer.' In any case, it was 'no part of the function of a professor to speak only in accents familiar to the administration.'

Some have argued that the Crowe case was not about academic freedom at all.[20] Can the writing of a private letter constitute an exercise of academic freedom? Initially, and provided the letter remains private, it would seem not. Here, however, it did not remain private. The whole point was that, with regard to the second dismissal at least, the contents of the letter were indeed the basis for the board's termination of Crowe's employment. The college administration itself made the issue one of academic freedom by putting Crowe on trial for his assumed views and not providing an opportunity for him to rebut or qualify their interpretation. Fowke and Laskin did not say that views such as those expressed by Crowe, if meant by him to be taken at face value, would necessarily be protected by the concept of academic freedom for a professor at a church-affiliated college. Their point was that the board and Crowe should have entered into a dialogue to ascertain his true intent. Only then could it be determined whether his views exceeded permissible bounds.

This concern about due process would resurface two decades later in one of Laskin's most important judgments, *Nicholson v. Haldimand-Norfolk Board of Commissioners of Police*.[21] In *Nicholson* the relevant legislation gave specified protections from arbitrary dismissal to constables with more than eighteen months' service, but was silent with regard to those with less service. The police board dismissed Nicholson without reasons and with no opportunity to state his case. Breaking with previous jurisprudence, Laskin said the board owed an elementary duty of fairness to Nicholson, obliging it to provide reasons and an opportunity to reply.[22] Crowe had been treated a little better, but not much. Crowe's first dismissal letter contained no reasons at all. Only six weeks later, in a letter circulated to all faculty at United College, did the president justify Crowe's dismissal on the basis of his 'expressed attitudes to the College,' his threats of legal action, and the 'aggressive belligerency' of his communications with the principal, the board, and the church. The circular denied that Crowe's letter was before the board or influenced its decision, but Laskin found there to be a 'decided unreality' about the latter assertion. The letter containing notice of the second 'peremptory' dismissal of 15 September did not provide reasons either, but 'was subsequently justified in a statement to the press as based on the contents of [Crowe's] private letter.' In all this long and sorry train of events, Laskin inquired, why had Professor Crowe not once been afforded an opportunity to meet with the president or the board to respond to their concerns about his behaviour?

Fowke's analysis of the security of tenure issue parallelled closely Laskin's treatment of academic freedom. He too pointed to the disparity between the legal definitions of tenure as reflected in university statutes and the common understanding held in the academic community. In practice, the 'boss and hired hand relationship is not accepted as an appropriate analogy for the treatment of faculty by the governing boards of Canadian universities,' whatever the formal law might say. 'Academic freedom and security of tenure are neither ends in themselves,' Fowke observed, 'nor the exactions of special privilege but merely conditions indispensable for the performance of higher education.' Security of tenure was 'prerequisite to academic freedom.' It was not difficult to define the minimum standards of treatment for a 'permanent' member of staff such as Crowe: immunity from dismissal except for just cause, with no adverse decision to be made without the opportunity to know and answer the charges being made. Like Laskin, Fowke agreed that a ground of dismissal constituting a violation of academic freedom could not constitute 'just cause.' United College could not rely on the views in the letter because it had never given Crowe a chance to comment on what it found offensive in them, while Crowe's protest at the principal's unauthorized retention, photostatting, and employment of his letter could not itself constitute just cause.

Laskin called Fowke's section nine on tenure 'a magnificent piece of analysis' and later told him that their association was 'one of the most rewarding of all my experiences in the academic community.'[23] They were troubled, however, by Crowe's refusal to allow publication of the offending letter. Laskin thought it essential on both issues, academic freedom and security of tenure.[24] Crowe disagreed, having been advised that a court might consider his remarks defamatory.[25] Laskin managed to put a brave face on it. Absent any opportunity for Professor Crowe to meet charges based on the content of the letter, the views expressed in it were irrelevant. The most Laskin would do was hint at what Crowe had said: 'It is stale enough, and safe enough, even for churchmen, to deplore religious hypocrisy or to doubt whether devotion to religious principle in words is satisfactory if there is no manifestation of the devotion in action in the world in which we live.' Replacing 'religion' with 'law' and 'churchmen' with 'lawyers,' these were exactly Laskin's sentiments about his own profession. Devotion to the text of the law should never become a pretext for ignoring its spirit.

On the eve of the CAUT executive council's consideration of the report, Crowe's three strongest supporters submitted their resignations to the board: Kenneth McNaught, Stewart Reid, and Richard Stingle. For Laskin there was an uncanny parallel with another trio of resignations nearly a decade earlier. At the CAUT council meeting at the King Edward Hotel in Toronto on 22–3 November, twenty faculty associations from Dalhousie to UBC unanimously endorsed the Fowke-Laskin report. On the Saturday evening, Laskin invited McNaught to his home on Warren Avenue for a drink. There, McNaught recalled, Laskin was much more approachable than the rather formidable figure who had conducted the inquiry. He expressed grave concern for those who had supported Harry Crowe in a conversation laced with '[n]ot a little black humour.'[26] The labour arbitrator knew all about retaliatory firings. The evening was the beginning of a long friendship between Bora and Peggy Laskin and Kenneth and Beverley McNaught. Kenneth's leftist politics, his irreverent outspokenness, and his principled stance appealed to Laskin. The McNaughts moved to Toronto the next year when Kenneth accepted a position in the department of history at the University of Toronto – another parallel to Laskin's own history.

The Fowke-Laskin report was released on the twenty-fourth to generally favourable reaction across the country. A steady haemorrhage of staff culminated in Principal Lockhart's own resignation on 6 December. When the survival of the college itself looked to be at stake, a sudden wave of sympathy for Lockhart caused a reaction against the 'intransigent' professors. Laskin was drawn into an attempt by church authorities in Toronto to forestall further acrimony, but it was over-taken by events in Winnipeg. Board member Gordon Churchill, minis-ter of trade and commerce in the Diefenbaker government, brokered a settlement obliging the board to withdraw the letters of dismissal and affirm Crowe's position in the college.[27] Harry Crowe did not expressly make reinstatement of his colleagues a condition of his return, but assumed it would occur. The board eventually agreed to ignore all the resignations except those of McNaught, Stingle, and Reid, but Crowe saw this as a breach of faith and resigned on 22 March. In all thirteen faculty members and three administrative staff left United in support of Crowe, out of a faculty of about fifty. Michiel Horn has suggested that the board was quite prepared to pay this price as a means of getting rid of the troublemakers.[28]

Most who left United found positions elsewhere without too much difficulty, and most crossed Laskin's path again. McNaught went to Toronto, as we have seen, and Stingle to the University of Saskatchewan. Crowe became research director with a railway union before re-enter-ing academe at York University's Atkinson College in 1966, where he encountered Laskin on the board of governors. Political scientist Michael Oliver moved to McGill, and later to Carleton as president, where he too found Bora Laskin on the board of governors. Stewart Reid moved to Ottawa to become the first permanent executive director of the CAUT. Suffering from terminal cancer, Reid served long enough to welcome Bora Laskin as vice-president of the CAUT in 1963, though not long enough to see him assume the presidency a year later. With Laskin's help Peggy Morrison found a position in the registrar's office at the University of Toronto. Lockhart's resignation was not accepted by the board and the campus regained its equilibrium surprisingly quickly after the turmoil of 1958–9. When United became the Univer-sity of Winnipeg in 1967 Lockhart became its first president. Unfortu-nately, Vernon Fowke's health declined rapidly after the inquiry and Laskin was saddened to hear of his death only six years later, at the age of fifty-eight.

The Fowke-Laskin report marked a key turning point not only in the history of academic freedom in Canada, but also in the self-image of Canadian academics. In reviewing the case a year later, the *Toronto Daily Star* headline summed it up: 'United College Aftermath: Profs Flex Their Muscles.' As a result of the CAUT's actions, 'Canadian university administrators noted the bulging professorial biceps and were impressed ... [They] know the professors will play rough if they're shoved in future.' The professor was no 'blinking, timid egghead. The faculty man can be rugged in asserting his rights.'[29] The 'his' was more appropriate than the writer knew, given the inferior remuneration for women faculty, and the dismal proportion of female faculty at Canadian universities. Nearly a decade would pass before the academic world began to take seriously the particularly disadvantaged position of women faculty. At a time when boards of governors and faculty were almost all male, the portrayal of the Crowe affair as a kind of gladiatorial contest was almost inevitable.

The testosterone-charged imagery in the press merely reflected the language used in the Fowke-Laskin report itself. The professors tapped into a gendered discourse first used widely during the English Civil War, and later in the American Revolution: men siding with royal authority were labelled 'docile,' 'subservient,' or 'supine' (and hence inappropriately effeminate), while those on the side of 'the people' were invested with the traditional male qualities of firmness, leadership, and strength. It was this subtext to the comments about Lockhart's lack of leadership that sympathizers found unacceptably humiliating to the beleaguered principal. They had a point. Laskin had good reason to be critical of Lockhart, but no excuse to insult him by thinly veiled jibes at his manhood. For someone who often preached the values of civility and courtesy, Laskin's language did not display the kind of restraint associated with an impartial investigation. A triumphalist and even vindictive tone mars the authors' analysis at certain points. As a test for his future judicial career, one would have to give Laskin a six out of ten on this effort.

The immediate outcome of the Crowe case was failure, as Crowe resigned and most of his sympathizers fled. In symbolic terms, however, it took on a life of its own as a great victory. Using the new platform provided by the CAUT, two widely respected professors had stood up to an arbitrary board and outlined clearly the moral economy of the university community. Knowing full well that the legal deck was stacked against them, Fowke and Laskin simply ignored the formal law and brilliantly turned the struggle into one for hearts and minds. They threw down the gauntlet to university administrations across the country: here are the conditions on which we will work, flout them at your peril. In the ongoing struggle within Canadian universities over wages, working conditions, academic freedom, and university governance, a victory in one area provided strategic leverage in another. The Crowe case was an enormous morale-booster for the entire Canadian professoriate. A chastened administration at United College became the first in the country to approve an agreement dealing with professorial salaries, benefits, conditions of employment, tenure, and academic freedom in 1959.

The Crowe case led the CAUT to create its own academic freedom and tenure committee in 1959. Bora Laskin declined to join 'so long as the last echoes of the Crowe case have not died away.'[30] He recommended his colleague J.B. Milner, who became chair in 1964.[31] The Fowke-Laskin model of a voluntary inquiry presided over by respected academics has proved to be an effective tool to safeguard academic freedom on Canadian campuses ever since.[32] Two years after J.B. Milner's sudden death in 1969 the CAUT instituted the Milner Award for Academic Freedom. Its first recipient was, appropriately, Mr Justice Bora Laskin.

Harry Crowe's letter catapulted Bora Laskin beyond the confines of the law faculty and made him an instant celebrity in the university world, smoothing his way to the presidency of the CAUT a few years later and solidifying his status as elder statesman at his own university. But the Crowe case was about much more than the employment status of university professors or even academic freedom. In the public mind, it was also about Human Rights. Crowe's fate came to be seen as a potent illustration of the need for more secure protection of individual rights against the power of large institutions. Just two weeks after the release of the report, Laskin spoke at a conference marking the tenth anniversary of the Universal Declaration of Human Rights.[33] The latest developments in the Crowe affair appeared in Ottawa newspapers alongside coverage of the conference, at which Laskin delivered a trenchant critique of the proposed Bill of Rights.[34] John Humphrey, the Canadian director of the Human Rights Division at the UN, who also spoke at the conference and at a similar one in Winnipeg, linked the events in his diary: '[t]he Crowe case at United College which has so worked up public opinion in Canada gave background to the Winnipeg proceedings, while in Ottawa interest in the proposed Canadian Bill of Rights made the conference more topical.'[35]

Bora Laskin was the person who connected these events into a single narrative. Already well-known for his record on labour issues and his battle with the benighted benchers, Laskin's advocacy of a stronger bill of rights and his role in the Crowe case now raised his public profile even higher. The Crowe inquiry was the crucible in which all these elements fused, transforming Laskin into one of the heroes of the post-war rights revolution. After 1958, he was no longer just a law professor–cum–labour arbitrator. He was a public figure sought out for high-profile tasks within and beyond the university. If the Crowe case marked a turning point in the history of academic freedom and professorial status in Canada, it also began a new chapter in the life of Bora Laskin.

On his return from sabbatical in 1962 Laskin was pursued by law professor and CAUT president A.W.R. 'Fred' Carrothers for the CAUT executive. As Carrothers explained to Frank Scott, he was worried that the 'first blush of enthusiasm for the organization has worn off.' The main issue was 'university government, but we must get on with a study on the economic status of the university professor, and this RCMP [campus surveillance] business can get a lot worse ... [T]hese are tricky times for CAUT, and we should get the strongest people we can for the executive (that is the principal reason why I went after Bora).'[36] Carrothers was much less enthusiastic about Scott's suggestion of Laskin's future Supreme Court colleague Jean Beetz as a future vice-president. According to Carrothers, Beetz had been a disaster as president of the Canadian Association of Law Teachers.[37] At the 1963 annual meeting held at Laval Laskin was duly elected vice-president.

Owing largely to the weakness of local faculty associations and the absence of codified procedures around hiring, discipline, and dismissal at most universities, the CAUT played a critical role in university life in the 1960s. Its research function was invaluable in a rapidly changing university environment. As the numbers of dues-paying faculty members shot up, the CAUT was able to flesh out its bare-bones establishment. In addition to a full-time executive director, the national office at 77 Metcalfe Street in Ottawa housed an administrative secretary, E.L. Southwell, a part-time secretary, and a full-time researcher, Witold Weynerowski. Stewart Reid was succeeded in May 1964 by another prairie academic, Percy Smith of the University of Saskatchewan. Two issues preoccupied Laskin during his tenure at the CAUT: a major study on university governance, and RCMP activities on Canadian campuses. The first involved mainly administrative legwork but the second required leadership, diplomacy, and tenacity.

University of Toronto president Claude Bissell could see where the professorial 'muscle flexing' would lead if unmet by some creative response.[38] As president of the National Conference of Canadian Universities and Colleges in 1962–3 he steered that body to accept Stewart Reid's idea for a joint study of Canadian university government. The

Ford Foundation subsidized it to the tune of $50,000 and the steering committee, on which Laskin sat, decided to name one American and one British commissioner to conduct the study. The British commissioner was to be Sir James Mountford, and the American, Robert A. Berdahl of San Francisco State College, author of a well-received study of British universities. When Mountford withdrew due to illness, Laskin was stuck with the task of finding a successor. He spent the next May in England doing so, and finally settled on Sir James Duff, sometime vice-chancellor of the University of Durham and vice-president of the BBC. At first glance Duff and Berdahl seemed an unlikely pair: Berdahl almost a caricature of the eager young American academic, Duff, thirty years older, 'a stout kindly English country squire' with a slow, deliberate manner. Yet, as Claude Bissell recalled, they got on 'famously.'[39]

To find Duff Laskin engaged in what might be called 'judge shopping.' With Bissell's approval, he sought someone prepared to look critically at the Canadian corporate board model. As the CAUT secretary E.L. Southwell confessed to Sir James Mountford after his withdrawal, there was a 'wide-spread assumption that the corporation set-up, with its lay boards, is the normal way to organize and run a university.' She knew most British academics would find this model undemocratic, but worried that 'there may be senior academics in Britain who would not care to recommend any radical revision which would "buck" the [Canadian] Establishment.' While, she hastened to add, this was to be an 'impartial investigation, with unbiased recommendations,' Southwell hoped that the report would be made 'by someone not only of stature in the education world but also with a real understanding of just what a university community should be.'[40]

Bora Laskin's own idea of 'what a university community should be' was much closer to the older European model of the self-governing community of scholars than to the North American model with its sharp division between academic (Senate) and financial (board) authority. Himself a member of the University of Toronto Senate for many years, Laskin was a staunch defender of the senatorial role in setting academic policy but advocated greater faculty control over budgetary matters in order to fulfil this function. Unlike his friend Fowke, who opposed lay boards altogether, Laskin preferred mixed boards whose lay members would ideally defer to the academics on major policy questions, guided by a strong and academically minded president.

The Duff-Berdahl Report hewed closely to Laskin's philosophy of university governance.[41] It diagnosed the problem as the near-total separation of powers between boards and senates, and recommended closer integration of the two. There should be faculty or senate representatives on boards of governors and possibly some token representatives of the board on senate. Student representation on either body was totally ignored, leading Sir James Duff himself to observe that the report seemed 'out of date almost before it appeared.'[42] The report was also deficient in its blithe assumption that once faculty members sat on boards they would actually have a voice in university government. With the addition of student members to senates and boards, and the diffusion of more consultative procedures surrounding faculty, decanal, and senior administrative appointments, Canadian university government rests today largely where Duff-Berdahl left it.

The debate over university governance unfolded in the early 1960s with all the drama of a church bake sale. Academics tried to shape public opinion through the standard tools of reports, public addresses, and strategic media coverage. A number of like-minded, left-leaning professors put together a collection called *A Place of Liberty: Essays on the Government of Canadian Universities, Dedicated to the Memory of Stewart Reid*, which contained a manifesto of sorts.[43] Governing boards were too powerful and unaccountable, and the gap between scholars and administrators should be ended 'as far as possible.' Edited by George Whalley of the Queen's University department of English, contributors included Frank Scott, Frank Underhill, Vernon Fowke, and Max Cohen, now dean of the McGill Faculty of Law. Notably, the volume included essays from Quebec scholars Paul Lacoste and Pierre Dansereau. Laskin contributed an appendix summarizing the few decisions rendered by Canadian courts on academic freedom and tenure; his conclusion echoed that in the Crowe case: 'the principles laid down [by the courts] do not comport with the views generally held by the academic community.'[44] The most radical suggestion in the book was Whalley's advocacy of elections for presidents and board members, as 'a reasonable restraint upon inbreeding and ... self-perpetuation.'[45] Boards were mostly unreceptive to these overtures until the eruption of the student power movement of the later 1960s, which posed a more fundamental challenge to authority structures than the idealism of *A Place of Liberty* or the tired bromides of Duff-Berdahl. By then Bora Laskin was on the other side of the fence, chairman of one board of governors and member of another. In a world suddenly turned upside down, Laskin would find himself struggling to maintain the status quo rather than advocating reform.

The key weakness in Duff-Berdahl, and in Laskin's own views, lay in leaving the dual spheres model largely intact. Laskin, like Frank Scott, thought boards with faculty representation would ultimately become constitutional monarchs, using their fiscal powers largely to implement the academic policy agreed on by the senate.[46] The view was not far-fetched at the time. The power of boards was temporarily on the wane in the 1960s as munificent government support made their fiscal powers less significant. In the later 1960s business ideology itself was suddenly thrown on the defensive by a counter-cultural movement emphasizing the links between North American industry and the Vietnam war. This setback for the business board model proved to be a transient phenomenon. The fiscal and fund-raising power of boards was critical to the reshaping of Canadian universities in the 1970s, '80s, and '90s as state financing went into steady decline. Student and faculty representation on boards became largely window dressing, as the real power withdrew into a smaller executive circle of administrators and key board members. Faculty reacted to a threatening environment by forming labour unions at many universities and largely abandoning any effort to penetrate the governance structure. For Bora Laskin these developments represented a swapping of professional status for that of mere employees, and a betrayal of everything he had fought for. He told the CAUT so in no uncertain terms – to the great discomfiture of his audience – when he was invited to address their twenty-fifth anniversary dinner in May 1976.[47] It is not clear whether, in the new fiscal and political climate, he had any solutions to propose consistent with his philosophy of university governance.

Bora Laskin's two years on the CAUT executive coincided with the awakening of concerns about the presence of counter-subversion activities by RCMP officers on Canadian campuses. The RCMP had always tried to keep tabs on suspected campus Communists without arousing much public indignation. The emergence of the nuclear disarmament movement caused the RCMP to recruit informants on various campuses in the early 1960s. In public Minister of Justice Davie Fulton defended the force, but privately he 'ordered a halt to secret security investigations on campus, including the recruitment of new sources, although the RCMP was allowed to continue receiving intelligence from existing ones.'[48] His successor Donald Fleming refused to meet with CAUT representatives to discuss their 'farfetched' concerns.[49]

Further allegations of RCMP attempts to recruit sources on campus surfaced in the fall of 1962, but inquiries by the CAUT were met with contradictory responses. When a young NDP MP from British Columbia, Thomas Berger, asked in Parliament about the nature of RCMP activities on campus, the official reply was: 'Members of the RCMP are not engaged in interviewing students and faculty members at Canadian universities about the political views and political activities of other students and faculty members.' No sooner had the official denial been made, than Commissioner Harvison of the RCMP admitted in an interview with the Canadian University Press that the force was indeed engaged in monitoring the Communist presence in various campus organizations.[50]

Two weeks after the Harvison interview the Diefenbaker government fell, and the CAUT decided to bide its time until Lester Pearson's team had had a chance to settle in. When Bora Laskin came on to the CAUT executive in June, he eagerly took on the RCMP file. First he shepherded through CAUT Council a resolution advising CAUT members that they were not compelled to reply to RCMP questions on the political or religious beliefs, activities, and associations of colleagues and students. It urged them not to reply orally to such questions, but if they chose to reply, to do so only in writing.[51] Laskin then sought the assistance of the new Liberal member for Northumberland, Pauline Jewett, to secure a meeting with the Prime Minister and the new minister of justice, Lionel Chevrier. A professor at Carleton University with a civil libertarian bent, Jewett was happy to act as intermediary between the CAUT and the government on this issue. Within a month Laskin, Stewart Reid, and Jewett met with Pearson, Chevrier, and Gordon Robertson, clerk of the privy council, to discuss RCMP activities. Laskin provided Chevrier with a list of recommended actions regarding both the RCMP's general security and intelligence activities, and its investigations on Canadian campuses. On the former question, the CAUT advocated investigation by an independent commission of inquiry into the 'present jurisdiction, procedures, records, qualifications, and training, of the S[ecurity] & I[ntelligence] section of the RCMP,' together with the establishment of a tribunal where persons who felt maligned could test the validity of the RCMP's conclusions. As for campus activities, the list of 'recommendations' sounded more like a list of demands: 'no general surveillance, no questioning of members of suspected organisations, no recruiting of informers, no communication of suspicions to other parties.'[52]

Laskin and Reid reported back to the CAUT that they had 'received a cordial and sympathetic hearing and were satisfied that the Government appreciated the special position of universities and the essentiality of a climate conducive to freedom of thought and discussion.' Pearson and Chevrier admitted that mistakes had been made to the detriment of innocent persons, but hoped that 'procedures and techniques could be developed to avoid errors' in the future.[53] New procedures governing security clearances in the civil service were announced by Pearson in a speech on 25 October 1963. They supposedly allowed employees the right to learn the reasons for their alleged unreliability, to present their side of the story, and to appear before a review tribunal, but these changes did not address the situation on university campuses.

A second meeting with the prime minister and Commissioner G.B. McLellan of the RCMP did not go so well. Pearson and McLellan played the good-cop bad-cop game, Pearson emollient and reassuring, McLellan stern and inflexible. According to Pearson the government was anxiously seeking the proper balance between the protection of individual rights and the fight against subversion. On every point of CAUT concern, however, McLellan refused to budge. Would the force limit itself to using signed statements by individuals? No, that would impede persons from speaking frankly. Would the RCMP agree to notify university presidents of investigations involving security screening on their campuses? With regard to security screening, probably, but with regard to subversion, no. Were faculty members under investigation informed of the fact? No. Does the RCMP allow officers to ask members of the university community about the beliefs of other members? No, but 'many university people, both faculty members and students, come forward and volunteer information,' and the force reserved the right to accept it. Were dossiers maintained on persons other than known Communists, such as members of the Combined Universities Campaign for Nuclear Disarmament (CUCND)? McLellan replied that there was 'no special interest in the CUCND or any other particular campus organization,' carefully avoiding the question about individuals.[54]

Laskin and Reid reacted somewhat differently to this meeting. Laskin wanted to believe that the political authorities were in control, and was inclined to give credence to Pearson's assurances. Reid was more cynical. In preparing a draft report on the meeting, he confessed that he had 'been perhaps more critical than you would like us to be,' but was 'just a little suspicious that we're being put off with friendliness and pious platitudes.' '[N]ow's the time to put a little pressure on Pearson,' he advised. 'He's such a timid little man – and in the tug of war that's going on now in the Liberal party, he's apt to think of Pickersgill and Chevrier as having more vote-getting appeal than they really do have.' As for McLellan, Reid was 'convinced that we'll get nowhere with him.' This was literally Stewart Reid's last word on the subject: he died three days later.[55]

After some months and several redrafts, Laskin and the Prime Minister's Office agreed on an account of the meeting. Both sides thought an arrangement had been reached. The CAUT believed there would be no further security investigations on campuses except those involving the screening of persons applying for certain government positions. The RCMP thought Fulton's ban on the recruiting of sources was still in effect. Steve Hewitt's interpretation of the 'arrangement' coincides with Stewart Reid's: it was 'nothing more than an exercise in public relations.' The tentative boundaries set in 1961 and 1963 were routinely exceeded by the force. 'It didn't fucking matter,' according to a former security service member interviewed by Hewitt. 'If we wanted the information, we'd get it.'[56] Even in the one area where the force did feel constrained – the recruitment of sources on campus – they managed to find an alternate route. When conducting investigations connected with security screening for employment, it was relatively easy to get interviewees to 'volunteer' information on other matters. No one had said the RCMP could not accept information offered up by a source.

The case of Professor Irving Glass soon made Laskin realize he had been too eager to accept the government's assurances on security matters. A member of the Institute for Aerospace Studies at Toronto, Glass wished to attend a conference in Florida in the fall of 1964. The Defence Research Board refused to give him either the necessary clearance or any reasons for denying it. Since he was not a member of the civil service he had no right to confront the case against him. Writing to Pauline Jewett, Laskin regretted that they had not pressed this point in their second meeting with Pearson. He believed that university researchers who needed such clearances should benefit from the same review process as civil servants.[57] A month later Laskin was shocked to hear Donald S. Macdonald, parliamentary secretary to the minister of justice, rise in the House to backtrack on the nature of security clearance procedures for civil servants. There was, Macdonald said, no right to appear before a review board after all, and he justified this with reference to the supposed British practice. Laskin discovered that the British practice did allow employees to appear personally before a tribunal.

Although denied counsel, the employee could call others to testify as to his or her reliability and character. Laskin expressed the CAUT's concern about Macdonald's statements to Pearson, and urged him to clarify or reform security clearance procedures.[58]

The activities of Bora Laskin and the CAUT on university governance reform were themselves subject to RCMP scrutiny. Inspector J.E.M. Barrett reported to Deputy Commissioner J.H. Lemieux, in response to the latter's request, that there was actually 'no indication that the subject [Stewart Reid] is connected with or a member of the Communist Party.'[59] When Laskin advocated in an October 1964 talk that 'the dominant voice [in university government] should be that of the academic,' an RCMP investigator in the audience expressed grave concern. 'Academics are notoriously inefficient administrators,' he reported, 'a great many of them being on an intellectual plan [sic] which they consider to be above trivial administrative detail. If the "wrong" type of academic were to gain a position on the board of governors which is responsible for the staffing of a University, he could then influence the board toward the hiring of other undesirables. Should the CAUT be successful in their attempt it could be the "thin edge of the wedge."'[60] In the world-view of the RCMP in the early 1960s, any proposal for reform of an existing institution was potentially subversive.

Did the efforts of Laskin and the CAUT efforts really achieve anything? It is easy to be cynical. The RCMP appears to have ignored the few restrictions on it when it wanted information badly enough. But what if the CAUT had not persisted in protesting possible threats to academic freedom and to civil liberties in general? What if the force felt it had carte blanche? The CAUT's efforts created some pressure on politicians to keep the force accountable. The 1961 and 1963 protocols at least contributed to a nascent sense within the RCMP that it had to act in accordance with the rule of law, even if it chose at times to flout that imperative. Their later campaign to have the restrictions officially removed – briefly successful in the wake of the October crisis – in itself suggests a belief that their activities were constrained in some way. If the RCMP operated, as Hewitt says, 'not in a complete vacuum but in a partial one,' Canadians through their political representatives seem to have been content for matters to continue that way. Laskin and the CAUT at least signalled a potential problem with RCMP powers, one that would not be fully investigated for another fifteen years.

PART IV

Transitions

13

Elder Statesman

Bora Laskin had taught full-time without a break for twenty years before applying for sabbatical leave for the year 1961–2. Now on the cusp of fifty, Bora and Peggy felt able to pause and take stock. Wisely, they decided to leave Toronto and spend the year based in London, taking Barbara with them while John stayed in Toronto to start university. Sabbatical leaves were granted on an ad hoc basis at this time, while salary arrangements ranged from full salary to no salary. Laskin was given half his $15,000 salary, topped up with a $4,500 Canada Council grant, one of just four awarded to faculty at the University of Toronto in that year. In addition, his travel expenses were paid as the first recipient of the Butterworths Overseas Legal Fellowship.[1] Laskin settled upon a project with a somewhat old-fashioned ring in an increasingly youth-oriented society: he would investigate the influence of the major decisions of the Privy Council on the development of Canadian constitutional law.

Laskin had never been outside North America in his entire life. Modernist and legal nationalist that he was, he had rather mixed feelings about the English legal tradition. He admired the pragmatic flexibility of the common law and its role in upholding liberal values, and respected the careful analysis displayed in many English judgments dealing with private law. On the whole, though, he tended to see the English influence on Canadian law as somewhat baneful in its conservatism and its elevation of precedent over policy. After the abolition of

Privy Council appeals, he had observed with some relish that it was 'possible for the first time to contemplate deviation of Canadian law from English law in all its branches.'[2] The year in London marked a softening of these attitudes. He and Peggy fell in love with England and would return many times in the years ahead. And as Laskin made contacts with British legal academics, he gradually adopted a more positive view of English law and its influence on Canada. The sabbatical was the first step on the road to his book *The British Tradition in Canadian Law*, initially presented by Laskin as the 1969 Hamlyn Lectures at the Inner Temple. Laskin's change of heart was reflected at the national level in the heightened interest in British discussions of the 'law and morals' issues of the 1960s. The 1957 Wolfenden Committee's recommendations regarding the decriminalization of homosexual offences were enormously influential in the Canadian debates leading to decriminalization in 1969, while the relaxation of the British abortion law in 1967 and the suspension, then abolition, of capital punishment, were also followed in Canada.

As well as preparing for the year away, Laskin had to attend to another move. The faculty was vacating Glendon Hall and moving at last into its permanent home, Flavelle House. Laskin's effects were moved into his new office even though he would not settle into it until the return from Britain. Just before the Laskins left Toronto, the Canadian Jewish Congress held a reception at the Primrose Club 'honouring Bora Laskin on the occasion of his departure abroad' – a symbol of his stature in the Jewish community as well as a quaint reminder of a vanished era.[3] Finally, in early October, they were off. The Laskins first stopped in Paris, where they found the city immobilized by a strike. When Laskin lamented not being able to use the Métro, Caesar Wright could not resist teasing his colleague. It was 'very salutary for an expert in the field of labour law to appreciate, as a member of the travelling public, all the hell-raising that these trade unions can cause.'[4] Once in London, Bora and Peggy settled into a flat at the tony address of 247 Knightsbridge. Bora had arranged to be a visiting scholar at the Institute for Advanced Legal Studies of the University of London, where he shared an office with Ralph Johnson, a young law professor from Seattle. Anne Johnson and Peggy Laskin embarked on sightseeing and shopping trips together, and the two couples dined often over the course of the year. It was an ideal time to be in London. The long years of wartime privation over, the city was basking in relative affluence and entering a period of renewed cultural dynamism. Swinging London was just around the corner.

The Institute was a research centre on the European model, providing an extensive library and intellectual home for scholars and graduate students but with minimal teaching functions. It occupied two Georgian buildings on Russell Square in the heart of Bloomsbury, walking distance from 'legal London' – the precincts along Chancery Lane where the Inns of Court and the Law Courts are located. The Institute possessed one of the best law libraries in Britain, although at some 65,000 volumes in 1960 it was not much bigger than the University of Toronto Law Library's collection of 50,000 tomes. Laskin reported jestingly to Wright in November that his dean should be proud of his diligence in reading transcripts and factums in a lonely corner of the Institute's library. Although violently opposed to the creation of such a free-standing institute in Canada, Laskin had no objection to it in the very different British context.

The Institute's executive director was Professor J.N.D. (later Sir Norman) Anderson, a distinguished scholar of Islamic law who was also head of the School of Oriental and African Studies. The secretary and librarian of the Institute, Howard Drake, played an important administrative role given Professor Anderson's multiple responsibilities. They made no particular demands on Laskin but he was sometimes asked to lecture by other groups, as when students at the London School of Economics asked him to give them a talk on the Canadian Bill of Rights.[5] The Institute welcomed Laskin and Johnson and their wives at a tea on 9 November, at which Laskin was looking forward to meeting the London law teaching crowd.

The Laskins spent a quiet fall developing a domestic rhythm and exploring London. For Bora, with no teaching, no labour arbitrations, no opinion work, no headnoting, no university committees, and no community commitments, it was the first real breathing space of his adult life. One can imagine him restless and disoriented at first, as he tried to adjust to a more relaxed pace. The weather was unusually bright and mild until the very end of the year. Snow on 31 December turned into slush, then froze over, providing Bora and Peggy an excuse to stay in on New Year's Eve. They were alone for the first time in years, as Barbara was away for the holidays until mid-January. A note to Wright early in the new year revealed Laskin in a reflective mood, anxious that he might be enjoying his freedom too much: would he ever be able to return to his accustomed pace of work? Frank Scott had written a few times about the proposed constitutional amendment formula, but the prime minister was calling a halt to discussions for a while. The Canadian papers said that Quebec was objecting to the proposals but Laskin thought Fulton had already conceded too much.[6]

The second semester saw Laskin's pace pick up significantly. Invitations flowed in, and he gave a series of lectures at British law schools, visiting Southampton and Bristol early in the year, Belfast and Edinburgh in April, and Oxford in May. Professor G.W. Keeton asked him to contribute the volume on Canada to a series on the laws and constitutions of Commonwealth countries. Laskin planned to compose the part on the Canadian constitution and farm out the chapters on the provincial legal systems to local contributors. During his stay he also became acquainted with L.C.B. 'Jim' Gower and Stanley de Smith, authorities on company law and administrative law respectively. Gower identified a steady stream of possible candidates for law appointments at Toronto whose names Laskin duly channelled to Caesar Wright. African developments in the era of decolonization elicited great interest at the Institute, and Laskin soon caught the bug. He wrote Caesar in support of Ted McWhinney's proposal on comparative studies in federalism and the emergent nations, and stayed in contact with his colleague A.B. Weston, who was spending the year in Tanganyika as it became independent Tanzania. Gower was about to leave the London School of Economics to take a job as adviser on legal education to the Nigerian government. Laskin seemed impressed with Gower's conviction that Westerners could help, and might be able to assist other countries to avoid Ghana's fate.[7]

One of the unwritten rules of sabbaticals is that plans always change. Laskin's research was not going all that well. Transcripts of counsel's arguments before the Privy Council were scarce and the law reporters destroyed their notes after ten years.[8] However, an invitation to a symposium in Chicago on federalism and the new nations of Africa, probably via Stanley de Smith, led him in another direction. In his paper 'Some International Legal Aspects of Federalism: The Experience of Canada' Laskin deplored the 'unfortunate' position of the federal government with regard to its treaty-making power.[9] Predictably, he preferred an 'omnicompetent' treaty power in the federal government rather than one dependent on some degree of provincial participation. Frank Scott, now dean at McGill, also attended the event and reported to Laskin his recent experience arguing the *Lady Chatterley's Lover* obscenity case at the Supreme Court of Canada. A few weeks later Laskin wrote Scott a congratulatory note after reading in *The Times* about his victory.[10] In addition to Africa, the emergence of the European Common Market also caught Laskin's attention. He advised Wright to beef up their library with relevant materials – but just those in English. While broadening his horizons Laskin also began to plan a course in civil liberties, embracing both domestic and international law. Wright and Abel pushed the proposal through the curriculum committee in spite of some concern about the possibility of Laskin 'empire-building' in the field of constitutional law.[11]

Caesar Wright's long gossipy letters were a great hit with Bora and Peggy. After its long peregrinations the faculty had finally settled near Queen's Park in the magnificent early twentieth-century mansion built by business magnate Sir Joseph Flavelle. Although Laskin and Wright complained long and loud about the proposed premises (both wanted a new building), Wright confided to Laskin after a visit to the new law building at the University of Western Ontario that it was 'not too bad, although we smugly felt that we had something much better and would have something infinitely better if we could only persuade the authorities here to finish the job they started so many months ago.'[12] Conflicts with John Willis, low-grade but irritating, were a constant theme: Willis interfered in the library, raised hell about being forced onto the curriculum committee, and was constantly at loggerheads with Al Abel. (Willis had gone to UBC from Halifax in 1957, then returned to Toronto in 1959.) On the positive side, applications were up and Wright had narrowly avoided having to section the first-year class for reasons of space. He was lobbying for two positions but with only one confirmed, hired Richard Risk, then doing graduate work at Harvard. Wright approved of Risk's interest in Canadian legal history but while 'anxious to get something of this nature into our first year,' he had run into a road block among the faculty and put the idea on hold.[13]

Wright was angling for a centre of criminology at Toronto, and attended a meeting convoked by Attorney-General Kelso Roberts to discuss its location. Ivan Rand, retired from the Supreme Court of Canada and founding dean of the new law school at Western Ontario, said he 'was not interested in Criminology – that it had nothing to do with law at all and was on the mere periphery.' To Wright this was like 'listening to a Bencher *circa* 1935.' Afterwards Wright advised Roberts how to avoid offending any of the existing law schools. He had 'to bring in an outsider to run an Institute; that the outsider was one Edwards;

that he should be appointed Director of an Institute of Criminology at the University of Toronto; and if he did that, we were willing to see that [Edwards] was appointed Professor of this Faculty.'[14] Wright's instructions were followed to the letter. In July 1963 Professor John Llewelyn Edwards, a sprightly and scholarly Welshman then at Dalhousie Law School, arrived in Toronto as founding director of the Centre of Criminology with a cross-appointment in law. Less clear was the faculty's role in a proposed institute of industrial relations. The dean feared a plot 'to get industrial relations centred in the Business school,' but by the end of the year only a weak Industrial Relations Centre had been created.[15]

Wright had welcome news for his friend towards the end of the academic year. The university had given Wright $3,000 towards salary increases for the entire staff, and as dean he recommended an increase of $500 for Bora, or one-sixth of the total amount, bringing his salary to $15,500. 'By the time you get back you will probably need it,' Wright observed, to which Laskin gave his hearty assent. John would be joining them soon to spend the month of June on the continent. Bora and Peggy felt the trip would be worth it in spite of the expense. Then they would return to England for a few weeks before returning home. Laskin concluded the letter with a startling prediction. Having waited two decades to undertake this trip, he said, they wanted to make the most of it because he did not expect to live another twenty years. At this point Laskin was only forty-nine years old and in excellent health, and the context does not suggest a jest. He likely had in mind his own parents, who died at sixty-three and seventy-five, and was soberly assessing his own life expectancy. This sense of the brevity of life may help to explain his enormous drive and sense of urgency. The prophecy was sadly accurate: Bora Laskin would live only another twenty-two years.[16]

The Laskin-Wright sabbatical correspondence provides a rare glimpse of Laskin in a more relaxed mode. Among his friends outside Toronto, his epistolary exchanges with Frank Scott were desultory; only with Morris Schumiatcher did he carry on a sustained correspondence verging on the intimate. During this precious sabbatical year, Laskin had the leisure to write for the sheer pleasure of communication. Given this context, Laskin's letters reveal more in their omissions than their content. They contain some humour and occasional moments of self-revelation, but mostly transmit information rather than opinion. There are few of the general observations on British life, even on British legal life, that one might expect of a sabbaticant abroad. This correspondence illustrates just how strongly Laskin maintained the barrier between his public and private selves. Even to his lifelong friend Caesar Wright, Laskin did not reveal much of his inner self on paper.

Wright's letters sparkle by contrast, even though he adopts the voice of a jaded administrator who believes that 'we have made considerable progress this year ... despite some of the noblest efforts of some of our colleagues to the contrary.'[17] The year 1961–2 represented a watershed of sorts in Wright's career. Having won the battle with the benchers in 1957, he went on to battle the university authorities for proper accommodation, staff, and library facilities for a rapidly growing student body. In 1961, with the move to Flavelle House completed, the construction of the cherished moot court room underway, and the library's growth and autonomy finally assured, Wright felt his mission had been accomplished. His one final aspiration was an appointment either as chief justice of Ontario or to the Supreme Court of Canada. As a lifelong Liberal, Wright's chances of an appointment by the Diefenbaker government were slim. With the sudden death in 1959 of his friend Sidney Smith, his principal advocate in Diefenbaker's cabinet, they diminished to nil.

Was the sabbatical year a turning point in the Laskin-Wright friendship as well? Both the correspondence and Laskin's subsequent actions suggest a subtle shift in the balance of power between them. Having lived to some extent in Wright's shadow virtually all his adult life, Laskin now seemed to need Wright less than Wright needed Laskin. Laskin was now exploring broader intellectual horizons, while Wright coasted on his record. Indebted to Wright ever since the latter recommended his student to Harvard, and Wright's staunchly loyal 'first lieutenant' throughout the dark years after 1949, Laskin had carved out an independent identity and public image. His career was on the ascendant, while Wright's star was past its zenith. Yet after thirteen years as dean, Wright still gave no hint of retiring. Upon his return from Britain, Laskin plunged into a round of extramural engagements that kept him mostly outside the law faculty, while a moody and frustrated Caesar Wright paced about Flavelle House, as one colleague recalled, 'like a lion in a cage.'[18]

For the next three years Laskin would channel his enormous energies outside the strictly legal sphere to university and public affairs. The catalogue of these activities is daunting: chair (1962–3) of the Association of Teaching Staff at the University of Toronto; vice-president (1963–

4) and president (1964–5) of the Canadian Association of University Teachers; organizer of the Duff-Berdahl inquiry into the governance of Canadian universities (1963–4); and chair of President Claude Bissell's Committee on the School of Graduate Studies (1963–5). In spite of these involvements, Laskin did not abandon his old interests in labour law, civil liberties, and constitutional law. The Robarts government appointed him to conduct a public inquiry into Ontario's *Industrial Standards Act* in 1962–3, and this was followed by a high-profile inquiry into the affairs of the Canadian actors' union (ACTRA). He was also much sought after as a speaker and adviser when constitutional reform appeared on the national agenda in the wake of the Quiet Revolution.

Soon after his return, Laskin was approached to chair the Association of Teaching Staff (ATS) at the University of Toronto. Founded in 1942, ATS only began to address salary issues in 1949–50 in the wake of postwar inflation. Between 1946 and 1950 the cost of living in Toronto rose 30 per cent but the salary scale did not rise at all, and income tax bit to the tune of 12 per cent instead of the pre-war 1.5 per cent. Salary discussions in the 1950s went like this: ATS 'would ask the president to support faculty requests in his dealings with the Board of Governors. The President would reply courteously but evasively. The Board would eventually decide on salaries for the coming year; the President would announce this decision. The faculty association would usually thank the President for his efforts, often expressing perfunctory gratitude with a solicitation for more next time.'[19] Nonetheless, the professors recovered much of their purchasing power over the 1950s – a 20 per cent raise in 1951 was followed by a 40 per cent scale increase implemented between 1957 and 1960. These gains resulted mainly from two exogenous forces: a growing scarcity of professors in the face of a burgeoning student body, and the initiation of federal grants to universities in 1951, which began at one dollar per head of population and rose sharply thereafter.

These large increases appear impressive but were less so for one particular group of faculty. Female academics were consistently underpaid relative to their male colleagues in similar positions, and with the ATS executive made up of senior male professors such as Laskin the issue was seldom raised in salary discussions. Professor C.B. Macpherson, married to noted feminist Kay Macpherson, chaired an ATS committee that inquired about gendered salary discrepancies in 1954, but to no avail. After several internal inquiries and pay adjustments in the 1970s and 1980s, some retired female faculty started a class action lawsuit against the University in 2000.[20]

Chairing the association was a thankless task. As Laskin recalled years later, '[t]he Association really didn't have ... much of a bite because those were gentlemanly days.'[21] The ATS 'had no power at all – no collective agreement, no regular procedures for discussion, no negotiations,' and no money, no staff, and no premises.[22] 'Its only hope of affecting University policy was through the personal influence, mediation perhaps, of senior professors.'[23] With the settlement for 1962–3 only 2.5 per cent, the lowest in a number of years, giving a leadership role to the acknowledged dean of Canadian labour arbitrators must have seemed a master stroke. As of the summer of 1962, the scale of minimum salaries at the university had not changed from the 1957 scale increase; salary minima ranged from $5,500 for lecturers to $12,000 for full professors. ATS requested a substantial and immediate scale increase of 25 to 30 per cent in order to aid recruitment in a tight market and to allow the university 'to retain its distinctive and essential position as the leading institution of research and graduate study in Canada.' Laskin marshalled data showing the salary minima at Toronto to be virtually the same as those at all other large universities in the country, while average salaries at Laval and Alberta were higher than at Toronto.

At the outset President Bissell was prepared to recommend only half the requested increase. Laskin tried to remain firm and requested a meeting of the ATS executive with the board of governors. After meeting with the ATS on 15 November, Bissell took the unusual step of writing a personal letter to Laskin at his home address. Concerned about 'a serious problem in the relationship between the staff and the administration' he wanted 'to avoid the excessive formalization of discussion that inevitably leads to a hardening of positions on both sides.' Bissell challenged the assumption that the ATS had the right to deal directly with the board of governors, whose members did not wish to be drawn into formal salary negotiations. If the ATS regarded itself as 'constituting one source of advice to the President,' who in turn would deal with the board, the looming gulf between faculty and administration could be avoided.[24]

Laskin followed the president's shift into informality. The two met from time to time for dinner, where Laskin assured Bissell he would not hesitate to advocate any reasonable proposal coming from Simcoe Hall.[25] In the end Laskin's negotiating skills bore some fruit. ATS got much less than Laskin had been seeking, but more than in previous years: it achieved scale increases of between 5 and 8 per cent depending on rank. Salary floors effective 1 July 1963 would be $13,000 for professors, $9,500 for associate professors, and $7,500 for assistant professors. Laskin and Bissell had agreed to a one-year arrangement in the hope that a two- to three-year salary program could be agreed upon in 1963.

When Bissell reminded Laskin 'of the dangers of creating an employer-employee atmosphere' in the university context, he was preaching to the converted. Laskin viewed professors as independent professionals for whom the union model was totally inappropriate. In fact Laskin had already taken the position that deans might join the ATS, as there was no prohibition in its constitution.[26] '[W]e are employees neither of our Universities nor of our governments,' he said in another context. University teachers were 'a profession because we admit ... to a sense of public responsibility for establishing a climate of intellectual excellence in the community and because ... we insist on a certain liberty to determine the conditions upon which we will exercise our functions as a process of self-government.'[27] In spite of his spirited criticism of university boards of governors over the years, Laskin continued to believe that after a gentlemanly exchange of views they would see the justice of faculty demands and produce a fair settlement. His attitude was clearly shaped by his experience at Canada's wealthiest university during the longest period of economic growth in Canadian history, when government support of universities grew by leaps and bounds and market conditions favoured faculty. Not long after he left academe the factors in this equation would change dramatically, resulting in major changes to the organization of university labour relations which he could never countenance.

Such was Bissell's respect for Laskin that he appointed the law professor to chair a presidential committee to investigate all aspects of graduate studies at the University of Toronto. The standards for graduate work were uneven across different units and the university's corporate commitment to graduate work was somewhat uncertain. Bissell, prodded by his graduate dean-elect Ernest Sirluck, wanted to articulate, renew, and refine that commitment to position the university to 'maintain itself in the vanguard of human inquiry.'[28] Until the war, Canadian universities were widely viewed as ill-equipped to support graduate work of high quality; talented students should be sent abroad. Nonetheless, the University of Toronto began to build up reputable graduate programs and was unquestionably the pre-eminent centre for graduate study in Canada by 1960. The university was home to some two thousand graduate students, a figure expected to reach five thousand by 1970, and to nearly one-third of all doctoral students in Canada in the humanities and social sciences.

Outside events both welcome and ominous spurred the launching of such an inquiry. In 1963 the province announced a generous program of Ontario Graduate Fellowships in the humanities and social sciences, while funding for the sciences through the federal councils was also on the increase. The province was particularly concerned about an impending shortage of teachers at every level, while the federal government was more influenced by the Cold War. Laskin's report openly acknowledged 'the dramatic influence of Sputnik I in focussing governmental attention upon the need for increased financial support for graduate studies and research.'[29] To respond to these challenges, Bissell assembled what he called the 'strongest internal committee in the history of the University':[30] John Cairns (History), Harry Eastman (Political Economy), Kenneth Fisher (Zoology), Northrop Frye (English), Archibald Hallett (Physics), Charles Hanes (Medical Biochemistry), Robert McRae (Philosophy), John Polanyi (Chemistry), Ernest Sirluck (Graduate Studies), and William Winegard (Metallurgy), with Laskin as chair and Frances Ireland of the president's office as secretary. Sirluck has succinctly summed up the committee's work: 'the committee was appointed in December 1963, worked steadily for almost two years, held more than forty meetings, sent delegations to visit some twenty universities in the United States, six in Britain, and six in continental Europe, received seventy-eight group or individual submissions ..., and held numerous hearings on campus.'[31]

After some preliminary study the committee swung into high gear in the academic year 1964–5, and Laskin was assigned minimal teaching duties. Given the concurrent demands of his presidency of the CAUT he was seldom seen around the law school in this, his last year in academic life. At first the committee appeared to be stuck in a political quagmire: only Sirluck and two others were committed to a unitary model for graduate studies where the university's faculty of graduate studies would play a key role in the administration and quality assurance of programs delivered by individual faculties. Most committee members believed their unit should run its own show without inteference from the central university administration. Laskin refrained from stating his own opinion until near the end of the process. His neutrality facilitated a highly productive exchange, and eventually evolution, of views over the course of the year. Sirluck believed he at first leaned towards the pluralist model, as did Caesar Wright, who proposed an autonomous graduate law school on the Harvard model. Of course, as Sirluck pointed out to Laskin, Harvard was graduating over fifty master's students and half a dozen doctoral students annually in the early 1960s, while Toronto had conferred a grand total of only sixteen LLM degrees since 1949. He might also have said that the Harvard LLM was in most cases merely a further rather than a higher degree in law, aimed principally at foreign students who wanted some exposure to the U.S. legal system, not at building up a body of advanced scholarship.[32]

The site visits began in earnest in late 1964, just in time for committee members to be exposed to the beginnings of campus unrest in the United States. Laskin, Sirluck, and Hallett began with a visit to the University of California at Berkeley on 2 December. As they strolled across the campus they ran into a massive student demonstration that ended with the occupation of Sproul Hall, with the protesters urged on by the declamations of Mario Savio and the impassioned strains of 'We Shall Overcome' sung by Joan Baez. Faced with this spectacle, Laskin inquired loudly, '"As a dean, Ernest, what do you think of this?" [and] was delighted by the angry swivelling of heads.'[33] The next day they heard that the police had forcibly ejected the students and arrested over eight hundred of them – as it turned out, the largest mass arrest in U.S. history. In spite of his apparent flippancy, Laskin later remembered witnessing the beginnings of the Free Speech Movement as one of the most moving experiences of his life.[34] After these events the rest of the tour, to UCLA, Harvard, Yale, and MIT, was bound to be an anticlimax. On the question of unity versus plurality the U.S experience was varied: the California state universities had centralized supervision of graduate studies while the Ivy League schools tended to allow major academic units to administer their own graduate programs.

In the spring of 1965 Laskin and Sirluck embarked on a whirlwind tour of British and European universities. They arrived in London on 27 April and were joined by Charles Hanes for visits to Oxford, Cambridge, Birmingham, and the University of London. Later Sirluck and Laskin were expected in Edinburgh but could only get seats on a plane to Glasgow. Arriving on a Sunday, they needed to take a taxi to Edinburgh to arrive in time for their meetings, a request 'nearly incomprehensible to the driver and the Glaswegians who had informed us that we'd have to wait until Monday morning for a train.'[35] In Scotland Sirluck found Laskin still highly sceptical about the rationale for a unitary graduate faculty, but saw him thaw somewhat during the course of their continental visit.

The European trip was of the 'if this is Tuesday it must be Belgium' variety, with visits to Paris, Rome, Munich, Leyden, Amsterdam, and Copenhagen between 6 and 21 May. Laskin prepared summaries of the visits for the committee, but they are mostly factual and contain virtually no evaluative comments. Sirluck recalled how appalled he and Laskin were with the disorganization at the University of Rome. Huge classrooms were filled mainly with place-sitters employed by the registered students to avoid the black mark recorded against them for vacant seats, while graduate students seemed totally at the mercy of their assigned professor. Elsewhere they found graduate study disorganized (Paris), unambitious (Munich), or too disengaged from the university (Copenhagen). Only in the Netherlands did they find a degree of institutional coordination of graduate studies likely to stimulate the best quality work and provide sufficient safeguards for students.

The two men had little time for touristic activities but as fellow Jews were especially interested to experience post-war German culture. They made a point of visiting the Munich Bier Garten, the birthplace of Nazism, and had the uneasy feeling that Nazi sentiments had not been entirely extinguished. Their unease deepened after attending one of the German night clubs notorious for their lurid displays of sexuality, more overt than were common in North America at the time. Although Rabbi Abraham Feinberg and his successor Gunther Plaut found more positive aspects of German culture to report to Canadian audiences after their visits in the early 1960s, Sirluck and Laskin came away with a sense of discomfort about the direction of post-war German society. The embrace of materialism and sensuality – so well portrayed in Fassbinder's film *Maria von Braun* – seemed an attempt to forget about the horrors inflicted by Germany on the world just two decades earlier.

True to his nature, Laskin drafted the entire report himself. He would bring each chapter to the committee for discussion, and accepted many suggestions for revision, but he never ceased to regard himself as the father of the report. In Sirluck's view, this was partly because 'his conscience would not allow him to hide from Caesar ... [H]e knew that Caesar would be distressed by it ... but he didn't think he ought to hide behind the committee.'[36] As the members discussed particular problems, the desirability of a unitary model gradually became more and more evident. Given the increasing significance of public funding, the committee came to agree that '[t]here is an obvious need, from the standpoint of relations with the government, for the President to be able to command a view of graduate studies as a whole.'[37] Maintaining Toronto's pre-eminent national position also required strong institutional champions beyond the faculty level for the financial and human resources necessary to conduct advanced study and research. A reinforced School of Graduate Studies was part of the answer. So was adequate recognition of graduate teaching. The report insisted that it could no longer be seen as an uncredited add-on to undergraduate teaching. At the same time, the report eschewed any policy of entrenched salary differentials between those primarily engaged in graduate versus undergraduate teaching.

Improving the graduate student experience was also a major concern. With characteristic bluntness Laskin pronounced current graduate accommodation 'wholly unsatisfactory' and warned that without swift remedial action, plans to expand graduate education would be 'irreparably frustrated.'[38] In his criticism of the inadequacy of the Graduate Students' Union, one recalls his own frustration at the law faculty's long isolation at Glendon Hall. Without proper social facilities, graduate students had failed to develop any sense of solidarity; in this failure 'is sunk the best chance the University has of maintaining an intellectual interchange above our many specializations, as well as the best chance the students will ever have of being liberated from narrowness by the free encounter of minds with widely divergent presuppositions.'[39] Here, perhaps, was an echo of W.P.M. Kennedy's ideal of the 'clash of disciplines.'

Laskin's timing was impeccable. The report was virtually drafted when his appointment to the Ontario Court of Appeal was announced in the late summer of 1965. At first it produced 'widespread controversy': some saw it as a power grab by the central administration. When the Graduate Council initially received the report a battle royal was eagerly anticipated but in the face of Mr Justice Laskin's persuasive presentation opposition dissipated. The report's main recommendations were all accepted and have guided the provision of graduate studies at the university ever since. Within the Ministry of University Affairs, however, bureaucrats expressed dismay that the report displayed 'little or no concern as to where the necessary funds are supposed to be acquired.'[40]

Laskin's role on the committee led to a friendship with Ernest Sirluck, whose origins as a first-generation Jewish boy from rural Manitoba were similar to Laskin's own. And there was a familial connection of sorts: Charles Laskin had roomed at a fraternity house managed by Sirluck in pre-war Winnipeg. Sirluck soon found another job for Laskin: chairman of the board of the newly created Ontario Institute for Studies in Education (OISE). There was much uneasiness within the University of Toronto over the spectre of 'a free-standing institute capable of churning out limitless numbers of higher degrees without control,' but the minister of education's plan to appoint as chair of the OISE board a teachers' federation official 'with little knowledge of universities' caused even more alarm. At a tense interview, Sirluck told William Davis that he would refuse to recommend recognition of OISE's Department of Educational Theory if the proposed candidate were appointed. When the minister requested another name, Sirluck suggested Bora Laskin, with whom he had already discussed the matter. Davis brightened immediately: 'Well, he'd be wonderful: he was my teacher.'[41]

The years between the return from sabbatical and Laskin's appointment to the bench were in some respects golden years for Bora and Peggy. Their children were growing up, with John doing his first degree at the University of Toronto and Barbara entering high school. They were affluent enough to purchase the finer things in life – elegant clothes, fine furnishings for their home, original pieces of art, European holidays. Like the wives of many workaholic legal figures, Peggy would have preferred to travel more, to spend more time just relaxing with her husband. But she accepted Bora's need to be constantly engaged as a fundamental part of his nature, and carved out an independent life for herself. Fortunately, her bachelor brother Sam visited frequently, helping out with odd jobs around the house and remaining an affectionate uncle to John and Barbara. Peggy kept an impeccable household, and with David Spencer's assistance became knowledgeable about antiques. She enjoyed gardening at their Warren Avenue home, practised yoga, and volunteered with the Cancer Society and the Clarke Institute of Psychiatry. Always aloof from organized Judaism, Peggy was probably glad when Bora extricated himself from most of his Temple commitments after the sabbatical. During their year away Rabbi Feinberg had retired, and was replaced by Rabbi Gunther Plaut.

Whenever Peggy could drag Bora away from his work, they enjoyed a fairly active social life. The senior members of the law faculty and their spouses saw quite a bit of one another, and some former students such as Charles and Anne Dubin and Eddie Goodman and his wife Suzanne were also part of the Laskins' circle. The early 1960s were a kind of sociological oasis in which the civility and decorum of pre-war society were still observed, while the snobbishness and exclusiveness of the old order were on the wane. As Rabbi Feinberg put it in 1964, 'Canadian afternoon-tea society is a disintegrating bastion of Anglo-Saxondom engaged in a rearguard battle to preserve some remnants of its moth-eaten ermine.'[42] Socializing between Jew and non-Jew was becoming more acceptable, but could still lead to some discomfort. After a soirée in 1965 honouring Bora Laskin's twenty-five years in teaching, where about half those in attendance were Jewish, Marie Wright remarked to Jean Milner that 'she was beginning to feel slightly anti-Semitic,' embarrassed at the fervency of some of the testimonials to Laskin. Milner disagreed with the dean's spouse, confiding to her diary that she liked the 'warmth and emotion' of such events, so different from Anglo-Canadian modes of social intercourse.[43]

Stimulated by the Shumiatchers, David Spencer, and Peggy, Laskin took an increasing interest in the visual arts, one he would soon invoke in a high-profile obscenity case when on the Court of Appeal. He was part of a group who invited the late President Kennedy's adviser on the arts, Arthur Schlesinger, to give a talk at the University of Toronto on 'Government and the Arts' in 1965. Schlesinger's subsequent behaviour unfortunately soured Laskin's satisfaction with the event. He and Peggy hosted a reception at their home for people to meet the speaker, but Schlesinger declined to mingle and remained in seclusion in the den until his flight was ready to leave. The honorarium, he explained, covered the talk itself but not subsequent socializing.[44]

Brother Saul was flourishing back home in Port Arthur. He and Adele had five children, and the furniture business was booming in the long years of post-war affluence. Politics beckoned: Saul served first as a Port Arthur alderman from 1958 to 1962, then mayor until 1969, always working for amalgamation of the twin cities. In the 1963 general election Saul ran as a Liberal in his home riding. He lost out to Douglas Fisher of the New Democratic Party (newly emerged from the old CCF), who had been so impressed with Bora Laskin's oratory as a high school student. Fisher was also impressed with Saul's 'fair play and social responsibility,' and when he decided to get out of politics, 'tried to signal Saul that he should run again, but he didn't catch the signal.'[45] Saul also helped turn Lakehead Technical Institute into Lakehead University in 1965. Bora's visits to his brother tended to accompany northern arbitrations these days. In sad testimony to the post-war decline of the Lakehead Jewish community, he came loaded with bagels, knishes, and other delicacies since the closing of the local Jewish bakery.

Laskin also retained an active interest in the children of Lakehead friends who had migrated to Toronto. In the 1950s a lawyer named Gerard Weiler frequently argued the employer side before him on arbitrations in the forest product industry in northern Ontario. When the Weiler family moved next door to Saul Laskin the two families became very friendly. Weiler's son was about to launch into a doctorate in philosophy at the University of Toronto in the spring of 1961, but he preferred to see his son study law. The young man was resisting his father's pressure because he understood legal education to be thoroughly vocational and black-letter. Gerard asked Bora Laskin to intercede. He invited a wide-eyed young Weiler to lunch at the Faculty Club and demolished his ideas about legal education. Legal education was becoming a serious intellectual experience, said Laskin, and would in turn transform the legal profession and the judiciary. He conveyed a sense of excitement about the study of law, which afforded a blend of general theory and the solution of real-world problems. As for practical advice: 'go to law school here, just like I did, and then go to Harvard Law School to get your LL.M. – you can do it in legal philosophy – and then you can come back here and teach.'[46] Paul Weiler followed Laskin's advice almost to the letter (he did law at Osgoode rather than Toronto), and did him one better: eventually he became a professor at Laskin's beloved Harvard Law School after teaching at Osgoode Hall Law School and serving on the B.C. Labour Relations Board. His 1974 work *In the Last Resort* was the first book-length critical assessment of the Supreme Court. It coincided with Laskin's appointment as chief justice and echoed much of his own dissatisfaction with the Court.

For one of Laskin's oldest friends, the 1960s took on a nightmarish quality. His first LLM student, Morris Shumiatcher, had gone into private practice after leaving the Saskatchewan public service in 1950. A man of enormous energy, ambition, and social commitment, Shumiatcher had developed a very successful practice in Regina and a high profile right across western Canada. Bora and Peggy adored his wife Jacqueline, an Anglo-French beauty who managed her husband's office, stimulated his interest in the visual arts and world travel, and transformed their home into a salon where people from all walks of life could mingle to enjoy stimulating conversation and fine food. Socially, the Shumiatchers were smart, stylish, and prominent. By the legal world, Morris was perceived as unconventional, flamboyant, and something of a gadfly.

As in some Greek tragedy, this upward trajectory could not last. In 1962 Morris was charged with conspiracy to defraud the public in connection with some advice he had given a corporate client, and he was disbarred in 1964. Lawyers often walk a fine line when providing advice to businesses about how to arrange their affairs. Had Morris crossed the line? He fought fiercely to show that he had not, insisting that his only wrong was to offend some prominent political and legal figures who carried on a vendetta against him.[47] Many judges on the Saskatchewan courts thought he was being unfairly harassed, including Emmett Hall, Laskin's future judicial colleague.[48] Laskin agreed. When Morris's troubles began, he and Jacqui sought Laskin's advice. The two men spent an afternoon in the Toronto law library, studying the authorities and discussing strategy. For the next five years, their meetings were 'etched by crises and bedevilled by frenzies,'[49] but when it was all over Morris was forever grateful for his friend's 'wise counsel' and 'great courage.'[50]

The Saskatchewan Court of Appeal quashed Morris's committal for conspiracy on the basis of manifest error by the trial judge.[51] His disbarment was revoked but the Law Society of Saskatchewan began to investigate new complaints and suspended him for six months in September 1966. The Court of Appeal quashed the unanimous decision of thirteen benchers for lack of evidence, and when leave to appeal to the Supreme Court of Canada was refused, Morris's troubles were finally over.[52] Laskin was shocked and saddened at what he saw as the vindictiveness and meanness of the Law Society.[53] His friend's traumatic experience was a sober reminder of how individuals could be suddenly destroyed by powerful groups, over-zealous prosecutors and abusive state officials – and of the role of the courts as a last beacon of hope for those caught in such predicaments. When a judge, Laskin often dissented in cases where professional disciplinary bodies breached his exacting standards of procedural fairness, but over time his rigorous approach has come to prevail.

After returning from London Bora Laskin saw less and less of his law colleagues. He introduced his new course in civil liberties in 1962–3, but otherwise seemed strangely silent at a time of increasing ferment in Canadian legal education. The intellectual terrain he had begun to mark out on his sabbatical remained mostly untilled: Ted McWhinney rather than Laskin occupied the field of comparative federalism, the ideas about EEC law remained undeveloped, the work on the Privy Council came to nought, and the volume on the development of the Canadian constitution never appeared. The latter was an especially frustrating enterprise that ground on for four years before Laskin, by now on the bench, was forced to conclude that half his contributors would never produce.[54] To this day the series on Commonwealth constitutions contains a gap where volume three, the ghostly Canada volume, should be. These false starts were partly due to Laskin's extra-curricular activities, but reflect too the limitations of the vision of legal education and scholarship shared by him and his contemporaries. The vision was oriented to close analysis and interpretation of legal texts, and a modest amount of policy analysis, but seldom to larger questions of the place of law in social relations, the economy, or in national history. W.P.M. Kennedy had embraced such a vision but the professional law schools of the post-war period had almost succeeded in stamping it out. With the departure of F.E. La Brie in 1963, Laskin himself remained the last survivor of the Kennedy era.

In the years after the sabbatical, it is almost as if the law faculty had become too small a stage. For someone of Laskin's talents and relentless drive, that is not surprising. He moved easily into the world of national university affairs with his presidency of the CAUT, and was named a Fellow of the Royal Society of Canada in 1964. The restless professor also became something of a roving commission of inquiry. His investigation into the *Industrial Standards Act* began when classes ended in the fall of 1962 and carried through the winter. He submitted his final report in July 1963 and most of its recommendations were implemented in 1964.[55] In February 1963 the provincial government appointed him as a mediator in a highly charged dispute in the forest industry in northern Ontario that left three people dead.[56] Laskin next conducted an inquiry into allegations of mismanagement against the president and general secretary of the Association of Canadian Television and Radio Artists (ACTRA) early in 1964. The charges were made by Percy Saltzman, the man who inaugurated television broadcasting in Canada by reading the weather report on 8 September 1952, but Laskin found them mostly unsubstantiated.[57]

The attraction of these external involvements for Laskin is understandable, but was there a push factor as well? Was he frustrated by Wright's unwillingness to step down? Everyone viewed Laskin as the heir-apparent, as did Wright himself. When it appeared that Wright might become chief justice of Ontario in 1957, he told Laskin, 'I guess you will be taking over here.'[58] Laskin's sense of decorum and loyalty prevented any public expression of disaffection, but in private he harboured concerns about Caesar's leadership. At a faculty council meeting in 1963 David Kilgour voiced some criticisms of Wright's authoritarian manner. No one dared to join him, but no one leapt to Wright's defence either, and the dean stormed out of the meeting. That evening, some young loyalists on faculty decided to visit Wright to cheer him up. They asked Dick Risk to join them, which he did. Laskin later told Risk he had been unwise. If Caesar had been left to 'stew' for a while, said Laskin, he might have accepted that it was time for him to share some power, or stop being obstructive.[59] But he did not. It was as if the deanship had swallowed up Caesar Wright: in giving it up the true Wizard of Oz would be revealed.

Even if Laskin had become dean, it is unlikely he would have had any different vision to implement. The vision of legal education prevailing when he departed for the bench deviated not one iota from that of 1949. At the end of the Wright-Laskin era, the curriculum was ossified, graduate work in law moribund, the research profile uneven, and teaching methods static. Big changes were underway in the late 1960s and the impetus for all of them came from a newly energized Osgoode Hall Law School,[60] not from the University of Toronto. In 1969 Gerald Le Dain, Osgoode's swashbuckling new dean, would persuade the benchers to allow the law schools to adopt a largely optional curriculum in upper years after a compulsory first year. Clinical legal education burst upon the scene in 1971 with the establishment of the Osgoode-affiliated Parkdale Legal Services Clinic, but Toronto's efforts in this field would be modest by comparison. Even Wright's much-vaunted library was soon dwarfed by the vast and magnificent collection being assembled at Osgoode, still the best centre for legal research in the Commonwealth.

Once the revolutionary heroes of 1949, a generation later Wright, Laskin, and Willis had become almost a new ancien regime. Their personal reputations were high, and they were still associated with the use of law as a force for progressive social change, but an idealistic younger generation was trying urgently to implement their ideals more directly in the classroom, the curriculum, the clinic, and the courtroom. And few of them could be found at the University of Toronto. Two migrations soon after Laskin's departure for the bench showed clearly the divergent identities of the two institutions. With the affiliation to York University secured in 1965, the 'progressives' migrated to Osgoode while three men less in sympathy with the new ideology – Derek Mendes da Costa, Alan Mewett, and Desmond Morton – shifted to the University of Toronto. Overnight, Toronto was thrown on the defensive, suddenly suspect in the eyes of a less deferential generation as a bastion of privilege and reservoir of conservative views on law.

Had he become dean, there was little Laskin could have done to change the course of the faculty even if he had wanted to do so. While not unsympathetic to the developments at Osgoode, it seems unlikely he would have replicated them at Toronto. His experience might have been uncomfortably similar to that of Frank Scott, who spent three unhappy years as dean of law at McGill (1961–4), alienating colleagues and students alike with his 'outmoded authoritarianism.'[61] As it was, with his promotion in the faculty dependent on Caesar's whim, Laskin increasingly sought responsibility and recognition elsewhere. When a door opened on an entirely different life in 1965, he stepped confidently through it, with no regrets.

May 1965 was full of beginnings and endings. On the twenty-sixth there was a fête organized by Harry Arthurs to honour Laskin's quarter-century of teaching. It was a jolly occasion, full of warm and funny impromptu testimonials from family, friends, and colleagues. A few days later Laskin's many contributions to scholarship and university affairs were recognized by his first honorary degree. Fittingly, it came from Queen's. The associations were many: the Queen's faculty association had first complained to the CAUT about Harry Crowe's dismissal; Queen's had been the centre of the *Place of Liberty* project; J.A. Corry, now principal, had represented the universities in the deal reached with the Law Society of Upper Canada in 1957; and Dan Soberman in the law faculty had written the report on tenure commissioned by the CAUT during Laskin's presidency, while W.L. Lederman and other Queen's scholars shared Laskin's interests in constitutional law and civil liberties. The degree from Queen's would be the first and only one he received as an academic; the next twenty-five would be conferred during his judicial career. As Bora Laskin strode across the stage on that fine May morning in Kingston, he accepted the vicarious thanks of the entire Canadian academic community for his vigorous defence and promotion of its interests. None of them knew it yet, but he was also silently saying goodbye.

14

The Accidental Judge

After being named chief justice of Canada, Bora Laskin observed in an interview with CBC journalist Elizabeth Gray that he never expected his initial appointment to the Ontario Court of Appeal. 'But there are accidents in life,' he continued, 'and I have developed what I call a theory of accidentalism. All you can do is live with it.'[1] Laskin's appointment to the Ontario Court of Appeal in September 1965 and his elevation to the Supreme Court of Canada in March 1970 were the product of a very particular set of events at a specific historical moment: the Pearson-Trudeau years of the late 1960s. Trudeau's vision of a just society built upon Pearson's expansion of the Canadian welfare state, and promoted a new understanding of where the state should be active and where it should let individuals make their own choices. This vision permeated the important legislative initiatives of the day: the *Divorce Act, 1968*, Criminal Code reform, the *Official Languages Act*, and the rationalization of the welfare state (including state-funded health care and the spread of legal aid) that followed the adoption of the Canada Assistance Plan in 1966. Citizens had more leeway to make decisions in intimate matters such as sexual activity, birth control, abortion, and divorce. In some respects these legal changes only confirmed new social practices taking root in post-war society, but in others – the decriminalization of abortion and homosexual acts, the moratorium on capital punishment – the law actually moved ahead of public opinion. For a brief moment, legal reform was seen as implementing a new social vision across a broad spectrum of human activity, rather than a hesitant and incremental response to new conditions in particular areas of social or economic life.

As a non-partisan, an academic, and a Jew, Laskin's appointment in 1965 was virtually unprecedented. Only a few years earlier, any one of these characteristics would have sufficed to torpedo a candidate for judicial appointment. Now, they added up to a winning curriculum vitae. Laskin was not the first Jew appointed to the Supreme Court of Ontario; that honour went to Abraham Lieff, appointed to the High Court shortly after Lester Pearson took office with a minority government in the spring of 1963. Nor was Laskin the first full-time academic appointed to the bench in Canada; that honour went to Vincent Macdonald, dean of Dalhousie Law School at the time of his appointment to the Nova Scotia Supreme Court in 1950 by Louis St Laurent. But both Lieff and Macdonald had been active in the Liberal Party, a fact that muted the novelty of their appointments. In Laskin's case, not only was his lack of public involvement with the governing party highly unusual in a judicial candidate, so too was his vocal criticism of the government on issues ranging from the RCMP presence on university campuses to the constitutional amending formula.

At one level, Laskin's appointment was a desperate attempt to bring some lustre to a troubled government whose reputation on justice issues was badly tarnished. But Canadian governments had been plagued by corruption before and not appointed candidates such as Bora Laskin to the bench. Now, his appointment was made possible by the sudden and urgent desire for change in all aspects of Canadian life, insistently articulated through a new rights-oriented discourse. This rights consciousness put the Canadian judiciary under a spotlight to which they were entirely unaccustomed. With the model of a newly activist U.S. Supreme Court constantly present in the media, Canadians began to believe that a forceful and enlightened judiciary could protect citizens better than (and sometimes from) sluggish, myopic, or over-zealous governments. The mysterious process of judicial appointment, hitherto veiled in secrecy and lubricated by patronage considerations, began to attract critical attention even within the governing party. A disgruntled William Angus, a law professor at the University of Alberta and member of the Alberta Liberal federal campaign committee, wrote to Pearson in 1965 to 'protest in the strongest possible terms against the succession of partisan political appointments to the bench of the province of Alberta since your government took office.'[2]

In the spring of 1965 the Pearson government was only two years old, but precocious with scandal. The worst centred on the case of Montreal mobster Lucien Rivard. When the United States sought his extradition for trial on charges of heroin smuggling, the U.S. government lawyer said he was offered large bribes by two ministerial aides to secure Rivard's release on bail. The opposition gleefully exploited rumours about Rivard's ties to Liberal organizers in Quebec when no charges were laid after an RCMP investigation. An inquiry by the Hon. Frédéric Dorion, chief justice of the Superior Court of Quebec, was given an added fillip by Rivard's escape from prison in March 1965. When Dorion's report criticized minister of Justice Guy Favreau for acting without full information in deciding not to lay charges against the two men, he resigned his cabinet post.[3]

Two federally appointed judges were also in trouble. In the fall of 1964 Justice Leo Landreville of the Ontario High Court, a St Laurent appointee, was under police investigation regarding some questionable stock dealings undertaken while mayor of North Bay. Landreville survived the preliminary inquiry but was seen to have 'fatally impaired his position and authority as a judge.'[4] Many newspapers called for his resignation or for a full-blown inquiry. Justice Adrien Meunier of the Quebec Superior Court was in even deeper trouble. In October 1964 he was convicted of perjury committed while a lawyer in the context of a fraudulent bankruptcy case. Meunier had been the Liberal member for Montreal Papineau from 1953 to 1963, when he stepped down to make way for Guy Favreau. Six months after the election Meunier received his judicial appointment, allegedly despite strong objections by the Quebec bar.[5]

In the midst of this gloom, party strategists were frantic for some good news. In Ottawa national Liberal organizer Keith Davey presided over a network of activists such as Jerahmiel (Jerry) Grafstein, president of the Toronto Young Liberals and recent graduate of the Wright law school.[6] He had absorbed the gospel of law reform from Wright and Laskin but regarded the dean as his mentor more than Professor Laskin. In the spring of 1965 Grafstein began lobbying in Ottawa to have Wright appointed to the Ontario Court of Appeal. Wright warned him that he had made too many enemies, and he was right. Superior court appointments required the support of the cabinet ministers from the province in question, but Joe Greene and Judy LaMarsh were members of that cantankerous class of veterans at Osgoode who had chafed under Wright's perceived tyranny. They were not about to reward him with a judicial appointment.

Grafstein returned to Toronto somewhat crestfallen, and broke the news to Wright at Flavelle House. The dean paused, then observed: 'You could try it for Bora.' The lightbulb went on. Here was a man well known for his integrity and lack of connection to economic or political power, respected as a labour arbitrator, university man, and constitutional authority. What better way for the Liberals to counter the sleaze factor that dogged their every move? Wright advised Grafstein to secure Laskin's consent in advance of an approach by the government, and warned him not to reveal Wright's own role. Grafstein found his former professor in his office and engaged him in a long discussion about the Court of Appeal before coming around to the sensitive topic of a possible appointment. At first Laskin resisted, saying he would not be involved in any way and would not promote himself for a judicial post, but eventually agreed to let his name go forward. Grafstein secretly reported the result to Wright, then went to Ottawa to work on Keith Davey.

Davey said he would give his right arm for some favourable press coverage, and if a Laskin appointment would do the trick, so be it. Apparently he held no grudge against his former professor in spite of failing first-year law in 1950. Laskin had advised him not to repeat but to get into politics straightaway if that was his ultimate goal.[7] Davey was persuaded by Grafstein that the public was ready for a progressive candidate who represented a break with tradition. For Grafstein's generation, the Ontario Court of Appeal was perceived as uncreative, precedent-bound, even reactionary. Its decision in *Noble v. Wolf and Alley* was seen as an ignoble and shocking retreat from the far-sighted progressivism of Mackay's judgment in *Drummond Wren*; many Jewish lawyers thought *Noble* carried more than a whiff of anti-Semitism. Wright and Laskin had never expressly articulated that view to their students, but had criticized the Court of Appeal's formalistic and conservative approach to many legal issues. It was a bellwether of the upcoming youth revolution that the discontent of a young lawyer like Grafstein was not only considered legitimate but carried some weight in the corridors of power.

There were other hurdles on the way, and Grafstein tried to surmount them all. First he met with the senior Ontario minister, Solicitor-General Lawrence Pennell. He, Greene, and LaMarsh were more receptive to Laskin than to Wright, and only Paul Martin Sr was initially resistant. Martin was pushing a candidate from his home constituency – he had a candidate from Essex County for every federal job in Canada – but even he came around eventually. Grafstein took the precaution of consulting the prime minister, who had no objection to Laskin and agreed to abide by the decision of the Ontario ministers. Pearson had been able to take the measure of the man through his meetings with Laskin as president of the CAUT on the RCMP campus surveillance issue; he and Laskin had also communicated on the constitutional amending formula, and Pearson had assisted Saul Laskin in his unsuccessful campaign for a Lakehead seat in 1963.

While this discreet lobbying was going on, the parliamentary secretary to the minister of justice was sizing up candidates for several Ontario judgeships about to become vacant. Donald S. Macdonald wrote on 7 April to Favreau and to all the Ontario ministers, noting adverse public reaction to recent appointments perceived to be motivated by patronage rather than merit; he urged the government to 'overcome this feeling by making a number of first-class appointments to the vacancies now existing.' This led him to recommend filling a High Court vacancy with someone 'not only [un]connected with Liberal politics but even publicly in opposition to them,' such as Ted Jolliffe, a former leader of the Ontario NDP, or John Osler, whose NDP politics were well known.[8] The government might be suddenly receptive to unusual suggestions, but the Ontario cabinet clique blanched at this one. A Jolliffe appointment was still beyond the pale and even Osler, scion of a venerable Upper Canadian legal dynasty, would have to wait for Pierre Trudeau to appoint him to the High Court in 1968.

As for the Court of Appeal, Macdonald had encountered critiques similar to those voiced by Grafstein: there was 'a strong feeling among the profession that the court is too thin on talent.' Wilfrid Roach had just retired on 1 April and Colin Gibson was expected to retire by the end of June, with the former position labelled as Catholic, the latter Protestant. Macdonald recommended Toronto barrister Brendan O'Brien for the 'Catholic' slot, but suggested the promotion of High Court judge Gregory Evans if O'Brien would not accept. For the Gibson slot, Macdonald recommended Bora Laskin. Leaders of the bar such as B.J. MacKinnon and Walter Williston both favoured him. His outstanding record as an academic and arbitrator 'would add real intellectual strength to the Court of Appeal [and] [h]is appointment would also help to right the imbalance which now exists with only one Jew on the Supreme

Court of Ontario out of 33 [judges].' In spite of the professor's public opposition to the proposed amending formula, Macdonald believed 'it would be to our political advantage with the Bar, the academic community and the Jewish community to appoint Mr. Laskin to the Court of Appeal in mid-summer.'[9]

Laskin's engagement with the law as a force for progressive change had long consigned him to the periphery of the legal profession. Now it singled him out as the man of the hour, as the epic scandals of the Pearson era soured the Canadian public on patronage appointments. Even before the scandals, however, reform of the judicial appointment process had emerged as an issue within professional bodies such as the Canadian Bar Association and the Canadian Association of Law Teachers.[10] These initiatives were a direct result of the 'rights revolution' in post-war society. Whatever the deficiencies of the Canadian Bill of Rights – and they were many – it, along with the example of the Warren Court, helped to create among Canadians a new consciousness of the role of the judiciary in protecting their 'rights.' The Supreme Court of Canada's civil liberties decisions of the 1950s also raised expectations, but by the mid-1960s judges such as Ivan Rand and James Estey were long gone. Diefenbaker's appointments created a much more conservative (and Conservative) court, around which an air of dismay settled like a chilly fog in the overheated 1960s.

The hue and cry about judicial appointments was also being raised by the rapidly increasing fraternity of legal academics. The boom in legal education gave law professors a certain cachet in Canadian society, and they were beginning to sound a new theme in their letters to the prime minister: Canadian courts needed judges drawn from academe, they insisted, in order to adjust the law creatively in response to social expectations. This refrain represented a break with the British tradition, where academics were never promoted to the bench; when Lord Denning heard of Laskin's appointment to the Supreme Court, he pronounced it a ridiculous idea.[11] Canadian professors inevitably invoked the great exemplars of the academic tradition on the U.S. Supreme Court. Writing to Pearson in 1963, Allen Linden lamented that Canada had 'no judges to stand in the company of Brandeis, Holmes, Frankfurter and Stone,' and promoted the U.S. custom of appointing one academic to the Supreme Court.[12] A professor at Osgoode, Linden was joined by Laskin's University of Toronto colleague Mark Mac-Guigan. Self-interest may have played some role in these pleas, but in the main they illustrated the expectations raised by the rights revolution and the growing faith in judicial activism and law reform as the appropriate response.

The Canadian academic touted most by these and other writers was Cecil Augustus Wright. For Linden he was 'the foremost legal scholar in Canada today,' for MacGuigan 'the greatest legal mind of his generation.' Sidney Smith, recommending to John Diefenbaker Wright's appointment as chief justice of Ontario in 1957, compared him to Oliver Wendell Holmes.[13] While, as Wright well knew, he had powerful enemies blocking his own judicial appointment, he paved the way for other academics to follow. The powers in Ottawa were not immediately won over by these professorial pleas. Pearson passed on Linden's letter to the minister of justice, Lionel Chevrier (a 1928 Osgoode graduate), to tepid response. Academic excellence was one factor to take into account in the appointment of judges, but he was 'not prepared to recommend that it be given primacy.' There would, moreover, 'be considerable divergence of opinion amongst lawyers and judges on the merits of the proposal.'[14] That was an understatement, but one made in 1963 in the first flush of electoral victory, when rewarding political supporters was a prime consideration. Two years later, in a more challenging political context, the same arguments would seem much more cogent.

What of the Jewish factor in Bora Laskin's appointment? Jews had been named to provincial superior courts much earlier in other provinces. Laskin's friend Sam Freedman went to the Manitoba Court of Queen's Bench in 1952. Why had Ontario been so slow? A kind of chicken-and-egg effect operated, whereby major firms denied positions to Jews, who then lacked powerful contacts to advocate their promotion to the bench. The Ontario court structure also contained some institutional constraints absent elsewhere. Quebec had no county court as did Ontario, and the Superior Court (the trial court equivalent to the Ontario High Court) was thus twice as large as Ontario's. Existing positions in Quebec and Ontario (and elsewhere) were always labelled as Catholic or Protestant, but new positions provided an element of flexibility, and they were more frequently created in Quebec than in Ontario.[15] When Harry Batshaw became the first Jewish appointee to the Quebec Superior Court in 1950, he assumed a newly created position and thus antagonized neither of the two Christian camps. Change came slowly, however, and Jewish lawyers who aspired to the bench continued to be held hostage to Protestant-Catholic rivalries for many years.

One might ask why Pearson settled on Abraham Lieff rather than

Bora Laskin as the first Jewish appointee to the Supreme Court of Ontario. In July 1963 he wrote to a disappointed lobbyist for another candidate to explain his choice. 'It was decided that there should be a judge of the Jewish race appointed. I think you will agree we couldn't have found a better one than Abe Lieff.'[16] Strongly held religious prejudice was waning, but in other respects Lieff's was a 'business as usual' appointment. One of the first Jewish lawyers in Ottawa, Lieff had long been active in the Liberal Party and owed his appointment as a magistrate in the 1930s to the Mitch Hepburn government. His wife Sadie Lazarovitch was also a lawyer and the two of them appeared frequently before the Senate divorce committee prior to the 1968 reform.[17] Lieff was deeply devoted to the human side of the law, to the sensitive resolution of some of the most emotionally charged disputes individuals can experience, and he became widely respected for his expertise in family law.

By the summer of 1965, 'business as usual' was no longer good enough. Pearson was away in Britain during the 'rather acrimonious debate' triggered by a bill amending the *Judges Act* to create two new positions on the High Court of Ontario. Donald Macdonald reported to Pearson on 6 July how the opposition parties 'all attacked the government very strongly in connection with the two unhappy instances' of Justices Landreville and Meunier. In Macdonald's view 'the events of recent days' had only strengthened his view 'that absolutely outstanding individuals should be appointed to the Ontario Supreme Court in defiance of partisan political considerations.' Then he hammered home his personal recommendation for Bora Laskin: in spite of his criticisms of the government, Laskin was 'one of the outstanding academic lawyers in Canada today and his appointment would be hailed not only by his fellow university law teachers, but by senior members of the profession and by members of the public who pay attention to these things.'[18] Macdonald's struggle to overcome the tradition of partisan appointments provides a marked contrast to the only passage in Pearson's memoirs dealing with judgeships – where he chastely denies that any factor besides merit played a role during his watch.[19]

The cabinet duly approved the appointment, but Jerry Grafstein then got a frantic call from Lawrence Pennell: how could he reach the candidate?[20] Bora and Peggy had left Canada on 21 June and would return from Europe on 23 August – a long holiday by Laskin standards. Grafstein eventually tracked them down and a call was placed to the Italian restaurant in London where they were dining with holidaying

Judy and Martin Friedland, whom Wright had just lured to Toronto.[21] Ever discreet, Bora did not tell his guests what the call was about, and the Laskins continued their holiday on the continent. Bora sent Percy Smith a postcard from Italy, provoking the following reply: 'I was delighted to have your card from Florence, and did in fact give some thought to the possible implications of the scene depicted. Clearly it suggests that you and Peggy are having a perfectly dreamy summer.'[22] Bora could be intense, he could be driven, but he could also surrender without regret to the sensuality of an Italian summer.

Jerry Grafstein had predicted the press coverage correctly. The appointment was officially announced on 24 August and even the *Toronto Telegram*, usually highly critical of the Liberals, came out with a favourable article on page one. The *Globe and Mail* noted that Laskin was one of a handful of law professors to be appointed to the bench. 'But to call him an academic is to limit him too severely. There has never been the aura of the ivory tower about Bora Laskin.' Laskin's labour arbitration work was cited in evidence, but the *Globe* went on to observe that it was his 'views as one of the country's foremost constitutional experts which attract most attention as he ascends the Bench.'[23] Jim Milner sent a batch of clippings to Frank Scott, observing that 'the newspaper approval of this appointment far exceeded any to this time.' He continued in a more rueful vein. '[W]hile we rejoice for Bora, we do allow ourselves a moment of self-pity on the Faculty. We have lost an heir-apparent whose appointment was quite unconscious and quite taken for granted. There may be no successor, and if there is there will be considerable soul searching.'[24] Elsewhere in the university world there was also a sense of loss. Coincidentally Frank Scott had won the Molson Award in August, and a CAUT colleague wrote him to say 'I was almost as delighted by the announcement of the Molson award as I was stunned by Bora's departure from among us – and that is saying something!'[25] Other reactions were more mixed. When Peggy excitedly told her mother the news, Mrs Tenenbaum replied, 'that's very nice, dear, but I always said he should have been a rabbi.'

The Laskins returned to Canada the day before the appointment was announced. It was effective 1 September but the swearing in would not take place until the seventeenth. Laskin had a few short weeks to move out of Flavelle House and into his chambers at Osgoode Hall, tie up some loose ends, and respond to an avalanche of congratulatory mail. Naturally there was a good deal of socializing too. John and Dorothy Willis invited Bora and Peggy to dinner on 30 August, along with Jim and Jean Milner and David and Elizabeth Kilgour; there was 'an incredible spate of gossip about who will be dean if Caesar retires, say, next year.'[26] Martin and Judy Friedland held a sherry party on 18 September, and the Milners invited the Laskins for a party on the twenty-ninth to meet some English lawyers and town planners. On the home front important transitions were also taking place. Barbara was starting high school while John was on the verge of leaving for Britain where he would do graduate work at the London School of Economics before attending law school at the University of Toronto.

Morris Shumiatcher travelled from Saskatchewan to attend the swearing in, bringing a stone cut entitled 'Boy Feeding Birds' that Laskin arranged to hang in his chambers. Morris was surprised to find Peggy less ebullient than usual on this happy occasion. In fact, she had not been feeling well since their return from Europe, and was awaiting surgery with some trepidation. Just two weeks after her husband's swearing-in, she underwent a mastectomy after breast cancer was discovered. For Peggy at fifty-three, beautiful, elegant Peggy, the experience was devastating, the sense of mutilation even greater than the fear of metastasis.[27] Still a bit giddy after their idyllic summer and the excitement over Bora's judicial appointment, both of them were stunned by the news. For Laskin, the strain must have been intense. He could only manage a wooden letter to Morris Shumiatcher, conveying the bare news about Peggy's health before veering into an account of his new work at the court. He was distraught, but simply could not write intimately about such matters, even to one of his oldest friends who adored Peggy almost as much as he did.[28]

When Peggy's recovery was assured, the Laskins slowly resumed their social life and their travels. They were able to go south for a holiday that winter, and enjoyed several weeks in Britain in the summer of 1966 when Bora received an honorary degree from the University of Edinburgh. They stayed close to home the next summer aside from a visit to Expo 67, but visited Jasper in the spring of 1968 and spent several weeks in Britain again that summer. Laskin was also looking forward to visiting Nigeria for a constitutional law conference, but it was postponed several times and finally cancelled. Peggy was delighted to report to the Shumiatchers that Bora attended the Grey Cup game in Toronto that fall with his Calgary Stetson, his only Western-attired rival being the prime minister.[29] The Laskin household was augmented by the arrival of a poodle named Sucre (Suki). Bora had resisted the acquisition of a pet for years but once Suki arrived, he bonded instantly with the dog and looked forward to discussing confidential court matters with her on their daily walks.

The year Bora Laskin left his career as a legal educator was also the most tumultuous year in Ontario legal education since 1949. The demographic pressure that had forced the Law Society to open up legal education to Ontario universities in 1957 was now causing a crisis within Osgoode Hall Law School itself. Osgoode Hall simply could not hold the surging numbers of law students in addition to the vastly expanded numbers of graduates taking the bar admission course, and the province made it clear that no money would be forthcoming for an addition. Further, the province refused to support single-purpose educational institutions in the belief that multi-purpose institutions were more efficient. In December 1961, a month after stepping down as provincial premier, Leslie M. Frost bluntly told the benchers to consider seriously affiliating their law school with York University.[30] Initially the benchers were not keen, but when John Arnup became treasurer of the Law Society in 1964 he was determined to bring the matter to a speedy conclusion. Only two conditions would be stipulated: retention of the name Osgoode Hall in some form and the addition of Law Society representatives to the York Senate. Arnup wanted the transfer to take place as early as 1967, but in the end the agreement began in 1968 and the move to the York campus did not take place until 1969.[31] Arnup was not interested in haggling over details with York because the Law Society's real concern was its bargaining position with the province regarding funding for the bar admission program. By surrendering the law school, the Law Society hoped to get major grant support for the bar admission program – and did.[32]

Political and financial levers pushed Osgoode Hall Law School north to York University, but internal changes at Osgoode also encouraged the move. Allan Leal, who had succeeded C.E. Smalley-Baker as dean in 1958, completed Osgoode's transformation into a university-type law school during his mandate. Harry Arthurs confirmed that 'by 1965, ... the school's academic programme and philosophy were indistinguishable from those of the university law schools.'[33] When John Arnup announced the migration of the law school to York at a dinner meeting with the faculty at Osgoode Hall on St Patrick's Day 1965, however, all hell broke loose. Dean Leal and those faculty who viewed the courts and the common law as central to legal education wished to remain downtown in touch with the professional pulse. Those more interested in law reform, social policy, and interdisciplinary approaches were keen to set up on the *tabula rasa* of the new campus. The former group tended to be politically conservative, the latter liberal or socialist.

Leal first tried to interest Caesar Wright in taking in the Osgoode faculty at the University of Toronto, but Wright turned him down flat. Some Osgoode faculty led by Ian Baxter then redesigned the proposal as one which would see Wright's faculty merge with Osgoode over a ten-year period; both would become part of a new Law Centre, possibly reaffiliated with the University of Toronto. The new centre might house entities such as the Ontario Law Reform Commission and legal research institutes. Baxter wanted to raise the plan privately with Laskin first, believing his attitude was key.[34] The plan was bold, it was visionary, and it was unanimously rejected by the law faculty at Toronto. In retrospect it is probably just as well. The two faculties' different identities have provided for more intellectual and educational diversity than would have been possible in a unitary setting. As it was, Leal indicated he would not continue as dean and exited to the Ontario Law Reform Commission. Several disgruntled Osgoode faculty went to the University of Toronto and the remaining idealists went on to York, where they hoped to create not just a new building but a new kind of legal education aimed at a new type of law student. Alan Mewett, who migrated from Osgoode to Toronto at this time, was not comfortable with Osgoode's desire to use the law as a tool to effect social change and assist disadvantaged groups. He used to sum up the differences between the two schools for his students by declaring that 'there is one law for the rich and one for the poor, and that is why we are at the University of Toronto.'[35]

Bora Laskin was not directly involved in the ferment at Osgoode, but his translation to the bench did not mean the end of his involvement in either legal education or university affairs. He continued to be involved in both, but in a new capacity: service on the board of governors of both York University and the Ontario Institute for Studies in Education (OISE). Laskin was named to the York board in January 1967 but Murray Ross was already relying on him as a member of the search committee for the new dean at Osgoode. Laskin forwarded names of possible candidates to Ross but as of February 1967 the situation looked bleak. An offer was made to Robert Mckay, associate dean at the New York University School of Law, but he declined when offered the deanship of his own faculty. Ross then told Laskin he was thinking of Max Cohen, who was just finishing a term as dean at McGill.[36]

At this point Peggy Laskin jogged her husband's memory about a Montreal legal academic who had impressed them both.[37] Gerald Eric Le Dain had served in the war, graduated from McGill Law with the gold medal in 1949, then shuttled back and forth between St James Street and teaching at McGill. The search committee was dazzled by him, and he was an inspired choice for Osgoode at a critical moment: Le Dain's experience in a prominent corporate counsel setting afforded him instant legitimacy with the bar, his teaching and scholarship in public law fields endeared him to the faculty, and his service as counsel to Quebec Attorney-General Claude Wagner on several constitutional files had given him a high public profile. In 1969, the same year he was named a Commission of Inquiry into the Non-medical Use of Drugs, Le Dain persuaded the Law Society to grant full curricular control to the law schools after first year.

While Osgoode was searching for a dean in 1966–7, so – at long last – was Toronto. Claude Bissell sought Bora Laskin's counsel, meeting with him in his chambers at Osgoode Hall early in September 1966. He came away with the impression that there was poor communication between the senior staff and dean on the one hand, and the younger men on the other, with the latter feeling left out of the development of faculty policy. This was not entirely accurate. Some of the younger men were fervid Wright loyalists, while some middling to senior faculty were quite disaffected. Wright and Willis continued to grind away at each other, McWhinney had just left for McGill partly as a result of conflict with Wright, and even the affable Milner's tolerance was wearing thin. The curriculum was 'in need of revision since it was introduced 16 years ago,' but Wright had rejected the report of the committee charged with reforming it. What was to be done? Nothing. Bissell concluded with the humane observation that 'the present Dean is incapable of serving in any capacity except as Dean [and] his prestige is such that termination two years before he is 65, and in reasonably good health, will be harmful to the Faculty, and to him.' The discontent in the ranks should be overcome 'by requesting from the Dean *and his staff* a report on the future development of this Faculty of Law.'[38]

Yet only weeks later, Bissell set in motion the train of events leading to Wright's resignation. The age of lifetime deanships had ended, he announced; deans would be appointed for a term of seven years, and those having served longer should consider stepping aside. Caesar Wright took umbrage at the change, but agreed to leave as of 30 June 1967. Possibly he was relieved to have an official excuse to resign.

Wright confided worries about his health to his young colleague Ronald St John Macdonald, whom he had hired away from Western Ontario when Laskin went on sabbatical in 1961.[39] Although only sixty-two, Wright's lifestyle was a checklist of risk factors for high blood pressure: heavy smoking, little exercise, and a steady diet of roast beef, Yorkshire pudding, and Scotch.

The search committee produced a shortlist of two: Jim Milner, the most senior man after John Willis, and Ronald Macdonald, who had been teaching barely a decade. Unknown to most people, Bora Laskin was briefly a shadow candidate. Al Abel approached Laskin privately to see if he would be interested in resigning from the bench and returning to the law faculty as dean, but was met with a negative reply.[40] Laskin was not the type to look back once he had moved on. He had worked hard to establish his legitimacy with his new brethren, was enjoying the work in spite of some frustrations, and was beginning to achieve some recognition. Besides, even in the eighteen months since his appointment, campuses across North America were becoming contentious, conflict-ridden hot spots, far removed from the relatively quiet havens in which Laskin had spent his academic life. A year later Laskin confided to Morris Shumiatcher that he felt he had left the university at the right moment, and wondered if he would have been able to understand it if he had stayed.[41]

If the faculty could not have Bora Laskin, Jim Milner was probably the next closest article. The two were close friends, and Milner had succeeded to Bora's role as a defender of academic freedom within the CAUT. He was well liked by the students, respected by his colleagues, and a man of considerable culture and erudition, but Bissell accepted the search committee's unanimous recommendation of the man perceived as the 'youth candidate,' Ronald St John Macdonald. It would not be the last time that two expatriate Nova Scotians competed for the deanship of a Toronto law school (two decades later it would be Osgoode's turn). Macdonald had attended Dalhousie Law School after service in the navy and followed up with LLM degrees from both the University of London and Harvard. A fervent believer in the Pearsonian tradition of Canadian leadership in world affairs, he devoted himself to international law, serving as the Canadian representative to the UN General Assembly in 1965 and 1966. He was on the verge of resigning from the university and remaining in New York when the deanship was offered to him.[42]

Macdonald's appointment was announced on 30 March, Gerald Le

Dain's as dean of Osgoode on 10 April, and on 24 April Caesar Wright died of a massive cerebral haemorrhage. The end was 'sad and very sudden,' Jim Milner wrote to a friend, '[o]ne week he was in the office, full of beans, the next week he was in the hospital for a checkup, and the next he was dead.'[43] Claude Bissell's observation had become a prediction: Wright was indeed 'incapable of serving in any capacity except as Dean.' Convocation Hall was full for the funeral, and all the faculty were honorary pallbearers. Prayers were read by an Anglican and a Catholic priest, 'but there was no music,' Jean Milner recorded, and 'the empty chairs behind, usually bright with academic robes, made it all rather drab and sombre. However we went to the [Wrights'] apartment afterwards and had a rather astonishing cocktail party.'[44] Cross-currents of emotion flowed through the crowd: sympathy for Marie Wright, who had made satisfying her difficult husband her life's work, guilty relief that the irascible Caesar was gone at last, and a buoyant optimism about the future of legal education and of Canada itself in this springtime of the country's centennial year.

For Bora Laskin, Wright's death represented a passage from life to myth. Initially mentor, teacher, and father-figure for Laskin, Wright later became a trusted friend and colleague. The special bond of loyalty forged between the two men in the crucible of 1949 survived even the irritations of Wright's last difficult years. A heroic myth gradually replaced the man in Laskin's mind, such that he would not allow a word to be said against Wright. In paying tribute to his friend in his 1982 Cecil Wright Lecture, delivered only two years before his own death, Laskin publicly chastised two authors present in the audience who had stated in print that Wright had resigned 'in a huff.' 'That,' he admonished, 'was an unworthy assessment – indeed a distortion of the events that led [us] to resign.'[45] When the abashed authors spoke to Laskin about this later, he told them there were worse things than being criticized by the chief justice of Canada.[46]

Laskin's membership on the York board of governors marked another important transition in his life. There and on the bench Laskin went from being a critical outsider to an insider, but the outlet of dissenting judgments in the Court of Appeal allowed Laskin to preserve his intellectual freedom to some extent. The board of York provided no such flexibility – he would have to work in harness with the other members. After his appointment to the bench it was natural for Laskin to be asked to join university boards and he had, after all, advocated the presence of faculty members on them. York's constitution at least conformed to the Duff-Berdahl ideal in not excluding faculty representatives, but in fact none served on the board during Laskin's tenure. In addition, the chance to keep a watching brief on the affairs of the new Osgoode Hall Law School as it joined York University was undoubtedly very tempting.

Service on the York board exposed Laskin to a new stratum of society – the movers and shakers of the business community. Murray Ross had made a particular effort to secure the services of the most senior figures on Bay Street to give his infant university a head start: the board was 'a homogeneous group, almost a "club".'[47] Thus Laskin joined Allan Lambert and John Proctor, two of the top men at the Bank of Nova Scotia and the Toronto-Dominion Bank respectively; Bert Gerstein, founder of People's Credit Jewellers (as it then was); and John D. Leitch, president of Upper Canada Shipping and son-in-law of Chief Justice Cartwright, among other captains of industry and finance. Founding chair of the board Robert Winters became president of Brazilian Light and Power (later Brascan) and was now in Pearson's cabinet as minister of trade and commerce, but would lose the leadership of the Liberal Party to outsider Pierre Trudeau in April 1968. The sole woman on the board was Signy Eaton, whose husband John David managed the Eaton empire, and her responsibilities related primarily to the aesthetic development of the campus. Laskin's labour background left him rather suspicious of corporate leaders. Ross saw him as 'fundamentally ... more at home with the faculty than with businessmen,'[48] and Laskin's work on the board reflected this. He preferred dealing with senate and students, not the bricks and mortar issues that the other members of the board enjoyed.

Laskin was no mere figurehead on the board. A year into his tenure Murray Ross asked him to chair a presidential committee 'to consider the broad subject of what is appropriate and what is inappropriate behaviour for various members of the University community, and to suggest what might be defined as the rights and obligations of the University and the various members of the University community.' The large committee included a young professor named Edward Broadbent, but he resigned from it after being elected as the NDP MP for Oshawa-Whitby in June of 1968. The seemingly bland mandate veiled the serious disquiet felt by university administrators in North America and Europe at the turbulence springing up on one campus after another. In December 1967 York witnessed student protests against on-campus recruiting by companies producing weapons for the Vietnam war. Ross moved quickly to ban such recruiting, and announced the appointment of Laskin's committee a few weeks later. University officials were on tenterhooks after *les évènements* of May 1968 in Paris, but York's students remained relatively quiet through the rest of the 1960s.

Student protest did not bother Laskin provided it did not involve violence or harassment of others holding different views – though if it did, he could be merciless. For him, to be passionate about one's ideas was to be human, and to seek to communicate them vigorously by all legitimate means was especially appropriate for students in the early years of their intellectual life. He had been deeply moved, not threatened, by the Free Speech demonstrations at Berkeley. Ross's appointment was a smart one. Laskin possessed high credibility with both senior faculty and university administrators, and he had a way with students. He happened to receive an honorary degree from the University of New Brunswick in the fall of 1968 at the height of the so-called Strax Affair. Strax was a professor of anarchist bent whose dispute with the university over library privileges had escalated into a state of siege on campus. His student supporters decided to picket the convocation procession as it wound its stately way across the campus. When Laskin saw the protesters he could not resist stepping out of the line and talking with them. He listened courteously and after he rejoined the procession one student was heard to remark, 'If they were all like that, we wouldn't have to be doing this.'[49]

Laskin submitted the committee's report, 'Freedom and Responsibility in the University,' in November 1969. As with the graduate studies report at Toronto, he clearly drafted it personally. It was mainly a summing-up of Laskin's long-held views on the nature of a university as 'a place of liberty.' The university was 'not a market-place – even of ideas[, but] a vibrant shared experience in a life devoted to intellect and imagination.'[50] Free inquiry could only flourish with a minimum of formal restrictions, but Laskin's commitment to 'the civility of University relationships' led him to rely mostly on self-policing. It was time to get rid of the paternalistic *in loco parentis* rule that had traditionally framed the relationship between university and student: the university was now a community of faculty and students, not a hierarchical institution for the governance of students alone. Internal courts should deal with university-related misconduct by any university citizen, but the report doubted the value of a detailed code of conduct. '[I]t is enough to enunciate such general standards as the duty to refrain from destruction of property, from invasion of premises, from violence, ... from unjustified interference with the conduct of classes or meetings [and the like].'[51] Laskin's lawyerly concern with jurisdictional issues was evident in much of the report. It dealt in some detail with the proper relationship between domestic university tribunals and the ordinary courts; Laskin denied that concurrent actions represented 'double jeopardy' as each proceeding served a different end. Where sit-ins or other behaviour disrupted classes or movement on campus, however, the report suggested calling in the police immediately rather than invoking the civil machinery of restraining orders.

It was not students but faculty with whom relations were most strained, as Laskin had ample occasion to observe while chairing the search for a successor to Murray Ross. The almost surreal misadventures of this tortured search process provide a perfect microcosm of academic life in the later 1960s. The search committee included three board members, three members elected by senate, three students, and the president of the York Faculty Association. Women's role in university democracy was not yet an issue: the ten members of the search committee were all men and the position profile developed for the presidency invariably referred to the candidate as male (Laskin's *Freedom and Responsibility* committee was also all male).

The *York University Act* gave the board the power to appoint a president 'after consultation with the senate,' but was silent as to the form of consultation. There was no initial agreement about how the search committee would report to the board or the senate, but it began its work in the hope that a process would be agreed upon in due course. The two leading candidates were perceived to be John Saywell, dean of arts, and Jim Gillies, dean of the faculty of administrative studies and former vice-president of York. Saywell was quickly identified as the senate candidate, Gillies as the board candidate, and indeed the board strongly favoured Gillies. It was the tenor of the times that Gillies, with many contacts in the private sector, would be seen by many faculty members as too business-oriented and not a 'pure' academic. Laskin may well have shared this view, as Ross hints in his memoirs. When the dean of science reported to the committee that in his view Gillies was a poor administrator, that clinched it: Gillies's name was left off the list and Laskin submitted a list of three names in confidence to the board on 27 November: Saywell, Michael Oliver of McGill (and part of the United College exodus after the Crowe affair), and Albert Allen of the University of Toronto.

With that, Laskin left for England to give the Hamlyn Lectures. As the senate and board haggled over reporting procedures, someone on the committee leaked his report to the *Globe and Mail* on 9 December. The search process unravelled immediately. First Oliver withdrew his name because he was also a candidate for the principalship of McGill, then Saywell withdrew. In his view the closed nature of the search process had led to a 'flood of rumour, fabrications and slander [circulating] on the campus over the past few months.'[52] The board was furious, Laskin disgusted, and York appeared ridiculous in the public eye. Laskin wanted the whole committee to resign but the board persuaded him to stay on in view of time pressures. The second phase of the search turned out to be even more acrimonious than the first, and resulted in the appointment of the least controversial, and probably least suitable, candidate on a short list of four (Allen, Gillies, Saywell, and David Slater of Queen's).[53] Slater's difficult tenure, which coincided with large cuts in provincial grants, lasted only two years.[54] By the time Slater accepted the offer Laskin had been named to the Supreme Court of Canada, but the frustrating search process meant that he left the board on a sour note.

Laskin's period as chairman of the board of governors of the Ontario Institute for Studies in Education (OISE) also had its frustrating moments but in the end was perhaps more satisfying. It was exciting presiding over the birth of such an innovative institution, even though its novelty created its own tensions and problems. OISE was supposed to be oriented to 'developmental research,' to generate new ideas that could be implemented directly in Ontario schools at a time when the whole educational system was under review. This mandate was not well understood outside or even inside OISE, where many faculty were more comfortable with traditional kinds of scholarly research aimed at peer-reviewed publications. Governance issues also simmered under the surface. OISE's statute was a bare-bones piece of legislation creating it as a corporate entity with a board of governors, and not much more. Even the Academic Council, functionally the equivalent of a university senate, was formally a creature of the board, although in practice it soon operated as the major policy-initiating body at the Institute. The board's formal omnipotence was still irksome to faculty, while the board feared a more powerful council might take OISE in unforeseen directions. To head off an impasse, the board wisely appointed a special committee on governance in 1968 to make recommendations for reform. It suggested fleshing out the governance structure to more closely resemble a university, with a statutorily based senate, and a reorganization of the Institute to ensure the developmental aspect of its mandate was accomplished.[55]

The OISE board, made up almost entirely of teachers, educational administrators, and representatives of other universities, could not have been more different from that of York. With thirty-five members it was rather unwieldy, so the real work had to be done by an executive committee. Board meetings and executive committee meetings each occupied a full day a month, and undoubtedly required hours of preparation. OISE rewarded Laskin with an honorary degree in 1975, invoking for the first time its previously unexercised degree-granting powers. Laskin enjoyed the prestige of serving on two university boards, but he certainly paid dearly for it out of what could have been his leisure time. He would never serve on the board of his alma mater. There was little love lost between him and the University of Toronto board of governors, and it is unlikely he was ever seriously canvassed as a possible candidate.

When Bora Laskin attended a conference of U.S., British, and Canadian law professors at New York University in 1960, he had felt rather at sea, remained tongue-tied, and did not make much of an impression. Frank Scott reported his disappointment to Lon Fuller at Harvard: 'we [the Canadians] had far too many silent bodies; ... Bora Laskin, one of our ablest teachers and scholars, ... somehow did not feel able to participate in the public discussions.'[56] This inauspicious international debut did not hold him back later on. Once on the bench, Laskin was in demand at legal gatherings on both sides of the Atlantic. In October 1968 he participated in a conference at New York University School of Law commemorating the centenary of the fourteenth amendment to the U.S. constitution, where he appeared at the podium alongside such luminaries as Earl Warren, Abe Fortas, and Lord Denning.[57] The source of the invitation was probably NYU's dean, Robert Mckay, whom Laskin had met as a candidate for the deanship at Osgoode. Not that Laskin's contacts gave him any unearned advantage. When such gatherings were looking for a representative of the Canadian judiciary, there was scarcely a credible candidate since Ivan Rand's retirement.

The fourteenth amendment conference was notable for two things, one highly public, the other totally unnoticed at the time. On the second day of the conference Lyndon Johnson withdrew Fortas's nomination as chief justice of the United States in succession to Warren when it became clear the Senate would not confirm him. Fortas was thus a

Laskin *manqué*. The two men were the same age, first generation sons of immigrant Russian Jewry who rose from the frontier (Fortas was from Tennessee) to the summit of their professions. Fortas went to the Supreme Court just a month before Laskin went to the bench, but would resign in disgrace in May 1969 over an ethical lapse.[58] Laskin was probably intrigued by Fortas but would not have approved of his continuing as an adviser to President Johnson after ascending the bench. The unheralded event at the conference was a passage in Laskin's talk on Canadian constitutionalism. When speaking of the amending process, he observed that 'amendment depends on formal British action – taken, however, only at the behest of national authorities. It remains, of course, a matter of internal politics whether an amendment can be safely sought without the consent of the provincial governments.' Whether provincial consent was a legal requirement or merely a political advantage was exactly the issue the Supreme Court of Canada would be called upon to decide a dozen years later in the *Patriation Reference*, but no one discovered that Laskin had already put his views on the record extra-judicially.

When Laskin gave the Hamlyn Lectures at the Inner Temple in December 1969 he was in very select company indeed. With Lord Denning inaugurating them in 1949, the annual lectures were usually given by British academics or judges and treated large themes in the common law. Laskin was the first Canadian and only the second North American to be asked to speak – Dean Erwin Griswold of Harvard preceded him. One might have expected a lecture on the revolution in labour law in the post-war world, on human rights, or even on federalism. Laskin chose instead to speak on *The British Tradition in Canadian Law*, a topic some found almost colonial in its genuflection to the English heritage. His concern with displaying 'civility' to his hosts probably explains the choice. Laskin's mentor Felix Frankfurter had also shown a marked Anglophilic turn, and similar deference, in his later years. Distinction came with a price however: Laskin was obliged to stay home most of the summer to complete the lectures for a late July deadline, and then had to lecture at the first annual national judges' seminar in Toronto. Peggy, feeling cheated of a proper summer holiday, was not amused.[59]

By 1969 Laskin's professional fame had spread far and wide in the common law world. Within Canada, his cachet was symbolized by his role at Frank Scott's seventieth birthday party on 19 September. The legal, literary, and political elites of (mostly anglophone) Canada were all in attendance, including the prime minister, who got off the best one-liner of the evening: 'We are all Frankophiles here.' Senator Carl Goldenberg chaired the event but asked Laskin to make the presentation of a Karsh portrait of Scott to the Faculty of Law. His succinct and heartfelt speech was a worthy tribute to its subject.[60] As with his last few years at the university, it seemed as if Laskin was again pacing on a stage several sizes too small. If he was fit to lecture alongside Earl Warren and address the cream of the British legal establishment on its own turf, how much longer could he be confined to the Ontario Court of Appeal?

15

Ontario Court of Appeal

Laskin's nine brethren were a crusty old lot, with emphasis on the 'old.' Aside from Gregory Evans, who was a year younger than Laskin and joined the court at the same time, and James Laidlaw McLennan, who was only four years older than Laskin, the rest were all born at the turn of the twentieth century. Most had been on the court for many years, two since 1946. One of these was John Bell Aylesworth, the dominant personality on the court, whom Laskin knew from the days of wartime conciliation boards when Aylesworth was counsel for Ford Motor Company. Aylesworth never let anyone forget that he had articled with his uncle, the redoubtable Sir Allen Aylesworth (1854–1952), who had been a member of Laurier's cabinet. Three members of the court were veterans of the First World War, and George Argo McGillivray also served in the Second. Only one had had a political career. Dana Porter, a long-serving member of the provincial cabinet and attorney-general of Ontario from 1949 to 1955, was named directly to the office of chief justice of Ontario in 1958, frustrating Caesar Wright's ambitions. He was also a member of the University of Toronto board of governors during the years when Laskin was feeling highly aggrieved at that body. Whatever tensions existed between him and Laskin did not last long, as Porter died in office in May 1967. He was succeeded by George Gale, also a long-serving member of the Ontario Supreme Court, who is generally well remembered as chief justice. Laskin's colleagues were good lawyers by the standards of their day, but their age and seniority made them less than receptive to the fresh ideas represented by 'the professor.'

Among these new colleagues there was, one may imagine, some scepticism about Laskin's appointment. After all, much of the positive press coverage was implicitly a criticism of the Court of Appeal's incumbent judges. And Laskin himself had delivered at times bracing critiques of the decisions of this and other courts. In the last quarter-century Canadian judges have become inured to such criticism and have even welcomed it on occasion, but in the mid-1960s vigorous criticism of the judges by lawyers or legal academics was viewed as highly improper. Laskin's public critique had opened up an important new avenue of judicial accountability, but it was not one initially welcomed by the judges themselves.

Laskin immediately found his new job fascinating, but on a personal level his integration into the court was anything but smooth. He was too discreet to commit his frustrations to paper, but confided in his friends Ernest Sirluck and Morris Shumiatcher. Senior counsel such as Bud Estey knew the court well and also had occasion to observe Laskin's 'probationary' period. For someone used to discussing ideas, Laskin found the transition a shock. The atmosphere at the court was not an intellectual one: rather, a grinding, relentless work ethic prevailed. Hearing the next case, writing the next opinion, churning out the judgments, these were the prime concerns. The court was run like a corporate law office, with a corresponding emphasis on hierarchy and productivity. It was virtually an all-male world, with a rough and tumble edge to it. Relations with counsel were often tense and combative, as the judges sometimes lashed out at lawyers who were relatively powerless to reply. Bud Estey, no shrinking violet himself, described the Court of Appeal of the 1960s as a 'firing line,' adding that he still shuddered to think of the experience over thirty years later.[1] The judges would have said they wanted to cut through silly arguments and avoid wasting time; counsel saw a court unreceptive to creative argumentation who seemed to define justice exclusively in terms of speed and conformity to precedent. Laskin saw interchange with counsel as a continuation of discussions with his best students, not a contest of wills. He did not emulate the techniques of the senior judges and for the most part tried to treat counsel with civility.

As a full-time academic who had virtually never appeared in court or even practised as a solicitor, Laskin suffered from an immediate legitimacy problem. He was an unknown quantity, and his colleagues feared the worst of this legal intellectual. Like the new recruit to a seasoned regiment, Laskin had to run faster and further than anyone else to prove his mettle. There were many parallels between Laskin's reception and that afforded Bertha Wilson, the first woman appointed to the court a decade later. In some respects Laskin may have had a worse time of it because he had no mentor to ease his entry into the court, and the pressure to 'fit in' was all the stronger for remaining unverbalized. Bertha Wilson was enormously assisted by John Arnup, coincidentally Laskin's successor on the Court of Appeal, and Chief Justice Gale also gave her valuable support.[2] An additional problem for Laskin arose from a concern that he should not sit on cases involving legal topics on which he had expressed himself in print. If followed literally, this practice would have disqualified Laskin from a wide range of cases and made more work for the other judges, but eventually a modus vivendi was found. According to Bud Estey, Laskin 'had a very unhappy time on that court until he demonstrated to Aylesworth that he could crank out the volume.'[3] Laskin soon proved he did not need to take any productivity lessons from Aylesworth or anyone else, and worked extra to cover for ill colleagues.

Other sources of tension were not so easily resolved. One minor but significant irritant for Laskin was the judges' practice of retiring to the University Club in the late afternoon for a rubber of bridge. The club, unconnected to the University of Toronto in spite of its name, did not admit Jews as members although they could be signed in as guests. This precluded Laskin from taking his turn as host, but his brethren seem not to have sensed the invidiousness of the distinction, and Laskin felt unable to raise the issue. On an ideological plane, the most marked difference between Laskin and his colleagues lay in the field of criminal law. Here Laskin was somewhat vulnerable because this was one of the few areas he had not studied in depth. His civil libertarian tendencies were obvious, however, and he wrote his most high-profile dissents in these years in the field of criminal law. His colleagues saw themselves as guardians of law and order and espoused what came to be called a 'crime control' approach to the criminal law, as opposed to Laskin's 'due process' model.[4] One of Laskin's senior colleagues told him to his face, 'your trouble as a judge is that you are afraid to let the weight of the law come down on the accused.' Laskin admitted to his friend Ernest Sirluck that the criticism had some validity.[5] Fortunately Laskin was not faced with decisions involving capital punishment, which was suspended soon after he joined the bench.

Even after Laskin gained some legitimacy with his colleagues, he still found himself frustrated with what he regarded as result-oriented jurisprudence. Morris Shumiatcher tried to console him by letter after Laskin unburdened himself in a conversation in July 1967. 'How could it be otherwise?' Morris wondered. 'Your present criticisms are no different from those which you have expressed over the years ... [O]nly now ... your vantage point has changed and possibly your worst suspicions have been proved well-founded. The courts have always selected the facts which they have wanted to select in order to reach the result which they think fit and proper.'[6]

The 1960s were a turning point in the work of appellate courts across Canada. In the first half of the twentieth century most of their work had involved the review of private law matters. Business disputes, the workings of the land market, dispositions of wealth within the family, and liability for accidents took up most of the court's time. Before the advent of legal aid, appeals in criminal matters were not frequent, the law of taxation was in its infancy, and the only public law entities regularly before the court were municipal institutions. The rapid growth of the economy after the war led to increasing governmental intervention and a corresponding shift to public law. In the 1950s Toronto was the fastest growing city in North America, spawning a complex web of planning, zoning, and expropriation law to guide the urban development process there and elsewhere in the province. The powers of new and newly empowered administrative agencies such as the Ontario Labour Relations Board and the Ontario Municipal Board had to be defined. Legal aid brought more appeals in criminal law matters. Private law still formed the bulk of the work in appellate courts, but the proportion of public law work was steadily increasing.

Much of this new work required finding the appropriate balance of state and individual rights. This balancing typically arose in one of two main contexts. In the first, the individual encountered state power directly in the form an expropriating agency, a provider of public services, or a public sector employer. Here the courts were often called upon to establish the ground rules for procedures to be followed by state agencies in their dealings with citizens where their constituent legislation was unclear or silent. In these situations, Laskin generally held the state to a high standard of procedural fairness and interpreted any legislative ambiguities in favour of the individual. In the second context, a state-created regulatory body was vested with the power to adjust the interests of opposing groups: labour boards, human rights tribunals, planning authorities, and the like. This situation was more complex because there were two or more sets of private interests at stake. Interfering with the decisions of these statutory decision makers would benefit one set of private interests at the expense of another. Although these bodies were typically given large amounts of discretion to carry out their tasks, Canadian courts in the past had often been accused of imposing court-based norms and procedures on them. For Laskin the legal modernist, educating his colleagues about the virtues of deference was high on his agenda.

In situations where the individual met state power directly, Laskin and his colleagues were generally in agreement. In *R. v. Pringle, ex parte Mills*, a Jamaican citizen was allowed to enter Canada for six weeks as a visitor. During that time he applied for permanent admission but before any decision was made on the application the six weeks ran out. The immigration authorities then arrested Pringle and made an order to deport him; it was upheld by the Immigration Appeal Board and a motion to quash the order was refused by Justice Lieff. Proceeding in this way ignored section 7(3) of the *Immigration Act*, which deemed someone in Pringle's position to be a 'person seeking admission to Canada' and thereby entitled to an examination on his application. The authorities claimed the section gave them a discretion as to whether such an examination should be held, but Laskin would have none of it, labelling their argument 'desperate.' '[A]pplicants,' he said, 'have a right to regularity of procedure prescribed under the Act.' Adverting to the 'floodgates' argument raised by the government, Laskin replied that he saw 'nothing baneful if every temporary visitor should decide to seek permanent admission. Does it matter whether the immigration officers are busier inside Canada than at the border or ports of entry? An examination must be given; it is the right of every immigrant.'[7] Laskin's decision did not guarantee that Pringle's application would be successful, but it at least ensured that his right to proper adjudication on it could not be short-circuited through deportation.

Laskin had little patience when public authorities advanced economic arguments to deny basic rights or services to individuals. In *Holmberg v. Public Utilities Commission of Sault Ste. Marie*, a homeowner was left literally out in the cold by a decision not to supply his home with water or electricity. Holmberg had the misfortune to build the only house in a projected subdivision where the developer had defaulted on an obligation to test the water main and to construct a secondary power line and transformer. Upon being requested to supply water and power to the house in question, the Public Utilities Commission (PUC) cited cost factors in denying the application. The *Public Utilities Act* imposed a duty on the PUC to supply water, and Laskin held that it was 'not entitled to cast the burden on the applicants [for the developer's default], especially when ... it did not appoint an inspector as provided by the subdivision agreement respecting installation of the water-main.' Nor did the developer's default shield the PUC from providing electricity 'unless there is no supply line at all from which it can be provided.'[8] Laskin clearly felt that the risk of the developer's default could be better absorbed by a public body than an individual.

These were unanimous decisions, but one core area of state-individual interaction where Laskin and his colleagues disagreed, somewhat surprisingly, was in the interpretation of expropriation legislation. Laskin dissented on several occasions in favour of the landowner, perhaps a result of his family's small-business background or his experience as a professor of real property or both. One might have expected the other judges to leap to the defence of property owners more readily than Laskin. These decisions fit nonetheless with his general approach to administrative law and criminal law, which put a heavy burden on the state to deal fairly with individuals. In one case where the claimant was seeking to elicit on discovery information about previous valuations obtained by the expropriating ministry, Laskin would have required the department to provide them. In his view, the 'unique position of expert appraisal in expropriation proceedings' was sufficient to adopt a more liberal rule on access to such valuations.[9] In two other cases Laskin found that the failure of the expropriating authority to make an offer of compensation within statutory delays entitled the claimants to interest on the award even though they had remained in possession for some months. These cases were consistent with his legal modernism in that the expropriating agency was not an expert tribunal commanding deference, but simply a public body in an adversarial relationship with a land-owning citizen. If acquisition of the land was in the public interest, there was no reason that an individual citizen should suffer under-compensation by cheese-paring bureaucrats.

These cases came up at the very end of Laskin's service on the Court of Appeal, and provided the occasion for him to declare his views on *stare decisis*. In *Re Judson and Governors of the University of Toronto* Laskin had dissented on a point regarding an award of interest under the

Expropriation Act.[10] A similar case came up shortly thereafter and Laskin dissented again. 'My persistence in dissent gives me some unease,' he confessed, 'but since I do not subscribe to a doctrine of *stare decisis* binding upon the members of this Court in respect of its own decisions, I must perforce stay with my dissenting view until I am myself persuaded that it is wrong or I am compelled so to agree by reason of a judgment of the Supreme Court of Canada on the point. I believe dissents have survival value, at least in the Court in which they are delivered, and they would have none if a majority decision of the Court was enough to erode them.'[11] And survive they did: his dissents in both cases, delivered just days before his appointment to the Supreme Court, were upheld there.[12]

Laskin's concern to protect the individual from state power also extended to professional licensing and disciplinary bodies exercising statutory powers. Here he demanded very high standards of procedural fairness, higher than those his colleagues were willing to support. Laskin had occasion to make his views known in a case where the discipline committee of the Council of the College of Physicians and Surgeons had reprimanded a member for unauthorized advertising. When an appeal was taken to the full council, some members of the committee sat on it. Justices Schroeder, McGillivray, and Laskin all agreed this was wrong, but a majority of the court simply remitted the matter to the council to decide the appeal without the discipline committee members. For Laskin, that was a Pyrrhic victory for the appellant; he declared the council had disqualified itself on this file and the court itself should make the final decision.[13] This decision presaged Laskin's 'glorious dissent' while on the Supreme Court of Canada in a very similar case involving the Law Society of Upper Canada.[14]

It was in the second public law context, where the issue of the degree of deference to be afforded to administrative agencies and labour arbitrators was raised, that Laskin and his colleagues were more often divided, though not perhaps as much as one might have expected. Laskin dissented in three of the nineteen labour relations cases on which he sat, and in two of these the court's proper stance to labour board or arbitrator rulings was the issue. He had been on the court less than a year when he had occasion to lecture his colleagues on the need to take a 'hands-off' approach to the Canada Labour Relations Board, even in a case where he felt the board had exercised poor judgment in not requiring an employer to post notices of an application for certification on its premises. Such an omission did not mean it had exceeded its jurisdiction, however: 'I believe that a Court must be wary not to translate into a question of jurisdiction its objections to the manner in which the Board has exercised its powers. We are dealing with statutory tribunals for whose constitution and for whose endowment of powers the Legislature is responsible; and the statutory prescriptions are no less the law of the land than is the common law which has been, in many such instances, either set aside completely or deflected.'[15] In the end his colleagues agreed in the result though they expressly disclaimed agreeing with all his reasoning. He was less successful in a later case involving the Ontario Labour Relations Board, where some disgruntled employees had challenged the board's decision to certify a union without a vote. They argued the board had erred in deciding the effective date of union membership for a number of employees, and persuaded Justices Kelly and McLennan to overturn the board's decision.[16] Laskin dissented. He had more success in *R. v. Arthurs, ex parte Port Arthur Shipbuilding*, where he and Dalton Wells formed a majority in upholding an award by Harry Arthurs.[17] Some employees were discharged for taking a job with another employer in anticipation of a lay-off which did not materialize, and phoning in sick to cover their absence. Arthurs found the dismissal was not 'just' within the meaning of the collective agreement and ordered suspension without pay instead. This was a tempting target for Laskin's management-oriented colleagues, but he was finally succeeding in convincing some of them of his modernist approach to arbitrator autonomy.

In regulatory contexts outside of labour law, Laskin and his brethren tended to agree on the need for fair procedures, but did not overjudicialize the work of tribunals whose work involved a considerable policy element. One of the most important of these tribunals was the Ontario Municipal Board, the body charged with overseeing the orderly expansion of urban and rural municipalities at a time of unparalleled growth – and the subject of Laskin's long-ago Harvard LLM thesis. The Court of Appeal consistently held that the board was required to act judicially only in the sense that parties were entitled to a fair hearing. Ultimately its work involved policy considerations beyond challenge by developers or municipalities.[18] If the OMB gave all sides a fair chance to state their case before approving a developer's decision to, in Joni Mitchell's words, 'pave Paradise and put up a parking lot,' well, Paradise would be duly paved.

Perhaps Laskin's most surprising victory was persuading his colleagues of the validity of a deferential approach to administrative tribunals in the human rights field. In *Bell v. Ontario Human Rights Commission* a trial judge had issued a writ of prohibition to prevent Professor Walter Tarnopolsky from hearing a complaint of discrimination pursuant to his appointment as a board of inquiry under the *Ontario Human Rights Code*. Mr Bell, who was black, complained that a landlord had discriminated against him in refusing to rent an upstairs flat to him when it was in fact vacant. The landlord's defence was that the unit was not 'self-contained.' Such units were excluded from the purview of the Code, the landlord argued, and the board of inquiry would be acting without jurisdiction if he proceeded with the inquiry. Writing for a bench of three, Laskin said the proper course was to let the board of inquiry interpret the phrase 'self-contained' and apply it to the facts as found; the respondent would still be able to apply for judicial review afterwards if he disagreed with the board's interpretation.[19]

Although Laskin tended to protect 'the little guy' in cases pitting an individual against a government agency, this attitude did not carry over into any general pro-plaintiff attitude in private law matters. His upholding of existing law, even when it led to harsh results, is perhaps clearest in his torts decisions. In *Harris v. Toronto Transit Commission*,[20] a thirteen-year-old boy stuck his arm out of a bus window even though he saw the 'Keep Arm In' sign. As the bus pulled away from the curb it grazed a steel pole and the boy's arm was crushed between the pole and the bus. The trial judge apportioned liability equally but the Court of Appeal reversed, exonerating the defendant entirely. It was the plaintiff's 'carelessness for his own safety ... that was the operative cause of the accident,' declared Laskin. In *Wong Aviation Ltd. and National Trust Co.*,[21] a man rented an airplane from the plaintiff company for a half-hour solo flight, flew off, and was never heard from again. Eventually he was declared dead. The company sued the man's estate for breach of the bailment contract, relying on the usual rule in such cases: where the chattel disappears the onus is on the bailee to disprove negligence. Speaking for the court, Laskin applied the existing law and allowed recovery for the value of the plane. The Supreme Court of Canada reversed, stating that the policy rationale for imposing the burden of proof on the bailee – the assumption that the bailee was in the best position to explain what happened – did not apply where the bailee had disappeared with the chattel and the bailee's executor had no knowledge of the circumstances.[22] Here was a case – admittedly rare – where the Supreme Court of Canada entertained the kind of policy analysis one might have expected Laskin to invoke.

Perhaps Laskin's most notorious private law decision involved a ruling on the commencement of a limitation period. A woman hired a notary public to represent her in the drafting of a separation agreement, by which the husband obliged himself to transfer to her sole title to a house. The deed to the house was registered in May 1959 but in September 1960 the husband asserted a claim to the property which was upheld by a judgment in 1965. The plaintiff sued the notary public in negligence on 5 April 1966. Laskin noted that whether the claim was framed in contract or tort the relevant limitation period was six years. He held that the period began to run from the time the services were rendered, that is May 1959, not from the time the plaintiff had notice that they might have been ill performed; the plaintiff's claim was thus statute-barred. While acknowledging that it might 'appear to be harsh to visit upon the plaintiff the consequence flowing from [this] holding,' this was 'the result of the formulation of the statute and of the course of decisions thereon respecting breaches of duty by persons undertaking to render skilled or personal service.'[23] Where the law was clear and consistently applied, there was no warrant for the courts to disregard it merely because they disagreed with its policy. *Schwebel v. Telekes* is an important decision in the Laskin repertoire because it demonstrates his respect for both precedent and legislative policy when the latter was clearly discernible. For Laskin judicial activism was warranted in precise situations, but not a panacea for every injustice.

Laskin got little chance at the Court of Appeal to display his expertise in constitutional law, but when such points came up his colleagues were happy to let him write. In fact, he wrote for a unanimous panel on each of the three occasions when constitutional law issues were raised. Two dealt with the validity of statutes relating to divorce procedure. One was of minor importance,[24] but *Papp v. Papp*, in which Laskin upheld the constitutional validity of the corollary relief provisions of the federal *Divorce Act, 1968*, has become a cornerstone of the administration of family law in Canada.[25] The third posed complex questions about the interaction of federal and provincial legislation in the context of bankruptcy. In *Ontario (Attorney General) v. Wentworth Insurance*, Laskin was faced with provincial legislation purporting to deal with the distribution of securities deposited by an insurance company with the government as a condition of obtaining a licence in Ontario, upon the company's insolvency. He found parts of the federal *Winding-up Act* to conflict with provisions of the provincial *Insurance Act* and declared the latter invalid.[26]

If Laskin's brethren had feared an overly academic approach to opinion writing from their new colleague, they need not have worried.
Many of his decisions were similar to theirs in methodology and general approach. Laskin was not one for large generalizations, overt references to legal theory, or even much policy analysis. His decisions were
carefully crafted, always stating the issues narrowly, setting out the
existing law, and then examining whether the lower court had either
misapprehended or misapplied it. They were models of common law
reasoning: brisk, concise, and not deciding more than required to resolve the issues at hand. A case in point was his decision in an alimony
case, *Johnstone v. Johnstone*. Laskin found there was no 'arbitrary rule'
entitling a wife to alimony in the amount of one-half or any set fraction
of the combined incomes of the couple, but that 'where the parties are
of advancing years and have no present ... dependants, it is only reasonable that the wife be not relegated to a lower standard of living than
that of her husband.'[27] In other words the wife in the instant case was
entitled to half the parties' joint income, but Laskin was not going to
declare any general principle of equality in the alimony context. The
message seemed to be 'equality if necessary, but not necessarily equality.' This case is illustrative not only of Laskin's general approach to
judging, but also to gender issues. In a public law context Laskin usually advocated the equality of the sexes, as would be seen in his Supreme Court dissent in *Lavell*, but in private law, especially in matters
of 'pure' family law, he did not articulate clearly a standard of sexual
equality.[28]

Yet, if Laskin and his colleagues shared similar techniques and sought
to advance similar values in private law adjudication especially, there
were some significant methodological and value-based differences between Laskin and his colleagues. He referred to U.S. case law and
academic writing considerably more often than his brethren, though
not frequently in any absolute sense, and usually on novel points where
Canadian law was underdeveloped. In *Hellenius v. Lees*, for example,
Laskin dissented and would have ordered a new trial in a tire blow-out
case where a paying passenger was left a quadriplegic.[29] Justices Gale
and Kelly referred only to the facts and cited no law at all, while Laskin
referred to U.S. and English law, to academic authority from both
jurisdictions, and also to Caesar Wright's article on *res ipsa loquitur*.[30]
Laskin often found the existing law to be ambiguous rather than unsatisfactory. He would find opposing lines of authority on the same point,
allowing him to choose the one he found more in line with contempo-

rary values and policy goals. In those infrequent cases where the law was both clear and clearly unsatisfactory, Laskin did not hesitate either to overrule bad precedents or to develop the law in a more positive direction if that was possible.

Some have wondered why Laskin was not more bold in his approach to the law, both in the Court of Appeal and later in the Supreme Court of Canada. On the surface at least, there is a certain disjunction between the critiques Laskin voiced in his academic writing and his performance as a judge. One interpretation is that he felt his initial lack of legitimacy on the Court of Appeal so keenly that he hewed to a fairly conservative line. Laskin himself admitted this to some extent in a 1975 interview, where he said, 'I am not as free-wheeling as when I was a professor, maybe it is another way of saying I can't be as reckless as I was when I was a professor.'[31] Another view might be that in the face of the upheavals of the later 1960s, Laskin appreciated more deeply the role of law as a vital conservative force. Such interpretations only become necessary if one accepts that there was indeed some cleavage between Laskin's professorial and judicial performances. In my view such a disjunction exists but has been much overstated. It focuses only on the daytime Laskin, and forgets the night-time Laskin. The professorial Laskin who attracted public attention was critical of the courts on particular issues of public law: federalism, the appropriate extent of judicial review, the treatment of labour. He commented only occasionally in his writings on the vast subterranean river of private law that nourishes daily life: the law of contracts (including the individual contract of employment), property, mortgages, inheritance, family relations, agency, partnership, corporations, and liability for accidents. Yet he was intimately familiar with all these areas through his night-time work.

Laskin internalized the structure and ethos of the common law by scribbling headnotes at night in his basement for nearly thirty years. He did this partly (at first) to earn money, partly because of the prestige associated with it, and partly (he would have said) to keep up with the law. But at some level he continued to devote a lot of time to the enterprise because he believed in its importance. He believed the courts played an essential role not just in shielding the individual from domination by larger economic and political forces, but also in their less glamorous role of articulating and adjusting the common law. By following the 'everyday' work of the courts so closely, Laskin absorbed a few simple lessons that characterized his own judicial work. The common law has the capacity for growth but it is essentially conservative. A heavy burden rests on the proponent of change. It is unwise to pronounce on issues not raised directly by the facts at hand, lest one fetter the law's flexibility for the future.

Laskin's reputation as a dissenting judge started in the Court of Appeal, and in fact he disagreed with his colleagues in 17 per cent of the reported decisions in which he took part during his four and a half years there. Such a rate was probably high for an appellate judge at the time, and Laskin seemed to take pride that this was so. When his former CAUT colleague Percy Smith visited him at Osgoode Hall, Smith reported that Laskin observed 'wryly, "since I came to the bench, I have written more dissenting opinions than all my fellow judges together."'[32] It would be a mistake to see Laskin as in fundamental disagreement with his colleagues on all issues. Rather, his dissents were concentrated in particular areas: a third of all his dissents were in the field of criminal law, one-tenth each in labour law and torts, and the rest displayed no particular pattern. Laskin's agreement with his brethren encompassed large areas of the law: in property law, family law, corporate and commercial law, even in administrative law, Laskin seldom dissented. It was not the quantity of Laskin's dissents, but the way in which a few of them captured the *zeitgeist* that contributed to the Laskin myth. Both of his most celebrated dissents, in *R. v. Cameron* and *R. v. Horsburgh*, centred on sexuality when social and legal attitudes were in a rapid state of flux. And both happened to come up in his first year on the court, an accident of timing which helped fix in the public mind the image of Bora Laskin as a great dissenter and a liberal prophet.

R. v. Horsburgh involved the explosive subject of adolescent sexuality.[33] As the baby boom generation reached puberty in a society less constrained by religious and social convention than in pre-war days, public anxiety about adolescent sexual mores ran high. When journalist Pierre Berton wrote in *Maclean's* in 1963 that he hoped his daughters would have sex in a comfortable bed rather than the back seat of a car, the resulting backlash led to his being fired.[34] It was not a good omen for a well-intentioned but naive small-town minister named Russell D. Horsburgh, who also became a sacrificial lamb for a generation of scandalized parents. At a time when public discussion of sexuality was in its infancy, the Horsburgh saga provided opportunities for both public titillation and for the opening of a serious dialogue on a previously taboo subject. It even inspired a play, put on by Toronto's feisty Theatre Passe Muraille a decade after the events in question.[35]

The Rev. Mr Horsburgh was ordained as a minister in 1947 and had served in northern Ontario, Hamilton, and Waterloo before beginning his pastorate at Park Street United Church in Chatham in 1961. He was in his early forties, and married with two stepsons when he arrived in the small, conservative southwestern Ontario city. Located on the Thames River in the middle of a rich agricultural hinterland, Chatham functioned as a service centre to a large rural population. The city was home to several food processing plants and proximity to Detroit gave it a role in the manufacture of automobile parts. It was a prosperous city, without cultural pretension, perhaps best known in the mid-1960s as the town from which Sylvia Fricker fled to launch a successful career as a folk-singer with her husband Ian Tyson. Just a few miles from Chatham was Dresden, terminus of the underground railway a century earlier and the locus of some of the battles against anti-black discrimination of the early 1950s. Chatham too had its black population and race would be an important subtext to the Horsburgh story.

Even one of Horsburgh's warmest supporters admitted that 'this traditionally conservative city was ill-prepared for his advent. Within the first eighteen months of his ministry [Horsburgh] had introduced a weekly dance for teenagers, initiated the Youth Anonymous programme for young people who had experienced legal difficulty, and had, furthermore, received negroes into full church membership – all of which were entirely unprecedented in Park Street United Church.'[36] Chatham's social elite were not amused by the fact that Horsburgh 'took the church to the street and brought the street into the church,' and the governing board had little chance to caution Horsburgh because he never consulted them before adopting his next eye-popping innovation: 'he just went bulling ahead.' A liberal parish in a major urban centre would have looked askance at Horsburgh's hurricane of activity in the early 1960s. At Park Street United, it was simply beyond the pale. The sudden mixing of races in what was perceived as the highly charged sexual atmosphere of teen dances was particularly shocking to the congregation. Even Rabbi Abraham Feinberg, probably the most liberal clergyman in Canada in the 1960s, found Horsburgh's approach unwise. As part of his ecumenical outreach, Horsburgh had invited the rabbi to give a lecture-sermon in Chatham. Afterwards, the minister revealed his plan for 'a lecture-discussion course on sex, directed particularly at the young.' Feinberg 'listened to the glowing prospectus with mounting astonishment. What naivete! Suicidal!' It was this 'unromantic unrealism,' the rabbi believed, that 'drove [Horsburgh] from pulpit to prison.'[37]

Horsburgh had concocted a volatile mixture, and it did not take long to explode in his face. In 1964 he was tried on eight counts of contributing to the juvenile delinquency of a number of fourteen- and fifteen-year-olds. None of the charges alleged that Horsburgh himself had had sexual relations with the adolescents, nor that he watched them. Rather, he was alleged to have incited adolescents to engage in sex with each other. Horsburgh was said to have told Robert Miller 'that there was nothing wrong with the said child having intercourse [and] explaining to [him] how to have sexual intercourse without hurting the girl [and] indicating to [him] to take the said girl to [a church-owned] apartment for sexual intercourse.' At the trial, held at Chatham before Juvenile Court Judge W.H. Fox, Horsburgh denied all the allegations but was found guilty and sentenced to one year in prison on each of five counts, the terms to run concurrently. The case was considered so sensational that the producers of CBC TV's *This Hour Has Seven Days* had to defy their managers in order to air their treatment of it, and the *Chatham Daily News* apologized to its readers for having to cover the story.

On 25 June 1965 Justice Moorhouse of the High Court dismissed an appeal by Horsburgh. Horsburgh then appealed to the Court of Appeal, where he was represented by Charles Dubin. A bench consisting of Chief Justice Dana Porter, Gregory Evans and a recently elevated Bora Laskin heard the appeal in October and delivered judgment on 10 December. Evans found that while the trial judge had made some errors, no substantial miscarriage of justice had occurred. He saw the whole case in terms of credibility and was disinclined to interfere with the trial judge's findings in this regard. Laskin took a different tack, asserting that the trial judge had committed two legal errors of sufficient gravity to require a new trial. First, the evidence of the adolescents should have been treated as that of accomplices rather than independent witnesses. The boys could have been charged under the Criminal Code with having intercourse with underage females, an offence to which Horsburgh would have been a party if the allegations of encouragement were proved. Laskin adopted a broad definition of accomplice as 'one who is concerned with another or others in committing or attempting to commit any criminal offence.' The second error in the trial related to the charges involving the girls. Insofar as their complaints led to the charges against Horsburgh, their evidence should be treated in the same way as that of all complainants in sexual cases; the trier of fact should be warned that it is dangerous to convict on uncorroborated evidence. As the trial judge approached the case on the basis that the adolescents' evidence was that of independent witnesses and did not require corroboration, he fell into serious error. Laskin would have ordered a new trial with a directed acquittal since the Crown had adduced no corroborative evidence.

In this, his first major dissent, Laskin stated his views clearly and forcefully, but without overt passion or lofty rhetoric. The only point where he permitted himself a short lecture to the gallery was on the somewhat tangential issue of the test for competency of witnesses. The majority accepted uncritically the doctrine that competency to testify under oath depended on a witness showing a 'belief in God and a belief in a future state of rewards and punishments.' This emphasis on 'divine retribution (as an exclusive test) rather than earthly justice as the consequences of false testimony,' Laskin retorted, 'is highly talismanic. The common law deserves better than that at the hands of the judiciary in the 20th century.' This comment succinctly conveys both Laskin's modernist jurisprudence and his conception of the judicial role. The common law no longer needed talismans and rituals. It had outgrown first its primitive and then its formalist period and now derived its legitimacy from its commitment to reason and its responsiveness to contemporary social conditions. As a Jew Laskin would be sensitive to the common law's universalization of Christianity, but his objections to this formulation of the witness competency test went beyond his Judaism. He objected to the belief in divine retribution as an 'exclusive test.' In other words, the courts needed to fashion a test rooted in the pluralist nature of Canadian society, where some citizens had no religious belief and the beliefs of others did not extend to accepting the inevitability of other-worldly punishment.

Justice Evans displayed the same schizophrenic attitude to the behaviour of the youth in this case as did the public at large. They were quick to castigate the young people for their precocious sexual activities, but could not quite believe that such activities could have occurred without the guidance or encouragement of an adult. Evans observed drily that 'the evidence of all these witnesses clearly indicates that their worldly experience was rather extensive and, it is to be hoped beyond the norm for high school students.'[38] Yet he could not conceive of the young witnesses as having sufficient agency to be accomplices, and painted them as passive figures led astray by Horsburgh. Laskin quickly cut through this ambiguity, observing 'they cannot have it both ways.' If the sworn evidence of the young witnesses was to be treated as if it were that of a fully competent adult, 'then *a fortiori* should they as witnesses be subject to the same cautions that limit adult accomplices or adult complainants in sexual cases.'[39] Laskin's judgment remained squarely focused on the central issue of fairness to the accused. He was not disposed to share in the witch-hunt mentality surrounding the Horsburgh trial. Bringing his academic scepticism to the judicial arena, Laskin emphasized inconsistencies in the young witnesses' evidence ignored by the trial judge. At one point, Laskin noted, the trial judge asked himself 'why would these youngsters tell the story they did tell about the accused if it was not true?'[40] Clearly they had an incentive to blame an adult for behaviour that could have landed them in trouble socially and legally. It was also troubling that Horsburgh's counsel sought leave to introduce before the appeal court evidence from two of the witnesses who sought to contradict what they had said at trial, even though all three judges rejected the application.

Laskin's scepticism was well warranted. He could not have failed to note that in the parade of character witnesses for Horsburgh, there was only one from Chatham; all the others came from his prior parishes. To say Horsburgh was unpopular with his congregation in Chatham was a towering understatement. The scandal could be seen as a useful way to rid Park Street United of a 'turbulent priest.' In a book written after his eventual acquittal, Horsburgh alleged that the 'old guard' framed him, and that police exerted improper pressure on the young witnesses. According to him, one of the witnesses 'was under a charge of rape[,] [o]ne girl was promised a shortened reformatory term, which she was serving for unmanageability at the time of my trial [and] [a]nother boy was waiting to be charged for theft.'[41] Given the many examples in subsequent decades of wrongful convictions as a result of police pressure on young witnesses, and of young persons acting in concert to instigate charges of a sexual nature against adults, the necessity of Laskin's cautionary approach has been put beyond question.

Laskin's dissent on a point of law ensured that Horsburgh could appeal to the Supreme Court of Canada. In a four-three ruling, the Court upheld him on the point dealing with accomplice evidence, and ordered a new trial. His vindication on this point meant that he would be a man to watch in the future. The majority actually went further than Laskin, stating that a young person could be charged with aiding and abetting another juvenile in committing an act of delinquency. This put it beyond doubt that the witnesses should be treated as accomplices. As Martland put it, 'all the material evidence tendered to establish that the appellant aided and abetted at the commission of delinquencies was given by persons who had knowingly and wilfully committed those very delinquencies.'[42] At the new trial the Crown's case collapsed. Of the fourteen original witnesses, only three were called. The Court found that the evidence presented did not even require a reply by the defence, and Horsburgh was acquitted of the one count brought by the Crown.[43] After writing a book in his own defence, Horsburgh fell ill and died of cancer in 1971.

The Supreme Court's decision was unexpected. The Court was not noted in the 1960s for generous interpretations of the rights of accused persons, and Justices Hall, Spence, and Cartwright often wrote minority decisions in such cases. On this seven-man bench, Martland was the swing vote who wrote the majority decision upholding Laskin's dissent. Possibly the defendant's status as a clergyman led Martland to scrutinize this criminal case more closely than he usually did. Being upheld in the Supreme Court was quite a coup for Laskin, but in view of his later elevation to the chief justiceship over Martland's head it was highly ironic that Martland himself should have contributed to the emerging Laskin legend.

In *Horsburgh* Laskin's concerns about fairness to the accused arguably had some validity. In other cases involving sex offences, his desire to ensure a high standard of protection for defendants appeared to ignore the interests of female victims. Shortly after his appointment he sat on an appeal from a conviction for indecent assault on an eleven-year-old girl. One ground of appeal was that while exploring the voluntariness of a statement to the police given by the accused, the trial judge had asked him directly whether the statement was true. A previous decision of the Court of Appeal had decided that it was not reversible error for a trial judge to pose that question, but Laskin still dissented from the majority decision upholding the conviction.[44] More troubling was his dissent in a case where a man fraudulently posing as a physician had been convicted of indecent assault for carrying out intimate examinations of female 'patients.'[45] Laskin seemed to sympathize more with the accused than the victims, calling the situation 'an unusual one, strange and perhaps also sad by reason of the accused's self-delusion.'[46] He would have acquitted based on a very narrow interpretation of section 141(2) of the Criminal Code, which stated that consent to what would otherwise be an indecent assault would be vitiated by 'false and fraudulent representations as to the nature and quality of the act.' He found the Crown's concession that the accused had done only what a fully trained physician would have done to negate the fraudulent nature of the representations. Laskin thought an assault had occurred, but not an indecent one. His focus on the specific actions divorced from their larger context was at odds with his usual approach to statutory or even common law interpretation, but consistent with a pre-feminist approach to law where women's interests were seldom treated with the same rigour or seriousness as men's.

Not long after the Court of Appeal heard argument in *Horsburgh*, another sexually charged case began to work its way through the courts. On 25 November 1965 Toronto art gallery owner Dorothy Cameron was convicted before Magistrate F.C. Hayes of exposing to public view seven obscene pictures in an exhibition entitled 'EROS 65' and fined fifty dollars on each count. Five were by Robert Markle, a Mohawk artist whose work hung in the National Gallery of Canada.[47] (An erotic drawing by the exhibition's best-known artist, Harold Town, somehow escaped police attention, leading one waggish journalist to suggest Town was suffering from a case of subpoena envy.) One of the impugned works showed a single nude female 'in an attitude of sexual invitation,' several showed two females engaged in sexual activity, one showed a male and female in the act of sexual intercourse, and one portrayed a female nude grasping a nude male's penis with her hand. Such an exhibit was a startling precedent: when the National Gallery put on a major retrospective of Canadian art in 1967, it included one nude among some three hundred works. It was not that Canadian artists did not paint nudes or treat erotic themes, they just kept them safely hidden in their studios. Cameron bravely sought to expose to view a hitherto invisible category of Canadian art.

The charges caused a stir in a city determinedly trying to shed its dowdy image as the 'Belfast of Canada.' Toronto in the mid-1960s boasted a half-dozen prestigious commercial galleries, each serving a particular niche market and evidence of an expanding and diverse public appetite for visual art. Among these, Dorothy Cameron's eponymous gallery at 840 Yonge Street catered to the WASP avant-garde, and Cameron herself had a high profile in Toronto society. She was also a staunch supporter of 'her' artists and prepared to defend their interests to the utmost when they came under attack – though the media tended to portray her as hysterical in this regard. The opening of EROS 65 was a 'fashionable crush,' according to journalist Kildare Dobbs. Under pink floodlights, Rosedale ladies sipped pink champagne and 'stared bravely at graphics and drawings celebrating more or less explicitly the theme of physical love.' Pierre Berton announced proudly that Toronto had at last grown up, but later events proved his statement to be somewhat premature.[48] A young Crown prosecutor named Peter Rickaby in attendance at the opening was disturbed by what he saw, and informed the police.[49] Six months later Cameron found herself in the midst of 'the most celebrated, the most bizarre, and the most distressing event of her professional life,' as she was prosecuted by Rickaby on obscenity charges in Old City Hall's notorious courtroom C, the 'women's court.'[50] A relic of the Progressive era's concern to separate female offenders from rough male criminals, courtroom C was usually host to sex trade workers, addicts, and shoplifters, among whom Dorothy Cameron cut a most unusual figure in her mink and heirloom diamond brooch.

At the trial five expert witnesses were called to testify to the artistic merit of the works; the Crown called no expert evidence. Art critic Robert Fulford attended the trial and labelled it 'a comedy of mutual incomprehension.' To art critics of the 1960s content was nothing and form was everything. Cameron's show was clearly about content, but the critics denied that the works were erotic at all. When asked about a painting clearly depicting oral sex between two women, the director of the Art Gallery of Toronto 'professed to see ... only "the pattern of dark and light, ... [t]he flame-like figures as they flicker across the surface, ... an emphasis on pattern."'[51] Hayes was not impressed with such seemingly evasive testimony. He found that 'the search for artistic merit cannot be allowed as an excuse to exceed the bounds set by the definition of obscenity,' and concluded he could come to 'no other impression than [that] the dominant characteristic in each exhibit is the exploitation of sex.'[52] The 'undue exploitation of sex' was the new definition of obscenity adopted in a 1959 amendment to the Criminal Code, replacing the old Hicklin test of 'depravity and corruption.' The Supreme Court of Canada had recently ruled that contemporary Canadian standards should be applied in determining what was 'undue,' but Hayes found the pictures in question to exceed those standards. Cameron soon found herself treated as a public heroine and with the aid of a public subscription fund, she appealed.

The seriousness with which the Court of Appeal considered the proceeding was revealed when five of its members showed up on the bench. The bar rallied behind Dorothy Cameron; her counsel at trial, Meredith Fleming, was joined for the appeal by Walter Williston and his junior Julian Porter, son of Chief Justice Dana Porter. There was considerable media interest in the appeal, and journalist June Callwood recalled attending with a small placard that read 'freedom of speech.' While strolling down the corridors of Osgoode Hall during a break in the argument she ran into Laskin, who asked her what she was doing there. 'I'm here to see justice done,' she said diplomatically, conscious of the sign she was holding. He flashed her a grin and said 'Good for you' before proceeding on his way.[53]

The final decision was not a surprise: four of Laskin's colleagues agreed with the decision of Magistrate Hayes. Writing for the majority, Justice Aylesworth was 'left in no doubt as to their [i.e., the works] being obscene. They lie not in any gray area of doubt; they are of base purpose and their obscenity is flagrant.'[54] For him, the display of such works was corrosive of the moral life of the community and their suppression by the state was entirely legitimate as a kind of self-defence. This has always been the justification of obscenity legislation, but the perennial difficulty with administering it is to know at what point freedom of expression might be legitimately restricted. The majority of the Court of Appeal could be read as prohibiting any visual representation of acts of a sexual nature. If the drawing of a single nude female 'in an attitude of sexual invitation' was deemed to be flagrantly obscene, it is difficult to imagine any naturalistic portrayal of a sexual theme that would not be.

It was left to Bora Laskin to mention the one word not uttered by any of the other judges: love. Where the other judges saw only 'genitalia' and licentious exploitation of a sexual theme, Laskin observed that 'love as a theme, whether in literature or in art, and in all of its manifestations, is hardly a novelty.'[55] He confirmed what the majority seemed to deny, that 'the human figure, singly or multiplied, expressing love in any of its known forms, is a permissible theme for a novel and for a picture.'[56] Whether the works had treated that theme in a permissible way depended on the relatively new doctrine of community standards. Laskin was quick to point out the policy issues at stake: obscenity law 'must take account of the value that we place on freedom of expression exercised in serious vein. We exercise this freedom because of a conviction, supported by experience, that individual creativity, whether in the arts or in the humanities or in science or in technology, constitutes our social capital; in art, it gives measure to our culture.'[57] Laskin's long immersion in the university environment clearly influenced his views on the fundamental value of free expression.

For Laskin, the determination of community standards was an exercise in declaring 'what Canadian society should have to tolerate at a particular point in time.'[58] Such a conclusion had to rest on evidence of some kind, and he was scathing in his remarks on the magistrate's rejection of the expert evidence in favour of his own untutored reaction. Laskin was not above engaging in a little amateur criticism of his own, however, as he gamely adopted the formalist critical stance of the experts. After viewing the drawings several times, he reported, '[t]he result was that any gross sexual aspect became dissolved in the forms of the figures, in their movements and spatial position, and in the relationship achieved against the background of the tones of the drawings. To me, at any rate, some of the Markle drawings have an abstract character.'[59] While Hayes was entitled to reject the expert evidence for the defence, said Laskin, he could not 'on an entirely subjective appraisal find that the Crown had proved its case beyond a reasonable doubt[,] especially ... where artistic merit ha[d] been clearly shown.'[60] Parliament's decision to substitute a new definition of obscenity for the discredited Hicklin test inevitably meant 'a change in the kind of evidence, information and materials receivable by a Court.'

Both Laskin's university background and his modernist jurisprudence led him to emphasize the role of experts in evaluating artistic merit, which was relevant to the issue of community standards. He quoted William O. Douglas of the U.S. Supreme Court, who in the recent Fanny Hill case had stated flatly that judges were incompetent to render judgment on the worth of fiction, and had to rely on experts for an evaluation of literary merit and historical significance. In assessing this evidence, Laskin urged courts to focus on the temporal dimension of community standards, to be concerned not 'with where we have been but rather to be alert to where we are going.'[61] As generals are criticized for always preparing for the last war rather than the next one, Laskin encouraged judges to orient themselves to present-day attitudes and realities rather than spent precedents.

Laskin's dissent in Cameron was as perfectly attuned to the emerging ethos of sexual liberation as his judicial brethren were out of tune with it, and public discourse was not yet complicated by the feminist critique of the artistic 'male gaze.' Cameron's counsel applied for leave to appeal to the Supreme Court but it appears Laskin unwittingly let them down. He had not taken care to frame his dissent around a point of law, which would have given Cameron an appeal as of right to the Supreme Court. Leave to appeal was refused in spite of the court's landmark holding in Brodie v. The Queen in 1962 that D.H. Lawrence's Lady Chatterley's Lover was not obscene. In that case, Frank Scott had persuaded the court to adopt many of the points reiterated by Laskin in his dissent.[62] The Court of Appeal itself had applied *Brodie* in 1964 when it found *Fanny Hill* not to be obscene.[63] The apparent backtracking in *Cameron* was probably based on the more visceral reaction of the judges to visual art as opposed to literature.

It was not until shortly after Laskin's death that the Supreme Court of Canada made another definitive ruling on obscenity. In *Towne Cinema Theatres v. The Queen*,[64] the Court for the most part adopted Laskin's dissent in *Cameron* as authoritative. It agreed with him that trial judges cannot rely on their own subjective opinions in assessing community standards of tolerance, nor can they reject expert evidence without giving reasons. Somewhat illogically, however, the majority said that the Crown was not obliged to introduce evidence, expert or otherwise, on the issue of community standards. The works in question could 'speak for themselves' in grounding an obscenity conviction. Justices Wilson and McIntyre dissented on this point and would have followed Laskin's suggestion that there was an onus on the Crown to introduce some evidence of community standards. On the whole, the difference is probably not significant because the thrust of the decision is to ensure a reasoned rather than emotional response by the trier of fact in obscenity cases.

Aside from his dissents in *Horsburgh* and *Cameron* and some of his decisions on deference to administrative tribunals or labour arbitrators, Laskin's time on the Court of Appeal produced few decisions with a lasting impact. That is not surprising given the make-up of the court's caseload at the time. Few division of powers cases came up, the Bill of Rights was seldom pleaded, and much of the court's work involved fine-tuning the law rather than declaring broad principles. Laskin's public profile was enhanced by a few high-profile dissents, but the media were of course not interested in the bulk of his ordinary judicial work. Analysis of the latter reveals a deep commitment to a liberal world-view leavened by respect for state initiatives designed to redress imbalances in the private sphere. Where the common law still reigned, Laskin took it seriously: individuals had a duty to look out for their own interests, and had only themselves to blame if they did not. He could be moved by the plight of the vulnerable, but set a high bar: mere youth, as in *Harris v. TTC*, or inexperience, as in *Schwebel v. Telekes*, was not sufficient to temper the result dictated by the common law. Laskin was also very conscious of the line between the judicial and legislative roles. In *Johnstone*, where he had the chance to enunciate a policy of gender equality in the awarding of alimony, he did not, preferring to await legislative action. Where the individual confronted the state directly, whether in the criminal law setting or in areas such as expropriation or deportation, Laskin set a very high standard for the conduct of government officials. At the same time, where government had chosen to vest authority over a particular field in a statutory decision maker, he counselled a deferential attitude and had some success in persuading his colleagues to adopt this view.

PART V

The Supreme Court of Canada

16

On to Ottawa

When Frank Scott heard of Bora Laskin's appointment to the Supreme Court of Canada, he wrote immediately to his friend. 'This is the best news since the death of Lord Haldane,' he exulted, 'or, to be more humane, since the Radio case. Of course it should have happened, but in Canada so few things seem to work out the way they should.' With 'Drybones, ... Bora on the Supreme Court ... maybe the Liberals can win the Quebec election and turn federalist!' Then, in a more serious vein: 'Nobody knows what we may be in for over the next few years, but whatever it may be the courts have a critical role to play, the Supreme Court above all. There has not been a creative mind there since Rand left. I speak principally, of course, of public law decisions, but these are what really count in the making of a free society ... May we hold together long enough as a country for you to have a chance to make your proper impact.'[1]

Where Laskin's initial appointment to the Court of Appeal had been seen as startling – an academic! a non-partisan! a Jew! – Trudeau's elevation of Laskin to the Supreme Court was seen as bold and innovative. It made an unambiguous statement about the need to broaden the pool of candidates for the top court. The *Globe* found Trudeau's move a 'most encouraging [sign of a] trend away from using appointments as rewards for political services rendered [to] the party in power.' A feature story displayed the surtitle 'No practice as lawyer' above the heading 'An architect of legal thought,' but journalist Michael Enright expressed no dismay at Laskin's lack of practical experience.[2] Trudeau himself had been an outsider to the political process five years earlier, and seemed to prove that someone unconnected to the political establishment might provide inspired leadership in a time of rapid change. Laskin's lack of ties to vested interests, whether political, professional, or corporate, resonated with the idealism of the late 1960s. With existing institutions and modes of thought under attack, Canadians were ready to give philosopher-jurists, like philosopher prime ministers, a try. Laskin's Judaism was mentioned only in passing by the media, but its significance was perhaps all the more powerful for that. The appointment of a Jew to Canada's highest court possessed a symbolism similar to Thurgood Marshall's appointment to the U.S. Supreme Court three years before. It broke the French-English Catholic-Protestant stranglehold on the Court, and provided dramatic recognition of the contributions of Canadians not belonging to the two European 'founding nations.' Laskin was also similar to Marshall in another way: he was not just a 'token Jew' but someone who had been deeply involved in advancing human rights protection in Canada, as Marshall had been involved as chief counsel to the NAACP.

Laskin's general approach to law and legal interpretation generated as much interest as his stance on particular issues. In comparing Laskin's 'creative mind' to Ivan Rand's, Frank Scott meant to highlight the commitment of both men to principle and policy rather than precedent. In the context of the Supreme Court's work, this meant rethinking its traditional role as a simple forum for settling disputes and urging it to play a more important role in developing the law. The Minister of Justice, John Turner, echoed Scott's endorsement of a more 'creative' role for the Court. In the *Globe and Mail*'s interpretation, this meant the Court 'will continue making policy decisions but it will do so in different way. It will discuss the policies and instead of trying to find a legal precedent to hang the judgment on, it will concentrate much more on developing philosophical arguments. It will become a court less concerned with the law books and more concerned with social and political theories.' The modernist note Laskin had sounded for thirty years suddenly appealed to a more iconoclastic generation. Using language borrowed from south of the border, Enright painted the new judge as 'a legal activist, uncomfortable within the restrictions of precedent and tradition, anxious to push the law toward social issues.'

This theme was not present in the commentary on Laskin's 1965 appointment to the Court of Appeal, but reflected the reputation he had acquired there. His progressive image contrasted sharply with that of his future colleagues. 'Our Supreme Court is too cautious,' lamented the *Toronto Daily Star* in 1967. 'The U.S. [Supreme] Court is active, powerful, not afraid of controversy, and a great force for reform and progress. The Canadian court is passive, ultra-cautious, and plays a very limited role in the life of the nation.' Its weakness had 'aggravated many of the problems of our national life,' from the 'uncertain division between federal and provincial authority, the backwardness of our legal system, and the lack of a firm foundation for civil liberties.'[3] These were new and somewhat unreasonable expectations to place on the Supreme Court. Canadians suddenly expected their highest court to follow the lead of the Warren Court even though it existed under very different constitutional arrangements. Bora Laskin's record in the Court of Appeal, especially his high-profile dissents in *Horsburgh* and *Cameron*, suggested he might be able to help jolt the Supreme Court out of its perceived inertia.

Inevitably, there was speculation about the impact of Laskin's well-known views on federalism on the Court. The *Globe* wondered whether 'Mr. Justice Laskin has been appointed with the aim of beginning a transformation of the Court's style and its attitudes toward expansion of federal powers.'[4] The early Trudeau years had seen not so much an expansion of federal power as a greater willingness on Ottawa's part to enlarge its role in areas where its authority had lay unexercised. The best example of this was the enactment of the *Divorce Act, 1968*. Where earlier politicians had only dared tinker with this sensitive area of unquestioned federal competence, Trudeau finally gave Canada a uniform divorce law from coast to coast, superseding a confusing pastiche of provincial codes. Once the federal beast was roused, observers naturally wondered where it would stop, especially when John Turner was quoted as saying that 'the federal government should be more aggressive in flexing its constitutional muscle.'[5]

Supreme Court appointments are a prime ministerial prerogative, but occasionally he or she will rely heavily on the views of the minister of justice. While John Turner is emphatic that in Laskin's case Trudeau took the initiative, Turner himself approved of the choice.[6] He had hitched his own political star to the cause of law reform and was pleased to have a judge on the Supreme Court who could lend intellectual ballast to his position. Others were alarmed at the rhetoric surrounding the Laskin appointment. A.S. Patillo, president of the Canadian Bar Association, voiced his concern before a packed courtroom when

Chief Justice Fauteux and Mr Justice Laskin received the customary welcoming remarks from leaders of the bar on 28 April. He did not agree with those who 'advocated that the Canadian court follow in the footsteps of the U.S. Supreme Court and make law rather than interpret it.' It should simply hear appeals and 'should not get mixed up in the legislative process.' Parliament's role should not be usurped by activist judges.[7] Public disagreement between the minister of justice and the president of the CBA was a far cry from the usual platitudes expressed on such occasions.

Four other men were reported to have been considered for the position vacated by Chief Justice Cartwright: John J. Robinette, John Arnup, G. Arthur Martin, and Mr Justice Maurice Lacourcière of the High Court of Ontario. The first three were said not to be interested in an appointment to the Supreme Court of Canada.[8] Within weeks John Arnup was appointed to replace Laskin on the Ontario Court of Appeal, where he served happily for fifteen years.[9] As with many of Toronto's best counsel, the disadvantages of a move to Ottawa outweighed any prestige to be gained by serving on Canada's highest court. Consideration of Lacourcière suggests that Trudeau flirted with the idea of balancing D.C. Abbott, the Quebec anglophone on the Court, with a francophone from English Canada. Such an appointment would have conformed nicely to Trudeau's vision of Canada, but in the end naming Laskin proved even more attractive.

More about the exact circumstances of Laskin's appointment may be revealed when the Turner and Trudeau papers are opened, but even without them it is not difficult to understand why Trudeau wanted Bora Laskin on the Supreme Court. Unlike 1965, when Laskin's appointment was provoked by a peculiar combination of political circumstances, in 1970 he was a perfectly obvious choice for Pierre Elliott Trudeau. Although their familial, social, and cultural backgrounds were radically different, the two men were similar in many ways. Both were intellectuals with a strong desire to shape their society, and both were missionaries of legal modernism. Both cherished free inquiry, and had chosen the university as the only setting where they could flourish intellectually with the least possible restraint. Both saw greater protection for individual rights as an antidote to the outmoded claims of ethnic nationalism. Both remained aloof from partisan politics, Laskin permanently, Trudeau until his mid-forties (though he had been identified publicly with the NDP before joining the Liberals). Both wanted the federal government to play a greater role in national life than it had

previously done. Both rejected Quebec's claims for constitutional recognition as excessive. If Laskin had not existed in 1970, Trudeau would
have had to invent him.

Trudeau had also witnessed the rising of Bora Laskin's star since his
appointment to the Court of Appeal. By 1970 he was probably Canada's
best-known judge elsewhere in the common law world: he had shared a
podium with Earl Warren in New York in 1968, and given the Hamlyn
Lectures in London in 1969. Just days after his appointment to the
Supreme Court he was in New York again, this time as one of fifteen
judges from around the world invited to discuss the future of the World
Court.[10] Then as now, there is no better way of achieving status within
Canada than achieving it outside Canada. Also, Trudeau did not share
the traditionally exclusive attitude of Ottawa society towards Jews,
which was only just beginning to relax in the late 1960s. On the contrary, he was very much at ease in Jewish company and named many
Jews to high positions, including Herb Gray as Canada's first Jewish
federal cabinet minister.[11]

Laskin himself was jubilant at his promotion, as he confessed in
replying to a congratulatory letter from his old friends, the New
Brunswick artists Molly Lamb Bobak and Bruno Bobak.[12] His response
to Frank Scott was more muted. The odd sequence of events that placed
him on the Supreme Court, Laskin mused, could not have been predicted even a decade earlier. He then became surprisingly benignant on
the subject of Lord Haldane. Even the House of Lords was now becoming less strictly bound by precedent, he observed, so that Haldane's
legacy need not imprison Canadians forever. At one level, Laskin seemed
to be claiming victory in the war against *stare decisis*; Haldane's past
victories were now irrelevant. At another level, his air of detachment
suggested membership in an exclusive club which precluded casting
aspersions on fellow judges.

As with his appointment to the Ontario Court of Appeal, the excitement surrounding the new judge was implicitly a criticism of the Court's
sitting members, and they would have been less than human if they did
not feel somewhat slighted. Some sense of contrast was due to Laskin's
relative youth and vigour. The average age of the judges just before
Laskin's appointment was nearly sixty-eight. At fifty-seven, Laskin
reduced the average to sixty-five, but this was still a relatively old court
at a time when age had suddenly become a liability. Age alone was not
an accurate predictor of a judge's place on the ideological spectrum,
however, nor was political affiliation. Laskin's closest colleague on the

Court during his early years was Emmett Hall, who was also the Court's oldest member at seventy-two and a Conservative. The day after the Conservatives' election win in 1957, Diefenbaker telephoned Hall to offer him the chief justiceship of the Saskatchewan Court of Queen's Bench; he was promoted to chief justice of the province in 1961 and the next year to the Supreme Court. Hall was a Red Tory, or 'Establishment Radical,' as his first biographer has called him.[13] A devoted civil libertarian and a stout defender of the welfare state, in 1935 he had assisted in the defence of the two dozen young men charged for their part in the Regina riot. In 1965 Hall's Royal Commission on Health Services recommended the adoption of a universal, compulsory, tax-financed insurance program for medical and hospital care, making him the architect of Canada's modern medicare system. The 1968 Hall-Dennis Report on public education in Ontario, *Living and Learning*, has been less well received by posterity.[14]

Laskin had some acquaintance with the other two Ontario judges, Wishart Spence and Wilfred Judson. Spence's social background was much more typical of the Canadian judiciary of the time than Laskin's. Raised in the affluent Rosedale district of Toronto, his father was a well-connected Liberal lawyer appointed to the Senate in 1928, his mother the daughter of a woollen manufacturer. Spence's academic trajectory was almost identical to Laskin's: a BA in Political Science from the University of Toronto, attendance at Osgoode, then an LLM at Harvard in 1929. Laskin had him as a teacher of bankruptcy law at Osgoode Hall Law School. In 1942 Spence became head of the Regional Rental Office of the Wartime Prices and Trade Board and was appointed to the High Court of Ontario in 1950. The newly installed Pearson government named Spence to the Ontario seat vacated by the sudden death of Chief Justice Patrick Kerwin in February 1963.

Known as a firm no-nonsense trial judge, Spence presided over some sixty capital cases before his move to Ottawa. He let himself be persuaded by Pearson to conduct a royal commission into the Gerda Munsinger affair in 1966, even though the Court had just decided not to accept such invitations because of the possible impairment of judicial independence. When Spence sheepishly told Robert Taschereau of his decision, he recalled, the chief justice 'was just as happy as if I had told him I had taken rat poison.'[15] Spence's own reputation and that of the Supreme Court were diminished by his participation in the sex-and-spy circus.[16] In time, the controversy died down and Spence emerged as a clear liberal voice on the Court in the 1970s, aligning himself with Laskin in many decisions raising civil liberties issues.

Laskin knew Wilfred Judson from Toronto legal circles.[17] He came from a working-class English background, emigrated to Canada as a young man, and was employed as a Latin teacher before turning to the study of law. His appointment to the High Court of Justice came in 1951, just one year after Spence's. It was unusual for a St-Laurent appointee to be noticed by Diefenbaker, but the prime minister elevated him to the Supreme Court in 1958, reassured no doubt by his social and political conservatism. Judson would have been happiest as a classical scholar, and was devoted to English legal history. Wishart Spence acknowledged that Judson was 'terse, very terse,' but Douglas Abbott thought he had the best legal mind of any judge of his day, ranking him even above Ivan Rand.[18] Surprisingly, Judson wrote one of the first Supreme Court decisions to depart from established authority as laid down by the House of Lords.[19] For this he would have earned Laskin's admiration, even if he presented a less than exciting profile to the general public.

Douglas Charles Abbott was the senior judge after Chief Justice Fauteux. A Montreal anglophone, he served as minister of finance under St-Laurent and was named directly to the Supreme Court from the cabinet in 1954 when he left political life. No such appointment had occurred since 1911 and it has not been repeated since Abbott's elevation (though senior party officials desperately tried to interest John Diefenbaker in the chief justiceship on Kerwin's death in 1963). The appointment contributed to an emerging current of discontent with the role of political partisanship in judicial selection. Abbott nonetheless acquired a certain reputation with the progressive legal community in Canada as a result of his remarks in some of the celebrated civil liberties decisions of the 1950s. Invoking the implied bill of rights argument, he was the only judge to state that interference with freedom of religion was beyond the constitutional authority of both federal and provincial legislatures.[20] He also shared Laskin's critique of the Privy Council's constitutional jurisprudence: 'Haldane, Atkin and Watson buggered Sir John MacDonald's ideas as to what the Canadian constitution should be.' As a former federal minister of finance, his belief that the Privy Council had 'used the property and civil rights provision to completely emasculate the powers of the federal government' was perhaps not surprising.[21] At seventy-one, Abbott was the next oldest judge after Emmett Hall.

Ronald Martland and Roland Ritchie were Diefenbaker appointees with a long record of Conservative Party activity. Both men had studied law at Oxford, at Hertford and Pembroke respectively, and both

were strongly Anglophile through family tradition and personal incli-
nation. Born in England, Martland came to Canada at age four with
his parents when they settled in Edmonton.[22] The Haligonian Ritchie
came from Nova Scotian legal dynasties on both sides of his family,
for whom England was still 'home.' Martland enjoyed a brilliant
academic career at Oxford between 1928 and 1932, winning double
firsts and the Vinerian Prize before returning to Edmonton, where he
practised mainly as a corporate solicitor. After Oxford Ritchie practised as a litigator and business lawyer with leading firms in Halifax.
During the war he suffered a severe head injury in a motorcycle
accident in France and spent months recuperating in England. Ritchie
was left with a condition similar to epilepsy and remained prone to
seizures all his life, but kept it a family secret because he feared
discrimination by employers.[23]

Martland and Ritchie were highly competent legal professionals but
as judges they espoused a rather unimaginative approach to the common law. Martland went so far as to confess being 'troubled with the
idea of a judicial philosophy. I can't say that after 24 years I have ever
formulated one.'[24] When Martland's legal conservatism was joined to
his rock-solid social conservatism, the result was unlikely to favour any
kind of innovation. He had loved about Oxford exactly what philosopher George Grant had found 'disappointing' during his brief study of
law there in 1939: 'it is merely stating the law, never asking what it is (as
the basis), never asking why it is as it is, never asking what it ought to
be.'[25] Ritchie's values were somewhat more liberal than Martland's.
He was the swing vote in *Brodie, Dansky and Rubin v. The Queen*, for
example, in which the Court found the novel *Lady Chatterley's Lover* not
to be obscene by a vote of five to four, with Martland voting in the
minority.[26] And when Laskin joined the Court Ritchie was still basking
in the attention his judgment in *Drybones* had garnered. He had used
the Canadian Bill of Rights to declare inoperative a section of the *Indian
Act* imposing harsher penalties for Indians found to be 'intoxicated off a
reserve' than for non-Indians in similar circumstances.[27]

For the most part Laskin respected Martland's and Ritchie's knowledge of substantive law; in many areas of private law their decisions
were almost interchangeable. The major difference between them,
legally speaking, lay in Laskin's greater willingness to harness the
creative power of the common law instead of waiting for legislative
reform of outdated precepts. This authority was to be used sparingly,
but he could wield it to powerful effect when he chose to do so. In

public law Laskin diverged more noticeably from the duo, but this was largely a function of their very different values and life experiences. Martland and Ritchie came from relatively privileged backgrounds and showed a certain complacency about the social and legal status quo. Laskin had been almost a professional critic of legal institutions, and was more likely to take seriously the position of the underdog in cases involving criminal law or over-reaching state action.

Louis-Philippe Pigeon's academic and law reform credentials were of long standing. As early as 1945 he had written an essay entitled 'Nécessité d'une évolution du droit civil' arguing for root and branch reform of the Civil Code and Quebec law in general. Making a point articulated more explosively by artists and intellectuals in the *Refus global* of 1948, Pigeon alleged Quebec law had been too long ossified by a powerful form of ancestor worship.[28] As legal adviser to Premier Jean Lesage in the 1960s, he had been able to carry some of his ideas into action. Laskin appreciated Pigeon's mastery of the substantive law and found his respect for federal constitutional powers (highly unusual in a late-twentieth-century Quebec judge) congenial, though the two differed substantially on the extent of the federal 'peace, order and good government' power.[29] Aside from that, the two seldom found themselves on opposite sides of a decision except in criminal law matters. While many of the Quebec judges found the Supreme Court monastic and Ottawa stultifying, the atmosphere was ideal for Pigeon; he was a rather idiosyncratic 'loner' for whom social life was not especially important.[30]

Laskin took his oaths on 2 April and sat briefly before going off on his New York junket. Fortunately the term was almost over. With several outstanding Court of Appeal judgments, Laskin worked quickly to finish them, then took a week's holiday with Peggy to relax.[31] The spring term commenced on the twenty-eighth with the official welcoming of both the new puisne judge and the new chief justice. Laskin was in high spirits as Peggy, family members, and friends, and his law clerk gathered in his chambers before the ceremony began. The swearing in took place at 10:00 a.m. in Chief Justice Fauteux's chambers before the other red-robed judges, family members and guests. Laskin was attired in John Cartwright's robes, passed down by tradition from incumbent to successor. As a symbol of change in post-war Canada, this ritual exchange was almost too perfect. On a May morning in 1945 John Cartwright had put forward an argument, prepared with Laskin's help, that an anti-Semitic restrictive covenant was contrary to public policy. *Re Drummond Wren* was the opening salvo in the campaign for better human rights protection in Canada. Now, a quarter-century later almost to the day, Cartwright literally passed on his mantle to the Supreme Court's first Jewish member.

At 10:30, after the judges took their places on the high bench in the sombre but elegant audience room, the registrar read the letters patent of the chief justice and the new member of the Court. There followed remarks by Mr Justice Abbott, as the senior puisne judge, the minister of justice, and leaders of the bar.[32] The remarks of W.G. Howland, treasurer of the Law Society of Upper Canada, were surprisingly generous. After citing a famous passage from Laskin's writings – 'Empiricism not dogmatism, imagination rather than literalism, are the qualities through which the judges can give their Court the stamp of personality' – Howland expressed the confidence of the Ontario bar that 'the stamp of his personality, his sense of social consciousness and his broad knowledge of the field of constitutional law will play a significant role in ... the days ahead.'[33]

The two judges' differing backgrounds pointed up the changes beginning to affect the Canadian social hierarchy. Gérald Fauteux was as perfect a representative of the elite of 'old Canada' as one might find. The son of a physician, grandson of Honoré Mercier and nephew of Sir Lomer Gouin, both premiers of Quebec, Fauteux was also the brother of Gaspard Fauteux, a former speaker of the House of Commons and lieutenant-governor of Quebec. While on the Supreme Court, Fauteux was named first dean of the University of Ottawa Faculty of Law.[34] He was unquestionably a talented man, especially in his chosen field of criminal law, but his family connections had certainly not harmed his career. Alongside him sat Bora Laskin, first-generation son of Russian immigrants, who had barely made it onto the bottom rung of the Canadian establishment with his faculty appointment at the University of Toronto the year after the cornerstone of the Supreme Court building was laid. Perhaps unconsciously wanting to endow Laskin with the pedigree he lacked, John Turner referred to him as 'an Elizabethan gentleman' in his welcoming remarks. W.G. Howland found a gracious way to acknowledge his Judaism, observing that 'in an age when we are striving for ecumenicity it is most appropriate that this representation [of the various Christian denominations] has been broadened to include the Jewish faith.'[35] That, Laskin might have mused wryly, was as close to an apology as the Law Society would ever make for its long tolerance of exclusionary practices by the bar.

Within weeks of his arrival Laskin signalled in subtle – and perhaps not so subtle – ways that he would not conform automatically to the culture of the Court. He rarely followed the traditional routine of going to the Rideau Club for lunch, for example. While it is possible that he disliked its traditional Anglo-centred exclusiveness – the club had only just abandoned its exclusion of Jews from membership, thanks to the efforts of Emmett Hall and others, and women would not be admitted as members until 1974 – he had socialized with his brethren at the exclusive University Club while at the Court of Appeal. Such practices are an important way of integrating new members into a group, but Laskin seemed to resist the process. He had a parade of visitors in his first months on the Court, more it seemed than all the other judges put together.[36] Some of these visitors came to help relieve the loneliness Laskin was believed to be suffering during his first months in Ottawa without Peggy. Harry Arthurs urged June Callwood to visit for this reason, and she did so while in Ottawa on other business. After wandering about the Supreme Court for a while she ran into Emmett Hall, whom she knew, and he offered to show her to Laskin's office. To do so they took a short-cut through the audience chamber, which Callwood had never seen before. Awed by the silence and solemnity of the room, she asked, 'Is there any passion here?' 'Oh no,' replied Hall, 'we're all old men.'[37] She then proceeded to visit Laskin on the pretext of asking him why the federal government couldn't do more to alleviate child poverty, and got a lecture on the division of powers.

Laskin's gregariousness suggested an attempt to break with the rather monastic traditions of the Court, and represented the beginnings of a personal crusade to make the institution better known to Canadians. The traditional isolation and reserve of the judiciary serve an important function in preserving their impartiality but, as Laskin recognized, they can be taken too far. Laskin greatly admired John Cartwright, but disagreed entirely with the antiquated image the chief chose to project. A visitor to Cartwright's chambers found he 'created a rather Victorian or Edwardian atmosphere, quite like the famous SPY cartoons of the British legal great.'[38] Even upon his retirement Cartwright refused to be interviewed, in spite of pleas by the editor of the *Globe and Mail*, who wanted to build a long feature story around such an interview.[39] Laskin also had to deal with outmoded ideas among some of his colleagues as to the appropriate use of academic authority. One can only imagine his reaction when he heard of a colleague reminding a lawyer that the Court declined to receive citations from living authors – the author in this case being one Professor Bora Laskin![40]

Laskin also made his mark at the outset in his treatment of the clerks. In 1967 the judges had first been authorized to hire recent law graduates to assist them with research. Emmett Hall and Ronald Martland researched the U.S. Supreme Court clerkship program and were keen to emulate it in Ottawa. Justice William J. Brennan of the U.S. Supreme Court reported to Martland that he found his clerks 'invaluable and stimulating. They provide a conduit to current scholarly thinking in the major law schools, besides being very bright young men [sic] who are very helpful.' Brennan's clerks digested the applications for review of lower court judgments, did extra research on some files, and worked closely with him in the organization and composition of his decisions.[41] At first the judges resisted. In 1967–8 only five opted to take a clerk; in the following year each judge was assigned one. As the world outside exploded with political violence, youthful rebellion, and counter-cultural chaos, the judges of the Supreme Court plodded along with assumptions appropriate to the world of 'Upstairs, Downstairs.' All the clerks were installed in an area directly off the boiler room on the third floor of the building. That in itself was probably inescapable given space constraints (a number of clerks still work in those quarters). More problematic was the installation of a directory board in the clerks' quarters with nine flashing lights, activated by a button in each judge's office, for summoning the clerks.

Laskin was appalled by this contraption and never used it, preferring to have his court attendant find his clerk or seek him out personally (telephones for the clerks came later). He inherited Chief Justice Cartwright's clerk, Mohan Singh Jawl of Victoria, a UBC law graduate who had done an LLM at the London School of Economics before arriving at the Court. Jawl was doubly fortunate in his principals, but their personal styles were quite different. Where meetings with Cartwright were formal and to the point, Jawl's interaction with Laskin was more spontaneous and wide-ranging. Laskin encouraged him to volunteer his own opinions, and enjoyed engaging in debate with him; sometimes their meetings became almost a one-on-one tutorial. Laskin alerted Jawl to cases he should attend, introduced him to notable lawyers, discussed his career plans, pressed books on him from his own library, introduced him to family and friends, and corresponded with him long after Jawl's brief tenure ended.[42] Laskin early on became a kind of godfather to all the clerks, and was the only judge who deigned to visit them in their own quarters. Louise Arbour, later a justice on the Court, clerked for Justice Pigeon in 1971–2 and still recalls a thrill running through the room when Laskin made one of his unannounced visits.[43] To the younger generation he was heroic for his willingness to speak out against injustice and his resistance to received ideas, and iconic in representing everything the new generation thought Canadian law should be.

Laskin ended his first year on the Court with two honorary degrees, one from Dalhousie and one from the Law Society of Upper Canada. With his promotion to the Supreme Court, the Law Society could no longer ignore its old gadfly. Forty years earlier Laskin had barely been able to enroll as a student-at-law at Osgoode Hall for want of a principal; now he was receiving the highest honour the benchers could bestow. With this honour, his love-hate relationship with the Law Society of Upper Canada finally achieved a state of equilibrium.

Although excited by Laskin's promotion, Bora and Peggy were reluctant to leave their home in Toronto 'for the unknown and questionable blessings of Ottawa,' as Morris Shumiatcher put it.[44] For the time being Laskin rented an apartment at 400 Stewart Street. That spring and summer had an unsettled feeling as Bora and Peggy contemplated leaving the city they had called home for forty years. Then beloved Sucre's death cast a pall over the family. The dog had been left in the care of relatives while the family attended Laskin's swearing-in ceremony in Ottawa, and was accidentally poisoned. When told of her death, 'he just became very silent.'[45] Unfortunately, greater calamities lay in store that summer. On 25 August Laskin's younger brother Charles died in Toronto at the age of fifty-five.[46] Only days after this blow, another struck. One morning Peggy awoke dizzy and disoriented. Her distraught spouse called both the ambulance and the fire department for assistance. Peggy was rushed to hospital where she underwent surgery to remove a brain tumour. Jean Milner summed it up: 'first they lost the dog, then Bora's brother, then they almost lost Peggy.'[47] It was a cruel and uncanny coincidence considering Peggy's first illness at the time of her husband's appointment to the Court of Appeal. The surgery was successful, and Morris wrote encouragingly: '[y]ou looked just delightful and if someone had removed the antiseptic props, I would be sure that you were holding a levee in Louis' palace at

Versailles.'[48] Always elegant even in adversity, Peggy wore a silk turban for some time to cover her hair loss. Once home, her recovery proceeded slowly.[49]

Domestic drama preceded national disaster that fall. Preoccupied as he was with Peggy's health, Laskin must have felt his world was crashing down around him when the October crisis burst upon the country a month after her operation. The kidnapping of James Cross by the Front de Libération du Québec on 5 October launched a nightmarish sequence of events: the kidnapping of Quebec Labour Minister Pierre Laporte on the tenth, the posting of hundreds of armed troops in Montreal and Ottawa, invocation of the *War Measures Act* in the early hours of the sixteenth, the discovery of Laporte's body on the eighteenth, the arrest and detention without charge of hundreds of Quebeckers held without bail. The atmosphere in Ottawa was not as hysterical as in Montreal but it was still grim, with as many as a thousand armed soldiers patrolling the streets. A soldier with a loaded rifle was assigned to remain within the Supreme Court at all times, over the strenuous objections of Chief Justice Fauteux.[50] How Laskin reacted to Pierre Trudeau's invocation of the *War Measures Act* must remain a mystery for now. With even staunch civil libertarians such as Frank Scott, Eugene Forsey, Samuel Freedman, and Thérèse Casgrain supporting it, Trudeau's action likely gained Laskin's private approval.

Crisis or no crisis, the Supreme Court began its fall session as usual on the first Tuesday in October. The judges attended the prorogation of Parliament on the seventh and the opening of the new session on the eighth, then got on with two and a half months of hearings. The term was very busy and by December Laskin was looking forward to a month at home in Toronto with Peggy. She had made considerable progress in her recovery by the time he returned to Ottawa, and national life returned slowly to normal as well. James Cross was freed on 3 December, his kidnappers were found and flown to Cuba, and Laporte's abductors were arrested soon after.

In spite of his concerns about Peggy's health, Laskin kept up his usual round of extra-curricular activities. Over the holidays he began working on two papers he agreed to give at the Canadian Judicial Conference in Vancouver in August.[51] This was yet another way in which Laskin sought to break down the isolation of the Court. The Canadian Judicial Conference began in the later 1960s as a spin-off from the National Conference of Chief Justices, an annual gathering inaugurated in 1964 and at first devoted solely to criminal law. As its ambit expanded to non-criminal issues, an informal continuing education program for federally appointed puisne judges also developed.[52] The Supreme Court judges had stayed away from both these conferences in spite of repeated invitations, and the organizers were desperate to get them to come. Hall and Laskin decided to break the ice.[53]

Laskin's paper on 'Developments in the Law of Evidence' was unremarkable except for his obvious unhappiness with the controversial decision in R. v. Wray, heard just before he arrived at the Court and handed down in June. The case arose out of a murder near Peterborough, Ontario. A day-long police interrogation of the adolescent accused resulted in a confession determined to be coerced and hence inadmissible. Wray confessed to throwing the murder weapon in a swamp, whence it was retrieved by the police. Expert evidence showed the bullet in question to have come from the recovered rifle. The Crown sought to introduce the gun as evidence as well as the part of the otherwise inadmissible confession that led them to it. The trial judge ruled the latter evidence inadmissible because it would operate unfairly against the accused and would also tend to bring the administration of justice into disrepute, in line with the 'fruit of the forbidden tree' doctrine then emerging in the United States. With no evidence to connect the murder weapon to the accused, and all the remaining evidence circumstantial, the trial judge directed an acquittal and the Ontario Court of Appeal affirmed. A majority of the Supreme Court reversed and ordered a new trial. Evidence which operated *unfortunately* for the accused did not necessarily operate *unfairly* as that term had been defined in earlier cases, said Martland; and in any case Canadian judges possessed no discretion to exclude evidence that would bring the administration of justice into disrepute. Laskin concluded his paper by asking whether the rule should be reconsidered. Suggesting reconsideration of a major ruling less than two months' old was highly unusual, especially when proposed by a novice judge far junior to the author of the precedent in question. The collision course between Martland and Laskin was clearly marked out.[54]

Even more of a coup was the presence at the fall meeting of the chief justices in Regina of Chief Justice Fauteux, who had been persuaded to attend in part through the efforts of Hall and Laskin. The main agenda item was the proposed Canadian Judicial Council, a new statutory body empowered to investigate allegations of misconduct made against federally appointed judges. The chief justice of Canada was supposed to chair the council, but Fauteux held serious reservations about the whole scheme. For some years provincial chief justices had been trying to develop a mechanism to give them some control over errant or incapable judges on their own courts. The Landreville debacle pointed to a gap in the law, and created some political impetus for the judges' work.[55] The constitution provided for judges of superior courts to be removed on a joint address to both houses of Parliament but created no machinery for preparing such an address, nor did it contemplate judicial misbehaviour meriting less drastic measures. Wilbur Jackett, then president of the Exchequer Court of Canada, drafted the necessary amendments to the *Judges Act* and managed to dispel Fauteux's unease. John Turner presented the scheme to Parliament later in the fall, and the chief justice presided over the first meeting of the council in Ottawa on 10 December.[56] Laskin would fill the same role in turn, with Chief Justice Ted Culliton of Saskatchewan at his right hand.

Laskin could not resist keeping up his contacts with the university world, joining the board of governors of Carleton University in November 1970. After his disastrous experience at York his willingness to serve is rather surprising, but it did allow him to meet some of Ottawa's inner circle: mandarin Sylvia Ostry, Bank of Canada president Louis Rasminsky, and senior lawyers such as Hyman Soloway and G.E. Beament. Laskin also joined his fellow activist from the human rights struggles of the 1950s, Kalmen Kaplansky.[57] The Laskins became good friends with the Rasminskys, and Bora would deliver the eulogy at Lyla's death in 1976. A second university position he could hardly refuse: the chancellorship of Lakehead University in his home town of Thunder Bay. Laskin's brother had been instrumental in getting the university up and running, and offering the post to Bora was a way of thanking Saul as well as raising the profile of the new institution. Laskin was installed as chancellor at the 29 May 1971 convocation and for the next several years, until illness intervened in the late 1970s, presided over the graduation ceremonies of Ontario's northernmost university.[58]

After their almost annual sojourns in Europe in the 1960s, the Laskins settled into a pattern of a January vacation in Florida and summer holidays in Canada, usually tacked onto a judges' seminar where Bora was giving a paper. Occasionally they also managed a quick trip to the south during the Court's Easter break. In 1971 the Shumiatchers finally succeeded in persuading the Laskins to spend some time at their favourite holiday spot near Lake Louise. To Morris, Lake O'Hara was 'without question, the world's most beautiful lake.' The resort offered simple cabins on an Alpine meadow near the lake, a dining room with excellent food prepared by Swiss chefs, spectacular mountain scenery including a view of the Victoria glacier, and 'not much to do except walk, hike and fish.' Bora and Peggy were a very urban couple without any deep need to commune with nature, and Peggy was not well enough to do much hiking, but they succumbed to Morris's enthusiasm and appear to have enjoyed the holiday.[59]

The spring and summer of 1972 were a blur of activity. In April came the Laskins' first trip to Israel, where Bora delivered the Lionel Cohen lecture at the law faculty of the Hebrew University of Jerusalem. His Yiddish came in handy when he found that the dean of the law faculty spoke little English: 'Laskin and he chatted away merrily in the *mamaloshen.*'[60] Laskin's talk, 'The Institutional Character of the Judge,' represented the fullest account of his conception of the role of a judge in the common law world that he ever committed to paper. Coming close to the mid-point of his judicial career, its reflections reveal its author's increasing awareness of the constraints of the judicial role, and a conse- quent tempering of some of his earlier views on judicial individuality. As he confessed at the outset: 'When I took my seat on the Supreme Court of Canada I told [the audience] that I had no one to answer to save my own conscience and my personal standards of integrity. The euphoria of the occasion was my excuse for a touch of hyperbole. My previous judicial experience had already taught me better; what I said was not the whole story.'[61] The rest of the story, it appeared, was the way in which established patterns of judicial behaviour, the constraints of *stare decisis*, and the monitoring function of an appellate hierarchy, combined to reduce the scope for heroic action by a single judge. Laskin's audience may have wondered whether he was speaking auto- biographically when he made the following observation about the iso- lation of judges on a final appellate court. 'Fresh faces that appear when vacancies occur ... may not be a sufficient tonic when it is remembered that the new incumbent joins an established institution; the existing complement is more likely to absorb him than he them.'[62] If Laskin feared he was losing his edge, he needn't have worried: the dissents he would write in the next few years would be among his most memorable.

There followed three honorary degrees in May (Alberta, Manitoba – where Laskin's friend Ernest Sirluck was now president – and York). Then Barbara graduated from the University of Toronto, just before her marriage on 4 June to Timothy Plumptre. The groom's father, Wynne Plumptre, now principal of Scarborough College, was a young lecturer in economics when Laskin was a student. His mother, Beryl Plumptre, would soon be better known as the chair of the Food Prices Review Board set up as part of Trudeau's anti-inflation measures. The public confrontations of this formidably proper matron and the homespun but combative agriculture minister Eugene Whelan provided Canadians with some welcome comic relief in the mid-1970s. The bride chose a romantic location for the ceremony – a forest glade adjoining her father-in-law's residence on the college grounds – and to the relief of all, the weather cooperated. Rabbi Feinberg was summoned from California as no local rabbi would preside over a mixed marriage, while the other celebrant was the groom's brother-in-law, an Anglican canon attached to Winchester Cathedral.[63] Bora and Peggy were delighted that the new couple would make their home in Ottawa, where Barbara worked for the Canada Council.

No sooner was the wedding over than Bora and Peggy began preparing for the final move to Ottawa. They had arranged to take over Emmett and Belle Hall's apartment in Champlain Towers, a penthouse with magnificent views on all sides. Jean Milner found the Laskins nonetheless 'torn to bits because they are going to have to sell the house.'[64] In August they added a week's holiday to the annual judicial seminar in Halifax, but it was spoiled when Peggy suffered a gallbladder attack. After surgery back in Ottawa she found the large airy rooms of their new home ideal surroundings for her recovery. They also showed off to perfection the paintings, objets d'art, and antique furniture she and Bora had collected over the years. Morris Shumiatcher was duly impressed when he visited for the first time. 'It was like the Muscovites opening the Hermitage to the public. I never knew that you had so many beautiful hidden treasures.'[65] The Laskins were also joined on Rideau Terrace by Max and Isle Cohen. Coincidentally, just a month after Laskin was named chief justice Cohen was appointed Canadian chairman of the International Joint Commission, the Canada-U.S. body created in 1909 to monitor water quality on the Great Lakes. Both had come an unimaginable distance since the 1930s, when they commiserated over breaking through the wall of prejudice confronting them in the legal community.

Emmett Hall and Laskin were great allies on the Court, and Laskin must have been anxious about his successor when Hall retired in February 1973.[66] As usual, a quiet skirmish broke out as to which of the four western provinces should provide his replacement. With Martland from Alberta and Hall having occupied Saskatchewan's turn on the rota, it came down to Manitoba or British Columbia. Hall had replaced British Columbian Charles Locke, suggesting Manitoba should be looked to next. Brian Dickson of the Manitoba Court of Appeal was duly appointed in March but Thomas Berger had been briefly considered and Hall tried to advance his candidacy. As he reported to Berger, when it came time to decide, 'Mr. [James] Richardson, whose weight in the Cabinet has been increasing, carried the day and Manitoba got the call.'[67] Perhaps it was just as well. In view of later events, the prospect of Bora Laskin and Thomas Berger sitting concurrently on the Supreme Court of Canada is a historical counter-factual too surreal to contemplate.[68]

Brian Dickson and Bora Laskin were both the eldest sons of immigrants to Canada, but in other respects their personal backgrounds and paths to the law were radically different. Dickson's parents were Protestant Irish; his mother was one of the first female graduates of Trinity College Dublin, while his father quickly rose through the ranks of the Bank of British North America after they settled on the prairies. Brian Dickson won the gold medal at law school, then worked at an insurance company when Manitoba law firms were not hiring anyone. During a distinguished war career overseas he lost a leg during a 'friendly fire' incident. After marrying the daughter of a wealthy grain magnate Dickson embarked on a successful career in corporate law with the Winnipeg firm of Aikins, Macaulay and Company, then the largest law firm in western Canada.[69] His work there involved more business than law, and he had quite a bit of catching up to do when he was named to the Manitoba Court of Queen's Bench in 1963. Promotion to the Court of Appeal followed in 1967. Supreme Court judges traditionally came from the professional elite but were seldom wealthy men. Dickson was, and he brought to the Court a lifestyle more appropriate to the English landed gentry, albeit with a prairie twist. As the former registrar of the Court, Ken Campbell, informed Emmett Hall, 'Brian Dickson has bought a large property at Lucerne Quebec. He is bringing down a number of horses and a buffalo; that really is something new for a judge of the Supreme Court of Canada.'[70]

Dickson's social, ideological, and jurisprudential background appeared to put him at the opposite end of the spectrum from Bora Laskin, and certainly the two disagreed frequently on the division of powers under the constitution, Dickson being much more receptive to provincial arguments than Laskin. But the new appointee, at first intimidated by Laskin's encyclopaedic knowledge of the law and his formidable intellect, gradually and somewhat unexpectedly found himself drawn into Laskin's orbit.[71] Dickson's initial sense of inadequacy and his perfectionism caused him to work harder than most of the other judges, and he was notorious among his clerks for writing a dozen drafts of a judgment before attaining a version he felt comfortable circulating. Dickson felt free to contact them at any hour of the day or night to discuss a point or ask for more research (Laskin's clerks had a much easier time). Dickson's quasi-apprenticeship under Laskin would serve him in good stead when he succeeded his friend as chief justice in 1984 and guided the Court through its early years of Charter jurisprudence.

In spite of their differing backgrounds and some important cleavages on constitutional law, Laskin and Dickson shared a similar approach to judicial decision making. Dickson's judgments were always characterized by a search for principle, not a simple quest for precedent, and he was not afraid to innovate within limits. He respected academics, though he sometimes urged them to do more and better work, and possessed little of the anti-intellectualism sometimes on display in the corporate bar. On civil liberties issues, particularly in the criminal law area, Dickson eventually fitted into the dissenting spot vacated by Emmett Hall, but not before he had spent two or three years on the Court. The Hall-Laskin-Spence triad eventually became the famed 'LSD' group: Laskin, Spence, and Dickson. During the somewhat fractious years ahead, Dickson would be a voice of calm and reason and one of Laskin's valued supporters. The intellectual partnership of the enlightened corporate solicitor and the former labour activist proved to be a fruitful one. Their jointly developed approach to public law, discussed in chapter 21, continues to anchor much of the Canadian jurisprudence in the field.

17

Early Promise

The 1970s saw important debates in Canadian society translated into legal form and argued before the Supreme Court. New issues such as gender equality, gay rights, and aboriginal entitlements appeared alongside more traditional ones such as the division of powers, the role of the courts in defining criminal procedure, the relationship between the courts and administrative agencies, and the continuing adjustment of the common law. There were few division of powers cases for Laskin to sink his teeth into during his first few years on the Court: many more would arise after he became chief justice late in 1973. Before 1975 the Court did not have control over its docket and was obliged to hear appeals in any case where the matter in question involved more than $10,000, regardless of the significance of the legal issues raised. Its caseload included much more private law than in later years, and some of Laskin's best-known decisions from these years dealt with private law: *Highway Properties v. Kelly Douglas, Canadian Aero Service Ltd. v. O'Malley*, and *Murdoch v. Murdoch*.[1] In public law his best-known decision from his early years is probably his dissent in *Attorney General of Canada v. Lavell; Isaac v. Bédard*, in which he invoked the equality guarantee of the Canadian Bill of Rights to declare inoperative a provision of the *Indian Act* depriving native women of Indian status when they married non-Indian men.[2] Another less well-known but important dissent involved a contempt of court charge where Laskin felt the trial judge had acted outrageously in disciplining a lawyer who was probably ill rather than in contempt. *R. v. McKeown* shows Laskin trying to use his position in the appellate hierarchy to set standards for judicial behaviour, a theme that would preoccupy him in later years as chief justice.[3]

Laskin's decisions at the Supreme Court began to take on a bolder quality than they had in the Court of Appeal. His promotion seemed to make him more confident; no doubt he was conscious of the higher expectations of the public and the legal profession aroused by his elevation. Laskin tried to teach by example, to show his colleagues how to get beyond the dispute-settlement approach to judging and to remould the contours of the law in appropriate cases instead of just applying it. Surprisingly, he was able to persuade a majority of his colleagues to support some of his early law reform efforts. It was almost as if they were waiting for someone to show them how. Laskin's early successes tended to be in the realm of private law; in public law his perceived heterodoxy kept him in the minority on many issues. Where the rights of accused persons were concerned, or the degree of deference to be afforded to labour arbitrators and administrative tribunals, important differences separated Laskin from his colleagues. These will be dealt with in a subsequent chapter; the present chapter will focus on Laskin's early private law adjudication, and his approach to women's rights and aboriginal claims.

One of Laskin's first cases involved a claim by a landlord against a commercial tenant in a Vancouver shopping mall who had abandoned the leased premises. The tenant carried on a supermarket business that was meant to be the anchor store in the mall. It had signed a fifteen-year lease and covenanted to carry on business for that period, but repudiated the lease after three years of mediocre returns. When this caused some of the mall's other tenants to depart, the landlord resumed possession of the premises and sued the tenant for prospective losses suffered over the full term of the lease. In an ordinary commercial contract situation such damages would be recoverable, but in the landlord-tenant context the common law had long restricted recovery to the unpaid rent over the course of the lease minus any rent actually received from a subsequent tenant. Consequential losses such as those incurred here were not recognized. The conceptualization of the landlord's interest as an estate in land – a property interest – suggested that once the landlord had accepted the repudiation of the lease, there was nothing left upon which to base damages. Laskin noted 'some questioning of this persistent ascendancy of a concept that antedated the development of the law of contracts in English law and has been transformed in its social and economic aspects by urban living and by commercial practice.'[4] Both Australia and the United States had allowed recovery for consequential losses by the landlord, and even in England doubts had been cast on the traditional doctrine.

Speaking for a unanimous panel of five judges, Laskin overruled a recent Ontario Court of Appeal decision applying the old law, and allowed the landlord's appeal. 'It was no longer sensible to pretend,' he declared, 'that a commercial lease ... is simply a conveyance and not also a contract. It is equally untenable to persist in denying resort to the full armoury of remedies ordinarily available to redress repudiation of covenants, merely because the covenants may be associated with an estate in land.'[5] Where the common law had created the problem, it could also fashion a solution according to Laskin's judicial philosophy. Jacob Ziegel calls this Laskin's most significant decision in contract law, and doubts whether there would have been even a majority in favour of reversing the old law 'in the absence of Laskin's masterful opinion.'[6]

Laskin again spoke for a unanimous panel of five judges in another business law case, *Canadian Aero Service Ltd. v. O'Malley. Canaero*, as it is popularly known, remains one of Laskin's most-cited judgments.[7] It addresses important questions relating to the ethical standards expected of senior corporate officers who learn of valuable opportunities while employed with one company, then exploit them for personal gain after their departure. The context was the competition over free-flowing government aid money directed to newly independent Third World countries in the 1960s. O'Malley and one Zarzycki were respectively president and vice-president of Canaero, a company specializing in topographical mapping and geophysical exploration. In that capacity they learned of, and pursued on behalf of the company for some years, a possible contract to conduct aerial mapping of parts of Guyana to be funded by the government of Canada. The two men then incorporated a company called Terra Surveys on 6 August 1966, resigned from Canaero in mid-August, and almost immediately secured the $2.3 million contract for Terra. At issue was the nature and extent of any duty owed by the two executives to Canaero, and whether it had been breached. Corporate directors are held to a strict standard of fiduciary duty with respect to their company, such that they cannot be seen to let their personal interest and their corporate duty conflict, but there was some debate about the exact parameters of this duty.

In light of the increasing attention paid to the standards of conduct of corporate officers in the intervening years, the liability of O'Malley and Zarzycki may seem obvious. Yet both the trial judge and the Ontario Court of Appeal had dismissed Canaero's claim. The trial judge found that the two men were indeed fiduciaries vis-à-vis Canaero, but that the scope of their duty did not extend to cover the acts in question. He seemed to regard the misuse of confidential information as necessary to establish a breach of fiduciary duty, and found no such misuse on the facts. The Court of Appeal denied that the two executives were even fiduciaries, holding them to be mere employees of the company unrestricted in their right to compete once they had resigned from it. Lurking in the background were some Supreme Court precedents which had seemed to countenance similar free-wheeling behaviour by corporate directors in the mining industry. Existing law seemed to protect the fundamental liberal ethic of competition more vigorously than the expectations by shareholders of ethical conduct by their company's officers.

Laskin cut through these contradictions in a careful and lucid judgment. Senior officers such as O'Malley and Zarzycki were undoubtedly fiduciaries according to both academic authority and the trend of case law; here Laskin cited his friend L.C.B. Gower to this effect. As to the extent of their duties, Laskin noted the 'pervasiveness of a strict ethic in this area of law,' thereby trying to reduce the effect of the looser Supreme Court precedents, and summed up the applicable rule: 'this ethic disqualifies a director or senior officer from usurping for himself or diverting to another person or company with whom or with which he is associated a maturing business opportunity which his company is actively pursuing; he is also precluded from so acting even after his resignation where [it] may fairly be said to have been prompted or influenced by a wish to acquire for himself the opportunity sought by the company, or where it was his position with the company rather than a fresh initiative that led him to the opportunity which he later acquired.'[8] The formulation is classic Laskin: a broad statement with plenty of wiggle room to take account of possible factual variations. One might debate what was a 'maturing' business opportunity, 'actively' pursued, or what a 'fresh initiative' might be, but these would have to be assessed in each new factual context. On the whole, the decision 'has had a very beneficial effect in discouraging any dilution in the high standards of probity and loyalty expected of corporate management.'[9]

Laskin's long immersion in labour law had left him with a certain scepticism about business leaders which Murray Ross had noticed when Laskin joined the board of governors of York Unviersity. Given his background, it is not surprising that Laskin pounced on *Canaero* as an opportunity to promote a vision of ethical corporate behaviour. It is perhaps more surprising that his colleagues joined him, but in both *Highway Properties* and *Canaero* Laskin clearly demonstrated his basic commitment to the free market and corporate capitalism, albeit within a framework of public regulation and judicial scrutiny designed to curb its most undesirable aspects. In *Highway Properties* he assimilated the consequences of lease repudiation to the general rule for the protection of expectation damages in contract, while in *Canaero* he could be seen as reminding his audience that shareholders were as much a part of corporate capitalism as directors and managers. One could even interpret *Canaero* in law and economics terms: it was not efficient to allow Terra Surveys to free-ride on the efforts of O'Malley and Zarzycki for which Canaero had paid. At another level one can see *Canaero* as inspired by the principled approach taken by Laskin's parents in their own business activities during his youth. The stringent application of the fiduciary duty, said Laskin, was 'a necessary supplement in the public interest, of statutory regulation and accountability which themselves are, at one and the same time, an acknowledgment of the importance of the corporation in the life of the community and of the need to compel obedience by it and by its promoters, directors and managers to norms of exemplary behaviour.'[10] In Laskin's universe, power always attracted responsibility.

Laskin was probably assisted in his thinking in *Canaero* by the arguments of Charles Dubin, who was counsel for the plaintiff. Another counsel was Charles H. Locke, a former Supreme Court judge who had gone into practice in Ontario after being compulsorily retired from the Court in 1962. The judges were unlikely to have been pleased with their former colleague's decision to appear before them as an advocate. Certainly the benchers of the Law Society of Upper Canada were highly affronted by the practice, believing that former judges appeared to clients to possess an unfair advantage even if that was not the case in fact; eventually the Law Society passed a rule restricting the practice of retired judges. Locke, now in his mid-eighties, represented James Wells, a lawyer who had advised O'Malley and Zarzycki and had become a shareholder in Terra Surveys. Laskin agreed with the dismissal of the action against Wells on the basis that he owed no fiduciary duty to Canaero nor could he be said to have conspired against it with his clients to deprive it of a benefit.

If Laskin's colleagues were content to agree with him when he upheld the fundamentals of corporate capitalism, they disagreed strongly on many other issues. One went to the very heart of the role of an appellate judge – how zealously should higher courts police the behaviour of lower courts? Laskin was often annoyed by the way his colleagues would slap down labour arbitrators and administrative tribunals without a moment's hesitation, but rode easily on lower court judges even when they had behaved outrageously. An example of such conduct arose early in Laskin's tenure, involving a lawyer named C.G. McKeown.[11] McKeown had failed to appear before Judge Walter Martin on 9 and 10 September 1969 as counsel for a client charged as an habitual criminal, and was cited by the judge for contempt. He had been at the courthouse but each time had felt too ill to proceed, and witnesses had observed him there walking unsteadily and muttering to himself. On the evening of the tenth McKeown's doctor had diagnosed him with diabetes and he remained under his care for the next two weeks. The judge cited McKeown for contempt and at a hearing on the twenty-fifth, Laskin observed, 'proceeded entirely *suo motu*, no one appearing on behalf of the Attorney-General to conduct the proceedings. He [Martin] called three witnesses (in addition to making a statement of facts of his own) and examined them.' Martin concluded that McKeown had not appeared because he was under the influence of drugs or alcohol, in spite of the testimony of McKeown's doctor that the symptoms he had displayed in the courthouse were consistent with diabetes. Martin rejected the doctor's evidence in favour of that of the lay witnesses and found McKeown guilty of contempt in the face of the court.

McKeown then found himself in a Catch-22 situation. In cases of summary conviction for contempt in the face of the court, section 9 of the Criminal Code allowed an appeal only against the punishment imposed, not the conviction itself; in the case of other contempts, both conviction and punishment could be appealed. McKeown appealed the conviction to the Court of Appeal, hoping to convince the court that his contempt, if any, had not been in the face of the court. That court quashed the appeal without recorded reasons. Martland, speaking for himself, the chief justice, and Judson, dismissed McKeown's appeal in a judgment of less than a page. For the majority, the only question was whether there was some evidence on which Judge Martin could find that the contempt had been committed in the face of the court. For a criminal offence, this was a marked departure from the usual standard of proof required. The judges seemed untroubled by the inquisitorial manner in which Martin had proceeded, acting as judge, prosecutor, and witness, and rejecting out of hand any evidence that did not conform to his pre-conceived views of what had happened. The majority were content to apply the law like a mathematical formula, without delving beneath the surface of the arguments.

Both Spence and Laskin wrote separate dissenting judgments. Spence's was relatively restrained, Laskin's full of outrage. Spence denied that an appeal court could be bound by the trial judge's characterization of the contempt as one committed in the face of the court. Where, as here, the key evidence of justification lay outside the court's direct knowledge, the contempt was a 'hybrid' one. An appeal lay properly to the Court of Appeal and beyond, but Spence disagreed with Laskin's conclusion that the appellant should be discharged of any taint of contempt. Spence would have sent the matter to the attorney-general for him to consider the taking of proceedings by indictment for the alleged contempt – though it is clear he expected no such indictment to be laid once the attorney-general reviewed the facts of the case.

Laskin began by recalling the purpose and function of contempt proceedings. They were not concerned with the 'protection of the personal dignity of the judge or the honour of the Court' but were rather 'a sanction to serve the administration of justice in the public interest.'[12] He then entered into a long historical review of the distinction between contempts in the face of the court and others. There being few Commonwealth precedents, he considered several American cases on the subject, and concluded by adopting the dissenting views of Justice Roger Traynor, later chief justice of California, in a 1962 case.[13] He agreed with Traynor that the classification of contempts was 'merely a semantic device for differentiating contempts that can be adjudicated summarily from those that can be adjudicated only after adequate notice and hearing.' This kind of functional analysis was still rarely encountered in the Supreme Court, and it was rarer still to cite the reasons of a dissenting American judge as authoritative.

According to a functional analysis, contempts in the face of the court were simply those where all the relevant facts were within the direct knowledge of the court. Here it was clear that many relevant facts were outside Judge Martin's knowledge as he had to call witnesses to testify to matters outside the courtroom. Thus the judge had no jurisdiction to proceed in the way he did. Laskin then entered into a minute scrutiny of the transcript, highlighting each and every error committed by Judge Martin in his handling of the case. Spence clearly felt this was uncalled for, but Laskin had no hesitation in upbraiding a judge who had deviated so spectacularly from the fundamentals of due process in a case where a lawyer's professional life was on the line. Laskin observed that 'the rules of natural justice that judges have so firmly fashioned for non-curial tribunals must have equal validity for them.'[14] More pointedly, he declared that Judge Martin showed no awareness of the obligation to meet the standard of proof beyond a reasonable doubt, and 'in his findings of fact relied on an exaggerated estimate of power to pass on credibility without providing any rational basis for so doing.'[15] Laskin was a strong believer in expert knowledge and could not countenance a judge rejecting medical evidence without any explanation. In view of the laconic response of the Ontario Court of Appeal and Laskin's own colleagues to this egregious behaviour, Laskin must have felt he needed to speak out strongly. Morris Shumiatcher congratulated his friend on a 'magnificent' judgment, and in reply Laskin hoped that it might slow down precipitate action by trial judges in future.[16] Even if he did not convince his colleagues, his dissent may have sparked a change in the law. The next year, Parliament changed the Criminal Code so as to allow an appeal against a conviction for contempt as well as against the sentence.[17]

In *McKeown* Laskin displayed many of the characteristics that would characterize his best Supreme Court judgments: a wide-ranging search for principle rather than a mere recitation of precedent; a clear attempt to link the purpose and function of legal doctrine with its formulation and application; and a sensitive appreciation of the human context out of which particular disputes emerged. This quest for justice rather than mere law resonated widely with the public and continued to enhance the 'Laskin legend.' *McKeown* also illustrated why Laskin sometimes grated on his fellow judges, in the Supreme Court and elsewhere. When he trained his critical intelligence on lower court judges he could be merciless, contrary to existing traditions of judicial courtesy. In this Laskin's harsh treatment of Principal Lockhart in the Fowke-Laskin Report had been an accurate harbinger of things to come. The mini-lectures in some of his decisions were sometimes interpreted as grandstanding at a time when academic flourishes were still suspect among judges. And in later years, when some of Laskin's own decisions were questioned, he showed himself incapable of accepting the kind of criticism he had often inflicted on others.

Aboriginal claims posed very difficult questions for Laskin. His legal modernism was in principle opposed to the kind of group identity claimed by aboriginal people (or Quebeckers, for that matter), with all its historical and cultural baggage and its claims of distinct legal status. The path of modernism was the path the Jews had taken, and it seemed to show that a plunge into the dynamic mainstream of North American life was not necessarily incompatible with the retention of cultural traditions, provided they were kept firmly in the private sphere. Many aboriginal claims seemed to feature a strong undertow of anti-modernism, an attempt to restore a vanished era or to assert ancient rights in a new and very different context. The opposing pull of modernity was most fully on view in the 1969 federal government white paper that advocated scrapping the *Indian Act* and getting rid of special status for native peoples, with the goal of accepting them as full members of Canadian society. Faced with this stark either-or choice, native leaders preferred to opt for the status quo, at least for the time being.

Laskin's strong commitment to equality and to modernism meant that his sympathies lay with the white paper, as would be evident in a number of his decisions involving aboriginal claimants. The one seeming exception to this pattern is Laskin's role in *Calder v. Attorney General of British Columbia*, the keystone of Canadian case law on aboriginal title and one of the Court's most important decisions of the twentieth century.[18] One of the two principal sets of reasons was written by Laskin's friend Emmett Hall, and represented his swan song at the Court. The Nisga'a people asserted title to a large part of northwestern British Columbia which they had never surrendered by treaty. In 1969 they sought a declaration against the Crown in right of British Columbia clarifying their land rights, but the attorney-general refused them permission to bring their action, as then required under B.C. law. Undeterred, Vancouver lawyer Thomas Berger argued their claim at both the trial and appeal level. A few years earlier he had persuaded both the B.C. Court of Appeal and the Supreme Court of Canada to affirm the continuing validity of an 1854 treaty long ignored by the provincial government.[19] There were few treaties in British Columbia, however, and recognition of the contested doctrine of common law aboriginal rights was the key goal of First Nations in that province. In *Calder*, the B.C. Court of Appeal denied the existence of any doctrine of aboriginal title, and said even if it existed, pre-Confederation laws of the colony of British Columbia had extinguished it in the case of the Nisga'a. Berger argued the case before the Supreme Court for an entire week in November-December 1971. During that week John Turner kept trying to reach him by telephone to offer him a position on the B.C. Supreme Court, but Berger put off responding so as to remain focused on his argument. Afterwards he returned the call, accepted the offer; and was sworn in on 5 February 1972.[20] Had Berger's promotion occurred a little earlier one wonders whether, deprived of his argument, the Supreme Court would have ruled the same way in *Calder*.

Hall was not able to begin writing in earnest until the summer recess, when he returned to Saskatoon, but he remained in close touch with Laskin by mail as he composed his judgment. On 7 September he sent Laskin a large portion of his draft reasons and was 'looking forward to discussing many aspects of the proposed judgment.'[21] Spence agreed with Hall but did not work closely with him on the judgment as Laskin did. Canadian courts had never ruled definitively on the status of aboriginal claims to land in areas unaffected by treaty where the occupants could demonstrate continuous possession back to pre-European times. According to the B.C. Court of Appeal aboriginal peoples had only a moral entitlement to 'their' land. This broadly held view underpinned the 1969 white paper.[22]

Thus it came as a shock to the government when six out of seven judges in *Calder* accepted Berger's argument. Justice Minister Otto Lang at first suggested he might ask the Court to reconsider its ruling, but this came to nought.[23] Both Judson and Hall expressed the essence of 'Indian title' with refreshing simplicity. '[W]hen the settlers came,' said Judson, 'the Indians were there, organized in societies and occupying the land as their forefathers had done for centuries. This is what Indian title means.' Hall said simply that long possession was *prima facie* proof of ownership at common law. The Nisga'a had been in possession since time immemorial according to the anthropological evidence, and were 'a distinctive cultural entity with concepts of ownership indigenous to their culture and capable of articulation under the common law.' Judson and Hall differed on one crucial point: Judson accepted a doctrine of *implicit* extinction of aboriginal title, and found it satisfied in this case, while Hall demanded that extinguishment be expressed in clear and plain language. The seventh judge, Pigeon, expressed no opinion on the main issue, holding that the Nisga'a claimed failed liminally because of the failure to obtain the attorney-general's fiat. In fact, Pigeon had said he agreed with Hall's draft decision and Hall even changed a few things to suit him; only at the last minute did he change his mind. Kenneth Campbell, the Court's former registrar, thought Pigeon 'must have been thinking of la Belle Province and the Indians in the James Bay area.'[24]

Technically, the Nisga'a lost four to three, but the *Montreal Gazette* recognized its impact with the headline 'Case Denied, Cause Gained.'[25] With six Supreme Court judges recognizing the doctrine of common law aboriginal title, the federal government had to take notice. On 8 August 1973 the Minister of Indian Affairs, Jean Chrétien, reversed long-standing policy and declared the willingness of the government to settle native land claims in all non-treaty areas of Canada. Nearly three decades later, on 11 May 2000, the Nisga'a Treaty came into force, and many new treaties have also been signed in other parts of Canada. It is almost impossible to overstate the significance of *Calder* on the evolving status of the First Nations in Canada. It not only opened a new era of treaty-making in Canada, but also sent out a new message about the courts' duty to take aboriginal claims seriously. Without *Calder*, it is difficult to imagine the decision in *Guerin*, just over a decade later.[26] In *Guerin* the Supreme Court defined the historic trust-like relationship between the Crown and the First Nations for the first time as a powerful fiduciary duty rather than an unenforceable political trust. *Calder* also resonated internationally: it was cited with approval in *Mabo v. Queensland*, the 1992 Australian decision reversing the long-standing denial of aboriginal title to any part of the continent.[27] Hall's reasons in *Calder* are now recognized as a classic of Canadian jurisprudence, but the role of Laskin and Berger in assisting in their development also deserves recognition.

The Supreme Court's decision in *Calder* accepted the historical possession of lands by the First Nations as entitling them to certain rights possessed by no other Canadians, at least in their traditional territories. How did Laskin reconcile this with his legal modernism, which, like Trudeau's, was not very receptive to claims for special status by particular groups? Laskin's dislike of separate military courts, for example, would result in a strong dissent in 1980 based on their denial of equality before the law (as he saw it) under the Canadian Bill of Rights.[28] And Laskin was never sympathetic to Quebec's claims to distinct status under the Canadian constitution. But recognizing aboriginal title did not necessarily involve a further acceptance of a distinct status for aboriginal peoples. The entitlement to land could be seen as providing a long-denied economic basis for native society, one native leaders might rely on to improve the material conditions and educational attainments of their people – and lead them, possibly, into modernity.

In other decisions dealing with the rights of native peoples, Laskin displayed either a neutral or an overtly hostile approach to the whole system of Indian status created by the *Indian Act*. In *Lavell*, discussed in more detail below, Laskin was merely agnostic; he did not challenge the *Indian Act* as such, merely the gender bias contained within it. Whatever rules for status the Act created for men, they should be the same for women. In *Natural Parents v. Superintendent of Child Welfare*, he again expressed neutrality in stating that a British Columbia law on adoption could not interfere with the status of Indian children when adopted by non-Indian parents.[29]

In *Attorney General of Canada v. Canard*, Laskin confronted the question of Indian status head-on.[30] Brian Dickson had written the judgment appealed from while on the Manitoba Court of Appeal, holding a section of the *Indian Act* inoperative on the basis that it contravened the equality before the law guarantee contained in section 1(b) of the Canadian Bill of Rights. The provision in question vested all authority with respect to the estates of deceased Indians in the minister of Indian Affairs. After the death of her husband in a road accident, Flora Canard tried to deal with his estate and to commence a wrongful-death suit against the party responsible, only to find that Indian Affairs had already appointed someone to do so. At the Supreme Court a majority allowed the government's appeal from Dickson's judgment in her favour.[31] In doing so, they adopted the 'valid federal objective' test, recently articulated by the Court in a case called *Burnshine*, in order to neutralize Canard's Bill of Rights argument.[32] The majority were probably motivated by a concern that the entire *Indian Act* might be invalidated if plaintiffs were allowed to succeed in cases such as *Lavell* and *Canard*. In their defence, it might be observed that the Bill of Rights had no 'reasonable limits' clause allowing the courts to uphold legislation which might appear facially discriminatory. In attempting to separate legitimate from illegitimate legislative distinctions, the majority erred strongly on the side of caution. For Laskin this was just not good enough. The obvious discrimination against spouses of aboriginal persons raised his hackles, as he observed that Parliament had put 'a legal road-block in the way of one particular racial group, placing that group in a position of inequality before the law.'[33]

This paternalistic provision certainly appeared discriminatory on its face. It is less clear whether the *Indian Act* system as a whole could survive the kind of scrutiny Laskin's powerful deployment of section 1(b) equality analysis might entail. In the Manitoba Court of Appeal, Dickson had at least sought to limit his reasoning to those provisions of the *Indian Act* outside the 'core' of Indian identity. Laskin imposed no such limitations in his reasons and even seemed to deny their validity. He restated the majority decision in *Lavell* as having decided that 'the Indian Act is a self-contained code which if it exhibits any dissonance with the Canadian Bill of Rights is justified by the very fact that Indians have been designated as a special class for which Parliament may legislate. I did not accept that view in *Lavell* and I do not accept it now, because I do not regard the mere grant of legislative power as itself authorizing Parliament to offend against [the] protections in the Canadian Bill of Rights.'[34] If Parliament wished to insulate the *Indian Act*, said Laskin, let it provide that it was to operate notwithstanding the Canadian Bill of Rights. His embrace of equality was based on an 'equality as sameness' model that would have erased all legislative distinctions between Indian and non-Indian in Canada if pursued to its logical conclusion – an end result that remains controversial in the aboriginal community today. If neither the majority nor the minority seemed to provide a satisfactory discussion of this thorny issue, it is probably because the Canadian Bill of Rights and the *Indian Act were* irreconcilable if the Bill of Rights was to be given any real force.

Laskin's lack of enthusiasm for historically based aboriginal claims was evident again in a 1979 case, *Jack v. The Queen*.[35] It dealt with a dispute over the meaning of article 13 of the 1871 Terms of Union under which British Columbia had joined Confederation, a provision that obliged the federal government to pursue a 'policy as liberal as that hitherto pursued by the British Columbia government.' After federal fisheries officials closed particular rivers to salmon fishing, a number of Indians were charged with fishing, admittedly for food. In a brief majority judgment Laskin said simply that nothing in article 13 'could possibly operate as an inhibition on federal legislative power in relation to fisheries.' In a lone dissent, Dickson went into the historical evidence in a very thorough fashion, trying to discern the policy of the colonial British Columbia government. For the first time he advanced the idea that any ambiguity in legislative or treaty texts should be resolved in favour of native peoples. He also set out the hierarchy of claims over limited fish resources that would inform his later judgment in *Sparrow v. The Queen:*[36] (1) conservation; (2) Indian food fishing; (3) non-Indian commercial fishing; and (4) non-Indian sport fishing.

Jack revealed Dickson as the intellectual father of the Court's path-breaking jurisprudence on aboriginal peoples in the 1980s and '90s. It would be interesting to know how Laskin would have responded to Dickson's reasons in a case like *Guerin*, which totally transformed the legal relationship between the federal government and aboriginal peoples in Canada. His earlier decisions suggest he would have tried to find some less dramatic way to emphasize the government's obligations to aboriginal peoples. He would likely have been attracted by a solution based on contract, which implies a relationship of equals, rather than a fiduciary relationship, with its overtones of paternalism and inequality. But then again, he might have been persuaded by the reasoning of Brian Dickson, for whom he developed great respect. The philosophical differences between the two men on this issue were probably fuelled by their respective experiences with aboriginal persons. Growing up on the prairies, and again as a judge in Manitoba, Dickson had much more direct exposure to aboriginal persons than Laskin had had. Native people occupied the fringes of society at the Lakehead, and Laskin is unlikely to have encountered them except as urban outcasts. Laskin's few decisions in this area have an air of abstraction, while Dickson's are informed by a more sympathetic and historically grounded view of aboriginal peoples.

The revival of the women's movement in the 1960s led to sweeping demands for social and legal reform throughout the Western world. The *Divorce Act, 1968*, introducing 'no-fault' divorce after a three-year separation, and the reform of the abortion laws in 1969 were two early victories in this campaign, and the appointment of the Royal Commission on the Status of Women in 1967 was a third. When the commission reported in 1970 it made almost five hundred recommendations aimed at advancing women's equality, many of which required legal change.[37] Women began entering law school in droves, creating a new generation of female lawyer-activists, and women's issues were catapulted to the front page in a way not seen since the suffrage campaigns of the 1910s. When the *Toronto Star* looked back at the events of 1973 in a year-end review, it called the year one of 'triumph and tragedy' for women.[38] The 'triumph' was the appointment of Margaret Birch as the first woman cabinet minister in Ontario, while the 'tragedy' label was fixed on two decisions of the Supreme Court: *Lavell* and *Murdoch*. These cases dealt with the rights of married women in very different contexts, and Laskin dissented in both. Although an unlikely harbinger of female emancipation, Laskin saw these opinions, along with his dissent in *Morgenthaler* the next year, lauded as major breakthroughs by women (and some men) across the country. Dickson recalled later that 'Bora ... was declared the folk hero of Canada, ... whereas the others were somewhat criticized and denigrated.'[39] In fact, Laskin thought *Lavell* and *Murdoch* had been major factors in his subsequent appointment as chief justice.[40]

In *Murdoch v. Murdoch*, the Supreme Court had to decide on the property rights of an Alberta ranching couple who had always taken title to their farms in the husband's name.[41] The doctrine of 'separate property' then in force declared such assets to belong to the named owner unless the other spouse could prove a contribution to their acquisition or maintenance. Further, the spouse had to show that any share in the asset was the result of an explicit or implicit agreement. Earlier decisions of lower courts had provided relief from the sometimes harsh consequences of separate property by finding an implicit partnership-type agreement between farming couples. Irene Murdoch argued that her labour, both in running the farm while her husband was away on business, and in working alongside him when he was home, should entitle her to a share in the farms. The circumstances propelling Irene to separate from her husband did not appear in the court proceedings. When the couple quarrelled over whether to sell their farms and start over in a different business, Alex Murdoch assaulted his wife, breaking her jaw in three places. He took her to the hospital, but on her return she found the door locked and her credit cut off at local stores. Irene worked as a cleaning woman to supplement the $200 monthly support Alex was obliged to pay, but was left with the medical bills from her fractured jaw and the $3,500 court costs from her unsuccessful court proceedings.[42] In a later divorce action, however, she received a $60,000 settlement as lump sum support.[43]

Ronald Martland earned the undying enmity of the women's movement by citing and agreeing with the trial judge's finding that Irene Murdoch's contribution was just 'what the average farm wife did' and not such as to entitle her to a share in any of the farms. Laskin, alone in dissent, disagreed with this characterization but went further: even if no agreement existed, relief might be provided by way of a constructive trust imposed to remedy the unjust enrichment the husband would otherwise enjoy. This was legally controversial, as unjust enrichment was not a widely invoked head of liability at the time, and was usually reserved for cases where a pre-existing fiduciary relationship existed, such as between a principal and agent.

Laskin acknowledged that legislative reform was probably in order, 'but the better way,' he observed, 'is not the only way.' In his view, Irene Murdoch was entitled to a share of the farm assets, the exact amount to be quantified after a reference back to the trial judge. The decision illustrates both Laskin's creativity and his sense of restraint. By employing an existing doctrine in a new context to redress a perceived injustice, Laskin innovated within parameters well understood in the common law. As in his alimony decision in the Ontario Court of Appeal, however, he did not enunciate any principle of spousal equality. The constructive trust allowed judges considerable discretion in assessing the extent of redress, and was accompanied by no presumption of equal sharing. Laskin made very clear that the new remedy was based on property law, not matrimonial law: it was 'unnecessary ... to invoke present-day thinking as to the co-equality of the spouses to support an apportionment in favour of the wife.'44 Such a radical change in the law, in Laskin's view, was best left to the legislature. Women seeking redress on the ground of unjust enrichment would have to amass clear evidence proving their non-domestic contributions to their husbands' increase in net worth – an expensive and time-consuming process in most cases. They might also encounter gender bias on the part of the virtually all-male judiciary who would be exercising a highly discretionary jurisdiction. When another prairie farm wife, Helen Rathwell, sought a half-share of properties registered in her husband's name after receiving $250 in monthly support payments, the trial judge rejected her claim with the words: 'she's not going to get it both ways ... Somebody has to defend the men from the present mode of the women's liberation movement.'45

Laskin's dissent was warmly received by the women's movement in Canada at the time, and if their spokespersons noted its essentially conservative nature they kept it to themselves. As Carol Rogerson has observed, Laskin drew a very clear line between 'extraordinary' labour such as that performed by Irene Murdoch on the farm itself, and 'ordinary house-keeping duties,' which 'might be said to be merely a reflection of the marriage bond.'46 The vast majority of wives were still engaged in 'ordinary house-keeping duties' and married to wage-earning men. Few had the opportunity to contribute to the farms or businesses of their husbands. Laskin's dissent in *Murdoch* had little to offer most women, but its psychological impact was enormous and it contributed to a growing campaign to change matrimonial property laws. The fact that even one judge on the Supreme Court of Canada could state that the labour of wives should not be taken for granted was seen as a huge step forward. By the early 1980s all provincial legislatures had taken the step Laskin had hinted they should take. They declared marriage to be a partnership with deemed equal contributions by both spouses, regardless of their form, and a presumed equal division, on marriage termination, of the principal matrimonial assets or their increase in value over the course of the marriage.

Some provinces proceeded directly to this model, but others arrived at it by stages. Both British Columbia and Ontario passed laws in the 1970s instituting only a partial marital partnership, and Laskin wrote in one case arising under each of these transitional laws. In the British Columbia case *Harper v. Harper*, the statute in question gave the courts a broad power to allocate assets in a reasonable manner between spouses on marriage termination.[47] Hazel Harper, who had borne seven children during a twenty-year 'traditional' marriage, asked for half the matrimonial home. Laskin, writing for the majority, awarded her one-third but without articulating any justification, while Estey in dissent would have given her half. In the Ontario case *Leatherdale v. Leatherdale*, the relevant Act provided for equal sharing of 'matrimonial assets' but no sharing of 'non-matrimonial assets' unless some contribution could be proved by the spouse not holding title.[48] As in *Murdoch*, Laskin refused to find that domestic labour alone could constitute a contribution to non-matrimonial assets. Even where a statute gave the court extensive powers to reorder matrimonial property relations, Laskin refused to use it to articulate a presumption of spousal equality. His legal conception of family remained fairly traditional, treating it as 'a unit of economic security for its dependants [wherein] women's domestic services ... are appropriately rewarded through an award of support' rather than a division of property.[49] Yet, 'its ideals contained a transformative potential.'[50]

The potential of Laskin's unleashing of unjust enrichment and the constructive trust in his dissent in *Murdoch* was realized within a few years. Only five years later, in another case involving a farm couple, Dickson wrote for a five-four majority upholding the claim of Helen Rathwell. It was possible to distinguish *Murdoch* because of some financial contributions made by Mrs Rathwell but, declared Dickson, 'to the extent that *Murdoch* stands for the proposition that a wife's labour cannot constitute a contribution in money's worth and to the extent that

Murdoch stands in the way of recognition of constructive trust as a powerful remedial instrument for redress of injustice, I would not, with utmost respect, follow *Murdoch*.'[51] It was still only 'extraordinary' labour that was being rewarded, but that was better than nothing. Soon the legislatures took over the job of reforming matrimonial property law, but none of the new legislation covered unmarried couples, even those who had cohabited for a lengthy period in a marital-type relationship. In *Pettkus v. Becker* in 1980, Dickson secured a six-three majority (including Laskin) for his decision awarding Rosa Becker half the assets accumulated during twenty years of cohabitation and joint efforts with her common-law husband, Lothar Pettkus.[52] In *Pettkus*, the majority declared that the doctrine of unjust enrichment and its remedial handmaiden the constructive trust were of general application in Canadian law, and not restricted to familial disputes. In a 1993 Supreme Court decision, the 'domestic/non-domestic' labour dichotomy was finally overcome, when a 'traditional' wife in a common-law relationship was awarded half the assets built up by the couple over their relationship.[53]

The second 'tragedy' noted by the *Toronto Star* in 1973 was the Supreme Court's decision in *Attorney General of Canada v. Lavell; Isaac v. Bédard*.[54] *Lavell* was the most important case involving women's rights to come before the Court since the *Persons* case in 1929, and it raised a highly charged issue: the *Indian Act*'s deprivation of native women's status (and that of their children) upon their marriage to non-Indian spouses, when native men could marry non-Indians with no loss of status. Jeannette Lavell and Yvonne Bédard had begun separate actions which were consolidated for hearing at the Court. Lavell, a member of the Wikwemikong Band of Manitoulin Island in Lake Huron, had married a non-native man and been struck from the Indian Register. Her loss of status propelled her into activism: she became one of the founding members of the Ontario Native Women's Association and later served on the executive of the Native Women's Association of Canada. Her appeal to the Federal Court of Appeal from the registrar's action was successful: Justice Thurlow, writing for the Court, applied the *Drybones* precedent to find the relevant section of the *Indian Act* inoperative. The case of Yvonne Bédard, born on the Six Nations Reserve near Brantford, was more complex. She had married a non-Indian in 1964, had two children by him, and moved off the reserve. After separating from him in 1970, Bédard returned to the reserve to live in a house left to her in her mother's will. When the band council obliged her to dispose of the property, she transferred it to her brother, who allowed her to continue to live there. The band council passed a resolution authorizing the issuance of a notice to quit to Bédard, but it had not yet been served on her when she commenced her action challenging her removal from the register. Justice Osler of the High Court of Ontario followed the Federal Court of Appeal decision in *Lavell* and held that the actions of the band council were without effect.

The fault lines of gender were clearly evident as counsel proceeded to make their arguments: male-led Indian organizations across Canada supported the attorney-general of Canada's arguments for the status quo, while a diverse range of women's organizations, both Indian and non-Indian, intervened in support of Jeannette Lavell and Yvonne Bédard. The latter included the University Women's Club of Toronto, University Women Graduates Ltd., and the North Toronto Business and Professional Women's Club. Unusually, counsel for the interveners were both women: Margaret Hyndman, Laskin's near-contemporary at Osgoode Hall in the 1930s, and Frances Smookler. This was one of the first occasions when Euro-Canadian women joined their aboriginal sisters in a national campaign to promote a cause seen as affecting all women, even though its immediate impact was felt only by aboriginal women. The issue had immense symbolic and practical significance for both sides. The 'loss-of-status' provision had been in the *Indian Act* for over a century. With housing in chronically short supply on reserves, establishing a list of band members was crucial to band governance and the allocation of benefits. A sudden expansion in the numbers of those able to claim status would have posed immense difficulties for band councils and created immediate social conflict. On the other hand, the litigation itself showed how native women's lives were subject not just to the immense power of Indian Affairs, but also to the authority of native men who seemed to work hand-in-glove with the bureaucrats to maintain the 'system.' The issue was hugely complex and not really suited to adjudication in all-or-nothing fashion by a court with little in the way of empirical evidence upon which to base its opinions. Even after section 15 of the Charter came into force and section 12 of the *Indian Act* was repealed, the particular form of the new gender-neutral definitions of status remain controversial in many quarters.

In a five-four decision, the Supreme Court allowed the appeals by the government of Canada. In his majority judgment, Roland Ritchie purported to distinguish his landmark opinion in *Drybones* by observing that 'equality before the law' meant only equality in the administration and enforcement of the law, not in the construction of legal categories under the *Indian Act*. To find such an anemic definition of equality before the law Ritchie had to go back to the writings of the nineteenth-century English jurist Albert Venn Dicey, whose approach, as academics such as Walter Tarnopolsky noted, 'is now considered outdated even by the followers of Dicey.'[55] The majority seemed unable to focus on the specific issue before them; much of Ritchie's decision was 'devoted to setting up shibboleths and then elaborately and repeatedly striking them down.'[56] Few found it convincing. Laskin, writing also for Abbott, Spence, and Hall, refused to sanction this departure from *Drybones*. The 'statutory excommunication of Indian women' was, in his view, a clear example of discrimination on the basis of sex, proscribed by the Bill of Rights. For Laskin the idea that 'a differentiation on the basis of sex is not offensive to the Canadian Bill of Rights where that differentiation operates only among Indians under the Indian Act [would] compound racial inequality even beyond the point that the *Drybones* case found unacceptable.'[57]

Laskin's sweeping application of the equality clause was not without its critics. Counsel for the government urged the Court to adopt the 'reasonable classification' test used at that time by the U.S. Supreme Court in scrutinizing legislative distinctions attacked under the equal protection clause. The majority did not need to do so because it found there to be no discrimination in any case. But Laskin rejected the U.S. test as of 'marginal relevance': 'the Canadian Bill of Rights itself enumerates prohibited classifications which the judiciary is bound to respect.' Moreover, Laskin doubted whether discrimination on the basis of sex, 'where as here it has no biological or physiological rationale, could be sustained as a reasonable classification.'[58] Walter Tarnopolsky thought Laskin was wrong to reject the 'reasonable classification' test. Clearly Parliament had the authority to define Indian status, and based on existing social practice and on gendered distinctions in many laws, it might not be unreasonable to use gender as a marker for Indian status. Laskin might well have replied that such gendered legal distinctions were themselves based on long-standing social practices now seen as discriminatory.

With new ideas about gender equality just beginning to achieve prominence, Laskin's views in *Murdoch* and *Lavell* seemed to be on the cutting edge. Certainly his 1974 dissent in the *Morgentaler* case, upholding a woman's right to decide on an abortion in consultation with her doctor, was a bold position on a highly controversial issue. His

stance on gender was always more nuanced than it was portrayed,
however. Contrasting *Murdoch* and Laskin's other family law decisions
with *Lavell* shows him as a strong proponent of gender equality in the
public sphere but not within the private sphere of the family. The
thread that runs through his family law decisions is the desire to curb
certain kinds of exploitation of wives by husbands, but not to interfere
otherwise with the dynamics of 'traditional' households. Gender was
the one place in Laskin's mental universe where the writ of modernity
did not run unimpeded. Even within the public sphere, the very large
caveat of possible 'biological or physiological rationale[s]' for differential treatment of women mentioned by Laskin in *Lavell* leads one to
wonder how he would have reacted to claims of discrimination based
on maternity. Unfortunately, Laskin was too ill to participate in what
would have been the acid test of his views on this point: *Bliss v. Attorney
General of Canada*.[59] In this unanimous – and notorious – decision by
what was still an all-male bench, the Supreme Court held that the
denial of unemployment insurance benefits to pregnant women when
they were available to other workers did not constitute sex discrimination. In sexual assault cases, Laskin's 'due process' model of criminal
justice predisposed him to favour the accused and to give short shrift to
the interests of female victims.[60] Seen from a present-day perspective,
Laskin's record on achieving equal justice for men and women seems
rather mixed. In his own day, however, Laskin's dissents in *Murdoch*,
Lavell and, after he became chief justice, *Morgenthaler* and *Canard*, were
rightly seen as ground-breaking. They encouraged legislative change in
the direction of sexual equality and emboldened women's groups to
bring other issues before the courts when the legislative route appeared
to be blocked. Although expressed in dissent, the intellectual force of
Laskin's ideas exerted a broad and persuasive influence on public
opinion at a key moment in Canadian social history.

As 1973 drew to a close Bora Laskin's status as the conscience of the
Supreme Court was secure. He was the first Supreme Court judge since
Ivan Rand retired in 1959 to possess any substantial public profile
beyond the legal profession. Only Emmett Hall was in any way compa-
rable, and his public recognition had resulted mostly from his work as a
royal commissioner than as a judge, buttressed by his dissent in the
Stephen Truscott case. Laskin seemed able to speak the language of
justice rather than the dry jargon of the law, and to embody changing
Canadian values, especially those of the young. In the public mind, his

role in Canada's judicial life mirrored Pierre Trudeau's in its political life – here was someone impatient with outdated ideas, anxious to lead Canadians into a more just and tolerant era, a person of broad understanding and large vision. Laskin was comfortable in this role, and as far as he knew it would continue indefinitely – but the next episode in his 'accidental career' was already in the making.

18

Chief Justice

In December 1973 Bora had prepared a surprise for Peggy: two weeks in Hawaii during the January recess. Morris Shumiatcher was in on the secret, and on 18 December he wrote to his friend: 'You must tell me about the hugs and kisses that Peggy will bestow upon you when you will have told her of your arrangements to go to Honolulu next month.'[1] The eighteenth was the last sitting day that term, and judgments were to be delivered on Friday the twenty-first. Then, after a week's rest, the tropical holiday beckoned. Laskin did not know that a bigger surprise awaited him: before month's end he would be chief justice of Canada.

It all happened so quickly. Chief Justice Fauteux, at seventy-three, was expected to remain in office for another two years, and had given no intimation of an early departure. Suddenly, on 19 December, he announced he would retire before Christmas. He had given a little advance warning to the government before going public, but apparently none to his colleagues apart from Martland. Pierre Trudeau, preoccupied with impending fatherhood, threw the matter into the lap of the Minister of Justice, Otto Lang. Lang had created the new position of adviser on judicial appointments that spring, and named his former executive assistant Ed Ratushny to it. By doing so, Lang intended to obtain some independent information on the candidates proposed for the many judicial vacancies constantly arising across the country. Otherwise, the minister was at the mercy of those lobbying for one candidate or another, unable to assess objectively their relative merits.[2]

Only two candidates appeared to be seriously in the running, Ronald Martland and Bora Laskin, but Ratushny found a deep polarization of opinion in his rapid sounding of professional opinion.[3] Martland had three things going for him: convention, strong support from western Canada, and a conservative view of the common law and the judicial function that appealed particularly to the older generation of professional leaders. Laskin's support was strongest among academically minded lawyers, the labour and criminal defence bar, and the younger generation. According to a firm but not invariable tradition, Martland should have succeeded Fauteux as the senior judge. The last time the convention was not respected occurred in 1924, when Francis Anglin was named chief justice instead of the more senior Lyman Duff because of Mackenzie King's concerns about Duff's excessive drinking. The media did not appear to be unduly interested in the succession, except for the Ottawa *Citizen*, which declared that Fauteux's resignation 'provides an opportunity to elevate the most brilliant of [the Court's] members, Mr. Justice Bora Laskin, to the post of chief justice – and to strengthen the liberal forces on this bench. We look for more legal brilliance, more diligence and more humanity in the judgments of our highest court.'[4]

Precedent alone was enough for many lawyers to prefer Martland, and even the iconoclastic Pierre Trudeau appeared to lean in that direction. Otto Lang had the impression that Trudeau was expecting him to recommend Martland's promotion, and would have accepted it. When Lang recommended Laskin instead, Trudeau was first intrigued, then delighted.[5] Lang was reported to have telephoned Laskin on Christmas Eve to ask if he would be willing to allow his name to go forward to Trudeau. Startled and surprised, Laskin nonetheless agreed immediately. Declining was not an option, he told a reporter later: 'that wouldn't be part of my code.'[6] Lang communicated Laskin's assent to Trudeau's office since the prime minister himself was with his wife Margaret, who was giving birth to Alexandre (Sacha), their second Christmas Day baby boy. On the twenty-seventh Trudeau telephoned Laskin with the formal offer, and that evening Bora and Peggy entertained friends at a champagne reception at their Champlain Towers penthouse before the news was made public on Friday the twenty-eighth. Laskin's abode atop one of Ottawa's most exclusive residences now mirrored his position at the pinnacle of the Canadian judiciary.

Editorial opinion in the Toronto papers was highly favourable. Geoffrey Stevens of the *Globe* called Laskin's elevation 'one of the happiest and most exciting selections made by the Trudeau Government in its 68 months in office,'[7] while Richard Gwyn of the *Toronto Star* looked to the new chief justice to fill the 'intellectual vacuum at the Supreme Court.'[8] In the wake of Laskin's highly publicized dissents in *Murdoch* and *Lavell*, the women of Canada were said to be 'quietly rejoicing.'[9] Georges Angers, writing in Quebec City's *Le Soleil*, was fairly critical of Laskin's perceived centralist bias, but found little reaction in Quebec: 'le silence du Québec, traditionnellement autonomiste, a été étonnant.' He also mentioned Laskin's liberal tendencies but observed, insightfully, that one could not expect the Supreme Court suddenly to mimic the Warren Court: 'les traditions institutionnelles canadiennes sont trop solidement enracinées pour que l'action du nouveau juge en chef puisse dépasser le cap du réformisme.'[10] Elsewhere, including the Court itself, the decision to elevate Laskin over Martland was controversial. Newspaper pundits saw Laskin's appointment variously as an attempt to politicize the Court and undermine judicial independence, a slap in the face for western Canada, a misguided endorsement of U.S.-style judicial activism, or a concession to the NDP by a minority government dependent on their support.

The reality was much simpler. Automatic promotion of the senior judge had produced no fewer than three chief justices over the past decade, all of them elderly, cautious, and unlikely to inject fresh ideas into the Court. Earlier in the century such a pattern would have evoked little comment, but the pace of change in the 1960s produced different expectations about the role of a chief justice. Paul Weiler was about to come out with *In the Last Resort*, a devastatingly critical analysis of the Court and its jurisprudence, but he had already foreshadowed its contents in article form. Otto Lang was well aware of the criticism of the Court in both academic and popular circles, and decided it was time to take a hard look at the alleged convention of promotion by seniority. He had already resisted application of the convention in the case of nominations to provincial superior courts. Addressing the Vancouver Bar Association a few months later, he disagreed categorically with the argument that a failure to appoint the senior judge as chief justice of a court compromised judicial independence: 'for us blindly to follow such an approach, would be an irresponsible abdication of our duties.' Lang saw 'no merit in artificially limiting the range of possible choices for the position of chief justice,' and reserved the right to appoint a chief justice directly from the bar. In fact, of ten chief justice appointments in the previous year (including Laskin's) only one had been the senior judge in his court.[11]

Lang himself was a career legal academic before wafting into the House of Commons on the wings of Trudeaumania in 1968. He began teaching at the age of twenty-three at the University of Saskatchewan, where Laskin's cousin Balfour had been a classmate, and in 1961 became the youngest law dean in Canadian history at twenty-nine. For Lang's generation, Laskin was a heroic figure who epitomized the same dynamic modernism in law represented by Pierre Trudeau in politics. Ed Ratushny too was predisposed to consider Laskin favourably. A student at Saskatchewan during Lang's tenure as dean, he was summoned to Ottawa as Lang's executive assistant when he joined the cabinet in 1968. Ratushny was then hired at the new University of Windsor Faculty of Law by another Saskatchewan native, Dean Walter Tarnopolsky, in 1970. With the decision on the new chief justice in the hands of three legal academics – Trudeau, Lang, and Ratushny – there was little doubt which candidate they would favour.

Lang had met with Martland to let him know the proposed course of action before the news became public, and although the judge accepted the news stoically Lang was not surprised to hear later on of his surprise and disappointment. Martland was too much of a gentleman to seek to undermine the new chief, but he remained suspicious of Laskin and never recovered from the blow to his self-esteem. In an interview a year after Laskin's death, Martland's bitterness was still painfully evident. Fauteux confided that he had recommended Martland to the prime minister as his successor, and Martland admitted to being shocked when informed by Otto Lang that he would not get the nod. 'It was an indication that certainly the government did not think much about my capacity, when they broke a long tradition to pass over me ... [I]t was a bit humiliating.' Martland interpreted the choice of Laskin as due to pressure from those who wanted 'a more American type of court' and to the vigorous criticism of his own decision in *Murdoch* the previous fall. '[A]lso, from the point of view of the Prime Minister it was no discredit to be the one who appointed the first Jewish Chief Justice.' While Martland did not criticize Laskin for taking the position when offered, he opined that 'he must have had his eye on it from the time he first went to the Ontario Court of Appeal[;] he wanted it, and if it was offered to him, I knew that he would snap it up. And that would be natural.' He confessed that '[i]t is rather unkind to say it, but I did hear from people who knew members of the Court, that the Court of Appeal was delighted when he moved on to Ottawa.'[12] John Arnup, who replaced Laskin on the Court of Appeal, denies that such sentiments existed and attributes Martland's willingness to believe such gossip to his own rivalry with Laskin.[13]

It was Martland's misfortune to embody everything Laskin had fought against for his entire adult life, and Laskin's to personify a type of legal modernism Martland found intolerable. Both were civil to each other, but the two men could never really work in harness. They stood on opposite sides of a divide that had grown into a gulf over the course of the twentieth century. For Martland, the colonial boy who won double firsts and carried off the Vinerian Prize at Oxford, loyalty to the English model remained engraved on his psyche to the end of his days. His judicial hero was Duff, whom he thought 'brilliant'; Laskin found him highly over-rated, and idolized Rand, Cardozo, and Frankfurter. When asked who he thought were the most talented of his judicial colleagues, Martland named Pigeon, Judson, and Cartwright – pointedly not Laskin. Martland distrusted legal academics and did not believe they made good judges. 'A law professor can sound off in the classroom on any subject and in any manner that he likes, and the more colourful his comments, why the better he is going to be liked by his students, and he becomes a great success.' Martland accused Laskin of a 'consciousness of intellectual superiority which develops in the classroom and ... which showed through.' With Cartwright, there had been no such 'manifestation of arrogance.' Martland saw evidence of this attitude in Laskin's comments about the decisions of lower courts: 'he was not conscious of how much hurt there could be inflicted [as] happened with some of the Court judgments reflecting on what had been done in lower tribunals, that indicated they were hardly up to par and so on. You don't do that. You shouldn't. It doesn't help anyone.'[14]

In the days following the announcement of Laskin's promotion, rumours circulated of possible resignations at the Court. Two judges were 'reliably reported' to have considered quitting.[15] If true, Martland and Ritchie would have been the obvious candidates, but it is doubtful if these reports were more than speculation. Roland Ritchie was close to Martland and might have been very upset by the rupture of tradition, but it would have been an expensive protest: he had another year to go before reaching the fifteen years' service required to retire on full pension. What would the resignations of Martland and Ritchie have achieved in any case, except an opportunity for Trudeau to pack the Court with even more like-minded candidates? The rumours likely arose through exaggeration of stories of discontent at the Court, but they are of interest nonetheless as illustrative of the difficult atmosphere prevailing as Laskin assumed office.

As the New Year dawned, Ottawa was abuzz with a sense of renewal. A new baby at Sussex Drive, a new chief justice, two new Supreme Court judges appointed on 1 January, and soon a new governor-general as well. Roland Michener's last official act was the swearing in of the new chief justice on the morning of 7 January. The ceremony at the time was very brief and held in private at Government House. Barely ten people were in attendance: the prime minister, the governor-general and two of his staff, a handful of cabinet ministers, and the clerk of the privy council Gordon Robertson. At noon Laskin and his executive secretary Benoît Godbout were summoned to the governor-general's study. Just before his arrival Michener had signed an instrument of advice appointing Laskin, now titled 'the Right Honourable,' to be a member of the Queen's Privy Council for Canada. The candidate then put his hand on a Bible and swore an oath of office, an oath of allegiance, and the privy councillor's oath, repeating after each one, 'So help me God.' A few signatures later, and it was all over. When he emerged Laskin made a few remarks to reporters on a favourite theme: pay more attention to the work of the Court, he admonished. When asked whether he considered himself a 'liberal,' Laskin dodged the question and agreed with Trudeau, who suggested the new chief justice did not believe in such labels. That evening the Laskins attended a state dinner for the retiring vice-regal couple.[16] The one flaw in the proceedings was a misprint on Laskin's instrument of appointment, which showed the year as 1873 instead of 1973. Some years later Laskin pointed this out to his Caribbean friend Sir Fred Phillips when he was visiting Ottawa. He asked Laskin what he proposed to do about the error. 'Absolutely nothing,' he replied. 'In years to come posterity will be able to judge the inefficiency of the bureaucracy in such matters in the twentieth century. But for now, I will apply the maxim, *falsa demonstratio non nocet.*'[17]

A week later it was Laskin's turn to swear in Jules Léger as the new incumbent. Unlike Laskin's own swearing in, the pageantry attached to the induction of a new governor-general is public and elaborate, though only a few hundred spectators, mostly civil servants, braved the cold to take part in the event. Laskin was met by government limousine at Champlain Towers, in which he made his way to the Peace Tower accompanied by a police escort; Peggy was chauffeured separately.

Standing at the top of the steps below the Peace Tower, Laskin received a general salute from the Guard of Honour before entering the rotunda of Parliament. He was then conducted to the chambers of the Speaker of the Senate by the Gentleman Usher of the Black Rod, where the swearing-in ceremony began at 11:00 a.m. with two trumpet fanfares and two twenty-one-gun salutes. Ronald Martland administered the oath to the new governor-general, though it is not clear whether this was the normal procedure or an attempt by Laskin to give his disappointed rival a prominent role on this occasion.[18]

The new governor-general came from a distinguished, cultured, and deeply spiritual Quebec family; his younger brother Paul-Émile, named Cardinal Léger in 1953, gave up his position as archbishop of Montreal in 1967 to pursue missionary work in Africa. Jules Léger had studied law at Montreal and the Sorbonne before entering upon a diplomatic career crowned by ambassadorial postings in Europe and Mexico. His remarks after his swearing in might well serve as a capsule history of Canadian law and indeed of Bora Laskin's own approach to law. Observing that Canada has been formed and sometimes deformed by English, French, and American influences, he said, '[i]n the past, we have had to yield to them, because the strength to resist was not forthcoming in a young and scattered people, disunited and hungry for new technology. But now we have the strength, the numbers and the self-confidence to choose what suits us, to assimilate it and give it originality, thus creating a civilization of many cultures – the only kind that can survive in the world today – as we learn that we need very little gasoline to explore the highways of the soul.'[19] As both academic and judge, Bora Laskin had shown himself willing to turn away from acquired habits and ideas, to choose from among different legal traditions what was necessary for a changing Canada, and to impress upon Canadian law the stamp of originality. In welcoming the Queen's new representative, Trudeau picked up Léger's reference to the recent oil crisis, noting that threats to the natural environment had convinced Canadians 'that squandering material resources is not a luxury of the Canadian way of life – but a threat to it.' In the years ahead the Supreme Court would make its first decisions involving what was only just beginning to be called environmental law.

The role and many of the duties of the chief justice of Canada are prescribed by convention rather than law. The *Supreme Court Act* merely states that the chief justice of the Supreme Court shall be styled the chief justice of Canada. It does not say that while in the sanctum of the Court the chief justice is merely first among equals, the chief justice plays a considerably more elevated role when representing the Court to the outside world. After leading the relatively anonymous and monkish life of a puisne judge of the Supreme Court, the transition to the much more high-profile role of chief justice can be somewhat jarring. The incumbent occupies the third position in the Table of Precedence, after the governor-general and the prime minister, far above the puisne judges, who rank below cabinet ministers, ambassadors, and ecclesiastical dignitaries. Formal distinctions between the chief justice and his colleagues are tangible but hardly invidious. Since 1968 the chief justice has been styled 'the Right Honourable,' in contrast to the justices who are merely 'Honourable.'[20] Chief justices, but not the puisne judges, are sworn as privy councillors.[21] The chief justice was entitled to a salary of $47,000 in 1974, $5,000 higher than that of his colleagues, though this would rise dramatically to $65,000 effective 1 April 1975, with the puisnes receiving $60,000. Neither the formal nor the informal distinctions were important to most of Laskin's colleagues but they did rankle with some, such as Louis-Philippe de Grandpré and his successor Yves Pratte. Both thought a justice of the Supreme Court should occupy a more elevated place in Ottawa society, and wanted the chief justice to share around among his colleagues the invitations that came his way.[22] The most important statutory duty of the chief justice of Canada, aside from presiding over the Supreme Court itself, is to chair the Canadian Judicial Council, the disciplinary body composed of the chief justices of all Canadian superior courts. The chief justice is also *ex officio* the chair of the Order of Canada, and presides over the selection process.

In becoming chief justice, Bora Laskin became titular head of a staff of approximately sixty, but the registrar and deputy registrar were effectively the chief managers of the staff complement. Laskin had to deal with three registrars: François des Rivières until 1977, then Gérard Bertrand for 1977–8, and finally Bernard Hofley.[23] Laskin was not especially interested in administration and was content to allow the registrar to continue with established routines. The staff included ten secretaries to the justices, nine law clerks, nine court attendants, library staff, and registrar's office staff, including those responsible for the production of the *Supreme Court Reports*. There was an employee with the title of executive secretary to the chief justice, but the position appeared to be a sinecure. The real power in the chief justice's office was Micheline Rochon, who combined the roles of executive assistant, secretary, translator, and gatekeeper. Given Laskin's own lack of interest in administrative matters and Ms Rochon's capable nature and unshakeable loyalty, his reliance on her had its positive side, but sometimes it was difficult to know where Bora Laskin ended and Ms Rochon began. She became known as Madame Justice Rochon within the Court, partly out of affection, partly out of exasperation; in the later years of Laskin's illness she would become fiercely protective of him.

The office occupied by the chief justice is undoubtedly one of the most desirable in Ottawa; its magnificent location, warm wood panelling, and elegantly understated furnishings combine to produce a suitably contemplative ambience. Octagonal in shape, it occupies the northeast corner of the second floor, facing both the Ottawa River and Parliament Hill. The warmth of the interior offices contrasts sharply with both the enormous marble-columned entrance lobby and the severe exterior of the Supreme Court building. The rigorous façade of the granite edifice designed by Ernest Cormier is barely relieved by several narrow windows and a few small gables poking out of the copper roof. The vast lawn, the monumental steps leading into the building, the intimidating lobby – all seem designed to evoke awe before the lofty detachment of Justice. Previous occupants of the chief justice's office seem to have relished the insularity provided by their physical surroundings. Bora Laskin would be the first to try to establish some direct connection with the citizenry served by the Court, to make it truly a court 'of and for Canadians' rather than a distant symbol.

Term began on Tuesday, 22 January, and more ceremonials attended the swearing in of two new judges. With two Quebec vacancies to fill, Trudeau was able to plant one foot firmly on either side of the great gulf separating Laskin and Martland. Jean-Marie Philémon Joseph Beetz represented the Laskin tradition: Beetz was a legal scholar, professor for twenty years at the faculty of law at the Université de Montréal and its dean from 1968–70, and had been special constitutional adviser to Pierre Trudeau before his appointment to the Quebec Court of Appeal early in 1973. Laskin and Beetz had met numerous times through the Canadian Association of Law Teachers. Fifteen years younger than Laskin, Beetz noted later that he and his generation of academics regarded Laskin 'comme un pionnier et un modèle, et même comme un héros, donnant l'exemple de la fermeté de conviction, du courage, de la générosité, du sacrifice, de l'excellence et de la science la plus haute.'[24] Erudite, profoundly cultured, and extraordinarily capable in both official languages, Beetz's spoken French was so vivid and exquisite that interpreters sometimes despaired of conveying its richness. Beetz had a reputation as a fairly strong Quebec nationalist in the early 1960s but had gravitated more and more into Trudeau's orbit as the decade progressed; even so, he and Laskin would often disagree on matters touching the constitutional division of powers.

Louis-Philippe de Grandpré was the choice of the practising bar of Quebec, having been president of the bars of Montreal and Quebec in 1968 and 1969 and president of the Canadian Bar Association in 1972–3. A career litigator, he had appeared often before the Supreme Court and knew many of the judges fairly well. Gérald Fauteux and Louis-Philippe Pigeon had persuaded him that a seat on the Supreme Court would provide a fitting conclusion to his brilliant career as an advocate when Ed Ratushny sounded him out in the fall of 1973 about a possible appointment. Unfortunately he found the life of a Supreme Court judge entirely different from his expectations and lasted less than four years before resigning. His relations with Laskin may be guessed from his words of praise for Gérald Fauteux, whose judicial opinions possessed 'moins de philosophie et plus de droit' than those of others.[25] De Grandpré was not impressed with legal academics to begin with, and felt especially irked at what he perceived to be Laskin's relegation of judges with a practical background to second-class status at the Court.

In addition to welcoming the two new judges, the Court released a decision that seemed to illustrate the promise of what would soon come to be called the Laskin Court. *Thorson v. Attorney General of Canada* dealt with the question of a citizen's standing to challenge the constitutionality of legislation.[26] The challenger in this case was not exactly Jane Q. Public. Joseph Thorarinn Thorson was a Manitoba lawyer of Icelandic heritage who had been a Rhodes Scholar, dean of law at Manitoba in the 1920s, and a minister in Mackenzie King's government during the war before being appointed president (chief justice) of the Exchequer Court in 1942. He had served as the last ad hoc judge of the Supreme Court of Canada on several occasions in 1944 and wrote a decision for the Court.[27] Mandatorily retired in 1964 after twenty-one years of judicial service, Thorson returned to practice and had argued his own case before the Supreme Court at the age of eighty-four. Thorson was notorious for two things while a judge: intolerable delays in rendering judgments, and outspoken pronouncements on political issues. When he proudly sent to John Diefenbaker a newspaper clipping reporting his remarks at a public meeting in 1961 opposing the stationing of nuclear-equipped weapons in Canada, the prime minister alerted the minister of justice. An exasperated Davie Fulton wrote to Thorson to express surprise at his public comments 'on matters so closely connected with government policy,' and suggested 'that a more fruitful area of endeavour would be to concentrate on such judgments as you may have in arrears at the present time, which I am informed, include cases heard as long ago as 1958.'[28] Now Thorson had brought a taxpayer class action to contest the constitutional validity of the *Official Languages Act* and the legality of the expenditures made thereunder.

The existing law on standing was clear: a citizen had to show exceptional prejudice distinct from the impugned law's effects on the general population in order to be granted standing to challenge it. This strict rule, based on the supposed 'grave inconvenience and public disorder' that would result from a more liberal rule, was embodied in a 1924 Supreme Court decision of Justice Duff called *Smith v. Attorney General of Ontario*.[29] The trial judge dismissed Thorson's claim for standing and the Ontario Court of Appeal did not even call on counsel for the government. Laskin saw clearly the problem involved in applying the existing law: by its very nature the *Official Languages Act* could not be said to cause exceptional prejudice to any individual or class of persons, thus forever insulating it from judicial review. He did not exactly overrule Duff's decision, but distinguished it, cast doubt on its reasoning, and then formulated a new rule. Laskin noted that the *Official Languages Act* was not a regulatory statute such as the *Canada Temperance Act*, which the claimant had sought to challenge in *Smith*. The *Official Languages Act* 'creates no offences and imposes no penalties; there are no duties laid upon members of the public.'[30] No one could thus suffer 'exceptional prejudice' as required by *Smith*. Laskin then queried Duff's reasoning, based as it was on English authorities inapplicable in a federal state such as Canada. Unlike England, where the doctrine of supremacy of Parliament rules, in Canada all legislation must conform to the constitution: 'it would be strange and, indeed, alarming, if there was no way in which a question of alleged excess of legislative power, a matter traditionally within the scope of the judicial process, could be made the subject of adjudication.'[31] In a typically discursive opinion, Laskin ranged over American and Australian precedents (both jurisdictions had recently liberalized their rules on standing in taxpayer suits) in addition to English and Canadian ones. He did not throw open the floodgates entirely: there would be no automatic right to standing, rather a broad judicial discretion to grant it where there was a 'justiciable issue.' Laskin did not elaborate on how justiciability should be assessed, leaving that for further development by case law.

One writer has called the *Thorson* decision 'the first clearly declared, and one of the most pronounced, law reform decisions rendered by the Supreme Court of Canada.'[32] Delivered on the opening day of the first term of Laskin's chief justiceship, the timing could not have been more perfect. Under Laskin's guidance, the Court seemed to reach out to Canadians, to promise more access to its process by ordinary citizens. What is most surprising about *Thorson* is that Laskin secured a six-three majority for his shake-up of the law. In a short dissenting opinion, Judson (joined by Abbott and Fauteux) said Duff's 1924 decision was controlling – period. Why Martland and Ritchie signed on to Laskin's judgment is something of a mystery, especially given Martland's near-worship of Duff, but presumably Laskin's careful attempt to distinguish rather than overrule *Smith* was found to be persuasive. *Thorson* made waves beyond Canadian shores, a development of which Laskin was very proud. The English Court of Appeal referred to *Thorson* briefly in liberalizing the rules on standing in 1976,[33] while a year later Lord Denning embraced it enthusiastically in *Gouriet v. Union of Post Office Workers.*[34]

In the end, Thorson won a Pyrrhic victory. In a similar case launched by the notoriously Francophobic mayor of Moncton, Leonard Jones, the Supreme Court of Canada unanimously upheld the validity of the *Official Languages Act*, with Laskin writing for the Court.[35] Undaunted, Thorson went on to argue his last case before the Supreme Court at the age of eighty-seven, again losing in a unanimous decision dismissing an appeal from the $1 million tax reassessment of a former Manitoba MP and MLA.[36]

Determined to provide a good example, Laskin set himself a punishing pace during his first year in office. He sat on ninety cases in calendar 1974 and wrote in nearly half of them – forty-four decisions – the highest number he would ever author in a single year. During this year the Court's most important case was unquestionably *Morgentaler v. The Queen.*[37] The appeal was unusual in the amount of public attention it attracted, in the number of interveners (six) the Court had allowed to participate, and in the nature of the arguments made by Dr Morgentaler's counsel. In all respects *Morgentaler* looked forward to a new era in the history of the Supreme Court, one in which it would be more fully engaged in issues of major import to Canadian citizens. On the first day of the four-day hearing in early October, eighty spectators jammed into a courtroom designed for forty, while two red-coated Mounties kept a large overflow crowd at bay in the lobby. One intrepid reporter in the courtroom 'pulled a folding camp stool from a bag and used it throughout the afternoon.'[38]

Dr Henry Morgentaler, a Polish-born Holocaust survivor, had admittedly performed six to seven thousand abortions in his free-standing Montreal clinic without the authorization of a hospital therapeutic abortion committee. Performing an abortion remained a criminal offence, but a 1969 Criminal Code amendment by the Trudeau government provided a defence where such a committee had certified that a continuation of the pregnancy would endanger the life or health of the mother. Unable to raise this defence, Morgentaler's lawyer pleaded three others: a violation of equality before the law under section 1(b) of the Canadian Bill of Rights; the common law defence of necessity; and section 45 of the Criminal Code, which exempted from criminal responsibility anyone performing a surgical operation if the same was done with reasonable care and skill and it was 'reasonable to perform the operation, having regard to the state of health of the person at the time ... and to all the circumstances of the case.' The trial judge had left the last two defences to the jury, who acquitted. The Quebec Court of Appeal ruled that there was no evidence to go to the jury, and substituted a conviction. Its right to do so, as well as the correctness of its decision on the merits, was challenged by Morgentaler.

The first item of business was a challenge by Morgentaler's lawyer, Claude-Armand Sheppard, to the presence of Justice Louis-Philippe de Grandpré on the panel. In view of recent public anti-abortion statements made by the justice prior to his appointment, Sheppard suggested there was at least an appearance of bias and requested the judge to recuse himself. De Grandpré did not appear during these discussions and after a forty-minute adjournment Laskin announced that he and the other seven judges found no impropriety in his joining them. Laskin's brief judgment tried to draw a bright line between a judge's views on the morality of abortion and its legality, one Morgentaler's supporters were unlikely to find convincing.

Morgentaler initially expressed optimism about the outcome of the court decision, but his views shifted when the Court announced that counsel for the province of Quebec did not need to reply to the arguments on the Bill of Rights presented by Sheppard and two of the interveners, the Canadian Civil Liberties Association and the Foundation for Women in Crisis. The Court had agreed that these arguments could not succeed, and Laskin would explain the reasoning of the Court in what was otherwise a dissenting judgment on his part. Sheppard had tried to argue that the vast disparity in access to abortion services across Canada amounted to a denial of equality before the law, but to accept this, Laskin said, would involve the courts in 'supervising the administrative efficiency of legislation [and] evaluating the regional or national organization of its administration.' This they could not do 'in the absence of any touchstone in the legislation itself which would indicate a violation of s. 1(b).' Sheppard also tried to draw on the reasoning of the U.S. Supreme Court in *Roe v. Wade*, decided the previous year, to inform the interpretation of the Bill of Rights, but Laskin resisted this in view of the different constitutional arrangements in the two countries. While Laskin was more receptive to Bill of Rights arguments than most of his colleagues, he was most likely to accept them where obvious infringements of traditional criminal law safeguards were involved, or where legislation itself created different standards of treatment for different classes of persons, as in *Lavell*. The arguments being made in *Morgentaler* were highly sophisticated compared to those previously brought before the Court in Bill of Rights cases. They would see more success in the post-Charter era, not least in the second round of Morgentaler litigation which resulted in the invalidation of the Criminal Code provisions dealing with abortion.[39]

While rejecting Morgentaler's Bill of Rights arguments, Laskin was receptive to the other defences advanced and he also deprecated the Quebec Court of Appeal's substitution of a conviction for the jury acquittal. While admitting the Court of Appeal had the power to do so, Laskin believed it should not be invoked except in the most extraordinary situation. No one, he observed, had been able to produce a single previous instance of a court having exercised the power. Initially, it appeared Laskin's views would attract a majority of the Court, probably all the judges except Martland and de Grandpré. Then Brian Dickson began to have second thoughts. He feared the highly subjective aspects of the necessity defence, and reluctantly agreed with Pigeon that the Criminal Code gave the Quebec Court of Appeal the power to substitute a guilty verdict for a jury acquittal; he chose not to interrogate the limits of that power. Dickson's doubts became the nucleus of the majority decision, leaving Laskin in the minority with Spence and, somewhat surprisingly, Judson.[40]

With regard to the defence of necessity Laskin concluded, contrary to the Quebec Court of Appeal, that there was sufficient evidence to go to a jury. Necessity has never been precisely defined in the common law, but encompasses the idea that breaking the law is sometimes justified in an urgent situation to avoid an immediate physical harm. In framing his decision on this point, Laskin reviewed in some detail the circumstances of the young woman whose abortion was the subject of the charge. Verona Robinson was 'a twenty-six year old unmarried female who had come to Canada from a foreign country [Sierra Leone] in 1972 on a student visa. She was without family or close friends in Canada, ineligible to take employment and also ineligible for Medicare benefits ... Throughout the period following her apprehension and the confirmation of her pregnancy, and until the abortion performed by the appellant, she was anxious, unable to eat or sleep properly, prone to vomiting and quite depressed.'[41] Robinson had tried unsuccessfully to get an appointment for an abortion at five different Montreal hospitals, and had finally got an appointment for a date two weeks after she met Dr Morgentaler, though she did not disclose that to him.

The Court of Appeal had been of the view that to make out the defence of necessity Morgentaler had to show that it was impossible for Robinson to get a lawful abortion; in view of the scheduled appointment, there was no impossibility. For Laskin, this ignored the 'evidence of the accused that he feared that the pregnant woman would do something foolish unless she was given immediate professional medical attention to relieve her condition and her anxiety. The jury was entitled ... to consider this evidence as raising an emergency situation in the light of the fact that the woman was a friendless stranger in this country, adrift more or less in an unfamiliar urban locality.'[42] Under these circumstances it was for the jury to say whether the harm to be avoided was immediate and physical and whether the situation was urgent enough to make a possible resort to a hospital abortion ineffective to avert it.

Laskin was here employing a technique that would later be dignified with the name of 'contextualism.' In effect he was trying to situate himself as precisely as possible in the position of both Robinson and Morgentaler, and inviting the reader to do the same, in order to ask, 'under these circumstances, what would you do?' For Laskin, the law had to be sensitive to the realities of the situation in which the parties found themselves, making a careful assessment of the facts imperative. Pigeon did not refer to any of the evidence, while Dickson merely reproduced portions of the transcript rather than trying to articulate Robinson's plight in his own words, as Laskin did. In light of the future hospital appointment, Dickson conceded only that there was 'some evidence of urgency' as time passed, but no evidence that it was impossible for Robinson to get an abortion. He thus took a more stringent view of the defence of necessity than Laskin. For Dickson, it was very difficult to get past his visceral reaction that Morgentaler had broken the law plain and simple, and had to be brought to account if respect for the law was to be preserved. Respect for the law was very high up on Laskin's list of values but it had to be reconciled with his modernist quest for responsive law. His re-articulation of the defence of necessity was aimed precisely at effecting that reconciliation. Another factor that probably played a role for Laskin was his traditional respect for professional expert opinion, itself an aspect of his modernism. Here a duly qualified physician possessed of vast experience in assessing the state of women in Robinson's situation had given evidence which, if accepted, showed that he believed she was in a desperate state and at risk to 'do something foolish.' For Laskin this was not a mere subjective opinion, as it seemed to be for Dickson, but a professional opinion based on experience and observation, one that deserved to go to the jury.

When the decision was released in March 1975 the majority decision came in for no little criticism, mainly for acquiescing in the overturning of the jury verdict. In retirement Dickson himself agreed that this had been unwise and the Court would have done better to order a new trial.[43] Parliament soon amended the Criminal Code to remove the power of courts of appeal to substitute convictions for jury acquittals. Morgentaler was tried on two subsequent occasions but acquitted both times by juries, and the new Parti Québécois government announced late in 1976 that it would cease to enforce the federal abortion law. Two commentators were rather prescient: the *Globe and Mail* urged Parliament to 'clean up the abortion law by taking it right out of the Criminal Code,'[44] while Claude-Armand Sheppard was only a decade out when he predicted that 'in five years, the offence [Morgentaler] was jailed for will not be on the books.'[45] Bora Laskin might well have declined to go this far, but when the second Morgentaler case came before the Court he was not there to provide an opinion.

The year 1974 had more surprises in store. On 8 June, less than six months after Laskin had sworn in the country's twenty-first governor-general, Jules Léger suffered a severe stroke. He was confined to hospital until the nineteenth but it was clear from the outset that he would not be capable of exercising any official functions for some time. While the chief justice and his colleagues can depute for the governor-general for some matters, such as giving the royal assent to legislation, the deputy cannot open Parliament or perform certain other state functions. When the governor-general is incapacitated or expected to be out of the country for a lengthy period, the appointment of an administrator is required. The protocol people at Rideau Hall were in a tizzy. The 1947 Letters Patent constituting the office of governor-general apparently provided for no discretion; Laskin should have been sworn in immediately as administrator once Léger's incapacity was apparent, but the government dithered until 2 July.[46]

Léger's illness could not have come at a worse time. Laskin was still a novice as Chief Justice, and was trying to keep up his accustomed pace of hearings and opinion writing in addition to his new administrative tasks. The last thing he needed was the drain of additional duties, ceremonial or not. These began even before the official swearing in with the visit of the Queen Mother on 25 June. Laskin welcomed the royal arrival in Toronto as she descended from her white Boeing 707 in the pelting rain, and saw her off six days later.[47] Did he reflect on the first time his orbit had intersected with hers? In May 1939 Laskin was hanging around the University of Toronto, with no real job and rather uncertain prospects, as the King and Queen were delivered by limousine to Hart House for a gala luncheon before being whisked away to continue their tour. Their next stop was Ottawa, where the Queen laid the cornerstone of the new Supreme Court of Building. Thirty-five years later, Bora Laskin presided in that building as chief justice of Canada, and he greeted the Queen Mother as the embodiment of the country.

More important duties loomed on the horizon. There was a definite possibility that Laskin would have to exercise the one remnant of political power in the hands of the governor-general: deciding which leader should be asked to form a new government when an election fails to produce a majority for any party. The country was in the midst of an electoral campaign, with 8 July set as polling day. Trudeau's Liberals had a minority government, David Lewis's New Democratic Party held the balance of power, and Stanfield's Conservatives formed a strong opposition. Morris Shumiatcher teased Laskin afterwards that he had feared another King-Byng constitutional crisis, but the Liberals' clear majority in the election obviated any such scenario. Shumiatcher regretted that he had not run in a local seat, then mused wistfully: 'with the Liberals in office and a seat opening on our Court of Appeal in the fall, I may yet be a candidate for a seat that I should find more to my liking.' Laskin agreed that he would be a good candidate but made no undertaking to plead his friend's cause.[48]

Just as the Hawaiian vacation evaporated with the sudden elevation to the chief justiceship, so the Laskins' summer plans were thrown askew with the new state responsibilities. A trip to England, the Laskins' favourite vacation spot, had to be put off. They were able to steal only three days of holiday when attending the meeting of the International Bar Association in Vancouver in late July – Bora was needed back in Ottawa to swear in the new cabinet ministers. In mid-August, with summer on the wane, Laskin wrote that he and Peggy hoped to get away to New Hampshire for a few days.[49] It was not until January that they managed to escape to Arizona for a proper vacation.

Having sworn in the new government in the summer, it was Laskin's duty to preside over the opening of Parliament in September. Canada had never had a Jewish governor-general, so no one noticed that the date set for the event, 26 September, fell on Yom Kippur. When Laskin protested he would be unable to officiate on that day, the event was moved to Monday the thirtieth.[50] Normally the governor-general would arrive in an open landau on (with any luck) a sunny fall morning, enter the House of Commons, and read the Speech from the Throne. As the day approached, however, the authorities grew nervous about the possible presence of a group of native protesters. A group calling itself the Native People's Caravan had left Vancouver on 15 September, proclaiming its intention to cross Canada and arrive at the opening of Parliament in order to present native grievances to the government. The Caravan leaders had spoken only in terms of peaceful petitioning, but the presence of members of the radical American Indian Movement (AIM) put the RCMP on edge.[51] No doubt they also had in mind the invasion of Parliament by striking railway workers not long before.

The emergence of native militancy was considered by police to be the greatest security threat in North America in the early 1970s. Many clashes occurred in the United States between elected tribal governments, supported by the state and sometimes maintained in power through corrupt means, and a revived traditionalist force that found expression in AIM. The occupation of the village of Wounded Knee, South Dakota, by Sioux traditionalists and their AIM supporters led to a three-month blockade by the FBI and two deaths in the spring of 1973. The stand-down was peaceful but federal authorities had been on the verge of ending the siege by invasive means.[52] Similar tensions arose in Canada as well. In the summer of 1974 blockades were erected in

Kenora, Ontario and Cache Creek, British Columbia, by traditionalist 'warrior societies' as native people turned increasingly to direct action to dramatize their situation. These actions were seen as successful, but native leaders believed an appeal to the public would be more effective if pursued through peaceful means. Thus emerged the Native People's Caravan, modelled in part on the On To Ottawa trek by the unemployed forty years before.

Late on the evening of the twenty-ninth between one and two hundred Caravaners, men, women and children, arrived and occupied the empty Carbide Mills Building on Victoria Island in the Ottawa River. They awoke to a cold clear morning and began their mile-long march to present their petition to Parliament. Along the way they were joined by Montagnais people from Quebec who came to protest the lack of progress on the James Bay treaty, and by members of the Communist Party of Canada (Marxist-Leninist). The protesters first met a line of RCMP officers about fifty metres in front of the entrance to the Centre Block. After some scuffling they managed to break through in an attempt to bring their petition to the main entrance, but the RCMP then re-established the line. They stood facing the demonstrators four men deep, arms locked, creating a *cordon sanitaire* within which the traditional parliamentary ritual could proceed unimpeded, albeit tinged with the surreal. The music of the Canadian Forces Band leading the honour guard mingled with the sound of native drumming and chanting as all awaited the arrival of the Administrator of Canada. The open landau had been dispensed with, and Laskin emerged from the governor-general's limousine to review the guard from a red-carpeted pedestal. As the salute ended, 'the grim-faced Chief Justice turned quickly and made his way into the Parliament Buildings,' accompanied by Peggy and escorted by two RCMP officers.[53] While he read the Speech from the Throne inside the House of Commons, the protesters made their own speeches outside and demanded a meeting with the prime minister. Their grievances have a depressing ring thirty years later: inadequate health services, substandard educational facilities, deplorable housing conditions, and over-representation of native people in prisons and mental institutions.

No one came to meet with the Caravaners, but when Laskin emerged from Parliament they hoped he would speak to them. Instead, he ignored them – constitutionally, he could do nothing else. The band struck up 'God Save the Queen,' but was drowned out by a renewed chorus of chanting, drumming, and booing. As the Laskins drove off, the crowd surged forward, throwing the front line against the barricades and precipitating a violent reaction by the police, who included a fully equipped riot squad. Some natives replied with sticks and stones but most were unarmed and suffered a severe drubbing. Caravan leaders accused the RCMP of fomenting the melée as payback for Kenora and Cache Creek, in an effort 'to intimidate us, to break our spirit, to teach us a lesson, and to drive off non-native support.'[54] If this was the intention of the RCMP, it backfired; many observers saw the protesters as victims rather than aggressors, while the next day's *Toronto Star* and *Ottawa Citizen* called for an independent inquiry into the incident.

As one whose entire life had been devoted to the peaceful resolution of disputes, for whom the words 'decorum' and 'civility' held vital meaning, Bora Laskin could not but recoil at the sight of violence at the symbolic heart of the Canadian body politic. Undoubtedly he had his own ideas about where responsibility for this debacle lay, but shared them only with family and possibly a few intimates. In contrast to all the causes Laskin had been associated with over the years, where progress through the democratic process had been dramatic, that of the native people of Canada had never known such success. Native people had been peacefully petitioning for redress of their grievances since well before Confederation, and had precious little to show for it. Governments showered money on every conceivable purpose in the 1960s, and the general standard of living rose by leaps and bounds, yet the position of the native people seemed static or worse, their legitimate claims unaddressed. The Native Caravaners appear not to have come to Parliament Hill with violent intentions, but without the dramatic confrontations of the 1970s it is doubtful whether native rights would have been guaranteed in the *Constitution Act* of 1982. The opinion of the Supreme Court in *Calder* had provided for the first time some solid legal basis for the claims of native people. The Native Caravan and associated protests tried to create the political will to capitalize on that victory, and for once they had history on their side. The first demand of the Caravaners was that 'the hereditary and treaty rights of all Native Peoples in Canada, including Indian, Metis, Non-status and Inuit, must be recognized.' That demand, in almost those words, became part of the patriation package in 1981 and found expression as section 35 of the *Constitution Act*, 1982.

After six months of ceremonial functions added to his already heavy workload as chief justice, 'His Excellency' was undoubtedly glad to return the reins of state to Jules Léger on 6 December. At an age when most people are wistfully contemplating retirement, Bora Laskin had just experienced what was probably the most demanding year of his life. To all outward appearances he had thrived on it, and he was enjoying a honeymoon period with the media. Laskin kept up his usual rate of dissents (about one-fifth of all cases he sat on), but aside from his high-profile dissent in *Morgentaler*, another in *Law Society of Upper Canada v. French* (discussed below), and some ongoing disagreements about the use of the Bill of Rights in criminal cases, many of Laskin's dissents in this year involved points of interpretation on which reasonable people might differ, rather than a fundamental clash of values. Those clashes were most likely to arise in cases raising federalism issues, and by chance none was heard in 1974. Ironically, the rate of Laskin's dissents declined after 1974 but when he did differ with his colleagues in the later 1970s, passionate disagreements over the division of powers or civil liberties were usually at play.

19

The Laskin Court

With his first year as chief justice behind him, Laskin's second was in some ways easier. He was no longer the administrator of Canada, and, more importantly, the long-sought amendment to the *Supreme Court Act* giving the Court control over its own docket came into force on 27 January 1975.[1] With a few exceptions, the Court would now have to hear appeals only in cases where a panel of three judges found that an issue of sufficient public or legal importance had arisen. The Court still heard 160 cases in 1975, but Laskin sat on only half of them (seventy-seven), and wrote in only twenty-eight. After peaking at forty-six judgments in 1974, his annual production would remain in the high twenties thereafter. With the new leave system fully operational in 1976, the number of cases heard declined significantly, to an average of 121 per year from the court years 1976–7 to 1981–2 inclusive, then to 89 and 77 in 1982–3 and 1983–4.[2] The decline would have been steeper if not for Laskin himself, who often insisted on bringing up a case out of personal interest – much to the chagrin of his colleagues.[3] The lower number of cases heard did not reduce the work of the Court substantially, however, because of Laskin's practice of sitting with a full bench or a bench of seven, rather than the quorum of five. The larger bench was partly a response to the greater importance of the cases heard, but it also precluded Laskin from being charged with manipulating the composition of smaller panels. With these changes, the Court became much more a public law court. Criminal law and administrative law would form the bulk of its docket, with private law matters attracting attention only when significant differences between provincial courts of appeal required resolution.[4] Constitutional law appeals remained infrequent in absolute numbers but were virtually guaranteed leave when it was sought.

After taking virtually no vacation in 1974, the Laskins were able to take several in 1975: ten days in Arizona in January, two weeks in Florida in April, a few days in Vancouver in the spring when Laskin received an honorary degree from Simon Fraser University, a long-postponed return to England in July, and several days in Quebec City in August.[5] The Canadian Bar Association annual meeting was held there that summer, and Laskin attended along with all his confreres to mark the centenary of the Supreme Court. Official events took up much of his time, but he and Peggy found time for a private dinner with the Shumiatchers. Morris found his friends looking rested and relaxed after an apparently enjoyable summer.[6] In the fall, however, Laskin was back to his accustomed routine of working every night except one.[7]

Back in Ottawa, Laskin was preoccupied with the centenary celebrations to be held on 26–7 September. Apropos of this event, Paul Weiler had observed wryly but accurately: '[a] strange thing happened to the Supreme Court of Canada on the way to the celebration of this, its centennial year: the public discovered that the court exists.'[8] Laskin accordingly planned the event as a 'coming of age' ceremony for the Court, one more oriented to the future than to the past. The centrepiece of the event was a symposium held at the new Lester B. Pearson Building on the theme 'The Role and Functions of Final Appellate Courts.' There were only three main speakers in addition to Laskin himself, each associated with the highest tribunal in his particular country. The Lord Chancellor Lord Elwyn-Jones attended from the United Kingdom, M. Marie-Daniel-Albert Monguilan, president of the Cour de cassation, from France, and Associate Justice Byron R. White from the Supreme Court of the United States. The chosen theme and the identity of the speakers revealed the public relations nature of the event. No academics were invited to speak as principals, not even Paul Weiler, who had written the only book-length analysis of the Court's work. Constructing the event around foreign judges who could be relied on to know nothing of Canada was much safer, and was presumably meant to illustrate that the Supreme Court was about to enter the juridical big leagues. With so few speakers, the symposium proceeded at a leisurely pace before about two hundred persons. On Friday evening the guests were treated to an entertainment at the National Arts Centre featuring a potpourri of legally themed music, readings, and sketches. The tongue-in-cheek nature of the event was highlighted by the program, drawn up as a lawyer's account with a fraction of a billable hour beside each item of the performance. The conference closed with a banquet hosted by the governor-general and Madame Léger, a token of thanks to the Laskins for having assumed the vice-regal role the previous year.

On the surface, the celebrations came off very nicely, a tribute both to Laskin and the Court. Underneath, there were problems, due largely to Laskin's lack of sensitivity to the Quebec judges and his non-consultative management style. The lack of participation of Laskin's colleagues in the proceedings immediately stands out, in contrast to the 125th anniversary symposium held in 2000, where each of the judges chaired one of the nine sessions at the event. The message projected was that only Laskin himself represented and embodied the Court. Laskin also did a poor job of representing an officially bilingual and bicultural institution. According to Jules Deschênes, who attended the ceremonies as chief justice of the Superior Court of Quebec, Laskin did not say one word of French either in introducing the speakers or in the text of his remarks. Appalled, Deschênes barely restrained himself from leaping up to repair the error; he saw in this omission not only a lack of courtesy but an affront to the francophone population of Canada.[9] If Laskin felt his French unequal to the task at that point, he could have called upon Louis-Philippe Pigeon to join with him in welcoming the guests.

The gaffe only confirmed the perils of Laskin's failure to consult his brethren in planning such events. When Laskin did have to rely on one of his brethren for assistance, he seemed to resent it. He planned to have Chief Justice Warren Burger attend, but Burger declined and said none of his judges could be spared for the event. On hearing of this, Louis-Philippe de Grandpré used contacts in the American Bar Association, developed while he was president of the Canadian Bar Association, to persuade Burger to allow Byron White to come. According to de Grandpré, Laskin regarded this circuitous move as inappropriate: 'il ne m'a jamais pardonné.'[10] White would probably not have been Laskin's first choice. Known for his dissents in *Miranda v. State of Arizona* and *Roe v. Wade*, he seemed to have more in common with Martland than Laskin in spite of being a Kennedy appointee. Laskin might have preferred to engage him on the subject of football: 'Whizzer White' had been the highest paid professional football player in North America before attending Yale Law School.[11]

The problems evident in Laskin's management of the centenary event remained throughout his tenure as chief justice. In part these resulted from his lack of administrative experience and in part from his own personality, but the structure of the Court itself and the circumstances of his promotion also played a role. Laskin had spent practically his whole life playing the role of a 'constructive subversive,' in the words of his friend 'Buzz' Woods. He had been a tireless critic, taking on institutions, judges, legal dogma, or the Law Society with equal passion and verve. Even his eight years as a puisne judge did not really change this. While adapting to some extent to institutional norms, Laskin's image, both in his own mind and in the public eye, was that of a fearless internal critic, a loyal opposition within the judiciary itself. Now, with his appointment as chief justice at the age of sixty-one, Laskin suddenly had to shift gears. He not only represented the public face of the Supreme Court of Canada and symbolized the entire Canadian judiciary, but was also responsible for making the Supreme Court 'work' in both its judicial functions and its everyday operations. It is not surprising that he encountered difficulty in filling this new role. It is also true that the Supreme Court of Canada poses particular managerial challenges because of the diversity of its membership. Provincial courts of appeal traditionally have been rather homogeneous: their members tend to have known each other, to be products of the same local legal culture. There is no such uniformity at the Supreme Court of Canada, which of necessity reflects all parts of the country, and in particular recognizes Canada's bilingual and bijuridical nature.

Good management consists in making people feel they are a valued part of a common enterprise, through symbolic measures, appropriate recognition, interpretation of feedback, and the actual organization of work. Without any management experience to draw upon – he had never been a dean, for example, or a managing partner in a law firm – Laskin developed a rather erratic approach to his new role. With regard to the organization of the purely judicial work of the Court, or in relation to highly symbolic events such as the centenary, Laskin displayed a take-charge, top-down management style. He tended not to seek or take advice, and seemed to model his leadership on Caesar Wright. This was particularly irksome to some of the Quebec judges, who felt Laskin did not treat them with sufficient respect. The root of this dispute was not language as such, but differing cultural expectations about the exercise of authority. According to Bud Estey, 'Bora got the francophones pretty annoyed by the way he ... would treat them like he did the rest of us. Which was ... when he wanted something it was ordered, it wasn't asked, he would tell you what to do ... It didn't bother me, I thought it was the right way to do it, ... but Pratte, he quit over that, essentially.'[12] Laskin's treatment of Jean Beetz was especially egregious. Beetz wrote extremely clear, articulate, and carefully reasoned judgments, but was chronically slow about producing them. Laskin worked extremely quickly and simply could not understand how Beetz could take so long. His response was to scold Beetz in front of his colleagues at the conference table, much to their discomfiture as well as that of the offending judge.[13] These outbursts, predictably, did little to accelerate the production rate of Beetz's judicial prose. Laskin's style did not offend all the Quebec judges, however. Pigeon's worldview was extremely hierarchical – it was said his law clerks would never dare to sit in his presence until invited to do so – and he seemed to accept Laskin's exercise of authority without complaint.

With regard to the day-to-day management of the Court, by contrast, Laskin had a more laissez-faire style; he was content to let established routines run their course until some crisis arose. When that happened he reverted to a rather peremptory – to use one of his favourite words – style, as with his treatment of Beetz. The registrar of the Court was in effect its chief executive officer, and Laskin relied heavily on him in most administrative matters. Ms Rochon also played an increasing role over the years. A continuing annoyance was the delay in the publication of the *Supreme Court Reports*. Their lethargic production (when compared to the *Federal Court Reports*) outraged Laskin. The latter, he noted acerbically to registrar Bernard Hofley, appeared more quickly even though the Federal Court devoted fewer resources to them, but Laskin never succeeded in getting the registrar to generate them with the speed he desired.[14]

Laskin probably had little innate desire to innovate administratively, but even if he had, he felt constrained in introducing new ways of doing things by the possible opposition of Ronald Martland. He told Bud Estey once, ruefully, that it was not enough to be the chief justice of Canada, one had to be the most senior judge if one wanted to accomplish change at the Court.[15] Creating a sense of collegiality out of the disparate group of individuals at the Court, especially given Martland's sense of grievance, was not easy, but Laskin's style did not make it any easier. It was not in his nature to provide the social lubricant that might have allowed the judges to interact more smoothly. Having established his independence as a puisne judge by declining to lunch with his colleagues at the Rideau Club, he continued to join them only very infrequently for a Friday lunch. Perhaps he belatedly came to realize the importance of such signals, since late in his tenure he succeeded in establishing a dining room for the judges in the Supreme Court building. In the end, however, it is the intellectual leadership of the chief justice that really matters, and for which Bora Laskin will be remembered. Laskin's U.S. contemporary Warren Burger, by contrast, was widely regarded as an administrative wizard but an intellectual lightweight.[16]

There are differing views as to the appropriate role of a chief justice. Some think the chief should try to achieve unanimity, or at least strong majorities, on as many decisions as possible, so that the law will be clear. Others believe it is inappropriate for the chief in particular to seek to influence the opinions of his or her colleagues. Under this model, a judge's individual responsibility to interpret the law precludes any substantial negotiation with fellow judges about the content of a judgment. This is the English model, where the usual practice was for judges to write their opinions in such total isolation that the majority opinion was not clear until the judgments were actually delivered. The Canadian model has usually involved some circulation of draft opinions, and some give and take between the judges. Laskin's own practice signals a fairly dramatic shift in his ideas. A year after becoming chief justice Laskin's rate of dissents began to decline steadily, and after 1979, steeply. The last five years of his tenure saw him much more concerned to achieve consensus among his colleagues. It is difficult to single out one factor which might account for this change. Media criticism began in earnest in the late 1970s and may have played a role. It is also hard to discount the effect of the serious health problems Laskin began to experience in 1978–9, both in sapping his energy and in directing his mind towards the possible legacy of 'the Laskin Court.' Finally, the simple passage of time may have caused Laskin to 'bond' more with his colleagues, and to allow them to see some of their worst fears about him allayed.

During Laskin's tenure as chief justice the Supreme Court building provided quarters to the Federal Court of Canada – a relatively recent creation. Prior to 1971, most matters of federal law were litigated in the provincial superior courts. With the enormous growth of the federal government in the 1950s and '60s some felt that a more uniform approach to federal law was needed, particularly in the area of judicial review of federal administrative tribunals such as the Canada Labour Relations Board and the Immigration Appeal Board. Wilbur Jackett, the president of the Exchequer Court – a relatively minor court with a highly specialized jurisdiction in certain areas of federal law such as patents, maritime law, taxation, and claims against the Crown in right of Canada – drafted an act replacing it with a much expanded Federal Court of Canada, and persuaded Justice Minister John Turner to support it. The court would be a bilingual national court with local facilities in each province, allowing non-Ottawa counsel to deal with it directly and reducing the expense to litigants. The judges would go out on circuit across the country but reside in Ottawa, both to provide the consistency and collegiality necessary in a national court, and to avoid the creation of local fiefdoms by individual judges. Lawyers would never know which judge to expect and could not tailor their pleadings accordingly. The court was duly created and began sitting on 1 June 1971, with Jackett as its chief justice.[17]

The judges of the Supreme Court were somewhat uneasy about this new force in the land being created under their very noses. That unease turned to envy and even antipathy when it became clear that Jackett's superb administrative skills and excellent connections in the civil service enabled him to obtain better financial, human, and physical resources for his court than the Supreme Court itself possessed. Judges of different court levels can be acutely conscious of even minor differences in status, and the judges of the Supreme Court proved no exception to the rule. Laskin's soon-to-be colleague Bud Estey, Jackett himself and other contemporaries observed that Laskin seemed 'noticeably envious of Jackett's administrative ability and the quickness with which he could make things happen.'[18] Friction quickly arose between the two courts over their shared physical space and the metaphysical space occupied by the Federal Court in the Canadian legal order.

Jackett had started work with the Department of Justice in 1939, when he had been chosen over Bora Laskin (and a hundred other applicants) for a junior position as legal officer. He became deputy minister (1957–60), then resigned to become general counsel to CPR; he knew he stood a better chance of being appointed to a judgeship from the private sector than from within government. With his long immersion in Ottawa and his seven years' service as president of the Exchequer Court before its rebirth as the Federal Court, it is not surprising that Jackett's skills and experience seemed intimidating. He was the consummate Ottawa insider and a highly experienced administrator, while Laskin was very much an outsider and possessed almost no administrative experience. Instead of trying to learn from Jackett, however, Laskin only became more deeply resentful over the years. Jackett, a short compact man 'like a little wrestler' with a rough and blunt exterior, seemed to bring out Laskin's worst competitive instincts. It is almost as if he assumed his rugby persona from Fort William to deal with this perceived external threat. The jurisdictional tussles between the Supreme Court and the Federal Court during Laskin's tenure as chief justice are impossible to understand without appreciating the personal tensions bubbling beneath the surface of the legal texts.

The problem lay in interpreting the bland words of section 101 of the *British North America Act*, which granted Parliament the authority to provide for 'the Establishment of any additional Courts for the better Administration of the Laws of Canada.'[19] To what extent could Parliament create new courts which would take away the traditional jurisdiction of the provincial superior courts? Until the creation of the Federal Court of Canada, judicial review of federal administrative bodies such as the Immigration Appeal Board and the Canada Labour Relations Board was carried on by the provincial superior courts – Laskin had sat on a number of such cases while on the Ontario Court of Appeal. Afterwards, all such authority was vested in the Federal Court, and the Ontario judges did not like it one bit. There were good reasons for the change: given the locus of most federal boards in Ottawa, the Ontario Court of Appeal was becoming the de facto creator of federal administrative law for all of Canada, a result with no compelling legal or policy rationale, and one distinctly unpopular in Quebec and western Canada. But the Federal Court had its own legitimacy problems. For many lawyers and judges, it created a perception of bias for the federal government to create its own courts to adjudicate claims against itself and its agencies. Members of the Supreme Court and the provincial superior courts were of course federally appointed, but existed to interpret and apply all Canadian law, whether federal or provincial. They did not see themselves, and were not perceived, as 'federal' courts in the same sense as the Federal Court of Canada, which existed only to administer federal law. In a series of decisions under Laskin, the Supreme Court interpreted section 101 to say that the Federal Court's jurisdiction could not be co-extensive with federal legislative authority in the abstract – only where Parliament had actually exercised its authority by passing a law could the Federal Court be given power to administer it. Thus disputes over a contract to build a federal penitentiary[20] and a contract to build a rail car marine terminal (an area of federal jurisdiction)[21] were found not to be cognizable in the Federal Court because only the provincial law of contract was involved. In both cases the Supreme Court overturned a unanimous panel of the Federal Court of Appeal. The Federal Court's own historian characterizes these unanimous decisions of the Supreme Court as having correctly 'reset the constitutional balance of legislative power between the provinces and Ottawa' after some over-reaching by the Federal Court.[22] At the time, however, the sharp tone of Laskin's reasons and the edgy personal dynamic between some members of the two courts ensured that the Supreme Court was seen as having administered a severe rebuke to the Federal Court.

These tensions became spectacularly evident in an admiralty case dealing with a ship called the *Capricorn*.[23] A dispute over the ownership of the *Capricorn* in the spring of 1973 led to the arrest of the ship in Quebec City. The plaintiff alleged it had bought the ship and wished to preserve it from the claims of a corporation to whom the original owner had wrongfully sold the ship a second time. On 1 October Justice Louis Pratte of the Trial Division ordered the original owner and the subsequent purchaser to be added as parties to the action, but neither party had any presence in Canada. When the plaintiff applied for permission to serve them outside the jurisdiction (both were Liberian corporations), Pratte denied it in a judgment dated 12 November. The Federal Court of Appeal upheld his decision and an appeal to the Supreme Court of Canada was heard by a bench of five judges. Four judges overturned the decisions below, but Laskin dissented in a lengthy judgment containing an unprecedented personal attack on Jackett's method of proceeding in the case. To do this, he had sent for the court file from the Federal Court registry, containing documents not part of the official record in the case and thus not properly before the Supreme Court. Jackett had noticed that the parties had not appealed from Pratte's decision of 1 October on the motion within the designated limitation period. He had written a memorandum to the parties stating his desire to avoid sending a panel of three judges to Quebec City to hear an appeal that would inevitably be quashed, but affirming his willingness to do so if there was any real argument to the contrary. The appellant in due course discontinued its appeal, but Laskin interpreted this in a sinister fashion, labelling Jackett's memo 'extraordinary' and implying that he had bullied the parties into accepting his view of the matter. Laskin also seemed to think that Jackett had tried to 'short-circuit' the appeal of the 1 October decision in order to preclude an appeal to the Supreme Court.

Jackett was 'devastated' by Laskin's open criticism and only with great difficulty was he dissuaded by his friends from resigning on the spot. Perhaps Martland was thinking of this incident in particular when he criticized Laskin for being unaware of the effect his intemperate language might have on lower court judges. Jackett interpreted the remarks of the chief justice of Canada as tantamount to a vote of no confidence in his abilities. Bud Estey, though not yet on the Supreme Court of Canada, was friends with both men and heard from both at great length on the subject. He felt both shared some of the blame for their inability to interact in a productive fashion. While Laskin felt personally slighted by the praise lavished on Jackett as an administrator, Jackett seems to have been unable to interpret Laskin's remarks in this case and his restrictive stance on Federal Court jurisdiction in general as a genuine disagreement about law and procedure. Jackett was known to be a very forceful judge and in his drive for efficiency might well have intimidated counsel on some occasions. He was known for writing out decisions in advance of the hearing and rendering them on the spot after oral argument concluded. Laskin was not totally wrong in sensing that Jackett's case management techniques could verge on the dictatorial, but he turned what might have been a discreet and salutary warning into a virtual public whipping. The decision in the *Capricorn* case was one factor, though probably not the most important one, provoking Jackett's early retirement in 1979 at the age of sixty-five.

This incident illustrates a character trait noticed by many after Laskin became chief justice. In spite of being a lifelong champion of free expression and a vigorous critic of all societal institutions including the courts, he became extraordinarily sensitive to any perceived slights on himself or his office. Laskin took his symbolic role highly seriously, perhaps too seriously, and took any criticism of the Court or its administration personally. He did not have the thick skin of the seasoned manager, and when criticized he would never engage directly with the critic. He would either ignore the incident totally or, in some cases, use his position to lash out at the offender so as to preclude any reply. The incident with Jackett would be repeated on a more dramatic scale when Justice Thomas Berger ran afoul of Laskin's notions of judicial ethics in 1982. Examples of this sort of behaviour can also be found on a more minor level. A former associate recalls meeting Laskin on two separate occasions at legal functions in Toronto. Both times the individual tried to explore with Laskin an apparent inconsistency between something he had said as a law professor and one of his recent decisions. Even allowing for the somewhat importunate nature of such a question, many people in Laskin's position would have waved off the inquiry in a humorous fashion, or invoked judicial ethics to justify avoiding a reply. In both instances Laskin became visibly roiled, turned on his heel, and stalked away without a word.

If Laskin isolated himself from his colleagues to some extent as chief justice, he also continued to find himself in the minority on many substantive law issues, at least during the first half of his tenure. His dissent rate before he became chief justice always hovered around 20 per cent, and it remained so in 1974 before dropping to 13 per cent in 1975 and falling slowly after that to about 10 per cent, with one spike back to 18 per cent in 1979. Some of Laskin's friends worried about the difficulty of his position during his early years as chief justice, and did what they could to promote candidates for the Court who might work better with him. In May 1975 Emmett Hall wrote to Senator Carl Goldenberg that Laskin was 'as you know, ... somewhat isolated at the moment,' and raised the possibility of 'getting some one on the Supreme Court who could and would work in harmony with Bora.'[24] The candidate Hall had in mind was Pat Hartt, an Ontario judge who had been seconded to head up the Law Reform Commission of Canada in 1972, but Hall's campaign came to naught.

No new judge arrived until Wilfred Judson was compulsorily retired on 20 July 1977, and his replacement provoked some controversy behind the scenes. Minister of Justice Ron Basford asked Bud Estey, who had just been appointed chief justice of Ontario in December 1976, for the names of three suitable candidates (either judges or lawyers) for the vacancy.[25] Estey duly complied but Basford then told him that 'the prime minister had been advised that [he] was the man they needed.' He even pursued Estey to a Canadian Judicial Council meeting in Whitehorse to lobby him to accept the appointment. According to Estey's account, Basford said, 'We have got troubles which I am not going to burden you with, we are going to solve them, we are going to solve them within the next two days, and I need your consent.' In spite of Ruth Estey's tearful protestation against moving to Ottawa, her husband accepted the appointment. He himself protested that he was not keen to go, but one should probably take these protestations with a grain of salt. Gregarious, relentlessly energetic, and well-respected by the bar, Bud Estey was a highly popular chief justice of Ontario. He had been at this job less than a year and was supremely at home in Toronto. When asked why he accepted, he cited a sense of loyalty to Bora Laskin – 'I wouldn't have gone if Bora hadn't been there' – and a sense of duty to the country: 'I went because from wartime I was used to going where the country needed me and I didn't want to get into a row with the prime minister.'[26]

Ronald Martland and Brian Dickson's accounts of the succession to Judson complement Estey's. Martland reported that Laskin was 'very much involved in the appointment which went to Bud Estey. Ron Basford ... wanted to appoint Pierre Genest, now [1985] Treasurer of the Law Society; Bora wanted Charlie Dubin. Then Trudeau said, get somebody you can both agree on.' At this point, Dickson invited Laskin and 'a senior cabinet minister' to a Sunday lunch at Marchmont, his country estate. As Dickson told his biographers, 'the minister and the chief justice went for a walk along the shore and came back about two hours later all smiles. Estey's appointment was announced the next day.'[27] It appears that Estey had emerged as a compromise candidate. Laskin's good friend Charles Dubin had been named to the Ontario Court of Appeal in 1973, but both Martland and de Grandpré regarded Laskin's lobbying on his behalf as unseemly. Martland observed that upon his own retirement in 1982, Laskin 'did a stout bit of argument on Charles Dubin's behalf to succeed me,' but the appointment went to Bertha Wilson.[28]

Presumably Dubin was one of the three names recommended by Estey; he was certainly very highly regarded and went on to become chief justice of Ontario in 1990. For some the reason why he did not emerge as the successor to Judson was obvious enough. In Louis-Philippe de Grandpré's opinion, 'que sur un groupe de neuf juges, deux soient juifs, quelque soit leur intelligence, ca m'étonne un peu.'[29] He regarded Laskin's pro-Dubin campaign as doomed from the start for this reason. Perhaps the operative comparison was not so much with the nine judges, but the fact that of three judges from Ontario, two would have been Jewish. In a culture long accustomed to a delicate balance between Protestant and Catholic interests, a Jewish candidate could still be the odd one out. It is worth noting in this context that the Court would wait nearly twenty years after Bora Laskin's death to welcome its next Jewish member. Justice Morris Fish of Quebec was appointed to the Court in 2003, followed closely by Justice Rosalie Abella of Ontario in 2004.

Charles Dubin appeared before the Supreme Court from time to time, and one of his appearances provided Laskin with one of his favourite stories. Once, before Laskin's elevation to the Court, Dubin had taken a case to the Supreme Court of Canada. It was a novel point, but Dubin had given his client a very positive opinion about the chances of success based on his analysis of the underlying principles. Unfortunately, he lost. Some years later he had an identical case, but this time he was on the opposite side of it. Dubin explained to his client that he had argued the previous case and lost, but was certain of victory this time since the cases were indistinguishable. The trial judge and the Court of Appeal agreed with him that the Supreme Court decision was controlling and binding. By this time Laskin had been appointed to the Court. During argument, Dubin agreed that in principle the appellant's argument was very persuasive. Indeed it had been the very argument he had put to the Court years earlier, 'but Your Lordships showed me that I was wrong.' Laskin delighted in quoting the punchline of Dubin's story: 'and then they showed me I was wrong again.' The Court, led by Laskin, decided not to follow its previous decision. Dubin was placed in the awkward position of having to explain to his new client how he could lose both sides of the same issue in the same Court.[30]

The appointment of Bud Estey to the Supreme Court provided Laskin with the friend and confidant he had not had since Emmett Hall's retirement in 1973. Laskin was on good terms with Spence and Dickson but his relations with them lacked the spark that existed between him and Estey. In the late 1940s and '50s Estey had often appeared as counsel before arbitrator Laskin or sat as a management nominee on tripartite boards chaired by him. Estey had great respect for Laskin's talents as an arbitrator, and Laskin grew to admire the abilities of this feisty, quick-thinking lawyer. While Estey was often impatient with law professors, he felt Laskin combined an acute legal mind with a solid grasp of the practical realities of labour relations. Having attended both the University of Saskatchewan College of Law and Harvard Law School, Estey also supported Laskin's crusade for a more academic approach to legal education.

Estey shared Laskin's passion for responsive law but was less concerned about how precisely to reconcile the need for change with existing precedent. If the law needed to change to serve 'the community' better, he was quite prepared to knock down, ignore, or somersault over any precedent that might stand in the way. This trait and his volatile personality caused some to view Estey as a loose cannon, but he was a pillar of strength to Laskin on the Court, and he was the only judge in whom both Martland and Laskin would confide. Estey's prairie roots and hard-nosed practitioner's persona appealed to Martland even though their personalities and judicial philosophies were different. Laskin knew Estey's approach to law largely mirrored his own, and valued his friendship and his judgment. Their dissent in the *Patriation Reference* bears witness to the fundamental similarity of their legal and constitutional visions.

Estey appreciated Laskin's strengths and tolerated his weaknesses. An admirer of Laskin's intellectual leadership, he was prepared to overlook the chief's lack of interest in administration even though it drove him crazy at times. Estey realized Laskin rubbed some of his colleagues the wrong way and tried to intercede occasionally, albeit to little observable effect. During Laskin's later illnesses, Estey grew increasingly protective of his friend. After Laskin's death Estey grew increasingly disaffected with the Court and resigned in a most ungracious way in 1988. While his disagreement with the direction of the early Charter cases largely explains this trajectory, there is also little doubt that without Bora as captain, the Supreme Court team had lost its appeal.

Bud Estey's arrival on the Court was followed two days later by the departure of Louis-Philippe de Grandpré and his replacement by Yves Pratte, the former chairman of Air Canada. There was no little irony in Estey and Pratte arriving on the Court within days of each other, as Estey had just written a commission of inquiry report critical of Pratte's management of the airline. Pratte did not seem unduly perturbed by this, as the two played tennis weekly while on the Court, and Estey respected Pratte's judicial talents more than his managerial ability. But Pratte's stay was short-lived – only a year and a half. He left for many of the same reasons as de Grandpré: after their high-flying careers and busy social lives in Montreal, the Supreme Court seemed a dull backwater, and Laskin's blunt management style a provocation.

By the time Pratte resigned from the Court on 30 June 1979, the world had turned upside down in Ottawa. The Liberals were out and the Conservatives were now in power with a minority government. On 24 September Julien Chouinard became Joe Clark's only appointment to the Supreme Court. It was not easy for the Conservatives to find a credible candidate from Quebec but they succeeded admirably with Chouinard. A Rhodes Scholar and former deputy minister of justice, he held the top post in the Quebec public service before his appointment to the Quebec Court of Appeal in 1975. As secretary to Robert Bourassa's cabinet, he made the fateful call to mandarin Gordon Robertson in October 1970 that triggered Trudeau's decision to invoke the *War Measures Act*. He was a man of few words but possessed an excellent legal mind, and his organizational skills were such that Laskin began to delegate some administrative tasks to him. Early on Chouinard was touted as a possible successor if the government were to follow the usual French-English rotation of the chief justiceship. Unfortunately Chouinard did not live long enough to make a major contribution: he died of cancer in 1987 at the age of fifty-eight.

On 1 January 1979 a replacement was named for Wishart Spence, who had turned seventy-five the previous month. Spence's official retirement ceremony provided a neat illustration of the low profile of the Supreme Court aside from its chief justice. Justice Minister Marc Lalonde came to the Court to deliver some words of appreciation to the retiring judge. He said all the right things – with his eyes fixed unwaveringly on Roland Ritchie. Even the body language of the other bemused judges could not straighten out the confused minister.[31] Normally Spence's appointment should have come from Ontario but the British Columbia lobby managed to convince the government that it was their 'turn.' It was agreed to hold the Ontario position in abeyance until Martland retired, allowing a British Columbia nominee to succeed Spence. The candidate turned out to be similar to Spence in many ways. William McIntyre was raised in Saskatchewan and had been at university with Bud Estey in Saskatoon. After war service overseas he settled into a law practice in Victoria and was named to the B.C. Supreme Court in 1967, then the Court of Appeal in 1973. Like Spence he was firm, direct, pragmatic, and a strong defender of civil liberties; he was also unalterably opposed to capital punishment.[32] Like Estey, his resignation in 1989 would also be largely attributable to his unease with the direction of the early Charter jurisprudence.

The number of honours Laskin received while chief justice was not especially striking – one or two honorary degrees per year – but their provenance was more international and more interdisciplinary than those conferred on any previous judge of the Supreme Court. McGill and the University of Ottawa were the first off the mark in 1974, and at McGill it was Frank Scott who read the citation. In 1975 Laskin accepted degrees from two institutions without law faculties: OISE, in recognition of his service as the founding chair of its board of governors; and Simon Fraser University, where his old friend Pauline Jewett was now president and his former colleague Ted McWhinney a professor of political science. The next year the University of Victoria invited him to come and bless its new law school, where the inaugural class was just finishing its first year. He also travelled to London as president of the Bentham Club, an honour previously bestowed upon Lord Denning. The club, composed of the alumni and faculty of the University of London, selects a president each year whose sole duty is the delivery of a public lecture at the Club's annual dinner. Brian Dickson was in attendance, along with Canada's high commissioner. Paul Martin noted that Laskin began his address with the traditional salutation, 'Mr. Bentham, My lords, ladies and gentlemen.' Also traditional was the subsequent reception in the Housman Room, where, 'in a glass case, is the skeleton, without head, of Jeremy Bentham ... wearing the clothes he had on at the time of death.'[33] Laskin's talk on 'English Law in Canadian Courts since the Abolition of Privy Council Appeals' ended with the bracing conclusion that 'English decisions will have to compete on merit for consideration with decisions in Canada as well as decisions elsewhere' – a pithy summary of his own approach to the search for authority.[34]

In August 1976 the Laskins travelled to Israel for the second and last time. The Canadian Friends of the Hebrew University of Jerusalem had been lobbying the University to recognize Laskin ever since his elevation to the chief justiceship, and the university finally held a special convocation to honour him. Laskin was especially grateful to receive his first degree in philosophy, saying he regarded it 'as a challenge to work yet to be done as well as an affirmation, generously given, that I have been on the right track.' He also declared his intention to 'draw nourishment for my own Jewish roots for the rest of my life from the privilege I have been given of claiming association with this community of scholars.'[35] The Laskins enjoyed travelling with their friend Nathan Nemetz, now the chief justice of the British Columbia Supreme Court, who was also being honoured by the university at the same ceremony. As they toured the Mount Scopus campus, Bora and Peggy were amazed at its physical development since their last visit four years earlier.

Further honours from Jewish institutions followed the next year: an honorary LLD from Yeshiva University in New York in May, and a Doctor of Humane Letters from Hebrew Union College in Cincinnati in June. The ceremony at Yeshiva coincided with the first anniversary of the university's new Benjamin N. Cardozo School of Law. Of all the honours Laskin received, it would be hard to equal sharing the podium at the New York Hilton Hotel with two other chief justices, Warren E. Burger of the United States and Joel Sussman of Israel, before a thousand distinguished guests. (Curiously, after welcoming a long line of stellar Jewish jurists in the first half of the twentieth century, the U.S. Supreme Court had had no Jewish judge since Abe Fortas resigned in disgrace in 1969, and there would not be one again until President Clinton's appointment of Ruth Bader Ginsburg in 1993.) Even in this august company, Laskin's sense of duty did not allow him to bask in this moment of glory. The ceremony was held on Sunday, 1 May, but Laskin had to return to Ottawa late in the evening after the convocation dinner because the Court was sitting on Monday.[36] He and Peggy did take a vacation in Australia after Bora addressed an Australian legal convention in Sydney in July.[37]

Carleton University recognized Laskin in part for his service on their board of governors at their convocation on 13 November 1978. As President Michael Oliver read the citation, both would have thought of their meeting thirty years before under very different circumstances, when Oliver was a junior professor of at United College about to flee after the Crowe controversy. Events at Carleton illustrated the sea change in Canadian university affairs since the palmy times of Laskin's final years as a university professor. President Oliver had decided to deal with severe budget cuts in the early 1970s by reducing the number of junior faculty members. As a result, in 1974 Carleton professors became the first in Ontario to establish a faculty union, a step Laskin deplored.

It is hard to know which honour Laskin would have cherished more, his degree from Yeshiva University, or his 1979 recognition by Harvard. It is believed that Al Abel was the main instigator of this honour, which Laskin received along with ten others on 7 June.[38] After regular academic degrees were conferred in Harvard Yard, each candidate stood in the brilliant sunshine on the south portico of the Memorial Church to receive his or her degree. This time Laskin's fellow honorands included Sir Isaiah Berlin, who shared his Riga birthplace with Laskin's mother, Milton Friedman, the Rev. Mr Desmond Tutu (not yet an archbishop), Jacques-Yves Cousteau, and Chancellor Helmut Schmidt of West Germany. In the audience of twenty thousand was Laskin's friend Paul Weiler, Mackenzie King Visiting Professor at Harvard and soon to be a faculty member at the law school. Laskin's advice had been crucial in Weiler's life twenty-five years earlier, and more recently he had recommended Weiler for the Harvard position to President Derek Bok. Weiler proved to be a disappointment only in shifting his loyalties from Laskin's beloved New York Yankees to the Boston Red Sox after his move to Harvard.[39]

Unfortunately, Al Abel was not in the audience to witness his friend's triumph. He had died in a tragic accident a year earlier: a furnace malfunction had filled his house with carbon monoxide and Abel was asphyxiated as he sat reading in his study. Laskin gave a short but moving eulogy at a memorial service at Hart House attended by hundreds of former students and colleagues.[40] Only to Al would Laskin entrust the preparation of the fourth edition of his constitutional law text.[41] Abel quixotically removed the section on civil liberties, causing such howls of protest from readers that it was hastily restored in a revised fourth edition; John Laskin wrote the new version of the section.[42] The move to Ottawa meant the two men saw each other much less often, and Laskin's elevation to the Supreme Court seemed to intimidate Abel. He disagreed strongly with Laskin's decision in *Morgan v. Prince Edward Island*, upholding provincial legislation imposing ownership ceilings of coastal property on non-residents, but did not feel able to say so. A friend urged him to raise it with Laskin, predicting the chief justice would not allow a professional disagreement to taint their friendship.[43] Abel did manage to be moderately critical in print of Laskin's decision in the *Anti-Inflation Act Reference*.[44]

Abel's death on 6 May 1978 preceded Laskin's first serious illness by less than two weeks, and it is hard not to make a symbolic linkage between the two events. It is almost as if, in his shock and grief, Laskin let down his guard for a fatal moment The relentless workaholic suddenly stopped to reflect on the meaning of life, and in that instant of doubt and hesitation the worm of ill health penetrated Laskin's defences. Once inside, it could never be purged.

As Bora Laskin observed his sixty-fifth birthday on 5 October 1977 he felt in anything but a celebratory mood. Peggy had been in hospital in Toronto almost the entire month of September, and emerged on crutches. After a week with her sister in Toronto, she arrived back in Ottawa on the ninth. She was well enough to spend the end of year recess in Florida, where Bora joined her on 21 December.[45] He seemed his usual fit and energetic self during the winter session, but as the Easter session advanced he became more and more fatigued. On 18 May he received the twenty-eighth annual Humanitarian Award from the Beth Sholom

Brotherhood in Toronto, but the next day he was admitted to the Toronto Western Hospital suffering from exhaustion and angina. A heart 'disturbance' resulted in by-pass surgery on 1 June, and Laskin remained in hospital until the 8th of July. A number of complications delayed his recovery, including a serious post-operative infection. 'Everything that could have gone wrong seems to have gone wrong,' he reported to Morris Shumiatcher by telephone, and upon his release he was still suffering from phlebitis.[46] Laskin asked Bud Estey to pinch-hit for him on outstanding Canadian Judicial Council matters, but could not totally sever himself from his work; his law clerk William Braithwaite was summoned more than once to his hospital bedside to discuss draft judgments.[47] The spectre of ill health that had stalked Peggy for years now advanced relentlessly on both of them. One or the other would be ill or in convalescence for the rest of their lives. Wishart Spence's observation about Bora was equally apposite when applied to Peggy: 'He went through in those six years what would have made most people simply retire to their beds and stay there. And he kept fighting back.'[48]

In what would become a familiar pattern with each new medical crisis, the press soon began to speculate about Laskin's retirement.[49] Had the journalists really known Bora Laskin, they would have realized how illusory an option voluntary retirement was for him, no matter what his state of health. He continued to regard each new ailment as yet another obstacle to be surmounted in due course and never seems to have seriously considered retiring. This first encounter with major surgery did force Laskin to slow down considerably, however. By mid-August he was still resting in the hope of being well enough to resume his duties in the fall. He had lost twenty-five pounds and the phlebitis in his leg was still bothering him.[50] Morris Shumiatcher wrote an enthusiastic if perhaps ill-timed letter to Laskin urging him to build some physical fitness facilities into the Court building. 'The U.S. justices had a great gym built into the courthouse and many of them are reported to use it ... [M]ore important than secretaries and security staff – maybe even libraries – is a place where you can do things to keep physically fit. Do build the gym, Bora! You owe it to yourself and to the constitutional health of the judges ... and the country.'[51] Shumiatcher himself was a fitness addict and all-round outdoorsman. He enjoyed hunting and hiking, and ran marathons long before it became mandatory for lawyers to do so. Laskin, by contrast, confined his physical activity to walking and to sessions on an exercise bicycle in his chambers, but it is unlikely that a more demanding regimen would have had much impact on his multiple medical problems.

Laskin was back in the office in September and resumed his normal sitting schedule when the Court opened on 3 October. He seemed in good health that fall and into the winter, and had many lively interchanges with his law clerk, Wayne MacKay. MacKay even managed to negotiate a raise for the law clerks, the first in a long time, from $15,000 to $18,000 per year. Nonetheless, by late winter Laskin seemed to slow down markedly. Ted Culliton visited Laskin on Judicial Council business in March 1979 and was shocked at his demeanour. As he reported to Morris Shumiatcher, he was 'very concerned that Bora appeared to be very tired and in much need of a rest'; he also gingerly raised with Peggy the possibility of Bora taking leave from the Court for some months.[52] At the end of March Laskin was admitted to hospital in Toronto with alarming symptoms: he had taken on eighteen pounds of fluid in a week and seemed to be swelling uncontrollably. Tests revealed Laskin to be suffering from Addison's Disease, a rare autoimmune ailment afflicting about four in every 100,000 persons, in which the adrenal glands are destroyed by misguided antibodies. These glands produce cortisol and aldosterone, two hormones which regulate water and salt absorption. Dehydration is a key symptom, along with nausea, fatigue, low blood pressure, and irritability. The condition also causes a build-up of melanin in the skin, such that Addison's sufferers often appear to have a deep tan. Laskin's fluid build-up may have been the result of an initial overdose of medication to counteract the dehydration of Addison's.[53]

The treatment for Addison's Disease is straightforward: oral cortisone is taken to replace the hormones the body can no longer produce on its own. Daily cortisone can control the symptoms satisfactorily, but Addison's also weakens the immune system. Laskin became more prone to infection, and required more time for recovery when he fell ill. His friends continued to urge him to take leave from the Court. Morris Shumiatcher tried to get at Bora through Peggy, but she knew her husband too well to try to persuade him to take a leave of absence. Bora would be depressed if he couldn't do his job, she said in a telephone call to Morris. If he couldn't sit, it would be like sending him into exile.[54]

Laskin slowly recovered and began to sit again in May. His concession to his friends' urgings to slow down was to plan a holiday in Vancouver in August before attending the opening of the new courthouse on 5 September. Nathan Nemetz, promoted to Chief Justice of

British Columbia in January, had planned a lavish round of ceremonies to mark the opening of Arthur Erickson's stunning ziggurat in glass, including a special convocation at UBC where Lord Denning, Laskin, and former Chief Justice Thibaudeau Rinfret would receive honorary degrees. Unfortunately, the wild card of Laskin's ill health would force Nemetz to alter his plans at the last minute. On 22 August Laskin was admitted to St Paul's Hospital in Vancouver for an emergency hernia operation. Nine days later he was discovered to have a strangulated bowel and required surgery again. Neither of these in itself was a matter for grave concern, but Laskin then fell prey to a severe infection. He went into a steep decline, required surgery again, and had to remain in hospital for three months.[55]

Not until the end of November was Laskin strong enough to be released, and for a time he could only get around with the aid of a walker before progressing to a cane. Estey tried to cheer him up on his return to Ottawa by teasing him about a 'mental lapse,' referring to 'the story abroad that you were displeased with the outcome of the Grey Cup game which obviously shows some kind of mental collapse.'[56] (Laskin's favoured Montreal Alouettes had lost the Cup to the Edmonton Eskimos.) The humour was a little close to the line, but Laskin responded in kind. One of his first priorities on his return was to meet with his law clerks Clarke Hunter and Philippe Lalonde. Authorization had been granted for an additional clerk for the chief justice the previous year, but the two had been seconded to other duties in view of their principal's illness. Laskin descended very slowly from the upper level of his apartment, frail and gaunt, and apologized profusely for his absence. He gradually recovered his strength and was well enough to attend the dinner on 7 January hosted by the governor-general and Mrs Schreyer to honour the retirement of senior mandarin Gordon Robertson.[57] When the term began later in the month Laskin returned to work, albeit in somewhat fragile condition. His physician had ordered a regime of half-days but this soon escalated to full days in spite of the best efforts of both Peggy and Micheline Rochon.[58]

Laskin's illness in 1979 marked a shift in his relationship with his clerks. In earlier years he had been reasonably close with them and worked them fairly hard. Laskin almost never accepted editing suggestions from his clerks – he told Clarke Hunter 'you just can't change a man's style' – but there was nonetheless a certain sense of partnership about the enterprise. Laskin genuinely wanted to know his clerks' views and would debate particular points of law with them, even though the likelihood of his altering his own views was slim. After 1979–80 Laskin tended to be less demanding, more avuncular, and more prone to reminiscence. His selection process never changed, however. He made up his mind based mainly on the student's academic record, before seeing the candidate; the interview was only a formality, to ensure there was no obvious incompatibility. When interviewing University of Ottawa student John Manley in 1975, Laskin observed 'your B in Constitutional Law fairly bruises me, Mr. Manley,' to which the nervous candidate replied that he too had found it bruising. (Manley got the job.)[59] In the fall of 1979 when Laskin was too ill to hire his own clerks he delegated the task to Bud Estey. The result was the chief justice's first woman clerk, Kathy de Jong, along with Neil Finkelstein, who would later edit the fifth (and seemingly final) edition of Laskin's constitutional law text. Laskin always stressed with his clerks the necessity of maintaining confidentiality about the Court's business. He was horrified by the appearance of *The Brethren*, a gossipy look at the inner workings of the U.S. Supreme Court based on interviews with former clerks and justices, and made a point of discussing it with all the clerks after he returned to the Court early in 1980.

Laskin's health problems in 1978–9 marked the end of his honeymoon with the media. Commentary did not turn uniformly negative, but divergent views emerged. Some sharply critical voices provided a stark contrast to the unalloyed enthusiasm displayed in the early years of Laskin's tenure. Laskin both reaped the rewards and ran the risks of encouraging more media coverage of the Court and making himself more available to journalists. A July 1974 cover story in *Maclean's* painted Laskin as a flawless latter-day Solomon, and went so far as to label him a *tzaddik* – a saintly figure in Jewish lore. An unprecedented television documentary on the series *Private Lives* featured a long interview between journalist Peter Desbarats and Laskin on 8 October 1976. Laskin was described in the opening voice-over as a 'controversial, colourful and warm' person, not beholden to wealth or power in any way, and was shown driving his own car to work. The interview, held in Laskin's chambers, covered the well-worn topics of Laskin's baseball career in Thunder Bay, his special relationship with his dog, his Judaism, and his talent for baking date squares. Once the conversation turned to the legal order, Desbarats became more aggressive in his questioning and Laskin a little more defensive. On the theme of the isolation of judges, Laskin conceded it might be possible to remain a judge for too long, but noted that judicial sabbaticals had been suggested as a possible remedy. Desbarats pooh-poohed this, saying the university was the last place one should go to keep in touch with people, then suggested irreverently 'maybe we should use the Chinese solution – send you out to the fields for a time.' Laskin ignored this suggestion and closed with what he saw as the Court's mission: 'it is important to keep the law up to date, keeping in mind Parliament has the last say except in constitutional matters. We feel a responsibility to make advances in line with our conception of what society will tolerate.' On the whole Laskin came across as earnest, humane, and disarmingly uncomfortable under the camera's scrutiny, providing a more human face to a somewhat remote institution.[60]

By the later 1970s some were lauding Laskin's achievements at the Court. 'The road to social justice is slow and hard but the driver is up to it' opined Alan Fotheringham in the fall of 1978. A 'quiet revolution' had been going on, '[p]ractically unnoticed by the public and editorial writers[:] the Rt Hon CJ of Canada from Thunder Bay, with those piercing eyeballs and singular cheek bones, has transformed the nature of the court that rules over us all; ... the Laskin court has begun to shape our social attitudes, our morals, our way of looking at one another. Laskin is not another dry interpreter of dusty text and precedents; he is a translator of the shifting mood of a changing nation and in his own way, he is shaping our perceptions and our attitudes just as much, if not more, than a clutch of legislators.'[61] George Radwanski of the *Financial Times* also paid tribute to Laskin in 1979, calling him 'an attractive personification of what most people would want their top jurists to be – a manifestly brilliant man of striking warmth and unpretentiousness, but with an aura of dignity which leaves no doubt that his lack of aloofness is never to be mistaken for weakness.' If the Court's record on the protection of human rights and civil liberties remained unsatisfactory, that was 'through no fault of the chief justice,' who cast only one of nine votes. Radwanski remained optimistic that Laskin's 'eloquent, forceful dissents ... constitute a process of intellectual leadership that may well bear fruit in later years; the dissenting opinions of this decade may well form the basis for the majorities of the next.'[62]

Others were neutral or downright hostile about Laskin's performance. The cover of *Maclean's* 12 February 1979 issue featured a shadowy Laskin rising above a Supreme Court building riven in two, with the caption 'Repairing a court divided.' While Laskin had made 'every effort to minimize the increasingly visible and sharp differences between himself and the majority on the court,' noted Barbara Amiel, 'the differences remain substantial and apply in every area of law.' Her conclusion – reasonably accurate as it turned out – was that real change would have to await the entrenchment of a bill of rights. Eight months later, Elizabeth Gray let fly in *Maclean's* in an article titled 'The supreme and inaccessible court,' but her criticisms were unfair or uninformed in many respects. She seemed to think Laskin's 'surprisingly weak administrative record' was responsible for the continued conservative ascendancy at the Court, when the two had little to do with one another. And she berated Laskin for his 'failure to influence court appointments,' referring to Charles Dubin's non-appointment, when the role of a chief justice is to be consulted and no more. Gray was on more solid ground in finding fault with Laskin's approach to the media. She admitted media coverage was still inadequate, but pointed to Laskin's failure to 'create a more open system.' There were still no press seats in the courtroom, no simultaneous interpretation for the public, no media liaison officer. Supposedly one had been hired but lasted only a year before the position was dropped, and in that time she had seen Laskin only twice. Journalists wanted to improve their coverage but Laskin seemed unable or unwilling to give them some of the tools they needed. Gray's sources suggested Laskin held back from change because of his 'obsessive fear of offending his more conservative brothers.'[63]

The year 1980 marked two milestones at the Court: the retirement in February of Louis-Philippe Pigeon; and in September the fifteenth anniversary of Laskin's appointment as a judge. On 28 March Antonio Lamer was appointed as Pigeon's replacement. Trudeau had been minister of justice when Pigeon was appointed thirteen years earlier, and gained the right to appoint his successor by his defeat of the short-lived Clark government the previous month. Lamer was seconded from the Quebec Superior Court to the Law Reform Commission of Canada, becoming its vice-chair in 1976. In that capacity he met Laskin a half-dozen times a year in the mid-seventies to discuss the commission's work. With his background in law reform and his earlier part-time teaching at the Université de Montréal Lamer was the kind of appointment Laskin welcomed, and he may well have recommended Lamer's promotion. Forty-six-year-old Antonio Lamer and fifty-one-year-old Julien Chouinard now constituted the 'youth wing' of the Court, in contrast to the increasingly aged and infirm common law judges.

Fifteen years' judicial service permits retirement on a full pension, and some of Laskin's friends hoped he would seize the opportunity. To Antonio Lamer, who had not seen him recently, the chief justice 'was not the Bora Laskin I had known.'[64] Two years of almost constant health problems had taken a shocking toll. The haggard figure who returned to the Court after his long illness in the west looked at least fifteen years older than the smiling and healthy figure on the cover of *Maclean's* in 1974. Pension or no pension, however, Laskin was not about to retire. He stayed on partly out of a sense of duty, partly out of a sense of pride. Retirement also meant imagining some other life, and that, Bora Laskin could no longer do. Like his mentor Caesar Wright he had allowed his own identity to become submerged in that of his office, and like Wright he would die in harness.

Even if Laskin toyed with the idea of retiring, the rekindling of the embers of constitutional reform would have dissuaded him. With the failure of the Quebec referendum in May 1980, a resurrected Pierre Trudeau put patriation of the constitution back on the front burner. It was clear to anyone that his mission was unlikely to succeed without the involvement of the Supreme Court at some point in the journey. Bora Laskin was not the type of man who could stand on the sidelines while such momentous events were unfolding. Besides, he seemed to have climbed out of the pit he found himself in back in January. Laskin would never have the same energy as before, but he had regained a good deal of strength over the course of the year. As the fall term commenced, and he observed his sixty-eighth birthday, he looked ahead with some optimism for the first time in a long while.

20

The Great Dissenter

'A judge never writes more freely than when he writes in dissent,' observed Bora Laskin in 1972.[1] And Canada has never had a chief justice who dissented as frequently, and freely, as Laskin himself. He was not completely isolated on the Court, however, and only rarely dissented alone. Whether joined by Hall and Spence in his early years on the Court, by Spence and Dickson later, or by Estey and Dickson in his last years, Laskin always spoke for an important subset of his colleagues even if they did not form a majority on a particular issue. Laskin and those who joined him in turn represented a significant body of opinion among academics, the legal profession, and the public. In his last years Laskin did begin to urge the Court to speak with a more united voice, but this was an aberration. From his days as a law professor when he had championed the right and duty of judges to dissent, Laskin seldom wavered from the view that the overt clash of ideas was necessary to move the law forward. Many of his dissents, especially in administrative law, became accepted orthodoxy in later years, while his concerns about criminal procedure were taken up in subsequent Charter jurisprudence. By contrast, Laskin's dissents in federalism cases were never adopted by his colleagues or by later courts. His pronounced penchant for centralist interpretation was displaced by the preference for balanced federalism displayed by his academic rival William Lederman and largely embraced by the Supreme Court. This chapter considers those areas, primarily constitutional law and criminal law, where Laskin and his colleagues had ongoing differences, while the next considers those fields, primarily in public law, where Laskin's views came to influence those of his colleagues.

Laskin's dissents in division of powers cases and in criminal law revealed a quite profound clash of values with many of his brethren. While a believer in ordered liberty, Laskin was heavily committed to law's role in expanding individual freedom, especially in the core areas of speech, thought, and association. Provincial enactments were more often challenged as contravening these values than federal laws, and Laskin would not hesitate to strike them down on federalism grounds – usually because he found them to conflict with the federal power over criminal law. In the criminal context, Laskin scrutinized minutely the actions of police and prosecutorial authorities, and constantly tried to rein in tactics he found to be oppressive or unfair to the accused. To accomplish this he employed two techniques. Laskin tried to broaden the scope of the common law, moving it away from the rather timid position of the English judiciary and towards the more aggressive American stance developed by the Warren Court; he also used the Canadian Bill of Rights more and more confidently over the years.

Most of Laskin's colleagues preferred to uphold state power and the powers of the police and state officials wherever possible. They adopted an expansive notion of concurrency that allowed a considerable overlap of federal and provincial authority. In criminal matters they were reluctant to alter the received English jurisprudence that minimized judicial authority to exclude evidence based on questionable police tactics. The majority were more in tune with Canadian history, with its legacy of parliamentary sovereignty, strong state power, and highly visible police agencies such as the RCMP. But this legacy entailed viewing Canadians as subjects ('British' subjects, to be precise) rather than citizens. Laskin was also a believer in parliamentary sovereignty and a strong state, but he believed both would function better if Canadians were autonomous, free-thinking citizens rather than loyal and deferential subjects. Inferentially, he was also concerned about the legitimacy of state institutions and policing agencies if they persisted in using heavy-handed tactics in carrying out their missions. Laskin's views did not represent a rejection of traditional Canadian values and institutions but a re-articulation of them, a forceful reminder that the state was not an end in itself but existed to enlarge the scope of the individual's potential. When the social movements of the 1960s put individual freedom back on the agenda, Laskin found a ready audience for his liberalism.

Sites where the individual met state power directly brought out the liberal side of Laskin, but the division of powers cases on economic regulation illustrated the continuing influence of his modernist views on the role of the state in curbing the liberty of some to advance the liberty of others. His commitment to a strong central government reflected his belief that state action was required to 'level the playing field' for the individual when economic power was more and more concentrated in large corporations. He remained convinced that the provinces could not perform this task as effectively as the federal government, but had little success in persuading his colleagues on this point.

The 1975 case of *Harrison v. Carswell* best reveals the gap between Laskin and his colleagues, even an increasingly sympathetic one such as Brian Dickson, on fundamental values, on the nature of law, and on the judicial role.[2] It continues to be taught in law schools precisely because it illustrates age-old debates about the law so vividly. The case did not deal with the division of powers but raised civil liberties issues of a quasi-constitutional nature. On the surface it was simply a private law dispute about the use of space in a shopping mall. Sophie Carswell was on a legal strike against her employer Dominion Stores, which occupied leased premises in the Polo Park Shopping Centre. Along with eleven others she picketed on the (mall-owned) sidewalk in front of these premises, and was asked by the shopping mall owner to leave. When Carswell refused she was charged under the *Petty Trespasses Act* of Manitoba and convicted at trial but a majority of the Manitoba Court of Appeal allowed her appeal.

With Dickson writing the majority judgment, the Supreme Court restored her conviction. At first he wanted simply to apply a recent precedent by the Court, and not to deal with the policy issue at all, but the strength of Laskin's dissent forced his hand.[3] Dickson admitted – Laskin got him to add this sentence to his judgment – a general creative power in common law courts, but denied in this instance that a court had any obligation to balance Carswell's right to free expression and peaceful picketing against the mall owner's property right. If the balance was to be struck differently, that was the responsibility of the legislator. The right to property was primordial, and not to be tampered with. Individuals had a right to enjoy property and not to be deprived thereof without express enactment. Resorting to the impersonal usage favoured by lawyers, he framed the question thus: 'if A is to be given the right to enter and remain on the land of B against the will of B – it would seem to me that such a change must be made by the enacting institution.'[4] Dickson's long experience as a corporate solicitor suggests a ready source for his adoption of this deferential stance towards existing property rights.

In his dissent Laskin in effect balanced the rights involved, but he did so in a careful and rather doctrinal way. In effect he tried to 'read down' the concept of possession, upon which the tort of trespass is based, so as to provide a defence to Carswell. Laskin the property lawyer came to the aid of Laskin the labour and constitutional lawyer. Possession had to be appreciated in each physical context, and the 'considerations which underlie the protection of private residences cannot apply to the same degree to a shopping centre in respect of its parking areas, roads and sidewalks.'[5] In other words, Laskin envisaged property, and hence possession, along a kind of spectrum. In the most private and intimate settings the power to exclude would be absolute, but in quasi-public premises, the power to exclude might be diminished. Here he proposed that 'members of the public are privileged visitors whose privilege is revocable only upon misbehaviour ... or by reason of unlawful activity.'[6]

As a rationalist and defender of ordered liberty, Laskin wanted a *reason* for the mall owner to be able to exclude people; if he could exclude Carswell, he could exclude anyone for any reason or no reason, provided he did not offend provincial human rights law. The right to exclude for any reason or no reason is of course a hallmark of the traditional definition of property, one Laskin was prepared to accept where the expectation of total control was high, as in a private home. But he resisted treating property as a 'one-size-fits-all' concept when it manifested itself in different ways in lived experience. Walking through a shopping mall is *not* the same as walking through someone's living room, in spite of the law's recognition of a formally identical property interest in the homeowner and the owner of the shopping mall. The extent to which some other interest competing with the property owner's should be recognized depended on the strength of that interest. Laskin had been part of the Court when it decided a few years earlier that a shopping mall owner could evict persons picketing on mall property in furtherance of a boycott on California grapes, but he distinguished that case from Carswell's based on the nature of the underlying interest at stake.[7] The grape boycott was a broad campaign aimed at many retailers, and its message could be conveyed in a number of ways. Sophie

Carswell could not exercise her right to picket elsewhere without seriously compromising its effectiveness.

Laskin made the same choice he had made as a labour arbitrator, when he decided that an employer had no right to prevent employees on a meal break from canvassing other employees about forming a union, provided they did so peacefully and without bothering their co-workers. Property alone was not a sufficient reason to shut down such activity.[8] In *Harrison* Laskin also advanced an analogy to the Quebec civil law doctrine of abuse of rights, probably suggested to him by Beetz who also signed the dissent along with Spence.

The decision attracted surprisingly little commentary at the time. Harry Arthurs had commented on the issue at the Court of Appeal level and did not write again on the Supreme Court's decision, but on balance favoured the approach adopted by Laskin.[9] Many years later Bertha Wilson expressed her own preference for Laskin's views, claiming his dissent as an early example of the 'contextualist' approach she had championed in the Supreme Court.[10] Paul Weiler admitted there were good arguments on both sides – if anything, he leaned towards Dickson's view – and was impressed that the issues had been thoroughly aired. Dickson had not just retreated into precedent but had offered a principled defence of judicial restraint in this particular context. Laskin was having an ameliorative effect on the majority's reasoning process even if he remained in dissent.[11]

Harrison v. Carswell exposed the fault-lines between the academic-cum-labour arbitrator and the representatives of the corporate managerial class who largely made up the Court's membership. Dickson's views did not remain static, however. While he probably would have decided this particular case in the same way even later in his tenure, on other issues he began to detach himself from the majority and to join Laskin in dissent. When *Harrison* was heard Dickson had been on the Court less than two years. Late in 1974 he would join Laskin for the first time in a dissent, and later in the 1970s he became a member of the 'LSD' triumvirate which regularly dissented on criminal law and civil liberties issues. Laskin's ability to persuade Dickson on some matters did not extend to issues relating to the division of powers: on these, Laskin the centralist and Dickson the supporter of provincial rights would remain far apart.

Laskin's appointment as chief justice coincided with a highly acrimonious period in the history of Canadian federalism. As Snell and Vaughan have noted, after 1974 'the Supreme Court was caught in the crossfires of federal-provincial disputes more frequently than in any previous period.'[12] No fewer than fourteen were heard in the 1976–7 year alone. It seemed as if the players were going out of their way to aggravate each other, with Manitoba even seeking to tax meals served on Air Canada while its planes crossed provincial airspace.[13] That at least was a slam-dunk for the federal government, and Laskin wrote for a unanimous Court in striking down the Manitoba taxing provisions. Other issues were much more important, and much more contentious: the sweeping powers claimed by Ottawa to combat inflation, the extent of provincial authority over criminal prosecutions, jurisdiction over private enterprises carrying out work on federally sponsored projects, the applicability of provincial law on Indian reserves, the authority of provincial film censors, and the capacity of cities to ban demonstrations. These cases fall into two categories: those involving straight federal-provincial conflicts, such as those over economic regulation, labour matters, and the administration of justice; and those where civil liberties issues arise in a division of powers context. In the first set of cases Laskin's views have mostly remained in the minority, while the civil libertarian concerns he expressed have been largely embraced in the Charter of Rights jurisprudence.

President Nixon's decision to de-link the American dollar from the price of gold in August 1971 set off an inflationary spiral that was particularly hard on Canada. Increased unemployment, decreasing productivity, and declining government revenues were further exacerbated by the oil crisis of 1973. Canada's economy was in serious trouble as a new word, 'stagflation,' entered the popular lexicon. After ridiculing Robert Stanfield's proposal for a ninety-day wage and price freeze in the July 1974 election campaign, Pierre Trudeau found himself needing to propose even more interventionist measures a year later. On Thanksgiving Day 1975 he announced on television the imposition of a comprehensive system of wage and price controls to be administered by a new Anti-Inflation Board. When passed in December, the legislation authorized the establishment of guidelines for the restraint of prices, profit margins, compensation, and dividends. The Act applied to the federal public sector, to private sector businesses employing more than five hundred persons, to suppliers of designated professional services, and to construction businesses employing more than twenty persons. Compensation of provincial public sector employees was not covered by the Act, though the government was authorized to enter into agreements with the provinces to bring them under its aegis.

Only British Columbia and Saskatchewan had not entered such agreements by the following spring, though Quebec had also created its own
Inflation Control Commission.

Early in 1976 the federal government referred to the Supreme Court
two questions: was the *Anti-Inflation Act* within the powers of the
Parliament of Canada? And was an agreement entered into between
Ontario and the federal government effective to bring the Act into force
with respect to the provincial public sector in that province? The unspo-
ken condition in the latter question was whether the agreement was
effective in spite of the absence of provincial legislation bringing the
agreement into force. Most other provinces had passed such legislation
but the minority government of William Davis could not because both
the Liberals and the NDP had publicly opposed it; he was thus forced
into relying on an executive decree alone to bring the federal Act into
force. Speaking for a unanimous Court on this point, Laskin made
short work of the arguments of Ontario counsel Roy McMurtry and of
D.W. Mundell, with whom he had had a spirited exchange on constitutional law two decades earlier. 'There is no principle in this country,' Laskin declared, 'that the Crown may legislate by proclamation
or order in council to bind citizens ... without the support of a statute
of the Legislature.'[14]

The courtroom seemed to be full of Laskin's former academic rivals.
William Lederman represented the union of Ontario teachers who were
challenging the federal legislation. As soon as he rose to speak, observer
Stephen Goudge recalled, 'he and Laskin got into a very, very significant tiff that had a personal edge to it that seemed to me to say, "This
goes back through years of academic debate that is now being replayed
in this courtroom."'[15] In spite of his general commitment to civility,
Laskin would abandon his polite demeanour with people whom he
found particularly threatening (William Lederman, Wilbur Jackett) or
dangerously wrong-headed (D.W. Mundell). He must have been aware
of the need to appear particularly even-handed in his treatment of
counsel with whom he had had significant principled disagreements,
but on these occasions his usual iron discipline deserted him.

The hearing lasted an entire week, featured more than two dozen
lawyers, and was virtually a dress rehearsal for the *Patriation Reference*
six years later. It was arguably the most important case decided by the
Supreme Court of Canada since the abolition of Privy Council appeals.
Dominating both hearings was the lordly figure of J.J. Robinette. Goudge,
who along with Ian Scott was counsel for the Ontario Public Service

Employees Union, remembered his masterful advocacy for the federal government: '[Robinette held] the courtroom spell-bound for about no more than I suspect an hour-and-a-half ... I remember being mesmerized by how simply he was able to put things ... The Court seemed to listen without a question, without a comment, as if they were being told what to do. [He had] the ability to make simple and comprehensible what we'd succeeded in making an unbelievably complicated case.'[16] In spite of the surface similarities between the two hearings, Robinette would succeed in the *Anti-Inflation Reference* but lose in the patriation battle.

On the principal question there was a majority of seven to two in favour of federal competence based on an interpretation of the peace, order, and good government (POGG) power limiting its use to national emergencies. In fact, the very speed with which the judges rendered their decision – a mere five weeks after the close of the hearing – suggested the existence of an emergency. Laskin would have been prepared to interpret the federal power more expansively, but his decision on this point attracted only three concurrences (Judson, Spence, and Dickson) and thus remained a minority view. Indeed, the federal government had refrained from framing the *Anti-Inflation Act* as emergency legislation, clearly hoping to justify it on a broad 'national concern' basis growing out of the POGG power.[17] The interpretation of the POGG clause had been at the heart of Laskin's views on the Canadian constitution ever since his first major scholarly foray into the field in 1947. In fact, one might call his plurality decision in the *Anti-Inflation Reference* '"Peace Order and Good Government Re-examined" Revisited.'[18] Laskin was determined to use this occasion to retain some vigour in a broader interpretation of POGG authorizing the federal government to legislate on matters of national concern other than emergencies. Unfortunately he seemed unable or unwilling to get beyond the tangle of precedent in order to identify clearly his policy preferences.

After tracing all the relevant Privy Council decisions from *Russell v. The Queen* in 1882 forward, Laskin ended up where he had in 1947, with the summing-up of Viscount Simon in the *Canada Temperance Federation* case.[19] Simon had distanced himself from the progressive narrowing of the POGG power evident in the intervening Privy Council jurisprudence, and expressly rejected the view that it could only be invoked in the case of an emergency. '[T]he true test,' according to Simon, 'must be found in the real subject matter of the legislation: if it is such that it goes beyond local or provincial concern or interests and must from its inherent nature be the concern of the Dominion as a whole (as, for example, in the *Aeronautics* case and the *Radio* case), then it will fall within the competence of the Dominion Parliament as a matter affecting the peace, order and good government of Canada, though it may in another respect touch on matters specially reserved to the provincial legislatures.'[20] At this point, Laskin abruptly shifted focus. Rather than refine or elaborate on the very general 'national concern' test proposed by Viscount Simon, he noted that even the opponents of the legislation had conceded its validity if it could be characterized as 'crisis legislation' (Laskin seemed reluctant to employ the more usual phrase, 'emergency legislation'). Thus, in the name of deciding no more than necessary, he turned to that issue.

Deciding whether an emergency existed involved considering a wealth of economic data submitted by all parties. *Re Anti-Inflation Act* marked the first time the Court had accepted and relied on such a quantity of extrinsic material. But there was a prior question: by what standard would the Court review the federal government's assertion that an emergency existed? Laskin set the bar fairly low, requiring only a 'rational basis' for the government's action. He seemed impressed by Statistics Canada data showing the purchasing power of the Canadian dollar as declining from a base of 100 in 1971 to 0.78 by September 1974 and 0.71 in September 1975, and by Canada's 10.9 and 10.8 per cent inflation rate in 1974 and 1975 respectively, but did not explain how these figures led to the conclusion that an emergency existed.

Justice Beetz's dissent, in which de Grandpré joined, proposed that POGG had two branches: an emergency power, resulting in the suspension of the normal division of powers under the constitution, and a power to legislate in respect of new matters of national concern not articulated in any of the enumerated heads of section 91 or 92. In his view, the legislation failed to pass muster on either branch. Where Parliament wished to invoke the emergency power, it had to do so expressly in the legislation, which it had not done here. Considered on a non-emergency basis, inflation was not sufficiently precise to be a valid head of federal authority, like aeronautics or radio regulation. It was rather 'an aggregate of several subjects some of which form a substantial part of provincial jurisdiction. It is totally lacking in specificity [and] so pervasive that it knows no bounds.'[21] As for the 'national concern' doctrine in general, Beetz declared that it was 'not difficult to speculate as to where this line of reasoning would lead: a fundamental feature of the Constitution, its federal nature, the distribution of powers between

Parliament and the provincial legislatures, would disappear not gradually but rapidly.'[22]

The use of economic data by the majority was widely regarded as a breakthrough for the Court even if Laskin did not explain clearly how it shaped his reasoning,[23] but in other respects his judgment is disappointing. One authoritative commentator declared that Laskin's 'rational basis' test for the emergency power was so weak as to 'make it almost impossible to challenge federal legislation on the gound that there is no emergency.'[24] Beetz's judgment is more analytically powerful, more persuasive in a purely intellectual sense. Laskin treats the 'national concern' doctrine in an almost entirely formalist fashion, providing no historical or functional grounding for his conclusions and citing virtually no academic writing. For this he was criticized by his friend Al Abel, who agreed that the federal residual power went beyond emergencies but thought Laskin had not articulated a convincing basis for its extension.[25] An astute court watcher, Peter Russell, thought the resort to formalism was deliberate. While the majority decision had 'the *appearance* of being based on narrow, technical, purely legal considerations, [the] preference for this style of jurisprudence is based on larger considerations of constitutional policy ... As a result,' he observed, 'Canadians cannot expect judicial reasoning to add very much to the country's stock of constitutional wisdom. The question remains whether this masking of judicial power is in itself a kind of constitutional wisdom.'[26] For Russell, the Court's need to preserve its legitimacy and impartiality in highly political federalism cases could justify a recourse to a more formal style of reasoning.

And while a victory was extremely important strategically for the federal government in the *Anti-Inflation Reference*, there is a sense in which Laskin's conception of POGG is mired in phantom controversies. Ever since the war the federal government had been constantly legislating on matters of national concern that were mainly in provincial jurisdiction, by using the spending power. None of the judgments even acknowledged this trend. In spite of these deficiencies, Laskin's attempt to keep a 'national concern' doctrine alive did bear some fruit after his death. In a 1988 case, his successor on the Court, Gerald Le Dain, wrote a majority decision upholding federal ocean pollution legislation on this basis.[27]

The differing approaches of Laskin and Beetz to constitutional interpretation were said by one scholar to be 'one of the most exciting developments ... in the whole of our constitutional jurisprudence.'[28]

Noel Lyon of Queen's University saw the two men as having articulated quite different models of federalism. For Laskin, the character of a given law has 'a chameleon tendency to take its colour from the circumstances of the day,' such that its 'matter' for purposes of the division of powers was rather fluid. Concurrency was thus the principal tool used by Laskin to reconcile federal versus provincial claims to authority. In Beetz's 'classical federalism' the content of the various heads of power was more hard-edged, and where Laskin saw concurrency Beetz saw an invasion of provincial power. Paraphrasing Beetz, Lyon said 'the concurrency of the Laskin Model looks like a one-way street in favour of central power and grand national schemes at the expense of local autonomy, distinctiveness and experience.' Speaking for many francophone legal academics in Quebec, Pierre Patenaude of the Université de Sherbrooke agreed with Lyon as to the stark opposition between the Laskin and Beetz philosophies, but was clearer about where his own sympathies lay. Beetz's approach to the interpretation of POGG, he asserted, was the only one compatible with federalism.[29]

In other areas of economic regulation, Laskin continued to argue for a more expansive federal trade and commerce power, but usually without success. In *Dominion Stores v. The Queen*,[30] he dissented from a decision quashing charges under federal apple grading regulations which the majority found to have been wrongly applied to intraprovincial transactions, while in *Labatt's Breweries* he dissented from the majority's decision to strike down a section of the federal *Food and Drug Act* restricting the content of light beer to 2.5 per cent.[31] Both of the majority decisions were written by Estey, and they reflect not so much a restrictive view of the trade and commerce power as a reaction to the proliferation of bureaucracy for its own sake. Estey was never as much a fan of concurrency as Laskin, as it often led to a duplication of federal and provincial effort he found wasteful.[32]

One case involving the trade and commerce power saw Laskin do something very uncharacteristic. In *MacDonald v. Vapor Canada*, speaking for a unanimous bench, he struck down a section of the federal *Trade Marks Act* – the first time a piece of federal legislation had been held ultra vires in decades.[33] In question was section 7 of the Act which, after prohibiting various kinds of misrepresentations about products likely to cause confusion with the wares of a competitor, concluded with a blanket prohibition on 'do[ing] any other act or adopt[ing] any other business practice contrary to honest industrial or commercial usage in Canada.' Penalties for contravening this provision included injunctive relief and the recovery of damages or profits. Section 7(e) could not be justified as providing a statutory cause of action to enforce existing trade marks, said Laskin. Rather, it purported to function as an extension of existing provincial laws regarding breach of confidence, unconscionable transactions, and the like, creating new rights between subject and subject available for private enforcement. This was exactly what previous case law had said could not be justified on the basis of the trade and commerce power.

Nonetheless, Laskin made some important dicta that breathed new life into that power after his death. Had the provision in question been part of a regulatory scheme administered by a federal agency and directed to trade or industry as a whole, he intimated in *Vapor*, the result might have been different. The Supreme Court gratefully put his suggestion to work in 1989 to uphold the federal *Competition Act*, which had previously been upheld as criminal law but had more recently been amended to provide for primarily civil remedies administered by a statutory tribunal.[34] It is not clear why the existence of a regulatory scheme alone should render constitutional that which would not otherwise be so, but the train of thought is consistent with Laskin's legal modernism, which always made a sharp distinction between the common law and statutory schemes for the enforcement of rights.

In a number of cases dealing with Indian reserves and federally owned property, Laskin's view of federalism drove him to try and develop an enclave theory insulating activities on such properties from provincial regulation. Laskin's textbook on constitutional law had stated baldly that 'provincial laws are inapplicable on a reservation' but he was never able to persuade a majority of his colleagues that he was right.[35] Thus in *Cardinal v. Attorney-General of Alberta* Laskin dissented from the majority decision that an Indian could be convicted under provincial legislation of selling moose meat to a non-Indian on a reserve,[36] while in *Four-B Manufacturing* he also dissented when the majority held provincial labour law applicable to an Indian-owned shoe-manufacturing business located on a reserve.[37] Provincial legislation is not allowed to go so far as to affect the very status of being Indian, however, and in *Natural Parents v. Superintendent of Child Welfare* Laskin spoke for a plurality in reading down a provincial adoption law; the law could permit non-Indian parents to adopt an Indian child, but could not deprive the child of his Indian status even though it severed the tie with his birth parents in other respects.[38]

The opposition between the Beetz and Laskin models of federalism was revealed again in cases where jurisdiction over labour matters on federal projects was at issue. In *Construction Montcalm v. Minimum Wage Commission* Quebec asserted the applicability of its minimum wage laws to workers helping to construct runways for the new Mirabel airport.[39] Beetz upheld Quebec's claim in a strong majority judgment joined by six other judges. Labour relations being in principle a provincial matter, Ottawa had to show its authority to be integral to the carrying on of a particular project if it was to oust provincial jurisdiction. For the majority that was not the case here: the construction of runways was sufficiently removed from the core subject matter of aeronautics to maintain provincial jurisdiction. Only Spence joined in Laskin's dissent, which rather gamely tried to demonstrate how constructing a runway directly impacted upon the aeronautics power.

The Beetz-Laskin opposition was soon made a triangular conversation by the increasing confidence of Brian Dickson's reasoning in federalism cases. Dickson became an exponent of William Lederman's views on balanced federalism, and tended to oscillate between joining Laskin and Beetz on particular issues. Lederman and Dickson had attended high school together in Regina, where they became good friends, and both served in the Royal Canadian Artillery in Britain and Europe during the war. Citations of Lederman's writings frequently appeared in Dickson's judgments, in contrast to Laskin's.[40] Dickson's views came to the fore in a series of cases on the limits of the provincial power over the administration of justice, where he clashed with Laskin.

The *British North America Act, 1867* gave power over criminal law, both substantive and procedural, to the federal government in section 91(27), but left authority over 'the Administration of Justice in the Province, including the Constitution, Maintenance, and Organization of Provincial Courts, both of Civil and of Criminal Jurisdiction' with the provinces pursuant to section 92(14). The provinces existing in 1867 and those that joined later already possessed an array of courts and administered justice on a day-to-day basis, and it was thought best to continue this arrangement. In spite of the obvious potential for conflict between these two heads of power, the parameters of section 92(14) had seldom been explored in previous cases. In *DiIorio v. Montreal Jail* the Court had to consider the constitutionality of Quebec legislation creating 'a state-sanctioned inquiry [into organized crime] by a public tribunal with compulsory and punitive powers against those refusing to co-operate in its proceedings,' as Laskin described it.[41] Two men who were committed to jail for refusing to testify challenged via habeas corpus the constitutionality of the commission's proceedings; Laskin admitted that if the commission was rightfully created, the power to punish via contempt had been legitimately exercised. His concerns, however, were far broader than any civil liberties issues underlying the division of powers question.

Writing for the majority, Dickson upheld the legislation. Clearly the inquiry involved criminal law in a general fashion but it had no mandate to alter the criminal law nor to convict or acquit. Where there were legitimate overlapping interests between federal and provincial powers, Dickson believed the proper course was to try and uphold both pieces of legislation. Here he was able to rely on a strong institutional tendency of the Court to favour concurrency in the post-war period. Laskin was also a supporter of concurrency in general, but he tended to advocate a strong and hard-edged federal criminal law power, probably because it was the one area where the Privy Council had not whittled down federal authority. It is a measure of his isolation on this point that his dissent attracted only one – surprising – concurrence, that of Louis-Philippe de Grandpré. Given the level of personal animosity and ideological difference between the two men, this joint dissent was probably a unique occurrence.

Laskin's dissent is premised on a 'thin-end-of-the-wedge' argument: if the province can do this, why could it not institute an inquiry into the operation of the bankruptcy laws, or into monopolistic practices in a province (dealt with by federal anti-combines legislation), or into federal penitentiaries located in a province, all of which he assumed to be equally invalid. His reasoning is unpersuasive because it conflates law and society, crime and criminal law. An inquiry into crime is not the same thing as an inquiry into the state of the criminal law, just as an inquiry into the rates and causes of bankruptcy in a province would not be an inquiry into the bankruptcy laws, nor an investigation into the prevalence of monopolistic practices an inquiry into anti-combines law. The causes and prevalence of crime, bankruptcy, and anti-competitive practices are eminently concerned with economic and social conditions within a given province, and may vary widely from one province to another. The federal government is unlikely to create an inquiry into organized crime in one province only, and it is not clear why a province thereby afflicted must await federal action which may never be forthcoming. Laskin's approach is a recipe for a vacuum in governance with potentially grave consequences. Only his penitentiaries example has some force, and then because of their very nature as federally created and operated institutions; any analogy with the criminal law as a whole breaks down. A province probably could not create such an inquiry even if, hypothetically, a given penitentiary had a high rate of escapes causing alarm in the immediate neighbourhood.

A later series of decisions on the proper locus of prosecutorial authority for various types of federal offences appeared to retreat from Dickson's view on provincial powers over the administration of justice and to embrace Laskin's. It was clear that provincial attorneys-general could enforce Criminal Code offences, but what about other federal offences? Did it matter if the offence was created pursuant to some other head of power? In *R. v. Hauser* the Court decided that offences created under other heads of power had to be prosecuted by federal officials, but to do so the majority had to characterize the *Narcotics Control Act* as legislation based on the POGG power rather than the criminal law power.[42] The decision was roundly criticized in this respect, and both Laskin and Dickson disagreed with it. Laskin was in hospital with his first illness and did not sit on *Hauser*, but later indicated his disagreement with the majority's reasoning on the constitutional basis for the *Narcotics Control Act*.[43] Dickson dissented, agreeing with Laskin that narcotics control legislation was properly characterized as an exercise of the criminal law power, but disagreeing with regard to who should prosecute such offences. For Dickson, federal prosecutorial authority was guaranteed only where non-criminal federal offences were at issue; as far as the ordinary criminal law went, prosecution fell to the provinces under their section 92(14) power.

Two decisions released on the same day, less than six months before Laskin's death, supported his expansive views on federal prosecutorial authority.[44] Both confirmed such authority for non-criminal federal offences – *Combines Investigation Act* and *Food and Drugs Act* offences were at issue in the two decisions. A Laskin-led majority in both cases went further and declared the same result would have flowed even if the offences had arisen from statutes based on the criminal law power. In *obiter* Laskin suggested the federal prosecutorial power was exclusive, mirroring Dickson's view that the provinces had exclusive power to prosecute criminal law offences. Peter Hogg suggests that concurrency is the better view in light of *DiIorio* and the long-standing tradition of provincial prosecution of Criminal Code offences. In practice concurrency operates, in that the federal Crown has delegated its authority over most offences to provincial attorneys-general. While concurrency entails a possibility that the federal government could take over all criminal prosecutions, Hogg believes this threat 'is adequately deterred by political forces.'[45] In the end Laskin won out on theory while Dickson had history and politics on his side. Once again Laskin's contribution to constitutional law was of a highly abstract nature, quite divorced from historical experience or the realities on the ground. He tended to reason based on his understanding of the first principles of constitutional law, rather than asking whether the status quo could be legitimated, as Dickson tended to do.

The occasions when Laskin upheld provincial powers were few and far between. The one time when he spoke for a unanimous Court upholding provincial legislation was the exception that proved the rule: *Morgan v. Prince Edward Island (Attorney General).*[46] For many years the province had been concerned about land acquisition by non-residents. In 1972 it passed legislation requiring cabinet approval for any acquisition of land by non-residents exceeding ten acres or shore frontage of over five chains. Non-residents in this context included both Canadian and non-Canadian citizens. Two U.S. citizens who were residents of the island challenged the law, arguing its invalidity on two grounds: that it was legislation dealing with the status of alienage, and that it conflicted with the provisions of the *Canadian Citizenship Act*. Citizenship, they urged, 'involved being at home in every province, [and] was a status under exclusive federal protection.'[47] At one level such an argument might have appealed to Laskin, whose preoccupation with the status of Canadian citizenship was well known. But the legislation in question did nothing to prevent or impede anyone from acquiring citizenship, nor did it affect free movement by anyone on and off the island. The counter-argument for the province was solidly anchored in the bedrock of property and civil rights. 'Absentee ownership of land in a province is a matter of legitimate provincial concern,' he observed, and in one of his few references to history in a constitutional case, noted the significance of landlordism in Prince Edward Island's past as adding force to its authority.[48]

In these pre-Charter days, the division of powers was one way to challenge provincial legislation that might be thought to trespass on civil liberties. In two such cases in the later 1970s Laskin's dissents attracted widespread attention: *Nova Scotia Board of Censors v. McNeil*[49] and *Attorney General for Canada and Dupond v. City of Montreal*.[50] Both cases featured plaintiffs possessed of the kind of rights consciousness which was becoming more evident in the Canada of the 1970s, encouraged by the Court's liberal approach to standing in *Thorson*.

When the Nova Scotia Board of Censors prohibited the film *Last Tango in Paris* from being shown in the province, Gerard McNeil, a newspaper editor from Dartmouth, challenged its authority. The board, endowed with unfettered powers to prohibit the public exhibition of films, gave no reasons for its decision. McNeil first went all the way to the Supreme Court to establish that he, like Thorson, had standing to challenge the law in question, and the Court agreed.[51] Then he had to go back to the Nova Scotia courts before eventually returning to the Supreme Court on the substantive issue. The Canadian Civil Liberties Association intervened, with Ed Ratushny appearing for them, and the federal government intervened on the side of McNeil, arguing that the province had trespassed on the criminal law power. A unanimous decision by four members of the Nova Scotia Appeal Division had agreed with McNeil, but the Supreme Court went five to four against him. Ritchie, who wrote the majority decision, was the swing vote. Interestingly he had also been the swing vote in the *Lady Chatterley's Lover* case in 1962, but on the side of freedom of expression. Here he parted company with Judson, who joined Laskin's dissent with Spence and Dickson. Whether Ritchie felt a distinction had to be drawn between visual and literary representations of sexuality, or whether his views changed over time, is impossible to know. Possibly there were class issues lurking beneath the surface: only the better sort of citizen was likely to read about the exploits of Oliver Mellors with Lady Chatterley, while a mass audience might attend the cinema to see Marlon Brando and Maria Schneider engaged in similar activities.

In any case, the majority decision is embarrassing, at first characterizing the legislation in question as simply the regulation of a business within the province, like shoe production or chocolate manufacturing. Then Ritchie virtually gave away the game in observing that he was 'satisfied that the Board is clothed with authority to fix its own local standards of morality in deciding whether a film is to be rejected or not for local viewing.'[52] Community standards were indeed relevant in the assessment of obscenity, but framing the matter in those terms virtually admitted the legislation to be about criminal law in pith and substance. One might concede that provinces should have the power to regulate the moral calibre of some local entertainments without running afoul of the criminal law power, but the problem in *McNeil* was the total absence of legislative or board-generated criteria defining how the board was to exercise its powers.[53]

Laskin's criminal law arguments were really a screen for more fundamental civil liberties concerns. A long concurring judgment by Macdonald J.A. in the Appeal Division denied the province the power to trench on fundamental freedoms, in a way that pointed to Charter decisions of the next decade. Laskin did not even bother to address the argument, knowing it was hopeless without an entrenched bill of rights, and restricted his remarks to the criminal law point. He was frustrated by the province's attempt to play cat-and-mouse by hiding behind the board's lack of reasons. Laskin virtually accused the board of bad faith, saying it could not 'shield its exercise of power by refusing to disclose the grounds upon which it has acted.'[54] A long review of other provinces' legislation was meant to illustrate a movement towards film classification rather than prohibition, suggesting that the province had ample power to exclude young persons from explicit or controversial films if that was the concern. Laskin was surely correct to observe that it was the potential powers of the board that would determine the constitutionality of its legislation, and on its face the board had powers to prohibit films for political or religious reasons as well as obscenity. 'All of this,' he observed sternly, 'is by way of prior determination, by way of anticipatory control of public taste.'[55] For someone with Laskin's commitment to free expression, there was scarcely a more egregious act.

McNeil and *Dupond* raised similar issues about the limits of provincial powers, and both were released on the same day, 19 January 1978. *Dupond* arose out of the unsettled conditions prevailing in Montreal in the late 1960s when separatist sentiment rose dramatically. In November 1969 the city imposed a thirty-day ban on demonstrations, on the ground that ninety-seven demonstrations, some with violence, had occurred in the previous ten months at an estimated cost to the city of some $7 million. This ordinance was passed under the authority of a by-law allowing the executive committee of city council to do so where it had reasonable grounds to believe 'that the holding of assemblies, parades, or gatherings will cause tumult, [or] endanger safety, peace or public order.' Ironically, the first casualty of the by-law was the Eaton's Santa Claus parade, which was not held in Montreal thereafter.[56] The plaintiff Claire Dupond had been trying to attack the by-law in the Quebec courts for seven long years, without success, nor did she enjoy a victory in Ottawa. A majority of six upheld the by-law, with the familiar LSD trio dissenting. Beetz wrote for the majority, but the decision does not possess his usual analytical force. Upon re-reading his reasons later, he confessed to his friend Andrée Lajoie, 'je me relis et je me vois devenir terriblement conservateur, mais c'est moi, cela, et je ne peux pas le renier.'[57] Beetz had been dean of law at the Université de Montréal during this tumultuous time and was horrified by the constant demonstrations both on and off campus. In fact he was a dean under siege, a rather shy scholar totally unsuited by temperament to deal with such a confrontational and politically charged context. In upholding the by-law he was content to quote *Hodge v. The Queen* from 1883, which endorsed municipal police powers 'calculated to preserve [peace] in the municipality, ... and repress ... disorderly and riotous conduct.'[58]

Laskin noted that the result in *Hodge* was justified as part of a valid liquor licensing scheme admittedly within provincial jurisdiction. But the by-law in question here was simply a 'mini-Criminal Code.' It tracked too closely the provisions of the Criminal Code dealing with unlawful assemblies and thus invaded the federal criminal law power. 'For constitutional purposes, provincial prohibitions to be valid have to be associated with a valid scheme of regulation as enforcements or reinforcements thereof, and are not sustainable as peremptory directions against forbidden conduct or behaviour.'[59] There were no considerations of traffic, public health, or sanitation in the present case, 'but a naked concern for the public peace and about anticipated violence.'[60] The city's concerns were legitimate, but Laskin noted the existence of extensive police powers of arrest without warrant in the Criminal Code as an important tool in its repertoire. He was troubled that persons who might gather for innocent purposes were prohibited from doing so because of a broad concern about violence. 'This is an invocation of a doctrine which should alarm free citizens even if it were invoked and applied under the authority of the Parliament of Canada, which has very wide power to enact criminal law.'[61] In *Dupond* it seems that Laskin the centralist trumped Laskin the legal modernist. In the administrative law context he always advocated deferring to those with the greatest knowledge of local context. Here he was not prepared to defer to the wisdom of local politicians acting in good faith in an extremely volatile context, even where they had restricted their interventions to a mere thirty-day period. It is also not clear why the fear of many citizens to use streets and parks could not suffice to justify characterizing the by-law as dealing with municipal property.

One intriguing aspect of both *McNeil* and *Dupond* is Laskin's reticence about analysing them in terms of the theory he had propounded as an academic: that civil liberties constituted a separate 'matter' for purposes of the division of powers, within exclusive federal jurisdiction and thus immune from provincial infringement. As Robert Sharpe has pointed out, these two cases were the perfect vehicles for this theory but Laskin refrained from raising his earlier ideas in them.[62] A year earlier he had treated the question as still open in a law school address, and the civil liberties chapter of the 1975 revised edition of his casebook, authored by his son, continued to advance Laskin's traditional position on the subject.[63] Macdonald J.A. in the Nova Scotia Appeal Division in *McNeil* had more or less adopted Laskin's theory, though without naming him as the source.

One can only speculate as to Laskin's reasoning. His basic views on federalism remained firmly fixed, and it seems unlikely that he had abandoned his earlier theory. Rather, he chose not to express it when there was an alternate way to reach the same result. Even though Laskin was an enthusiastic dissenter, he undoubtedly weighed the costs each time he did it. Pursuing an academic theory that had made virtually no impact on judicial thinking in the twenty years since its articulation risked making him look even more isolated than he actually was. It is also possible that Laskin floated his professorial approach by his co-dissenters, Spence and Dickson, and was discouraged from pursuing it. If it is true, as Peter Hogg observes, that 'Laskin C.J.'s view of the criminal law power as a substantial limitation on provincial power to enact penal laws finds little support in the numerous cases upholding [such] provincial laws,'[64] it is equally true that the Charter now allows the arguments for and against them to be framed in more appropriate terms than those provided by federalism.[65]

McNeil and *Dupond* caused great disappointment in media circles. Editorial writers lamented that 'civil rights are taking a beating,' as Ray Conlogue of the *Globe and Mail* wrote in a long article reacting to these and other recent decisions unreceptive to civil liberties concerns.[66] Ed Belobaba, a former Laskin clerk then teaching at Osgoode Hall Law School, was quoted as saying *Dupond* 'must have ripped into him [Laskin] emotionally, but I think he knows his view will win eventually.' As Conlogue observed resignedly, 'the future of civil rights in Canada will rest in large measure on the appointments made' in the next few years, and he was correct. The appointments of Estey and Pratte in 1977, replacing the relatively conservative Judson and de Grandpré, Antonio Lamer in 1980, replacing Pigeon, and Bertha Wilson in 1982, replacing Martland, helped shift the centre of gravity of the Court, while Laskin's own views seem to have shifted more to the centre after his illnesses in 1978–9. William McIntyre, who replaced Spence in early 1979, would be relatively conservative on some Charter equality issues but was cut from the Spence mould where traditional civil liberties were concerned.

If the civil liberties fallout from Laskin's approach to federalism was popular in liberal media circles, his general approach to the division of powers while on the bench has not found much support in academe. In the most extensive study of Laskin's federalism decisions published to date, Professor Katherine Swinton found them unsatisfactory in both style and substance. According to her he cast his judgments in a formalist style that allowed him to ignore or obscure the true provincial interests at stake, contrary to his constant exhortations while an academic about the need to identify policies and interests overtly.[67] It is hard to refute this claim, especially when this opacity did not feature nearly so prominently in Laskin's non-constitutional jurisprudence. In the latter he often went beyond precedential exegesis and clearly identified the real issues involved. This dichotomy demonstrates an unwillingness rather than an inability to address the interests involved. It is almost as if Laskin felt he could not articulate persuasively the policy reasons favouring federal authority, and turned to the discussion of precedents to fill the gap. Whatever the defects in Laskin's reasoning, however, Professor Swinton arguably understates his contribution by failing to look at him as part of the Court as a whole. If it is true that Laskin's strongly centralist take on federalism has not survived him, it is also true that the emergent 'balanced federalism' of the 1980s was a product of the clash of strongly centralist and strongly provincialist views present in the Laskin Court. It is as easy to wave the flag of local diversity as the flag of national concern. 'Balance' implies a consideration and reconciliation of both perspectives, and Laskin's strong views on federal power in both trade and commerce and criminal law influenced Brian Dickson and through him, the subsequent evolution of Canadian constitutional law.[68]

The judges who tended to favour provincial rights were also inclined to uphold the forces of law and order in the criminal law context. Laskin, meanwhile, continued to display the same concern with fairness in criminal procedure as he had in the Court of Appeal. Martland, Ritchie, and the Quebec judges were unwilling to recognize any judicial discretion to exclude illegally obtained evidence or to supervise police or prosecutorial practices in any way, while Laskin believed the courts had an inherent jurisdiction to protect their own process from abuse and to shield the individual from excessive zeal on the part of the Crown. Laskin often dissented on such issues with Spence and Hall, and later with Dickson and Estey. In *Rourke v. The Queen*, for example, the Court faced for the first time the question of whether delay by police authorities in bringing charges against an accused could result in a stay of proceedings by the trial court on the basis of an abuse of process.[69] Laskin was on the Ontario Court of Appeal when it had decided in *R. v. Osborn* that such a power existed, and had used it to quash a conviction.[70] On appeal the Supreme Court had restored the conviction, but as Laskin observed, 'no majority view emerged as to whether a Court could stay or dismiss criminal proceedings by reason of abuse of process.'[71] In *Rourke* a narrow five-four majority decided that there was no general discretionary power in courts of criminal jurisdiction to stay regularly instituted proceedings because the prosecution was allegedly oppressive. Although Laskin agreed in the result that the delay in this case was not oppressive, he strongly urged the recognition of such a power while admitting that it was 'one of special application [whose] exercise cannot be a random one.'[72] Laskin's oconcerns were ultimately addressed in section 11(b) of the Charter, conferring upon those charged with crimes a right 'to be tried within a reasonable time.'[73]

Oppressive tactics by the Crown also motivated Laskin in a case dealing with double-charging, though on this rare occasion he actually secured a five-four majority for his views. In *Kienapple v. The Queen*, the accused was charged and convicted on two counts involving a thirteen-year-old girl: rape contrary to section 143 of the Criminal Code and unlawful carnal knowledge of a female under the age of fourteen, contrary to section 146(1).[74] The jury convicted on both counts and the accused was sentenced to two concurrent terms of ten years. Given that both charges arose out of the same act, should the accused have been found guilty of the section 146 charge after having been found guilty of rape? Laskin thought not. Even though the second conviction had not resulted in an additional penalty to the accused, 'the better practice [was] to avoid multiple convictions.'[75] Laskin grounded the principle against successive prosecutions on 'the Court's power to protect an individual from an undue exercise by the Crown of its power to prosecute and punish.'[76] *Kienapple* remains significant as one of a cluster of rules all based on the same concerns as the Charter's express proscription of double jeopardy.

Entrapment techniques by police had concerned Laskin since his days on the Court of Appeal. There, in *R. v. Ormerod*, he had first speculated about the existence of such a defence in Canadian law, though he did not find it made out on the facts in that case.[77] As a Supreme Court judge he went into the issue in much more detail in *R. v. Kirzner*, though again he did not make a final pronouncement because he felt the factual foundation was missing.[78] He finally resolved his doubts when he signed on to Estey's strong dissenting opinion in *Amato v. The Queen*.[79] Estey urged the court not to lend its support to the state in situations where the police had inveigled an accused into committing a crime through persistent solicitation amounting to harassment. Entrapment was not a defence in the ordinary sense that it led to an acquittal, because the Crown could often establish all the elements of the offence; rather, a successful plea of entrapment should result in a judicial stay of proceedings. The Supreme Court of Canada expressly approved of the Estey-Laskin analysis a few years later in a post-Charter case; the use of entrapment techniques is now considered contrary to 'the principles of fundamental justice' under section 7 and a stay of proceedings will issue in appropriate cases.[80]

Similarly, Laskin joined Estey's dissent in *Rothman v. The Queen*, where police tricks were under review.[81] Where an accused suspected of drug offences made inculpatory comments to a police officer disguised as a fellow inmate, the two judges would have excluded the confession as tending to bring the administration of justice into disrepute. After the Charter, the Supreme Court has considered such conduct as violating section 7.[82] More generally, section 24(2) is a codification of the supervisory jurisdiction over excessive police and prosecutorial tactics that Laskin fought so long to establish: where evidence is obtained in breach of the Charter, it 'shall be excluded if it is established that, having regard to all the circumstances, the admission of it in the proceedings would bring the administration of justice into disrepute.'

In a number of cases Laskin was able to amplify his concerns about fairness to the accused by invoking the Canadian Bill of Rights. In *Curr v. The Queen* he agreed with the Court that the obligation to provide a breath sample in cases of suspected impaired driving did not contravene the privilege against self-incrimination affirmed in the Bill of Rights – even in the United States with its entrenched Bill of Rights such arguments had been rejected.[83] However in *Brownridge v. The Queen*

Laskin and five colleagues found the right to counsel guarantee contained in the Bill of Rights to have been infringed, and quashed a conviction for impaired driving where a police officer had refused to allow the accused to consult counsel during the two-hour period during which a breathalyzer test must be administered if the results are to be accepted in court.[84] 'The right to retain and instruct counsel without delay,' said Laskin, 'can only have meaning to an arrested or detained person if it is taken as raising a correlative obligation upon the police authorities to facilitate contact with counsel.'[85] The Court was not prepared to go so far as to exclude evidence acquired after a refusal by the police to allow counsel to be consulted, however, and this pushed Laskin back into dissent in a subsequent case on this point, *Hogan v. The Queen*.[86] He was vindicated in a case arising a week after the coming into force of the Charter, where a majority excluded a breath sample when a police officer had forgotten to inform a drunk driver of his right to counsel.[87] *Brownridge* and *Hogan* signalled a much greater interest by Laskin in the potential of the Bill of Rights than he had manifested as a law professor, one which would only increase throughout his tenure on the Court.[88]

Given Laskin's long experience in helping to draft and secure the passage of anti-discrimination legislation, it is not surprising that he was a stronger advocate of the equality clause in the Canadian Bill of Rights than most of his colleagues. The earliest opportunity for him to express his views came in *Lavell*, as discussed in chapter 17. The next came in *R. v. Burnshine*, where sentencing provisions exposing young offenders in British Columbia to longer sentences than adult offenders were attacked as infringing the equality guarantee contained in the Bill of Rights.[89] On the reading of the statute advanced by the Crown, young offenders could be sentenced to a combination of determinate and indeterminate sentences that might exceed the maximum fixed by the statute creating the offence. Laskin, with Spence and Dickson concurring, found the provisions to contravene equality before the law, but employed a less intrusive remedy than the Court had used in *Drybones*. Rather than declare the provisions in question inoperative, which presumably would have created a significant gap in the criminal law, Laskin 'read down' the impugned provisions to say that any combination of determinate and indeterminate sentences could not exceed the maximum imposed by the statute for a particular offence. The majority judgment by Martland adopted a theory of the Bill of Rights that not only retreated from *Drybones* but virtually ensured that the Bill could

never again be successfully invoked to challenge legislative classifications. As long as legislation was passed pursuant to a 'valid federal
objective,' said Martland, it must be deemed to operate in accordance
with the Bill of Rights. This was tantamount to saying that any federal
legislation valid in a division of powers sense could not be said to
contravene the Bill of Rights. In response to this anaemic reading of the
Bill of Rights, Laskin adopted his most expansive interpretation of its
equality guarantee a year later in *Attorney General of Canada v. Canard*,
as discussed in chapter 17.[90]

A case not dealing with the Bill of Rights but illustrative of how
Laskin's approach to equality diverged from that of his colleagues is
Gay Alliance Toward Equality v. Vancouver Sun, which is considered from
another perspective in the next chapter.[91] The *Sun* had refused a two-
line advertisement from a group advocating homosexual rights, solicit-
ing subscriptions for its newspaper *Gay Tide*. Upon complaint, a board
of inquiry under the B.C. Human Rights Code had found the *Sun* to
have discriminated against GATE without reasonable cause contrary to
section 3 of the Code, and ordered it to print the ad. A majority of the
B.C. Court of Appeal upheld the *Sun*'s appeal: Branca J.A. on the basis
that any bias by the newspaper against homosexuals was honestly held
and thus provided 'reasonable cause' for any discrimination; and
Robertson J.A. on the ground that it was reasonable for the newspaper
to refuse the ad because it might offend some customers and diminish
its business. Laskin dissented on the administrative law ground that the
Court should defer to the board of inquiry, no manifest error having
been shown, but he was obviously very troubled by the reasoning of the
B.C. Court of Appeal. Branca's argument he declared to be 'destructive
of the substance of s. 3,' while he found Robertson's permission to the
newspaper to hide behind its supposedly offended customers execrable.
If the learned judge was correct, 'a person who operates a service or
facility customarily available to the public can destroy the prohibition
against denial of its service ... by parading his apprehensions that he
will lose some business. Moreover, this would destroy the prohibition
not only in respect of a class of persons such as the appellant association, but against a complaining black person or a Catholic or any other
person in the categories mentioned in s. 3(2)(a) of the Code.'[92] These
were strong words but they reflected Laskin's fundamental commitment to equality, even with regard to individuals and groups not belonging to the traditional categories defined by race, religion, and sex.
Defined as an outsider for so many years because of his Judaism, Laskin

identified keenly with those who were victims of exclusionary practices, unlike his colleagues who came from more mainstream backgrounds. He had been close friends with a gay man, David Spencer, for
some forty years, and had no qualms about extending human rights
protection to homosexuals when permitted by the legislation. The B.C.
Human Rights Code was unusual at the time in that it did not contain a
closed list of forbidden categories of discrimination, but a blanket anti-
discrimination clause that could be applied to persons with a wide
range of characteristics. The majority in the Supreme Court were prepared to sacrifice equality on the altar of freedom of the press, a value
they were notably lax about protecting in other contexts. *Gay Alliance*
also illustrates Laskin's influence on Brian Dickson. Dickson had initially written a strong decision upholding the B.C. Court of Appeal, but
did a complete U-turn after Laskin responded critically to his initial
draft. Laskin persuaded Dickson that no threat to freedom of the press
was posed where the content of mere classified advertisements was at
stake, and that their usual deference to administrative tribunals should
be respected here.[93]

Laskin's final dissent in a Bill of Rights context came in a case posing
important questions about the interaction of civil and military justice.
In *MacKay v. The Queen*, a member of the Canadian Forces was tried by
a Standing Court Martial on charges under the *National Defence Act*, six
of which related to drug trafficking contrary to the *Narcotic Control
Act*.[94] He was found guilty and the Court Martial Appeal Court upheld
the convictions on five of the charges, as did a majority of the Supreme
Court. Joined by Estey, Laskin would have found inoperative those
provisions of the *National Defence Act* authorizing the trial of Forces
members by service tribunals of military personnel on charges under
the ordinary criminal law. Section 2(b) of the Bill of Rights required
Canadian law to be construed and applied so as to guarantee a 'fair and
public hearing by an independent and impartial tribunal.' In this case,
however, Laskin found 'the accused [to be] in the hands of his military
superiors in respect of the charges, the prosecution and the tribunal by
which he was tried.'[95] In his view, all Canadians were entitled to a trial
'before a court of justice, separate from the prosecution and free from
any suspicion of influence of or dependency on others.' In the case of
ordinary criminal charges laid against a member of the Forces, 'there is
nothing ... that calls for any special knowledge or special skill of a
superior officer, as would be the case if a strictly service or discipline
offence, relating to military activity, was involved.'[96] For similar rea-

sons, Laskin also found trial for ordinary criminal offences by a military tribunal to be a denial of equality before the law under the Bill of Rights.

The four veterans on the Court split three different ways. Ritchie wrote for the majority, who held that neither the guarantee of equality before the law nor of a trial by an independent and impartial tribunal was infringed when military tribunals tried members of the Forces for ordinary crimes. Dickson and McIntyre came up the middle, agreeing in the result but adding a caveat. They held that the Bill of Rights would render inoperative the provisions of the National Defence Act where 'the commission and nature of the offences had no necessary connection with the service,' but in their view, trafficking drugs within the military establishment was intimately related to issues of military discipline. The concurrence by Estey gave considerable weight to the dissent, given Laskin's lack of direct military experience. Estey's work with the Judge-Advocate General's office during the war had not endeared him to the system of military justice, and he was only too happy to try and restrict its ambit when the occasion arose.

MacKay is a case that looks backward and forward at the same time. It touches on one of Laskin's oldest preoccupations: the attributes of Canadian citizenship and the fundamental equality of all citizens. He accepted that the military were a separate class within Canadian society, justifying legal distinctions in some instances. But those distinctions were not to be extended one iota beyond what was absolutely necessary for the continued integrity and effectiveness of the military, lest the equality of members of the Forces and civilians be impaired. There are echoes too of his report *Freedom and Responsibility in the University*, which insisted on both the equal citizenship of students and faculty within the university and the limits of university tribunals when considered in light of the general law.

Perhaps because the issues raised were so close to Laskin's heart, his decision has an unusually tight focus compared to many of his more discursive judgments. It reviews only the key Bill of Rights decisions, and concludes that 'unless the *Drybones* case is to be overruled, its principle must be given effect here.'[97] *MacKay* looks forward too in the sense that it is almost a Charter case *avant la lettre*, one which demonstrates the readiness of the Court to tackle the greater responsibility shortly to be thrust upon them. In taking such a strong stand on equality before the law and the meaning of an independent and impartial tribunal, Laskin forced Dickson and McIntyre in effect to articulate a section 1 'reasonable limits' argument stating clearly the conditions under which military justice would be constitutionally acceptable. It is not surprising that neither Laskin's nor McIntyre's judgment is totally satisfactory on this point. Laskin conceded that prosecutions under military justice would be justified in some cases but was unable to articulate a clear test delineating the scope of this jurisdiction. McIntyre did pose a test, but it was so broad as to be of little use. According to him, service personnel could be tried by military courts for civilian offences where the offence was 'so connected with the service in its nature, and in the circumstances of its commission, that it would tend to affect the general standard of discipline and efficiency of the service.'[98] In post-Charter years the Court would return to this issue in a case called *R. v. Généreux*, where a court martial was found not to be 'an independent and impartial tribunal' within the meaning of section 11(d) of the Charter.[99] Like Laskin, the Court was troubled by the tribunal's lack of independence from superior officers and the appearance of bias caused by the appointment of tribunal members on a case-by-case basis.

It would be a mistake to label the reasons of a majority in a given decision as 'winning' and the minority as the 'losers.' Only for the immediate parties is that calculus significant. What is important over the long term for all judicial decisions is the quality of their reasoning. A poorly reasoned and unpersuasive majority decision can be sidelined subsequently by a compelling dissent. For Laskin, dissents were important for more than the voicing of principled disagreements about the law. They were a way of communicating directly with the disappointed litigants and the constituencies behind them: married women, as in *Murdoch*; disenfranchised native women, as in *Lavell*; proponents of free speech and artistic expression, as in *McNeil* and *Dupond*. Laskin's dissents validated the concerns of these groups; they showed that someone at the Supreme Court was listening, even if that someone did not speak for a majority. In this way Laskin lent legitimacy to a seemingly remote and indifferent institution, but his contribution went beyond this. He was not just waving from the sidelines, but was forcing the Court to grapple more directly and convincingly with the issues raised by litigants. In this process of 'challenge and response' lies much of Laskin's significance, and his legacy, to the Supreme Court. It was increasingly difficult for the other judges to rely on the opaque citation of precedent to justify their positions when Laskin crafted judgments in a more sophisticated and open-ended way. Where Laskin behaved most like his brethren, in his highly formalist reasoning in division of powers cases, he was least persuasive. Elsewhere, he was much more effective. Even if he was often in dissent, the positive reception accorded his views by the media and academics made at least some in the majority take notice. Older judges such as Martland and Ritchie were unlikely to change their views, but newer ones such as Dickson could be swayed.

21

Architect of Public Law

Laskin's principal success while at the Supreme Court was in the field of administrative law. Building on legal modernist ideas he had studied in the 1930s, then developed and applied during his long tenure as a labour arbitrator, he persuaded his colleagues to reorient their approach to the decisions of administrative tribunals and public officials. There were three main elements to Laskin's vision. First, he believed the courts should adopt a stance of deference to the decisions of statutory decision makers such as administrative tribunals and labour arbitrators. At the same time he subjected a wider range of actions by government officials to basic procedural fairness – the obligation to hear both sides before making a decision. Finally, he advocated the complete ouster of the common law in areas where statute had set up a comprehensive administrative scheme for the determination of rights in a given field of activity. Courts should defer to substantive determinations by administrative bodies, said Laskin, because complex social problems required the adjustment of competing interests by specialists familiar with the context in question. In a quid pro quo, statutory decision makers should ensure the fairness of their own procedures whenever they were making individualized decisions rather than setting broad policy. Laskin did not go so far as to say such bodies had to respect all the refinements of adversarial procedure developed in courts; they were granted a certain deference here too, and only a total absence of fair process or an egregious departure from expected procedural norms would suffice to set aside a decision. These three ideas remain at the heart of the judge-made part of Canadian administrative law, and it was Laskin, with Dickson's assistance, who put them there.

As seen earlier, initially the Court was not at all receptive to the idea that it should defer to the decisions of statutory decision makers. In *Bell Canada* in 1973, Laskin was in lonely dissent on this point.[1] The next year in *Metropolitan Toronto Police Association v. Metropolitan Toronto Board of Commissioners of Police*, Spence joined him in dissent, but only in part. Here Laskin sought to restore the decision of arbitrator Paul Weiler on the question of who was included for the purposes of check-off under a particular collective agreement.[2] The Ontario Court of Appeal and Laskin's colleagues decided that the agreement was 'perfectly unambiguous' and hence that Weiler had erred in using extrinsic evidence to interpret it. This misstep sufficed to quash the decision. Once Dickson joined the Court, he became a key convert to Laskin's cause. In the first year of his tenure he wrote for a unanimous panel of five, including Laskin, in allowing an appeal from a Saskatchewan Court of Appeal judgment quashing a decision of the province's labour board. The board had rejected an application for certification by a nurses' staff association on the ground that it contained mostly management nurses and was an employer-dominated organization. The Court of Appeal had quashed the decision because the board had not articulated its findings to the Court's satisfaction. Dickson's brief judgment was couched entirely in legal language and did not discuss the policy behind deferring to bodies such as labour boards; nor did it signal any major change in the Court's approach to judicial review in the short term.

A few years later Laskin and Spence joined a dissent by Dickson, in a case where the Federal Court of Appeal had overturned a decision of an adjudicator with the Public Service Staff Relations Board. The case concerned the proper characterization of the dismissal of Roland Jacmain, a probationary employee of the Commissioner of Official Languages. Jacmain had been chief of division of the complaints branch in the commissioner's office, but was himself a chronic complainer about office conditions. He complained about 'the files for which he was responsible, the calibre of work of the stenographic pool, the telephone service, the records service, the distribution of the mail and even about the "landscaped" arrangement of the office,' engaging in 'continual "Jeremiads"' on these subjects. Where a probationary employee was dismissed for cause, he or she had no right to refer the matter to adjudication, but if Jacmain had been subjected to a disciplinary dismissal, he could grieve the matter. He did grieve it based on the latter theory, and the adjudicator accepted his argument and set aside the dismissal. There seems little doubt that the employer could have dismissed Jacmain for cause had it laid the proper foundation, but it had not done so. Jacmain's letter of dismissal gave only one cause, and that was an earlier disciplinary suspension, itself subsequently revoked after a grievance. On this evidence the adjudicator found that the dismissal was disciplinary, but the Federal Court of Appeal disagreed with this conclusion and found the adjudicator to be without jurisdiction.

This was the classic case where the decision maker's jurisdiction to proceed depended on a preliminary finding. Demanding a standard of correctness on this preliminary finding would mean that every such conclusion by a statutory decision maker would be subject to judicial review. But this was just one aspect of the larger problem of the relationship of courts to statutory decision makers. Dickson summed up the problem:

> The intractable difficulty is this. It is hard to conceive that a legislature would create a tribunal and yet bestow on [it] an unlimited power to determine the extent of its jurisdiction. On the other hand, if the correctness of every detail upon which the jurisdiction of the tribunal depends is to be subject to re-trial in the Courts and the opinion of a judge substituted for that of the tribunal, then the special experience and knowledge of the members of such a tribunal and the advantage they have of hearing and seeing the witnesses may be lost. The power to review jurisdictional questions ... enables the Courts to check unlawful attempts at usurpation of power. But the Courts, in my opinion, should exercise restraint in declaring a tribunal to be without jurisdiction when it has reached its decision honestly and fairly and with due regard to the material before it. The Court should allow some latitude in its surveillance of jurisdictional findings. It should ask whether there is substantial evidence for decisions of fact and a rational basis for decisions of law, or mixed decisions of fact and law. The error must be manifest.[3]

Laskin had been hammering away at this theme ever since he joined the Ontario Court of Appeal, and he had now gained a major ally in Dickson. Still, after eight years on the Supreme Court he must have despaired of ever securing a majority. The big breakthrough came only eighteen months after *Jacmain*, when Dickson again took up Laskin's concerns and secured unanimous support for them in *C.U.P.E. Local 963 v. New Brunswick Liquor Corporation*.[4] In this landmark decision, Dickson articulated a new and deferential standard: courts should not intervene in a tribunal's decision unless it was 'patently unreasonable' with respect to those matters at the heart of its jurisdiction. Of course if a board found itself obliged to interpret and apply other laws in the course of its decision making, it would be held to a standard of correctness.[5] But where a board was on its home territory it was to be granted considerable latitude.

In *C.U.P.E.* Dickson went further than his previous judgments in explicitly articulating the policy reasons motivating deference. The dispute in the case was over the decision of the New Brunswick Liquor Corporation to use management employees as replacement workers during a legal strike by the union, a practice arguably forbidden by a section of the province's *Public Service Labour Relations Act*. The Public Service Labour Relations Board had interpreted the clause in the manner advocated by the union and upheld its complaint, but the New Brunswick Court of Appeal had quashed the decision as beyond the board's jurisdiction. Dickson noted that the 'Board is given broad powers – broader than those typically vested in a labour board – to supervise and administer the novel system of collective bargaining created by the [Act]. The Act calls for a delicate balance between the need to maintain public services, and the need to maintain collective bargaining. Considerable sensitivity and unique expertise on the part of Board members is all the more required if the twin purposes of the legislation are to be met.'[6] Laskin's concerns of the 1930s are all there: the balancing of interests, the sensitivity to local context, the valorization of specialized expertise.

In a case just after *C.U.P.E.*, the Court unanimously applied the new standard in restoring the decision of a labour arbitrator on his interpretation of a collective agreement provision (in the event, the decision went against the union). Laskin wrote a plurality decision in which he tried to clear away some troublesome undergrowth from old House of Lords decisions still being cited by some members of the Court, but the majority would not go quite this far.[7] In *Alberta Union of Provincial Employees v. Olds College*, Laskin spoke for a majority of seven in applying the *C.U.P.E.* standard even in a case where the board in question was not protected by a strong privative clause. Martland and Beetz rendered only a *pro forma* dissent, stating they agreed with the reasoning of the Court of Appeal decision being overturned by the majority.[8]

There are two unusual features of *C.U.P.E.*, and they may be related.[9] The first is that Dickson rather than Laskin wrote it. While Dickson had begun to write in the area, Laskin had consistently advocated the position taken in *C.U.P.E.* for over forty years, throughout his entire academic and judicial career. In a sense he owned the issue and might have been expected to write. A second odd feature is that the Court was unanimous, in contrast to many earlier split decisions on the standard for judicial review. If the decision is one Laskin should have written, it was probably more politically astute for Dickson to write it. Sometimes an unwelcome message becomes more palatable when communicated by a different speaker. The Court was well aware of Laskin's position on deference, but hearing Dickson, a more circumspect and centrist member of the Court, espouse it may have convinced some of the judges to evaluate it anew. Unanimity was also motivated by the lucky fact that the reasons of the New Brunswick Court of Appeal were hopeless – 'in irreconcilable conflict,' as Dickson himself noted. Justice Limerick had overturned the board on one interpretation of the clause in question, Justice Hughes on a totally opposite interpretation of the same clause, and the third judge had only concurred in the result. If ever there was a case showing the value of consistent interpretation by a specialist tribunal, this was it. The Court was apparently agreed after the hearing on the need to restore the board's decision, but some judges may not have realized just how far Dickson's decision represented a break with the Court's previous jurisprudence.[10] He cleverly presented the 'patently unreasonable' test as a natural outgrowth of earlier cases and did not overrule or even mention cases such as *Metropolitan Life* or *Bell v. Ontario Human Rights Commission*, which had taken a much more aggressive stand towards arbitrators and tribunals. He politely if somewhat unconvincingly distinguished *Jacmain* as dealing with the preliminary questions doctrine. Perhaps most importantly, he did not refer to any of Laskin's previous decisions in the Court of Appeal or his dissents in the Supreme Court, or to any of the voluminous academic literature on the question. If this was a strategic decision to sugar-coat a pill the Court was reluctant to swallow – though there is no direct evidence of this – it worked brilliantly.

Laskin's philosophy of deference carried over to the remedial powers of administrative bodies, an issue that had been close to his heart as a labour arbitrator. He was prepared to afford a wide latitude to such bodies in fashioning appropriate remedies to enforce their decisions. By the end of his tenure he was able to write a unanimous decision confirming the power of the Canada Labour Relations Board to order a union to admit certain persons to membership even though this power was not specifically granted in its constituent statute. In *Canada (Labour Relations Board) v. Halifax Longshoreman's Association* the board was seized of a complaint alleging arbitrariness by a union in its job referral system, contrary to its duties under the collective agreement. In 'very extensive reasons,' Laskin noted, the board 'gave ample chapter and verse for the unprincipled and discriminatory way in which the job referral system was administered, [finding] the union has been run and behaved more as a privileged exclusive club than a modern trade union.'[11] According to the board, the union had no written rules for membership, and operated on a secret ballot in a manner 'so far out of touch with a modern appreciation of [its task] that it is painful to us who deal with other unions on a daily basis.' Probably fearing retaliatory action against the complainants, the board ordered them admitted to the union. The Federal Court of Appeal found this action to be punitive rather than remedial and thus to exceed the board's jurisdiction. In a succinct judgment Laskin simply quoted *C.U.P.E.* and said the Court now found it 'more consonant with the legislative objectives involved in a case such as this to be more rather than less deferential to the discharge of difficult tasks by statutory tribunals like the Board.' The exercise of remedy here was 'bottomed squarely on the involvement of the complainants in an allegation of breach which was firmly established and which required redress and protection to them as individuals.'[12]

There seemed to be a division of labour between Laskin and Dickson on administrative law issues. Dickson took over Laskin's previous dissents and translated them into a majority on the deference issue in *C.U.P.E.*, and Laskin returned the favour for Dickson on the fairness issue in *Nicholson v. Haldimand-Norfolk Regional Board of Commissioners of Police*.[13] The issue it presented had been the subject of controversy at the Court for some years. When could an administrative body render a decision without affording an affected individual the right to notice and reply? The issue had been especially bedevilled in federal administrative law by a notorious provision of the Federal Court Act purporting to draw a bright line between reviewable 'quasi-judicial' decisions of federal boards, and unreviewable 'administrative' decisions, but the distinction was not limited to the federal context. Predictably, courts proceeded to try and pigeonhole each decision under review according to some doctrinal formula rather than looking at the real issues at stake.

In *Howarth v. National Parole Board*, Dickson had protested against this arid approach in reasons signed by Laskin and Spence, apparently the first time the three had joined together in dissent.[14] Howarth was a convicted armed robber charged with indecent assault while on parole. He denied the offence and the charges were dropped, but four days later the National Parole Board revoked his parole without prior notice or explanation. Dickson proposed that 'the seriousness of the consequences for the individual affected was the most important factor in determining whether the Parole Board had a duty to act fairly.'[15] He did not suggest Howarth was entitled to a full-blown hearing, but simply to know of the Board's proposed action and to be permitted to reply.

A year later Laskin wrote a dissent in another Parole Board case, in which Dickson joined.[16] Laskin turned up the pressure both by venting his outrage and by invoking the Canadian Bill of Rights, which had not been considered in *Howarth*. 'The uncontested facts,' he said, 'tend to shock from their mere narration.'[17] An inmate serving a three-year term had been caught in a Kafkaesque situation where his arrest while on parole, after it had been suspended without his knowledge and without reasons, resulted in a revocation of parole (again without reasons). The net result was that he served a longer sentence than his original term. In language unusual even for him Laskin castigated the board for its secrecy and lack of accountability. 'The plain fact is that the Board claims a tyrannical authority that I believe is without precedent among administrative agencies empowered to deal with a person's liberty. It claims an unfettered power to deal with an inmate, almost as if he were a mere puppet on a string.'[18] After reiterating Dickson's reasoning in *Howarth*, knowing the majority would not follow it, Laskin tried to bring in the Canadian Bill of Rights. He would have found a violation of both section 2(c)(i) (the right of an arrested person to be informed promptly of the reason for his arrest) and section 2(e) (the right to a fair hearing in accordance with the principles of fundamental justice). The majority did not blush to find that Mitchell had been informed of the reason for his arrest – the fact that his parole was suspended – even though he was not told the reason for the suspension.

Was there a contradiction between Laskin's invocation of tribunal sensitivity and expertise as a basis for judicial deference, and his willingness to castigate publicly a tribunal for failing to observe procedural fairness? The reconciliation is the familiar lawyer's distinction between substance and procedure. Laskin always advocated deference to an agency's substantive determinations on matters located at the heart of its mandate, and a certain amount of deference to the process adopted by an agency in the course of its decision making. But where an agency failed to adopt any fair process or adopted a transparently unfair one, there was no reason to defer where important economic or liberty interests were at stake. Laskin was not alone in making this distinction. He had heard J.A. Corry speak in very similar terms when giving an address at the official opening of Flavelle House as the new home of the law faculty in 1962. In a talk entitled 'The Future of Public Law' Corry had extolled the virtues of deference by courts engaged in judicial review, but at the same time stressed the importance of fair procedures in the administrative process. 'The real outrage of administrative action,' he observed, 'is not that our rights are circumscribed by public authority but that, in a variety of matters, it is done without a right to a hearing.'[19] Laskin put these views into action in his landmark decision in *Nicholson v. Haldimand-Norfolk Board of Police Commissioners*.[20] Along with Dickson's judgment in *C.U.P.E.* and Rand's in *Roncarelli v. Duplessis*, *Nicholson* is considered as part of the 'pantheon of great Canadian administrative law judgments.'[21]

Arthur Nicholson was engaged as a constable in March 1973 on a one-year probationary contract. In March 1974 the contract was renewed and he was promoted to constable second class. In June of that year his contract was terminated without prior notice. The relevant legislation allowed local police boards 'to dispense with the services of any constable within eighteen months of his becoming a constable.' The ex-constable sought to protest this action, and at first instance his application for judicial review of the board's decision was heard by the Divisional Court of Ontario. Laskin's former student and one-time rowing companion, Samuel Hughes, wrote its decision. Hughes agreed with Nicholson that a constable held an 'office' and was not party to a simple master-servant relationship. Further, he held that the duty of police boards to hold hearings when dismissing constables with more than eighteen months' service did not leave those with less seniority with no rights at all; rather, such persons were owed a basic duty of fairness. The Court of Appeal reversed, speaking through Laskin's successor there, John Arnup. Arnup agreed that Nicholson's position was properly characterized as an office, but found that constables with his degree of seniority had no statutory protection and were thus governed by the common law. At common law such an office was held at pleasure, hence Nicholson could find no protection there either. In February 1978 the Court heard argument on the appeal. Nicholson was represented by Ian Scott, a future attorney-general of Ontario and law partner of Andrew Brewin, a fellow traveller from Laskin's days in the labour and human rights movements. Scott recalled the case as 'an example of the most important kind of case that I did. Principles were at stake; new law had to be made for us to be successful; and wider social consequences would flow if the case could be won.'[22]

Laskin was doubtful at first about the merits of Scott's argument, but gradually came round to the view that *Nicholson* was an appropriate case for the approach Dickson had developed in *Howarth*. In a key part of the judgment, he described the duty of fairness as Dickson had, 'as a halfway house ... between the observance of natural justice and arbitrary removal.'[23] In fact Arnup's views were similar to the 'reserved management rights' doctrine often advanced by employers in the collective bargaining context, a doctrine always rejected by Laskin when he was a labour arbitrator. Just as employers tried to argue that anything not covered by the collective agreement remained within their power, so Arnup declared that constables of less than eighteen months' seniority were subject to the whims of management. Laskin's answer to Arnup was similar to the one he had developed long ago in the arbitration context. A comprehensive statutory scheme, aimed at covering police employment relations in their entirety, was not simply an add-on to the common law but a fresh start. Given the board's limited powers as a creature of statute, Laskin doubted whether the common law was relevant at all. Laskin received useful support for this idea by tracing the legislative history of the Police Act; he found that the words 'at pleasure,' formerly used to describe all members of a police force, had been removed from the Act in 1951. The words and the concept were now 'relics of Crown law which no longer govern the relations of police and Boards or Municipal Councils.'[24]

Having cleared away those obstacles, it was necessary to spell out affirmatively when a duty to act fairly would arise and what it entailed. Here Laskin relied on academic authority, itself stimulated by the dissent in *Howarth*. He paraphrased David Mullan of Queen's University: 'what rightly lies behind this emergence [i.e, of the duty to act fairly] is the realization that the classification of statutory functions as judicial, quasi-judicial or administrative is often very difficult, to say the least; and to endow some with procedural protection while denying others any at all would work injustice when the results of statutory decisions raise the same serious consequences for those adversely affected, regardless of the function in question.'[25] In keeping with Laskin's legal modernist project, it was important to reject mere labels and get on with identifying the true interests at stake. A probationary constable had an interest in continued employment sufficient to afford him the right to be told why his services were no longer required and to be given an opportunity to reply either orally or in writing. He was not entitled to a full in-person hearing, but as Laskin said, the right to be informed and to reply was important to ensure that the board had not acted upon some mistake or misperception. The parallels with the position of the untenured Harry Crowe in the United College affair, two decades earlier, were striking. In a sense *Nicholson* was the Crowe case all over again, only with an impact far beyond the university context. It remains one of Laskin's most-cited decisions, and its impact on Canadian administrative law has been profound.

Laskin often resorted to American authority when he wanted to introduce an innovation. *Nicholson* is unusual in his repertoire for the amount of English authority cited in support of a change in the law. With an earlier and more pervasive welfare state, English law had had to face these issues before Canada did. Even though Laskin determined that the statutory scheme had displaced the notion of office 'at pleasure' in the police context, he cited his friend S.A. de Smith for the point that even in England offices at pleasure were no longer held to be bereft of all procedural protections: 'public policy does not dictate that tenure of an office held at pleasure should be terminable without allowing its occupant any right to make prior representations on his own behalf: indeed, the unreviewability of the substantive grounds for removal indicates that procedural protection may be all the more necessary.'[26] English case law had been moving towards a synthesis expressed by Justice Robert Megarry in 1972 and now adopted by Laskin: 'in the sphere of the so-called quasi-judicial the rules of natural justice run, [while] in the administrative or executive field there is a general duty of fairness.'[27]

Nicholson, a five-four decision, demonstrated the significance of a changing bench. It was heard early in 1978, by which time Estey had replaced Judson. Judson might well have voted with Martland and the three Quebec judges to make a majority, whereas now they were left in the minority. By voting with the majority, Ritchie now became the swing vote. He and Martland usually voted the same way, but not always; what motivated him to switch to the Laskin team on this occasion is unknown. Normally Martland was content to follow English authority but here he chose to rely on older English authority and did not even attempt to distinguish the more recent decisions used by Laskin. His view was that a probationary employee had no protectable interest at all in continued employment: 'the only interest involved was that of the Board itself.'[28] Martland's reverence for English law was rooted in the common law he had studied at Oxford in the 1930s; he was not nearly as keen on the post-war expansion of the social security state produced by successive Labour governments in England.

In *Nicholson* Laskin was prepared to develop the common law of natural justice to assist in the interpretation of interests created by a statutory scheme. Whether the common law could continue to develop substantively in the face of a comprehensive legislative scheme for the creation and enforcement of rights was at issue in one of Laskin's most controversial decisions. In *Seneca College v. Bhadauria*, he spoke for the Court in refusing to recognize the existence of a new tort of racial discrimination.[29] Dr Pushpa Bhadauria was a highly qualified mathematician with seven years' teaching experience in that field in Ontario. On numerous occasions she had applied for positions at Seneca College, but never received an interview or an explanation as to why her applications were rejected. In fact, she alleged others with inferior qualifications were hired. Dr Bhadauria might have laid a complaint under the Ontario Human Rights Code but did not. Rather she commenced an ordinary action against the college alleging it was liable on the basis of a new tort of discrimination recognized by the common law. No one had ever tried to do this in Canada before. The college asked that the statement of claim be struck out as disclosing no reasonable cause of action and succeeded at trial, but the Ontario Court of Appeal reversed. Laskin's future colleague Bertha Wilson wrote that the growth of the common law was not impeded by the development of the Ontario Human Rights Code. 'While the fundamental human right we are concerned with is recognized by the Code' in its preamble, she said, 'it was not created by it.'[30] In reaching this result she cited *Drummond Wren*, which had used the public policy expressed in the 1944 *Racial Discrimination Act* to invalidate a discriminatory restrictive covenant. She then went on to hold, on the basis of *Ashby v. White* (1703), that 'where there is a right, there is a remedy,' and fashioned a new remedy, the tort of discrimination.[31]

There were many ironies here. Wilson was in effect relying on an argument Laskin himself had developed as a young law professor, one that had persuaded Keiller Mackay twenty-five years earlier. In *Bhadauria* he said coyly, 'I do not myself quarrel with the approach taken in *Re Drummond Wren*.' Now Laskin had to examine that argument as a judge, and to do so he could not ignore *Drummond Wren*'s effective overruling by the Court of Appeal in *Noble and Wolf v. Alley*, where it had upheld an anti-Semitic restrictive covenant. He had been furious at the court's decision in *Noble* at the time and disappointed that the Supreme Court had not seen fit to address *Noble*'s comments on public policy. Now, as a judge, he considered himself bound to apply *Noble* unless he could persuade his colleagues to overrule it. Clearly that was an option, but one he seems not to have seriously considered. I suggest he did not because he and his fellow activists in the Canadian Jewish Congress had accepted after *Noble* that Canadian courts would not develop the common law so as to prohibit discrimination. They threw all their resources into the legislative route and succeeded beyond their own expectations. Indeed, the preamble to the Ontario Human Rights Code cited by Wilson was there because Laskin had put it there, and he had put it there precisely to try and diminish the effect of *Noble and Wolf v. Alley*. To say, as Wilson had, that the Code recognized but did not create the right to be free from discrimination was a kind of natural law interpretation that was nonsense to anyone with Laskin's experience. The Jewish activists of the 1950s had proceeded on exactly the opposite assumption, and in light of the legislative occupation of the field since then there was no compelling reason to revisit *Noble*. It did not need to be over-ruled because it had now been completely superseded.

One strand in Laskin's reasoning in *Bhadauria* was based on his personal experience, another on his legal modernism. If not arising directly out of the common law, a tort of discrimination would have to be at least implicitly authorized by the Code. And what was the rationale for such a tort when the legislature had put in place an elaborate administrative and quasi-judicial scheme for the redress of discriminatory acts? Laskin and his colleagues in the Canadian Jewish Congress had lobbied for an administrative scheme because they believed, with some justice, that judges of the day were at worst racist and at best sceptical about the goals enshrined in the new human rights legislation. They wanted to develop a cadre of administrators who would develop some expertise in the manifestations, proof, and effects of discrimination, and to equip them with a whole array of tools beyond purely adversarial procedures. This legal modernist response would be imperilled if complainants could simply ignore the Code-based scheme and proceed directly to court. Wilson's decision threatened to create a two-tier system where well-heeled complainants would go directly to court while those with fewer resources would have to be content with the Ontario Human Rights Commission process. This could only undermine the latter in the long run.

Laskin's decision, agreed in by a unanimous bench of seven, was seen as controversial at the time and has remained so.[32] Wilson's decision had been received rapturously in the press and by the human rights community – in a manner reminiscent of some of Laskin's earlier decisions. The Supreme Court's decision appeared as a step backwards. Some were puzzled why the well-known advocate of human rights blocked what seemed to be a promising avenue for the redress of discrimination. Legal academic Ian Hunter thought *Bhadauria* showed 'the great dissenter [in] a particularly unaccustomed role.'[33] Others thought it showed a conservative turn in a chief justice bowed down by illness and overwork. Laskin was becoming more conservative in some ways, but *Bhadauria* is not at all an apt example. It is totally consistent with the legal modernist stance he had developed in the 1930s and adhered to ever since. In labour law and human rights matters in particular, Laskin constantly preached the virtues of civil servants' values over lawyers' values, to use a phrase employed by his friend John Willis.[34] He always sought to limit substantive judicial review of the decisions of statutory bodies charged with these mandates, and to characterize the statutes in question as a fresh start rendering recourse to the common law inappropriate and unnecessary. As James Walker has observed, Laskin's 1969 decision in *Bell v. Ontario Human Rights Commission* was a perfect predictor of his position in *Bhadauria*.[35]

A reader of Laskin's opinion in the *Gay Alliance* case just two years before *Bhadauria* would have seen the same philosophy at work. This was the case in which the *Vancouver Sun* had declined to print an advertisement from a gay rights group, a refusal found to be discriminatory by a board of inquiry under the B.C. Human Rights Act but not by the B.C. Court of Appeal. Laskin defined the issue in the opening words of his dissent not as a human rights matter but as involving 'a recurring question in administrative law, namely, the reviewability on questions allegedly of law or of jurisdiction, of the decision of a statutory tribunal.'[36] For Laskin, the case was all about whether the board of inquiry made an error in its interpretation of the phrase 'reasonable cause' as found in the B.C. Human Rights Code, and if so what should be done about it. What he found objectionable in the decision of Branca J.A. in the B.C. Court of Appeal was 'a direct substitution of the learned

judge's opinion for that of the board.'[37] For Laskin that was the unforgivable sin. The policy of the Act was 'plain and clear. Every person or
class of person is entitled to avail himself or themselves of such services
or facilities [i.e., those customarily available to the public] unless reasonable grounds are shown for denying them or discriminating in
respect of them.' Then came a barb directed at his colleagues: 'This
Court is obliged to enforce this policy regardless of whether it thinks it
to be ill-advised.'[38] You see, he might have said to his former colleagues
in the Canadian Jewish Congress, that is why we were right to keep
human rights out of the courts and put them in the hands of a tribunal.

The fact that Laskin was consistent is not necessarily a virtue if
conditions had changed since he first adopted his modernist stance. In
the 1960s and 1970s the administrative state was being attacked from
both the right and the left. The right saw it as stifling initiative, burden-
ing business unnecessarily, and running roughshod over individual
rights. The defence of individual rights as understood by the common
law reached its apotheosis in the mammoth three-volume report of the
Royal Commission Inquiry into Civil Rights in Ontario chaired by
James McRuer, a retired chief justice of the High Court of Ontario.
Volume one, authored largely by Laskin's old nemesis D.W. Mundell,
sounded a ringing endorsement of traditional lawyers' values and court-
based processes and revealed a corresponding suspicion of administrative agencies and their work. Some on the left were also beginning to
question the legacy of legal modernism. Increasing reliance on expert
administrators seemed to betoken less accountability and less democracy, as whole areas of life fell into a kind of technocratic maw. Observers on the left sometimes echoed the critiques of those on the right
regarding the apparent erosion of protections for the individual, but
they were more concerned about the bigger picture. Was the proliferation of expert agencies really to the advantage of workers, women,
minorities, and the poor? Or was it simply the erection of a kind of
buffer zone in which the state mediated and deflected the claims of
those groups, and behind which capital accumulation and inequality
could proceed more or less unimpeded? Sociologists and political scientists elaborated theories of agency 'capture,' arguing that administrators easily fell under the sway of sophisticated and talented business
advocates with whom they shared much in terms of social background
and education. This scepticism is in turn reflected in current historical
writing on the post-war administrative state, much of which is decid-
edly anti-celebratory in tone.[39]

It was evident by the late 1970s that the system administered by the Ontario Human Rights Commission was beginning to display serious problems, partly as a result of its own organization, partly a result of the ambient legal culture.[40] As its mission and its resources expanded it began to manifest a certain sluggishness and a preoccupation with its own procedures, interpreted by complainants as a lack of responsiveness. As its own internal processes became more complex, a backlog of complaints accumulated. Dr Bhadauria had in fact made twenty-two separate complaints to the commission with respect to previous job applications, and not one had proceeded to a board of inquiry. While court proceedings were far from speedy, a plaintiff in a civil suit could exert pressure at various points to hurry things along. In the human rights system a complainant had no control at all, and even if a board of inquiry was eventually appointed, commission counsel had carriage of the complaint. This was intended as a means of promoting access to the process for those unable to hire a lawyer, and it probably did have that effect to some degree. Still, it created an appearance of unaccountability to the population whom the commission was supposed to serve. Further delays were created by the extremely adversarial posture taken up by lawyers, especially where large corporations were respondents. A board of inquiry was typically presented with a flurry of objections to jurisdiction, disputes over the admissibility of evidence, and the like. Judicial review of a board's preliminary decision on one or more of these motions might have to be awaited before the board could even proceed to hear the substance of the complaint, though at least one board of inquiry has observed that the court's process was 'remarkably prompt in comparison with the human rights process.'[41]

Had Dr Bhadauria's counsel raised some of these problems as reasons for seeking to do an end run around the commission, would Laskin's response have been different? Probably not, at least not without hearing the commission's side of the story, which was not available in the proceedings between Seneca College and Dr Bhadauria. He would likely have replied that involving the courts was no panacea – witness the decision of the B.C. Court of Appeal in the *Gay Alliance* case just two years earlier. If an agency was broken it should be fixed, not ignored. Even Alan Borovoy of the Canadian Civil Liberties Association, initially positive about Wilson's decision, agreed with Laskin's approach after subsequent reflection.[42] Some indirect support for Laskin's views can be found in the report on the reform of the *Canadian Human Rights Act* commissioned by the minister of justice in 1999. The panel found many problems with the complaints process but its proposed solution was direct access to the Canadian Human Rights Tribunal, not to the courts.

The larger question about whether the rise of expert administrative agencies has been a boon or a bust is not one that can be answered here, or perhaps at all. It is difficult to generalize when there is such a vast range of agencies, both federal and provincial, with a perhaps equally vast range of competencies. Laskin's views were shaped not in the world of theory but by his own personal experiences of both the labour and human rights fields. He was a product of the 'bad old days' when the courts and the common law were the tools available for the resolution of such disputes. The results, as he saw them, were wasteful economic and even physical warfare in the form of recognition strikes, and racial discrimination praised as a legitimate form of social preference. In spite of attempts by him and others to urge the courts to reform the common law in a more progressive direction, they refused, with the notable, but isolated and ultimately discredited, example of *Drummond Wren*. The intervention of the state through the creation of specialized agencies to deal with both these areas of social conflict was seen as a blessing by Laskin and his contemporaries. Should they have foreseen the problems now laid at the door of industrial pluralism (the rise of a class of allegedly complacent union bureaucrats, the alienation and depoliticization of labour) or of human rights commissions (insulation of violators from timely remediation, alienation of target populations)? Inaction was not an option for Laskin's generation. If their solutions have in turn manifested their own problems, as they have, some responsibility rests on subsequent generations to address them, whether by incremental reform or a radical overhaul of the mechanisms created in the post-war decades.

The judicial arena was not one where Laskin could have addressed these larger questions even if he had wanted to do so. As a judge he remained largely faithful to the corpus of legal modernist ideas he had developed in his youth, and these were his most important legacy to the court. He came to a court initially unreceptive to such heresy. He left it fully converted, powerfully assisted by Brian Dickson in his missionary work. His message was one of principled rather than uncritical deference to administrative bodies in the core area of their mandate, balanced by an abiding concern for the observance of fair procedures where important individual rights were affected. Recent scholarship suggests that subsequent articulations of his test for review have sufficient flexibility to allow the courts to intervene in cases of inexperienced or relatively incapable boards, while respecting the integrity of those who are widely perceived to excel at their task.[43]

A development in Laskin's public law jurisprudence contemporaneous with his decision in *Bhadauria* provided more persuasive evidence of his alleged conservative shift. In 1977 while in Sydney he had given a talk on aspects of comparative constitutional law in the United States, Australia, and Canada. Much of it was anodyne, the kind of speech travelling judges give all the time. But then Laskin wandered into the case law on section 96 of the *British North America Act*, the article providing for federal appointment of the judges of the provincial supreme, county, and district courts. Here he said something so startling that a friend of Canadian law professor Harry Arthurs who happened to be in the audience contacted Arthurs immediately to report it. At first Laskin appeared to be critical of the fact that '[t]his appointing power [s. 96] was translated by judicial decision into a check on the assignment to provincial ... agencies or tribunals (whose members are provincial appointees) of judicial power exerciseable in a manner that would make them analogous to a superior, district or county court.' He noted that the Supreme Court had taken 'a pragmatic approach' to the functions of such tribunals and had been 'chary of a too conceptual assessment of s. 96.' But in concluding, his account took a sharp turn away from his usual defence of administrative agencies. 'It is obvious,' he said, 'that administrative agencies cannot escape making determinations of law in the course of their regulatory or quasi-judicial operations, and to deny them such leeway would weaken considerably their utility. *The reasonable compromise here is to deny them unreviewable authority to make such determinations, and equally to deny them power to determine finally the limits of their jurisdiction.* These are matters with which Canada is quite familiar without being bound by a strict separation of powers doctrine.'[44]

The maxim *a beau mentir qui vient de loin* (those who come from afar do not need to tell the truth) comes to mind. Laskin appeared to be presenting as an uncontroversial proposition that provincial governments were *constitutionally* precluded by section 96 from completely insulating their tribunals from judicial review by the superior courts. This was an argument he had railed against as an academic and even, speaking extra-judicially, while on the Ontario Court of Appeal.[45] Moreover, the position now being advanced by Laskin as settled doctrine was in fact quite uncertain in Canadian law in 1977.[46] It was true that

Canadian courts had traditionally been none too respectful of privative clauses purporting to oust judicial review, but it was a different matter altogether to say that even a perfectly drafted one would be unconstitutional. In a recent exchange in the *Canadian Bar Review*, Noel Lyon had argued for the position articulated by Laskin,[47] while Peter Hogg had argued that 's. 96 [was] too frail a foundation to support the building of a constitutionally-guaranteed administrative law.'[48] To add to the confusion, Laskin ended his talk by referring his audience to Hogg's article – but not Lyon's.

A few years later life imitated art: in *Crevier v. Québec (Attorney General)* Laskin carried the full court with him in support of the expansive interpretation of section 96 he had foreshadowed in Australia. The Quebec statute at issue was one creating the Professions Tribunal, a body of six provincial court judges vested with supervisory jurisdiction over some thirty-eight professional corporations including the bar. Each corporation had to establish a discipline committee, from which appeals could be made to the tribunal. Section 194 of the Act purported to insulate the tribunal completely from the remedies for excess of jurisdiction normally available in the Quebec superior courts. For the first time, Laskin wrote, 'this Court [declares] unequivocally that a provincially-constituted statutory tribunal cannot constitutionally be immunized from review of decisions on questions of jurisdiction.'[49] His position seemed difficult to reconcile with the legal modernist views he had long expressed. Making provincial appeal tribunals subject to attack via section 96 would tend to undermine the integrity of the administrative process and to spur governments to avoid them as policy instruments. If a province wanted to insulate fully a particular tribunal from judicial review, even for jurisdictional error, why should it be constitutionally prevented from doing so? The enlargement of the appointing power in section 96 into a substantive limit on provincial power is not in the least compelled by the wording of section 96 or the structure of the constitution. In *Crevier* the Court conceded that judicial review for 'ordinary' error of law by a tribunal could be ousted by clearly worded legislation, but not errors in defining the limits of the tribunal's own jurisdiction. Such errors, said Laskin, were 'not far removed from issues of constitutionality,' and it was universally admitted that judicial review of a tribunal's interpretation of a constitutional provision could not be precluded.

Viewed on its own, *Crevier* seems to reveal a more conservative Laskin, but in some ways it is actually quite consistent with his legal modernism.[50] The decision was virtually contemporaneous with *Bhadauria*, with its strong defence of the role of administrative agencies even to the exclusion of the courts where comprehensive tribunal-based schemes were created; and it came after the Supreme Court had signed on to deference in *C.U.P.E.* In this context *Crevier* represents a fine-tuning of Laskin's thinking on the allocation of responsibilities among different constitutional actors, not a wholesale retreat. For much of his life Laskin had focused on the question of what courts should not do. Now, when pushed by the proliferation of provincially appointed appeal tribunals, he had to consider what courts should do – was there any 'protected core' of jurisdiction for the provincial superior courts in Canada? The question was acute in the Quebec context, as revealed by the number of times statutes from that province were challenged on section 96 grounds. If the robust privative clause in the Professions Tribunal's statute survived scrutiny, it would likely spread to all Quebec appeal tribunals, and thence, possibly to many in English Canada. That could leave whole continents of provincial economic, social, and professional life to be finally adjudicated upon by locally paid judges without recourse to the superior courts. Laskin's modernism left him suspicious of leaving the final word on local disputes to the locals. For all his embrace of local knowledge and expertise in the tribunal context, he knew there was still the occasional possibility of a vendetta, a settling of scores by officials who should have known better. Where would Morris Shumiatcher have been if Saskatchewan had had a system similar to Quebec's Professions Tribunal? Would he have found justice at the hands of provincial court judges, appointed by the very attorney-general whom he alleged was on a crusade to destroy him?

It is no coincidence that a case on professional discipline would present the dilemma about the finality of tribunal decisions in its most acute form. Laskin always demanded the highest standards of procedural fairness when professionals were being disciplined or deprived of the right to practice. Early on in his Supreme Court career, in *R. v. McKeown*, he had lambasted a lower court judge for finding a lawyer in contempt after a hearing Laskin found lamentably flawed. A few years later, in *Law Society of Upper Canada v. French*, Laskin had been very concerned about what he saw as a biased discipline process.[51] In that case a solicitor had been found guilty of seven counts of professional misconduct by the discipline committee of the Law Society. He was given the chance to object when the report came before Convocation, the governing body of the society. Convocation confirmed the report and imposed a three-month suspension, but two members of the discipline committee took part in the meeting of Convocation at which this occurred, in spite of French's objection to their presence. French succeeded before Justice Osler in having the decision of Convocation quashed. Osler had ordered the report of the discipline committee remitted to Convocation for consideration without participation of any members of the committee, and the Court of Appeal had affirmed his order. The Law Society successfully appealed to the Supreme Court, where Spence wrote the majority opinion. The majority was persuaded that the specific exclusion of discipline committee members from Convocation in the case of an appeal from certain minor penalties, found in section 39 of the Act, meant that no such exclusion was mandated in the case of appeals from other penalties. In other words, they applied the maxim *expressio unius est exclusio alterius* (to express one thing implies exclusion of the other). Laskin was always wary of leaving important matters to be decided on such technical grounds. Surely, he said, there was all the more reason to exclude the discipline committee members when a more serious penalty was under consideration. At worst, this was an omission 'which cries for judicial intervention in accordance with accepted principles of administrative law.'[52]

If even the Law Society of Upper Canada could not be relied on to observe what Laskin felt was an elementary requirement of impartiality, then perhaps the escape route to the superior courts had to remain constitutionally unblocked after all. Many other statutory bodies, he might have reasoned, would be even less sensitive to basic requirements of due process and impartial decision making. For the rare situation where an agency really ran amok, Laskin felt Canadians needed a superior court insurance policy, and he provided one in *Crevier*. His defence of the provincial superior courts in the section 96 jurisprudence is also of a piece with his constant policing of the Federal Court's jurisdiction in the *McNamara Construction* line of cases.

Both these choices can be seen as motivated by self-interest, as creating a force field around the superior courts that no legislative harpoon could penetrate. If that view is taken, Laskin shares the blame with virtually all his Supreme Court colleagues, as decisions on both section 96 and Federal Court jurisdiction were often unanimous. Indeed, the Supreme Court has continued to develop in exuberant fashion the idea of a protected zone of provincial superior court jurisdiction since Laskin's death.[53] On this issue it would be accurate to see Laskin as articulating a widely held view in the Supreme Court and to some extent the provincial superior courts themselves, rather than converting them to his viewpoint. Seen in the wider context of his public law decision making, the allegation of self-interest seems unconvincing. It might be argued that it was only safe to decide a case such as *Crevier* once Laskin, with Dickson's assistance, had finally made respect for administrative agencies part of the institutional culture of the Canadian courts. It was only then that the truly exceptional nature of *Crevier* could be appreciated. Laskin's public law legacy was a complex one, articulated around his ideas about the proper allocation of institutional roles among actors in the Canadian constitutional system. It tried to ensure maximum flexibility for government actors to govern on behalf of the collectivity, but also to guarantee clear protections for the individual with important interests at stake.

In the immediate wake of his death, Laskin's administrative law contributions were not seen as particularly noteworthy. Some academic opinion castigated his reluctance to jettison the notoriously nebulous idea of 'jurisdiction' as the main organizing concept of Canadian administrative law, as had been done earlier in the United States. Laskin was said to bear some responsibility for the unsatisfactory state of administrative law wherein '[w]hat should be a matter of functional allocation of decision-making remains in Canada a complex and intimidating doctrinal morass.'[54] His decision in *Nicholson* was praised but its implications were 'far from clear.' In the twenty years since Laskin's death, his contribution can be seen more clearly. His legal modernist ideas served as the base for an approach to administrative law that would pay attention to the optimal allocation of responsibilities among different actors, without sacrificing the interests of the individual on the altar of efficiency or subscribing to exaggerated notions of deference.

22

Patriation

A few years after Laskin's death, the University of Toronto Faculty of Law rebuilt its library and renamed it the Bora Laskin Law Library. At a gala event on 21 March 1991 celebrating its official opening, former prime minister Pierre Trudeau addressed a large audience at Convocation Hall. The audience probably expected a pleasant blend of personal reminiscence and insightful analysis of Laskin's contribution to Canadian jurisprudence. What they got was a eulogy to the Laskin-Estey-McIntyre dissent in the *Patriation Reference*, and a blistering attack on the majority decision – a decision declaring the existence of a constitutional convention requiring 'substantial' provincial agreement before the federal government could make a request for an amendment to the Canadian constitution to the UK Parliament. After praising the minority decision as 'not only the better law but also the wiser counsel,' Trudeau went on to excoriate the majority judges: '[n]o doubt believing that a political agreement would be better for Canada than unilateral legal patriation, they blatantly manipulated the evidence before them so as to arrive at the desired result.'[1] Sitting in the front row of the dignitaries in attendance was none other than Brian Dickson, recently retired as chief justice of Canada and one of those subscribing to the decision so relentlessly pilloried by the former prime minister. In earlier days perhaps the confrontation would have led to a duel, but as it was, Dickson 'politely but firmly informed Trudeau that he rejected everything he had said' when the two men met after the talk.[2]

The only thing Dickson might have agreed with in Trudeau's speech was his description of the *Patriation Reference* as 'the most important decision [the Supreme Court] ever rendered or ever will render.'[3] The passionate emotions aroused by it a decade afterwards may have faded now, but the issues raised by it – the nature of Canadian federalism, the proper role of the judiciary in highly politicized cases, the nature of law itself – remain contested and by their nature can never be finally resolved. Bora Laskin, like Trudeau, hoped that the *Patriation Reference* would finally give some shape to fundamentals of the Canadian constitution that had long remained obscure. It was not to be. The Canadian constitution would continue to be a work in progress, a blend of hard law, soft convention, hopes, prayers, and luck.

Canada was the only country in the developed world in the later twentieth century still lacking the capacity to amend its constitution by a purely domestic process. The *British North America Act, 1867* was itself a British statute, as were all the amendments to it passed over the years. The *Statute of Westminster 1931*, passed when Bora Laskin was in his second year of university, made legal what had been a matter of political practice for some time: that is, that the British Parliament would not legislate for any of its former colonies except at their own behest. As Ivan Rand had expressed it, Westminster was a 'bare legislative trustee' of the Canadian constitution.[4] It was tolerably clear after 1931 that any request for amendment of the *British North America Act, 1867* had to come via the Dominion government, but it was not so clear what if any provincial consent had to be obtained by the Dominion before requesting amendments affecting provincial powers. Numerous attempts had been made in the post-war period to reach agreement on an amending formula in order to obviate recourse to Westminster, but all had ended in failure. After becoming prime minister, Pierre Trudeau had made the 'patriation' of the Canadian constitution one of his main objectives, preferably with an entrenched charter of rights and freedoms attached.

The election of the Parti Québécois government on 15 November 1976, avowedly devoted to the secession of Quebec from Canada, created obvious problems for the realization of these plans. Trudeau continued nonetheless with his 'magnificent obsession.'[5] First the federal government appointed the high-profile Pépin-Roberts Task Force on Canadian Unity to inject some vigour into the constitutional project. Its report, *A Time for Action*, served in turn as the basis for Bill C-60, which would have unilaterally amended the constitution by adding a charter of rights and transforming the Senate into a new House of the Federation. When asked to rule on the legality of the latter change, the Supreme Court stated unanimously that the federal government could not accomplish it by a simple statute.[6] Two more rounds of federal-provincial negotiations in the late 1970s, in which Trudeau tried to interest the premiers in a patriation/charter package in return for some expansion of provincial powers, came to naught. Then came the roller coaster of 1979–80: the Liberals' electoral defeat in May 1979, Trudeau's decision to step down as leader in November, the defeat of Prime Minister Joe Clark's minority government in December, Trudeau's return to the leadership and victory in the February 1980 election, and the loss of the first Quebec referendum by a sixty-forty margin on 20 May 1980.

With a mandate of at least four years stretching before him, and a huge amount of political good will in English Canada as a result of his decisive victory over the separatists, Trudeau decided to pursue the constitutional holy grail once again. This time, however, he would go over the heads of the premiers and speak directly to the Canadian people. Whatever the technical difficulties involved in bringing the constitution home, Trudeau gambled that the support of public opinion would ultimately ease his path. He seems not to have anticipated that a detour through the Supreme Court of Canada on the way to London would seriously complicate his game plan.

On 6 October 1980, the day after Bora Laskin's sixty-eighth birthday, Trudeau introduced his proposal for unilateral patriation in the House of Commons. The machinery involved a joint address by the Senate and House of Commons to the Queen, asking her to lay the enclosed draft bill before the Parliament at Westminster. In form the bill would be an amendment to the *British North America Act* incorporating the desired changes. These were anathema to most of the premiers: an entrenched bill of rights allowing the courts to strike down provincial (and federal) legislation that offended fundamental rights and freedoms, minority language education rights for the English in Quebec and in other provinces for francophones where numbers warranted, guaranteed labour mobility across the country, affirmation of aboriginal and treaty rights, and a constitutional amending formula. The latter even included the authority for the federal government to call a popular referendum in future cases where federal-provincial negotiations on constitutional amendments led to an impasse. Only Ontario's Bill Davis and New Brunswick's Richard Hatfield swallowed their reservations and supported the proposals.

Trudeau was determined to have his resolutions passed in the United Kingdom in time for a Canada Day ceremony in 1981, famously observing that the British MPs should 'hold their noses' and pass the bill. The dissenting premiers in turn adopted a two-pronged oppositional strategy, diplomatic in England and juridical in Canada. In London they wined and dined British MPs in the hope of persuading them to delay or even vote against the bill. This strategy bore fruit when a parliamentary committee chaired by Sir Anthony Kershaw reported – to the amazement of Canadian observers – that the UK Parliament would not 'accept unconditionally the constitutional validity of every request coming from the Canadian Parliament.' In Canada the premiers strategized about where legal challenges to the process might most profitably be launched and how the questions should be framed. Provincial governments cannot refer legal questions directly to the Supreme Court of Canada, but they can refer them to their own courts of appeal and proceeded to do so even before the resolutions were actually passed by the House and Senate in April 1981. The Quebec Court of Appeal was an obvious choice, supplemented by the Newfoundland Court of Appeal and the Manitoba Court of Appeal in order to provide western and eastern balance. The strategy was somewhat high-risk, because the courts might have said Trudeau's unilateral approach to Westminster was perfectly legal – as the Supreme Court ultimately did. By adding a question about the existence of constitutional conventions, the premiers hoped to muddy the waters and prevent the federal government from gaining a pure victory, and in this they enjoyed some success.

In the midst of all this manoeuvring, Laskin took a quick February vacation on the west coast in order to attend a symposium honouring Frank Scott, now eighty-one. The event at Simon Fraser University provided Laskin with a rare chance to unwind, perhaps to reflect on his own life, and even to display his acting talents. A skit developed by Timothy Porteous, director of the Canada Council, and Donald MacSween, director general of the National Arts Centre, centred on the appeal of one Wilbur Throckmorton to the Celestial Supreme Court. Throckmorton, a Cherubim Second Class, had been fired from the celestial public service as a result of creating Scott, who had disturbed its peaceful workings. His lawyers, the Archclerk Michael (played by Michael Pitfield, clerk to the Privy Council) and Saint Peter (played by Pierre Trudeau), advised Mr Justice Jehovah (Laskin) to 'hold his nose' and allow the appeal, in a pointed reference to Trudeau's recent remark. Laskin reinstated Throckmorton, observing that the issue turned on 'whether or not Scott has been good for Canada.'[7] Scott and Laskin seldom saw each other after Laskin went to the Supreme Court, and this may have been their last personal encounter, though not their last intellectual one: Scott's constitutional views would be cited with approval in the *Patriation Reference*. After the conference Laskin wrote to say how much he had enjoyed Scott's recent volume of collected poems, which his law clerks had given him as a Christmas gift.[8] Before long, Laskin would have more extended – and conflictual – dealings with another participant at the conference: the aftermath of the *Patriation Reference* would put Justice Thomas Berger of British Columbia and Bora Laskin on a collision course.

The respite was all too brief. Laskin was soon back at work, where he avidly followed the progress of the provincial reference cases. There were essentially three questions for the courts of appeal: did any of the proposed amendments in Trudeau's package affect federal-provincial relationships or provincial powers? If so, was the agreement of the provinces constitutionally required before the joint address could be presented by the Canadian government to the UK authorities? And if not required by the constitution itself, was there nonetheless a constitutional convention that the Canadian Parliament would not request the Queen to lay such a measure before the UK Parliament without provincial agreement? The Manitoba Court of Appeal was the first to answer the questions, in February. All of the judges agreed that provincial consent was not legally required but decided against the existence of a convention, with Chief Justice Samuel Freedman writing the majority opinion on this point. Next to report was the Newfoundland Court of Appeal, and its decision threw Trudeau's strict timetable into disarray: a panel of three judges unanimously found provincial consent to be required both legally and conventionally. The prime minister had accepted the advice of the deputy minister of justice that if either the Newfoundland or the Quebec court ruled against him, he should allow the Supreme Court to have the final say before proceeding to London.[9] By the time the Quebec Court of Appeal found in favour of the federal government by a four to one majority on 15 April, the Manitoba decision had already been appealed to the Supreme Court. Appeals in all three cases would be consolidated into one proceeding.

The Supreme Court moved with alacrity to hear the appeal, scheduling it to be heard barely two weeks after the Quebec Court of Appeal issued its decision. The press of lawyers, media, and extra security was unprecedented as the hearing unfolded over five days in late April and early May. Nearly forty black-gowned lawyers occupied all the central tables in the hearing room, leaving the press to crowd in along the sidelines on folding chairs. Attorney-General Roy McMurtry argued the case personally for Ontario, while the federal government retained J.J. Robinette as lead counsel for the Manitoba Reference, St John's lawyer (and future premier) Clyde Wells on the Newfoundland Reference, and Michel Robert, former *bâtonnier* of the Barreau du Québec (and future chief justice of Quebec) on the Quebec Reference. Aside from the provinces, only the Four Nations Confederacy (formerly the Manitoba Indian Brotherhood) appeared as an intervener. Aboriginal leaders had decided to attack the patriation plan in the British rather than the Canadian courts, and 132 First Nations sought a ruling from the High Court as to the legitimacy of Trudeau's plans to proceed without their consent.

Observers seemed to think that the Court would produce its decision within a month or so, perhaps recalling the Court's very quick turn-around in the *Anti-Inflation Reference*.[10] Even Trudeau shared this view, and later complained that Bora Laskin had let him down in not issuing the judgment earlier.[11] Had he known of Trudeau's views Laskin would have been furious with the prime minister's assumption that the chief justice would make the Court dance to the government's tune, even assuming he could muster his colleagues to do so. As it was, the shape of the judgment was discussed by the judges at conference after conference, contrary to their usual practice of devoting only one or at most two meetings to a given judgment.[12] When the summer recess began the judgment was still not ready, and some of the judges had accepted invitations to attend a series of lectures sponsored by the Cambridge Institute for Advanced Legal Studies. The Institute was a rather odd forum promoted by Anglophilic Cambridge alumnus Paul Martin, Sr while high commissioner to the United Kingdom. Its founders seemed concerned that 'since the abolition of appeals to the Privy Council there has been no active organization to maintain and continue the legal ties between Canada and the U.K.' – though if thirty years had gone by without such an organization, perhaps it was not a major priority for either Canadian or British lawyers.[13] The idea was to have a biennial series of lectures in Cambridge (or elsewhere) featuring high-profile speakers who would lure Canadian lawyers across the Atlantic. Attendance at the first lectures in 1979 had been rather sparse and the organizers were hoping for a better turnout in 1981. As an honorary patron, along with Lord Elwyn-Jones and Paul Martin himself, Laskin felt some obligation to attend.

Bora and Peggy decided to sail to England by ocean liner for the conference, hoping the sea voyage would provide a real break from the stress of the previous months.[14] Bud and Ruth Estey also attended the lectures in Cambridge, though Bud was far too impatient to sail anywhere. Laskin and Estey had already shared their similar ideas about the reference, and they spent hours in their college rooms discussing the case. One evening featured a discussion of the legal arguments in the case by a number of Canadian politicians, including Roy McMurtry, Roy Romanow, and Jean Chrétien. Laskin surprised Estey by expressing a desire to attend. Estey persuaded him that it would look very bad if they were present: they had heard the arguments and should not be receiving additional submissions extra-judicially.[15]

Back in Ottawa in September, the judges began to move into high gear to complete the judgment. Laskin was petrified about security as drafts of reasons circulated through the Supreme Court building. He refused to discuss the judgment with his clerks, leaving them rather put out because they knew the other judges discussed it with their clerks.[16] He did discuss his judgment with at least one of his previous clerks, however. After finishing at the Court Kathy de Jong had enrolled in the master of laws program at Harvard. She had just arrived and was having a nap in her room when the phone rang. It was Bora Laskin. He did not tell her exactly what he was going to do, but he seemed to need a sympathetic ear.[17]

As decision day loomed, arrangements were made for the televising of the event – a first for the Court but an inauspicious debut as it turned out. On the morning of 28 September law students and lawyers across the country gathered around their televisions as the chief justice began to read the decision. Unfortunately one audio hookup was left unconnected with the result that the decision was inaudible to the expectant audience. Laskin would undoubtedly have preferred a unanimous judgment but was forced to accept a rather fractured one. Its unusual form – a majority judgment on the legal question and another majority judgment, with a different group of judges, on the conventional question, rounded out with two- and three-judge dissents on both questions, made it almost impossible to digest quickly in any case.[18] True to form, Laskin never understood the needs of the electronic media for instant analysis. Had advance copies of the judgment been made available earlier in the morning to the media, informed commentary could have made up for the technical glitches that spoiled the event.

The answer to the first question was not much in debate: all nine judges agreed that the proposed Charter of Rights in particular would

impose significant restrictions on provincial (as well as federal) legislative power. On the second question, all the judges except Martland and
Ritchie agreed that there was no legal restriction on the power of the
Senate and House of Commons to adopt the resolution in question or to
cause it to be laid before the UK Parliament, even though the constitutional amendments contained within it might affect provincial powers.
The writer of the majority judgment is not identified but it bears clear
signs of Laskin's authorship. Many of his characteristic turns of phrase
are found in it, but it is likely that others added certain passages.
William McIntyre told his biographer that he made contributions to
both the majority judgment on the law and the minority judgment on
the conventional question.[19] It was on the third question that a more
significant division of opinion emerged. Six of the judges agreed that
even if there was nothing in the written Canadian constitution to prevent the two houses of Parliament from adopting the resolution, there
was a convention to the effect that Parliament would not proceed to
request constitutional changes via the UK Parliament without provincial agreement. A minority of three, Laskin, Estey, and McIntyre, interpreted 'provincial agreement' in the reference questions to mean
unanimous agreement and declared against any such convention. Their
six colleagues decided that a convention requiring 'substantial' provincial agreement had been established; they stated that the support of only
Ontario and New Brunswick was not substantial, but declined to specify
what number of provinces might be required to meet this threshold.

Constitutional conventions are political practices or usages which
find no expression either in statutes or in the common law of the constitution. In fact, many of the most important tenets of responsible
government arise from convention rather than law. For example, the
requirement for a government to tender its resignation should the
opposition win a majority at the polls arises from convention rather
than constitutional law. According to the majority on the third question, 'the main purpose of constitutional conventions is to ensure that
the legal framework of the constitution will be operated in accordance
with the prevailing constitutional values or principles of the period.'[20]
All the judges were agreed that the one 'striking peculiarity' of conventions is their non-enforceability by the courts. While the assent of the
governor-general or lieutenant-governor is legally required for all federal or provincial legislation, as a matter of convention that assent
cannot be refused. Yet occasionally the convention is broken: a recalcitrant lieutenant-governor of Prince Edward Island refused to sign a law

with which he profoundly disagreed in 1945. The courts could not recognize the law as valid without his signature, even though he had violated a convention in refusing it.[21]

If conventions are a matter of political practice rather than law, one might have expected the courts to refuse to rule on their existence (or non-existence). After all, courts only adjudicate based on the law of the land. Peter Hogg criticized the Supreme Court on this point, observing that 'the only justification for even considering the convention question would be to influence the political outcome.'[22] According to Hogg the convention issue was indeed non-justiciable and the Supreme Court should have refused to rule on it. The Laskin-Estey-McIntyre trio appeared to agree with him, but reluctantly felt drawn into expressing views on the matter because the majority had done so. '[O]rdinarily,' they said, 'the Court would not undertake to answer [such questions] for it is not the function of the Court to go beyond legal determinations.' Nonetheless, they felt 'obliged to answer the questions notwithstanding their extra-legal nature.'[23] It is notable that not just the Supreme Court but all thirteen judges in all the courts below, with the sole exception of Justice Hall in the Manitoba Court of Appeal, felt compelled to express views on the convention issue when they might have legitimately refused to rule on it. The unusual Canadian reference process, where the opinion of the courts is sought by federal and provincial governments in a quasi-political context, seems to have created a legal culture in which Canadian courts feel it is appropriate to provide quasi-political advice to governments, and not to restrict themselves to matters of strict law.

If the three dissenters agreed largely with the majority's statements on the general nature of conventions, they wished to distinguish clearly between their use in Britain and Canada. 'In a federal state where the essential feature of the constitution must be the distribution of powers between the two levels of government, each supreme in its own legislative sphere, constitutionality and legality must be synonymous, and conventional rules will be accorded less significance than they may have in the United Kingdom.'[24] In the United Kingdom many actions may be termed unconstitutional which are perfectly legal, given the traditional supremacy of the British Parliament. Reducing the availability of a jury trial for certain crimes, for example, might be described as 'unconstitutional' in Britain in the sense that it departs from long tradition, even though the legislation incorporating the change has been duly passed and cannot be challenged in the courts. The minority deprecated the majority's willingness to follow the British example by using the term 'unconstitutional' to describe the mere non-observance of a convention. There was more at stake here than linguistic usage. The label 'unconstitutional' is a powerful one in the public mind, and if the majority could use the term to describe Trudeau's actions, the provinces would clearly have won a significant victory in the public relations war.

The real nub of disagreement between the majority and the Laskin-Estey-McIntyre minority was over the nature of the convention of provincial agreement alleged to have been followed prior to requests for constitutional amendment. Here Laskin had made his views clear extra-judicially years earlier.[25] In 1964, he had praised the 'wise procedure' providing that '[o]nly the central government has the ear of the United Kingdom.' An amendment to the constitution could be secured whenever the federal government sought one, but 'such a decision must run the gauntlet of political forces which are particularly sensitive at the provincial level when issues of legislative power are concerned.'[26] The professor had not changed his mind after appointment to the bench. In the *Patriation Reference*, he admitted that the federal government might well wish to secure a measure of provincial consent for any proposed changes, but 'as a matter of good politics rather than as a constitutional requirement.'[27] Given that the essence of a convention resides in the relevant actors' sense of obligation to follow it, the minority placed particular emphasis on the statements of Mackenzie King in seeking the constitutional amendment regarding unemployment insurance in 1940. Unanimous consent of the provinces had been secured, but King observed that 'we have avoided the raising of a very critical constitutional question, namely, whether or not in amending the British North America Act it is absolutely necessary to secure the consent of all the provinces, or whether the consent of a certain number of provinces would of itself be sufficient.'[28] In other words, King had sought provincial consent to ease the passage of the amendment, but expressly disclaimed the legal necessity of doing so.

Further, the actions of the federal government in requesting constitutional amendments had not crystallized into a clear and predictable pattern of seeking either unanimous consent or some set threshold less than unanimity. The minority reviewed the history of constitutional amendments provided in a white paper prepared under the authority of Guy Favreau in 1965, and found in several instances that the federal government had proceeded to request constitutional amendments affecting provincial powers without their consent. The white paper had concluded somewhat confusingly that 'the Canadian Parliament will not request an amendment directly affecting federal-provincial relationships without prior consultation and agreement with the provinces,' but admitted that '[t]he nature and the degree of provincial participation in the amending process ... have not lent themselves to easy definition.'[29] It is hard to refute the minority's analysis that 'the very difficulty of fixing the degree of provincial participation ... prevents the formation or recognition of any convention.'[30]

Nonetheless, the majority found themselves seduced by the argument presented by Kenneth Lysyk, then dean of law at the University of British Columbia, and John Whyte of Queen's on behalf of the province of Saskatchewan. The two academics threw the majority the lifeline they were seeking, and they eagerly grasped it. It was not necessary to state the exact degree of provincial consent required, said the professors. A practice of seeking 'substantial' provincial consent had been proven, and clearly the consent of two provinces was not substantial by any standard. The Court could thus conclude that the federal government had violated a constitutional convention even though it could not state with any precision what the content of the convention was. Both on analytical and on policy grounds, it is hard to imagine Bora Laskin reacting with anything less than horror to this proposition. The only thing worse than the constitutional straitjacket he had deplored for so many years was a shape-shifting straitjacket of indeterminate size. In an interview given some years later, Bud Estey stated that it was Jean Beetz who had championed the Lysyk-Whyte proposal in the post-hearing discussions and gradually persuaded most of his colleagues to adopt it. 'He was the intellectual leader of the idea that we should soften the approach, make it possible, let everybody back down a wee bit, force another rung on the ladder for the aggressive feds who just wanted to snap it [off].'[31] According to Estey all the judges wanted the constitution to be patriated, and differed only on the mechanics. Although Estey had been a staunch member of the 'convention minority' in 1981, a dozen years later he permitted himself to wonder (with the benefit of hindsight) whether Beetz's approach was not the better one after all.

Whatever their effect on the law, these differences bore fruit in the political sphere. By handing both the federal and the provincial governments partial victories, the decision promoted one last round of bargaining by the parties, resulting in a new package announced on

5 November. The process by which the original 'gang of eight' became unstuck, resulting in the adherence of the anglophone provinces to the new deal and the isolation of Quebec, is well known and need not be repeated here.[32] The result gave Trudeau the 'substantial provincial support' required by the Supreme Court and guaranteed that British parliamentarians would not display any embarrassing hesitations when he showed up with a draft bill for them to pass. The English Court of Appeal obligingly ruled that any responsibilities once owed by the British Crown to aboriginal peoples had now devolved on the government of Canada, further quieting possible British anxieties.[33] Quebec immediately referred to its Court of Appeal the question of whether the province had a conventional veto owing to its distinct linguistic, cultural, and legal traditions, but that court denied the existence of any such veto just a week before the *Constitution Act, 1982* came into force, and the Supreme Court later upheld the decision.[34]

The new package of 5 November featured some alterations to Trudeau's original plan: the addition of the 'notwithstanding' clause allowing governments to override Charter rights, including sexual equality; the adoption of an amending formula more in tune with provincial desires, though with no compensation for provinces choosing to opt out of an amendment transferring a given power to Ottawa; the adoption of an 'affirmative-action' caveat to mobility rights in favour of provinces with above-average unemployment rates; and the dropping of any affirmation of aboriginal rights and of the referendum clause aimed at breaking future constitutional impasses. Women and aboriginal groups reacted strongly to the changes negatively affecting them, and succeeded in mobilizing sufficient public support to reinstate the status quo ante before Trudeau proceeded to Britain. No one spoke up for the referendum clause in the earlier package, and it quietly passed into history.

However unhappy Bora Laskin was with the divisions in the Court in the *Patriation Reference*, he was probably not too dissatisfied with the final political outcome. Although he had never clearly gone on record in favour of an entrenched charter of rights while an academic, his expansive interpretation of the Canadian Bill of Rights as a judge suggests that he gradually warmed to the idea. Part of the reason for his hesitation was his commitment to the fundamentals of parliamentary democracy: one of the strongest themes in his pre- and post-judicial writings is his respect for the boundaries between the legislative and judicial spheres. For Laskin judicial activism was a weapon which remained powerful only through sparing use, under very particular conditions. He would not have embraced the Charter as a tool for enlightened judges to show benighted politicians how to run the country; such thinking was totally foreign to him. It is hard to imagine him being too upset even about the notwithstanding clause, the *bête noire* of so many equality-seeking groups. Laskin's modernist thought had always stressed flexibility, the need to respond to new and unforeseen circumstances. The possibility of ill-advised but final judicial decisions on rights without any escape route was one he would have wished to avoid.

Kathy de Jong remembered the chief justice standing silhouetted in his office window which faced east towards Parliament Hill, 'talking about the great responsibility towards our country we had as lawyers. We had an obligation of service and an obligation to uphold the democratic process. He deeply respected his country and the parliamentary process. He wanted to convey to us that we were part of something bigger, and that we should keep that in mind.'[35] Judges too were part of 'something bigger.' The image of Laskin's silhouette superimposed on the Parliament buildings behind him is the perfect one to express his views on the role of judges, whether before or after the Charter. Even though the Charter would give them a larger role in the Canadian legal order, that duty was one to be exercised with due humility, keeping in mind that only Parliament was finally responsible to the Canadian people.

23

The Berger Affair

Indirectly, the *Patriation Reference* initiated a bitter controversy between two men whom many people would have identified as judicial twins: Bora Laskin and Thomas Berger. William McIntyre, who knew both of them well, thought 'there were [no] two judges in the Canadian judicial firmament who were more alike juridically than Laskin and Berger.'[1] The family resemblance was striking: Berger *was* in many respects a younger, west coast version of Bora Laskin. As a twenty-nine-year-old MP, Berger had spoken out in Parliament about the RCMP presence on university campuses when Laskin was pursuing the issue on behalf of the CAUT. As a labour arbitrator Berger had great admiration for Laskin's arbitral decisions and relied on them regularly. As a young lawyer, he had been involved principally with union-side labour law, criminal defence work, and the nascent field of native rights. He served as junior counsel to Frank Scott in a 1963 Supreme Court of Canada case where a union challenged B.C. legislation prohibiting the payment of union dues to political parties.[2] They lost the case four to three but became fast friends. Like Scott and Laskin, Berger admired Ivan Rand, calling him 'the greatest judge in Canadian history.' He was also counsel before the Supreme Court in two of the most important native rights cases in twentieth-century Canada, *R. v. White and Bob* and *Calder*; in the latter, he appeared before Laskin just before his own appointment to the Supreme Court of British Columbia. As a civil libertarian, defender of human rights, and labour advocate, Berger seemed cut from the Laskin mould. Yet by the time the 'Berger Affair' ended Laskin had succeeded in hounding Berger off the bench. His handling of the affair aroused widespread public indignation, quiet consternation in some quarters of the judiciary, and criticism from the academic community.[3]

Justice Thomas Berger had been following the constitutional saga closely. Given his experience as head of the Mackenzie Valley Pipeline Inquiry in 1974–7, he was particularly concerned that the rights of the native peoples be recognized in any new constitutional arrangements. The clause in the original 'unilateral' federal package approved by Parliament in April 1981 stated that 'the aboriginal and treaty rights of the aboriginal peoples of Canada are hereby recognized and affirmed.' Berger found this satisfactory and said so on 2 September 1981 at the annual meeting of the Canadian Bar Association in Vancouver. He also expressed his view as to the constitutional propriety of unilateral action by the federal government, in essence agreeing with what would be the Laskin-Estey-McIntyre position in the *Patriation Reference*. The majority judgment released on 28 September sent the federal government back into negotiations with the provinces, but the new package released on 5 November had dropped any mention of the rights of native peoples and gave Quebec no veto in the new amending formula. The day happened to be the twenty-sixth wedding anniversary of Thomas and Beverley Berger, and they spent it anxiously considering whether he should make any public statement.

Berger happened to be in Ottawa promoting his book *Fragile Freedoms: Human Rights and Dissent in Canada* on the tenth, and sent up a trial balloon. Calling the new deal 'mean-spirited,' he told the *Ottawa Citizen* he could hardly believe that the Indians, Inuit, and Métis people of Canada had been 'sacrificed.'[4] This statement was repeated on the CBC TV evening news, but it was the publication by the *Globe and Mail* of a speech Berger gave at the University of Guelph on the seventeenth that launched the controversy in earnest.[5] He lamented the omission of the Quebec veto and the repudiation of native rights, and urged the restoration of both. Justice G.A. Addy of the Federal Court wrote immediately to Bora Laskin in his capacity as chair of the Canadian Judicial Council to lay a formal complaint against Thomas Berger. Berger, he alleged, had 'not the faintest idea of the position and role of a judge in the British parliamentary system to-day.' Such misconduct, in Addy's view, 'would tend to cause far greater harm to the administration of justice than sleeping with a prostitute or driving whilst impaired.' The judge hastened to add he was not quarrelling with the content of Berger's views but rather with his having expressed them publicly.

No sooner had the letter arrived at Wellington Street than the prime minister entered the fray. While being interviewed on a television talk show in Vancouver on 24 November, Trudeau expressed frustration with Berger's intervention, saying 'I just regard this as the judiciary getting mixed into politics and I hope the judges will do something about it.' And they did. On 8 March the council resolved to appoint a committee of investigation to inquire, in private, into Justice Addy's complaint. This was the most serious matter the Canadian Judicial Council had faced in its ten-year existence and it revealed a serious divergence of views among its members. The chief justices of British Columbia, Nathan Nemetz and Allan McEachern, both supported Berger and dissented from the council's decision. A number of other judges stated at the outset their opposition to Berger's removal from office. McEachern become Berger's de facto advocate before the inquiry committee when he declined to appear before them. Berger's position was that no facts were in dispute: there was no need for an inquiry. He was also of the view that the council had no power to recommend any discipline short of removal from office.

In two letters to Bora Laskin, Berger defended himself by framing his action as a matter of conscience. 'I believe it is a mistake to think it is possible to place fences around a judge's conscience. These are matters that no tidy scheme of rules and regulations can encompass, for all judges are not cast from the same mould.' Laskin had stated at his own swearing in at the Court of Appeal that he was responsible only to his conscience, but he was of course thinking of his responsibility to interpret the law, not of extra-judicial pronouncements. Berger also invoked previous examples of judicial outspokenness: Justice Thorson's participation in the campaign for nuclear disarmament, Chief Justice Freedman's television appearance in October 1970 expressing support for the invocation of the *War Measures Act*, and Lord Denning's public observation in Vancouver in 1979 that trade unions were a threat to freedom in the United Kingdom. Allan McEachern developed this argument further before the committee of inquiry. He conceded the existence of a 'custom' of judicial abstention from making pronouncements on matters of political controversy, but denied that extra-judicial statements or conduct, short of criminal acts or serious moral turpitude, had ever been the basis for removal of a judge anywhere in the common law world.

Bert MacKinnon, associate chief justice of Ontario and chairman of the inquiry committee, sought legal advice from J.J. Robinette as to the extent of the council's powers to recommend discipline short of removal of a judge from the bench. He was of the view that the council, in reporting its 'conclusions' to the minister of justice, was not restricted to a finding that conduct by a judge did or did not justify removal from the bench. Given the objects underlying the creation of the council, it might express an opinion on a judge's conduct without necessarily recommending removal. With Robinette's letter in hand, it did not take the committee long to reach a conclusion. They found the principle of separation of powers in Canada to require judges to be 'divorced from all politics,' and rejected Berger's defence of 'conscience' as too amorphous to provide any sure guide to judicial behaviour. The proper recourse where a judge felt moved by conscience to speak out on a matter of great importance, according to the committee, was to resign and enter the arena of public debate shorn of his or her judicial mantle. Berger's 'unwise and inappropriate' action was sufficiently serious to recommend his removal from the bench but, acknowledging the prior existence of differing views on the subject, the committee declined to recommend removal. This was the first time in its existence that the council had been seised of such a question, and the committee was disinclined 'to set standards *ex post facto.*'

When the full council considered the report of the inquiry committee in May, it no doubt led to some heated discussion but Laskin was not part of it. He had been rushed to hospital on 21 April after suffering stroke-like symptoms at work and was not able to return to the bench until 7 June.[6] In fact his absence may have been crucial to the decision of the council to distance itself from the inquiry committee's most serious finding. According to the council, while Berger's 'actions were indiscreet, they constitute no basis for a recommendation that he be removed from office.' Laskin's later interventions suggested he agreed with the position of the inquiry committee, and he might have been able to sway the full council to his position had he been present. As it was, the council's resolution gave only a one-line explanation of its views by way of advice to judges: 'members of the Judiciary should avoid taking part in controversial political discussions except only in respect of matters that directly affect the operation of the courts.' This final resolution, together with the report of MacKinnon's committee and a variety of supporting documentation, was transmitted to the minister of justice, Jean Chrétien, on 31 May and laid before Parliament on 4 June. Unfortunately, Chrétien did not immediately seize the important distinction between the inquiry report and the final resolution. In comments to the media shortly after receiving the material, he seemed to indicate that the views of the committee had been fully adopted by the council. Chief Justice Gregory Evans of the High Court of Ontario also made public remarks that were open to that interpretation.

Berger was not given a copy of the committee report by the council. Even after Chief Justice McEachern provided him with one, these confusing public statements scarcely helped to clarify the council's already opaque resolution. Berger thus sought to obtain a clarification as to the relationship between the inquiry report and the final resolution by contacting Pierre Chamberland, the executive secretary to the council. When Bora Laskin learned of this he interpreted the inquiry as an attempt to intrude upon the confidentiality of Judicial Council deliberations, and fired off a blast expressing strong objection to Berger's action.[7] Svend Robinson, MP wrote to all members of the council urging them to make a statement clarifying the error made by Jean Chrétien in his public remarks. Laskin replied that if the minister had made an error it was no business of the council to correct. When Chief Justice Evans made a similar error in a public statement, Chief Justice of Alberta William McGillivray wrote to Laskin asking him to put the matter on the agenda for the next meeting of the council. He believed a statement should now be made for two reasons: a spokesman for the council itself had now made an error, and 'it is required as a matter of just plain fairness.'[8] It is unknown whether the matter reached the council agenda, but no such statement was ever made.

By mid-summer the controversy appeared to be winding down. Berger replied to Laskin's fiery letter expressing hope that he had recovered from his recent illness and recording his disagreement with the way the matter was handled, but agreeing that the matter was now at an end. Laskin, rather ominously, thanked Berger for his sympathy but said the press had manufactured reports of his illness (in fact, he himself had referred to his illness in a previous letter to Berger). He too agreed the matter was over. When McGillivray wrote to Laskin on 4 August he expressed the belief that 'most of the public have forgotten about the whole thing,' and Berger himself, writing to Frank Scott in July, also thought '[t]his crazy dispute with the Judicial Council seems to be behind me at last.'[9] Little did they know that as Laskin gathered his strength over the summer he was preparing to deliver the last word on the subject, the message he had been unable to convey earlier because of illness.

It had not gone unnoticed by Laskin that Berger had widespread support. In his home province, Berger was a local hero. The benchers of the Law Society of British Columbia passed a resolution on 27 May asking the Canadian Judicial Council to dismiss the complaint against him, and the newspapers were solidly behind him. The Canadian Civil Liberties Association (CCLA) had urged the council to examine the complaint 'with extreme circumspection, ... especially when his conduct was not anomalous when viewed in the context of how others have behaved.' If the council were to find some impropriety, the CCLA asked that no action be taken against Berger because Canadians would continue to trust him in the discharge of his judicial duties.[10] Laskin's old friend Emmett Hall was honorary president of the CCLA. He telephoned Berger at the height of the controversy to commiserate with him and said he felt like going to Ottawa and giving Bora a good shaking.[11] Editorials across the country were favourable to Berger, primarily because he had echoed public frustration with the politicians' about-face on aboriginal rights. Laskin would have been especially stung by the allegation that he and the council had thrown the book at Berger but had gone lightly on John Farris, the former chief justice of the British Columbia Supreme Court. In August 1978 Farris had been detected in a drug wire-tap as the client of a well-known Vancouver prostitute. According to journalist Allan Fotheringham, '[t]here was much to-ing and fro-ing between the high muckymucks of the B.C. legal system and Chief Justice Bora Laskin of the Supreme Court of Canada, and the then justice minister, Otto Lang, [with] the result that Farris was allowed to announce he was resigning on a date of his choosing.'[12]

Laskin had been asked to address the annual meeting of the Canadian Bar Association in Toronto on 2 September – a year to the day after Thomas Berger had addressed the same group in Vancouver and expressed his support for the patriation package as it then existed. Before a thousand lawyers and judges Laskin used the platform as a bully pulpit to lash out at Berger and those who had criticized the Judicial Council's ruling. He castigated 'some members of the press and some in public office' for believing that 'freedom of speech gave them the full scope of participation and comment on current political controversies.' 'Was there ever any such ignorance of both history and of principle?' he asked rhetorically. For Laskin, who had often said he lost half his freedom of speech when he became a judge and the other half when he became a chief justice, the position was stark and simple. A judge who feels so strongly on political issues that he must speak out 'is best advised to resign from the bench.' Berger 'was reactivating his Mackenzie Valley Pipeline Inquiry, a matter which was years behind him and should properly be left dormant for a political decision, if any, and not for his initiative in the midst of a sensitive political controversy.'[13] Someone rose after Laskin's jeremiad and said it was too bad Berger was not there to defend himself. 'This was greeted with substantial, perhaps significant, and certainly deserved applause.'[14]

A west coast newspaper carried the blunt and not wholly inaccurate headline: 'LASKIN CALLS BERGER IGNORANT.' With that, Berger realized he could not carry on as a judge. He made the decision that fall to resign the following summer, and wrote his letter of resignation to the Minister of Justice, Mark MacGuigan, on 25 April 1983. He was not in an enviable position in the short term. At the age of fifty and with less than twelve years' service on the bench he was ineligible for a pension, and the Law Society of British Columbia had fairly strict rules regarding the resumption of law practice by former judges. In the end the benchers allowed him to resume an unrestricted practice, providing only that he drop 'the Honourable' as a form of address since it might mislead clients. Given his popularity in British Columbia, it was not long before he had resumed a thriving professional life. Within days of his resignation he accepted an appointment as a commissioner to inquire into the workings of the Alaska Native Claims Settlement Act, renewing his ties with the Arctic land and people he had grown to love during the Mackenzie Valley inquiry.

Berger knew he was stepping into dangerous waters when he made his public statements in November 1981, but seemed genuinely surprised when the Judicial Council took Justice Addy's complaint seriously, and shocked when it found he had gone beyond the bounds of acceptable judicial behaviour. Perhaps he felt that someone with Bora Laskin's record as a civil libertarian would be hesitant to impose restrictions on free speech. If so, he did not reckon with the bright line Laskin drew between free speech in general and *judicial* free speech. For Laskin, the judicial role was endowed with a well-understood set of behavioural conventions. Among these, avoiding controversy on highly political topics not directly connected to the judiciary itself was second only to conviction for a major criminal offence on the list of prohibited judicial behaviours. For a judge to contravene such norms so overtly was simply unforgivable. Perhaps Laskin was even more likely to go after Berger precisely because of the underlying similarity of their political views. Laskin would not have wanted to be seen as going easy on Berger because of any such assumed compatibility. For Laskin the content of Berger's views on the constitutional question was absolutely irrelevant – the gravamen of the offence lay entirely in his manner of expressing them.

What is perhaps surprising in retrospect is the amount of support Berger received around the Judicial Council table. While the inquiry committee thought Berger's conduct merited removal from the bench, members of the full council believed 'that it amounted to an indiscretion only' in the words of Chief Justice McGillivray. It seems that a number of the chief justices of Canada did not make the razor-sharp distinction Laskin did between the content of Berger's views and his chosen forum, and were swayed by the intrinsic merit of the former. Even Frank Scott did not fully support the manner of Berger's intervention in the constitutional debate, in addition to being totally opposed to the substance of his views on the Quebec veto. In replying to an inquiry from Berger, Scott said he thought his friend had

> made a very powerful reply to all that part [of the committee of inquiry report] relating to Inuit [*sic*] claims, and their inclusion in the Charter. If the Government appointed you to investigate and report, ... then it seems hard for them to say you are wrong in protesting their removal from the constitutional guarantees. But even this argument is answerable by showing new facts had emerged which were not in evidence before you when you made your report: e.g., that the Government had a choice between dropping the Inuit or dropping Quebec ... Frankly, however, it makes me wonder whether judges should ever be asked to assume the chairmanship of policy-forming bodies, like Royal Commissions and others. If judges must be so used, then they must be extra-circumspect in their subsequent public utterances, confining themselves to explaining the meaning of their recommendations and related matters.[15]

Scott's understanding of acceptable judicial behaviour was similar to Laskin's: he was careful to say only that Berger had made a 'powerful reply' to the committee of inquiry, not that he endorsed his speaking out. Few people had a sense of injustice as acute as Frank Scott's. If he felt Berger had been harshly dealt with, he would have said so in no uncertain terms, especially in a private letter. Even within the Supreme Court, views were divided. William McIntyre thought Berger was wrong to speak out, while Brian Dickson told Laskin he disagreed with the way he handled the matter, later calling the chief's views on judicial free speech 'antediluvian.'[16]

Berger and his defenders were fond of pointing out examples of judicial pronouncements on highly political matters in Canada and elsewhere. Laskin himself had forcefully and publicly expressed his views on issues such as the constitutional amendment formula while on the Ontario Court of Appeal. Such examples were relevant to the issue of any extant conventions regarding judicial expression on extra-judicial matters, but they could in no way be determinative. All these examples dated from before the creation of the Canadian Judicial Council, when the sole standard of impermissible conduct was defined, in effect, procedurally. Only those actions sufficiently grave to justify a joint address to the Senate and House of Commons requesting removal of the miscreant judge were considered clearly unacceptable. Other lesser forms of misbehaviour might be considered unethical by many judges, but there was no body officially charged with ascertaining any such standards or enforcing them. With judicial 'capital punishment' as the sole official sanction, by definition the misbehaviour in question would have to be grave indeed. When the Landreville scandal and other lesser problems showed the impracticability of invoking the joint address mechanism, the Canadian Judicial Council was established to create a means of judicial self-policing. The power given to the council was purposefully broad, and not restricted to situations where a *prima facie* case for removal existed, for the good reason that it was the 'lesser' kinds of cases that had most troubled the judges involved in the creation of the council.[17] There was little merit in Berger's argument that the council had no jurisdiction over him.[18]

The second reason why previous cases of unpoliced judicial political speech could not be determinative is that this was merely the 'but he was speeding too' argument in a different guise. If the council had chosen not to investigate other complaints of such speech (though it is doubtful whether there had been any such complaints), that was not a good defence for Berger though it might be germane to a reduction in sentence. His conscience-based defence was also flawed, and the inquiry committee was right to reject it. Such a defence would truly 'vary with the Chancellor's foot,' making it impossible for the council to establish standards for it.

As noted earlier, Laskin was absent for the debate over what to do with the committee's report, though council members were undoubtedly aware of his general position on the matter. In view of his later intervention, it is clear that he was not happy with the council's decision to find Berger guilty of 'an indiscretion and no more.' He was nonetheless bound by the result and should have accepted it with good grace even if he thought it wrong. His decision to make a public *ad hominem* attack on Berger at the Canadian Bar Association meeting was unfair and completely unjustifiable. The matter had been settled, as Laskin himself said to Berger in June, but Laskin chose to rekindle the controversy for his own reasons. His thinly veiled call for Berger's resignation was, according to Berger himself, the 'key element' in his decision to step down.

What motivated Laskin to do an end run around the Judicial Council he himself chaired? In a sense Laskin was invoking the 'conscience' argument he had rejected in Berger's own case. Since he felt so strongly about the seriousness of Berger's impropriety, Laskin seemed to be saying, he was compelled to speak out about it even though the judicial body he chaired had rendered a quite different judgment. To state the argument, however, is to reject it – to employ one of Laskin's favourite locutions. Some have interpreted Laskin's behaviour as the result of illness, as if he would not 'normally' have done such a thing. This seems unpersuasive for two reasons. While Laskin was quite ill in the spring, he recovered from that crisis over the summer and was rarely absent from Court that fall. His health was generally declining and he was becoming much more irritable in these last years, but there is no reason to believe his decision to speak on 2 September was clouded by incapacity. Moreover, the attack on Berger was not 'abnormal' for Laskin. It was in fact characteristic of him when he felt put on the defensive. Laskin's attack on Berger was reminiscent of his treatment of Wilbur Jackett nearly a decade earlier, before any of his health problems arose. In both cases he reacted very strongly to the presence of a perceived competitor against whom he seemed to be losing a public relations battle. In both cases there was some basis for Laskin's critical views, but he reacted in an excessive and entirely inappropriate manner in venting his criticism. These incidents were the most obvious examples of Laskin's extreme sensitivity to any perceived slights on his office or his person.

While my interpretation of Laskin's behaviour emphasizes his masculine competitive nature, I do not exclude the possibility that unresolved doubts and insecurities about his Jewish identity may have played a role in these incidents. Some have suggested that the strain of trying 'to resolve the question of whether he was an insider or an outsider' explains the rather erratic behaviour of Felix Frankfurter while on the bench.[19] Without the evidence of private papers or the testimony of intimates, however, one remains in the realm of speculation. Still, it is worth noting that even a secular, liberal, virtually assimilated third-generation Jew such as H.L.A. Hart, holder of the Oxford Chair in Jurisprudence and one of the greatest legal theorists of the twentieth century, harboured such insecurities until the end of his life. To his American successor in the chair, Ronald Dworkin, he once observed that it was remarkable 'that no English person had held the chair in recent decades. Amazed, Dworkin replied, "But you are English." "No," [Hart] retorted, "I'm Jewish."'[20]

There is a coda to the Berger saga. In the spring of 1983 Laskin was furious when he got wind of plans by the *McGill Law Journal* to publish a series of documents on the Berger affair, including the report of the investigation committee, the final resolution of council, and various pieces of correspondence (though none by Laskin himself). His position was that Judicial Council matters were confidential. It is not clear how these documents found their way to the journal, but in all likelihood Berger himself sent them. Like most North American law journals the *McGill Law Journal* is a student-run enterprise, and the editor in 1982–3 was a student named Stephen Toope. Out of the blue Toope received a call from a very irate Bora Laskin, who tried to dissuade him from publishing the documents. When persuasion did not seem to work, Laskin told Toope that if he went ahead he would have no future in the law in Canada. Toope interpreted this as a threat, but Laskin may have seen himself as simply stating a fact – that no one would trust Toope after his involvement in what Laskin saw as a serious ethical breach. Even so it was pretty strong medicine for a chief justice to administer to a mere law student. Laskin next called Dean John Brierley to ask him to intervene but the dean replied that the journal was independent and there was nothing he could do. Brierley later told Toope that even if he could have intervened, he would not have done so. The journal went ahead and published the documents, and Laskin's prediction about Toope's future proved highly inaccurate – in due course he became dean of the McGill Faculty of Law.[21]

Thomas Berger, unsurprisingly, was left with a jaundiced view of Bora Laskin after this conflict. While acknowledging Laskin's 'formidable contribution to Canadian law,' he accused the chief justice of 'display[ing] a devotion to rank, status and hierarchy. Inside the skin of a civil libertarian was an authoritarian struggling to get out.'[22] This strikes me as an exaggerated assessment. It is true that Laskin displayed a more authoritarian side, and an unfortunate penchant for secrecy, once he became chief justice, but this characteristic was most in evidence on those comparatively rare occasions when he felt threatened by a competitor. Otherwise his civil libertarian commitments remained relatively intact.

24

Final Years

At a gathering of the judges in the early 1980s, Laskin wanted to express the hope that each of his colleagues would serve out their full term. Except that through a Freudian slip he said 'live out,' rather than 'serve out.'[1] His subconscious knew what his conscious mind refused to admit. Publicly Laskin continued to insist that he had no plans to retire before the age of seventy-five, and he retained a full agenda of court work and extra-curricular activities until some new health crisis intervened. The spring of 1982 was particularly thick with events, some with personal resonance, some political, some pulling his thoughts into the distant past, others propelling them into an amorphous future. On 10 March Laskin was fêted at a lunch at Massey College before giving the Cecil Wright memorial lecture, in which he paid warm tribute to his mentor and friend. Marie Wright had died only weeks before the event. The published version of this talk is unique among Laskin's writings for its personal reminiscences and emotional overtones; he virtually never spoke about such matters on the record. As he rose to speak to the overflow crowd in the moot court room, the 'thunderous standing ovation' and the ghosts of half a century nearly overwhelmed him. He paused with tears in his eyes, then announced, 'It's good to be home.'[2] Afterwards, Laskin mingled with students, attended a reception at Falconer Hall, and then dined with the faculty before returning to Ottawa late in the evening. Underneath the surface pleasantries, he was consumed with worry. Laskin had asked that Jean Milner be seated next to him at dinner, and he confided to her his concern about Peggy's health. Her cancer, once in remission, had spread to her bones and she was now having to learn to walk with crutches.[3]

On the thirtieth the newest member of the Court, Bertha Wilson, was sworn in under the glare of television cameras. It was only the second time the media had ever filmed the ceremony – the first was for Antonio Lamer in 1980 – but in the new Charter era it would certainly not be the last. Given his long service in the cause of human rights, one might have expected Laskin to welcome a woman to the Supreme Court. But his anxiety about Wilson's presence was 'painfully evident' at the reception following her swearing in. Just when he had begun to try and seek more consensus among his colleagues, he feared that Wilson's presence would make this goal unattainable. Earlier in the month Laskin had observed with grim satisfaction that Wilson would be put to work immediately after her swearing in, and so she was.[4] The case heard that afternoon was *Shell Oil Co. v. Commissioner of Patents*,[5] which Laskin assigned to Wilson to write; she knew nothing of patents but did not feel she could say so at her first Supreme Court conference. He continued to be defensive about her appointment. When speaking to peace activist Kay Macpherson after her induction into the Order of Canada that fall, Laskin was quick to assure her that 'merit, not sex, had counted in the appointment,' but somewhat inconsistently said 'the Minister of Justice had been insistent that a woman be appointed.' After he lamented that it was difficult to find qualified women candidates, Macpherson regretted she had not thought to reply, 'It must be equally difficult to find competent men.'[6]

Laskin had been asked to address the Bermudian bar in April but decided to pass in view of Peggy's health and his already crowded schedule.[7] On the sixth he went on an unusual excursion organized by Antonio Lamer. There had been discussion for some time about the desirability of more social outings for the judges as a morale-building exercise. As the junior judge prior to Bertha Wilson's appointment, Lamer had arranged a visit to a sugar bush in Ste-Thérèse de la Gatineau, about two hours from Ottawa on the Quebec side of the border. Most of the judges and their spouses attended, transported by chartered bus. The group stopped first at Maniwaki, where the mayor insisted on offering them a 'stirrup sherry' at a brief reception. He had also arranged for a chorus of local school children to sing some French songs for the visitors, including one specially written in honour of the chief justice. As Laskin listened to these delicate voices deliver this unexpected tribute, it touched a well of Yiddish sentimentality long capped by his formidably disciplined exterior. Tears rolled down his cheeks before the singing ended. The judges enjoyed their subsequent tramp about the sugar bush but the trip proved to be a one-off occasion.[8]

On a rainy 17 April Laskin watched the Parliament Hill ceremony where the Queen signed the proclamation bringing the *Constitution Act, 1982* into force, while on the twenty-first he was due to attend the investiture of a new group of members of the Order of Canada. This time the ceremony had a special resonance because Morris Shumiatcher was to be among those honoured. The Laskins attended a splendid dinner given by Morris and Jacqui at Le Chateauneuf in Hull the previous evening, but fate intervened to prevent Bora from attending the ceremony itself. On the twenty-first Laskin went to his office and met with his clerks Alan Young and Sheridan Scott. The Court was not sitting but Laskin was due to attend a lunch for a number of provincial chief justices to be given in the judges' newly opened dining room. Young immediately noticed something was wrong: Laskin seemed at a loss for words, and could only use the verb 'dealt with' even though it was not appropriate for what he wanted to say. One of the visiting judges suspected a stroke and arranged for an ambulance. Laskin remained at Ottawa Civic Hospital for two weeks, then returned home for a month of rest. The episode seems to have been precipitated by incorrect dosages of some of his medications. By the time Laskin returned to work the spring session was almost over, but he confidently predicted to Morris that he expected to be restored to good health by the end of the summer.[9]

Alas, there would be no complete restoration. In addition to his myriad existing health problems, Laskin had been diagnosed with myelofibrosis. The bone marrow of patients with this incurable, untreatable condition produces blood with too few red blood cells, causing severe anaemia and a host of other complications. Blood transfusions alleviate some of the symptoms but do not slow the progress of the disease. During his last few years on the Court, Laskin's colleagues recalled his moods and general health following a predictable cycle.[10] Just after a transfusion, he would be almost his old self in both body and spirit, but as time went on he would become increasingly weak and irritable. His irascibility became particularly noticeable in interchanges with counsel, but one of the few occasions when he nearly 'lost it' involved an extremely provocative litigant rather than counsel. Joe Borowski was a determined anti-abortion crusader on a self-appointed mission to abolish what he saw as Canada's excessively liberal laws on the subject. In the years immediately before the Charter of Rights and Freedoms was adopted, he sought to have the relevant sections of the Criminal Code struck down as abridging the right to life as guaranteed by the Canadian Bill of Rights. In May 1981 the Supreme Court heard the government of Canada's appeal from lower court rulings that confirmed Borowski's challenge could be heard in the Saskatchewan courts (the federal government argued that the Federal Court was the proper venue). By consent of counsel the Court agreed to consider the previously unaddressed issue of Borowski's standing. Borowski had been on a hunger strike to further his cause, but was persuaded to end it by his counsel Morris Shumiatcher, who advised that his appeal would be rendered moot if he died before the hearing. When Borowski attended the hearing in Ottawa, he was, as William McIntyre recalled,

> sitting in the back and looking like a ghost ... [S]omeone made a submission to the bench and Bora made a reply. It did not seem of any great consequence, but whatever it was, offended Borowski. He got up and began walking up the aisle, and Bora said, Mr. Borowski, you have to sit down. Borowski said he would be heard, and made some remark about a fascist court or a Nazi court, and there he was talking to a Jewish intellectual and accusing him of being Hitlerian. The colour drained right out of Bora's face and he told the ushers to take that man out. No one could have delivered a graver insult to Bora Laskin. Borowski was probably at the end of his tether at that time and could perhaps be excused. He was starved and obsessed and believed that he was a prophet of God, but it was the only time that I ever saw Bora getting close to ungovernable. It passed quickly and he had not said anything that it was not perfectly proper for a chief justice to say.[11]

Laskin might well have become 'ungovernable' if Borowski had completed his mission to approach the bench. It was rumoured that he had brought a bottle containing a preserved foetus, which he proposed to brandish before the judges to alert them to the 'reality' of abortion.[12] Notwithstanding his earlier expansive precedents on standing Laskin dissented, rather unconvincingly, with Antonio Lamer from the majority holding dismissing the appeal and confirming Borowski's standing to bring the challenge.[13]

In spite of his worsening health, Laskin coped reasonably well during his last full year on the Court, 1982–3. According to his clerks that year,

Ruth Sullivan and Dennis Klinck, he had only occasional brief absences. His general energy level seemed low, but he was still able to write judgments virtually overnight. On 2 October John and Barbara Laskin arranged a surprise party at the Four Seasons Hotel in honour of their father's seventieth birthday. Most of Laskin's colleagues were able to attend, in addition to retirees Wishart Spence, Ronald Martland and Louis-Philippe Pigeon, and some of Bora and Peggy's closest friends: Charles and Anne Dubin, Morris and Jacqui Shumiatcher, Nathan Nemetz. On his actual birthday, the fifth of the month, Laskin had a further surprise when all the Supreme Court staff gathered in his office to wish him happy birthday on his arrival. The judges also arranged a luncheon party for him in the new dining room, something they might not have dared to do while Martland was still on the Court. In January Bora and Peggy were well enough to splurge on a ten-day vacation in Las Vegas, where they joined their old friend David Spencer and his companion Bruno.[14] It is pleasantly unsettling to imagine the Laskins strolling about the heartland of American glitter and debauchery, as if on holiday from overly strict parents. In March they took a brief holiday in Florida where Bora was made an honorary member of the American College of Trial Lawyers after being introduced by Chief Justice Warren Burger.

In May Laskin visited the city of his birth for what would be the last time. He had been awarded an honorary degree by Lakehead University the previous spring, and the Education Building was to be renamed in his honour, but he was too ill to attend the ceremonies. Typically, Laskin felt duty bound to return in order to give the convocation address he had been unable to deliver earlier.[15] In obsessive fashion, he returned yet again to the topic of judicial free speech and the battle with Thomas Berger, who had resigned from the bench in April.

Laskin's final year on the Court was truly an *annus horribilis*. The pendulum swings of his myelofibrosis became more and more extreme, while he suffered increasing anxiety about Peggy's deteriorating health. Back pain forced Laskin to spend his and Peggy's forty-fifth wedding anniversary in the hospital in June 1983 and he remained there for some time. Ted Culliton found him depressed when calling on him at home in August.[16] Laskin returned to work in September in frail condition, trying to conserve his strength by arriving just before hearings began at 10:00 a.m. and leaving as soon as the Court rose in the afternoon. His clerks met with him only when called, which was not often. Micheline Rochon responded by guarding her boss's door even more ferociously than usual, keeping even the other judges out unless summoned by

Laskin. Only Bud Estey ignored her strictures and saw the chief whenever he liked. Part of what kept Laskin going was the chance to hear the
early Charter cases. The first significant one came forward that fall, and
Laskin was very keen to sit on it. He heard the argument in *Hunter v.
Southam* late in November but was unable to take part in the deliberations and did not live to see the judgment rendered.

Some incidents in the fall of 1983 revealed a chief justice in the throes
of a personality change induced by illness and possibly medication. In
that year thousands of Sikhs were fleeing the unrest in the Punjab that
would result in Indira Gandhi's raid on the Golden Temple in Amritsar
the next year and her assassination by her Sikh bodyguards. Many
sought refugee status in Canada, and twenty to thirty applications for
leave to appeal were being made to the Supreme Court every week that
fall from lower court denials of such claims. None was successful.
Laskin became obsessed with the idea that these were phony refugee
claims being put forward by unscrupulous immigration lawyers, and
expressed the view that 'these people should not be coming here.'[17] He
was upset enough to demand that the Law Society of Upper Canada
look into the matter, and insisted that Treasurer Laura Legge travel to
Ottawa to discuss the matter. Bud Estey was not convinced there was
anything wrong and wrote to Bertha Wilson and Antonio Lamer to ask
if they had noticed any irregularities in the processing of these appeals.
When they replied in the negative, Estey told Laskin there was no point
in summoning Ms Legge.[18] After Laskin's death, some of the clerks got
together and pointed out to Bud Estey that a number of these applications for leave to appeal presented interesting issues. Leave was granted
in several cases that were consolidated into one proceeding, known as
Singh v. Minister of Employment and Immigration. A unanimous bench
agreed that the existing refugee process, which did not afford an in-
person hearing to refugee claimants, was inadequate given the interests
at stake.[19] Given Laskin's own immigrant background and the empathy
with immigrants he demonstrated while on the Ontario Court of Appeal, he displayed an uncharacteristic antipathy towards this group of
claimants. Only extreme illness could have produced such a contrast
with his ordinary behaviour.

Laskin was not the only judge with health problems. Roland Ritchie
was also failing rapidly. On one occasion when they were both sitting,
Ritchie was seized with a coughing fit and disappeared below the
bench as he tried to shake it off. Laskin leaned over to help him but he
too began coughing and disappeared from view.[20] From the perspec-

tive of the audience it was almost a Punch and Judy show, but such quasi-comedy did not do much for the Court's image. Laskin could hardly urge Ritchie to retire when he would not contemplate it himself, and it was left to Brian Dickson to move in that direction soon after he became chief justice.

Laskin's judicial colleagues also suffered from his unpredictability during his last months in office. For the first time in his judicial career 'there were some absences that were not counted on,' according to William McIntyre. His irascibility with counsel became such that sometimes Brian Dickson had to intervene by saying 'the rest of us would like to hear what you have to say, counsel'[21] The situation was exacerbated by Laskin's refusal to discuss his health with his colleagues. Bud Estey knew a little more than the others, but even he did not know much.

After barely scraping through the fall of 1983, Laskin had to enter the hospital in December for a cataract operation. The operation was successful but he was too weak to return to work when the Court began to sit in January. Peggy too was declining quickly, but as Bud Estey observed after a visit to their apartment, 'she [was] hanging on for Bora.' To the end she rose above her own severe problems to try and assist her husband. As ever, Laskin saw his health problems as temporary setbacks and was planning a spring vacation in the Caribbean. He contacted his old friend Sir Fred Phillips in Barbados and asked him to make reservations at a suitable hotel, but sadly the Laskins were unable to make the trip.[22]

Early in 1984 a sea change was clearly underway in Ottawa as Trudeau's long reign reached its end. In contrast to the spirit of optimism a decade earlier, when an energetic new chief justice, a new governor-general, and a new baby at Sussex Drive had seemed to herald a buoyant new era, an aura of uncertainty pervaded the capital. Trudeau himself took his long walk in the snow on 29 February and announced he was stepping down after nearly sixteen years as prime minister. He had appointed one of his loyal lieutenants, Jeanne Sauvé, as governor-general in December, but she was felled by a respiratory infection in the new year and lay near death in an Ottawa hospital, too ill to be sworn in. Bora Laskin too was dying, though few outside his family and judicial colleagues realized it. When Laskin had not been at Court since December and had to be hospitalized again in February with pneumonia, it was clear that the end could not be far off. Brian Dickson quietly put in motion some arrangements he had made twice before when Laskin was very ill. Knowing that the Order of Canada does not make posthumous appointments, Dickson ensured that Laskin would be named secretly to the Order – as it turned out, less than two weeks before his death.[23]

All but a few insiders heard of the chief justice's death on the evening news on 26 March. The next day, Pierre Trudeau rose in Parliament to say that Canadians had 'lost one of their greatest champions of equity and fairness,' and concluded his tribute with the story of Laskin's famous home run in Thunder Bay. Opposition leader Brian Mulroney thought Laskin's 'supreme achievement was to shake the Court out of the straight-jacket of orthodoxy in which it had long operated.' NDP leader Ed Broadbent reminisced about the time he served with Laskin on the York University committee on 'Freedom and Responsibility in the University,' while the Minister of Justice, Mark MacGuigan, remembered their six years together as faculty members at the University of Toronto.[24] The parallels between Trudeau's and Laskin's careers were almost uncanny in spite of their very different origins. Trudeau, the child of privilege and product of two of Canada's founding European nations, and Laskin, the child of impoverished Russian immigrant Jews, had ended up at the summit of Canada's political and legal life. Both had left the academy at exactly the same time, with Laskin's appointment to the bench in September 1965 and Trudeau's entry into federal politics the same month. Both had been outsiders to the political and legal establishments when they became prime minister and chief justice respectively. Both had faced severe setbacks in 1979: Trudeau the loss of office and end of his marriage, Laskin a near-death experience. But both had bounced back.

Trudeau's offer of a state funeral was declined, but a compromise was worked out. Laskin's body lay in state in the marble splendour of the Supreme Court lobby until mid-morning on the twenty-eighth, as a procession of some five hundred dignitaries paid their respects to the family. Former governor-general Roland Michener, who had sworn in Laskin as chief justice, represented Edward Schreyer, who was out of the country. Propped up on a table beside Laskin's flag-draped coffin were his three highest awards: the Order of Canada, the Queen's Silver Jubilee Medal, and the Canadian Centennial Medal. Hundreds also attended the funeral service at the Chevra Kadhisha Synagogue in Ottawa, where Rabbi Gunther Plaut, Rabbi Feinberg's successor at Holy Blossom Temple, delivered the eulogy. Peggy attended but was too frail for the afternoon trip to Holy Blossom Memorial Park in

Scarborough. The brief burial service was conducted by Holy Blossom's senior rabbi, Dow Marmur, as raw March winds chilled those huddled about the grave site. They listened in silence as violinist Maurice Solway played his composition 'Prayer' as a final tribute to his fraternity friend of fifty years' standing.[25]

Few Canadian chief justices have died in office, though Patrick Kerwin had in 1963. His death warranted a modest obituary on page nine of the *Globe and Mail* and a small private funeral, whereas Laskin's death gave rise to nationwide mourning and an outpouring of editorial reflection on what he represented to Canada and Canadians.[26] The reaction in Quebec was much more generous than Laskin had any right to expect. The Parti Québécois Minister of Justice, Pierre-Marc Johnson, said that while his government disagreed with Laskin's centralizing view of federalism, he 'left a legacy worthy of inspiring a generation of jurists.' The Assemblée Nationale even passed a unanimous resolution of condolence.[27] An editorial in *Le Devoir* said not a word about Laskin's views on federalism, but praised his contribution to 'une conception évolutive du droit' and hoped that his example would inspire 'une génération plus nombreuse de juristes plaçant la justice au coeur de leur profession.'[28] The anglophone press also lauded Laskin's creative approach to the law, his independence of mind, and his compassion. Joan Cohen of the *Winnipeg Free Press* summed up the prevailing opinion: 'Whatever its talents, greatness is not a word that either lawyers or the public attach to the Laskin court as a court. But there is a wide view that it does attach to Laskin himself, and his writings for the court.'[29]

Bud Estey had been right about Peggy: she had indeed been 'hanging on for Bora.' Confined to a wheelchair, she barely managed to get through the funeral ceremonies. After it was all over, Peggy just gave up. A month after her husband's death she had to enter Ottawa General Hospital, where she died on 28 May.[30] As Bora Laskin had done for his friend Lyla Rasminsky, so Louis Rasminsky did for Peggy, as he delivered the eulogy at her funeral. For Morris Shumiatcher '[i]t was the saddest news, sadder in some ways than learning of the death of Bora because she was his heart-beat and his life net and to all, she was the blithe spirit of the family. She was beautiful and buoyant and brilliant from the first day that I was in Toronto in the fall of 1941 until the last time I saw her eight weeks ago.'[31] Months later, Shumiatcher reflected further on the deaths of his two friends, and urged the erection of a sculpture of both of them on the grounds of the Supreme Court. 'It should be of bronze and granite,' he mused, and 'must find its inspiration in the heart and brain of a renowned sculptor who knew both Peggy and Bora and understood and loved them well. [There should] be a tangible memorial that many generations of lawyers and litigants who will make their way across the green grass that surrounds the Supreme Court buildings will pause to see and there draw inspiration from the lives of a man and a woman whose personalities entered the hearts of countless of their friends, and colleagues, all of whom will claim Peggy and Bora as their own, and rightly so, because they gave so freely of themselves to all of us.'[32]

Epilogue

All his life Bora Laskin sought to move Canadian society in a different direction, to make it more tolerant, more just, more open to a diversity of ideas, more solicitous of the needs of the most disadvantaged and disenfranchised. Law and education were the tools he used to try and effect change. As an academic he participated in legislative reform campaigns and sought to influence the course of judicial decisions through his writing, as an arbitrator he was able to shape the lived experience of labour law, and as a judge he contributed directly to the development of Canadian jurisprudence. In a sense, however, all of this work was only a subset of Laskin's larger educational mission. From the time he took over the teaching of the Talmud Torah in Fort William as an adolescent until his last press interviews in which he sought to inform Canadians about the work of the Supreme Court, Laskin tried to educate and influence labour leaders, present and future lawyers, university boards, judges, politicians, the media, and the Canadian public.

Laskin must have been often disappointed, though, that his ideas were not adopted, his aspirations left unfulfilled. His agenda for the reform of university governance remained unimplemented, and he deplored the trend to faculty unionization. So many of his decisions on the Canadian Bill of Rights remained dissents, and the reinterpretation of federalism jurisprudence he had long advocated did not come to pass. Laskin was in the minority on the most important part of the decision on the *Patriation Reference*, the most important case heard by the Court in its history, and he never got to decide a single case under the Canadian Charter of Rights and Freedoms. At a personal level, too, the premature deaths of Bora and Peggy were cause for regret. They did not live to see their grandchildren, nor to congratulate their children on their successes. They would have been enormously proud to see John elevated to the Ontario Court of Appeal in 1994, and to know that Barbara would serve as a lay bencher of the Law Society of Upper Canada. The latter appointment would have provoked some mirth, no doubt, in view of Laskin's sometimes conflictual relations with that body.

Yet, seen in a longer perspective, Laskin's contribution as an academic, a labour arbitrator, and a judge was immense. His early activism in support of the union movement, and later in the cause of human rights, mark him out as one of those who helped hasten the arrival of modern Canada. As an academic, Laskin's role in university affairs at large has endured more than his scholarship, though the latter was important to his generation and inspired the next. His report on the Crowe case will always stand as a pivotal moment in the history of academic freedom in Canada, and of the university itself, while his report on graduate studies at the University of Toronto remains a monument to the importance of developing Canada's human capital. His approach to labour arbitration was crucial in redressing the heavy pro-management bias of contemporary labour law, and articulating human dignity as an important value in the workplace.

The quality of the judiciary as a whole improved markedly over the course of Laskin's years on the Supreme Court, in part because of the active interest he took in superior court appointments and the interest in them he generated in the media and the public. In effect, Laskin told the Canadian public that they had the right to expect more of their judicial officers, and told the judges not to rest on their laurels. A judicial appointment was the beginning of a new and demanding career, not a prelude to retirement. Laskin's critiques of the quality of judicial effort, both as an academic and as a judge, had some effect in urging governments to take the task of judicial appointments more seriously, even as it made him unpopular in certain quarters of the judiciary. A greater public profile and significant improvements in salary in turn made judicial appointments more attractive to talented candidates. The Ontario Court of Appeal Laskin left in 1970 was not well respected, but with the appointments of the early 1970s it soon came to be seen as the strongest provincial appeal court in the country, a reputation it retains to this day.[1] And appointments to the Supreme Court of Canada since Laskin's time have generally been considered to represent the best Canadian jurists and to be free of partisan considerations. It is hard to imagine a former prime minister or other politician being parachuted on to the Court, as was seriously contemplated in 1963 when the Conservatives were trying to remove John Diefenbaker from the political landscape.

In addition to Laskin's reshaping of public law, his most significant contribution resided in his general approach to decision making. Laskin became a judge at a time when the allure of the English heritage had faded in Canadian legal culture generally, but the judiciary itself seemed unwilling or unable to acknowledge this transition. Someone had to challenge this mindset, and Laskin eagerly took up the role. In doing so, however, he did not subscribe to any narrowly nationalist vision. He directed Canadian jurists to take their law from many sources, wherever the most persuasive reasoning could be found that was suitable to Canadian conditions. Nor did Laskin, as is sometimes said, 'Americanize' Canadian law: rather, he urged a serious consideration of American precedents in specific fields where economic or social similarities seemed compelling and where differing constitutional frameworks did not present an impediment to Canadian borrowing. He continued to learn from English law, to cite Australasian precedents, and on occasion to suggest the utility of Quebec civil law approaches in a common law context. Laskin did not invent this approach – indeed, it is one that arguably constitutes a fundamental feature of Canadian law, in contrast to other traditions which regard legal 'borrowing' as a threat to the integrity of 'national' law.[2] But he did revive it and re-legitimate it at a time when the courts seemed mired in a mechanical search for the closest English precedent. Laskin also cited academic writing more frequently than was commonly done at the time, and continued to contribute to legal scholarship after becoming a judge, a practice that had almost disappeared after the war. At the same time he urged his colleagues to be more open about the policy choices implicit in their decision making, though it is a fair critique of his decisions to observe that they did not always live up to his own exhortations.

Laskin also helped to shape legal and societal discourse about the concept of rights. At one level law is fundamentally about the protection of rights: property rights, the right to bodily integrity, the right to do what is not prevented by positive law, the right to test the legality of any deprivation of physical liberty by habeas corpus, and so on. Yet

Canada's model of rights protection was within the British parliamentary tradition, with its reliance on legislative supremacy, rather than the constitutional tradition of rights protection represented by the United States. Laskin was prepared to work within the British model by seeking the legislative creation and protection of rights in those areas, such as protection from discrimination, where the judges seemed incapable of reforming the common law. When the Canadian Bill of Rights provided a rather unusual add-on to the parliamentary system, he was not afraid to try and shape it into a quasi-constitutional document, especially where equality before the law and the safeguards of the criminal trial process were concerned. Laskin's Bill of Rights decisions seldom attracted a majority, but they helped to establish a climate of public expectation regarding the judicial protection of fundamental rights, and began the work of teasing out the meaning in specific situations of very broadly worded guarantees, work that continues under the Canadian Charter of Rights and Freedoms.

Many have speculated about how Laskin would have treated the rights guaranteed under the Charter. In criminal law matters it is likely he would have joined enthusiastically with the high standard of protection for defendants articulated by the jurisprudence under sections 7 through 14. In other areas I suspect he would have been rather more cautious than the Dickson court was, particularly in elaborating the limitations on rights that could be 'demonstrably justified in a free and democratic society' under section 1. For Laskin the legal modernist, the state was a friend, not an enemy, at least outside the realm of criminal prosecutions. It could over-reach itself, certainly, and its bureaucrats sometimes had to be restrained from unjustified interference in citizens' lives, but in general it was a force for good and its decisions entitled to respect. An acute recognition of the separation of powers as between the judicial, executive, and legislative branches was one of the strongest themes in Laskin's judicial decisions, and he had strong ideas about those areas where the judicial writ simply did not run.[3] While the Charter clearly altered those boundaries somewhat, it did not obliterate them. Laskin likely would not have approved of some of the early Charter jurisprudence, which appeared to set a high bar for the state to meet if any limitation on rights were to be upheld.[4] Gradually the Court has relaxed this requirement and exhibits a greater willingness to uphold legislation, especially where it is of an ameliorative or protective nature, even though it may infringe Charter rights in some respect.[5] As Laskin had warned of the dangers of a 'premature synthesis' in his early writing on administrative law, he would probably have resisted the temptation to articulate a conclusive test for the application of section one until the Court had had a good deal more experience with the Charter.

Laskin had his flaws, both as a judge and as a human being. For someone who constantly preached the virtues of free discussion and debate, his own ideas remained relatively impervious to change. In spite of some decisions in which he promoted the idea of gender equality, for example, Laskin never really seemed to accept that women might have a distinctive contribution to make to the legal profession or the judiciary. If anything he became even more convinced over time of the rightness of his own ideas. Once he had decided upon his approach to a particular case, he rarely sought or accepted input from either his clerks or his colleagues. He tended to write his decisions quickly and seldom revised them, even when it was tactfully suggested by his clerks that clarity might be enhanced by doing so. Identifying the ultimate *ratio decidendi* in a Laskin judgment is not always an easy task. Often the legal conclusion is hedged about with caveats arising from the particular facts of the case, such that the rule being enunciated is much narrower than at first appears, or the reasoning process skips over key steps which were clear in Laskin's mind but remain unarticulated in the judgment. For someone who wrote hundreds of judgments over two decades, there are relatively few quotable passages in Laskin's work. This lack of clarity has impaired the survival value of many of his decisions.

Laskin's passionate individualism was both a strength and a weakness. It enabled him to speak his mind fearlessly both as an academic and a judge, to resist the complacent conformity that has often characterized the legal profession and the judiciary. But it left him with few skills for managing people or institutions, and meant that he was apt to treat those with different ideas as rivals and competitors. His willingness to administer strong criticism to others was not matched by an ability to receive it gracefully. As chief justice he seemed increasingly to treat his office as evidence of his own infallibility. An unattractive authoritarian streak also became more evident over the course of his tenure, exacerbated no doubt by illness but not caused by it. Some people mellow with age while others, like Laskin, see some of their more negative traits distilled over time.

In the decades since Laskin's death, the Canadian judiciary has entered upon a kind of golden age. The Charter has focused more public attention upon the courts, especially but not exclusively the Supreme Court of Canada, and their work has become better known internationally than at any previous time in Canadian history. As many countries in eastern Europe, Asia, and Africa have sought to reform their economies and political systems, they have turned to Canada for assistance. Canada's strong tradition of judicial independence, its expertise in court administration, and its new constitutional jurisprudence have attracted interest in many parts of the world, and the advice of Canadian judges is frequently sought on such matters. Individual Canadian judges have been asked to take on some of the most difficult tasks in the world today. Former Supreme Court judge Louise Arbour is now the United Nations Commissioner for Human Rights, Canadian Philippe Kirsch was named as the first president of the International Criminal Court, and retired Supreme Court judge Peter Cory recently conducted an inquiry for the British and Irish governments into alleged official involvement in a number of killings in Northern Ireland. Laskin's attempt to 'put the stamp of [his] personality' upon the Supreme Court of Canada had an impact far beyond that which he could have imagined.

Laskin's work may have remained unfinished, but the power of the inchoate can sometimes exceed that of the final product. One-legged Terry Fox ran across only half of Canada before succumbing to cancer in 1980 but his example inspires thousands more each year.[6] A monument to Fox was erected not in Port Coquitlam, where he was raised, or in St John's, where he began his run, but on the outskirts of Thunder Bay, where his health failed and he could no longer continue. There are now many buildings, awards, and events named after Bora Laskin, but all of these inevitably suggest a degree of finality about his contribution to Canadian life. We would do better to think of him as a beginning, not an ending, to remember him as a person whose passion for the law and for his country continue to inform its unpredictable journey.

Notes

Introduction

1 [1984] 2 S.C.R. 145.
2 *Canadian Bar Review* 80 (2001): 241-80.
3 'Laskin and Civil Liberties,' *University of Toronto Law Journal* 35 (1985): 670.
4 See R.J. Sharpe and K. Roach, *Brian Dickson: A Judge's Journey* (Toronto: University of Toronto Press for the Osgoode Society 2003); E. Anderson, *Judging Bertha Wilson: Law as Large as Life* (Toronto: University of Toronto Press for the Osgoode Society 2001); W.H. McConnell, *William R. McIntyre: Paladin of the Common Law* (Montreal: McGill-Queen's University Press 2000).
5 F. Vaughan, *Aggressive in Pursuit: The Life of Emmett Hall* (Toronto: University of Toronto Press for the Osgoode Society 2004).
6 B. Cardozo, *The Nature of the Judicial Process* (New Haven: Yale University Press 1921).
7 'The Supreme Court of Canada: A Final Court of and for Canadians,' *Canadian Bar Review* 29 (1951): 1076.
8 'English Law in Canadian Courts since the Abolition of Privy Council Appeals,' *Current Legal Problems* 29 (1976): 25.
9 (Toronto: McClelland & Stewart 1999), 62.
10 In what follows I draw on recent historical work in the field of masculinity. See, e.g., M. Kimmel, *Manhood in America: A Cultural History* (New York: Free Press 1996); M. Carnes and C. Griffen, eds., *Meanings for Man-*

hood: Constructions of Masculinity in Victorian America (Chicago: University of Chicago Press 1990), especially Michael Grossberg's essay 'Institutionalizing Masculinity: The Law as a Masculine Profession.' Laurel Sefton MacDowell also uses masculinity as a prism through which to interpret the life of her subject, in *Renegade Lawyer: The Life of J.L. Cohen* (Toronto: University of Toronto Press for the Osgoode Society 2001).

11 *Canadian Jewish News*, 29 Jan. 1981.

12 *The Law Society of Upper Canada and Ontario's Lawyers, 1797–1997* (Toronto: University of Toronto Press for the Osgoode Society 1997), chap. 4.

13 I rely here on the extended account of his own life and career Laskin gave when interviewed by Professor Robin Harris of the University of Toronto in 1976 and 1977 (transcript at University of Toronto Archives [UTA]). These will be abbreviated as BLI 1976 and BLI 1977. I develop these ideas further in an unpublished paper, 'Bora Laskin Starting Out, Bora Laskin Looking Back: Narratives of Judicial Success' (2000).

Chapter 1: The Lakehead

1 Laskin told the story of his famous home run many times during his life, and Prime Minister Pierre Trudeau recounted it when paying tribute to the late chief justice the day after his death: *Hansard*, 27 Mar. 1984, 2464. For the Harry Arthurs anecdote, see *Maclean's*, July 1974.

2 J.D. Klier, *Russia Gathers Her Jews: The Origins of the 'Jewish Question' in Russia, 1772–1825* (Dekalb: Northern Illinois University Press 1986); Klier, *Imperial Russia's Jewish Question, 1855–1881* (Cambridge: Cambridge University Press 1995).

3 On the Jews of Latvia, see 'Riga,' *Encyclopedia Judaica*, vol. 14.

4 Bora Laskin's brother Saul Laskin has recounted the family's history as told to him by his parents in a variety of published accounts and unpublished interviews; see I. Abella, 'The Making of a Chief Justice: Bora Laskin, the Early Years,' *Law Society of Upper Canada Gazette* 24 (1990): 187–95 and in F.E. McArdle, ed., *The Cambridge Lectures 1989* (Montreal: Yvon Blais 1990); J. Gault, 'Doing Justice to Bora Laskin,' *Maclean's* (July 1974); A. Goldstein, 'History of the Laskin Family in Thunder Bay,' *Northern Mosaic* 6 (1986) (based on a 1985 talk by Saul Laskin to Thunder Bay Historical Society, audiotape available at Thunder Bay Historical Museum [TBHM]); Saul Laskin interview with O. Jagodnik, 4 May 1977, transcript at TBHM; Laskin biographical files, TBHM. I will refer to these compendiously as 'the family story.' The accounts of the Laskin and Zingel families in Russia are unverifiable but conform to what is known of the history of

the Jews in Russia in the nineteenth and early twentieth centuries. The date of Mendel (Max) Laskin's arrival in Canada is given variously as 1905 and 1906.

5 S.M. Dubnow, *History of the Jews in Russia and Poland from the Earliest Times until the Present Day* (Philadelphia: Jewish Publication Society of America 1916–20), 3 vols., 2: 348–57.

6 As quoted in B.W. Menning, *Bayonets Before Bullets: The Imperial Russian Army, 1861–1914* (Bloomington: Indiana University Press 1992), 152. In 1898 the Chinese had granted Russia a twenty-five-year lease on the port, located on Manchuria's Kwantung Peninsula. It was captured by the Japanese in November 1904.

7 On the role of Jewish troops in the Russo-Japanese War, see Dubnow, *History*, 3: 94–7.

8 The U.S. figures are reported in Klier, *Jewish Question*; the Canadian figures in B.G. Sack, *Canadian Jews: Early in This Century* (Montreal: Canadian Jewish Congress 1975), 43. On the early history of the Jews in Canada, see G. Tulchinsky, *Taking Root: The Origins of the Canadian Jewish Community* (Toronto: Lester Publishing 1992).

9 The policy of the Public Archives of Manitoba is to afford access to marriage records of any vintage only to descendants or next of kin of the parties.

10 I.I. Katz, 'Ezekiel Solomon: The First Jew in Michigan,' *Michigan History* (Lansing) 32 (1948): 247–56.

11 The preceding two paragraphs rely heavily on V. P. Lytwyn, 'The Anishinabeg and the Fur Trade,' in T.J. Tronrud and A.E. Epp, eds., *Thunder Bay: From Rivalry to Unity* (Thunder Bay: Thunder Bay Historical Museum Society 1995).

12 *Henderson's Port Arthur City Directory for 1907*, 166.

13 *Daily News* (Port Arthur), 31 Aug. 1912.

14 Cited in F.B. Scollie, 'Falling into Line: How Prince Arthur's Landing Became Port Arthur,' *Papers and Records* 13 (1985): note 32. Prince Arthur was named governor-general of Canada in March 1911.

15 J. Stafford, 'A Century of Growth at the Lakehead,' in Tronrud and Epp, eds., *From Rivalry to Unity*.

16 The movements and activities of the Laskin family have been derived from a variety of local sources such as assessment records held at the Thunder Bay City Archives, deeds and wills held at the Thunder Bay land titles office, city directories, and newspapers. Max Laskin's surname is occasionally misrecorded as 'Liski' or 'Luskin.' For the Westfort properties see Thunder Bay City Archives, assessment rolls TBA 231 (1908), 233 (1909), 237 (1910), 241 (1911); for the Ward One properties, see TBA 242

(1912), 246 (1913). Separate city directories were published for Fort William and Port Arthur until the early 1920s, when they merged in *Henderson's Twin Cities Fort William and Port Arthur City Directory*.

17 As to two daughters, see Saul Laskin interview, Jagodnik interview, 4 May 1977. AO, MS 935, reel 169 no. 030028 records the birth of a stillborn girl to Max and Bluma Laskin on 22 Jan. 1911. No record of another daughter has been found but it is possible that the death of an infant might have escaped registration.

18 On the history of the Jewish community at the Lakehead, see L.C. Hansen, 'The Decline of the Jewish Community in Thunder Bay: An Explanation' (MA thesis, University of Manitoba, 1977).

19 This was probably something of an exaggeration. The 1911 census recorded 343 Jews in both Port Arthur and Fort William together.

20 B.C. Kaganoff, *A Dictionary of Jewish Names and their History* (New York: Schocken Books 1977), 109, 113.

21 On Borah, see the entry in *Dictionary of American Biography* 12 (supplement 2); C.O. Johnson, *Borah of Idaho* (New York: Longmans, Green 1936); M.C. McKenna, *Borah* (Ann Arbor: University of Michigan Press 1961).

22 H.J. Abraham, *Justices and Presidents: A Political History of Appointments to the Supreme Court*, 3rd ed. (New York: Oxford University Press 1992), 205. Cardozo, a Sephardic Jew, was duly confirmed as a justice of the Supreme Court.

23 NA, Jacob Finkelman Papers, MG 31 E 27, vol. 10, Laskin to Finkelman, 7 Apr. 1937.

24 *Canadian Jewish News*, 5 Apr. 1984.

25 D. Telfer, ed., *The Best of Humboldt* (Humboldt, Sask.: *Humboldt Journal* 1982), 376–7.

26 Thunder Bay Land Registry Office, David William Butters and James Miller Butters deed of sale to Max Laskin, 14 Oct. 1913, inst. 1720A, lot 24, block 12, plan 54, City of Fort William.

27 *Report of a preliminary and general social survey of Fort William, March, 1913, directed by the Department of Temperance and Moral Reform of the Methodist Church and the Board of Service and Evangelism of the Presbyterian Church* (Fort William 1913).

28 4 Sept. 1912.

29 B. Muirhead, 'The Evolution of the Lakehead's Commercial and Transportation Infrastructure,' in Tronrud and Epp, eds., *From Rivalry to Unity*, 81–2.

30 S. High, 'Responding to White Encroachment: The Robinson-Superior Ojibwa and the Capitalist Labour Economy: 1880–1914,' *Papers and Records* 22 (1994): 23–39.

31 See generally D. Avery, *'Dangerous Foreigners': European Immigrant Workers and Labour Radicalism in Canada, 1896–1932* (Toronto: McClelland & Stewart 1979).

32 J. Morrison, 'The Organization of Labour at Thunder Bay,' in Tronrud and Epp, eds., *From Rivalry to Unity*. J. Mauro, *Thunder Bay: A History* (Thunder Bay: n.p. 1981). *Fort William Daily Times-Journal*, 8 Oct. 1912.

33 T.J. Tronrud, 'Building the Industrial City,' in Tronrud and Epp, eds., *From Rivalry to Unity*.

34 See abstract of title for lots 25 and 26, block 11, plan 54, City of Fort William, Thunder Bay Land Registry Office.

35 *Fort William Canada: Some Facts About It that Ought to Interest You* (Fort William Board of Trade 1917), AO pamph. 1917, no. 175.

36 Abella, 'The Making of a Chief Justice,' 192–3.

37 C. Wilkins, *Breakfast at the Hoito and Other Adventures in the Boreal Heartland* (Toronto: Natural Heritage 1997).

38 The *Israelite Press*, 20 Jan. 1920, notes Max's role in organizing a Chanukah party that raised eighty-two dollars to send to the victims of recent pogroms in Ukraine and Poland.

39 Abella, 'The Making of a Chief Justice, ' 192.

40 *Israelite Press* (Winnipeg), 30 Oct. 1925. Special thanks to Esther Leven of the Jewish Heritage Centre of Western Canada (Winnipeg) for translating this and other items of interest from the Yiddish. The Herzl Forest near Jerusalem was planted in memory of Zionist leader Theodor Herzl and symbolized the return of the Jews to Palestine in the early twentieth century.

41 R.D. Gidney, *From Hope to Harris: The Reshaping of Ontario Schools* (Toronto: University of Toronto Press 1999), 289.

42 Saul wanted to attend university but family circumstances and the intervention of the war did not permit it. He attended university in his retirement and acquired a BA degree from Lakehead University in his eighties.

43 P. Vervoort, '"This Magnificent Pile": Architectural Embellishments of Older School Buildings in Thunder Bay,' *Papers and Records* 21 (1993): 59.

44 'Observations on Secondary Education in Fort William and Port Arthur 1919–1932,' *Papers and Records* 8 (1980): 14.

45 The commercial and technical classes were sent to another school in the fall of 1930, when the school changed its name to Fort William Collegiate Institute, by which it is known today.

46 Interview with *Canadian Jewish News*, 29 Jan. 1981.

47 *Oracle 1930*, 12.

48 Ibid., 17.

49 22 Aug. 1930.
50 R. Lappage, 'The Competitive Spirit in Sports,' in Tronrud and Epp, *From Rivalry to Unity*. There is a family story to the effect that Laskin was scouted by the Chicago White Sox for their farm team, but in the absence of any professional baseball teams at the Lakehead in the 1920s the presence of scouts seems unlikely; cf. Abella, 'The Making of a Chief Justice,' 193.
51 *Toronto Sun*, 2 Jan. 1974 (commenting on Laskin's appointment as chief justice).
52 *Daily Times-Journal* (Fort William), 26 Apr. 1930.
53 I would like to thank Bora Laskin's contemporaries and friends Mandy Helper of Thunder Bay and the late Walter Clemens of Vancouver for sharing with me their memories of growing up in Port Arthur and Fort William respectively and providing some information about the activities of Bora Laskin and his family.
54 UTA, BLI 1976: 3.
55 S. Repo, 'Rosvall and Voutilainen: Two Union Men Who Never Died,' *Labour/Le Travail* 8/9 (Aut./Spr. 1981–2): 79–102; L.S. MacDowell, *Renegade Lawyer: The Life of J.L. Cohen* (Toronto: University of Toronto Press 2001), 45–53.
56 *Daily Times-Journal* (Fort William), 6 and 8 Aug. 1930.
57 *Daily Times-Journal* (Fort William), 22 Aug. 1930.

Chapter 2: Law School

1 BLI 1976; 6.
2 D. Vanek, *Fulfilment: Memoirs of a Criminal Court Judge* (Toronto: Dundurn Press for the Osgoode Society 1999), 68.
3 BLI 1976 at 5. Wilfred Gregory author interview, 26 Oct. 2000. Gregory was a classmate of Bora Laskin, and his son John would later clerk for Laskin in 1975–6.
4 Author interview with Abraham Acker, 17 Dec. 2000.
5 *Varsity*, 19 Oct. 1931. See also E. Einbinder, 'A Study of Attitudes towards Jews in Toronto' (MA thesis, University of Toronto, 1934), who found that 80 per cent of students polled said they would not admit Jews to their clubs.
6 *Varsity*, 21 Oct. 1931.
7 *Ibid.*
8 M.L. Friedland, *The University of Toronto: A History* (Toronto: University of Toronto Press 2002) at 352.

9 *Torontonensis 1931*, 432 shows Laskin as a member in 1930–1.
10 Sigma Alpha Mu Fraternity Papers, UTA, A73-0051/252/1035 (37). It seems to have been obliged to give up the house when it could not afford the winter supply of coal. An investigator from fraternity headquarters in New York was dismayed to find members meeting in each other's homes in 1935: Marianne Sanua, '"Going Greek": A Social History of Jewish College Fraternities in the United States, 1895–1945' (PhD dissertation, Columbia University, 1994), 272.
11 See generally Paul Axelrod, *Making a Middle Class: Student Life in English Canada in the Thirties* (Montreal and Kingston: McGill-Queen's University Press, 1990).
12 The term 'alumni' was used more frequently with reference to fraternities and sororities than to the university at large at this time.
13 Author interview with Martin Friedland, 28 May 2002.
14 Laskin's membership is noted in his entry in *Torontonensis 1933*.
15 I. Abella, 'The Making of a Chief Justice: Bora Laskin, the Early Years,' *Law Society of Upper Canada Gazette* 24 (1990): 187–95, refers to such letters but it is not clear if they survive.
16 Ibid.
17 NA, RG 30, vol. 13812, file 26225ME, CNR farm contracts between Bora Laskin and H. Adams. I thank Harriet Lewis for discussing this practice with me by e-mail in May 2003. Her father, Leo Lewis, was a fellow 'Sammy' and contemporary of Bora Laskin, and travelled to Toronto on the CNR from his home in Alberta on a similar arrangement.
18 *Addresses delivered before the Canadian Club, Toronto, Season 1930–31*, 178.
19 *Life Before Man* (New York: Warner Books 1979),122.
20 *Canada Law Times* 34 (1914): 151.
21 R.C.B. Risk, 'The Many Minds of W.P.M. Kennedy,' *University of Toronto Law Journal* 48 (1998): 353–86.
22 P.B. Waite, *Lord of Point Grey: Larry MacKenzie of U.B.C.* (Vancouver: UBC Press 1987).
23 UTA, Robert Falconer Papers, A67-0007/121, Kennedy to Falconer, 31 Jan. 1930.
24 B.C. Aural Legal History Project, transcript of 1984 interview with Gilbert D. Kennedy (son of W.P.M. Kennedy) at 19 (copy at UBC Library).
25 UTA, Falconer Papers, Kennedy to Falconer, 26 Feb. 1930 (emphasis in original).
26 'Law as a Social Science,' *South African Law Journal* 3 (1934) 100, as cited in Risk, 'Many Minds,' 371.
27 Cited in Risk, 'Many Minds,' 374.

28 UTA, President's Office (Cody), A68-0006/060, Kennedy to Cody, 30 Oct. 1943.

29 BLI 1976: 7.

30 Cited in Risk, 'Many Minds,' 371.

31 Ibid., 374.

32 UBC Archives, Norman A.M. MacKenzie Papers, 52/1, Laskin to MacKenzie 15 May 1970.

33 BLI 1976: 16.

34 *Torontonensis 1932*, 254.

35 UTA, Cecil Wright Papers, B82-0028/03, Kennedy to Wright, 20 Nov. 1930; n.d. reply by Wright. C.I. Kyer and J.E. Bickenbach, *The Fiercest Debate: Cecil A. Wright, the Benchers, and Legal Education in Ontario, 1923–1957* (Toronto: University of Toronto Press for the Osgoode Society 1987) discuss the talk and its impact at 108–9. R. Blake Brown sets it in the context of Wright's legal thought in 'Cecil A. Wright and the Foundations of Canadian Tort Law Scholarship,' *Saskatchewan Law Review* 64 (2001): 86–9.

36 The talk was published as 'An Extra-Legal Approach to Law,' *Canadian Bar Review* 10 (1932): 1–17.

37 R.C.B. Risk, 'Canadian Law Teachers in the 1930s: "When the World Was Turned Upside Down,"' *Dalhousie Law Journal* 27 (2004): 9.

38 The lectures were published as *Some Aspects of the Theories and Workings of Constitutional Law* (New York: Macmillan 1932). This quotation and those that follow are as cited by Risk in 'Many Minds,' 365–7.

39 As cited in Risk, 'Many Minds,' 367.

40 UTA, Wright Papers, B82-0028/003, Wright to Smith, 27 July 1933.

41 My account of this incident relies heavily on M. Horn, '"Free Speech Within the Law": The Letter of the Sixty-Eight Toronto Professors, 1931,' *Ontario History* 72, no. 1 (1980): 27–48 and his *Academic Freedom in Canada: A History* (Toronto: University of Toronto Press 1999), 88–93.

42 S.H. Hughes, *Steering the Course: A Memoir* (Montreal and Kingston: McGill-Queen's University Press 2000), 65. Samuel Hughes author interview, 30 Sept. 2000.

43 Entry on Laskin in *Torontonensis 1933*. On the 'Lit' generally, see Charles Levi, 'Where the Famous People Were?: The Origins, Activities and Future Careers of Student Leaders at University College, Toronto, 1854–1973' (PhD dissertation, York University, 1998).

44 *Varsity*, 2 Nov. 1932.

45 *Torontonensis 1933*.

46 *Varsity*, 12 Oct. 1932.

47 *Varsity*, 8 Feb. 1933.

48 *Varsity*, 16 Feb. 1933.
49 *Varsity*, 31 Jan. 1933.
50 *Varsity*, 23 Jan. 1933.
51 In May Laskin signed a document authorizing the registrar to accept his diploma at convocation: Bora Laskin graduate record file, UTA, A73-0026/220(11).

Chapter 3: Articling

1 C. Levitt and W. Shaffir, *The Riot at Christie Pits* (Toronto: Lester & Orpen Denys 1987). A recent novel makes the riot its focal point: K.X. Tulchinsky, *The Five Books of Moses Lapinsky* (Vancouver: Polestar 2003).
2 C. Moore, *The Law Society of Upper Canada and Ontario's Lawyers 1797–1997* (Toronto: University of Toronto Press 1997), 179, 199–201.
3 BLI 1976: 14.
4 Moore, *Law Society*, 201 n32.
5 Author interview with Samuel Gotfrid, 25 Oct. 1999.
6 This period is well treated in, Moore, *Law Society*, chap. 4.
7 Law Society of Upper Canada Archives, Past Member File no. 2693.
8 The Bennetts had anglicized their surname from their original Jewish name.
9 Samuel Gotfrid Osgoode Society interview (1990). Although Gotfrid's plight was not enviable, he could at least turn to established lawyers from his fraternity for assistance. Aspiring women lawyers could rarely rely on such connections, although they might in some cases be able to count on male lawyers to whom they had ties of family, faith, or community.
10 Ibid.
11 *Toronto Star* obituary, 13 July 1979; Law Society of Upper Canada Past Member File no. 4636.
12 John Arnup, then a junior at the predecessor firm of Weir & Foulds where W.W. Davidson worked, recounts this tale in *Middleton: The Beloved Judge* (Toronto: McClelland & Stewart 1988).
13 Membership in Davidson's firm can be tracked through *Might's City Directory*, relevant years.
14 John Arnup reminisces about this unpleasant task in his Osgoode Society interview (1982), 63.
15 Rufus Isaacs (1860–1935), named Lord Reading in 1914, served as Lord Chief Justice from 1913 to 1921 and resigned to become Viceroy of India (1921–5).
16 John Arnup Osgoode Society interview (1982), 117.

17 There is conflicting evidence as to whether the same mourning customs were observed on the death of George VI in 1952. If they were, it seems the observance was much more perfunctory. The Law Society minutes contain various references to the protocol to be observed on the monarch's death in 1936 but none in 1952.

18 BLI 1976: 14.

19 Moore, *Law Society*, 208.

20 *Felix Frankfurter Reminisces* (New York: Reynal & Co. 1960), 34–9. M. Davis, *Thurgood Marshall: Warrior at the Bar, Rebel on the Bench* (Secaucus, NJ: Carol Pub. Group 1992).

21 E. Anderson, *Judging Bertha Wilson: Law as Large as Life* (Toronto: University of Toronto Press 2001).

22 It is implausible that Laskin should have forgotten how he began his articles; he had a phenomenal memory and was normally extremely punctilious when dealing with factual matters, whether in court or out. Nor was there any rift with Gotfrid, with whom he remained on good terms for many years afterwards.

23 What follows is based largely on Curtis Cole's manuscript history of Osgoode Hall Law School, entitled 'In the Eye of the Storm' (1995); I.C. Kyer and J.E. Bickenbach, *The Fiercest Debate: Cecil A. Wright, the Benchers, and Legal Education in Ontario, 1923–1957* (Toronto: University of Toronto Press 1987); and B. Bucknall, T. Baldwin, and J.D. Lakin, 'Pedants, Practitioners, and Prophets: Legal Education at Osgoode Hall to 1957,' *Osgoode Hall Law Journal* 6 (1968): 138–229. I thank Dr Cole for allowing me to look at his manuscript.

24 See R.C.B. Risk, 'Canadian Law Teachers in the 1930s: "When the World was Turned Upside Down,"' *Dalhousie Law Journal* 27 (2004): 13–17 for a review of Falconbridge's career and scholarship.

25 BLI 1976: 20–1.

26 Author interview with Stanley Schiff, 14 Dec. 2002.

27 On Wright's scholarship see R.B. Brown, 'Cecil A. Wright and the Foundations of Canadian Tort Law Scholarship' *Saskatchewan Law Review* 64 (2001): 169–217; Risk, 'Canadian Law Teachers in the 1930s': 17–24.

28 BLI 1976: 19.

29 Ibid.

30 G.D. Finlayson, *John J. Robinette, Peerless Mentor: An Appreciation* (Toronto: Dundurn Group for the Osgoode Society 2003), 32–6.

31 Cited in Kyer and Bickenbach, *Fiercest Debate*, 101.

32 BLI 1976: 8.

33 BLI 1976: 64.

34 Law Society of Upper Canada Archives, Past Member file no. 2693.
35 *University of Toronto Calendar for 1935–36. Curriculum in Law.*
36 *Obiter Dicta*, 15 Feb. 1934.
37 *Obiter Dicta*, 15 Mar. 1934.
38 *Obiter Dicta*, 15 Feb. 1934; 15 Jan., 13 Feb., 18 Mar., 15 Apr., 15 Nov. 1935.
39 UTA, School of Law Papers, A82-0041/004, Macalister to W.P.M. Kennedy, 20 Feb. 1939.
40 BLI 1976: 56–7. See generally R.C.B. Risk, 'Volume I of the Journal: A Tribute and a Belated Review,' *University of Toronto Law Journal* 37 (1987): 193–211.
41 '"An Embarrassingly Severe and Masculine Atmosphere": Women, Gender and the Legal Profession at Osgoode Hall, 1920s–1960s,' *Canadian Journal of Law and Society* 11, no. 2 (1996): 35.
42 UTA, Peggy Gertrude Tenenbaum Graduate Record file, A73-0026-464(75); Sam Tenenbaum, A73-0026-464(77).
43 *Toronto Star*, 29 Jan. 1936.
44 A. Gillis, 'Searching for Uniformity: Differences in Legal Education Methods throughout Canada and their Effects' (unpublished paper, 2004, on file with the author).
45 A.Z. Reed, *Present-Day Law Schools in the United States and Canada* (New York: Carnegie Foundation 1928), 350.
46 *Obiter Dicta*, 15 Mar. 1935, 1.
47 *Canadian Bar Review* 12 (1934): 144–60; repr. *Obiter Dicta*, 15 Apr. 1935.
48 Cole, 'In the Eye of the Storm,' 204.
49 Moore, *Law Society*, 210.
50 *Obiter Dicta*, 15 Apr. 1936.
51 *Canadian Bar Bureau* 10 (1932): 2.
52 *Obiter Dicta*, 15 Apr. 1936.
53 *Canadian Bar Review* 12 (1934): 149.
54 *Obiter Dicta*, 15 Apr. 1936.
55 J. Auerbach, *Unequal Justice: Lawyers and Social Change in Modern America* (New York: Oxford University Press 1976); but see R. Stevens, *Law School: Legal Education in America from the 1850s to the 1980s* (Raleigh: University of North Carolina Press 1983) for a more complex account. In British Columbia members of the First Nations and Asians were directly discriminated against by the requirement that articling students be entitled to vote, which these groups were not; J. Brockman, 'Exclusionary Tactics: The History of Women and Visible Minorities in the Legal Profession in British Columbia,' in H. Foster and J. McLaren, *Essays in the History of Canadian Law VI: British Columbia and the Yukon* (Toronto: Osgoode Society 1995).

56 H.W. Arthurs, review of Auerbach, *University of Toronto Law Journal* 27
     (1977): 513–18; J.E. Bickenbach, 'Lawyers, Law Professors, and Racism in
     Ontario,' *Queen's Quarterly* 96, no. 3 (1989): 585–98.
57 Wright Papers, UTA, B82-0028/002, Wright to George Steer, 6 Nov. 1944.
58 *Obiter Dicta*, 17 Mar. 1936.
59 Ibid.
60 S.O. 1935, c. 28. NA, Jacob Finkelman Papers, MG 31 E 27/7, Margaret
     Mackintosh to Finkelman, 6 Aug. 1936, refers to Laskin's role as instructor
     at the WEA summer school.

Chapter 4: Harvard

1 Wright Papers, box 3, Laskin to Wright 29 Sept. 1936.
2 J. Monagan, *A Pleasant Institution* (Lanham, MD: University Press of
    America 2002), 118. Monagan, later a U.S. Congressman, was in his
    final year at Harvard Law School in 1936–7.
3 Wright Papers, box 3, Wright to Pound, 12 Feb. 1936.
4 Ibid., Pound to Wright, 26 Mar. 1936.
5 A few years later, Laskin's friend Max Cohen provided detailed informa-
    tion on living expenses in Cambridge based on his stay there in 1937–8.
    He reckoned at least $5 per week for a room, plus $1.25 to $1.50 per day
    for food: NA, Max Cohen Papers, MG 31, E24, Cohen to John I. Bird,
    12 Jan. 1939.
6 Saul Laskin interview with Olga Jagodnik, 4 May 1977, 6 (transcript at
    Thunder Bay Historical Museum, Thunder Bay, Ontario).
7 Wright Papers, box 3, Laskin to Wright, 29 Sept. 1936. Laskin initially
    reported to Wright that he had enrolled in Torts with Warren Seavey and
    in Quasi-contracts, but he must have dropped them as they do not appear
    on his transcript. I thank the registrar of Harvard Law School for provid-
    ing me with a copy of Laskin's transcript.
8 The phrase served as the title to E.H. Warren's memoir of his legal educa-
    tion at Harvard: *Spartan Education* (Boston: Haughton Mifflin, 1942).
9 BLI 1976: 23–4.
10 BLI 1976: 22.
11 G. Stevens, *Stanfield* (Toronto: McClelland & Steward 1973), 35.
12 See generally A.E. Sutherland, *The Law at Harvard: A History of Ideas and
     Men, 1817–1967* (Cambridge, MA: Belknap Press 1967); R. Stevens, *Law
     School: Legal Education in America from the 1850s to the 1980s* (Chapel Hill:
     University of North Carolina Press 1983); for a more critical view, J. Selig-

man, *The High Citadel: The Influence of Harvard Law School* (Boston: Houghton Mifflin 1978).

13 Unlike the situation in the post-war period, before 1940 the Harvard SJD program was seen as a desirable asset for would-be American law teachers; a 1933 'Report on Advanced Degrees in Law' revealed that 114 of the 196 students who had acquired the degree between 1912 and 1933, or 60 per cent, were employed in law teaching, virtually all at U.S. law schools.

14 Stevens, *Law School*, 159.

15 L. Kalman, *Legal Realism at Yale, 1927–1960* (Chapel Hill: University of North Carolina Press 1986).

16 Cited in M. Keller and P. Keller, *Making Harvard Modern: The Rise of America's University* (New York: Oxford University Press 2001), 113.

17 'Mechanical Jurisprudence,' *Columbia Law Review* 8 (1908): 609–10; see generally D. Wigdor, *Roscoe Pound: Philosopher of Law* (Westport, CT: Greenwood Press 1974) and N. Duxbury, *Patterns of American Jurisprudence* (Oxford: Clarendon Press 1995).

18 *The Future of the Common Law* (Cambridge: Harvard University Press 1937).

19 R.A. Cosgrove, *Our Lady the Common Law: An Anglo-American Legal Community, 1870–1930* (New York: New York University Press 1987). Pound had first asked Sir Lyman Duff to represent Canada, and then Justice Humphrey Mellish of the Supreme Court of Nova Scotia; both declined for reasons of health.

20 I thank Dick Risk for stimulating these ideas. See D. Lodge, *Consciousness and the Novel: Connected Essays* (Cambridge: Harvard University Press 2002).

21 Cited by Kalman, *Legal Realism at Yale*, 29.

22 Cited by Kalman, *Legal Realism at Yale*, 57.

23 Cited in Keller and Keller, *Making Harvard Modern*, 112–13.

24 Wright Papers, box 3, Laskin to Wright, 16 Jan. 1937.

25 L. Henkin, in E. Chadbourn, comp., *Felix Frankfurter, 1882–1965: An Intimate Portrait* (Cambridge: Harvard Law School Library 1982), ii.

26 Monagan, *A Pleasant Institution*, 137.

27 L. Baker, *Felix Frankfurter* (New York: Coward-McCann 1969); L. Baker, *Brandeis and Frankfurter: A Dual Biography* (New York: Harper & Row 1984); H.N. Hirsch, *The Enigma of Felix Frankfurter* (New York: Basic Books 1981); R. Burt, *Two Jewish Justices* (Berkeley: University of California Press 1988); M. Parrish, *Felix Frankfurter and His Times* (New York: Free Press 1982); M. Alexander, *Jazz Age Jews* (Princeton: Princeton University Press 2001).

28 N.L. Dawson, *Louis D. Brandeis, Felix Frankfurter, and the New Deal* (Hamden, CT: Archon Books 1980), 48.

29 F. Frankfurter and N. Greene, *The Labor Injunction* (New York: Macmillan 1930).

30 H.W. Arthurs, 'Woe Unto You, Judges: or How Reading Frankfurter and Greene, *The Labor Injunction*, Ruined Me as a Labour Lawyer and Made Me as an Academic,' *Journal of Law and Society* 29 (2002): 657–66.

31 Cited in Wigdor, *Roscoe Pound*, 250. On Pound's last years as dean, see also Kalman, *Legal Realism at Yale*, 55–62.

32 Harvard Law School Archives, Felix Frankfurter Papers, box 189, file 11; minutes of faculty meetings, 14 Dec. 1936, 18 Jan. 1937. I am grateful to David Warrington of Harvard Law Library Special Collections for making these available to me. M.G. Synnott, *The Half-Opened Door: Discrimination and Admissions at Harvard, Yale, and Princeton, 1900–1970* (Westport, CT: Greenwood Press 1979).

33 3 Mar. 1937. On the reduction in the failure rate, see Keller and Keller, *Making Harvard Modern*, 115.

34 Minutes of faculty meetings, 15 Feb., 1 Mar. 1937; Frankfurter Papers, box 189, file 3, memo dated 23 May 1927; 'Report on Advanced Degrees in Law' (Harvard Law School, Dec. 1933).

35 Minutes of faculty meeting, 1 Mar. 1937. On the four-year movement in general, see Stevens, *Law School*, 159.

36 On Wright's own experience at Harvard, see J.E. Bickenbach and C.I. Kyer, 'The Harvardization of Caesar Wright,' *University of Toronto Law Journal* 33 (1983): 162–83.

37 I thank Robert Gordon for this suggestion.

38 P. Girard, 'The Roots of a Professional Renaissance: Lawyers in Nova Scotia, 1850–1910,' *Manitoba Law Journal* 20 (1991): 148–80.

39 J. McLaren, 'The History of Legal Education in Common Law Canada,' in R. Matas and D. McCawley, eds., *Legal Education in Canada* (Montreal: Federation of Law Societies of Canada 1987), 111–45.

40 E. Hobsbawm, *Interesting Times: A Twentieth-Century Life* (London: Abacus 2002), 388.

41 Baker, *Frankfurter*, 187. The expression is also seen as 'the switch in time that saved nine.'

42 B. Laskin, 'Canadian Federalism: A Scott's Eye View in Prose and Poetry,' *McGill Law Journal* 14 (1968): 497. The most convenient summary of the 1937 decisions and their immediate impact is found in J. Saywell, *The Lawmakers: Judicial Power and the Shaping of Canadian Federalism* (Toronto: University of Toronto Press for the Osgoode Society 2002), 203–37.

43 *Harvard Crimson*, 8, 11, 15, 25 Mar. 1937; Baker, *Felix Frankfurter*, 180–91; Frankfurter Papers, Harvard Law School, box 189, file 11. For Abel's reminiscences, see his review of the published Roosevelt-Frankfurter correspondence, *University of Toronto Law Journal* 19 (1969): 97–100.

44 Frankfurter Papers, box 189, file 11.

45 NA, Jacob Finkelman Papers, MG 31 E 27/10.

46 Wright Papers, box 3, Wright to Laskin, 20 Nov. 1936.

47 *Re Millar*, [1938] S.C.R. 1, [1938] 1 D.L.R. 65; M.M. Orkin, *The Great Stork Derby* (Don Mills, ON: General Publishing 1981). The Supreme Court of Canada took a narrow approach to public policy and did not find the clause to exceed permissible bounds.

48 See chapter 11.

49 BLI 1976: 23.

50 UBC Archives, N.A.M. MacKenzie Papers, box 6/2, Davison to MacKenzie, 22 Feb. 1930.

51 Finkelman Papers, Laskin to Finkelman, 17 Jan. 1937.

52 B. Laskin, 'The Ontario Municipal Board' (LLM thesis, Harvard University, 1937), 3.

53 The main example is J. Willis, ed., *Canadian Boards at Work* (Toronto: Macmillan 1941).

54 I. Abella, 'The Making of a Chief Justice: Bora Laskin, the Early Years,' *Law Society of Upper Canada Gazette* 24 (1990): 193.

55 R.C.B. Risk, 'Here Be Cold and Tygers: A Map of Statutory Interpretation in Canada in the 1920s and 1930s,' *Saskatchewan Law Review* 63 (2000): 195–213; and his 'Canadian Law Teachers in the 1930s: "When the World Was Turned Upside Down,"' *Dalhousie Law Journal* 27 (2004): 1–54; see also R.B. Brown, 'The Canadian Legal Realists and Administrative Law Scholarship,' *Dalhousie Journal of Legal Studies* 9 (2000): 36–72, and Risk, 'Volume 1 of the Journal: A Tribute and a Belated Review,' *University of Toronto Law Journal* 37 (1987): 193–211.

56 Risk, 'The World Upside Down,' 48–52.

57 Ibid., 8.

58 Ibid., 9.

59 From Holmes's *The Common Law*, as cited in Laskin, 'Contracting Out,' 672.

60 *Canadian Bar Review* 15 (1937): 10–20.

61 *Canadian Bar Review* 15 (1937): 270–84.

62 *Canadian Bar Review* 16 (1938): 669–700.

63 'Picketing,' 11.

64 *Allied Amusements v. Reaney*, [1936] 3 W.W.R. 129 (Man. Q.B.).

65 245 N.Y. 260 (1927).

66 [1936] 2 W.W.R. 129 (Man. Q.B.).

67 'Labour Injunction,' 283.

68 J. Sangster, '"We No Longer Respect the Law": The Tilco Strike, Labour Injunctions, and the State,' *Labour/Le Travail* 53 (Spr. 2004): 56–87.

69 If Laskin did not address his disagreement with some aspects of realism in print, Caesar Wright did. See R.B. Brown, 'Cecil A. Wright and the Foundations of Canadian Tort Law Scholarship,' *Saskatchewan Law Review* 64 (2001): 188–9.

70 'The Institutional Character of the Judge,' *Israel Law Review* 7 (1972): 329–48.

71 On Frank's disagreements with Cardozo, see A. Kaufman, *Cardozo* (Cambridge: Harvard University Press 1998), 458–61.

72 Cf. P. Horwitz, 'Bora Laskin and the Legal Process School,' *Saskatchewan Law Review* 59 (1995): 77–96.

73 D. Réaume, 'The Judicial Philosophy of Bora Laskin,' *University of Toronto Law Journal* 35 (1985): 438–68.

74 *Canadian Bar Review* 16 (1938): 674.

75 Of all the essays on Laskin in *University of Toronto Law Journal* 35 (1985), Carol Rogerson's on Laskin's contribution to family law explores this tension most fully.

Chapter 5: Waiting

1 J.D. Arnup, *Middleton: The Beloved Judge* (Toronto: McClelland & Stewart 1988), chap. 15.

2 NA, Jacob Finkelman Papers, MG 31 E 27/8.

3 The salary figure is based on Laskin's recollection in BLI 1976: 29.

4 D. Vanek, *Fulfilment: Memoirs of a Criminal Court Judge* (Toronto: Dundurn Press 1999), 77–9. Vanek had digested contracts cases for Burroughs the year before Laskin.

5 BLI 1976: 30.

6 Wright Papers, box 3, Wright to Laskin, 6 Jan. 1938.

7 Cohen would make his career at McGill, where he succeeded Frank Scott as dean. How he met Laskin is unclear, but Charles Laskin in Winnipeg may have been the link.

8 Wright Papers, box 3, Wright to Sidney Smith, 20 May 1939.

9 Ibid.

10 Draft letter of recommendation from W.P.M. Kennedy, n.d. [1938], UTA, Faculty of Law Records, A82-0041/4.

11 R.W. Pound, *Chief Justice W.R. Jackett: By the Law of the Land* (Kingston and Montreal: McGill-Queen's University Press 1999), 50–1, 57 n19.

12 BLI 1976: 11.

13 I. Abella, 'The Making of a Chief Justice: Bora Laskin, The Early Years,' *Law Society of Upper Canada Gazette* 24 (1990): 190.

14 UTA, President's Office, box 32, file 5, Kennedy to Cody, 5 Jan. 1938.

15 UTA, School of Law Papers, box 3, Kennedy to Cronkite, 25 July 1936. On Hopkins, see R.B. Brown, 'The Canadian Legal Realists and Administrative Law Scholarship, 1930–1941,' *Dalhousie Journal of Legal Studies* 9 (2000): 36–72.

16 School of Law Papers, box 3, Auld to Kennedy 29 July 1936.

17 Ibid., Kennedy to Finkelman, 3 Aug. 1936.

18 Ibid., Kennedy to Gage, 3 Aug. 1936.

19 I. Abella, 'Oshawa 1937' in I. Abella, ed., *On Strike: Six Key Labour Struggles in Canada 1919–1949* (Toronto: James Lorimer 1975); J. Saywell, *'Just Call Me Mitch': The Life of Mitchell F. Hepburn* (Toronto: University of Toronto Press 1991).

20 J. Taylor, *Union Learning: Canadian Labour Education in the Twentieth Century* (Toronto: Thompson Publishing 2001), 23–9; I. Radforth and J. Sangster, '"A Link between Labour and Learning": The Workers' Educational Association in Ontario, 1917–1951,' *Labour/Le Travailleur* 8/9 (1981–2): 41–78; G. Friesen, 'Adult Education and Union Education: Aspects of English Canadian Cultural History in the 20th Century,' *Labour/Le Travail* 34 (1994): 163–88.

21 *Globe and Mail*, 17 Apr. 1935.

22 Interview with Drummond Wren, 29 Sept. 1976 (tapes at Special Collections, McMaster University, Hamilton, Ontario).

23 AO, WEA Papers, MU 3991, minutes of meetings, WEA Ontario and Toronto District, 18 Dec. 1937.

24 *Trade Unionist's Handbook*, 5.

25 Ibid., 7.

26 Ibid., 36–7.

27 Ibid., 8–9.

28 *Globe and Mail*, 7 Oct. 1937.

29 BLI 1976: 32.

30 Tapes of the original broadcasts do not survive, but transcripts can be found in NA, CBC Records, RG 41, vol. 184, file 11-18-3 (pt. 1). See generally M. Klee, '"Hands-off Labour Forum": The Making and Unmaking of National Working-class Radio Broadcasting in Canada, 1935–1944,' *Labour/Le Travail* 35 (1995): 107–32, to which I am indebted for the original reference to Laskin's involvement with this radio series.

31 CBC Records, D.W. Buchanan to Drummond Wren, 23 Dec. 1937.
32 Ibid., Macpherson to CBC, 30 Dec. 1937.
33 NA, RG 146, vol. 2863. Hundreds of pages covering the WEA from the 1930s to 1970 were made available to me through access to information requests 2002-00045 to 00049.
34 AO, WEA Papers, MU 4023, file 46, Laskin to Wren, 30 Aug. 1939.
35 B. Laskin, 'The Legal Status of Trade Unions in Canada,' in V. Anderson, ed., *Problems in Canadian Unity* (Toronto: Thomas Nelson & Sons 1938), 98.
36 Ibid., 102.
37 CBC Records, transcript of lecture 3.
38 It is true that after his appointment at the University of Toronto Laskin's relationship with the WEA became more overtly professional, but even then he continued to teach night courses for some years and to respond to Drummond Wren's requests for legal advice until at least 1944.
39 'Tavern Refusing to Serve Negro – Discrimination,' *Canadian Bar Review* 18 (1940): 314–16, commenting on *Christie v. York Corporation*, [1940] S.C.R. 139. *Christie* was heard on 10 May 1939 and the decision released on 9 December 1939.
40 The case is explored in detail by J.W. St G. Walker in *'Race,' Rights and the Law in the Supreme Court of Canada: Historical Case Studies* (Waterloo: Wilfrid Laurier University Press 1997), 122–81.
41 [1940] S.C.R. 139 at 152. Davis was the judge who attended the 1936 Harvard conference, and he also dissented when the Supreme Court found much of Bennett's New Deal legislation invalid.
42 Walker, *'Race,' Rights and the Law*, 164.
43 [1940] 1 D.L.R. 81.
44 UBC Archives, N.A.M. MacKenzie Papers, 19/1, Auld to MacKenzie, 15 Aug. 1940. What follows is treated briefly by Martin Friedland in *The University of Toronto*, 340–1.
45 UTA, School of Law Papers, box 3, draft letter of reference by Kennedy, n.d.
46 Ibid., box 4, Macalister to Kennedy, 22 June 1940.
47 AO, Cody Papers, MU 4965 file 7, Kennedy to Cody 11 Aug. 1940.
48 School of Law Papers, box 4.
49 UTA, Office of the President (Cody), box 3, Kennedy to Cody, 21 Sept. 1940.
50 School of Law Papers, box 4, Macalister to Kennedy, 5 Oct. 1940; reply 10 Dec. 1940.
51 *Macalister, or, Dying in the dark: a fiction based on what is known of his life and fate* (Kingston, ON: Quarry Press 1995).

52 Frank was the brother of J.W. Pickersgill, a cabinet minister in the St-Laurent and Pearson governments.

53 UBC Archives, MacKenzie Papers, 20/2, Laskin to MacKenzie, 27 Aug. 1940.

54 BLI 1976: 42.

55 UBC Archives, MacKenzie Papers, 19/6, Kennedy to MacKenzie, 4 Oct. 1940.

56 Ibid., Finkelman to MacKenzie, 15 Oct. 1940.

57 NA, Jacob Finkelman Papers, vol. 10, MacKenzie to Finkelman, 19 Oct. 1940.

58 Ibid., Finkelman to MacKenzie, 23 Oct. 1940.

59 Cited by R.A. Cosgrove, *Our Lady the Common Law: An Anglo-American Legal Community, 1870–1930* (New York: New York University Press 1987), 232. Frankfurter replied, 'I am not a Socialist, Marxian or otherwise, in any sense that has scientific or scholarly meaning.'

60 D.C. Masters, *Henry John Cody: An Outstanding Life* (Toronto: Dundurn Press 1995), 217–18.

61 See M. Horn, *Academic Freedom in Canada: A History* (Toronto: University of Toronto Press 1999), 165. Horn goes on to suggest a possible anti-Semitic motivation for Kennedy's request, which I discount for reasons discussed later in this paragraph.

62 R.D. Francis, *Frank H. Underhill: Intellectual Provocateur* (Toronto: University of Toronto Press 1986), 109–14.

63 Masters, *Cody*, 254–68.

64 UTA, President's Office (Cody), box 32, W.P.M. Kennedy to H.J. Cody, 5 Jan. 1938.

65 BLI 1976: 41–2.

66 Author interview with Ernest Sirluck, 30 Sept. 2000.

Chapter 6: Professor

1 As cited in P.B. Waite, *Lord of Point Grey: Larry MacKenzie of U.B.C.* (Vancouver: UBC Press 1987), 84.

2 *Canadian Bar Review* 21 (1943): 424–5. The book in question was G. Schwarzenberger's *International Law and Totalitarian Lawlessness* (London: J. Cape 1943).

3 School of Law Papers, box 4, Kennedy to Macdonald, 13 Sept. 1940.

4 AO, WEA Papers, MU 4023, Laskin to Drummond Wren, 1 Oct. 1940.

5 Norman A. MacKenzie Papers, 19/1, Auld to MacKenzie, 11 Dec. 1940.

6 School of Law Papers, box 5.

7 Norman A. MacKenzie Papers, 19/1, Auld to MacKenzie, 11 Dec. 1940.

8 *Alumni News* (Nov. 1942): 58.

9 On the wartime atmosphere at the university, see D.C. Masters, *Henry John Cody: An Outstanding Life* (Toronto: Dundurn Press 1995) and M.L. Friedland, *The University of Toronto: A History* (Toronto: University of Toronto Press 2002).

10 NA, F.R. Scott Papers, MG 30 D 211/29/16, reel 1290, Underhill to Scott, 4 Jan. 1941.

11 Masters, *Henry John Cody*, chap. 24; Friedland, *University of Toronto*, 348–50; M. Horn, *Academic Freedom in Canada: A History* (Toronto: University of Toronto Press 1999), 154–65; R.D. Francis, *Frank H. Underhill: Intellectual Provocateur* (Toronto: University of Toronto Press 1986), chap. 10.

12 Ramsay Cook, as cited in J. Fudge and E. Tucker, *Labour before the Law: The Regulation of Workers' Collective Action in Canada, 1900–1948* (Toronto: Oxford University Press 2001), 230.

13 *Re R. v. Burt*, [1941] O.W.N. 17.

14 *Canadian Bar Review* 19 (1941): 133–7.

15 School of Law Papers, box 5, Laskin to Kennedy, 29 July 1941 (thanking Kennedy for recent stay at Narrow Waters).

16 Gilbert Kennedy interview (1984), B.C. Aural Legal History Project, P.A.B.C.

17 D. Vanek, *Fulfillment: Memoirs of a Criminal Court Judge* (Toronto: Dundurn Press for the Osgoode Society 1999), 171.

18 Cody Papers, box 50, Kennedy to Cody, 22 Oct. 1941.

19 School of Law Papers, box 7; e-mail communication with Telford Georges, 26 Jan. 2001.

20 *Varsity*, 11 Mar. 1947.

21 School of Law Papers, box 7, Laskin to Kennedy, 19 July 1943.

22 Charles Bourne author interview, 19 Feb. 2001.

23 School of Law Papers, box 5, Laskin to Kennedy 15 June 1942.

24 Laskin vented his frustrations during this period in a book review of *The International Labour Code 1939* (Montreal: ILO 1941), *Canadian Bar Review* 20 (1942): 477–8.

25 *Labour before the Law*, 252.

26 Ibid., 262. See also L.S. MacDowell, *'Remember Kirkland Lake': The History and Effects of the Kirkland Lake Gold Miners' Strike, 1941–42* (Toronto: University of Toronto Press 1983).

27 *Journals of the Legislative Assembly of the Province of Ontario*, vol. 77, session 1943 part 2, app. no. 2: Report of the Select Committee of the Legislative Assembly Appointed to Inquire into Collective Bargaining between

Employers and Employees. See generally J. Willes, *The Ontario Labour Court, 1943–44* (Kingston, ON: Industrial Relations Centre, Queen's University 1979); L.S. MacDowell, 'The Formation of the Canadian Industrial Relations System during World War Two,' *Labour/Le Travilleur* 3 (1978): 175–96; *Labour before the Law*, 263–302. On Cohen's role see MacDowell, *Renegade Lawyer: The Life of J.L. Cohen* (Toronto: University of Toronto Press for the Osgoode Society 2001), 109–21.

28 *Canadian Bar Review* 21 (1943): 684–706.

29 S.O. 1943, c. 4. A new branch of the High Court called the Labour Court was created by an amendment to the Judicature Act, S.O. 1943, c. 11.

30 'Collective Bargaining in Ontario: A New Legislative Approach,' *Canadian Bar Review* 21 (1943): 692.

31 Cited in *Labour before the Law*, 272.

32 Ibid.

33 'Collective Bargaining in Ontario,' 693.

34 'Recent Labour Legislation in Canada' *Canadian Bar Review* 22 (1944): 783; also published as 'Industrial Relations and Social Security,' *Public Affairs* (Fall 1944): 48–54.

35 *Canadian Bar Review* 22 (1944): 784.

36 BLI 1976: 38. AO, Labour Court Papers, RG 7-60/6/59.

37 *Globe and Mail*, 10, 14 Sept. 1943. AO, Labour Court Papers, RG7-60/3/24. The application for certification was ultimately successful.

38 Cody Papers, box 60, Kennedy to Cody, 13 Sept. 1943 ('strictly confidential').

39 Ibid., Laskin to Cody, 5 July 1943.

40 BLI 1976: 38.

41 School of Law Papers, box 8, Fox to Kennedy, 2 Dec. 1944; Kennedy to Fox, 5 Dec. 1944.

42 Material in this and the following two paragraphs is drawn largely from J. Taylor, *Union Learning: Canadian Labour Education in the Twentieth Century* (Toronto: Thompson Publishing 2001), chap. 2.

43 AO, WEA Papers, F 1217-14/3, WEA Summer School 1942 brochure; WEA photo collection, AO 3914, 3947. A video clip from the 1942 summer school can be viewed at http://unionlearning.athabascau.ca (accessed 6 June 2002).

44 BLI 1976: 45. School of Law Papers, box 7, Kennedy to Laskin, 11 July 1943 ('congratulations on your promotion to Assistant Professor. The finance looks better than I hoped for (keep it private & confidential)').

45 Wright Papers, box 3, Wright to Sidney Smith, 20 May 1939.

46 School of Law Papers, box 7, Kennedy to Laskin, 14 Aug. 1943.

47 On what follows, see R.C.B. Risk, 'The Many Minds of W.P.M. Kennedy,' *University of Toronto Law Journal* 48 (1998): 370–6.

48 University of Toronto School of Law calendars, 1939–40 and subsequent years.

49 University of Manitoba Archives, UA 43, box 5, folder 10.

50 BLI 1976: 45–6.

51 School of Law Papers, box 7, Kennedy to Morris Shumiatcher, 22 Mar. 1941.

52 Personal communication from Judge Sandra Oxner, Provincial Court of Nova Scotia, a member of the 1982 delegation.

53 Correspondence in School of Law Papers, box 5. G.T. Tamaki, 'The Law Relating to Nationality in Canada' (LL thesis, University of Toronto, 1944). Given the difficult experience of Tamaki and his family, his thesis is remarkably restrained in its critique of the Canadian law of nationality. He observes only that 'it is perhaps not to the credit of Canada that natural-born and naturalized British subjects of Chinese, Japanese, or East Indian racial descent may exercise the full rights of citizenship in one province of Canada, and yet may not do so in another province of the same Dominion' (at 161).

54 *The Office of Governor-General: An Appreciation of the Significance of That Office in New Zealand* (Toronto: University of Toronto Press 1951).

55 His doctoral thesis was published with some revisions as F.E. LaBrie, *The Meaning of Income in the Law of Income Tax* (Toronto: University of Toronto Press 1948).

56 BLI 1976: 48–9.

57 BLI 1976: 25.

58 'Tests for the Validity of Legislation: What's the "Matter"?' *University of Toronto Law Journal* 11 (1955): 114–27.

59 P. Boyer, *A Passion for Justice: A Life of J.C. McRuer* (Toronto: University of Toronto Press for the Osgoode Society 1994), suggests that anti-Semitism in the Canadian Bar Association had something to do with Laskin's failure to become editor, but that is not the way I read the documents he cites. On the contrary, President E.K. Williams and Vice-President J.C. McRuer seem enthusiastic in private correspondence about the prospect of Laskin's editorship, and disappointed when he declines for the reasons cited in the text: AO, J.C. McRuer Papers, F 1329, box 16.

60 I would like to thank former Laskin clerk Wayne MacKay for providing me with a copy of the curriculum vitae used by Chief Justice Laskin.

61 BLI 1976: 56.

62 Ibid.

63 'Taxation and Situs: Company Shares,' *Canadian Bar Review* 19 (1941): 617–37.
64 See generally R.B. Brown, 'The Canadian Legal Realists and Administrative Law Scholarship, 1930–1941,' *Dalhousie Journal of Legal Studies* 9 (2000): 36–72.
65 J. Willis, ed., *Canadian Boards at Work* (Toronto: Macmillan 1941).
66 School of Law Papers, box 5, W.P.M. Kennedy to A. Gordon Burns, Manager, University of Toronto Press, 20 Apr. 1942.
67 UTA, Office of the President (Cody), box 3, Kennedy to Cody, 20 Sept. 1940. Presumably Kennedy did not see Laskin's WEA connection as problematic since it operated under university auspices.

Chapter 7: Osgoode

1 Law Society of Upper Canada, *Special Course of Lectures on Wartime Emergency Orders and Administrative Tribunals* (Toronto: Carswell 1943).
2 On the debate over legal education in Ontario during these years, see generally C.I. Kyer and J.E. Bickenbach, *The Fiercest Debate: Cecil A. Wright, the Benchers, and Legal Education in Ontario, 1923–1957* (Toronto: University of Toronto Press for the Osgoode Society 1987), chaps. 6–8; C. Moore, *The Law Society of Upper Canada and Ontario's Lawyers* (Toronto: University of Toronto Press for the Osgoode Society 1997), 227–33; C. Cole, 'In the Eye of the Storm,' chaps. 6–8 (unpublished manuscript, 1995).
3 *Fortnightly Law Journal* (1 Mar. 1944): 233.
4 Cited in Cole, 'In the Eye of the Storm,' 233.
5 Ibid., 231; UTA, School of Law Papers, box 7, memo from W.P.M. Kennedy to Council of School of Law, 20 Mar. 1944.
6 BLI 1977: 2–3.
7 This paragraph and the next rely heavily on Kyer and Bickenbach, *Fiercest Debate*, chap. 6.
8 Wright to Smith, 12 July 1945, as cited in Kyer and Bickenbach, *Fiercest Debate*, 168.
9 Kennedy to Smith, 18 July 1945, as cited in ibid., 170.
10 Albert Abel Papers, UTA B82-0014/017, Laskin to Abel, 27 Oct. 1947.
11 Robert Reid, a veteran of the air force, cited in Moore, *Law Society*, 228.
12 Oral information provided by Richard Moon, 2 June 2000, with respect to his father Alexander Moon, one of Laskin's students in the post-war years.
13 Cited in Cole, 'In the Eye of the Storm,' 236. The author was District Court Judge J.B. Moon of Parry Sound, father of Alexander Moon. In British Columbia a member of the Labour Progressive Party (a front for the

Communist Party) had been refused a call to the bar; *Martin v. Law Society of B.C.*, [1950] 3 D.L.R. 173.

14 S.H. Hughes, *Steering the Course: A Memoir* (Montreal and Kingston: McGill-Queen's University Press 2000), 125.

15 Law Society of Upper Canada Archives, 324/16-2-68(2).

16 He contributed three annual surveys of labour legislation to the *University of Toronto Law Journal* in 1947, 1948, and 1949, and in 1948 he cast a backward glance at the evolution of labour law in Canada over the previous quarter-century: 'Canadian Labour Law: 1923–47,' *Canadian Bar Review* 26 (1948): 286–307. These pieces were mostly descriptive.

17 *Canadian Bar Review* 25 (1947): 1054–87.

18 R.C.B. Risk, 'On the Road to Oz: Common Law Scholarship about Federalism after World War II,' *University of Toronto Law Journal* 51 (2001): 148.

19 See chapter 10.

20 School of Law Papers, box 9, Finkelman to Kennedy, 28 July 1945.

21 *University of Toronto Monthly* (Apr. 1947): 181.

22 BLI 1976: 65.

23 Kyer and Bickenbach, *Fiercest Debate*, 196–7.

24 *Obiter Dicta* (Oct. 1948): 9.

25 Eileen Mitchell Thomas Osgoode Society interview, 9 Dec. 1988, 62.

26 For what follows, see Cole, 'In the Eye of the Storm,' chap. 8, and Kyer and Bickenbach, *Fiercest Debate*, chap. 8.

27 BLI 1977: 12. See also NA, F.R. Scott Papers, MG 30 D 211/1/1, reel H-1211, Laskin to Scott, 30 Jan. 1948.

28 Dalhousie University Archives, Horace Read Papers, MS-2–322. Read, a Dalhousian with a doctoral degree from Harvard, was lured back to Dalhousie as dean in 1950.

29 F.R. Scott Papers, 211/24/7, reel 1284, Wright to Frank Scott, 20 Apr. 1948.

30 BLI 1977: 16.

31 BLI 1977: 8.

32 B. Laskin, 'Cecil A. Wright: A Personal Memoir,' *University of Toronto Law Journal* 33 (1983): 154.

33 BLI 1977: 9.

34 Law Society of Upper Canada Archives, 68/2-2-8, Denison to Mason, 24 Jan. 1949.

35 Communication cited in Kyer and Bickenbach, *Fiercest Debate*, 212.

36 BLI 1977: 13.

37 BLI 1977: 11.

38 Kyer and Bickenbach, *Fiercest Debate*, tread gingerly over this point, admitting at 215 that 'Wright, consciously or unconsciously, had provoked

the old-school benchers into taking a hard-line position,' but concluding that '[t]here is no clear evidence ... that Smith and Wright actually conspired in the way [contemporaries] suggested.' Having quoted the July 1945 letter at length in an earlier chapter, they do not refer to it again at this point.

39 *Globe and Mail*, 27, 29 Jan. 1949.
40 3 Feb. 1949.
41 Moore, *Law Society*, 231–2.
42 A.J. Hobbins, 'Designating the Dean of Law: Legal Education at McGill University and the Montreal Corporate and Professional Elite, 1946–1950,' *Dalhousie Law Journal* 27 (2004): 163–202. NA, F.R. Scott Papers, reel H-1211, Laskin to Scott, 30 Jan. 1948.
43 D. and L. Gibson, *Substantial Justice: Law and Lawyers in Manitoba 1670–1970* (Winnipeg: Peguis Publishers 1972), 283–90. The Manitoba Law School shifted from university to bar society control in 1931.

Chapter 8: Revolution

1 Eugene La Brie author interview, 1 Oct. 2000; D. Vanek, *Fulfillment: Memoirs of a Criminal Court Judge* (Toronto: Dundurn Press for the Osgoode Society 1999), 175–8.
2 C.I. Kyer and J.E. Bickenbach, *The Fiercest Debate: Cecil A. Wright, the Benchers, and Legal Education in Ontario, 1923–1957* (Toronto: University of Toronto Press for the Osgoode Society 1987), 222–3.
3 *University of Toronto Faculty of Law Calendar for 1949–50*, 9–10.
4 Eugene La Brie author interview, 1 Oct. 2000.
5 Kyer and Bickenbach, *Fiercest Debate*, 226.
6 See generally *Report to the Social Sciences and Humanities Research Council of Canada by the Consultative Group on Research and Education* (Ottawa: SSHRC, 1983) (commonly known as 'the Arthurs Report').
7 School of Law Papers, A82-0041/28, Kennedy to Wright, 2 Aug., 20 Aug., 4 Nov. 1953; Wright to Kennedy, 9 and 19 Apr. 1954.
8 R.C.B. Risk assures me that the name was never used during his time as a professor at the law school, 1962–98. The only remaining commemoration of Kennedy in the faculty appears to be the W.P.M. Kennedy silver medal for the student graduating with the second highest average.
9 Though R.C.B. Risk did provide an account of Kennedy's school in the 1999 issue of the alumni magazine *Nexus* devoted to the anniversary.
10 'Law Teachers and Law Teaching in Canada,' *Journal of the Society of Public Teachers of Law (n.s.)* 2 (1953): 115–21.

11 UTA, Office of the President (Sidney Smith) Papers, 111/04, Kennedy to Plucknett, 8 Mar. 1954.

12 Two years after Wright's death, when Laskin was reviewing the history of Canadian legal education in the Hamlyn Lectures he gave at the Inner Temple, he was able to be more generous about the pre-1949 course of studies at Toronto, although he still omitted to mention Kennedy's name. Noting that the English universities were 'much better off from the standpoint of scholarship and scholarly writing' as a result of their lack of ties to professional bodies, he observed: 'It was on this very basis that the University of Toronto offered a liberal arts and law programme for some two decades notwithstanding the refusal of the Law Society to credit any of the work for the right to practise': *The British Tradition in Canadian Law* (London: Stevens & Sons 1969), 85.

13 UTA, Office of the President (Sidney Smith) Papers, box 65, Wright to Smalley-Baker, 27 Dec. 1949, Smalley-Baker to Wright, 9 Jan. 1950.

14 I. Scott, *To Make a Difference: A Memoir* (Toronto: Stoddart 2001), 24.

15 *Daily Times-Journal* (Fort William), 24 Jan. 1950.

16 Last Will and Testament of Max Laskin dated 2 Oct. 1950, no. 4505 GR, Registry Division of Port Arthur.

17 *Daily Times-Journal* (Fort William), *News-Chronicle* (Port Arthur), 11 July 1955.

18 A.L. Feinberg, *Storm the Gates of Jericho* (Toronto: McClelland & Stewart 1964), 140.

19 Stanley Schiff author interview, 14 Dec. 2001. Schiff entered the law school in 1953, served on faculty 1958–60, went to Harvard for his LLM and practised for several years, then returned to the faculty in 1965 to replace Laskin when he went to the bench.

20 'Law Teachers and Law Teaching in Canada,' *Journal of the Society of Public Teachers of Law (n.s.)* 2 (1953): 119.

21 BLI 1977: 10.

22 UTA, Office of the President (Sidney Smith), 089/10, Willis to Wright, 29 Nov. 1951, Wright to Willis, 3 Dec. 1951.

23 Wright Papers, box 3, Wright to Griswold, 14 Apr. 1950.

24 *Globe and Mail*, 21 Mar. 1953.

25 Its main inadequacy was in the plumbing department. Caesar Wright complained to Sidney Smith in 1954 that 107 men and 5 women were obliged to share one urinal and one toilet, resulting in line-ups of 20 people at the morning break. The washroom was of necessity used by both sexes, which Wright regarded as a personal affront. 'As Dean of this School I am willing to suffer the personal indignities which the impoverished condition of the University apparently cannot remedy with regard

to the women's washroom. I cannot, and will not, cheerfully submit to a situation which deprives the students of this University of the common decencies of life which are to be found in even the poorest reform institutions.' UTA, Office of the President (Sidney Smith), 122/06, Wright to Smith, 1 Oct. 1954.

26 James A. Bridle et al., 'The University of Toronto Law School – A History 1843–1967' (unpublished ms., 1969), 62.

27 Author interview with Jean Milner, 20 May 2002.

28 Author interview with Stanley Schiff, 14 Dec. 2001.

29 Martin Friedland Osgoode Society interview, 6 Oct. 1999.

30 BLI 1977: 31.

31 J. McClennan, 'The Story of the Faculty of Law,' *Varsity Graduate* (June 1959): 96.

32 All references in this paragraph can be found in R. Blackburn, *Evolution of the Heart: A History of the University of Toronto Library Up to 1981* (Toronto: University of Toronto Library 1989), 259–61.

33 Author interview with R. St J. Macdonald, 2 Nov. 2000, recounting a conversation with Abel's brother at Abel's funeral.

34 'Legal Research,' *Canadian Bar Review* 34 (1956): 1108.

35 'Legal Research,' *Canadian Bar Review* 35 (1957): 117.

36 Ibid., 119.

37 NA, CALT Papers, MG 28 I 138, vol. 1.

38 CALT Papers, MG 28 I 138/1, minutes of annual meeting 1952.

39 There is no account of Mathews's talk in the account of the meeting in *Canadian Bar Review* 30 (1952): 608, but reference to it can be found in NA, CALT Papers, vol. 1, unofficial summary of 1952 meeting by G.W. Reed.

40 CALT Papers, vol. 3.

41 As cited by Bora Laskin, 'Law Teaching in Canada,' 115.

42 CALT Papers, vol. 3.

43 A pun on the name of former Supreme Court of Canada judge Pierre-Basile Mignault.

44 'Law Schools, Bars and Education,' *Canadian Bar Review* 31 (1953): 557.

45 Laskin, 'Law Teaching in Canada,' 117.

46 'The Law Teachers' Annual Meeting,' *Canadian Bar Review* 32 (1954): 664. Laskin's talk was probably the basis for 'Our Civil Liberties – The Role of the Supreme Court,' *Queen's Quarterly* 61 (1955): 456–71.

47 [1957] S.C.R. 285.

48 [1959] S.C.R. 121.

49 AO, Holy Blossom Temple Congregational Records 1856–1956, MS 290, reel 3.

50 Ibid.
51 Holy Blossom Temple Archives, Religious Education Committee/Board of Religious Education minutes 1954–60. I thank David Hart for making these available to me, and for discussing changes in religious education during these years.
52 Ibid., Board of Education minutes, 28 May 1958.
53 *Toronto Daily Star*, 6 June 1960.
54 NA, Heinz Warschauer Papers, MG 31 D, vol. 3, file 14.
55 Feinberg's *Sex and the Pulpit* (Toronto: Methuen 1981) contains a partial autobiography.
56 Kyer and Bickenbach, *Fiercest Debate*; Moore, *Law Society*; B. Bucknall et al., 'Pedants, Prophets and Practitioners,' *Osgoode Hall Law Journal* 6 (1968): 138–229.
57 Moore, *Law Society*, 258. In the end a mortgage was not required.
58 UTA, President's Papers (South), ATI-0011/06/012, Bell to Carson, 24 Nov. 1955.
59 BLI 1977: 30.

Chapter 9: Federalism

1 The literature on the Privy Council's role in Canadian constitutional interpretation is large, but there is only one comprehensive historical account: J. Saywell, *The Lawmakers: Judicial Power and the Shaping of Canadian Federalism* (Toronto: University of Toronto Press for the Osgoode Society 2002).
2 *Canadian Bar Review* 25 (1947): 1054–87.
3 [1947] A.C. 127 [sub nom. *Attorney-General for Ontario v. Attorney-General for Canada*].
4 [1947] A.C. 87.
5 [1946] A.C. 193.
6 'Peace, Order and Good Government,' 1054.
7 R.C.B. Risk, 'On the Road to Oz: Common Law Scholarship about Federalism after World War II,' *University of Toronto Law Journal* 51 (2001): 148–9.
8 'Peace, Order and Good Government,' 1080.
9 Ibid., 1075.
10 Ibid., 1076.
11 Ibid., 1079.
12 *O'Sullivan v. Noarlunga Meat Ltd. (No. 2)* (1956), 94 C.L.R. 367 at 375–6.
13 Cited in P. Ayres, *Owen Dixon* (Carlton, Victoria: Miegunyah Press 2003), 245. I thank Vaughan Black for drawing this book to my attention.

14 Law Society of Upper Canada Archives, Acc. no. 994.133/1, notes of Harriet A.L. Clark (constitutional law lecture notes, ca. 1945).

15 *Canadian Constitutional Law: Cases, Text and Notes on Distribution of Legislative Power* (Toronto: Carswell 1951); *Canadian Bar Review* 29 (1951): 1038–9.

16 Charles Holland Locke was on the Court from 1947 to 1962, and his colleague Ronald Martland spoke of his habits in an Osgoode Society interview, Oct. 1985.

17 'The Meaning of Provincial Autonomy,' *Canadian Bar Review* 29 (1951): 1134.

18 Ibid., 1135.

19 'Du pouvoir d'amendement constitutionnel au Canada,' *Canadian Bar Review* 29 (1951): 1136–79.

20 See the survey by W.S. Tarnopolsky in 'F.R. Scott: Civil Libertarian,' in S. Djwa and R. St J. Macdonald, *On F.R. Scott: Essays on His Contributions to Law, Literature, and Politics* (Kingston and Montreal: McGill-Queen's University Press 1983), 140.

21 Review by P. Wright, *Canadian Bar Review* 31 (1951): 213–15.

22 (Toronto: Butterworths 1981).

23 [1937] A.C. 326.

24 'Some International Legal Aspects of Federalism: the Experience of Canada,' in D.P. Currie, *Federalism and the New Nations of Africa* (Chicago: University of Chicago Press 1964), 400.

25 'The Provinces and International Agreements,' in Ontario Advisory Committee on Confederation, *Background Papers and Reports* (Ontario: Queen's Printer 1967), 101–13. The debate occurred on the Weekend Review show on CBC Radio on 25 April 1965; NA, CBC Radio fonds, acc. no. 1985–0268.

26 *University of Toronto Law Journal* 15 (1964): 506–10.

27 'Occupying the Field: Paramountcy in Penal Legislation,' *Canadian Bar Review* 41 (1963): 234–63.

28 'Jurisdictional Framework for Water Management,' in *Resources for Tomorrow* (Ottawa: R. Duhamel 1961). This was a volume of background papers for a major conference on natural resources held at Montreal in October 1961, itself an exercise in cooperative federalism.

29 The issue is reviewed in P. Hogg, *Constitutional Law of Canada*, 4th ed. (Scarborough, ON: Carswell 1997), 197–205.

30 'Administrative Law and the British North America Act,' *Harvard Law Review* 53 (1939): 251–81.

31 [1955] S.C.R. 454. Bora Laskin, 'Municipal Tax Assessment and Section 96 of the British North America Act: The Olympia Bowling Alleys Case,' *Canadian Bar Review* 33 (1955): 993–1017.

32　Ibid., 1010.

33　I thank my colleague Dianne Pothier for suggesting this to me.

34　B. Laskin, 'Tests for the Validity of Legislation: What's the "Matter"?' *University of Toronto Law Journal* 11 (1955): 114–27; Laskin was replying to D.W. Mundell, 'Tests for the Validity of Legislation under the British North America Act,' *Canadian Bar Review* 32 (1954): 813–43, and Mundell replied in *Canadian Bar Review* 33 (1955): 915–48.

35　NA, F.R. Scott Papers, reel 1223, Scott to Laskin, 19 Sept. 1955.

36　Personal communication from Harry Arthurs, 22 May 2002.

37　A.S. Abel, 'The Neglected Logic of 91 and 92,' *University of Toronto Law Journal* 19 (1969): 500–1.

38　F.R. Scott Papers, reel 1253, Scott to Abel, 5 Feb. 1970.

39　Risk, 'The Road to Oz.'

40　In 'The Balanced Interpretation of the Federal Distribution of Legislative Powers in Canada,' published in P.-A. Crépeau and C.B. Macpherson, *The Future of Canadian Federalism/ L'Avenir du fédéralisme canadien* (Toronto: University of Toronto Press 1965) Lederman developed ideas originally presented in 'Classification of Laws and the British North America Act,' in J.A. Corry, F.C. Cronkite, and E.F. Whitmore, eds., *Legal Essays in Honour of Arthur Moxon* (Toronto: University of Toronto Press 1953). Laskin's own 1955 article on the classification of laws was thought at the time to have been provoked by this 1953 piece by Lederman, but Laskin did not refer to it there.

41　Lederman, 'Balanced Interpretation,' 106, citing his 1953 article at 197–8.

42　W.R. Lederman, ed., *The Courts and the Canadian Constitution* (Toronto: McClelland & Stewart 1964). He chose to include Laskin's '"Peace, Order and Good Government" Re-examined' and 'The Supreme Court of Canada: A Final Court of and for Canadians.'

43　See below, chapter 21.

44　J. Whyte and W.R. Lederman, *Canadian Constitutional Law: Cases, Notes and Materials* (Toronto: Butterworths 1975).

45　'Our Civil Liberties: the Role of the Supreme Court,' *Queen's Quarterly* 61 (1955): 456–71. The idea of the four categories of liberty is more fully developed in 'An Inquiry into the Diefenbaker Bill of Rights,' *Canadian Bar Review* 37 (1959): 77–134. For a trenchant analysis, see R.J. Sharpe, 'Bora Laskin and Civil Liberties,' *University of Toronto Law Journal* 35 (1985): 632–71, upon which I rely in what follows.

46　[1951] S.C.R. 887. The decision was affirmed by the Privy Council, [1954] A.C. 541.

47　'Mr. Justice Rand and Canada's Federal Constitution,' *University of West-*

ern Ontario Law Review 18 (1979–80): 31, as reprinted in W.R. Lederman, *Continuing Canadian Constitutional Dilemmas* (Toronto: Butterworths 1981), 396.

48 *Winner*, [1951] S.C.R. 887 at 920.

49 Review of D. Schmeiser, *Civil Liberties in Canada* (Toronto: Oxford University Press 1964), in *University of Toronto Law Journal* 16 (1964): 201 (re companies); OJA, JPRC fonds, box 8/24, minutes of 29 Jan. 1957 meeting (re change of name).

50 Review of *Civil Liberties and Canadian Federalism* (Toronto: University of Toronto Press 1959), *University of Toronto Law Journal* 13 (1960): 289. N. Finkelstein 'Laskin's Four Classes of Liberty,' *Canadian Bar Review* 66 (1987): 227–66.

51 *Globe and Mail*, 11 Dec. 1958.

52 Cited in C. MacLennan, *Toward the Charter: Canadians and the Demand for a National Bill of Rights, 1929–1960* (Montreal and Kingston: McGill-Queen's University Press 2003), 131.

53 Jackett to Walker, 1 Dec. 1958, cited ibid., 138.

54 'Inquiry into the Diefenbaker Bill of Rights,' 134.

55 [1951] S.C.R. 255.

56 [1953] 2 S.C.R. 299.

57 [1957] S.C.R. 285.

58 [1959] S.C.R. 121. *Roncarelli* had been decided by the Supreme Court though not yet reported when Laskin published his 'Inquiry' piece; he had seen the decision in manuscript, undoubtedly via Frank Scott.

59 When interviewed in 1975 by CBC reporter Elizabeth Gray, Laskin named these decisions, minus *Switzman*, as those which had made the most powerful contribution to Canadian public law. Background interview for CBC Tuesday Night, 1975, audiotape at NA, ref. no. 276236.

60 'Inquiry into the Diefenbaker Bill of Rights,' 124.

61 [1963] S.C.R. 651.

62 'Freedom of Religion and the Lord's Day Act – The Canadian Bill of Rights and the Sunday Bowling Case,' *Canadian Bar Review* 42 (1964): 149.

63 [1970] S.C.R. 282.

64 The evidence comes from two sources. When I interviewed the late Justice Samuel Hughes, himself a Diefenbaker appointee to the Ontario High Court, he was quite insistent that Laskin was a candidate for a judicial appointment in 1958 but declined to provide further details. After Laskin's death the *Winnipeg Free Press*, 27 Mar. 1984, reported that 'John Diefenbaker was ready to appoint him to the Supreme Court in the early 1960s until he read an assessment of [the] Bill of Rights by Laskin.' Such infor-

mation might have come from Justice Samuel Freedman of Winnipeg, but
the source was not indicated. Allowing for a lack of clarity in some details,
the essentials of the story are the same.

65 NA, Diefenbaker Papers, MG 26 N, ser. VI, reel M-7948, 285035–36, 285042,
285060 (June-July 1958). NA, Pearson Papers, MG 26 N3/58/301 (Jan.-Feb.
1965); Senator J.J. Connolly and R.S. Malone of the *Winnipeg Free Press*
were the intermediaries.

66 NA, CALT Papers, MG 28 I 138, vol. 1. B. Laskin, 'Amendment of the
Constitution,' *University of Toronto Law Journal* 15 (1963): 190–4.

67 'Amendment of the Constitution: Applying the Fulton-Favreau Formula,'
McGill Law Journal 11 (1965): 2–18.

68 E. Whelan with R. Archbold, *Whelan: The Man in the Green Stetson*
(Toronto: Irwin Publishing 1986), 45–6. I thank Wade MacLauchlan for
drawing this reference to my attention.

69 I thank Sir Fred for sharing his recollections of Bora Laskin with me in a
communication dated 7 Jan. 2002, and for sending me a copy of his autobiography, *Caribbean Life and Culture: A Citizen Reflects* (Kingston, Jamaica:
Heinemann 1991). As a research fellow at McGill in 1964–5, Phillips
published two articles in Canadian journals: 'Politics and the Administration of Justice in Newly Independent Countries,' *University of Toronto Law
Journal* 16 (1966): 395–404, and 'A West Indian Looks at Canadian Federalism,' *McGill Law Journal* 11 (1965): 344–55, in which he thanks Laskin for
having read the manuscript in draft. Sir Fred unfortunately disposed of
his correspondence with Bora Laskin a few years before I contacted him.

70 R. Simeon and I. Robinson, *State, Society, and the Development of Canadian
Federalism* (Toronto: University of Toronto Press 1990), 83.

71 Ibid., 86.

72 'Reflections on the Canadian Constitution after the First Century,' *Canadian Bar Review* 45 (1967): 401.

73 D. Guest, *The Emergence of Social Security in Canada* (Vancouver: UBC Press
1980), 83.

74 D. Owram, *The Government Generation: Canadian Intellectuals and the State,
1900–1945* (Toronto: University of Toronto Press 1986), 221–53.

75 *Report of the Royal Commission on Dominion-Provincial Relations* (Ottawa:
Queen's Printer 1940).

76 Cited in Pigeon, 'Provincial Autonomy,' 1133.

77 Ibid.

78 The argument was made most extensively by J.R. Mallory, *Social Credit and
the Federal Power in Canada* (Toronto: University of Toronto Press 1954).

79 'Constitutional Trends and Federalism,' in A.R.M. Lower, ed., *Evolving Canadian Federalism* (Durham, NC: Duke University Press 1958), 92–125.
80 'Reflections on the Canadian Constitution,' 400.
81 Review of Crépeau and Macpherson, *The Future of Canadian Federalism/ L'Avenir du fédéralisme canadien, University of Toronto Law Journal* 16 (1965): 470–2.
82 Peter Russell author interview, 30 Apr. 2002.
83 As to Forsey, see F. Milligan, *Eugene A. Forsey: An Intellectual Biography* (Calgary: University of Calgary Press 2004), esp. at 218–33. D. Bercuson, *True Patriot: The Life of Brooke Claxton, 1898–1960* (Toronto: University of Toronto Press 1993).
84 B. Laskin, 'Canadian Federalism: A Scott's Eye View in Prose and Poetry,' *McGill Law Journal* 14 (1968): 497.
85 T. Kent, *A Public Purpose: An Experience of Liberal Opposition and Canadian Government* (Kingston and Montreal: McGill-Queen's University Press 1988), 267.

Chapter 10: Arbitrator

1 *Public Affairs* (Fall 1944): 49.
2 (1959), 10 L.A.C. 51 at 55.
3 J. Fudge and E. Tucker, *Labour before the Law* (Toronto: Oxford University Press 2001), 273.
4 The statistics are derived from the conciliation board reports reproduced in the monthly *Labour Gazette* for the relevant years.
5 Fudge and Tucker, *Labour before the Law*, 283–7. On the Windsor Strike, see H. Colling, *Ninety-Nine Days: The Ford Strike in Windsor, 1945* (Toronto: NC Press 1995).
6 Transcript of proceedings at Ford arbitration, 1946, NA, Rand Papers, MG 30 E77/1. I thank William Kaplan for bringing this reference to my attention.
7 *Pedlar People Ltd. and Local 2784, United Steel Workers of America, Labour Gazette* (Oct. 1944), 1231–3.
8 *Belleville-Sargeant and Company Ltd. and Local 426, UAW, Labour Gazette* (Nov. 1945): 1654.
9 *Ontario Malleable Iron Co. and Local 1817, United Steelworkers of America, Labour Gazette* (Sept. 1944): 1117–24; *Fittings, Ltd. and Local 1817, United Steelworkers of America, Labour Gazette* (Nov. 1944): 1343–54.
10 *Corbin Lock Co. and Local 426, UAW, Labour Gazette* (May 1945): 709–14.

11 *Dominion Glass and Local 251, UAW, Labour Gazette* (Oct. 1944): 1227.

12 *Public Affairs* (Fall 1944): 54–5.

13 *Wellesley Hospital and Local 204, Building Service Employees' International Union, Labour Gazette* (Sept. 1946): 769.

14 *Fittings, Ltd. and United Steelworkers of America, Local 1817, Labour Gazette* (Nov. 1944): 1343–54.

15 The calculations in this paragraph and the next are derived from Laskin's arbitration decisions as reported in *Labour Arbitration Cases* for the relevant years.

16 The following interpretation of Laskin's arbitral jurisprudence draws heavily on D. Beatty and B. Langille, 'Bora Laskin and Labour Law: From Vision to Legacy,' *University of Toronto Law Journal* 35 (1985): 672–727, with which I largely agree; see also W.L. Hunter, 'Bora Laskin and Labour Law: The Formative Years,' *Supreme Court Law Review* 6 (1984): 431–66.

17 *United Electrical, Radio & Machine Workers of America, Local 527 and Peterboro Lock Mfg. Co. Ltd.* (1953), 4 L.A.C. 1499 at 1502.

18 Langille and Beatty, 'Bora Laskin and Labour Law,' 689.

19 'The Protection of Interests by Statute and the Problem of "Contracting Out",' *Canadian Bar Review* 16 (1938): 699.

20 *United Electrical, Radio & Machine Workers of America and Canadian General Electric Co. Ltd.* (1951), 2 L.A.C. 917–22.

21 *United Electrical, Radio and Machine Workers of America and Canadian General Electric Co. Ltd.* (1951), 2 L.A.C. 910.

22 (1975), 62 D.L.R. (3d) 68 (S.C.C.). See the discussion in chapter 21.

23 *United Electrical, Radio, and Machine Workers of America, Local 524, and Canadian General Electric Co. Ltd.* (1951), 2 L.A.C. 688 at 691.

24 *United Packinghouse Workers, Local 114 and Canada Packers* (1958), 9 L.A.C. 200–4.

25 *United Brewery Workers, Local 304 and Molson's Brewery (Ontario) Ltd.* (1961), 11 L.A.C. 381–7.

26 *United Electrical, Radio and Machine Workers of America, Local 515 and Canadian General Electric Co. Ltd.* (1950), 2 L.A.C. 471–4; 'Problems of Procedure and Proof in Labour Arbitration,' *Canadian Public Administration* 5 (1962): 76.

27 *United Electrical, Radio and Machine Workers of America, Local 507 and Canadian General Electric Co. Ltd.* (1950), 2 L.A.C. 587–90.

28 A very modest equal pay statute passed by the Frost government in 1951 was not sought by either labour or human rights activists. See S. Tillotson, 'Human Rights Law as Prism: Women's Organizations, Unions, and Ontario's Female Employees Fair Remuneration Act, 1951,' *Canadian Historical Review* 72, no. 4 (1991): 532–57. C. Patrias and R. Frager, '"This Is

Our Country, These Are Our Rights": Minorities and the Origins of
Ontario's Human Rights Campaigns,' *Canadian Historical Review* 82, no. 1
(2001): 1–35.

29 *United Electrical, Radio & Machine Workers of America, Local 527 and Peterboro
Lock Mfg. Co.* (1953), 4 L.A.C. 1499–1506.

30 Ibid., 1503.

31 *Re United Steelworkers of America and Russelsteel Ltd.* (1966), 17 L.A.C. 253.
See also B. Langille, 'Equal Partnership in Canadian Labour Law,' *Osgoode
Hall Law Journal* 21 (1983): 496–536. I thank Dianne Pothier for alerting me
to the *Russelsteel* decision.

32 *International Union of Mine, Mill and Smelter Workers, Local 811 and Northern
Pigment Co.* (1948), 1 L.A.C. 216–22.

33 *United Electrical, Radio and Machine Workers of America, Local 514 and Amalgamated Electric Corp.* (1950), 2 L.A.C. 597–608

34 *Oil, Chemical & Atomic Workers and Polymer Corp. Ltd.* (1958), 10 L.A.C.
31–51.

35 *Oil, Chemical & Atomic Workers and Polymer Corp. Ltd.* (1959), 10 L.A.C. 51,
62.

36 *CGE and Local 507 United Electrical, Radio, and Machine Workers* (1952), 3
L.A.C. 1090.

37 Stanley Schiff author interview, 14 Dec. 2002. The words within quotation
marks must of course be a paraphrase of Laskin's outburst. The cases in
question were *Re U.P.W. and Quaker Oats Ltd.* (1954), 5 L.A.C. 1871 and *Re
U.E.W. and Canadian Westinghouse* (1954), 5 L.A.C. 1898.

38 (1961), 26 D.L.R. (2d) 609 (Ont. H.C.); (1961), 28 D.L.R. (2d) 81 (Ont. C.A.);
(1962), 33 D.L.R. (2d) 124 (S.C.C.).

39 'Tort Liability for Strikes in Canada: Some Problems of Judicial Workman-
ship,' *Canadian Bar Review* 38 (1960): 391.

40 'Certiorari to Labour Boards: The Apparent Futility of Privative Clauses,'
Canadian Bar Review 30 (1952): 986–1003. The early hostility of courts to
labour boards has been widely accepted as an article of faith, but for a
revisionist view see R.B. Brown, '"To Err Is Human, to Forgive Divine":
The Labour Relations Board and the Supreme Court of Nova Scotia, 1947–
1965,' in P. Girard, J. Phillips, and B. Cahill, *The Supreme Court of Nova
Scotia, 1754–2004: From Imperial Bastion to Provincial Oracle* (Toronto:
University of Toronto Press for the Osgoode Society 2004).

41 Wright Papers, box 3, MacDonald to Wright, 26 Feb. 1953; Wright to
MacDonald, 2 Mar. 1953.

42 See especially *R. v. Ontario Labour Relations Board, ex parte Metropolitan Life
Insurance Co.*, [1969] 1 O.R. 412, rev'd [1970] S.C.R. 425 (review of labour
board decision); and *Port Arthur Shipbuilding*, [1967] 2 O.R. 49, rev'd [1969]

S.C.R. 85 (review of labour arbitrator's decision). The arbitrator in the latter case was Harry Arthurs.

43 See Beatty and Langille, 'Bora Laskin and Labour Law,' 716–21 for a more detailed review.

44 *Report of the Attorney-General's Committee on the Process of Labour Arbitration in Ontario* (Toronto: 1962).

45 National Academy of Arbitrators, *Fifty Years in the World of Work* (Washington, DC: Bureau of National Affairs 1997), 37, 75–81.

46 I thank my former colleague Earl Palmer for discussing his early days in labour arbitration with me in July 2001. Palmer completed an LLM thesis on labour arbitration under Laskin at the University of Toronto in 1959–60 and did his first arbitration the following year. His later treatises on collective agreement arbitration became standard works.

47 *Falconbridge Nickel Mines Ltd.* (1958), 8 L.A.C. 276, 283.

48 H.W. Arthurs, 'Developing Industrial Citizenship: A Challenge for Canada's Second Century,' *Canadian Bar Review* 45 (1967): 786–830.

Chapter 11: Human Rights

1 *Daily Times-Journal* (Fort William), 26 Mar. 1946.

2 *Canadian Bar Review* 18 (1940): 504–6.

3 W. Kaplan, *State and Salvation: The Jehovah's Witnesses and Their Fight for Civil Rights* (Toronto: University of Toronto Press 1989), 260–1.

4 The role of Jewish activists is highlighted particularly in R. Lambertson, 'Activists in the Age of Rights: The Struggle for Human Rights in Canada, 1945–1960' (PhD dissertation, University of Victoria, 1998). See also C. Patrias and R. Frager, '"This Is Our Country, These Are Our Rights": Minorities and the Origins of Ontario's Human Rights Campaigns,' *Canadian Historical Review* 82, no. 1 (2001): 1–35; I. Abella, 'Jews, Human Rights, and the Making of a New Canada,' *Journal of the Canadian Historical Association* 11 (2000): 3–15; J.W. St G. Walker, 'The Jewish Phase in the Movement for Racial Equality in Canada,' *Canadian Ethnic Studies* 34, no. 1 (2002): 1–29; B. Kayfetz, 'On Community Relations in Ontario in the 1940s,' *Canadian Jewish Studies* 2 (1994): 60.

5 *In re Drummond Wren*, [1945] O.R. 778 (H.C.). Title to the land was presumably taken in the name of Drummond Wren personally because the WEA, as an unincorporated association, was incapable of doing so.

6 I draw on the discussion of *Drummond Wren* in J.W. St. G. Walker in *'Race,' Rights and the Law in the Supreme Court of Canada* (Toronto: Wilfrid Laurier University Press 1997), 202–5.

7 *Keily v. Monck* (1795), 3 Ridg. P.C. 205.

8 *Janson v. Driefontein Consolidated Mines*, [1902] A.C. 484 at 507; the key precedent was *Egerton v. Brownlow* (1853), 10 E.R. 359, which nonetheless invalidated a testamentary condition requiring the recipient to acquire a dukedom on pain of forfeiting an estate.

9 *Re Millar*, [1938] S.C.R. 1.

10 Laskin cited this passage from Holmes's *The Common Law* in 'The Protection of Interests by Statute and the Problem of "Contracting Out,"' *Canadian Bar Review* 16 (1938): 672.

11 J. Keiller Mackay Papers, St Francis Xavier University Archives, MG 28, Box 57/1 6862-6965. This file contains Justice Mackay's correspondence on *Drummond Wren*, and a copy of the transcript of John Cartwright's oral argument. See also the *Drummond Wren* case file in the Supreme Court of Ontario fonds, AO, RG 22-5801 docket 669 (1945).

12 *Hush Free Press*, 1 Dec. 1945.

13 'A Victory for Democracy: The Crucial Decision rendered by Mr. Justice Mackay in the SCO declaring void a restrictive land covenant in the case jointly conducted by the Workers' Educational Association and the Canadian Jewish Congress' (Toronto, n.d. [1945]), copy in Mackay Papers. The pamphlet records that counsel were assisted by Jacob Finkelman, 'Borah' Laskin, and Charles Dubin.

14 Walker, 'Race,' *Rights and the Law*, 204–5; the Mackay Papers contain correspondence from U.S. judges and lawyers seeking information about the case and whether it was appealed.

15 A copy of the deed conveying part of lot 5, plan 2969, township of East York, from Vanderbent to Wren, dated 15 June 1944, can be found in the *Drummond Wren* case file, supra note 11. Vanderbent's own deed to lot 4 and part of lot 5, dated 1 Sept. 1942, is registered as inst. no. 34872, Registry Division of the East and West Riding of County of York, Book G1, township of East York.

16 By deed dated 10 Sept. 1944 Vanderbent sold part of lot 5, plan 2969 to Sydney F. Lankin: inst. 40355, Registry Division of the East and West Riding of County of York, Book G1, Twp of E York. Omitting the covenant was not sufficient to discharge it, but it does suggest Vanderbent was not concerned to enforce. it.

17 CJC, Summary of Activities of the National Joint Public Relations Committee of the Canadian Jewish Congress and the B'nai Brith (1946), cited in Walker, 'Race,' *Rights and the Law*, 199.

18 Ontario Jewish Archives, Joint Community Relations Committee Collection, MG 8S, JPRC Correspondence 1947, Reel 1, file 34. I thank Ross

Lambertson for sharing this and a number of references to Bora Laskin he encountered in researching his PhD dissertation.

19 Ibid., JPRC Correspondence 1946, box 3, file 1; JPRC minutes 17 June 1946.
20 R. Alexander, 'FEP Legislation,' *Canadian Forum* (May 1948): 31–2. P.D. Moreno, *From Direct Action to Affirmative Action: Fair Employment Law and Policy in America, 1933–1972* (Baton Rouge: Louisiana State University Press 1997), 66–73.
21 OJA, JPRC Papers, box 3, file 2, JPRC minutes 17 Sept. 1947.
22 This paragraph draws heavily on Lambertson, 'Activists in the Age of Rights,' 379–98; see also Bruner, 'The Genesis of Ontario's Human Rights Legislation: A Study in Law Reform,' *University of Toronto Faculty of Law Review* 37 (1979): 236–53. The papers of the Jewish Labour Committee are at NA, MG 28 V 75. Those occupying the post of executive secretary were: Leslie Wismer (1947–8); Vivien Mahood (1948–50); Gordon Milling (1950–3); Donna Hill (1953–4); Sid Blum (1954–7); Alex Maxwell (1957–9); and A. Alan Borovoy (1959–67).
23 Jewish Labour Committee Papers, NA, MG 28 V 75, vol. 41.
24 Patrias and Frager, 'This Is Our Country,' 20.
25 Confidential memo, Saskatchewan Intelligence Section, 21 Feb. 1945, as reproduced in Rabbi Abraham Feinberg's RCMP file. All references in this paragraph come from this source. A copy of Rabbi Feinberg's RG 146 file, amounting to 1,100 heavily edited pages, was obtained by his daughter Sarah Jane Growe after his death. She allowed me to consult the file at her Toronto home, and discussed her father's activities with me on 22 May 2002. Ms Growe provides an overview of the file in the *Toronto Star*, 31 Dec. 1995. Reg Whitaker and Gary Marcuse provide context in *Cold War Canada: The Making of a National Insecurity State, 1945–1957* (Toronto: University of Toronto Press 1994), but the perception of Jewish subversion on the part of the security services is not explored.
26 *Information and Comment*, 1, no. 7 (June 1948): 9, copy in NA, Manfred Saalheimer Papers, MG 31 H 171 vol. 1. F.R. Scott made a similar proposal but in less detail in 'Dominion Jurisdiction Over Human Rights and Fundamental Freedoms,' *Canadian Bar Review* 27 (1949): 505–6.
27 M.A. Glendon, *A World Made New: Eleanor Roosevelt and the Universal Declaration of Human Rights* (New York: Random House 2001), xviii.
28 R. Graham, *Old Man Ontario: Leslie M. Frost* (Toronto: University of Toronto Press 1990).
29 [1948] O.R. 579. What follows draws largely on Walker's chapter on the case in *'Race,' Rights and the Law.*

30 [1949] O.R. 503.

31 Walker, 'Race,' *Rights and the Law*, 217, citing Ted Richmond's recollections of the hearing.

32 11 June 1949.

33 10 June 1949.

34 Walker, 'Race,' *Rights and the Law*, 225.

35 OJA, JPRC Correspondence, box 4, 1949 Minutes, 27 Sept. 1949.

36 I. Bushnell, *The Captive Court: A Study of the Supreme Court of Canada* (Montreal and Kingston: McGill-Queen's University Press 1992), 296. The Supreme Court not only overturned the conviction but said Boucher could not be tried again because sedition had to involve some attempt to overthrow governmental authority; Boucher's pamphlet attacked only the authority of the Catholic Church, not the state.

37 Bushnell, *Captive Court*, analyses the Supreme Court decision in *Noble* at 302–11.

38 Cited in Walker, 'Race,' *Rights and the Law*, 218.

39 The phrase is that of Donna Hill, executive secretary of the Toronto Joint Labour Committee for Human Rights; NA, MG 28 V 75, 41/71, Hill to Kalmen Kaplansky, 26 Mar. 1954.

40 Lambertson, 'Activists in the Age of Rights,' at 404. On the passage of the legislation of the 1950s, see, in addition to sources cited in note 4, H.A. Sohn, 'Human Rights Legislation in Ontario: A Study of Social Action' (DSW thesis, University of Toronto, 1975); Bruner, 'Genesis'; R.B. Howe, 'The Evolution of Human Rights Policy in Ontario,' *Canadian Journal of Political Science* 24, no. 4 (1991): 783–802; J.C. Bagnall, 'The Ontario Conservatives and the Development of Anti-Discrimination Policy: 1944–1962' (PhD dissertation, Queen's University, 1984).

41 1 Nov. 1948.

42 Graham, *Old Man Ontario*, 263.

43 OJA, JPRC fonds, box 3, 1950 minutes, 2 Mar. 1950.

44 S. Tillotson, 'Human Rights Law as Prism: Women's Organizations, Unions, and Ontario's Female Employees Fair Remuneration Act, 1951,' *Canadian Historical Review* 72, no. 4 (1991): 532–57. On the lack of interest in gender issues on the part of the 1950s human rights movement in Ontario, see Patrias and Frager, 'This Is Our Country.'

45 Bruner, 'Genesis,' 247.

46 OJA, JPRC Correspondence, box 3, Fair Employment Practices file B.

47 Bagnall, 'Ontario Conservatives,' 200.

48 Walker, 'Jewish Phase,' 17.

49 Bruner, 'Genesis,' 247.
50 P.N. Oliver, *Unlikely Tory: The Life and Politics of Allan Grossman* (Toronto: Lester & Orpen Dennys 1985), 59–77.
51 Moreno, *From Direct Action to Affirmative Action*, 2.
52 *Saturday Night* (May 1964): 15.
53 Walker, 'Jewish Phase,' 18.
54 I thank Shirley Tillotson for suggesting this to me.
55 OJA, JPRC correspondence, box 6, 7.
56 The campaign is covered in detail in Lambertson, 'Activists in the Age of Rights,' 399–418.
57 OJA, box 7, file 2.
58 Julius Isaac author interview, Federal Court of Appeal, 16 Nov. 2000.
59 S.O. 1960–61, c. 28, s. 2.
60 Stanley Schiff author interview, 14 Dec. 2001.
61 G.D. Finlayson, *John J. Robinette, Peerless Mentor: An Appeciation* (Toronto: Osgoode Society 2003), 43.
62 Law Society of Upper Canada Archives, Lawyers' Club fonds, M1. Christopher Moore, *The Law Society of Upper Canada and Ontario's Lawyers, 1797–1997* (Toronto: University of Toronto Press 1997), 267, gives the date of the change as 1958 but the minutes of the Club show it as 1952. Laskin's successor on the Court of Appeal, John Arnup, led the reform campaign.
63 OJA, box 6, minutes 4 Oct. 1955.
64 S.O. 1958, c. 70; S.O. 1960–61, c. 28, c. 63; S.O. 1961–62, c. 93.
65 Stanley Schiff interview, 14 Dec. 2001. Sydney Harris also recalled that 'people in Congress accorded him tremendous respect': author interview, 15 Dec. 2001.
66 OJA, JPRC Correspondence, box 11/9, M. Saalheimer to Fred Catzman, 19 July 1960. I thank Ross Lambertson for providing this reference.
67 D. Clément, 'Spies, Lies and a Commission: A Case Study in the Mobilization of the Canadian Civil Liberties Movement,' *Left History* 7, no. 2 (2000): 53–79.
68 *Canadian Bar Review* 30 (1952): 1080–3.
69 It is always difficult to prove a negative but Dominique Clément, who has investigated exhaustively the Canadian civil liberties community of the 1940s and '50s, has found no trace of Laskin; personal communication 24 Jan. 2002.
70 For a suggestive study of the social history of the Cold War in Canada, see R. Cavell, ed., *Love, Hate, and Fear in Canada's Cold War* (Toronto: University of Toronto Press 2004). For a brilliant fictional explanation of the social pressure to comform during a slightly later phase of the Cold War,

see Ann-Marie MacDonald, *The Way the Crow Flies* (Toronto: Random House 2003).

71 NA, Ministry of Labour fonds, RG 27, vol. 3504, file 1-10s-85; M.M. Maclean to A. McNamara, 28 Apr. 1948; A.H. Brown to T.W. Van Dusen, 7 Aug. 1958. On Wren's dismissal and the perceived Communist leanings of the WEA see Gilbert Jackson to Humphrey Mitchell, Minister of Labour, 31 Dec. 1947.

72 L.S. MacDowell, *Renegade Lawyer: The Life of J.L. Cohen* (Toronto: University of Toronto Press 2001), 223–76.

73 *Record of the Second Commonwealth and Empire Law Conference, Ottawa, September 14–21, 1960* (London: Sweet & Maxwell 1962), 129.

74 'An Inquiry into the Diefenbaker Bill of Rights,' *Canadian Bar Review* 37 (1959): 76–134; 'Canada's Bill of Rights: A Dilemma for the Courts?' *International and Comparative Law Quarterly* 11 (1962): 519–36; M.H. Fyfe, 'Some Legal Aspects of the Report of the Royal Commission on Espionage,' *Canadian Bar Review* 24 (1946): 777–84.

75 *Record of the Second Commonwealth and Empire Law Conference*, 131.

76 Author interview with June Callwood, 31 May 2002.

77 R. Putnam, *Bowling Alone: The Collapse and Revival of American Community* (New York: Simon & Schuster 2000), 17.

Chapter 12: Academic Freedom

1 This account relies heavily on the most thorough and objective account to date of the Crowe controversy, Michiel Horn's chapter 'The Crowe Caws' in his *Academic Freedom in Canada: A History* (Toronto: University of Toronto Press 1999). Two other sources give more partisan interpretations: K. McNaught, *Conscience and History: A Memoir* (Toronto: University of Toronto Press 1997), and A.G. Bedford, *The University of Winnipeg: A History of the Founding Colleges* (Toronto: University of Toronto Press 1976). McNaught was a strong Crowe supporter and Bedford stoutly defends the college and Principal Lockhart while admitting that Crowe did suffer an injustice.

2 Statutes of Manitoba 1937–38, c. 80.

3 Horn, *Academic Freedom*, 225–6, citing correspondence from Crowe.

4 The judgment is that of Horn, *Academic Freedom*, 228.

5 Ibid., 220.

6 Ibid., 222.

7 NA, CAUT Papers, MG 28 I 208/129, H.D. 'Buzz' Woods to Clarence Barber, n.d. [summer 1958].

8 *Conscience and History*, 90.

9 McNaught, *Conscience and History*, 119, recalls Frank Scott as having been the source of Laskin's name. Both Scott and Woods may have been consulted by Barber, but Barber's letter to Laskin on 12 Sept. states 'Woods has informed me that you have agreed to act as a member of Prof. Fowke's committee'; CAUT Papers, vol. 129.

10 McNaught, *Conscience and History*, 100.

11 CAUT Papers, vol. 129, Barber to Laskin, 12 Sept. 1958; Woods to Barber, n.d. [summer 1958]; Watson to Barber, 27 Aug. 1958; vol. 162, Laskin to Woods, 17 Sept. 1958.

12 *United Church Observer*, 1 Nov. 1958, 6.

13 CAUT Papers, vol. 129, Barber to Laskin, 2 Oct. 1958; vol. 162, Scott to Laskin, 24 Sept. 1958.

14 CAUT Papers, vol. 162, Laskin to Fowke, 20 Sept. 1958.

15 'Report of the Investigation by the Committee of the Canadian Association of University Teachers into the Dismissal of Professor H.S. Crowe by United College, Winnipeg, Manitoba' *CAUT Bulletin* 7 (1959): 13 (hereafter 'Fowke-Laskin Report').

16 CAUT Papers, vol. 163, Laskin to Fowke, 6 Feb. 1959.

17 McNaught, *Conscience and History*, 120.

18 Bedford, *University of Winnipeg*, omits any reference to this testimony.

19 CAUT Papers, vol. 162, Laskin to Fowke, 20 Oct., 16 Nov. 1958; Fowke to Laskin, 7 Nov. 1958.

20 Horn, *Academic Freedom*, reviews the debate at 235–6.

21 [1979] 1 S.C.R. 311. See below, chapter 21.

22 *Nicholson* did not extend such protections to all non-permanent employees, only those holding a 'public office' of some kind.

23 CAUT Papers, vol. 162, Laskin to Fowke, 16 Nov. 1958; vol. 163, Laskin to Fowke, 6 Feb. 1959.

24 CAUT Papers, vol. 162, Laskin to Fowke, 27 Oct. 1958.

25 Horn, *Academic Freedom*, 234.

26 McNaught, *Conscience and History*, 127.

27 Horn, *Academic Freedom*, 240.

28 Ibid., 242–3.

29 4 Apr. 1959.

30 Cited in Horn, *Academic Freedom*, 249.

31 Ibid., 246–51.

32 For a recent example, see J.H. Thompson, J. Downie, and P. Baird, *The Olivieri Report: The Complete Text of the Report of the Independent Inquiry Commissioned by the Canadian Association of University Teachers* (Toronto: J. Lorimer 2001).

33 See chapter 9.

34 His critique was a summary of that contained in his article 'An Inquiry into the Diefenbaker Bill of Rights,' *Canadian Bar Review* 37 (1959): 76–134.

35 A.J. Hobbins, ed., *On the Edge of Greatness: The Diaries of John Humphrey, First Director of the United Nations Division of Human Rights* (Montreal: McGill University Libraries 1994-), 4:42–3. I thank A.J. Hobbins for bringing this reference to my attention.

36 NA, F.R. Scott Papers, MG 30 D 211/45/4, Carrothers to Scott, 23 Jan. 1963.

37 Ibid., Scott to Carrothers, 25 Jan. 1963; Carrothers to Scott, 5 Feb. 1963.

38 C. Bissell, *Halfway up Parnassus* (Toronto: University of Toronto Press 1974), 117.

39 Ibid., 118.

40 CAUT Papers, vol. 138, Southwell to Mountford 11 May 1964. See also correspondence between Laskin and Percy Smith in vol. 20, canvassing various candidates according to how 'liberal' they were.

41 J. Duff and R.O. Berdahl, *University Government in Canada: Report of a Commission Sponsored by the Canadian Association of University Teachers and the Association of Universities and Colleges of Canada* (Toronto: University of Toronto Press 1966).

42 Cited in Bissell, *Halfway up Parnassus*, 121.

43 George Whalley, ed., *A Place of Liberty: Essays on the Government of Canadian Universities, Dedicated to the Memory of Stewart Reid* (Toronto and Vancouver: Clarke Irwin 1964).

44 Ibid., 177.

45 Ibid., 145.

46 Ibid., 27–37.

47 Personal communication from Roland Penner, Winnipeg, Manitoba, 16 Sept. 2002. Professor Penner was present at the dinner in his capacity as an executive member of the CAUT.

48 S. Hewitt, '"Information Believed True": RCMP Security Intelligence Activities on Canadian University Campuses and the Controversy Surrounding Them, 1961–1971,' *Canadian Historical Review* 81, no. 2 (2000) 191–228. This section relies heavily on Hewitt's findings and interpretation. See also his *Spying 101: The RCMP's Secret Activities at Canadian Universities, 1917–1997* (Toronto: University of Toronto Press 2002).

49 Hewitt, '"Information believed true."' See generally D. Fleming, *So Very Near: The Political Memoirs of the Honourable Donald M. Fleming*, vol. 2, *The Summit Years* (Toronto: McClelland & Stewart 1985), 543–4.

50 For a complete chronology of the CAUT's interest in RCMP activities down to the summer of 1963, see CAUT Papers, MG 28 I 208/164, file AFRT-RCMP no. 13-2.
51 *CAUT Bulletin* 12, no. 1 (Oct. 1963): 19.
52 Laskin and Reid to Chevrier, 31 July 1963, reproduced at *CAUT Bulletin* 12, no. 4 (Apr. 1964): 38–41.
53 'Memorandum concerning RCMP Activities on University Campuses,' in ibid., 36–8.
54 'RCMP Activities on University Campuses,' *CAUT Bulletin* 13, no. 1 (Oct. 1964): 54–9.
55 NA, CAUT Papers, MG 28 I 208/164, file 'AFRT-RCMP No. 13-2.'
56 Hewitt, 'Information Believed True.'
57 CAUT Papers, vol. 164, Laskin to Jewett, 14 Aug. 1964.
58 Ibid., Laskin to Pearson, 7 Jan. 1965; Pearson to Laskin, 8 Feb. 1965; Laskin to Pearson, 23 Feb. 1965.
59 NA, RCMP Papers, RG 146/59/96-A-00169, pt. 1, 28 June 1963.
60 Ibid., 22 Dec. 1964. Laskin's talk was reported in the *Varsity*, 7 Oct. 1964, a copy of which was appended to the report.

Chapter 13: Elder Statesman

1 *Varsity*, 3 Mar. 1961; Institute of Advanced Legal Studies, *Fifteenth Annual Report 1st August, 1961-31st July, 1962* (London: University of London 1962). I thank Barry A.K. Rider, Director of IALS, and Jules Winterton, its librarian, for assistance in sending this material.
2 'The Supreme Court of Canada: A Final Court of and for Canadians' *Canadian Bar Review* 29 (1951): 1069.
3 Canadian Jewish Congress Archives [CJCA], Laskin box, file 6, 30 Sept. 1961.
4 Wright Papers, box 3, Wright to Laskin, 31 Oct. 1961.
5 Ibid., Laskin to Wright, 8 Nov. 1961.
6 Ibid., Laskin to Wright, 3 Jan. 1962.
7 Ibid., Laskin to Wright 7 Feb. 1962. Soon after acceding to independence in 1957 with a quasi-federal constitution guaranteeing responsible government and multi-party democracy, Ghana had rapidly metamorphosed into a one-party unitary state under the near-dictatorship of Dr Nkrumah.
8 NA, F.R. Scott Papers, MG 30 D 211/52/6, Laskin to Scott, 23 Mar. 1962.
9 Published in D.P. Currie, ed., *Federalism and the New Nations of Africa* (Chicago: University of Chicago Press 1964).
10 F.R. Scott Papers, Laskin to Scott, 23 Mar. 1962.
11 Wright asked him to provide a 'rather flowery course description ... which

would give this somewhat of a different line than if it were another course in Constitutional Law ...'; UTA, Law School Papers, A82-0041/030, Wright to Laskin, 26 Jan. 1962. Laskin's sabbatical letters to Wright are in the Wright Papers, but Wright's to Laskin are mostly in the Law School Papers.

12 Ibid., Wright to Laskin, 31 Oct. 1961.

13 Law School Papers, Wright to Laskin, 5 Apr. 1962.

14 Ibid.

15 Ibid., Wright to Laskin, 26 Jan. 1962.

16 Law School Papers, Wright to Laskin, 5 Apr. 1962; Wright Papers, Laskin to Wright, 14 Apr. 1962.

17 Law School Papers, Wright to Laskin, 5 Apr. 1962.

18 Author interview with Edward McWhinney, 19 Feb. 2001.

19 W.H. Nelson, *The Search for Faculty Power: The History of the University of Toronto Faculty Association 1942–1992* (Toronto: Canadian Scholars' Press 1993), 12.

20 *Franklin v. University of Toronto*, [2001] O.J. No. 4321 (Sup. Ct. of Justice). Gans J. denied certification but suggested that the plaintiffs had strong individual claims. A negotiated settlement followed.

21 BLI 1977: 53.

22 Nelson, *Search for Faculty Power*, 19.

23 Ibid.

24 Bissell to Laskin, 23 Nov. 1962; Laskin to Bissell, 28 Nov. 1962. These letters do not appear to be part of the president's correspondence held at UTA. They, along with those referred to in note 26, were found at Simcoe Hall by Martin Friedland in preparing his history of the University of Toronto. I thank him for bringing them to my attention.

25 BLI 1977: 54.

26 Laskin to Bissell, 28 Nov. 1962; Bissell to Laskin, 4 and 10 Dec. 1962; Laskin to Bissell 11 Dec. 1962; E. Sirluck, *First Generation: An Autobiography* (Toronto: University of Toronto Press 1996), 221.

27 *CAUT Bulletin* 14:1 (October 1965): 11.

28 *Graduate Studies in the University of Toronto: Report of the President's Committee, 1964–65* (Toronto: University of Toronto Press 1965), 15 [hereafter, *GSUT*].

29 Ibid., 46. The launching of the Sputnik I satellite by the Soviet Union in 1957 shocked the West and gave rise to a perceived need to improve education in mathematics and the sciences at all levels.

30 C. Bissell, *Halfway up Parnassus* (Toronto: University of Toronto Press 1974), 80.

31 Sirluck, *First Generation*, 249. I rely heavily on Sirluck's account in what follows, supplemented by a personal interview on 30 Sept. 2000 and subsequent correspondence. The committee's own records can be found at UTA, A77-0019/062 (Bissell).

32 UTA, A77-0019/062 (Bissell), Sirluck to Laskin, 22 Oct. 1964.

33 Sirluck, *First Generation*, 250.

34 As related to Professor Peter Russell in the early 1980s; author interview with Peter Russell, 30 Apr. 2002. See generally R. Cohen and R.E. Zelnik, eds., *The Free Speech Movement: Reflections on Berkeley in the 1960s* (Berkeley: University of California Press 2002). The protest was spurred by the university's decision in the fall of 1964 to prohibit students from handing out informational pamphlets, setting up recruiting tables on campus, and organizing off-campus political activities.

35 Ernest Sirluck to the author, 30 Mar. 2001.

36 Author interview with Ernest Sirluck, 30 Sept. 2000.

37 *GSUT*, 21.

38 Ibid., 77.

39 Ibid., 78.

40 AO, RG 32-1-1, acc 15129/2A/6, E.E. Stewart, Assistant Deputy Minister, to Deputy Minister of University Affairs, 20 Jan. 1966.

41 Sirluck, *First Generation*, 254–6.

42 A.L. Feinberg, *Storm the Gates of Jericho* (Toronto: McClelland & Stewart 1964), 142.

43 Jean Milner diary, 26 May 1965.

44 Author interview with Peter Russell (one of the guests), 30 Apr. 2002. *Varsity*, 8 Feb. 1965.

45 *Toronto Sun*, 2 Jan. 1974.

46 Author interview with Paul Weiler, Oct. 2000.

47 Morris Shumiatcher's side of the story is recounted in a letter he wrote to C.A. Wright, 14 Dec. 1965 (Shumiatcher Papers, Saskatchewan Archives Board, 31.11.15.1 [hereafter, Shumiatcher Papers I]), in response to a frank but sensitive letter from Wright explaining that he felt unable to consider him for a position at the law faculty because of the publicity attendant on his recent misfortunes.

48 F. Vaughan, *Aggressive in Pursuit: The Life of Emmett Hall* (Toronto: University of Toronto Press for the Osgoode Society 2004), 100–2.

49 Shumiatcher Papers I, 31.11.15.1, Shumiatcher to Laskin, 14 Aug. 1967.

50 Shumiatcher Papers II, Shumiatcher to Peggy Laskin, 4 Apr. 1984 (personal collection of Jacqueline Shumiatcher).

51 *Schumiatcher v. Attorney General of Saskatchewan* (1964), 47 W.W.R. (n.s.) 57 (C.A.).

52 *Schumiatcher v. Law Society of Saskatchewan* (1967), 58 W.W.R. 465 (C.A.).

53 Shumiatcher Papers I, 31.11.5, Laskin to Shumiatcher, 28 Mar. 1967.

54 See Laskin's correspondence with Dalhousie's Dean Horace Read, one of the team who actually produced a chapter: Dalhousie University Archives, Faculty of Law Papers, MS-1-13 G 607. Laskin wrote Read on 31 Aug. 1966 that the project had to be abandoned.

55 *Report of the Committee of Inquiry into the Industrial Standards Act* (Toronto 1963).

56 *Globe and Mail*, 12, 13 Feb. 1963.

57 *Toronto Daily Star*, 4 Mar. 1964; *Globe and Mail*, 11 Dec. 1964. The total cost of the inquiry was over $16,000, including Laskin's fee of $2,100. For details of Laskin's involvement, see NA, ACTRA fonds, MG 28 I 217/33/12–14. I thank Stephen Waddell, executive director of ACTRA, for granting permission to look at the relevant files and supplying a copy of Laskin's report of 5 Aug. 1964.

58 Bora Laskin, 'Cecil A. Wright: A Personal Memoir,' *University of Toronto Law Journal* 33 (1983): 161.

59 Author interview with R.C.B. Risk, 17 Dec. 2001.

60 The transformation of Osgoode Hall Law School from a Law Society–run enterprise to a faculty affiliated with York University is discussed more fully in the next chapter.

61 S. Djwa, *The Politics of the Imagination: A Life of F.R. Scott* (Toronto: McClelland & Stewart 1987), 362.

Chapter 14: The Accidental Judge

1 Background interview for CBC Tuesday Night, 1975, audiotape at NA, ref. no. 276236.

2 NA, Pearson Papers, MG 26 N3/58/344, Angus to Pearson, 10 Mar. 1965.

3 *Special Public Inquiry 1964. Report of the Commissioner the Honourable Frédéric Dorion* (Ottawa: Queen's Printer 1965).

4 W. Kaplan, *Bad Judgment: The Case of Mr. Justice Leo A. Landreville* (Toronto: University of Toronto Press for the Osgoode Society 1996), 98.

5 *Globe and Mail*, 23 Oct. 1965.

6 What follows is based on a telephone interview with Senator Grafstein, 26 Mar. 2001.

7 K. Davey, *The Rainmaker: A Passion for Politics* (Toronto: Stoddart 1986), 8.

8 Pearson Papers, 160/346 Ont. 12, Macdonald Memorandum, 7 Apr. 1965.

9 Ibid.

10 See the review in W.H. Angus, 'Wanted – A New Method of Appointing

Judges,' *Chitty's Law Journal* 13, no. 9 (Sept. 1965): 249–51, 260; and his 'Judicial Selection in Canada: The Historical Perspective,' *Canadian Legal Studies* 1 (1967): 220–51.

11 Personal communication from Harry Arthurs, 22 May 2002, based on a meeting with Lord Denning in the 1970s.

12 Pearson Papers, 158/341.3 Ont, Linden to Pearson, 22 Apr. 1963; 158/346, MacGuigan to Pearson, 6 June 1964.

13 NA, Diefenbaker Papers, MG 26 M/XII/A/509, Smith to Diefenbaker, 28 Aug. 1957.

14 Pearson Papers, 158/341.3, Chevrier to Pearson, 29 Apr. 1963.

15 I thank Fred Kaufman, formerly of the Quebec Court of Appeal, for drawing this point to my attention.

16 Pearson Papers, 160/346 Ont. 12, Pearson to Robert Winters, 16 July 1963.

17 Author interview with Abraham Lieff, 14 Dec. 2000.

18 Pearson Papers, 160/346, Macdonald to Pearson, 6 July 1965.

19 *Mike: The Memoirs of the Right Honourable Lester B. Pearson*, vol. 3 (Toronto: University of Toronto Press 1975), 222–3: 'A bad judge can do a lot of damage. Thus, in the appointment of judges, my first and exclusive concern was judicial quality and capacity.'

20 On 7 July Lucien Cardin had replaced Guy Favreau as minister of justice, but as both were from Quebec they deferred to Pennell, the senior Ontario minister.

21 Martin Friedland Osgoode Society interview, 6 Oct. 1999.

22 NA, CAUT Papers, MG 28 I 208/146, Smith to Laskin, 5 Aug. 1965.

23 *Globe and Mail*, 25 Aug. 1965.

24 NA, F.R. Scott Papers, reel 1252, vol. 61/4, Milner to Scott, 5 Sept. 1965.

25 Ibid., 'Terry' to Scott, 31 Aug. 1965.

26 Jean Milner diary, 30 Aug. 1965.

27 Ibid., 25–6 Oct., 15 Dec. 1965.

28 Shumiatcher Papers I, R-1728, 31.11.5.2(1), Laskin to Shumiatcher, 29 Oct. 1965, Shumiatcher to Laskin, 10 Nov. 1965.

29 Shumiatcher Papers II, Peggy Laskin to M. and J. Shumiatcher, n.d. [early Dec. 1968].

30 Cited in C. Cole, 'In the Eye of the Storm' (unpublished manuscript, 1995), 332.

31 [York University Archives], Office of President, 1970–014/007/115, H.B.M. Best to M Ross, 22 Jan. 1965, reporting meeting with Arnup.

32 Cole, 'In the Eye of the Storm,' 333.

33 'The Affiliation of Osgoode Hall Law School with York University,'
   University of Toronto Law Journal 17 (1967): 197.

34 I.F.G. Baxter to Leal et al., 19 Mar. 1965, in the possession of Harry
   Arthurs, whom I thank for allowing me access.

35 *Nexus* (University of Toronto Law Alumni magazine), 1982.

36 YUA, Office of the President, 1977–013/014/353, Ross to Laskin, 14 Feb.
   1967; M. Ross, *The Way Must Be Tried: Memoirs of a University Man*
   (Toronto: Stoddart 1992), 115–16.

37 BLI 1977: 77.

38 UTA, Office of the President, A75-002/062, Memo to file, 7 Sept. 1966.

39 Ibid., Wright to Bissell, 30 Nov. 1966, Bissell to Wright, 5 Jan. 1967; R. St
   John Macdonald to the author, 10 July 2001.

40 Author interview with Edward McWhinney, 19 Feb. 2001.

41 Shumiatcher Papers I, 31.11.5.2(1), Laskin to Shumiatcher, 29 Feb. 1968.

42 Author interview with R. St John Macdonald, 2 Nov. 2000.

43 YUA, James Milner Fonds 1992–014/005/132, Milner to Frederick Phillips,
   7 July 1967.

44 Jean Milner diary, 26 Apr. 1967.

45 'Cecil A. Wright: A Personal Memoir,' *University of Toronto Law Journal* 33
   (1983): 154–5.

46 Email communication from I. Kyer, 1 May 2002, who along with J.E.
   Bickenbach was the author of the offending comment about Wright.

47 Ross, *The Way Must Be Tried*, 142.

48 Ibid., 148.

49 I thank Trevor Anderson, now at the University of Manitoba and present
   at the UNB convocation in question, for sharing this anecdote with me,
   23 May 2001.

50 *Freedom and Responsibility in the University. Report of the Presidential Committee on Rights and Responsibilities of Members of York University* (Toronto:
   University of Toronto Press 1970), 3.

51 Ibid., 38.

52 YUA, John Saywell Papers, 1982–014/001/05, Saywell to W.D. Farr,
   secretary to the University, 5 Jan. 1970; also published in York student
   newspaper *Excalibur* (Jan. 1970).

53 Ross, *The Way Must Be Tried*, gives a blow-by-blow account at 151–61.

54 Slater also had a connection to the Crowe case; he was to join the panel of
   inquiry with Laskin until United College challenged him because of an
   alleged conflict of interest.

55 UTA, OISE fonds, A2001-0024/100, Report of the Special Committee on
   Governance and Structure of OISE (Oct. 1969).

56 F.R. Scott Papers, MG 30 D 211/54/12, Scott to Fuller, 12 Sept. 1960 (reel H-1243).

57 B. Schwartz, ed., *The Fourteenth Amendment Centennial Volume* (New York: New York University Press 1970). Laskin's contribution was entitled 'Constitutionalism in Canada: Legislative Power and a Bill of Rights.'

58 L. Kalman, *Abe Fortas: A Biography* (New Haven: Yale University Press 1990).

59 Shumiatcher Papers II, Laskin to Shumiatcher, 24 Sept. 1969.

60 F.R. Scott Papers, MG 30 D 211/85/2.

Chapter 15: Ontario Court of Appeal

1   Author interview with W.Z. Estey, 28 Apr. 2000.

2   E. Anderson, *Judging Bertha Wilson: Law as Large as Life* (Toronto: University of Toronto Press 2001).

3   Author interview with W.Z. Estey, 28 Apr. 2000.

4   H.L. Packer framed the debate in this way in his *The Limits of the Criminal Sanction* (Stanford: Stanford University Press 1968), 149–73.

5   Author interview with Ernest Sirluck, 30 Sept. 2000.

6   Shumiatcher Papers I, 31.11.5.2, Shumiatcher to Laskin, 4 July 1967.

7   [1968] 2 O.R. 129 at 133.

8   [1966] 2 O.R. 675 at 682–3.

9   *Re Silverhill Realty Holdings and Minister of Highways for Ontario*, [1968] 1 O.R. 357 at 365.

10 [1970] 2 O.R. 371.

11 *Re Kalinin and Municipality of Metro Toronto*, [1970] 3 O.R. 536 at 540–1.

12 *Judson* was delivered on 17 Feb. and *Kalinin* on 17 Mar. 1970.

13 *Re Glassman and Council of the College of Physicians and Surgeons*, [1966] 2 O.R. 81.

14 *Law Society of Upper Canada v. French*, [1975] 2 S.C.R. 767. The appellation is that of Hudson Janisch, 'Bora Laskin and Administrative Law: an Unfinished Journey,' *University of Toronto Law Journal* 35 (1985): 575.

15 *R. v. Canada Labour Relations Board, ex parte Martin*, [1966] 2 O.R. 684 at 690.

16 *R. v. Ontario Labour Relations Board, ex parte Hannigan*, [1967] 2 O.R. 469. See also *R. v. Weiler, ex parte Hoar Transport*, [1968] 1 O.R. 705. The third labour case in which Laskin dissented, *Astgen v. Smith*, [1970] 1 O.R. 129, raised an issue of the proper procedure to be followed when two unions wished to merge. Laskin tried to facilitate the merger, his colleagues did not.

17 [1967] 2 O.R. 49.

18 See, e.g., *Cloverdale Shopping Centre and Twp of Etobicoke*, [1966] 2 O.R. 439.

19 [1970] 2 O.R. 683. At the Court of Appeal the case was called *R. v. Tarno-polsky, ex parte Bell.* The Supreme Court disagreed in a decision almost universally criticized by academic opinion; (1971), 18 D.L.R. (3d) 1.

20 [1966] 1 O.R. 763.

21 [1966] 2 O.R. 182.

22 *Sub nom. Taylor Estate v. Wong Aviation Ltd.,* [1969] S.C.R. 481.

23 [1967] 1 O.R. 541. Subsequent decisions of the Ontario Court of Appeal have significantly limited the scope of *Schwebel*, confining it to cases where negligence is alleged against someone exercising a 'common calling,' such as a notary or bailee: see *Robert Simpson Co. v. Foundation Co. of Canada* (1982), 36 O.R. (2d) 97.

24 *Adler v. Adler,* [1966] 1 O.R. 732.

25 *Papp v. Papp,* [1970] 1 O.R. 331. *Papp* was later endorsed by the Supreme Court of Canada in *Zacks v. Zacks,* [1973] S.C.R. 891. Laskin's decision meant that issues of post-divorce custody and support would be dealt with on the basis of uniform principles declared under the federal Act rather than varying from province to province.

26 [1968] 1 O.R. 730.

27 [1967] 1 O.R. 211.

28 See chapter 17.

29 [1971] 1 O.R. 273.

30 'Res ipsa Loquitur,' *Special Lectures of the Law Society of Upper Canada* (Toronto: Richard de Boo 1965). The Latin maxim ('the thing speaks for itself') is shorthand for a doctrine regarding the burden of proof in negligence cases.

31 Background interview for CBC Tuesday Night, 1975, audiotape at NA, ref. no. 276236.

32 *CAUT Bulletin,* May 1984, 22.

33 (1965), 55 D.L.R. (2d) 289 (C.A.).

34 *Globe and Mail,* 1 Dec. 2004.

35 B.J. Wylie, *The Horsburgh Scandal* (Windsor, ON: Black Moss Press 1981).

36 R.C. Smeaton, *The Horsburgh Affair: Disciple or Deviate?* (Toronto: Baxter Publishing 1966), 37.

37 R.D. Horsburgh, *From Pulpit to Prison: A Clergyman's Fight for Justice* (Toronto: Methuen 1969), 2.

38 *R. v. Horsburgh,* 297.

39 Ibid., 306.

40 Ibid., 311.

41 Horsburgh, *From Pulpit to Prison,* 88.

42 (1967), 63 D.L.R. (2d) 699 at 709 (S.C.C.).

43 Horsburgh, *From Pulpit to Prison*, 114–16.

44 *R. v. DeClercq*, [1966] 1 O.R. 674. The previous precedent was *R. v. La Plante*, [1958] O.W.N. 80.

45 *R. v. Maurantonio*, [1968] 1 O.R. 145.

46 Ibid., 146.

47 The Art Gallery of Ontario mounted a retrospective of Markle's work in 2003; see A. Hudson, *Woman as Goddess: Liberated Nudes by Robert Markle and Joyce Wieland* (Toronto: Art Gallery of Ontario 2003).

48 *Saturday Night* (Feb. 1966): 19–21; *Globe and Mail*, 22 May 1965.

49 Rickaby later became Crown attorney of York, and in 1977 served as prosecutor in the murder trial that followed the notorious paedophilic slaying of Yonge St shoe-shine boy Emmanuel Jacques: *Toronto Star* obituary, 10 Aug. 1995.

50 R. Fulford, *The Best Seat in the House: Memoirs of a Lucky Man* (Toronto: Collins 1988), 106–11.

51 Ibid., 105.

52 As cited in *R. v. Cameron*, [1966] 2 O.R. 777 at 784 (C.A.).

53 Author interview with June Callwood, 31 May 2002.

54 *R. v. Cameron*, at 788.

55 Ibid., 798.

56 Ibid., 808.

57 Ibid., 806.

58 Ibid., 805.

59 Ibid., 812.

60 Ibid., 808.

61 Ibid., 805.

62 *R. v. Brodie*, [1962] S.C.R. 681.

63 *R. v. C. Coles Co. Ltd.*, [1965] 1 O.R. 557.

64 [1985] 1 S.C.R. 494.

Chapter 16: On to Ottawa

1 NA, F.R. Scott Papers, MG 30 D 211/62/6, Scott to Laskin, 23 Mar. 1970.

2 21 Mar. 1970.

3 31 July 1967.

4 21 Mar. 1970.

5 Ibid.

6 Personal communication from John Turner, 17 May 2002. In Newfoundland and Quebec, only parliamentary divorce existed prior to the 1968 reform.

7 *Globe and Mail*, 29 Apr. 1970.

8 *Globe and Mail*, 21 Mar. 1970.

9 *Globe and Mail*, 18 Apr. 1970.

10 *NYU Center for International Studies Annual Report 1969–70*. I thank Katie Senft of the NYU Archives for assistance in locating this item.

11 S. Clarkson and C. McCall, *Trudeau and Our Times*, vol. 1 (Toronto: McClelland and Stewart 1991), 118.

12 NA, Molly Lamb Bobak and Bruno Bobak Fonds, MG 30 D378/5/12, Laskin to Bobaks, 10 Apr. 1970. The Laskins had met the Bobaks during the war in Toronto.

13 D. Gruending, *Emmett Hall: Establishment Radical* (Toronto: Macmillan 1985).

14 Hall's second biographer, Frederick Vaughan, covers these aspects of Hall's career extensively in *Aggressive in Pursuit: A Life of Emmett Hall* (Toronto: University of Toronto Press for the Osgoode Society 2004).

15 Osgoode Society interview with Hon. Wishart Flett Spence, Oct. 1985.

16 J.G. Snell and F. Vaughan, *The Supreme Court of Canada: History of the Institution* (Toronto: University of Toronto Press 1985), 230–2.

17 When Judson retired in 1977, Laskin remarked that he had known him 'longer than any other member of this Court; and it was borne in on me, even before I was called to the bar, how quickly he earned a solid reputation as a lawyer's lawyer'; copy at SCC library.

18 Interview with D.C. Abbott, 1 Mar. 1986. I am grateful to Randall Balcome for providing me with a copy of the transcript of this interview, which he conducted in connection with his contribution to *Supreme Court of Canada Decision-Making: The Benchmarks of Rand, Kerwin and Martland* (Toronto: Carswell 1990), co-authored with E.J. McBride and D.A. Russell.

19 *Fleming v. Atkinson*, [1959] S.C.R. 513.

20 *Switzman v. Elbling*, [1957] S.C.R. 285.

21 Abbott interview, 1 Mar. 1986.

22 For biographical details on Martland, see Dawn Russell's contribution to Balcome et al., *Benchmarks* at 253–9.

23 Author interview with Elizabeth Ritchie, 6 Sept. 2000. On Ritchie, see T. Stinson, 'Mr. Justice Roland Ritchie: A Biography,' *Dalhousie Law Journal* 17 (1994): 509–33.

24 Balcome et al., *Benchmarks*, 261.

25 W. Christian, *George Grant: A Biography* (Toronto: University of Toronto Press 1993), 57.

26 [1962] S.C.R. 681.

27 *R. v. Drybones*, [1970] S.C.R. 282.

28 Published in the series *Cahiers de la Faculté des sciences sociales* (Université Laval). It was republished in translation in the *Canadian Bar Review* 25 (1947): 955 with the earnest Laskinian title, 'The Necessity of Law Reform.'

29 L.-P. Pigeon, 'The Meaning of Provincial Autonomy,' *Canadian Bar Review* 29 (1951): 1126–35.

30 *Mélanges Louis-Philippe Pigeon* (Montreal: Wilson & Lafleur 1989), especially remarks by Chief Justice Brian Dickson at 49–51.

31 F.R. Scott Papers, 62/6, Laskin to Scott, 14 Apr. 1970.

32 NA, Emmett Hall Papers, MG 31 E 11/9/109, 'agenda for Tuesday April 28, 1970.'

33 [1970] *Law Society Gazette*, 99.

34 The faculty was very small at the time, allowing Fauteux to serve as dean on a part-time basis.

35 [1970] *Law Society Gazette*, 99.

36 Mohan Singh Jawl author interview, 2 Nov. 2000. Whether any past anti-Semitic practices by the club were an issue for Laskin is not known.

37 Author interview with June Callwood, 31 May 2002.

38 UBC Archives, N.A.M. MacKenzie Papers, 44/6, James Forrester Davidson to MacKenzie, 3 June 1969.

39 NA, Emmett Hall Papers, 9/109, R.J. Doyle to John Cartwright, 20 Jan. 1970 (copy in file).

40 Ibid., 2/13, Hall to George Curtis, 9 Dec. 1970. Hall observed that he did not agree with this policy and had asked his clerk Neil Brooks to prepare a memo on the subject.

41 Ibid., 7/81, Brennan to Ronald Martland, 18 Jan. 1966, attached to Martland to Hall, 24 Jan. 1966.

42 Mohan Singh Jawl author interview, 2 Nov. 2000.

43 Louise Arbour author interview, 18 Feb. 2002.

44 Shumiatcher Papers II, Morris Shumiatcher to Peggy and Bora Laskin, 14 Sept. 1970.

45 'Doing Justice to Bora Laskin,' *Maclean's* (July 1974).

46 *Globe and Mail*, 26 Aug. 1970.

47 Jean Milner diary, 20 Sept. 1970.

48 Shumiatcher Papers II, Morris Shumiatcher to Peggy and Bora Laskin, 14 Sept. 1970.

49 Shumiatcher Papers II, Laskin to Shumiatcher, 20 Jan. 1971. Author interview with Jacqui Shumiatcher, 9 Dec. 2001.

50 Ronald Martland Osgoode Society interview, Oct. 1985.

51 Shumiatcher Papers II, Laskin to Shumiatcher, 17 Dec. 1970, 20 Jan. 1971.

52 R.W. Pound, *Chief Justice W.R. Jackett: By the Law of the Land* (Montreal and Kingston: McGill-Queen's University Press 1999), 197–205.

53 NA, Emmett Hall Papers, 2/16, George Gale to Hall, 7 May 1971, Culliton to Hall, 4 Oct. 1971. A copy of Laskin's conference paper is in 2/15.

54 *R. v. Wray*, [1971] S.C.R. 272. Wray was convicted at his subsequent trial, and the conviction was upheld by both the Ontario Court of Appeal and a unanimous Supreme Court bench on which Laskin sat; *R. v. Wray (No. 2)*, [1974] S.C.R. 565.

55 W. Kaplan, *Bad Judgment: The Case of Mr. Justice Leo A. Landreville* (Toronto: Osgoode Society 1996).

56 On the creation of the council, see Pound, *Jackett*, 206–9.

57 Carleton University Archives, Acc. No. 1996-17.

58 Information supplied by Lakehead University Archives and the President's Office.

59 Shumiatcher Papers II, Laskin to Shumiatcher, 12 Sept. 1971.

60 *Canadian Jewish News*, 29 Jan. 1981.

61 *Israel Law Review* 7 (1972): 330.

62 Ibid., 339.

63 Shumiatcher Papers II, Laskin to Shumiatcher, 1 Aug. 1972.

64 Jean Milner diary, 1 Sept. 1972.

65 Shumiatcher Papers II, Shumiatcher to Laskin, 27 June 1973.

66 University of Saskatchewan Archives, Emmett Hall Papers, MG 70 S1/19, Laskin to Hall, 1 Mar. 1973. Their common friend Reva Gerstein wrote to Hall on his retirement, 'It was particularly heartwarming to see the mutual pleasure both you and Borah [sic] engender in each other. How fortunate that your time on the highest bench in the land overlapped.' Hall Papers, Gerstein to Hall, n.d. [ca. 1973].

67 Ibid., 1/6, Berger to Hall, 18 Apr. 1973; Hall to Berger, 1 May 1973. James Armstrong Richardson, the member for Winnipeg South, was minister of supply and services in the first Trudeau government.

68 See chapter 23.

69 R. Yalden, 'Before the Bench: Brian Dickson as Corporate Lawyer,' in D.J. Guth, ed., *Brian Dickson at the Supreme Court of Canada 1973–1990* (Winnipeg: Supreme Court Historical Society 1998).

70 NA, Emmett Hall Papers, Campbell to Hall, 25 Apr. 1973.

71 R.J. Sharpe and K. Roach, *Brian Dickson: A Judge's Journey* (Toronto: University of Toronto Press for the Osgoode Society 2003), chapters 7 and 8.

Chapter 17: Early Promise

1 Respectively, [1971] S.C.R. 562, [1974] S.C.R. 592, and [1975] 1 S.C.R. 423. In spite of the 1974 reporting date, *Canaero* was heard in May 1972 and the decision released in June 1973. Coincidentally the panel was the same as in

Highway Properties: Martland, Judson, Ritchie, Spence, and Laskin. *Murdoch* was heard on 22–3 March 1973 and the decision released on 2 October 1973.

2 [1974] 2 S.C.R. 1349.

3 [1971] S.C.R. 446.

4 *Highway Properties*, 569.

5 Ibid., 576.

6 'Laskin and Commercial, Contract and Corporate Law,' *University of Toronto Law Journal* 35 (1985): 405.

7 A search of a legal database revealed 391 citations to the end of 2004, almost all positive or neutral.

8 *Canaero*, 607.

9 Ziegel, 'Laskin and Commercial, Contract and Corporate Law,' 418.

10 *Canaero*, 610.

11 [1971] S.C.R. 446.

12 Ibid., 457.

13 *Chula v. Superior Court of California*, 368 P. 2d 107 (1962).

14 *McKeown*, 478.

15 Ibid., 479.

16 Shumiatcher Papers II, Shumiatcher to Laskin, 14 Apr. 1971, reply by Laskin, 23 Apr. 1971. The fact that McKeown does not appear to have been disciplined by the Law Society for his contempt of court conviction provides some indirect evidence that Laskin was correct in his assessment of the reason for the lawyer's absence from court.

17 S.C. 1972, c. 13, s. 4.

18 [1973] S.C.R. 313.

19 *R. v. White and Bob* (1964), 52 W.W.R. 193, 50 D.L.R. 193; [1965] S.C.R. vi.

20 C. Swayze, *Hard Choices: A Life of Tom Berger* (Vancouver and Toronto: Douglas & McIntyre 1987), 109–18. T.R. Berger, *One Man's Justice: A Life in the Law* (Vancouver and Toronto: Douglas & McIntyre 2002), 121–2.

21 NA, Emmett Hall Papers, MG 31 E 11/5/61, Hall to Laskin 7 Sept. 1972.

22 The story of the eclipse of the doctrine of aboriginal rights in British Columbia is well told by H. Foster, 'Letting Go the Bone: The Idea of Indian Title in British Columbia, 1849–1927,' in H. Foster and J. McLaren, eds., *Essays in the History of Canadian Law, vol. VI: British Columbia and the Yukon* (Toronto: University of Toronto Press for the Osgoode Society 1995).

23 *Globe and Mail*, 1 Feb. 1973.

24 University of Saskatchewan Archives, Emmett Hall Papers, MG 70 S1/1/6, Hall to T.G. Norris, 10 October 1974; Campbell to Hall, 25 Apr. 1973.

25 13 Feb. 1973.

26 *Guerin v. Canada*, [1984] 2 S.C.R. 335.

27 (1992),107 A.L.R. 1.

28 *MacKay v. The Queen*, [1980] 2 S.C.R. 370.

29 [1976] 2 S.C.R. 751.

30 [1976] 1 S.C.R. 170.

31 R.J. Sharpe and K. Roach, *Brian Dickson: A Judge's Journey* (Toronto: University of Toronto Press for the Osgoode Society 2003), 127–9.

32 [1975] 1 S.C.R. 693.

33 *Canard*, 177, quoting Dickson's judgment in the Court of Appeal.

34 *Canard*, 184.

35 [1980] 1 S.C.R. 294.

36 [1990] 1 S.C.R. 1075.

37 *Report of the Royal Commission on the Status of Women* (Ottawa: Information Canada 1970).

38 29 Dec. 1973.

39 Sharpe and Roach, *Brian Dickson*, 181.

40 Personal communication from Adrienne Clarkson, 7 Mar. 2003, reporting a conversation with Laskin shortly after his elevation.

41 [1975] 1 S.C.R. 423.

42 'The Human Stories behind the Irene Murdoch/Helen Rathwell Cases,' *Chatelaine* (Sept. 1974). I thank Veronica Girard for bringing this article to my attention. The Rathwell case was factually similar to *Murdoch*. It had been heard only at the trial level at the time this article was written, and Helen Rathwell's claim had been dismissed. It was later upheld in the Saskatchewan Court of Appeal and by the Supreme Court of Canada, [1978] 2 S.C.R. 436.

43 In legal terms, support is distinct from the division of property.

44 *Murdoch*, 451, and see C. Rogerson, 'From *Murdoch* to *Leatherdale*: The Uneven Course of Bora Laskin's Family Law Decisions,' *University of Toronto Law Journal* 35 (1985): 499–505.

45 As quoted in *Rathwell v. Rathwell*, [1976] 5 W.W.R. 148 at 159 (Sask. C.A.).

46 Rogerson, 'From *Murdoch* to *Leatherdale*,' 502–3, citing Laskin in *Murdoch*.

47 [1980] 1 S.C.R. 2.

48 [1982] 2 S.C.R. 743.

49 Rogerson, 'From *Murdoch* to *Leatherdale*,' 495.

50 Ibid., 485.

51 *Rathwell v. Rathwell*, [1978] 2 S.C.R. 436 at 465. Only Spence and Laskin agreed with this particular assertion by Dickson.

52 [1980] 2 S.C.R. 834.

53 *Peter v. Beblow*, [1993] 1 S.C.R. 980. In spite of this decision the law regarding the division of cohabitees' property remains somewhat unpredictable in its application.

54 [1974] 2 S.C.R. 1349. The hearing was held in February 1973 and the decision released on 27 August of the same year.

55 W.S. Tarnopolsky, *The Canadian Bill of Rights*, 2nd rev. ed. (Toronto: McClelland & Stewart 1975), 160.

56 Ibid., 149.

57 *Lavell*, 1383.

58 Ibid., 1387.

59 [1979] 1 S.C.R. 183.

60 See chapter 15.

Chapter 18: Chief Justice

1 Shumiatcher Papers II, Shumiatcher to Laskin, 18 Dec. 1973.

2 Author interview with Otto Lang, 22 May 2001.

3 Author interview with Ed Ratushny, 13 Feb. 2002.

4 24 Dec. 1973.

5 Author interview with Otto Lang, 22 May 2001.

6 *Toronto Star*, 29 Dec. 1973. The *Star* reports Lang's call as having been made on Christmas Eve, but it must have been made earlier. The recently released cabinet conclusions for 1973 show Laskin's appointment as chief justice confirmed at a cabinet meeting on the twentieth, and this is unlikely to have occurred without Laskin having expressed a willingness to take the post.

7 *Globe and Mail*, 29 Dec. 1973.

8 *Toronto Star*, 29 Dec. 1973.

9 *Globe and Mail*, 11 Jan. 1974 (letter to the editor from Joan Wallace of Vancouver Status of Women).

10 26 Jan. 1974. 'The silence of Quebec, traditionally autonomist, has been astonishing ... Canadian institutional traditions are too solidly entrenched for the actions of the new chief justice to amount to more than modest reformism.'

11 [B.C.] *Law Society Gazette* 8 (1974): 121 (address delivered 22 Mar. 1974).

12 Ronald Martland Osgoode Society interview, Oct. 1985.

13 Author interview with John Arnup, 3 Oct. 2000.

14 Ronald Martland Osgoode Society interview, Oct. 1985.

15 *Toronto Star*, 31 Dec. 1973.

16 *Globe and Mail*, 8 Jan. 1974.

17 Sir Fred Phillips to the author, 7 Jan. 2002. The Latin maxim is one applied in the law of wills, meaning 'an incorrect description does not invalidate [a legacy].'

18 *Globe and Mail*, 15 Jan. 1974.

19 Ibid.

20 Before 1949, the chief justice was often named to the Imperial Privy Council and hence styled the Right Honourable; after 1949 such appointments ceased and the chief justices were merely 'Honourable' until 1968, when the title 'Right Honourable' was restored to them; Antonio Lamer, 'A Brief History of the Court,' in *The Supreme Court of Canada and Its Justices* (Ottawa: Supreme Court of Canada 2000), 18.

21 Hence the puisne judges must petition the government to retain the title 'Honourable' upon retirement, while the chief justice does not.

22 L.-P. de Grandpré author interview, 19 Feb. 2002; Ronald Martland Osgoode Society interview, Oct. 1985.

23 Unfortunately Hofley became ill and died in office not long after Laskin, on 22 Jan. 1985.

24 Remarks by Jean Beetz at 2 Apr. 1984 memorial honouring Bora Laskin, Registrar's Papers, Supreme Court of Canada. See also *Mélanges Jean Beetz* (Montreal: Éditions Thémis 1995).

25 L.-P. de Grandpré author interview, 19 Feb. 2002.

26 [1975] 1 S.C.R. 138.

27 *City of Saskatoon v. Shaw*, [1945] S.C.R. 42. On Thorson's career, see I. Bushnell, *The Federal Court of Canada: A History, 1875–1992* (Toronto: Osgoode Society 1997), 124–5, 131.

28 NA, Diefenbaker Papers, MG 26N, ser. VI, micro no. 246348–49, Fulton to Thorson, 23 Nov. 1961. The clipping was from the *Winnipeg Tribune*, 6 Nov. 1961.

29 [1924] S.C.R. 331.

30 *Thorson*, 151.

31 Ibid., 145.

32 Bushnell, *Federal Court*, at 136; see also his discussion of the case in *The Captive Court: A Study of the Supreme Court of Canada* (Montreal and Kingston: McGill-Queen's University Press 1992), 395–9.

33 *R. v. London County Council, ex parte Blackburn*, [1976] 3 All E.R. 184 (C.A.).

34 [1977] 1 All E.R. 696 (C.A.). Laskin referred to both these endorsements when addressing a legal convention in Australia: *Australian Law Journal* 51 (1977): 450–1.

35 *Jones v. Attorney General of New Brunswick*, [1975] 2 S.C.R. 182. The case was heard in February 1974 and the decision released on 2 April.

36 *Smerchanski v. Minister of National Revenue*, [1977] 2 S.C.R. 23; the *Globe and Mail*, 30 June 1976, reported that Thorson had missed by weeks being the oldest lawyer ever to argue before the Supreme Court, the record being set by one W.C. Bentley of Charlottetown in 1960, who argued a case when aged nearly eighty-eight.

37 [1976] 1 S.C.R. 616.

38 *Globe and Mail*, 3 Oct. 1974.

39 *R. v. Morgentaler*, [1988] 1 S.C.R. 30.

40 On the evolution of the decision, see R.J. Sharpe and K. Roach, *Brian Dickson: A Judge's Journey* (Toronto: University of Toronto Press for the Osgoode Society 2003), 9–13.

41 *Morgentaler*, 638.

42 Ibid., 654.

43 Sharpe and Roach, *Brian Dickson*, 14.

44 29 Mar. 1975.

45 *Globe and Mail*, 27 Mar. 1975.

46 NA, Governor General of Canada Fonds, RG 7 Acc. no. 190-91/016/06/512–1.

47 *Globe and Mail*, 26 June 1974.

48 Shumiatcher Papers II, Shumiatcher to Laskin 12 July 1974; reply by Laskin, 14 Aug. 1974.

49 Ibid.

50 The shift caused a minor contretemps: see the letters to the editor, *Toronto Star*, 3 Aug. 1974.

51 What follows draws on an admittedly partisan but somewhat self-critical account by one of the leaders of the Caravan, Vern Harper, *Following the Red Path: The Native People's Caravan, 1974* (Toronto: NC Press 1979), supplemented by newspaper accounts. I thank Norman Zlotkin for drawing this book, and the entire episode, to my attention.

52 P.C. Smith and R.A. Warrior, *Like a Hurricane: The Indian Movement from Alcatraz to Wounded Knee* (New York: New Press 1996). Canadian Mi'kmaq activist Anna Mae Pictou Aquash was present at the 1973 occupation. She was later suspected by AIM of being an FBI informant, and was murdered in South Dakota in late 1975. Former AIM member Arlo Looking Cloud was convicted of her murder in February 2004, and at the time of writing his co-accused John Graham was in Canada fighting an attempt by the United States to extradite him. Catherine Martin's 2003 film *The Spirit of*

Annie Mae provides an excellent introduction to the native politics of the early 1970s.

53 *Globe and Mail*, 1 Oct. 1974.
54 Harper, *Following the Red Path*, 65.

Chapter 19: The Laskin Court

1 S.C. 1974–75–76, c. 18.
2 NA, W.Z. Estey Papers, MG 31/24/2.
3 William McIntyre author interview, 21 Feb. 2001.
4 P. McCormick, 'The Supervisory Role of the Supreme Court of Canada: Analysis of Appeals from Provincial Courts of Appeal, 1949–1990,' *Supreme Court Law Review* 3 (2d) (1992): 7 provides statistics showing the respective proportions of criminal and public law versus private law in the Laskin Court's caseload as 60:40, compared to 45:55 under the chief justices of the 1960s. Under Dickson the private law caseload would decline precipitously to 20 per cent. The exclusion of appeals from the Federal Court of Canada (approximately 15 per cent of the Supreme Court's caseload under Laskin) from these figures is unlikely to alter significantly the proportions shown by McCormick.
5 Shumiatcher Papers II, Peggy Laskin to Shumiatchers, 27 Dec. 1974; Shumiatcher to Laskins, 1 May 1975, 4 July 1975; Laskin to Shumiatcher, 13 Aug. 1975.
6 Ibid., Shumiatcher to Laskin, 2 Sept. 1975.
7 R. St J. Macdonald diary entry of 26 Sept. 1975, based on a conversation with Peggy Laskin at Supreme Court centenary celebration; I thank Professor Macdonald for sharing this entry with me.
8 'Of Judges and Scholars: Reflections in a Centennial Year,' *Canadian Bar Review* 53 (1975): 563.
9 J. Deschênes, *Sur la ligne de feu: autobiographie d'un juge en chef* (Montreal: Stanké 1988), 481–2.
10 L.-P. de Grandpré author interview, 19 Feb. 2002.
11 D.J. Hutchinson, *The Man Who Once Was Whizzer White: A Portrait of Justice Byron R. White* (New York: Free Press 1998).
12 W.Z. Estey Osgoode Society interview, 22 Sept. 1993, 78.
13 Ibid., 83; William McIntyre author interview, 21 Feb. 2001.
14 Supreme Court of Canada, Registrar's Collection, Laskin to Hofley, 6 Apr. 1981.
15 W.Z. Estey author interview, 28 Apr. 2000.

16 E. Maltz, *The Chief Justiceship of Warren Burger 1969–1986* (Columbia: University of South Carolina Press 2000). T.E. Yarborough, *The Burger Court: Justices, Rulings and Legacy* (Santa Barbara: ABC-CLIO 2000).

17 On the creation of the court, see R.W. Pound, *Chief Justice W.R. Jackett: By the Law of the Land* (Montreal and Kingston: McGill-Queen's University Press 1999), 213–5 and I. Bushnell, *The Federal Court of Canada: A History, 1875–1992* (Toronto: Osgoode Society 1997).

18 Pound, *Jackett*, 240, 267–8.

19 This paragraph relies on Bushnell, *Federal Court*, 195–247.

20 *McNamara Construction (Western) Ltd. v. The Queen*, [1977] 2 S.C.R. 654.

21 *Quebec North Shore Paper Co. v. Canadian Pacific Ltd.*, [1977] 2 S.C.R. 1054.

22 Bushnell, *Federal Court*, 244.

23 The following two paragraphs rely heavily on Pound, *Jackett*, at 263–70, supplemented by an interview with W.Z. Estey, 28 Apr. 2000.

24 University of Saskatchewan Archives, Emmett Hall Papers, MG 70 S1/1/8, Hall to Goldenberg, 30 May 1975.

25 On what follows, see W.Z. Estey Osgoode Society interview, 22 Sept. 1993, 66–72.

26 W.Z. Estey Osgoode Society 1979 interview.

27 R.J. Sharpe and K. Roach, *Brian Dickson: A Judge's Journey* (Toronto: University of Toronto Press for the Osgoode Society 2003), 186.

28 Ronald Martland Osgoode Society interview, Oct. 1985.

29 Author interview with L.-P. de Grandpré, 19 Feb. 2002.

30 Author interview with Clarke Hunter, 23 Oct. 2000.

31 *Maclean's*, 12 Feb. 1979.

32 W.H. McConnell, *William R. McIntyre: Paladin of the Common Law* (Montreal: McGill-Queen's University Press 2000).

33 W.R. Young, ed., *Paul Martin: The London Diaries 1975–1979* (Ottawa: University of Ottawa Press 1988), 130. The skeleton is encased in a wax effigy.

34 *Current Legal Problems* 29 (1976): 25.

35 'Address at the Special Convocation of the Hebrew University of Jerusalem held on Mount Scopus on Sunday, August 22, 1976' at 2. I thank Yael Wyant of the Faculty of Law, Hebrew University of Jerusalem for providing copies of correspondence with Chief Justice Laskin regarding his visit.

36 Yeshiva University Archives, Presidential Correspondence, Laskin to Norman Lamm, 25 Jan. 1977.

37 Laskin made some controversial remarks there on a point of constitutional law that are considered below in chapter 21.

38 Author interview with Edward McWhinney, 19 Feb. 2001.

39 *Harvard University Gazette*, 7 June 1979. Author interview with Paul Weiler, Oct. 2000.

40 See obituaries in *Toronto Star*, 10 May 1978, *Globe and Mail*, 9 May 1978.

41 UTA, Albert S. Abel Papers, B82-0014/17, Laskin to Abel, 27 May 1970, raising the possibility of Abel taking over the volume.

42 Ibid., Laskin to Abel, 13 Sept. 1973. Laskin agrees with some editorial excisions Abel has made but says nothing about the civil liberties section. See W.S. Tarnopolsky, 'F.R. Scott, Civil Libertarian,' in S. Djwa and R. St J. Macdonald, eds., *On F.R. Scott: Essays on His Contributions to Law, Literature, and Politics* (Kingston and Montreal: McGill-Queen's University Press 1983), 140.

43 Abel Papers, Marvin Lee to Abel, 17 July 1975.

44 'The Anti-Inflation Judgment: Right Answer to the Wrong Question?' *University of Toronto Law Journal* 26 (1976): 409–50.

45 Shumiatcher Papers II, Bora to Shumiatchers, 15 Sept. 1977; Peggy to Shumiatchers, 12 Oct. 1977; Bora to Shumiatchers, 20 Dec. 1977.

46 Shumiatcher Papers II, Shumiatcher to Laskin, 10 July 1978. Shumiatcher is repeating to Laskin the substance of an earlier telephone conversation between them.

47 Author interview with William Braithwaite, 7 Nov. 2000.

48 Wishart Flett Spence Osgoode Society interview, Oct. 1985.

49 *Toronto Star*, 3 July 1978.

50 Shumiatcher Papers II, Laskin to Shumiatcher, 17 Aug. 1978; Shumiatcher note to self re telephone call from Ted Culliton, 22 Aug. 1978.

51 Ibid., Shumiatcher to Laskin, 3 Sept. 1978.

52 Ibid., Morris Shumiatcher note to self 1 Apr. 1979 re telephone call to Peggy.

53 I thank Dr Carl Abbott of the Faculty of Medicine at Dalhousie for discussing with me the symptoms of Addison's Disease and the state of medical knowledge and treatment protocols in the late 1970s.

54 Shumiatcher Papers II, Shumiatcher note to self 1 Apr. 1979 re telephone call to Peggy.

55 *Toronto Star*, 29 Sept. 1979; *Winnipeg Tribune*, 22 Oct. 1979.

56 NA, W.Z. Estey Papers, MG 31–72/24/3, Estey to Laskin, 30 Nov. 1979, Laskin to Estey, 3 Dec. 1979.

57 G. Robertson, *Memoirs of a Very Civil Servant: Mackenzie King to Trudeau* (Toronto: University of Toronto Press 2000), 314.

58 Author interview with Clarke Hunter, 23 Oct. 2000; Philippe Lalonde author interview, 31 Oct. 2000.

59 John Manley to the author, 1 Aug. 2002.

60 Copy available at NA, ref. no. 234925.
61 *Maclean's*, 21 Aug. 1978, 56.
62 *Winnipeg Tribune*, 11 Sept. 1979.
63 *Maclean's*, 15 Oct. 1979.
64 Author interview with Antonio Lamer, 5 Sept. 2002.

Chapter 20: The Great Dissenter

1 'The Institutional Character of the Judge,' *Israel Law Review* 7 (1972): 340.
2 [1976] 2 S.C.R. 200.
3 R.J. Sharpe and K. Roach analyse the case from Dickson's point of view in *Brian Dickson: A Judge's Journey* (Toronto: University of Toronto Press for the Osgoode Society 2003), 148–53.
4 *Harrison*, 219.
5 Ibid., 207.
6 Ibid., 208.
7 *Peters v. The Queen* (1971), 17 D.L.R. (3d) 128 (S.C.C.).
8 See chapter 10.
9 H.W. Arthurs, 'Comment,' *Canadian Bar Review* 43 (1965): 357–63.
10 B. Wilson, 'We Didn't Volunteer,' *Policy Options* (Apr. 1999): 8–9.
11 P.C. Weiler, 'Of Judges and Scholars: Reflections in a Centennial Year,' *Canadian Bar Review* 53 (1975): 554–6.
12 J.G. Snell and F. Vaughan, *The Supreme Court of Canada: History of the Institution* (Toronto: University of Toronto Press for the Osgoode Society 1985), 233. The Court heard 158 division of powers cases in the Laskin-Dickson years (1970–89): K. Swinton, 'Dickson and Federalism: In Search of the Right Balance,' *Manitoba Law Journal* 20 (1991): 483–518.
13 *Manitoba v. Air Canada*, [1980] 2 S.C.R. 303.
14 *Re Anti-Inflation Act*, [1976] 2 S.C.R. 373 at 433.
15 G.D. Finlayson, *John J. Robinette, Peerless Mentor: An Appreciation* (Toronto: Osgoode Society 2003), 363. Goudge was representing the Ontario Public Sector Employees Union.
16 Ibid., 362.
17 P.H. Russell, 'The *Anti-Inflation* Case: The Anatomy of a Constitutional Decision,' *Canadian Public Administration* 20 (1977): 632–65.
18 See chapter 9.
19 [1946] A.C. 193.
20 As cited in *Re Anti-Inflation Act*, 416.
21 *Re Anti-Inflation Act*, 458.
22 Ibid., 445.

23 A.W. MacKay, 'The Supreme Court of Canada and Federalism: Does/
    Should Anyone Care Anymore?' *Canadian Bar Review* 80 (2001): 263.
24 P. Hogg, *Constitutional Law of Canada* (Scarborough, ON: Thomson 1997),
    17–26. Professor Hogg's fear that 'this means that the federal Parliament
    can use its emergency power almost at will' seems not to have been borne
    out by actual practice to date.
25 'The Anti-Inflation Judgment: Right Answer to the Wrong Question?'
    University of Toronto Law Journal 26 (1976): 409–50.
26 Russell, *'Anti-Inflation Case,'* 665.
27 *R. v. Crown Zellerbach*, [1988] 1 S.C.R. 401.
28 'The Anti-Inflation Act Reference: Two Models of Canadian Federalism,'
    Ottawa Law Review 9 (1977): 178.
29 'The Anti-Inflation Case: The Shutters are Closed But the Back Door is
    Wide Open,' *Osgoode Hall Law Journal* 15 (1977): 405.
30 [1980] 1 S.C.R. 844.
31 [1980] 1 S.C.R. 914.
32 I rely here on discussions with Justice Estey while serving as his law clerk
    in 1979–80.
33 [1977] 2 S.C.R. 134.
34 *General Motors v. City National Leasing*, [1989] 1 S.C.R. 641.
35 *Canadian Constitutional Law*, 4th ed. rev. (1975), 523. This position was
    abandoned by Laskin's clerk Neil Finkelstein in the posthumous fifth
    edition.
36 [1974] S.C.R. 695.
37 [1980] 1 S.C.R. 1031. Laskin's position finds some support in K. Wilkins,
    'Of Provinces and Section 35 Rights,' *Dalhousie Law Journal* 22 (1999):
    185–235.
38 [1976] 2 S.C.R. 751. All the judges reached this result by various routes.
39 [1979] 1 S.C.R. 754.
40 Sharpe and Roach, *Brian Dickson*, 38.
41 [1978] 1 S.C.R. 152 at 159.
42 [1979] 1 S.C.R. 984.
43 *Schneider v. The Queen*, [1982] 2 S.C.R. 112.
44 *Canada (Attorney General) v. CN Transportation*, [1983] 2 S.C.R. 206; *R. v.
    Wetmore*, [1983] 2 S.C.R. 284.
45 P. Hogg, *Constitutional Law of Canada* (Scarborough, ON: Thomson/
    Carswell 1997), 19-17.
46 [1976] 2 S.C.R. 349.
47 Ibid., 354–5.
48 Ibid., 358.

49 [1978] 2 S.C.R. 662.
50 [1978] 2 S.C.R. 770.
51 [1976] 2 S.C.R. 265.
52 *McNeil*, 691.
53 In her book *The Supreme Court and Canadian Federalism: The Laskin-Dickson Years* (Toronto: Carswell 1990), Katherine Swinton finds convincing the rationale of the majority decision in *McNeil* without noting that her judicial hero, Brian Dickson, joined Laskin in dissent.
54 *McNeil*, 672.
55 Ibid., 675.
56 *Le Devoir*, 21 Jan. 1978.
57 'Jean Beetz sur la société libre et démocratique,' *Revue Juridique Thémis* 28 (1998): 'On re-reading my reasons I find myself becoming terribly conservative, but that is the way I am and I cannot change it.'
58 As cited in *Dupond*, 791.
59 Ibid., 776.
60 Ibid., 779.
61 Ibid., 780.
62 R.J. Sharpe, 'Laskin and Civil Liberties,' *University of Toronto Law Journal* 35 (1985): 651–4.
63 B. Laskin, 'The Supreme Court and the Protection of Civil Liberties,' *Alberta Law Review* 14 (1976): 135–7.
64 P. Hogg, *Constitutional Law of Canada* (Scarborough, ON: Thomson 2002), s. 18. 11.
65 In *Re Ontario Film and Video Appreciation Society* (1984), 45 O.R. (2d) 80 the Ontario Court of Appeal held that a provincial censorship law violated the Charter without even mentioning *McNeil*.
66 13 May 1978.
67 'Bora Laskin and Federalism,' *University of Toronto Law Journal* 35 (1985): 353–91. A professor at the University of Toronto Faculty of Law and sometime labour arbitrator, Swinton again followed in Laskin's footsteps when she was named to the Ontario Court (General Division) in 1997.
68 See further MacKay, 'The Supreme Court of Canada and Federalism,' 260–3; and on Laskin's influence on Dickson in these fields, Sharpe and Roach, *Brian Dickson*, 155–8, 240–50.
69 [1978] 1 S.C.R. 1021.
70 [1969] 1 O.R. 152, rev'd. [1971] S.C.R. 184.
71 *Rourke*, 1029.
72 At 1040.
73 *R. v. Askov*, [1990] 2 S.C.R. 1199.

74 [1975] 1 S.C.R. 729.

75 Ibid., 751.

76 Ibid., 752.

77 [1969] 4 C.C.C. 3 (Ont. C.A.). On what follows, see J.Ll. Edwards, 'Bora
Laskin and the Criminal Law,' *University of Toronto Law Journal* 35 (1985):
325–52.

78 [1978] 2 S.C.R. 487.

79 [1982] 2 S.C.R. 418.

80 *R. v. Mack*, [1988] 2 S.C.R. 903. Lamer, who had joined Estey's dissent in
Amato, wrote for a unanimous Court.

81 [1981] 1 S.C.R. 640.

82 *R. v. Hebert*, [1990] 2 S.C.R. 151.

83 [1972] S.C.R. 889.

84 [1972] S.C.R. 926.

85 Ibid., 952–3.

86 [1975] 2 S.C.R. 574.

87 *R. v. Therens*, [1985] 1 S.C.R. 613.

88 Sharpe, 'Laskin and Civil Liberties.'

89 *R. v. Burnshine*, [1975] 1 S.C.R. 693.

90 [1976] 1 S.C.R. 170.

91 [1979] 2 S.C.R. 435.

92 Ibid., 445.

93 Sharpe and Roach, *Brian Dickson*, 406–7.

94 [1980] 2 S.C.R. 370.

95 *MacKay*, 380.

96 Ibid., 379.

97 Ibid., 386.

98 Ibid., 410.

99 [1992] 1 S.C.R. 259.

Chapter 21: Architect of Public Law

1 [1974] 1 S.C.R. 335 (decided in May 1973).

2 [1975] 1 S.C.R. 630. The case was heard and decided in 1974 though not
reported until the next year.

3 *Jacmain v. Attorney General of Canada and Public Service Staff Relations Board*,
[1978] 2 S.C.R. 15 at 29.

4 [1979] 2 S.C.R. 227.

5 *McLeod v. Egan*, [1975] 1 S.C.R. 517.

6 *C.U.P.E.*, 236.

7 *Volvo Canada Ltd. v. U.A.W., Local 720*, [1980] 1 S.C.R. 178.

8 [1982] 1 S.C.R. 923.

9 R.J. Sharpe and K. Roach discuss *C.U.P.E.* in *Brian Dickson: A Judge's Journey* (Toronto: University of Toronto Press for the Osgoode Society 2003), 173–5.

10 I thank Rollie Thompson, a Dickson clerk in 1978–9, for discussing his recollections of the decision-writing process in *C.U.P.E.* with me on 22 Sept. 2004.

11 [1983] 1 S.C.R. 245 at 250.

12 Ibid., 258. On the issue of remedial powers of boards, see also Laskin's judgment in *Tomko v. Nova Scotia (Labour Relations Board)*, [1977] 1 S.C.R. 112.

13 [1979] 1 S.C.R. 311.

14 [1976] 1 S.C.R. 453. Dickson's biographers identify *Howarth* as the first LSD dissent: *Brian Dickson*, 164.

15 *Brian Dickson*, 164.

16 *Mitchell v. The Queen*, [1976] 2 S.C.R. 570.

17 Ibid., 575.

18 Ibid., 577.

19 In R. St J. Macdonald, ed., *Changing Legal Objectives* (Toronto: University of Toronto Press 1963), 32.

20 [1979] 1 S.C.R. 62.

21 D. Dyzenhaus and E. Fox-Decent, 'Rethinking the Process/Substance Distinction: *Baker v. Canada*,' *University of Toronto Law Journal* 51 (2001): 195–242. The authors add *Baker*, a decision of Justice Claire L'Heureux-Dubé, as the fourth member of this exclusive club; see [1999] 2 S.C.R. 817.

22 I. Scott with N. McCormick, *To Make a Difference: A Memoir* (Toronto: Stoddart 2001), 66.

23 *Nicholson*, 321. As to Laskin's initial doubts, see Sharpe and Roach, *Brian Dickson*, 166.

24 *Nicholson*, 320.

25 'Fairness: The New Natural Justice,' *University of Toronto Law Journal* 25 (1975): 281, cited by Laskin in *Nicholson* at 325.

26 *Nicholson*, 323.

27 *Bates v. Lord Hailsham*, [1972] 1 W.L.R. 1373 (Q.B.).

28 *Nicholson*, 335.

29 [1981] 2 S.C.R. 181.

30 Per Justice Wilson in the Court of Appeal, as cited by Laskin in *Bhadauria*, 193.

31 For additional information on Dr Bhadauria, Wilson's decision, and the

reaction to it, see E. Anderson, *Judging Bertha Wilson: Law as Large as Life* (Toronto: University of Toronto Press for the Osgoode Society 2001), 121–4.

32 H. Kopyto, 'The Bhadauria Case: The Denial of the Right to Sue for Discrimination,' *Queen's Law Journal* 7 (1981): 146. See generally Walker, *'Race,' Rights and the Law in the Supreme Court of Canada* (Waterloo: Wilfrid Laurier Press for the Osgoode Society 1997), 237–40.

33 'The Stillborn Tort of Discrimination: *Bhadauria v. Board of Governors of Seneca College of Applied Arts and Technology*,' *Ottawa Law Review* 14 (1982): 226.

34 'The McRuer Report: Lawyers' Values and Civil Servants' Values,' *University of Toronto Law Journal* 18 (1968): 351.

35 Walker, *'Race,' Rights and the Law*, 240–1.

36 *Gay Alliance Toward Equality v. Vancouver Sun*, [1979] 2 S.C.R. 435 at 439.

37 Ibid., 444.

38 Ibid., 447.

39 This is particularly true in the field of labour history. See J. Fudge and E. Tucker, *Labour before the Law* (Toronto: Oxford University Press 2001); A. Finkel, 'The Cold War, Alberta Labour, and the Social Credit Regime,' in L.S. MacDowell and I. Radforth, eds., *Canadian Working Class History: Selected Readings* (Toronto: Canadian Scholars' Press 1992).

40 For a review of similar problems under the *Canadian Human Rights Act*, see *Promoting Equality: A New Vision* (Ottawa: Department of Justice 2000). This report was authored by the Canadian Human Rights Act Review Panel, chaired by the retired Justice Gérard La Forest of the Supreme Court of Canada.

41 *Mike Naraine and Ontario Human Rights Commission v. Ford Motor Company of Canada* (1996) 27 C.H.R.R. D/230: D/233 (per board of inquiry Constance Backhouse). The complaint in this matter was filed in 1985, and eight years elapsed before a board of inquiry was appointed.

42 A.A. Borovoy, *When Freedoms Collide* (Toronto: Lester & Orpen Dennys 1988), 224; Walker, *'Race,' Rights and the Law*, 238 n252.

43 W. Lahey and D. Ginn, 'After the Revolution: Being Pragmatic and Functional in Canada's Trial Courts and Courts of Appeal,' *Dalhousie Law Journal* 25 (2002): 259–354.

44 'Comparative Constitutional Law – Common Problems: Australia, Canada, United States of America,' *Australian Law Journal* 51 (1977): 457 (emphasis added).

45 B. Laskin, review of B.L. Strayer, *Judicial Review of Legislation in Canada* (Toronto: University of Toronto Press 1968), *University of Toronto Law Journal* 19 (1969): 86–9.

46 See the discussion in chapter 9.
47 'Comment,' *Canadian Bar Review* 49 (1971): 365.
48 'Is Judicial Review Guaranteed by the British North America Act?' *Canadian Bar Review* 54 (1976): 730.
49 [1981] 2 S.C.R. 220 at 236.
50 David Mullan traces the mutations in Laskin's thought on the subject in 'The Constitutional Position of Canada's Administrative Appeal Tribunals,' *Ottawa Law Review* 14 (1982): 239–69.
51 [1975] 2 S.C.R. 767.
52 Ibid., 773.
53 *MacMillan Bloedel v. Simpson*, [1995] 4 S.C.R. 725.
54 H. Janisch, 'Bora Laskin and Administrative Law: An Unfinished Journey,' *University of Toronto Law Journal* 35 (1985): 570–1.

Chapter 22: Patriation

1 P.E. Trudeau, 'Convocation Speech at the Opening of the Bora Laskin Law Library,' *University of Toronto Law Journal* 41 (1991): 302–3.
2 R.J. Sharpe and K. Roach, *Brian Dickson: A Judge's Journey* (Toronto: University of Toronto Press for the Osgoode Society 2003), 279.
3 Trudeau, 'Convocation Speech,' 296.
4 'Some Aspects of Canadian Constitutionalism,' *Canadian Bar Review* 38 (1960): 134–62 (delivered as the Oliver Wendell Holmes Lecture at Harvard Law School on 26 Feb. 1960).
5 C. McCall and S. Clarkson, *Trudeau and Our Times, vol. I: The Magnificent Obsession* (Toronto: McClelland & Stewart 1990).
6 *Reference re Legislative Authority of Parliament to Alter or Replace the Senate*, [1980] 1 S.C.R. 54.
7 S. Djwa, *A Life of F.R. Scott: The Politics of the Imagination* (Montreal: McGill-Queen's University Press 1987), 443.
8 F.R. Scott Papers, 83/25, Laskin to Scott, 4 Mar. 1982. Scott would outlive Laskin, but by less than a year; he died in January 1985.
9 McCall and Clarkson, *Magnificent Obsession*, 346–7.
10 *Globe and Mail*, 5 May 1981.
11 McCall and Clarkson, *Magnificent Obsession*, 350.
12 Sharpe and Roach, *Brian Dickson*, 269.
13 On the founding and progress of the Institute, see E.M. Culliton Papers, Saskatchewan Archives Board, R-1516, III.4.a, b. The quotation is from an undated 1978 document in the file.
14 Shumiatcher Papers II, Peggy Laskin to Shumiatchers, n.d. [July-Aug. 1981].

15 W.Z. Estey Osgoode Society interview, 4 Nov. 1993, 159.

16 Alan Young author interview, 10 Oct. 2000.

17 Kathy (de Jong) Tomaszewski author interview, 27 Mar. 2001.

18 *Reference re the Amendment of the Constitution of Canada*, [1981] 1 S.C.R. 753 [hereafter, *Patriation Reference*].

19 W.H. McConnell, *William R. McIntyre: Paladin of the Common Law* (Montreal: McGill-Queen's University Press 2000), 106.

20 *Patriation Reference*, 880.

21 *Gallant v. The King*, [1949] 2 D.L.R. 425.

22 *Canadian Bar Review* 60 (1982): 314.

23 *Patriation Reference*, 849.

24 *Patriation Reference*, 852.

25 See above, chapter 14.

26 B. Laskin, 'Amendment of the Constitution,' *University of Toronto Law Journal* 15 (1964): 190.

27 *Patriation Reference*, 866.

28 *Hansard*, 1940, 1117.

29 As cited in *Patriation Reference*, 870.

30 Ibid., 871.

31 W.Z. Estey Osgoode Society interview, 4 Nov. 1993, 162–3.

32 For an insiders' account, see R. Romanow, J. Whyte, and H. Leeson, *Canada ... Notwithstanding: The Making of the Constitution 1976–1982* (Toronto: Carswell/Methuen 1984).

33 *Manuel v. Attorney-General*, [1982] 3 W.L.R. 821.

34 *Re Objection to a Resolution to Amend the Constitution*, [1982] 2 S.C.R. 793.

35 Kathy (de Jong) Tomaszewski author interview, 27 Mar. 2001.

Chapter 23: The Berger Affair

1 William McIntyre author interview, 21 Feb. 2001.

2 *Imperial Oil v. Oil, Chemical and Atomic Workers Union*, [1963] S.C.R. 584.

3 Berger has recently reviewed the matter in his autobiography, *One Man's Justice: A Life in the Law* (Vancouver: Douglas & McIntyre 2002), 146–64, and it was previously treated by his biographer; C. Swayze, *Hard Choices: A Life of Tom Berger* (Vancouver: Douglas & McIntyre 1987), 172–91. Most of the major documents can be found in *McGill Law Journal* 28 (1983): 378–436. Only those not found there are footnoted in what follows.

4 10 Nov. 1981.

5 18 Nov. 1981.

6 See chapter 24.

7 Thomas Berger Papers, UBC Archives, 28/6, Laskin to Berger, 17 June 1982. Berger reprints Laskin's letter in full in his autobiography at 157–8.
8 Ibid., 30/6, McGillivray to Laskin, 4 Aug. 1982.
9 Ibid., 30/6, Berger to Scott, 12 July 1982.
10 Walter Pitman, president, CCLA, to Bora Laskin, 25 May 1982, copy in Berger Papers, 30/6.
11 Thomas Berger author interview, 21 Feb. 2001.
12 *Gazette* (Montreal), 8 June 1982.
13 *Globe and Mail*, 3 Sept. 1982; Swayze, *Hard Choices*, 189. A text of Laskin's speech can be found in the Berger Papers, 29/7.
14 *Globe and Mail*, 4 Sept. 1982.
15 Berger Papers, 30/6, Scott to Berger, 23 June 1982.
16 William McIntyre author interview, 21 Feb. 2001; R.J. Sharpe and K. Roach, *Brian Dickson: A Judge's Journey* (Toronto: University of Toronto Press for the Osgoode Society 2003), 365–66.
17 R.W. Pound, *Chief Justice W.R. Jackett: By the Law of the Land* (Montreal: McGill-Queen's University Press 1999), 206–9.
18 A contrary view is expressed by Jeremy Webber, 'The Limits to Judges' Free Speech: A Comment on the Report of the Committee of Investigation into the Conduct of the Hon. Mr. Justice Berger,' *McGill Law Journal* 29 (1984): 369–404.
19 H.N. Hirsch, *The Enigma of Felix Frankfurter* (New York: Basic Books 1981), 23.
20 N. Lacey, *A Life of H.L.A. Hart: The Nightmare and the Noble Dream* (Oxford and New York: Oxford University Press 2004), 271.
21 Stephen Toope author interview, 19 Feb. 2002. Former Dean Brierley died before I could interview him about his conversation with Laskin.
22 *One Man's Justice*, 163.

Chapter 24: Final Years

1 W.Z. Estey author interview, 28 Apr. 2000.
2 R.C.B. Risk and J.R.S. Prichard, 'Introduction,' *University of Toronto Law Journal* 35 (1985): 321–2.
3 Jean Milner author interview, 20 May 2002.
4 Shumiatcher Papers II, Laskin to Shumiatcher, 7 Mar. 1982. E. Anderson, *Judging Bertha Wilson: Law as Large as Life* (Toronto: University of Toronto Press for the Osgoode Society 2001), 150–1.
5 [1982] 2 S.C.R. 536.
6 K. Macpherson, *When in Doubt, Do Both: The Times of My Life* (Toronto:

University of Toronto Press 1994), 243–4. Macpherson's husband, the political theorist C.B. Macpherson, had spent his career at the University of Toronto.

7 Shumiatcher Papers II, Laskin to Shumiatcher, 7 Mar. 1982.

8 Antonio Lamer author interview, 5 Sept. 2002. *Le Droit* (Hull, Quebec), 7 Apr. 1982.

9 Shumiatcher Papers II, Laskin to Shumiatcher, 14 June 1982. Alan Young author interview, 10 Oct. 2000. *Globe and Mail*, 24, 25 June 1982.

10 Author interview with William McIntyre, 21 Feb. 2001; Author interview with W.Z. Estey, 28 Apr. 2000.

11 Author interview with William McIntyre, 21 Feb. 2001. Shumiatcher referred gingerly to the incident a few weeks later, after Bora had suffered a stroke-like episode and been forbidden from working: 'What bad luck, Bora, after our dinner, to have been packed off for tests and banished from the court for six weeks. Obviously, your doctor has treated you more rigorously than you treated my friend and client, Joe Borowski.' Shumiatcher to Laskin, 18 May 1982, Shumiatcher Papers II.

12 Private information.

13 *Minister of Justice and Minister of Finance v. Borowski*, [1981] 2 S.C.R. 575. Borowski's case was never heard on the merits, having been overtaken by the enactment of the Charter of Rights.

14 *Ottawa Citizen*, 7 Oct. 1982; Shumiatcher Papers I, 31.11.5.2(2), Barbara Laskin to Shumiatchers, n.d. [late 1982].

15 *Thunder Bay Chronicle-Journal*, 27 Mar. 1984.

16 Shumiatcher Papers II, Morris Shumiatcher note to self re conversation with Ted Culliton, 11 August 1983; Peggy Laskin to Shumiatchers, 23 June 1983.

17 Private information.

18 NA, Estey Papers, MG 31–72/24/3, Estey to Wilson and Lamer, 7 Nov. 1983; Estey to Laskin, 18 Nov. 1983.

19 [1985] 1 S.C.R. 177. The bench of six split evenly: Wilson wrote a judgment declaring that the existing procedure offended the Canadian Charter of Rights and Freedoms, while Beetz found it to contravene the Canadian Bill of Rights.

20 Private information.

21 Private information.

22 Sir Fred Phillips to the author, 7 Jan. 2002.

23 *Globe and Mail*, 29 Mar. 1984.

24 *Hansard*, 27 Mar. 1984, 2464–6.

25 *Globe and Mail*, 29 Mar. 1984.

26 *Globe and Mail*, 4 Feb. 1963.
27 *Montreal Gazette*, 28 Mar. 1984.
28 29 Mar. 1984.
29 29 Mar. 1984.
30 *Ottawa Citizen*, 29 May 1984.
31 Shumiatcher Papers I, 31.11.5.2(1), memo to file, 29 May 1984.
32 Ibid., Shumiatcher to John Laskin and Barbara Laskin Plumptre, 14 Aug. 1984.

Epilogue

1 G. Finlayson, *John J. Robinette, Peerless Mentor: An Appreciation* (Toronto: Dundurn Group for the Osgoode Society 2003), 200.
2 H.P. Glenn, 'Persuasive Authority,' *McGill Law Journal* 32 (1987): 261–97.
3 D. Réaume, 'The Judicial Philosophy of Bora Laskin,' *University of Toronto Law Journal* 35 (1985): 464–6.
4 *R. v. Oakes*, [1986] 1 S.C.R. 103.
5 *Irwin Toy v. Quebec (Attorney General)*, [1989] 1 S.C.R. 927 (provincial ban on advertising directed at children under the age of thirteen upheld in spite of impact on freedom of expression).
6 The *Globe and Mail*, 20 Sept. 2004, reported that participation records continue to be broken across Canada including, interestingly, in Quebec. Some $340 million for cancer research has been raised under the banner of the Terry Fox Run since his death, and the event is held in fifty countries. A second monument to Fox was erected directly across from the Parliament Buildings in Ottawa in 1998.

Illustration Credits

Archives of Ontario: Holy Blossom Temple, c. 1950 (F 1405, 23-83, MSR 7037 #3, I0005805).

Art Gallery of Ontario: Robert Nelson Markle, Canadian 1936–1990, Charcoal and tempera on paper, 89.1 × 58.4 cm, *Paramour (1965)*, Art Gallery of Ontario, Toronto. Purchased with funds donated by AGO Members, 2001.

Canadian Association of University Teachers: Bora Laskin receiving Milner Award (copy provided courtesy of Jean Milner).

CP Images: Andy Clark photo of Pierre Trudeau consoling Peggy Laskin and Barbara Laskin Plumptre, 1984.

Harvard Law School Library, Special Collections Department, Art & Visual Materials: Felix Frankfurter, 1935.

Harvard University Archives: Bora Laskin receiving honorary degree (HUP-SF Commencement 1979, folder 2, #22a); Langdell Hall (HUV Langdell Hall, folder 3, #4a).

Jacqueline Shumiatcher personal collection: Laskins and Shumiatchers at Lake O'Hara.

Lakehead University, Chancellor Paterson Library: Laskin family c. 1919 (*Northern Mosaic* 10, no. 3 (July-September 1986)).

Law Society of Upper Canada Archives, Photograph collection: Graduation photo of Bora Laskin 1936 (P469); resignation of Laskin et al. from Osgoode Hall Law School, 1949 (P41).

Library and Archives Canada: Supreme Court judges, Governor General and Madame Léger, 1978 (E002713266, reproduced with kind permission of Anne Roland, registrar of the Supreme Court of Canada); cartoon by Duncan Macpherson (reproduction by kind permission of Mrs Dorothy Macpherson).

Hon. R. Roy McMurtry personal collection: Bora Laskin receiving Beth Sholom Brotherhood Humanitarian Award.

Murray Mosher Photography: Colin Price photo of Bora and Peggy Laskin at home.

Thunder Bay Historical Museum Society: Laskin as editor of yearbook (*Oracle*, 1930); Laskin on the rugby team (*Oracle*, 1929).

University of Toronto Archives: rowing team (A65-0004/1045); W.P.M. Kennedy (A1978-0041/011(48)); F.C. Auld (A1978-0041/001(27)); N.A.M. MacKenzie (A1978-0041/014(25)); Jacob Finkelman (A1978-0041/007(08)); moot club (A65-0004/047(31)); Peggy Tenenbaum Laskin (A1973-0026); Bora Laskin, ca 1960 (photo by Ballad & Jarrett, A1978-0041/012(52); Bora Laskin receiving honorary degree from OISE (photo by Robert Lonsdale, A1978-0041/012(52)).

University of Toronto, Faculty of Law: Law school at 45 St. George St.; Baldwin House.

Windsor Star: Conciliation Board; Ford Motor Company of Canada representatives.

Index

1981 David H. Flaherty, ed., *Essays in the History of Canadian Law: Volume I*
1982 Marion MacRae and Anthony Adamson, *Cornerstones of Order: Court-houses and Town Halls of Ontario, 1784–1914*
1983 David H. Flaherty, ed., *Essays in the History of Canadian Law: Volume II*
1984 Patrick Brode, *Sir John Beverley Robinson: Bone and Sinew of the Compact*
      David Williams, *Duff: A Life in the Law*
1985 James Snell and Frederick Vaughan, *The Supreme Court of Canada: History of the Institution*
1986 Paul Romney, *Mr Attorney: The Attorney General for Ontario in Court, Cabinet, and Legislature, 1791–1899*
      Martin Friedland, *The Case of Valentine Shortis: A True Story of Crime and Politics in Canada*
1987 C. Ian Kyer and Jerome Bickenbach, *The Fiercest Debate: Cecil A. Wright, the Benchers, and Legal Education in Ontario, 1923–1957*
1988 Robert Sharpe, *The Last Day, the Last Hour: The Currie Libel Trial*
      John D. Arnup, *Middleton: The Beloved Judge*
1989 Desmond Brown, *The Genesis of the Canadian Criminal Code of 1892*
      Patrick Brode, *The Odyssey of John Anderson*
1990 Philip Girard and Jim Phillips, eds., *Essays in the History of Canadian Law: Volume III – Nova Scotia*
      Carol Wilton, ed., *Essays in the History of Canadian Law: Volume IV – Beyond the Law: Lawyers and Business in Canada, 1830–1930*
1991 Constance Backhouse, *Petticoats and Prejudice: Women and Law in Nineteenth- Century Canada*
1992 Brendan O'Brien, *Speedy Justice: The Tragic Last Voyage of His Majesty's Vessel Speedy*
      Robert Fraser, ed., *Provincial Justice: Upper Canadian Legal Portraits from the Dictionary of Canadian Biography*
1993 Greg Marquis, *Policing Canada's Century: A History of the Canadian Association of Chiefs of Police*
      F. Murray Greenwood, *Legacies of Fear: Law and Politics in Quebec in the Era of the French Revolution*
1994 Patrick Boyer, *A Passion for Justice: The Legacy of James Chalmers McRuer*
      Charles Pullen, *The Life and Times of Arthur Maloney: The Last of the Tribunes*
      Jim Phillips, Tina Loo, and Susan Lewthwaite, eds., *Essays in the History of Canadian Law: Volume V – Crime and Criminal Justice*
      Brian Young, *The Politics of Codification: The Lower Canadian Civil Code of 1866*
1995 David Williams, *Just Lawyers: Seven Portraits*

Hamar Foster and John McLaren, eds., Essays in the History of Canadian Law: Volume VI – British Columbia and the Yukon
W.H. Morrow, ed., Northern Justice: The Memoirs of Mr Justice William G. Morrow
Beverley Boissery, *A Deep Sense of Wrong: The Treason, Trials and Transportation to New South Wales of Lower Canadian Rebels after the 1838 Rebellion*

1996 Carol Wilton, ed., *Essays in the History of Canadian Law: Volume VII – Inside the Law: Canadian Law Firms in Historical Perspective*
William Kaplan, *Bad Judgment: The Case of Mr Justice Leo A. Landreville*
F. Murray Greenwood and Barry Wright, eds., *Canadian State Trials: Volume I – Law, Politics, and Security Measures, 1608–1837*

1997 James W. St.G. Walker, *'Race,' Rights, and the Law in the Supreme Court of Canada: Historical Case Studies*
Lori Chambers, *Married Women and Property Law in Victorian Ontario*
Patrick Brode, *Casual Slaughters and Accidental Judgments: Canadian War Crimes and Prosecutions, 1944–1948*
Ian Bushnell, *A History of the Federal Court of Canada, 1875–1992*

1998 Sidney Harring, *White Man's Law: Native People in Nineteenth-Century Canadian Jurisprudence*
Peter Oliver, *'Terror to Evil-Doers': Prisons and Punishments in Nineteenth-Century Ontario*

1999 Constance Backhouse, *Colour-Coded: A Legal History of Racism in Canada, 1900–1950*
G. Blaine Baker and Jim Phillips, eds., *Essays in the History of Canadian Law: Volume VIII – In Honour of R.C.B. Risk*
Richard W. Pound, *Chief Justice W.R. Jackett: By the Law of the Land*
David Vanek, *Fulfilment: Memoirs of a Criminal Court Judge*

2000 Barry Cahill, *The Thousandth Man: A Biography of James McGregor Stewart*
A.B. McKillop, *The Spinster and the Prophet: Florence Deeks, H.G. Wells, and the Mystery of the Purloined Past*
Beverley Boissery and F. Murray Greenwood, *Uncertain Justice: Canadian Women and Capital Punishment*
Bruce Ziff, *Unforeseen Legacies: Reuben Wells Leonard and the Leonard Foundation Trust*

2001 Ellen Anderson, *Judging Bertha Wilson: Law as Large as Life*
Judy Fudge and Eric Tucker, *Labour before the Law: The Regulation of Workers' Collective Action in Canada, 1900–1948*
Laurel Sefton MacDowell, *Renegade Lawyer: The Life of J.L. Cohen*

2002 John T. Saywell, *The Lawmakers: Judicial Power and the Shaping of Canadian Federalism*
Patrick Brode, *Courted and Abandoned: Seduction in Canadian Law*
David Murray, *Colonial Justice: Justice, Morality, and Crime in the Niagara District, 1791–1849*